Oxford Biblical Studies Online

FREE 6-month subscription with purchase of a new book—a $180 value!

Oxford Biblical Studies Online provides unrivalled access to six essential Oxford editions of the Bible alongside commentary and annotations from study Bibles, seamlessly combined with reference material and primary texts.

Online access to the finest scholarship in Biblical Studies includes . . .

- Nearly 5,000 A–Z articles, from Abel to Zion, including exclusive content from the forthcoming Oxford Encyclopaedia of the Bible, integrated with chapter-based scholarly works
- Maps and illustrations
- Interactive timelines and bibliography
- Tools and resources are available to aid research at any level

To activate your FREE 6-month subscription to Oxford Biblical Studies Online, go to https://ams.oup.com/order/OBSO4TEXTBKSCRIP and follow the instructions for entering your activation code, printed in the box on the right.

For customers outside the Americas, please go to https://subscriberservices.sams.oup.com/token to enter this code.

Please note that your subscription will start as soon as the activation code is entered. *This offer expires June 15, 2016.*

www.oxfordbiblicalstudies.com

MY14886133173343

OXFORD
UNIVERSITY PRESS

A Brief Introduction
to
THE NEW TESTAMENT

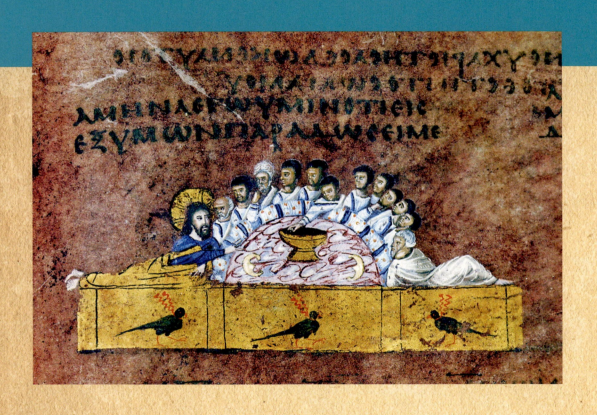

A Brief Introduction
to
THE NEW TESTAMENT

THIRD EDITION

Bart D. Ehrman

**UNIVERSITY OF NORTH CAROLINA
AT CHAPEL HILL**

New York   Oxford
OXFORD UNIVERSITY PRESS

Oxford University Press is a department of the University of Oxford. It furthers
the University's objective of excellence in research, scholarship, and education by
publishing worldwide.

Oxford New York
Auckland   Cape Town   Dar es Salaam   Hong Kong   Karachi
Kuala Lumpur   Madrid   Melbourne   Mexico City   Nairobi
New Delhi   Shanghai   Taipei   Toronto

With offices in
Argentina   Austria   Brazil   Chile   Czech Republic   France   Greece
Guatemala   Hungary   Italy   Japan   Poland   Portugal   Singapore
South Korea   Switzerland   Thailand   Turkey   Ukraine   Vietnam

Oxford is a registered trade mark of Oxford University Press in the UK and certain
other countries.

Published in the United States of America by
Oxford University Press
198 Madison Avenue, New York, NY 10016

For titles covered by Section 112 of the US Higher Education Opportunity Act,
please visit www.oup.com/us/he for the latest information about pricing and
alternate formats.

Library of Congress Cataloging-in-Publication Data
Ehrman, Bart D.
    A brief introduction to the New Testament / Bart D. Ehrman. — 3rd ed.
        p. cm.
    Includes bibliographical references and index.
    ISBN 978-0-19-986230-6
1.   Bible. N.T.—Introductions.   I. Title.
    BS2330.3.E37 2013
    225.6'1—dc23

                                                    2012027626

Printing number: 9 8 7 6 5 4 3 2

Printed in the United States of America
on acid-free paper

To My Students at Rutgers
and the University of North Carolina at Chapel Hill

BRIEF CONTENTS

CONTENTS

6 Jesus, the Jewish Messiah: The Gospel according to Matthew 77

7 Jesus, the Rejected Prophet: The Gospel according to Luke 95

8 Jesus, the Man Sent from Heaven: The Gospel according to John 112

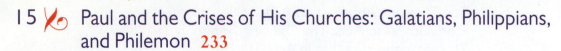

MAPS, TIME LINES, AND DIAGRAMS

MAPS

TIME LINES AND DIAGRAMS

BOXES

Writing textbooks can be enormously gratifying—one of our jobs as research scholars, after all, is to communicate with the world at large. But it also provides a range of unforeseen challenges. I have found the most difficult to be knowing how to balance the desire to leave well enough alone with the need to keep scholarship up to date.

Professors often object to the constant updating of textbooks. I completely understand the objection: I have myself been in the university classroom for twenty-seven years. At the same time, no one wants a textbook that presents knowledge that is out of date. For years I taught a subject in a cognate field—here unnamed, to protect the innocent (or the guilty)—using a textbook that had not been revised in light of advances in the field. It was the best-written textbook available, however, and students liked reading it. Since it was not my own field, I did not realize until much later that the information in the book was twenty years out of date. How does a textbook manage to keep from being dated? Only by being revised. And so, here we have a revision of my *Brief Introduction to the New Testament*.

NEW TO THIS EDITION

❖ Where I am aware of important advances in scholarship in the New Testament, I have tried to make the book au courant. My own research in the past few years has involved textual criticism, early Christian forgery, and the historical Jesus (most particularly, the historical evidence that he existed, something about which most students— at least the ones I run across—have little doubt to begin with). I have made appropriate changes in my discussions at these places in particular. But I have also updated the bibliographies to make them as useful as possible, while being keenly aware that the newest thing off the press may not be the best thing. In fact, a classic in the field is usually a classic for good reason, whereas a work that sees itself as cutting edge may in fact be as dull as a butter knife. In any event, I have tried to update the bibliographies to represent current scholarship, making them as useful as possible for students who want to understand the respective subfields.

❖ I have added a number of important "boxes" throughout the book: some on textual criticism, dealing with specific textual problems that students really do need to know about if they want to claim to have a decent historical understanding of the New Testament; others on forgery and the historical Jesus; others on important noncanonical texts, such as the Proto-Gospel of James, that students should at least have *heard* of.

❖ I have also modified one of the most important pedagogical features of the book. In the second edition I ended each chapter with a set of study questions. For the most part, these asked students to summarize what they had learned. I have decided that such questions are really not the most useful. It is far better to urge students to interact with the material, particularly in contexts that will be familiar to them. To that end I have replaced the study questions with a new kind of box that I call **"Take a Stand."** In them students are asked to imagine a completely plausible situation in which they need to make a case for a particular way of understanding the material covered in the chapter. Usually they are given a choice about how to respond, but in every case they are instructed to back up their views with historical evidence. Often they are asked to do so in conversation with a roommate or a friend, while discussing religion in general or the New Testament in particular. Sometimes they are to imagine being involved in a class debate. I mean for these hypothetical situations to be interesting, believable, and productive for thinking about the issues raised in the chapter and the evidence that is required to deal with them responsibly. I can imagine these questions forming the basis of essay questions or quizzes for the course. But most important, they are meant to urge the student to learn the material that has been covered in the chapter, to recognize its importance, and to develop the ability to interact with it in a thoughtful and compelling way.

RESOURCES FOR INSTRUCTORS & STUDENTS

This text is accompanied by a robust package of supplemental material for both students and instructors.

- ❖ The Instructor's Manual on CD (9780199862313) includes updated Media Resources, Chapter Summaries, Key Terms, Pedagogical Suggestions, PowerPoint lecture outlines, and a Test Bank with multiple-choice and essay questions.
- ❖ On the Companion Website (www.oup.com/us/ehrman), instructors can find most of the material from the Instructor's Manual on CD, password protected. Resources for students include links to Media Resources, interactive Self-Quizzes, Reading Guides, Flash Cards, and Maps.

There now remains only the happy task of thanking a number of scholars who have selflessly provided assistance for my revision of the book. I have spoken with none of these scholars directly, but they all have responded to my editor's request to evaluate the strengths and weaknesses of the book in its second iteration. Most of them responded at considerable length, giving me very much indeed to think about. I am in their debt. These biblical scholars are

- ❖ James Barker at Roanoke College
- ❖ Kenneth Beals at Mary Baldwin College
- ❖ Larry Dunlop at Marymount College
- ❖ Douglas Hume at Pfeiffer University
- ❖ Benjamin Murphy at Florida State University
- ❖ Susan Setta at Northeastern University
- ❖ Scott Shauf at Gardner-Webb University
- ❖ Karen Valdivia at University of San Diego and Cuyamaca College
- ❖ and two readers who have chosen to remain anonymous.

Finally I would like to thank Kristin Maffei, associate editor at Oxford University Press, for her diligence and hard work in bringing this new revision to fruition, and to my good friend Robert Miller, senior executive editor at OUP, whose exceptional efforts have made the world of textbook publishing a better and happier place.

Of the making of revisions, there is no end. I continually want to make this book better, more accessible, more usable. I think several changes have made this second edition much better than the first. Most obvious is the publisher's move to a four-color edition, which vastly improves both the appearance and readability of the text. Other changes have been somewhat minor—the rewriting of some portions, the renaming of the boxes throughout, the addition of several new boxes (for example, on the newly discovered Gospel of Judas) and the deletion of ones that seemed less germane, and so on. Among the major improvements are two significant organizational changes. Most teachers have not followed my suggestion of studying the book of Acts immediately after the Gospel of Luke, so I have reverted to a more traditional order, dealing with Acts after all the Gospels (instead of before John) and after the discussion of the historical Jesus; similarly, I have now moved the discussion of the Johannine epistles out of the chapter on the Fourth Gospel and placed it in its more natural (and canonical) place, among the other general epistles. I believe both changes make the book tighter and easier to use in the classroom. The final major change is the addition of a photo essay on the manuscripts of the New Testament at the end, intended to give students a sense of the kinds of material remains we have for the "original" text of the New Testament and of the numerous alterations made to that text over the course of the centuries.

Once again I am grateful to my outside readers, who went to great lengths in order to suggest ways to improve the book. In particular I would like to acknowledge the following for their insightful comments and suggestions: Jason BeDuhn of Northern Arizona University; Christopher Franks of High Point University; Chris "the man" Frilingos of Michigan State University; Nancy Hardesty of Clemson University; Davina Lopez of Eckerd College; Bradley Nystrom of California State University, Sacramento; Ken Stenstrup of Saint Mary's University of Minnesota; and Ronald Williams of Gardner-Webb University. I am especially indebted to Sarah Calabi, associate editor at Oxford University Press, for all her hard work on this new edition, and, above all, to Robert Miller, my editor at Oxford University Press and friend at home, who both pushes along and leads the way.

I n 1997 I published *The New Testament: A Historical Introduction to the Early Christian Writings*. This college-level textbook, now in its third edition, appears to have found a niche in the market. But it did not fill another niche, and that is the reason for the present book, *A Brief Introduction to the New Testament*. The truth is that some teachers find the more substantial treatment of the earlier book too demanding for their students: even though they like its historical approach, appreciate its style of presentation, and are committed to its contextual and comparative focus, these teachers feel obliged, for the sake of their students, to use a textbook that provides less material to digest, easier access to the issues, and more pedagogical aids.

And so I decided, in conversation with my editor, Robert Miller, to produce a briefer version of the book, not to replace the other but to provide a simpler alternative to it. I mean for this book to continue to present the best of New Testament (NT) scholarship in an interesting and competent way. I have tried to keep the book readable and clear. And I have worked to make the complicated tasks of NT scholarship understandable, accessible, and even fascinating to the beginner.

At the same time, I have wanted to retain the distinctive approach and flavor of the longer discussion. And so, I continue to see the orientation of this book as (*a*) historical, rather than literary-critical or theological; (*b*) contextual, in focusing on the historical and cultural milieux of the NT writings, both within the Greco-Roman world and among all the surviving early Christian literature; (*c*) comparative, in emphasizing the rich and fertile diversity of the early Christians and their writings; and (*d*) critical, in that I present arguments and evidence for the views I present, rather than simply "state the facts" as I see them.

For those who are familiar with the other book, some of the major changes will be evident. I have cut back on my treatment of the historical Jesus (from three chapters to one); I have relocated my discussion of the Jewish context to the early part of the book; I have continued to include discussion of noncanonical Christian literature, but in a new kind of box scattered throughout the text rather than in separate chapters; and I have condensed and simplified a large number of discussions, including, for example, my reflections on the genre of the Gospels as ancient biographies and the Synoptic Problem.

Most noticeably, I have significantly increased the number of pedagogical features. In addition to the **"What to Expect" précis** that begin each chapter and the **"At a Glance" summaries** of all major discussions, I have (*a*) provided a list of **Key Terms** for each chapter, each of which is highlighted at its first occurrence; (*b*) supplied **Questions for Study and Reflection** at the end of each chapter (these serve more or less as study guides to the chapters); and (*c*) included a greatly expanded **Glossary**.

I would like to thank Robert Miller, my friend and inimitable editor, who encouraged me to do this project and pushed me along the way. I have dedicated the volume to all the undergraduate students I have had at Rutgers and Chapel Hill, all of whom, in their own way, have helped teach me how to teach.

ACKNOWLEDGMENTS

I would like to acknowledge my gratitude to previous scholars whose labors make such introductory textbooks possible.

Most of the quotations of the Bible, including the Apocrypha, are drawn from the New Revised Standard Version. Some, however, represent my own translations.

The reconstruction of the Testimonium Flavium in Chapter 13 comes from John Meier, *A Marginal Jew: Rethinking the Historical Jesus,* vol. 1, Anchor Bible Reference Library (New York: Doubleday, 1991), p. 61.

The correspondence between Paul and Seneca in Chapter 18 is taken from Edgar Hennecke, *New Testament Apocrypha,* ed. Wilhelm Schneemelcher, trans. R. McL. Wilson, vol. 2 (Philadelphia: Westminster Press, 1965). The material from Fronto in Chapter 19 comes from *The Octavius of Marcus Minucius Felix,* ed. and trans. G. W. Clark (Mahwah, N.J.: Newman, 1974); the inscription from the Lanuvium burial society, also in Chapter 19, comes from N. Lewis and M. Rheinhold, *Roman Civilization*, vol. 2 (New York: Columbia University Press, 1955).

NOTES ON SUGGESTIONS FOR FURTHER READING

The bibliographical suggestions at the end of each chapter are meant to guide beginning students who are interested in pursuing one or more of the issues raised in this book. To avoid overwhelming the student with the enormous quantity of literature in the field, for most chapters I have limited myself to seven or eight entries (more for longer chapters, fewer for shorter ones). All the entries are books, rather than articles, and each is briefly annotated. Some of the entries are more suitable for advanced students, and they are indicated as such. For most chapters I have included at least one work that introduces or embraces a markedly different perspective from the one that I present. I have not included any biblical commentaries in the lists, although students should be urged to consult these, either one-volume works such as the *Harper's Bible Commentary*, the *Jerome Biblical Commentary*, and the *Oxford Bible Commentary*, or commentaries on individual books, as found in the Anchor Bible, Hermeneia, Interpretation, and New International Commentary series.

For some of the issues that I discuss, there are no adequate full-length treatments for beginning-level students to turn to, but there are excellent discussions of virtually everything having to do with the New Testament in Bible dictionaries that are readily available in most college libraries. Students should browse through the articles in such one-volume works as the *Harper's Bible Dictionary* and the *Mercer Dictionary of the Bible*. In particular, they should become intimately familiar with the impressive six-volume *Anchor Bible Dictionary*, which has become a major resource for students at all levels.

There are numerous online resources available for the study of the New Testament. The difficulty with Web pages generally, of course, is that anyone—trained professional, interested amateur, well-meaning crank—can construct one, and often it is difficult, if not impossible, for the student to know whether the information provided is reliable, disputed, or zany. One other difficulty is that Web pages come and go like summer storms. Rather than provide an entire list of useful pages, then, I have chosen to recommend just one, which I believe will be around for a very long time and which provides trustworthy scholarly information (through carefully chosen links) on just about everything one might want to know about the New Testament. This is the page created and maintained by Dr. Mark Goodacre at Duke University: www.ntgateway.com.

CREDITS

Frontispiece: Alinari/Art Resource, NY. Fig. 1.1: British Library. Fig. 2.1: Numismatic Museum, Athens/Hellenic Republic Ministry of Culture. Fig. 2.4: Scala/Art Resource, NY. Fig. 2.5: Forum, Pompeii/Erich Lessing/Art Resource, NY. Fig. 2.6: Louvre/Alinari/Art Resource, NY. Fig. 3.1: Ritmeyer Archaeological Design, England. Fig. 3.2: Eric M. Meyers. Fig. 3.3: British Museum. Fig. 3.5: Israel Museum, Jerusalem. Fig. 4.3: The Art Archive/Archaeological Museum, Piraeus/Gianni Dagli Orti. Fig. 5.2: The Art Archive/Collection Dagli Orti. Fig. 5.4: British Museum. Fig. 6.1: British Museum. Fig. 6.2: British Museum/Art Resource, NY. Fig. 7.1: Alinari/Art Resource, NY. Fig. 7.2: Staatsbibliothek, Munich/Foto Marburg/Art Resource, NY. Fig. 7.3: Erich Lessing/Art Resource, NY. Fig. 8.2: Erich Lessing/Art Resource, NY. Fig. 8.3: Réunion des Musées Nationaux/Art Resource, NY. Fig. 9.1: akg-images/André Held. Fig. 9.3: Scala/Art Resource, NY. Fig. 9.4: Scala/Art Resource, NY. Fig. 10.1: Dr. Jürgen Zangenberg. Fig. 10.2: Scala/Art Resource, NY. Fig. 11.2: akg-images/André Held. Fig. 11.3: Sonia Halliday Photographs. Fig. 11.4: V&A Images, London/Art Resource, NY. Fig. 12.2: University of Michigan. Fig. 12.4: Copyright 2012 property of Dr. Carl Rasmussen, www.HolyLandPhotos.org. Fig. 13.1 Scala/Art Resource, NY. Fig. 13.2: Vanni/Art Resource, NY. Fig. 13.3: C. M. Dixon/Ancient Art & Architecture Collection Ltd. Fig. 13.4: Scala/Art Resource, NY. Fig. 14.1: André Held. Fig. 14.2: Scala/Art Resource, NY. Fig. 14.3: Bart D. Ehrman. Fig. 14.4: akg-images/André Held. Fig. 15.2: Robert Miller. Fig. 15.3: Petit Palais, Musée des Beaux-Arts de la Ville de Paris. Fig. 16.1: Scala/Art Resource, NY. Fig. 16.2: Photo by Fred Anderegg. Fig. 17.1: British Library. Fig. 17.2: akg-images/André Held. Fig. 17.3: Alinari/Art Resource, NY. Fig. 18.1: Scala/Art Resource, NY. Fig. 18.2: Catacomb of Priscilla, Rome/Scala/Art Resource, NY. Fig. 18.3: Robert Miller. Fig. 19.1: British Museum. Fig. 19.2: Scala/Art Resource, NY. Fig. 19.3: Classical Numismatic Group, Inc., www.cngcoins.com. Fig. 19.4: Gilles Mermet/Art Resource, NY. Fig. 21.2: Hirmer Verlag München. Fig. 21.3: akg-images/André Held. Figure 21.4: Robert Turcan.

Photo Essay 1: Ancient Manuscripts of the New Testament (between pages 45 and 46)

Fig. 1: Reproduced by courtesy of the University Librarian and Director, The John Rylands University Library, The University of Manchester; Fig. 2: Digitally Reproduced with the Permission of the Papyrology Collection, Graduate Library, University of Michigan; Fig. 3: By permission of the British Library; Fig. 4: Biblioteca Apostolica Vaticana; Fig. 5: University of Cambridge, University Library; Fig. 6: Stiftsbibliotheck St. Gallen; Fig. 7: Leningrad State Public Library; Fig. 8: Biblioteca Apostolica Vaticana.

Photo Essay 2: The Material World of Jesus and the Gospels (between pages 164 and 165)

Fig. 1: Scala/Art Resource, NY. Fig. 2: Erich Lessing/Art Resource, NY. Fig. 3: Erich Lessing/Art Resource, NY. Fig. 4: Archaeological Exploration of Sardis/Harvard University. Fig. 5: SEF/Art Resource, NY. Fig. 6: Bart Ehrman. Fig. 7: Bart Ehrman. Fig. 8a (Psalm scroll): The Israel Museum, Jerusalem. Fig. 8b (copper scrolls): Courtesy Israel Antiquities Authority. Fig. 9: Bart Ehrman. Fig. 10: Erich Lessing/Art Resource, NY. Fig. 11: Courtesy Israel Antiquities Authority. Fig. 12: The Israel Museum, Jerusalem. Fig. 13: The Israel Museum, Jerusalem. Fig. 14: The Israel Museum, Jerusalem.

	History of Hellenistic and Roman Times	History of Palestine	History of Christianity
800 B.C.E.	753 B.C.E. Traditional date for the founding of Rome		
700 B.C.E.			
600 B.C.E.		587–586 B.C.E. Final conquest of Jerusalem by the Babylonians, destruction of the Temple, Jewish leaders taken into exile 559–332 B.C.E. Palestine ruled by the Persians	
	510 B.C.E. Expulsion of kings from Rome and beginning of Roman Republic		
500 B.C.E.			
400 B.C.E.	332–323 B.C.E. Conquests of Alexander the Great	333–332 B.C.E. Palestine conquered by Alexander the Great	
300 B.C.E.	264–241, 218–202, and 149–146 B.C.E. Punic Wars, Rome against Carthage for domination of the Mediterranean	300–198 B.C.E. Palestine ruled by the Ptolemies (of Egypt)	
200 B.C.E.		198–142 B.C.E. Palestine ruled by the Seleucids (of Syria)	

History of Hellenistic and Roman Times	History of Palestine	History of Christianity
	**167–142** B.C.E. The Maccabean revolt	
	142–63 B.C.E. Palestine ruled by the Hasmoneans, formation of the Jewish sects: the Pharisees, Sadducees, and Essenes	
100 B.C.E.		
44 B.C.E. Assassination of Julius Caesar	**63** B.C.E. Palestine conquered by Roman General Pompey	
	40–4 B.C.E. Herod made king of the Jews by the Romans	
27 B.C.E. Octavian (Caesar Augustus), emperor; beginning of Roman Empire	**4** B.C.E. The Birth of Jesus	**4** B.C.E. The Birth of Jesus
		4 B.C.E.–**30** C.E. Life of Jesus
1 C.E.		
14–37 Tiberius, emperor	**4–6** Judea ruled by Herod's son Archelaus	**27–30?** Public Ministry of Jesus
37–41 Caligula, emperor	**4–39** Galilee ruled by Herod's son Antipas	**30?** Crucifixion of Jesus
	6–41 Judea governed by Roman Prefects (Pontius Pilate, prefect in 26–30 C.E.)	**30–120** Oral Traditions of Jesus and initial spread of Christianity throughout the empire
41–54 Claudius, emperor	**41–44** Agrippa 1, king over most of Palestine	**31–32??** Conversion of Paul
	44–66 Most of Palestine ruled by Roman procurators	**34–64** Paul's missionary activities
54–68 Nero, emperor		
68–69 Year of four emperors	**66–70** First Jewish revolt	**49** 1 Thessalonians, Paul's earliest letter and the earliest surviving Christian Writing

History of Hellenistic and Roman Times	History of Palestine	History of Christianity
		49–62 Paul's letters
69–79 Vespasian, emperor		**64** Death of Paul and Peter
		65–70 Gospel of Mark
	70 Destruction of Jerusalem/Temple	
79–81 Titus, emperor		**80–85** Gospels of Matthew and Luke
81–96 Domitian, emperor		**80–110** Deutero-Pauline Epistles, Pastoral Epistles, General Epistles
		90–95 Gospel of John
96–98 Nerva, emperor		**95** 1 Clement
		95–100 Book of Revelation
98–117 Trajan, emperor		

History of Hellenistic and Roman Times	History of Palestine	History of Christianity
100 C.E.		
117–138 Hadrian, emperor	**132–135** Second Jewish revolt (under Simon bar Cochba)	**100** The Didache
		110 Letters of Ignatius
		100–130 Rise of Gnosticism
		110–120 Gospels of Thomas and Peter
		120–140 Shepherd of Hermas, Apocalypse of Peter
		130 Epistle of Barnabas
		130–150 Rise of Marcionites
		155 Martyrdom of Polycarp

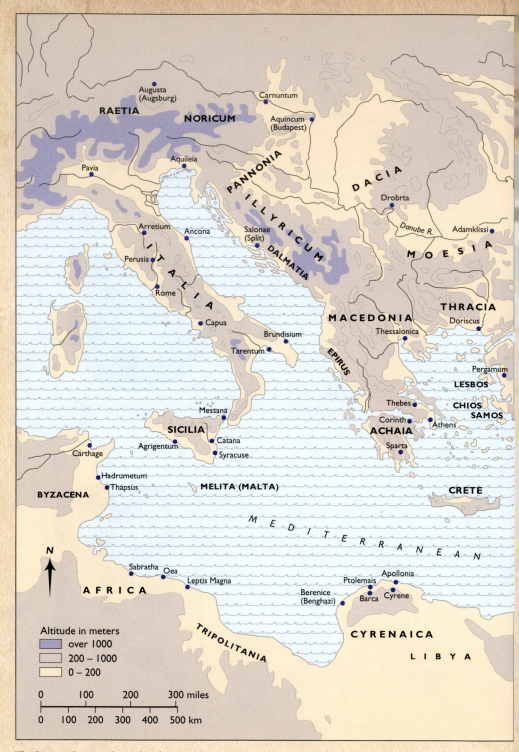

RAETIA

Augusta
(Augsburg)

NORICUM

Carnuntum

Aquincum
(Budapest)

PANNONIA

DACIA

Pavia

Aquileia

ILLYRICUM

Drobrta

Danube R.

Adamklissi

Arretium

Ancona

Salonae
(Split)

DALMATIA

MOESIA

I
T
A
L
I
A

Perusia

Rome

MACEDONIA

THRACIA

Doriscus

Thessalonica

Capua

Brundisium

EPIRUS

Pergamum

Tarentum

LESBOS

Messana

Thebes

CHIOS

SAMOS

SICILIA

Catana

Corinth

Athens

Agrigentum

Syracuse

ACHAIA

Carthage

Sparta

CRETE

Hadrumetum

Thapsus

MELITA (MALTA)

BYZACENA

M E D I T E R R A N E A N

N

Sabratha

Oea

Apollonia

AFRICA

Leptis Magna

Ptolemais

Berenice
(Benghazi)

Barca

Cyrene

Altitude in meters

over 1000

200 – 1000

0 – 200

TRIPOLITANIA

CYRENAICA

LIBYA

| 0 | 100 | | 200 | | 300 miles |

| 0 | 100 | 200 | 300 | 400 | 500 km |

The Roman Empire: Central and Eastern Provinces.

BLACK SEA

Tomis (Costanza)

Odessus (Varna)

Apollonia (Sozopol)

Sinope

Trapezus
(Trebizond)

ARMENIA

BITHNIA-PONTUS

Nicomedia
(Izmit)

Byzantium

Ancyra

GALATIA

CAPPADOCIA

Nyssa

COMMAGENE

MESOPOTAMIA

Stratonicea

Samosata

Sardis

Cyrrhus

Zeugma

Smyrna

ASIA

Tarsus

Ephesus

CILICIA

Aphrodisias

Antioch

Tralles

Alabanda

Aspendus

Side

Aleppo

Dura
Europos

Xanthus

SYRIA

Apamea

Palmyra

Tigris R.

Laodicea

Euphrates R.

RHODES

CYPRUS

Salamis

Paphos

Citium

Berytus

Baalbek

Curium

Damascus

Tyre

PHOENICIA

Bostra

SEA

JUDAEA

Gerasa

Joppa

Jerusalem

Gaza

Alexandria

Pelusium

Masada

ARABIA

Petra

Memphis

SINAI

EGYPT

Nile R.

RED SEA

Introduction

WHAT IS THE NEW TESTAMENT?

WHAT TO EXPECT

This chapter is concerned with some hard but intriguing questions that many people have never thought to ask about the New Testament: Where did this book—or, rather, this collection of books—come from? How did the twenty-seven books of the New Testament get gathered together into a "canon," a collection of authoritative books? Why were these books included in the Scriptures, but other Christian books—some of them written at the same time—not? Who made the decisions? On what grounds? And when?

What is the New Testament? The short answer is that it is the second part of the Christian Bible, which along with the **Old Testament** (see box 1.1), is considered by Christians to be the sacred **canon** (see box 1.2) of Scripture. And why should we study it? Because it is the most frequently purchased, commonly read, passionately believed, and widely misunderstood book in the history of Western civilization.

Christianity is the largest religion in the world today, with some 2 billion adherents. Throughout the history of Western civilization for the past 2,000 years, the Christian church has been by far the most powerful and influential institution—not just religiously but also socially, culturally, economically, and politically. And the New Testament is the book that stands at the foundation of this religion. Whether you are a Christian believer

or not, whether you have a personal attachment to the New Testament or not, whether you base your life on the teachings of Jesus or not, the New Testament has profoundly affected your life and will continue to play an enormous role in the world in which you, and all of us, live.

This textbook on the New Testament is not written only for believers, but for all people of all kinds. And so, I will not be approaching our study from a particular theological point of view (e.g., Baptist, Episcopalian, Catholic, Jewish, Muslim, atheist; see the excursus at the end of this chapter). I will be approaching it from a historical perspective, asking what we can know about the teachings of the New Testament, the authors of its books, the times within which they wrote, and the issues they were trying to address. My assumption throughout is that this kind of historical investigation into

BOX 1.1 The Hebrew Bible and the Christian Old Testament

The terms "Jewish Scriptures" and "Hebrew Bible" both refer to the collection of books considered sacred in the religion of Judaism, books that were written almost entirely in Hebrew. Many of these writings were regarded as holy even before Jesus' day, especially the first five books of Moses, known as the Torah or Law.

About a century after Jesus, the collection of books into the Hebrew Scriptures was more or less fixed. Altogether, the collection comprised twenty-four different books. Because of a different way of counting them, they number thirty-nine books in English translation (the twelve minor prophets in English Bibles, for example, count as only one book in the Hebrew Bible).

Christians have long referred to these books as the "Old Testament," to set them apart from the books of the "New Testament" (the new set of books that reveal God's will to his people). Throughout our study, I will use the term "Old Testament" only when referring explicitly to Christian views; otherwise, I will call these books the Jewish Scriptures or Hebrew Bible.

Even within Christianity there are different numbers of books included in the "Old Testament." The Roman Catholic Church, for example, accepts an additional twelve books (or parts of books)—including such works as Tobit, Judith, 1 and 2 Maccabees—which they call "Deuterocanonical" (meaning that they came into the canon at a later time than the books of the Hebrew Bible). Protestant Christians usually call these books the "Apocrypha." Since they did not form part of the Hebrew Bible, I do not include them in this chart or discuss them at any length.

The Hebrew Bible

The Torah (5 books)
Genesis
Exodus
Leviticus
Numbers
Deuteronomy

The Prophets (8 books)
Former Prophets
Joshua
Judges
Samuel (counts as 1 book)
Kings (counts as 1 book)
Later Prophets
Isaiah
Jeremiah
Ezekiel
The Twelve
(count as 1 book)
Hosea
Joel
Amos

Obadiah
Jonah
Micah
Nahum
Habakkuk
Zephaniah
Haggai
Zechariah
Malachi

The Writings (11 books)
Job
Psalms
Proverbs
Ruth
Song of Solomon
Ecclesiastes
Lamentations
Esther
Daniel
Ezra-Nehemiah (1 book)
Chronicles (1 book)

The Christian "Old Testament"

The Pentateuch (5 books)
Genesis
Exodus
Leviticus
Numbers
Deuteronomy

Historical Books (12 books)
Joshua
Judges
Ruth
1 and 2 Samuel
1 and 2 Kings
1 and 2 Chronicles
Ezra
Nehemiah
Esther

Poetry and Wisdom Books (5 books)
Job
Psalms
Proverbs
Ecclesiastes
Song of Solomon

Prophetic Books (17 books)
Major Prophets
Isaiah
Jeremiah
Lamentations
Ezekiel
Daniel
Minor Prophets
Hosea
Joel
Amos
Obadiah
Jonah
Micah
Nahum
Habakkuk
Zephaniah
Haggai
Zechariah
Malachi

ANOTHER GLIMPSE INTO THE PAST

BOX 1.2   The Canon of Scripture

The English term "canon" comes from a Greek word that originally meant "ruler" or "measuring rod." A canon was used to make straight lines or to measure distances. When applied to a group of books, it refers to a recognized body of literature. Thus, for example, the canon of Shakespeare refers to all of Shakespeare's authentic writings.

With reference to the Bible, the term canon denotes the collection of books that are accepted as authoritative by a religious body. Thus, for example, we can speak of the canon of the Jewish Scriptures or the canon of the New Testament.

---

the New Testament will be valuable for all people, believer and nonbeliever alike.

We will begin in this chapter by considering some basic information about the New Testament, seeing how the books within it came to be collected together into a canon of Scripture, and then considering whether we actually have the original books of the New Testament themselves, or only later copies of them, occasionally modified by the ancient scribes who did the copying.

THE NEW TESTAMENT: SOME BASIC INFORMATION

The New Testament contains twenty-seven books, written in Greek, by fifteen or sixteen different authors, who were addressing other Christian individuals or communities between the years 50 and 120 C.E. (see box 1.3). As we will see, it is difficult to know whether any of these books was written by Jesus' own disciples.

The first four books are **"Gospels,"** a term that literally means "good news." The four Gospels of the New Testament proclaim the good news by telling stories about the life and death of Jesus— his birth, ministry, miracles, teaching, last days, crucifixion, and resurrection. These books are traditionally ascribed to Matthew, Mark, Luke, and John. Christians of the second century claimed that two of these authors were disciples of Jesus: Matthew, the tax collector mentioned in the First Gospel (Matt 9:9), and John, the beloved disciple

who appears in the Fourth (e.g., John 19:26). The other two were reportedly written by associates of famous apostles: Mark, the secretary of Peter, and Luke, the traveling companion of Paul. This second-century tradition does not go back to the Gospels themselves; the titles in our Bibles (e.g., "The Gospel according to Matthew") were not found in the original texts of these books. Instead, their authors chose to remain anonymous.

The next book in the New Testament is the **Acts of the Apostles,** written by the same author as the Third Gospel (whom modern scholars continue to call Luke even though we are not certain of his identity). This book is a sequel to the Gospel in that it describes the history of early Christianity beginning with events immediately after Jesus' death; it is chiefly concerned to show how the religion was disseminated throughout parts of the Roman Empire, among Gentiles as well as Jews, principally through the missionary labors of the apostle Paul. Thus, whereas the Gospels portray the *beginnings* of Christianity (through the life and death of Jesus), the book of Acts portrays the *spread* of Christianity (through the work of his apostles).

The next section of the New Testament comprises twenty-one **"epistles,"** that is, letters written by Christian leaders to various communities and individuals. Not all these epistles are, strictly speaking, items of personal correspondence. The book of Hebrews, for example, appears to be an early Christian sermon, and the epistle of 1 John is a kind of Christian tractate. Nonetheless, all twenty-one of these books are traditionally called

ANOTHER GLIMPSE INTO THE PAST

BOX 1.3 The Common Era and Before the Common Era

Most students will be accustomed to dating ancient events as either A.D. (which does not stand for "After Death," but for "anno domini," Latin for "year of our Lord") or B.C. ("Before Christ"). This terminology may make sense for Christians, for whom A.D. 1996 is indeed "the year of our Lord 1996." It makes less sense, though, for Jews, Muslims, and others for whom Jesus is not the "Lord" or the "Christ."

Scholars have therefore begun to use a different set of abbreviations as more inclusive of others outside the Christian tradition. In this book I will follow the alternative designations of C.E. ("the **Common Era**," meaning common to people of all faiths who utilize the traditional Western calendar) and B.C.E. ("**Before the Common Era**"). In terms of the older abbreviations, then, C.E. corresponds to A.D. and B.C.E. to B.C.

epistles. Thirteen of them claim to be written by the apostle Paul; in some cases, scholars have come to question this claim. In any event, most of these letters, whether by Paul or others, address theological or practical problems that have arisen in the Christian communities they address. Thus, whereas the Gospels describe the beginnings of Christianity and the book of Acts its spread, the epistles are more directly focused on Christian beliefs, practices, and ethics.

Finally, the New Testament concludes with the Book of Revelation, the first surviving instance of a Christian **apocalypse.** This book was written by a prophet named John, who describes the course of future events leading up to the destruction of this world and the appearance of the world to come. As such, it is principally concerned with the culmination of Christianity.

OTHER EARLY CHRISTIAN WRITINGS

The books I have just described were not the only writings of the early Christians, nor were they originally collected into a body of literature called the "New Testament." We know of other Christian writings that have not survived from antiquity. For example, the apostle Paul, in his first letter to the Corinthians, refers to an earlier writing that he had sent them (1 Cor 5:9) and alludes to a letter that

they themselves had sent him (7:1). Unfortunately, this correspondence is lost.

Other noncanonical writings, however, have survived. The best known of them are by authors collectively called the **"Apostolic Fathers."** These were Christians living in the early second century, whose writings were considered authoritative in some Christian circles, some of them on a par with the writings of the Gospels or Paul. In fact, some of our ancient manuscripts of the New Testament include writings of the Apostolic Fathers as if they belonged to the canon. Other, previously unknown, Christian writings were discovered only within the twentieth century. Some of these writings clearly stand at odds with those within the New Testament; some of them appear to have been used as sacred scripture by certain groups of Christians. A number of them claim to be written by apostles. The most spectacular find occurred in 1945 near the town of **Nag Hammadi,** Egypt, where some peasants digging for fertilizer accidentally uncovered a jar containing thirteen fragmentary books in leather bindings. The books contain anthologies of literature, some fifty-two treatises altogether, written in the ancient Egyptian language called Coptic. Whereas the books themselves were manufactured in the mid-fourth century C.E. (we know this because some of the bindings were strengthened with pieces of scratch paper that were dated), the treatises that they contain are much older: some of them are mentioned by name by authors living in the second century. Before this

ANOTHER GLIMPSE INTO THE PAST

BOX 1.4   The Layout of the New Testament

Gospels: The Beginnings of Christianity (4 books)
Matthew
Mark
Luke
John

Acts: The Spread of Christianity (1 book)
The Acts of the Apostles

Epistles: The Beliefs, Practices, and Ethics of Christianity (21 books)

Pauline Epistles (13 books)
Romans
1 and 2 Corinthians
Galatians
Ephesians

Philippians
Colossians
1 and 2 Thessalonians
1 and 2 Timothy
Titus
Philemon

General Epistles (8 books)
Hebrews
James
1 and 2 Peter
1, 2, and 3 John
Jude

Apocalypse: The Culmination of Christianity (1 book)
The Revelation of John

This schematic arrangement is somewhat simplified. All of the New Testament books, for example (not just the epistles), are concerned with Christian beliefs, practices, and ethics, and Paul's epistles are in some ways more reflective of Christian beginnings than the Gospels. Nonetheless, this basic orientation to the New Testament writings can at least get us started in our understanding of the early Christian literature.

discovery, we knew that these books existed, but we didn't know what was in them.

What kind of books are they? Included in the collection are epistles, apocalypses, and collections of secret teachings. Yet more intriguing are the several Gospels that it contains, including one allegedly written by the apostle Philip and another attributed to Didymus Judas Thomas, thought by some early Christians to be Jesus' twin brother. These books were accepted as Scripture by *some* groups of early Christians.

Why were they—and other books like them—finally rejected from the canon of Scripture, and others accepted? Who made the decisions about which books to include? When did these decisions get made? And on what grounds?

THE DEVELOPMENT OF THE CHRISTIAN CANON

Christians did not invent the idea of collecting authoritative writings together into a sacred canon of Scripture. In this they had a precedent. For even though most of the other religions in the Roman Empire did not use written documents as authorities for their religious beliefs and practices, Judaism did.

Jesus and his followers were themselves Jews who were conversant with the ancient writings that were eventually canonized into the Hebrew Scriptures. Although most scholars now think that a hard-and-fast canon of Jewish Scripture did not yet exist in Jesus' own day, it appears that most

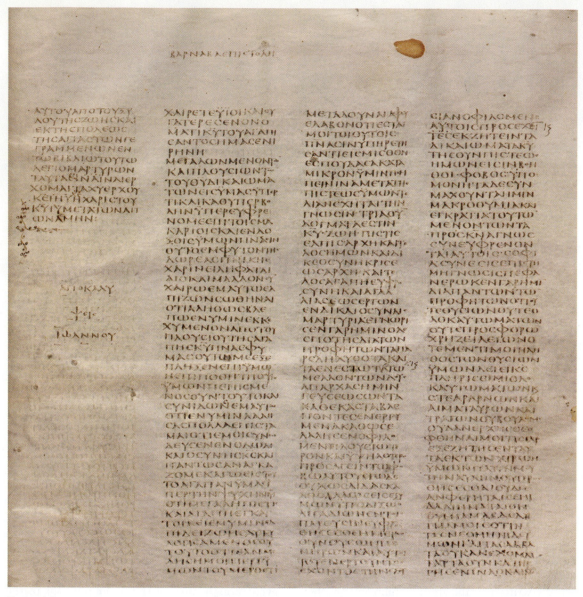

Figure 1.1 Codex Sinaiticus, the oldest surviving manuscript of the entire New Testament. This fourth-century manuscript includes *The Shepherd* of Hermas and the *Epistle of Barnabas* (the first page of which is pictured here), books that were considered part of the New Testament by some Christians for several centuries.

Jews did subscribe to the special authority of the Torah (i.e., the first five books of the Hebrew Bible, see box 1.1). Also, many Jews accepted the authority of the Prophets as well. These writings include the books of Joshua through 2 Kings in our English Bibles, as well as the more familiar prophets Isaiah, Jeremiah, Ezekiel, and the twelve minor prophets. According to our earliest accounts, Jesus himself quoted from some of these books; we can assume that he accepted them as authoritative.

Thus Christianity had its beginning in the proclamation of a Jewish teacher, who ascribed authority to written documents. Moreover, we know that Jesus' followers considered his own teachings to be authoritative. Near the end of the first century, Christians were citing Jesus' words and calling them "Scripture" (e.g., 1 Tim 5:18). It is striking that in some early Christian circles the correct interpretation of Jesus' teachings was thought to be the key to eternal life (e.g., see John 6:68 and *Gosp. Thom.* 1). Furthermore, some of Jesus' followers, such as the apostle Paul, understood themselves to be authoritative spokespersons for the truth. Other Christians granted them this claim. The book of 2 Peter, for example, includes Paul's own letters among the "Scriptures" (2 Pet 3:16).

Thus by the beginning of the second century, some Christians were ascribing authority to the words of Jesus and the writings of his apostles. There were nonetheless heated debates concerning which apostles were true to Jesus' own teachings, and a number of writings that claimed to be written by apostles were thought by some Christians to be forgeries.

It appears then that our New Testament emerged out of the conflicts among Christian groups, and that the dominance of the position that eventually "won out" was what led to the development of the Christian canon as we have it. It is no accident that Gospels that were deemed **"heretical"** (i.e., false)—for instance, the *Gospel of Peter* or the *Gospel of Philip*—did not make it into the New Testament. This is not to say, however, that the canon of Scripture was firmly set by the end of the second century. Indeed, it is a striking fact of history that even though the four Gospels were widely considered authoritative by proto-orthodox Christians then—along with Acts, most of the Pauline epistles, and several of the longer general epistles—the collection of our twenty-seven books was not finalized until much later. For throughout the second, third, and fourth centuries, proto-orthodox Christians continued to debate the acceptability of some of the other books. The arguments centered on (*a*) whether the books in question were ancient (some Christians wanted to include *The Shepherd* of Hermas, for example; others insisted that it was penned after the age of the apostles); (*b*) whether they were written by apostles (some wanted to include Hebrews on the grounds that Paul wrote it; others insisted that he did not); and (*c*) whether they were widely accepted among proto-orthodox congregations as containing correct Christian teaching (many Christians, for example, disputed the doctrine of the end times found in the book of Revelation).

Contrary to what one might expect, it was not until the year 367 C.E., almost two and a half centuries after the last New Testament book was written, that any Christian of record named our current twenty-seven books as the authoritative canon of Scripture. The author of this list was **Athanasius,** the powerful bishop of Alexandria, Egypt. Some scholars believe that this pronouncement on his part, and his accompanying proscription of heretical books, led monks of a nearby monastery to hide the Gnostic writings discovered 1,600 years later by bedouin near Nag Hammadi, Egypt.

IMPLICATIONS FOR OUR STUDY

Understanding the process by which the New Testament canon came into being raises a highly significant issue. The various books of the New Testament are typically read as standing in essential harmony with one another. But do the books of the New Testament agree in every major way? Or are they thought to agree only because they have been placed together, side by side, in an authoritative collection that is venerated as sacred Scripture? Is it possible that when these books are read in their original settings, rather than their canonical context, they stand at real tension with one another?

These are among the most difficult and controversial issues that we will address in our study of the New Testament writings. In order to anticipate my approach, I might simply point out that historians who have carefully examined the New Testament have found that its authors do, in fact, embody remarkably diverse points of view. These scholars have concluded that the most fruitful way to interpret the New Testament authors is to read them individually rather than collectively. Each author should be allowed to have his own say,* and should not be too quickly reconciled

---

*Throughout this book I will be using the masculine pronoun to refer to the authors of the early Christian literature, simply because I think all of them were males. For discussion of some of the relevant issues, see Chapter 18 and box 4.1.

with the point of view of another. For example, we should not assume that Paul would always say exactly what Matthew would, or that Matthew would agree in every particular with John, and so on. Following this principle, scholars have been struck by the rich diversity represented within the pages of the New Testament. This point cannot be stressed enough. The diversity of Christianity did not begin in the modern period, as some people unreflectively assume (cf. all the groups that call themselves Christian: Greek Orthodox, Roman Catholic, Southern Baptist, Methodists, Mormons, Seventh-Day Adventists, and so on!). The diversity of Christianity is already evident in the earliest writings that have survived from the Christians of antiquity, most of which are preserved within the canon of the New Testament.

In this book, we will approach the writings of the New Testament from this historical perspective, looking at each author's work individually, rather than allowing the shape of the later Christian canon to determine the meaning of all its constituent parts.

THE NEW TESTAMENT: ONE OTHER SET OF PROBLEMS

We have seen that the New Testament did not emerge as a single collection of twenty-seven books immediately, but that different groups of early Christians had different collections of sacred books. In some ways, however, the problem of the New Testament canon is even more complicated than that. For not only did different Christian communities have different books—they had different versions of the *same* books.

They had different versions because of the way books were transmitted in an age before Internet access, desktop publishing, word processors, photocopiers, and printing presses. Books in the ancient world could not be mass produced. They were copied by hand, one page, one sentence, one word, one letter at a time. There was no other way to do it. Since books were copied by hand, there was always the possibility that **scribes** would make mistakes and intentional changes in a book—any and every time it was copied. Moreover, when a new

copy was itself copied, the mistakes and changes that the earlier scribe (copyist) made would have been reproduced, while the new scribe would introduce some mistakes and changes of his own. When that copy was then copied, more changes would be introduced. And so it went.

Unfortunately, we do not have the originals of any of the books of the New Testament, or the first copies, or the copies of the first copies. What we have are copies made much later—in most cases hundreds of years later.

Many thousands of these later copies of the New Testament survive today: by last count (as of 2011), we have some 5,800 copies in the original Greek language of the New Testament. This number includes not only complete copies of all the books of the New Testament, but also fragmentary copies with just a few verses on them. Some of these smaller fragments are no larger than a credit card. Among all the surviving copies, some very few were produced in the second and third centuries: our earliest is a scrap containing portions of verses from the Gospel of John, just 30–40 years after the book's original composition. We begin to get more numerous copies of the New Testament in the fourth and later centuries. By far the vast majority of our copies come from the ninth century and later.

This means that even though we have lots of copies of the New Testament—more copies than for any other book from antiquity—we do not have very many *early* copies. That is a problem because there are so many differences among the copies that we do have. These differences show convincingly that scribes occasionally changed the words they were copying. Some scribes changed them rarely, others far more frequently. How often were the words of the New Testament changed? The reality is that no one knows: no one has yet been able to count all the differences among our manuscripts. What is striking is that of the 5,800 or so Greek copies of the New Testament that we have, no two of them are exactly alike in all their details. Some scholars have estimated that among these copies there are some 200,000 differences—most of them minor, but some of them quite significant. Other scholars suggest that there are 300,000 differences, or 400,000, or more. But possibly it is easiest to

Figure 1.2 This is an image of several pages of P⁴⁵, the earliest surviving (though fragmentary) copy of the Gospel of Luke, from the early third century.

put the matter in comparative terms: there are more differences in our manuscripts that there are words in the New Testament.

It should be of some comfort to learn, however, that the vast majority of the differences in our manuscripts are insignificant, immaterial, and do not matter for anything. A large number of them simply show that scribes in antiquity could spell no better than most people can today (every change of spelling of a word counts as a difference). Scribes sometimes not only misspelled words, they also accidentally left out words, or lines, or entire pages; other times they copied the same words or lines twice. At other times they changed the text not by accident but because they wanted to do so, adding a verse or even an entire story that they thought would "improve" the text or taking away a verse or removing a passage that they thought was difficult to understand. In some instances, these were important passages.

Our Gospel of Mark today, for example, ends with twelve verses in which Jesus appears to his disciples after he was raised from the dead (without these verses, the disciples would never come to believe in the resurrection in Mark's Gospel). Those verses are missing from some of our earliest and most important manuscripts, however.

Scholars today almost universally think that a later scribe added the entire passage (see box 5.6). Or as another example: one of the most familiar stories of the Gospels is from the Gospel of John, the story of Jesus and the woman taken in adultery, where Jesus says his famous words: "Let the one without sin among you be the first to cast a stone at her." But this story is not found in the earliest and best manuscripts of the Gospel. Here again, scholars are thoroughly unified in thinking that one or more scribes added the story to the Gospel (see box 8.3). So, too, with the one passage of the New Testament that explicitly states the doctrine of the Trinity (that there are three beings who are God, but the three are One) is undoubtedly a later addition to the text (1 John 5:7–8; see box 1.5). This is also the case in the one passage where Jesus, before being arrested, is said to have been "sweating blood" (Luke 22:43–44; see box 7.5). A good many more significant changes could be mentioned. What is somewhat more daunting is the fact that in a number of instances we simply do not *know* what the original text said, because the evidence can be interpreted in various ways.

The problem scholars have, then, is this: since we do not have any of the earliest copies of the NT books (say, copies of copies of the originals—let

ANOTHER GLIMPSE INTO THE PAST

BOX 1.5　Is The Doctrine of the Trinity Explicitly Taught in the New Testament?

Theologians have pointed to a number of passages in the New Testament to support their view that God is triune: three persons—the Father, Son, and Holy Spirit—who are together only *one* God. This doctrine of the Trinity, however, is never explicitly stated in the Bible—except in some late manuscripts of one intriguing passage: 1 John 5:7–8. Throughout the Latin Middle Ages, it was thought that this text read as follows: "There are three that bear witness in heaven, the Father, the Word, and the Holy Spirit, and these three are one." There it is! The doctrine of the Trinity. But this passage was found only in Latin manuscripts, not in Greek manuscripts of the New Testament (except manuscripts from after the fifteenth century, that may have taken the passage from the Latin).

When the first edition of the *Greek New Testament* was published in 1516, its editor, a scholar named Erasmus, did not include this verse, to the outrage of his theological enemies, who maintained that he had maliciously removed the Trinity from the Bible. Erasmus replied that he could not find the passage in any of the Greek manuscripts that he knew. And then, as the story goes, he went on to make an incautious challenge: he told his opponents that if they could produce a Greek manuscript with the passage, he would include it in his next edition of the New Testament. In response, his opponents, literally, *produced* a manuscript—or, at least, had one produced! Someone copied out the book of 1 John in Greek and added the passage and then presented it to Erasmus. True to his word, Erasmus included the passage in his next edition. And it was this edition that was ultimately at the foundation of the King James Translation that became so important for the history of the Bible in English. The verse is still found in the King James Bible, even though it is not found in more recent and more reliable translations. And that's why an older generation of English Bible readers assumed that the Bible explicitly taught the doctrine of the Trinity, even though the passage was not found in *any* Greek manuscript for well over a thousand years.

AT A GLANCE

BOX 1.6　The New Testament Canon

1. Early Christianity was not the unified monolith that modern people sometimes assume. It was, in fact, extremely diverse.

2. This diversity was manifest in a wide range of writings, only some of which have come down to us in the New Testament.

3. The New Testament canon was formed by Christians who wanted to show that their views were grounded in the writings of Jesus' own apostles.

4. Whether these writings actually represented the views of Jesus' own apostles, however, was in some instances debated for decades, even centuries.

5. A historical approach to these writings allows each book to speak for itself, without assuming they are all saying the same thing.

6. This approach will allow us to see the diversity of early Christianity more clearly, already in its earliest writings.

alone the originals themselves), and since all the copies that we do have contain mistakes and changes, we have to try to reconstruct what the authors of the New Testament originally wrote. In most instances, scholars are unified in thinking that the author probably wrote a verse in this or

that way. But in other instances, we simply do not know—or at least, scholars do not agree. This is one of the many issues that we will be dealing with throughout our study, as we try to understand the New Testament and the message that it delivered to its original audience.

EXCURSUS

Some Additional Reflections: The Historian and the Believer

Most of the people interested in the New Testament, at least in modern American culture, are Christians who have been taught that it is the inspired word of God. If you yourself belong to this camp, then you may find the historical perspective that I have mapped out in this chapter somewhat difficult to accept, in that it may seem to stand at odds with what you have been taught to believe (for example, about how we got our canon of the New Testament). If so, then it is for you in particular that I want to provide these brief additional reflections.

Here is the question: how can a Christian who is committed to the Bible affirm that its authors have a wide range of perspectives, and that they sometimes disagree with one another? I can address the question by stressing that this book is a historical introduction to the early Christian writings, principally those found in the New Testament, rather than a confessional one. This is an important distinction because the New Testament has always been much more than a book for Christian believers. It is also an important cultural artifact, a collection of writings that stands at the foundation of much of our Western civilization and heritage. These books came into existence at a distant point in time and have been transmitted through the ages until today. In other words, in addition to being documents of faith, these books are rooted in history; they were written in particular historical contexts and have always been read within particular historical contexts. For this reason, they can be studied not only by believers for their theological significance but also by historians (whether or not they happen to be believers) for their historical significance.

Historians deal with past events that are matters of the public record. The public record consists of human actions and world events—things that anyone can see or experience. Historians try to reconstruct what probably happened in the past on the basis of data that can be examined and evaluated by every interested observer of every persuasion. Access to these data does not depend on presuppositions or beliefs about God. This means that historians, as historians, have no privileged access to what happens in the supernatural realm; they have access only to what happens in this, our natural world. The historian's conclusions should, in theory, be accessible and acceptable to everyone, whether the person is a Hindu, a Buddhist, a Muslim, a Jew, a Christian, an atheist, a pagan, or anything else.

To illustrate the point: historians can tell you the similarities and differences between the worldviews of Mohandas Gandhi and Martin Luther King Jr., but they cannot use their historical knowledge to tell you that Gandhi's belief in God was wrong or that Martin Luther King's was right. This judgment is not part of the public record and depends on theological assumptions and personal beliefs that are not shared by everyone conducting the investigation. Historians can describe to you what happened during the conflicts between Catholics and Lutherans in sixteenth-century Germany; they cannot use their historical knowledge to tell you which side God was on. Likewise, historians can explain what probably happened at Jesus' crucifixion, but they cannot use their historical knowledge to tell you that he was crucified for the sins of the world.

(continued)

EXCURSUS *(continued)*

Does that mean that historians cannot be believers? No, it means that if historians tell you that Martin Luther King Jr. had a better theology than Gandhi, or that God was on the side of the Protestants instead of the Catholics, or that Jesus was crucified for the sins of the world, they are telling you this not in their capacity as historians but in their capacity as believers. Believers are interested in knowing about God, about how to behave, about what to believe, about the ultimate meaning of life. The historical disciplines cannot supply them with this kind of information. Historians who work within the constraints of this discipline are limited to describing, to the best of their abilities, what probably happened in the past.

Many such historians, including a large number of those mentioned in the bibliographies scattered throughout this book, find historical research to be completely compatible with—even crucial for—traditional theological beliefs; others find it to be incompatible. This is an issue that you yourself may want to deal with, as you grapple intelligently with how the historical approach to the New Testament affects positively, negatively, or not at all your faith commitments. I should be clear at the outset,

though, that as the author of this book, I will neither tell you how to resolve this issue nor urge you to adopt any particular set of theological convictions. My approach instead will be strictly historical, trying to understand the writings of the early Christians from the standpoint of the professional historian who uses whatever evidence happens to survive in order to reconstruct what probably happened in the past.

That is to say, I am not going to convince you either to believe or to disbelieve the Gospel of John; I will describe how it came into existence and discuss what its message was. I am not going to persuade you that Jesus really was or was not the Son of God; I will try to establish what he said and did based on the historical data that are available. I am not going to discuss whether the Bible is or is not the inspired word of God; I will show how we got this collection of books and indicate what they say and reflect on how scholars have interpreted them. This kind of information may well be of some use to the reader who happens to be a believer; but it will certainly be useful to one—believer or not—who is interested in history, especially the history of early Christianity and its literature.

TAKE A STAND

1. You are discussing religion with your roommate, who tells you that Christians have always had the same New Testament from day one, that all Christians have always considered the same twenty-seven books as *the* books of the New Testament since the beginning of the church. How do you respond?

2. A classmate informs you that since there are so many copies of the New Testament available today, we can know for certain what the authors originally wrote. Do you agree or not? State your reasons.

3. You are in the undergraduate library and you overhear two people in an argument about the Bible. One student is insisting that no one can really understand the New Testament except a Christian who believes in it, the other is claiming that it is possible for anyone to understand it from a historical perspective. What view do you take, and why?

SUGGESTIONS FOR FURTHER READING

Bauer, Walter. *Orthodoxy and Heresy in Earliest Christianity.* Trans. Robert Kraft et al. Ed. Robert Kraft and Gerhard Krodel. Philadelphia: Fortress, 1971. The classic study of the wide-ranging diversity of second- and third-century Christianity, suitable only for more advanced students.

Dunn, James D. G. *Unity and Diversity in the New Testament: An Inquiry into the Character of Earliest Christianity,* 3d ed. London: SCM Press, 2006. A very informative discussion that applies Bauer's view of early Christian diversity to the New Testament itself; highly recommended for students who have already completed a course in New Testament.

Ehrman, Bart D. *Lost Christianities: The Battles for Scripture and the Faiths We Never Knew.* New York: Oxford University Press, 2003. An examination of the early conflicts among various Christian groups (Ebionites, Marcionites, Gnostics, proto-orthodox) and the various "Scriptures" they produced—including noncanonical Gospels, Acts, Epistles, and Apocalypses. For popular audiences.

Ehrman, Bart D. *Lost Scriptures: Books that Did Not Make It Into the New Testament.* New York: Oxford University Press, 2003. Translations, with brief introductions, of various writings that were considered scripture by some early Christian groups but that eventually were not included in the canon.

Ehrman, Bart D. *Misquoting Jesus: The Story Behind Who Changed the Bible and Why.* San Francisco: HarperSanFrancisco. 2006. A popular discussion of the changes found in our surviving manuscripts of the New Testament, and of scholars' efforts to find the "original" text.

Gamble, Harry. *The New Testament Canon: Its Making and Meaning.* Eugene, Ore.: Wipf and Stock, 2002. A clearly written and informative overview of the formation of the New Testament canon.

Jefford, Clayton. *Reading the Apostolic Fathers: An Introduction.* Grand Rapids, Mich.: Baker, 1996. An introduction to the writings of the Apostolic Fathers; suitable for beginning-level students.

Lewis, Nicola Denzey. *Introduction to "Gnosticism": Ancient Voices, Christian Worlds.* New York: Oxford University Press, 2012. A full discussion of the "gnostic" writings discovered near Nag Hammadi, Egypt, in 1945; for beginning-level students.

Metzger, Bruce M. *The Canon of the New Testament: Its Origin, Development and Significance.* Oxford: Clarendon Press, 1987. The authoritative discussion of the formation of the canon, for advanced students.

KEY TERMS

Acts of the Apostles	B.C.E., Before the	epistles	Jewish Scriptures
apocalypse	Common Era	Gospel	Nag Hammadi
Apocrypha	canon	Hebrew Bible	Old Testament
Apostolic Fathers	C.E., Common Era	heresy	scribes
Athanasius			

2

The Environment of Early Christian Traditions

THE GRECO-ROMAN WORLD

WHAT TO EXPECT

You can't understand something if you take it out of its context. And so we begin our study by situating the New Testament in its own world, rather than assuming that it fits neatly into ours. This chapter explores the ancient Greco-Roman world in which the New Testament was written, with special emphasis on religions in that world.

THE PROBLEM OF BEGINNINGS

Where does one begin a study of the New Testament? One might be inclined to begin with the Gospel of Matthew. This, however, is probably not the best choice: even though Matthew is the first book in the canon, it was not the first to be written. Indeed, as we will see later, it was probably not even the first Gospel to be written.

The first New Testament book to be written was probably 1 Thessalonians, one of the letters penned by the apostle Paul. For this reason, some teachers begin their courses on the New Testament with the life and writings of Paul. While this choice makes better sense than beginning with Matthew, it has problems of its own. Paul lived after Jesus and based many of his teachings on his belief in Jesus' death and resurrection. Would it not make better sense, then, to begin with the life and teachings of Jesus?

The problem with beginning with Jesus is that we do not have any writings from him, and the Gospels that record his words and deeds were written long after the fact, indeed, even after Paul. To be sure, during Paul's lifetime Christians were talking—and some perhaps even writing—about Jesus, telling what he said and did, recounting his conflicts, and explaining his fate. Unfortunately, we do not have direct access to these older traditions. We know them only insofar as they were written down later, especially in the Gospels. This means, somewhat ironically, that if we want to begin with the earliest and most important figure in the New Testament, we have to start with documents that were written relatively late.

But this is not the only problem with beginning our study with the traditions about Jesus. What is even more problematic is that these first-century traditions do not "translate" easily into the twenty-first century, where our commonsense assumptions, worldviews, values, and priorities are quite different from those shared by the early followers of Jesus. Contrary to what many people think, it is very difficult for us today to understand the original meanings of the sayings of Jesus and the stories about him. This is one reason why modern people have such deeply rooted disagreements over how to interpret the New Testament. It comes from a different world. And many of the ideas and attitudes and values that we take for granted today as common sense would have made no sense in that world; that is, they would have been "nonsense."

In the early Christian world, there was no such thing as a middle class as we know it, let alone a Protestant work ethic, with all of its promises of education and prosperity for those who labor hard. In that world, only a few persons belonged to the upper class; nearly everyone else was in the lower. Few people had any hope for social mobility, slaves made up perhaps a third of the total population in major urban areas, and many of the poor were worse off than the enslaved. There were no cures for most diseases. Many babies died, and adult women had to bear, on average, five children simply to keep the population constant. Most people were uneducated, and 90 percent could not read. Travel was slow and dangerous, and long trips were rare; most people never ventured far from home during their lives. In the world of early Christianity, everyone, except most Jews, believed in a multiplicity of gods; they knew that divine beings of all sorts were constantly involved with their everyday lives, bringing rain, health, and peace—or their opposites.

People living in the ancient world would have understood the stories about Jesus in light of these realities. This applies not only to how they reacted to these stories and integrated them into their own worldviews but even to how, on the very basic level, they understood what the stories meant. For you can understand something only in light of what you already know.

Let me illustrate the point through a modern example. When I was in college in the 1970s, I drove an Austin Healey Sprite. Today this fact does not impress most of my students, who have never heard of an Austin Healey Sprite. If I want to explain to them what it was, I have to do so in terms

that they already know. I usually begin by telling them that the Sprite was the same car as the MG Midget. What if they have never heard of a Midget? I tell them that it was a 1970s version of the BMW Z4. This is a car they generally know. If they don't, I might tell them that the Sprite was a sports car. What if they don't know what that is? I explain: it's a small two-seat convertible that sits low to the ground and is generally considered sporty. What if they don't know what a convertible is or a two-seater? What if they don't know what a car is? "Well, a car is like a horseless carriage." My explanation, however, assumes that they know what carriages are and what relation horses generally have to them. And if they don't?

My point is that we can understand something only in light of what we already know. Imagine how you yourself might explain an elephant to someone who had never seen one, or a roller coaster, or a kumquat. What, though, has any of this to do with the New Testament? For one thing, it explains why I think that the most sensible place to begin our study is with the life of a famous man who lived nearly 2,000 years ago in a remote part of the Roman Empire.

ONE REMARKABLE LIFE

From the beginning his mother knew that he was no ordinary person. Prior to his birth, a heavenly figure appeared to her, announcing that her son would not be a mere mortal but would himself be divine. This prophecy was confirmed by the miraculous character of his birth, a birth accompanied by supernatural signs. The boy was already recognized as a spiritual authority in his youth; his discussions with recognized experts showed his superior knowledge of all things religious. As an adult he left home to engage in an itinerant preaching ministry. He went from village to town with his message of good news, proclaiming that people should forgo their concerns for the material things of this life, such as how to dress and what to eat. They should instead be concerned with their eternal souls.

He gathered around him a number of disciples who were amazed by his teaching and his flawless character. They became convinced that he was no

ANOTHER GLIMPSE INTO THE PAST

BOX 2.1 Pagan and Gentile

Throughout our discussions I will be using the terms **"pagan"** and **"Gentile."** When historians use the term "pagan," they do not assign negative connotations to it (as you may do when using it in reference, say, to your roommate or next-door neighbor). When used of the Greco-Roman world, the term simply designates a person who subscribed to any of the polythe-istic religions, that is, anyone who was neither a Jew nor a Christian. The term "paganism," then, refers to the wide range of ancient polytheistic religions other than Judaism and Christianity. The term "Gentile" designates someone who is not a Jew, whether the person is pagan or Christian. It, too, carries no negative connotations.

ordinary man but was the Son of God. Their faith received striking confirmation in the miraculous things that he did. He could reportedly predict the future, heal the sick, cast out demons, and raise the dead. Not everyone proved friendly, however. At the end of his life, his enemies trumped up charges against him, and he was placed on trial before Roman authorities for crimes against the state.

Even after he departed this realm, however, he did not forsake his devoted followers. Some claimed that he had ascended bodily into heaven; others said that he had appeared to them, alive, afterward, that they had talked with him and touched him and become convinced that he could not be bound by death. A number of his followers spread the good news about this man, recounting what they had seen him say and do. Eventually some of these accounts came to be written down in books that circulated throughout the empire.

But I doubt that you have ever read them. In fact, I suspect you have never heard the name of this miracle-working "Son of God." The man I have been referring to is the great neo-Pythagorean teacher and pagan (see box 2.1) holy man of the first century C.E., **Apollonius of Tyana**, a worshiper of the Roman gods, whose life and teachings are still available for us in the writings of his later (third-century) follower Philostratus, in his book *The Life of Apollonius.*

Apollonius lived at about the time of Jesus. Even though they never met, the reports about their lives were in many ways similar. At a later time, Jesus' followers argued that Jesus was the miracle-working Son of God, and that Apollonius was an impostor, a magician, and a fraud. Perhaps not surprisingly, Apollonius's followers made just the opposite claim, asserting that he was the miracle-working Son of God, and that Jesus was a fraud.

What is remarkable is that these were not the only two persons in the Greco-Roman world who were thought to have been supernaturally endowed as teachers and miracle workers. In fact,

Figure 2.1 A Roman coin from around the time of Jesus, with the likeness of Caesar Augustus and a Latin inscription, "Augustus, Son of the Divinized Caesar." If Julius Caesar, the adopted father of Augustus, was a god, what does that make Augustus?

we know from the tantalizing but fragmentary records that have survived that numerous other persons were also said to have performed miracles, to have calmed the storm and multiplied the loaves, to have told the future and healed the sick, to have cast out demons and raised the dead, to have been supernaturally born and taken up into heaven at the end of their life. Even though Jesus may be the only miracle-working Son of God that we know about in our world, he was one of many talked about in the first century.

Clearly, then, if we want to study the early traditions told about Jesus, traditions that are our only access to the man himself, we have to begin by situating them in their original context in the Greco-Roman world (see box 2.2). The stories about Jesus

---

ANOTHER GLIMPSE INTO THE PAST

BOX 2.2   The Greco-Roman World

The "Greco-Roman world" is a term that historians use to describe the lands surrounding the Mediterranean from the time of **Alexander the Great** through the first three or four centuries of the Roman Empire (see box 2.3).

Alexander was arguably the most significant world conqueror in the history of Western civilization. Born in 356 B.C.E., he succeeded to the throne of Macedonia as a twenty year old when his father, King Philip II, was assassinated. Alexander was single-minded in his desire to conquer the lands of the eastern Mediterranean. A brilliant military strategist, he quickly and boldly—some would say ruthlessly—overran Greece to the south and drove his armies along the coastal regions of Asia Minor (modern-day Turkey) to the East, into Palestine (as the land of "Israel" came to be known in antiquity), and then into Egypt. He finally marched into the heart of the Persian Empire, overthrowing the Persian monarch Darius and extending his territories as far away as modern-day India.

Alexander is particularly significant in the history of Western civilization because of his decision to impress a kind of cultural unity upon the conquered lands of the eastern Mediterranean. In his youth he had been trained in Greece by the great philosopher Aristotle and became convinced that Greek culture was superior to all others. As a conqueror he actively promoted the use of the Greek language throughout his domain and built Greek-style cities, with gymnasiums, theaters, and public baths, to serve as administrative and commercial centers. Moreover, he generally encouraged the adoption of Greek culture and religion throughout his cities, especially among the upper classes. Historians have named this cultural process "Hellenization," after the Greek word for Greece, *Hellas*.

Upon Alexander's untimely death at the age of thirty-three (323 B.C.E.), his realm was divided among his leading generals. During their reigns and those of their successors, Hellenism (i.e., Greek culture) continued to flourish in major urban centers around the eastern Mediterranean (less so in rural areas). Throughout this period, as political boundaries shifted and kings and kingdoms came and went, a person could travel from one part of Alexander's former domain to the other and still communicate with the local inhabitants by speaking the lingua franca of the day, Greek. Moreover, such a person could feel relatively at home in most major cities, amidst Greek customs, institutions, traditions, and religions. Thus, more than at any time in previous history, the eastern Mediterranean that emerged in Alexander's wake experienced a form of cultural unity and cosmopolitanism (a "cosmopolite" is a "citizen of the world," as opposed to a person who belongs only to one locality).

The Roman Empire arose in the context of the **Hellenistic world** and took full advantage of its unity, promoting the use of the Greek language, accepting aspects of Greek culture, and even taking over features of the Greek religion, to the point that the Greek and Roman gods came to be thought of as the same, only with different names. This complex unity achieved culturally through **Hellenization** and politically through the conquests of Rome is summed up by the term *Greco-Roman world*.

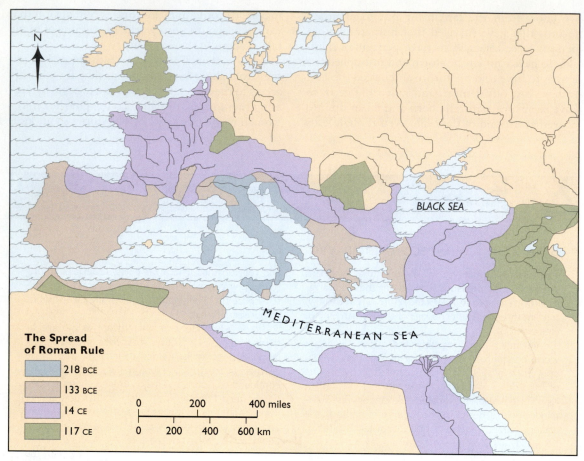

Figure 2.2 The Spread of Roman Rule.

were told among people who could make sense of them, and the sense they made of them in a world populated with divine beings may have been different from the sense that we make of them in our foreign world.

We will begin our reflections by discussing ancient "pagan" religions (see box 2.1), since it was primarily among pagans that Christians told most of their stories and acquired most of their converts when the books of the New Testament were being written. We will then turn to consider early Judaism, one of the distinctive religions of the Greco-Roman world, the religion of the earliest Christians and of Jesus himself.

THE ENVIRONMENT OF THE NEW TESTAMENT: RELIGIONS IN THE GRECO-ROMAN WORLD

Greco-Roman Religiosity: A Basic Sketch

Odd as it may seem, to understand the nature and function of religion in the Greco-Roman world, we have to abandon almost all our own notions about religion today. What do twenty-first-century Americans think of when they think about organized religion? The following list is by no means exhaustive, but it does include a number of popular notions held by many people in our society (although not by all people, of course, for our world is fantastically diverse):

1. Religious organization and hierarchy (e.g., the Christian denominations and their leaders, whether a pope, a Methodist bishop, or the leader of the Southern Baptist convention)
2. Doctrinal statements (e.g., the creeds said in churches, the basic beliefs endorsed by all believers)
3. Ethical commitments (i.e., religiously motivated guidelines for conducting one's daily interactions with others)
4. Sacred written authorities (e.g., the Hebrew Bible or the New Testament or the Koran)
5. Beliefs about the afterlife (which for some people in our time is *the* reason for being religious)
6. The separation of church and state (an important element in American politics *and* religion)
7. Exclusive commitments (e.g., a member of a Baptist church cannot also be a Hare Krishna, just as a practicing Jew cannot be a Mormon)

One of the most striking and startling aspects of ancient religion is that outside Judaism, none of these features applies. In the so-called pagan religions of the Roman Empire, there were no national or international religious organizations with elected or appointed leaders who had jurisdiction over the various local cults. There were no creedal statements or, indeed, any necessary articles of faith whatsoever for devotees. Whereas ethics were generally as important to people then as they are today, daily ethical demands played virtually no role in the practice of religion itself. Pagan religions were never centered on sacred writings to guide the individual's beliefs and practices. Many people evidently did not hold a firm belief in life after death; those who did, so far as we can tell, did not generally become more religious as a result. And there was no such thing as separation of church and state; on the contrary, since the gods made the state great, the state responded by encouraging and sponsoring the worship of the gods. Finally, virtually no one in the pagan world argued that if you

worshiped one god, you could not also worship another: exclusive adherence to one cult was practically unknown.

How can we fathom a set of religions so different from our own? Since we can only understand something in light of what we already know, we can begin by considering a series of contrasts between modern and ancient religions, somewhat along the lines I have already laid out.

Polytheism Instead of Monotheism. Modern religions in the West (Judaism, Christianity, and Islam) are **monotheistic**, advocating belief in one Divine Being. For most modern Westerners, it is simply common sense to think that (if God exists) there is one God and only one God. For persons in the ancient world, however, this was nonsense. Everyone knew that there were many gods, of all sorts and descriptions, of all functions and locations: gods of the field and forest, gods of the rivers and streams, gods of the household and courtyard, gods of the crops and weather, gods of healing, gods of fertility, gods of war, gods of love.

The belief in many gods came down from prehistoric times; in the Greco-Roman world, nearly everybody took their existence for granted. Not that everybody worshiped the same gods. On the contrary, many gods were localized deities of a certain place or a certain family. With the conquest of villages, towns, and countries by other villages, towns, and countries, local gods sometimes spread to other regions, occasionally becoming national or international. Sometimes conquered peoples would accept the gods of their conquerors, either by substituting them for their own (since the gods of the victors were, after all, demonstrably more powerful), by using the new names for their old gods (which is simply another mode of substitution), or by adding the new gods to those that they already worshiped.

There were of course the "Great Gods" who were worshiped throughout different portions of the Mediterranean. These included the gods mentioned by the ancient poets Homer and Hesiod. The writings of these ancients—for example, Homer's *Iliad* and *Odyssey*—were not considered to be some kind of Scriptural authority in the way the Bible was for Jews and later for Christians, but they were good stories that people told and enjoyed hearing, even if they did sometimes portray the gods in a somewhat unfavorable light as conducting themselves in wild and capricious ways.

How did the average person understand the relationship of the great gods to those of their own locality? Recent scholarship has shown that in the Greco-Roman world, the divine realm was seen as a kind of pyramid of power, with the few but mightiest god(s) at the top and the more numerous but less powerful deities at the bottom (see figure 2.3). Some of the most highly educated thinkers—for example, philosophers and their students—maintained that at the very peak of the pyramid was one almighty God, whether understood to be the Greek Zeus, the Roman Jupiter, or some unknown and unknowable God, so powerful as to be beyond human comprehension. This God was ultimately responsible for the world and for all that happens in it; ironically, however, he was so powerful that he was all but inaccessible to mere mortals.

The pyramid's next tier represented the powerful gods worshiped in different localities throughout the empire. Among Greek people, these gods would include Poseidon, Hera, Aphrodite, Artemis, Dionysus, and others of Greek myth; in Roman circles they would be identified by their Latin names: Neptune, Juno, Venus, Diana, and Bacchus. These gods were thought to be incredibly powerful and altogether worthy of worship and praise. Many of them were associated with significant functions of human society. For example, Ares (Latin Mars) was the god of war, Aphrodite (Venus) was the god-

dess of love, and Dionysus (Bacchus) was the god of wine.

Below this tier was another inhabited by lesser gods, including the local deities who had more limited powers (although they were still far beyond anything humans could imagine) but who were in more direct contact with human affairs. Included on this tier were the *daimonia*. This Greek term is hard to translate into English. The cognate term "demons" carries the wrong connotation altogether, for the *daimonia* were not evil fallen angels who temporarily inhabited human bodies, forcing them to do all sorts of nasty things. To be sure, some of them were dangerous, but for the most part they were relatively indifferent to human activities and so had to be persuaded, through cultic acts, to behave in ways that would lead to benefit rather than harm.

In addition, most people had their own family gods—for example, in Roman religion, each household worshiped divine beings called Penates, who had oversight of the pantry and foodstuffs, as well as deities called Lares (sometimes thought of as the spirits of the family's ancestors), who protected the house and its inhabitants, and each family had a personal deity, a kind of guardian angel called a "genius," thought to reside in the head of the household. Family gods were regularly represented through household shrines (see figure 2.4) and worshiped through prayers and simple acts of piety.

Finally, on the bottom level of the divine pyramid was a range of divine beings who more or less bridged the gap between mortals and the gods. Included here were humans who, at their deaths, had been divinized (i.e., made immortal, like the gods). These were typically great men, philosophers or warriors, whose extraordinary deeds won them special favors from the gods at death as well as in life. Also found here were demigods, individuals said to have been born to the union of a god or goddess with a mortal, as found, for instance, in a number of Greek and Roman myths and folktales. This final category is of particular interest for us because it included select human beings who were widely believed to have been far more than human, including great philosophers like Pythagoras, whose wisdom was thought by some to be inexplicable if merely human; powerful athletes like

Figure 2.3 The Divine Pyramid as Understood in Greco-Roman Religion.

The
One God

The Great Gods

Daimonia, local gods, etc.

Divine beings, demigods, immortals, heroes

Humans

Figure 2.4 Inhabitants of the Greco-Roman world worshiped a variety of gods in their homes; here is a shrine that depicts the family's guardian spirit (genius), flanked by two household gods (lares), with a snake representing a divinity.

Heracles, whose strength was far beyond the mere mortal; and great rulers like Alexander of Macedonia, whose power to affect human lives was nearly divine.

Some people considered the Roman emperor to be this kind of divine being. He was not the one God, or even one of the Olympians. Indeed, from the divine perspective he was very much a subordinate. But from the human point of view, he was fantastically powerful, himself divine, and for some inhabitants of the empire worthy of worship and praise. Also included among such beings were Apollonius of Tyana and other so-called sons of God, whose supernatural teachings and miraculous deeds demonstrated their divine lineage.

Pagans who heard stories about Jesus and his miracles would have had no difficulty understanding what they meant. Among other things, they meant that Jesus was himself divine, a divine man come to earth.

Present Life Instead of Afterlife. Many people in the modern world are motivated in their religious commitments by a belief in the afterlife. Fear-ing eternal torment or longing for eternal bliss, they turn to religion as a way of securing happiness after death.

This view would have made little sense to most people in the ancient world. Recent studies of ancient gravestone inscriptions, in fact, suggest that whereas some people subscribed to a notion of the afterlife, as we will see later when we consider the mystery cults, the majority did not. (One of the most common abbreviations on Roman tombstones [like our R.I.P. = "Rest in Peace"] was a six-letter code that stood for the Latin phrase "I was not, I am not, I care not"!) Moreover, of those who did, most believed that it involved some kind of vague shadowy existence that was to be postponed as long as possible at all costs, a netherworld to which all people were destined, whether moral or immoral, faithful or unfaithful. And yet nearly everyone in the ancient world believed in the gods and participated in religion.

For most ancient persons, religion was not the way to guarantee an afterlife; it was a way to secure life in the here and now. For the majority of people in the ancient world, life was constantly lived on the edge. There was nothing like modern medication to prevent and cure disease; a tooth abscess would frequently prove fatal. There were no modern surgical methods and only primitive forms of anesthesia; women often died in childbirth, and simple operations could be hellish nightmares. There were no modern methods of agriculture and limited possibilities for irrigation; a minor drought one year could lead to a poor village's starvation the next. There were no modern modes of transportation: in rural areas, food distribution was limited at best. War, famine, disease, poverty—the eternal blights of the human race—were constant and perennial concerns of ancient persons. And, of course, all the anxieties of personal relations were very much alive as well; ancient persons too knew the tragic loss of a child or friend, fear for personal safety, unrequited love.

In a world that is helpless against the elements, the gods play a major role. They supply rain for the crops, fertility for the animals, children for the family. They bring victory in war and prosperity in peace. They heal the sick and comfort the downtrodden. They provide security and hope and love.

Figure 2.5 Many inhabitants of the Roman Empire offered worship to the "genius" (ruling spirit) of the emperor as god, as seen in this depiction of a sacrifice taken from an altar before the temple of the emperor Vespasian in Pompeii. Notice the priest on the right holding a sledgehammer with which to stun the sacrificial bull before another priest slices its throat.

These are things beyond the control of mere mortals; they can come only from the gods.

Cultic Acts Rather than Doctrine. But how could the powerful and immortal gods be influenced to provide what was needed in this life? The gods were not impressed by anyone's beliefs about them, nor did they require people to say the proper creed or acknowledge the proper "truths." Odd as this may seem to us moderns, doctrine played virtually no role in these religions: it scarcely mattered what people believed. What mattered was how people showed their devotion to the gods. The gods wanted to be worshiped through proper cultic acts.

The English term **"cult"** derives from the Latin term for "care." The ancient concept of *cultus deorum* thus referred to the "care of the gods" (cf.

the English word "agriculture," meaning the "care of the fields"). How, then, did one "care" for the gods? How did one attend to them so as to secure their favor? For the ancient person the answer was simple: through prayer and sacrifice. Local and family deities had their own established cults. Daily cultic acts might involve pouring out a little wine before a meal in honor of one of the family gods or saying a prayer for favor. Periodic festivals would be celebrated in which a group of worshipers would sacrifice an animal, or have a local priest do so, while set prayers were spoken. The inedible parts of the animal would be burned to the god, the rest would be prepared and eaten by the participants in a picnic-like atmosphere.

Throughout the empire, special festival days were set aside for the worship of the state gods.

ANOTHER GLIMPSE INTO THE PAST

BOX 2.3   The Roman Empire

The traditional date for the founding of Rome is 753 B.C.E. Rome began as a small farming village that grew over time into a city spread over a large area that included the "seven hills of Rome." For nearly 250 years Rome was ruled by local kings, whose abuses led to their ouster in 510 B.C.E. For nearly half a millenium thereafter, Rome was a republic governed by an aristocratic oligarchy called the Senate, which was made up of the wealthiest and most influential members of its highest class.

As it refined its political and legislative systems, Rome also grew strong militarily, eventually conquering and colonizing the entire Italian peninsula and then, after three protracted wars against the city of Carthage in North Africa, known as the Punic Wars (264–241 B.C.E., 218–202 B.C.E., and 149–146 B.C.E.), acquiring control of the entire Mediterranean region.

The late republic period saw an increasing number of internal struggles for power, many of them violent, as prominent generals and politicians attempted to seize control of the government. When **Julius Caesar** tried to become a dictator, he was assassinated in 44 B.C.E. The Republic (ruled by the Senate) was not finally transformed into an empire (ruled by an emperor) until Caesar's great-nephew and adopted son **Octavian**, a wealthy aristocrat and Rome's most successful general, brought a bloody end to the civil wars that had racked the city. Octavian assumed full control in the year 27 B.C.E.

Even after this time, the Senate continued to exist and to oversee aspects of the immense Roman bureaucracy, which included the governance of provinces that eventually stretched from Spain to Syria. Official posts were sometimes delegated to members of the "equestrian" class as well. These persons had a lower rank and less wealth than senators, but they were nonetheless members of the landed aristocracy. But with the inauguration of the reign of Octavian, who soon assumed the name Caesar Augustus (roughly meaning "the most revered emperor"), there was one ultimate ruler over Rome, an emperor who wielded virtually supreme power. Emperors who succeeded Caesar Augustus after his death in 14 C.E. were of various temperaments and abilities. For the period of our study, they include the following:

Tiberius (14–37 C.E.)

Caligula (37–41 C.E.)

Claudius (41–54 C.E.)

Nero (54–68 C.E.)

Four different emperors in the tumultuous year of 68–69 C.E. included, finally,

Vespasian (69–79 C.E.)

Titus (79–81 C.E.)

Domitian (81–96 C.E.)

Nerva (96–98 C.E.)

Trajan (98–117 C.E.)

Hadrian (117–138 C.E.)

These were the powerful gods who had shown favor to Rome and made it great. People worshiped them to secure their continued favor and patronage. Great celebrations in the capital city itself would follow standard rituals by priests trained in the sacred traditions, who would perform the required sacrifices and say the established prayers in precisely the same way year after year. The Romans generally assumed that if religious practices worked, they must be right and must be retained. That they did work was plain for all to see—in the grandeur and power of Rome itself.

Moreover, it was possible to know for certain whether a particular cultic act had proved acceptable to the gods, for the gods would say so. One of the standard religious practices of the Romans that seems most bizarre to modern persons involved the art of "extispicy"—the reading of a sacrificial animal's entrails (Latin *exta*) by a specially trained priest (a "haruspex") to determine whether the

Figure 2.6 A depiction of the practice of extispicy from an ancient altar. Notice the priest who is stooped over to examine the entrails of the recently sacrificed bull to discern whether the sacrifice has been acceptable to the gods.

god(s) had accepted the sacrifice. If the entrails were not perfect—for example, if they were not healthy, or the right size, or in the proper place—then the rite was to be performed again.

The practice of extispicy shows that Roman religion was not simply a one-way street in which the worshiper tried to placate the gods. The gods had ways of communicating with humans as well. They did so through various modes of **"divination"** (ways of discerning the divine will). Roman priests called **"augurs,"** for instance, were trained in interpreting the flights or eating habits of birds ("taking the auspices") to determine whether the gods were in favor of a projected action on the part of the state, such as a military expedition. For private direction from the god, there were sacred places called **"oracles,"** where people perplexed about their own

future could come to address a question to a god, whose priestess would enter into a trance, become filled with the divine spirit, and deliver a response, sometimes written down by an attendant, often in poetic verse. Sometimes the gods communicated by more natural means, for example, by sending a thunderclap or a dream as a sign.

Thus there was close interaction between the divine and human realms in the ancient world. The gods spoke to humans through dreams and oracles and physical signs, and humans served the gods, securing their favor through prayers and sacrifices.

Church and State Together Instead of Separated. In the Greco-Roman world there was no separation between the function of the state and the performance of religion. Quite the contrary, government and religion both functioned, theoretically, to secure the same ends of making life prosperous, meaningful, and happy. The gods brought peace and prosperity and made the state great. In turn, the state sponsored and encouraged the worship of the gods. For this reason, state priesthoods in the Roman Empire were (to use our modern terminology) political appointments. The priests of the leading priestly "colleges" in Rome were senators and other leading officials. Temples were dedicated to the gods because of great military victories, the temple staff was supplied by the state, and celebrations were overseen by the government.

The emperor encouraged the cult of the gods, and in some parts of the empire (although not in the city of Rome itself) he himself was recognized as divine. At first, emperors were worshiped only after they had died and were proclaimed by the Senate to have become divinized. Outside Rome, however, even during the New Testament period, living emperors came to be worshiped as the divine "Savior" of the empire. These divine men had brought deliverance from the evils that threatened the well-being of the state. Some of the emperors discouraged this practice, but officials in the provinces sometimes promoted it (see box 2.4). Thus, local cults devoted to the emperor existed throughout much of Asia Minor when the apostle Paul arrived with his word of the Savior Jesus. By the second century, cities throughout the empire held celebrations in which sacrifices were made on behalf of the emperor or his

"genius," that is, the divine spirit that ruled over his family (see figure 2.5).

The political implications of this kind of worship may seem clear to us, living so many centuries later. The belief that the gods were directly involved in the Roman state surely helped to secure the peace of the empire. One might rebel against a powerful mortal, but who would take up arms against a god?

Tolerance Instead of Intolerance. Because of the ill-fated experience of the early Christians, who were occasionally persecuted by the Roman authorities, many people today assume that Romans were by and large intolerant when it came to religion. Nothing could be further from the truth. Certainly, refusing to perform a sacrifice to the gods on behalf of the emperor, or refusing to throw some incense on the altar to his genius, might cause trouble. This refusal would be seen as a political statement (again, to use our modern terms), a vote of no confidence or, even worse, open defiance of the power of the state and the even greater power of the gods who made it great. Moreover, since everyone knew that there were lots of gods, all of whom deserved worship, it made little sense to refuse to take part in cultic acts.

Basic tolerance was one of the central aspects of ancient Greco-Roman religion. Unlike some forms of Christianity that eventually arose in its midst, the empire's other religions were altogether forebearing of one another. There was no reason that everyone should worship the same gods any more than everyone should have the same friends.

ANOTHER GLIMPSE INTO THE PAST

BOX 2.4 Rulers as Divine Saviors

The Roman emperor was often paid homage as a divine being, the "Savior" of the human race. Consider the following inscription set up in honor of Gaius Julius Caesar Germanicus, otherwise known to history as the emperor Caligula, by the city council of Ephesus in Asia Minor, around 38 C.E.:

The council and the people (of the Ephesians and other Greek) cities, which dwell in Asia and the nations (acknowledge) Gaius Julius, the son of Gaius Caesar, as High Priest and Absolute Ruler, . . . the God Visible who is born of (the Gods) Ares and Aphrodite, the shared Savior of human life.

All the gods deserved to be worshiped in ways appropriate to them. Thus when people visited or relocated to a new place, they would typically begin to worship the gods who were known there; sometimes they would continue to worship their own gods as well. The various religious rites were by and large tolerated; local practices were honored, and those who worshiped the state gods did not try to drive out their opposition. There was no sense of exclusivity in Greco-Roman religions, no sense that my gods are real and yours are false, that you must convert to my gods or be punished.

In conclusion, religions in the Greco-Roman world were quite different from religion as we know it today. Virtually everyone participated in religion in that world, and, with the exception of Judaism, all the religions in the Roman Empire were **polytheistic**. Those who worshiped the gods did so through prayers and cultic acts of sacrifice. Worship was thought to secure the favor of the gods, which was needed not to gain a happy afterlife but to live well and happily in the here and now. These religions were not concerned with doctrine and ethics, and none of them made any claims to being the one and only true religion. In all these respects, the religious world into which Christianity was born was remarkably dissimilar to the religious world of our day.

AT A GLANCE

BOX 2.5 The World of Early Christianity

Almost all religions in the Roman Empire were

1. Polytheistic: worshiping many gods.

2. Concerned with the present life instead of the afterlife.

3. Focused on cultic acts of worship rather than doctrines (what to believe) or ethics (how to behave).

4. Closely connected with the political state.

5. Tolerant of other religions and nonexclusivistic (i.e., none of them insisted that it was right and that all others were wrong).

TAKE A STAND

1. Suppose you are talking with a friend who insists that Jesus was completely unique: no one else in history was called the son of God, able to heal the sick, cast out demons, and raise the dead. How do you respond?

2. Pretend that you are a pagan living in the Roman world and you want to show why Christianity is an inferior religion. Make your case.

3. Your cousin tells you that the main features of every religion, past and present, are doctrine, ethics, and a belief in the afterlife. Do you agree? If not, why not?

SUGGESTIONS FOR FURTHER READING

Anthologies of Texts

Cartlidge, David R., and David L. Dungan, eds. *Documents for the Study of the Gospels.* 2d ed. Philadelphia: Fortress, 1994. Presents a valuable selection of ancient literary texts that are closely parallel to the New Testament Gospels, including portions of Philostratus's *Life of Apollonius.*

Lane, Eugene, and Ramsey MacMullen, eds. *Paganism and Christianity: 100–425 C.E.: A Sourcebook.* 3d ed. Philadelphia: Fortress, 2005. A handy anthology of ancient texts that deal specifically with religion in the Greco-Roman world.

Lefkowitz, Mary R., and Maureen B. Fant, eds. *Women's Lives in Greece and Rome: A Source Book in Translation.* 3d ed. Baltimore: Johns Hopkins University Press, 2005. A superb collection of ancient texts illuminating all the major aspects of women's lives in the Greco-Roman world.

Shelton, Jo-Ann, ed. *As the Romans Did: A Source Book in Roman Social History.* 2d ed. New York: Oxford University Press, 1998. A very useful anthology of ancient texts dealing with every major aspect of life in the Roman world, including religion.

Warrior, Valerie. *Roman Religion: A Sourcebook.* Newburyport, Mass: Focus, 2009. A helpful collection of texts dealing with every important facet of Roman religion.

Studies of Greco-Roman "Pagan" Religions

Beard, Mary, John North, and Simon Price. *Religions of Rome.* Cambridge and New York: Cambridge University Press, 1998. An up-to-date discussion of Roman religion by three eminent scholars in the field.

Howatson, M. C., ed. *Oxford Companion to Classical Literature.* 3d ed. Oxford: Oxford University Press, 2011. For quick reference to names, myths, literary works, events, and other aspects of the ancient Greek and Roman worlds, this work is an indispensable tool for beginning students.

Klauck, Hans-Joseph. *The Religious Context of Early Christianity: A Guide to Greco-Roman Religions.* Philadelphia: Fortress, 2003. An introduction to the religions of the Greco-Roman world for students of the New Testament and early Christianity.

Lane Fox, Robin. *Pagans and Christians.* New York: Alfred A. Knopf, 1987. A long but fascinating discussion of the relationship of pagans and Christians during the first centuries of Christianity, valuable especially for its brilliant sketch of what it meant to be a pagan in the second and third centuries of the Common Era.

MacMullen, Ramsey. *Paganism in the Roman Empire.* New Haven, Conn.: Yale University, 1981. An authoritative discussion of the nature of Roman religion, for somewhat more advanced students.

Rives, James. *Religion in the Roman Empire.* Malden, Mass.: Wiley-Blackwell, 2006. A clearly written and up-to-date overview of religion in the Roman world at the time of early Christianity, written by one of the world's foremost scholars in the field. An ideal place to begin for students.

 ## KEY TERMS

Alexander the Great	*daimonia*	Hellenistic world	Octavian
Apollonius of Tyana	divination	Hellenization	oracles
augurs	Gentile	Julius Caesar	pagan
cult	Greco-Roman world	monotheism	polytheism
cultus deorum			

3

The Environment of Early Christian Traditions

THE WORLD OF ANCIENT JUDAISM

WHAT TO EXPECT

In this chapter we focus on the one aspect of the context of the New Testament that is most important for understanding Jesus and his followers: ancient Judaism. We will see what Jews in the ancient world believed and how they worshiped. And we will examine some of the political struggles that Jews experienced in Palestine, leading to widely different understandings of Judaism at the time Christianity appeared in the world.

O f all the religions of the Greco-Roman world, it is reasonable to think that Judaism is the most important for understanding Jesus and his early followers. Jesus himself was a Jew, as were his disciples. He was born to Jewish parents and raised in a Jewish culture; he worshiped the Jewish God, learned the Jewish Scriptures, kept Jewish customs, became a Jewish teacher, and preached to Jewish crowds. He was executed for allegedly claiming to be the Jewish king. What did it mean to be a Jew in the first century of the Roman Empire?

I will postpone discussion of specific aspects of Judaism in Jesus' homeland of **Palestine** to the second half of this chapter. There we will see how the rich diversity of early Christianity and of Greco-Roman religion were matched by that of early Judaism. Some scholars have been so struck by this diversity that they opt to speak of early Judaisms rather than early Judaism. Even with this diversity, however, people in the ancient world appear to have meant something in particular when they called somebody a Jew. What might that have been?

Judaism was everywhere understood to be one of the religions of the Roman Empire. Contrary to what many people think, Judaism was not absolutely unique and unlike other Greco-Roman religions. In fact most people in the ancient world recognized it to be an ancient form of cultic devotion similar to others in many ways. Of course there were distinctive features, but every religion, not just Judaism, was distinctive.

Like other Greco-Roman religions, Judaism included the belief in a higher realm in which there was a powerful deity who could benefit humans and who showed special favor to those who worshiped him in ways prescribed from antiquity. The principal cultic acts of this religion involved animal sacrifice and prayer. Sacrifices were performed by priests in a sacred temple (located in Jerusalem) and according to prescribed rituals.

Portions of the animal, for most sacrifices, would be burned in honor of the deity. The priest would skin, prepare, and sometimes cook the carcass; for some sacrifices the worshiper would then take it, or parts of it, home to eat with his family and friends as a feast. Prayers were an important part of the worship of the Jewish God, usually addressing personal and communal needs (e.g., peace, fertility, prosperity, health). In many fundamental respects, then, Judaism was comparable to other Greco-Roman religions. In other important ways, however, it was different.

MONOTHEISM: THE BELIEF IN THE ONE TRUE GOD

As we have seen, virtually all the religions in the empire were polytheistic. Before Christianity, Judaism alone was committed to the notion that there was one and only one true God who was to be worshiped and praised. To be sure, the difference between Jews and pagans on this score should not be blown out of proportion, as if they were absolutely dissimilar. We have already observed that some pagans, chiefly some philosophers and their followers, also believed that there was one chief deity who was ultimately responsible for the world and what happens within it, whether Zeus, Jupiter, or whoever else was thought to occupy the peak of the divine pyramid. The other gods, including the *daimonia* and the demigods, were of less power and eminence. Jews, too, believed that there were immortal beings, far greater in power than humans, who existed somewhere between them and the true God. In the modern world we might call these beings angels and archangels; for ancient Jews they also included such beings as the "cherubim" and "seraphim."

The key difference between Jews and persons of other religions, then, was not that Jews denied the existence of a hierarchy of supernatural beings; the difference was that Jews as a rule insisted that only the one Creator God, the supreme deity himself, was to be worshiped. Moreover, this one God was not the unknown and unknowable deity of some philosophers, nor was he the Greek Zeus or the Roman Jupiter. He was the God of the Jews, who

was so holy—so far removed from anything that anyone could think or say—that even his name was not to be pronounced. Originally, this deity, like many others in the Greco-Roman world, was a local god who was worshiped in the land of Judea (or Judah, as it was earlier called). Those who worshiped this God were the people who lived there, the Judeans, whence we get the term "Jew."

About 550 years before Jesus, a large number of the Judeans were forced to leave their homeland because of a military, political, and economic crisis spawned by the invasion of the Babylonians. Many of those who relocated in places like Babylonia and Egypt retained their belief in the God of their homeland and continued to worship him in the ancient ways, maintaining the various customs followed in Judea—except, of course, that they could not worship in the Temple in Jerusalem (neither, however, could the Jerusalemites themselves for the better part of a century, because the building lay in ruin). Hence, by the Greco-Roman period, being a Jew meant worshiping the God of the Judeans, that is, the God of Israel. Jews scattered throughout the world, away from Judea, were said to live in the **"Diaspora,"** a term that literally means "dispersion." By the time of Jesus, there were far more Jews in the Diaspora than in Palestine. By some estimates, Jews made up 7 percent of the total population of the Roman Empire, which is usually set at around 60 million in the first century. Only a fraction of these lived in the Jewish homeland. Some scholars calculate that in the days of Jesus, twice as many Jews lived in Egypt as in all of Palestine itself.

Most of the Jews in the Diaspora stopped speaking Hebrew, the ancient tongue of Judea. By the second century before Jesus, many Jews read (or heard) their Scriptures only in Greek translation (see box 3.1), the so-called **Septuagint** translation.

Thus a distinctive feature of Jews around the world was that they did not worship a god of their own locality but the one God of their distant homeland, the God of Israel, and no other. Moreover, they claimed that this God had shown them special favor. For most non-Jews this was thought to be an audacious claim (even though Romans, as we have seen, made similar claims about their own gods). Jews nonetheless maintained that the one God, the creator of heaven and earth, was

ANOTHER GLIMPSE INTO THE PAST

BOX 3.1   The Septuagint: The Hebrew Bible in Greek

Since the vast majority of Jews in the first century lived outside Palestine, they no longer spoke Aramaic or read Hebrew, but spoke the local language wherever they lived, with the more highly educated among them also speaking Greek—the lingua franca of the Roman world.

This posed a problem for reading the Jewish Scriptures, since they were written in Hebrew. And so, as one might expect, Greek-speaking Jews in the Diaspora prepared translations of Scripture, different translations at different times and places. The one translation we are best informed about, which became by far the most widely used, is called the Septuagint (often abbreviated as LXX). The name comes from the Latin term *septuaginta,* which means "seventy." This is a shorthand reference to the legend that the translation was made by seventy (or, as usually stated, seventy-two) Jewish translators.

The legend is best known from a fascinating document called the "Letter of Aristeas," allegedly written in the third century B.C.E. According to Aristeas, when the king of Egypt, Ptolemy II (285–247 B.C.E.), decided to expand his library to 500,000 volumes and wanted to include every important piece of literature in it,

he conferred with his chief librarian, Demetrius, who informed him that one major gap in his holdings was the sacred laws of the Jews. Ptolemy immediately sent a letter to the Jewish high priest in Jerusalem requesting assistance in procuring a copy in translation.

In response, the high priest sent seventy-two translators, six from each of the twelve tribes of Israel, to Egypt. They were feasted (for seven days!) by their host, who questioned them about their religion and then secluded them to do their work of translation. Miraculously, they completed the work to perfection in exactly seventy-two days.

This entertaining account appears to refer only to the translation of the first five books of the Jewish Scriptures (the Pentateuch). But eventually, by the second century B.C.E., all the books were translated, and they became the form of Scripture familiar to Jews throughout the Diaspora. The Septuagint became the Scriptures for the early Christians as well, who treated it as an authoritative text down to its very words. It is the Septuagint, not the Hebrew Scripture, that is quoted by the authors of the New Testament, most of whom did not know Hebrew but were thoroughly trained in Greek.

---

uniquely their God. Hence, the second distinctive aspect of Judaism: their belief in the pact that God had made with Israel, or, using their own term, the **"covenant."**

THE COVENANT: ISRAEL'S PACT WITH ITS GOD

Most Jews were committed to the belief that the one true God had entered into a special relationship with them in the ancient past. God had chosen Israel from among all the other nations of the earth to be his special people. As part of his agreement with them, he promised that he, the creator and sustainer of all things, would protect and defend them in all their adversities.

Jews had ancient stories that told how God had fulfilled this promise. The most important were stories connected with the Exodus of the children of Israel from their slavery in Egypt, stories that eventually came to be embodied in the Jewish Scriptures. According to the ancient accounts, Israel had been maliciously subjected to forced labor for 400 years. God heard their cries and sent a savior, Moses, whose miraculous deeds compelled the king of Egypt to release them from bondage. Thus God delivered his people from slavery, destroying the powerful Egyptian army in the process, and brought them through trial and tribulation to the Promised Land. After they did battle with the nations who possessed the land, they entered in and became a great nation.

In light of God's actions on their behalf, Jews maintained that he had chosen them and made a covenant with them to be their God. That was his side of the agreement. In exchange, Jews were to obey his laws, laws pertaining to how they were to worship him and behave toward one another. As we will see, Jews as a rule did not consider this Law of God an onerous burden. Quite the contrary, the Law was God's greatest gift to his people. The existence of this divinely given Law, and the Jews' commitment to follow it, is then a third distinctive aspect of this religion.

THE LAW: ISRAEL'S COVENANTAL OBLIGATIONS

The English word "law" is a rather wooden translation of the Hebrew term **"Torah,"** which is perhaps better rendered "guidance" or "direction." Ancient Jews sometimes used the word to refer to the set of laws that Moses received on Mount Sinai, as recorded in the books of Exodus, Leviticus, Numbers, and Deuteronomy. It was also used, however, to refer to these books themselves, along with their companion volume Genesis. These are the heart and soul of the Jewish Scriptures; today they are also sometimes called the **"Pentateuch"** (meaning "the five scrolls"). These books record the Jewish traditions of creation and primeval history, including the stories about Adam and Eve, Noah's ark, and the Tower of Babel, as well as the stories surrounding the Jewish Patriarchs and Matriarchs: Abraham and Sarah, Isaac and Rebecca, Jacob and Leah and Rachel, and the twelve fathers of the twelve tribes of Israel, that is, Judah and his brothers. In addition, they narrate the traditions about Moses, the Exodus from Egypt, and the wanderings in the wilderness prior to the entry into the Promised Land. In particular, they contain the actual laws that God is said to have delivered to Moses on Mount Sinai after the Exodus from Egypt, laws that were to govern the worship of the Jews and their actions within their community, including, for example, the Ten Commandments.

Christians today frequently misunderstand the intent and purpose of this Jewish Law. It is not the case that ancient Jews (or modern ones, for that matter) generally thought that they had to keep all the laws in order to earn God's favor. This was not a religion of "works" that required one to follow a long list of do's and don'ts in order to find salvation. Quite the contrary, ancient Jews were committed to following the Law because they had already been shown favor by God. The Jews were chosen to be God's special people, and the Law was given to show them how to live up to this calling. For this reason, keeping the Law was not a dreaded task that everyone hated; Jews typically considered the Law a great joy to uphold.

The Law consisted of rules pertaining to both cultic and communal life, with regulations on how to worship God properly and on how to live with one's neighbor. In the context of the first-century world, most of these laws would not have seemed out of the ordinary. Jews were not to commit murder or steal or bear false witness, they were to make restitution when they or something they owned did damage to a neighbor, and they were to perform sacrifices to God following certain set practices. Even though other cults did not have written rules and regulations governing ethical behavior, there was nothing unusual in people wanting to encourage such activities. Other Jewish laws, however, did strike outsiders as peculiar. Jews, for example, were commanded to circumcise their baby boys—an act that they interpreted as the "sign of the covenant," for it showed that they (or at least the males among them) were distinct from all other nations as God's chosen people. Even though several other peoples (e.g., Egyptian priests) also practiced circumcision, Jews in the empire were occasionally maligned for it, since the practice seemed to most Greeks and Romans to involve nothing short of forced mutilation.

Jews were also commanded not to work on the seventh day of the week, the Sabbath, but to keep it holy. Even though pagans observed periodic festivals in honor of their own gods, it was otherwise unheard of to take a weekly vacation from work. For the Jews this was a great good: for one day in seven they could relax with family and friends, enjoy a special meal, and join in a communal service of worship to their God. To some

pagan observers, however, the custom showed that Jews were naturally lazy. Other laws that led to widespread derision involved the Jews' dietary restrictions. God had for some mysterious reason commanded Jews not to eat certain kinds of food, including pork and shellfish, common foods among other peoples in the Mediterranean region. This struck many outsiders as bizarre and superstitious.

Most Jews did not consider these laws (even the dietary ones) to be picayune requirements that few people wanted to follow and that nobody could. For comparison, consider the ancient Jewish legal code in light of our own. We, too, for example, have laws against consuming certain edible substances (especially certain liquids, powders, and tablets). And our own legal system is far more complicated than anything available to the ancient Jew, indeed far more complicated than the average citizen can possibly understand (just consider our tax laws!). By comparison with modern law, the law embodied in the Jewish Torah was not particularly harsh or onerous or complicated. And for ancient Jews, it was not the law of political bureaucrats; it was the law of God. Keeping it was a great joy because doing so showed that the Jews were the elect people of God.

TEMPLE AND SYNAGOGUE: ISRAEL'S PLACES OF WORSHIP

Most Jews in the first century worshiped twice a day in their homes, recalling some of God's commandments and praying. In addition, there were two particularly important institutions for Jewish worship: the **Temple** in Jerusalem, where the animal sacrifices so central to the prescriptions of the Torah were to be performed, and the local synagogues, where Jews throughout the empire could worship God by studying and discussing the Law in the context of communal gathering and prayers.

The Jewish Temple

Jewish practices of animal sacrifice do not appear to have been so different from those of other ancient religions. Moreover, the Jewish Temple itself was not unlike other temples; it was a sacred structure in which the deity was believed to dwell, where worshipers could come to perform cultic acts in his honor and in hopes of receiving divine benefits as a result. At the same time, the Jewish Temple was known to be one of the grandest in the world of antiquity, spoken of with praise and admiration even by those who were not among

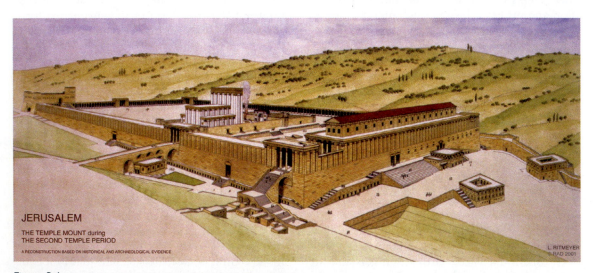

Figure 3.1 A pictorial reconstruction of the Jewish Temple in Jerusalem.

its devotees. In the days of Jesus, the Temple complex encompassed an area roughly 500 yards by 325 yards, large enough, as one modern scholar has pointed out, to enclose twenty-five football fields (see Sanders 1992). From the outside, its stone walls rose 100 feet from the street, as high as a modern ten-story building. No mortar had been used in its construction; instead, the stones, some of them 50 yards in length, had been carefully cut to fit together neatly. The gates into the temple were 45 feet high by 44 feet wide (with two doors, 22 feet wide, in each); one ancient source indicates that 200 men were required to close them each evening. From all of our ancient descriptions, the Temple complex appears to have been a fantastically beautiful set of buildings made with the best materials money could buy, including gold, which overlaid extensive portions of the structures. As you might imagine, its construction was an immense feat; when it was completed in 63 C.E., 18,000 local workers were reportedly left unemployed. It was destroyed just seven years later at the climax of the Jewish war against Rome, never to be built again.

One of the things that made the Jerusalem Temple unique in the Greco-Roman world is that in the opinion of most Jews of the period, it was to be the only temple for the God of Israel. Whereas numerous temples could be devoted to any of the pagan gods, this God would receive sacrifices only in the Temple in Jerusalem. Jews from around the world, even those who never set foot inside, paid an annual tax to help defray the costs of its upkeep and administration. In no small measure, this special reverence for the place derived from the belief that God himself dwelt in the Temple, in a special room called the **"Holy of Holies."** (God was in heaven, of course, and everywhere on earth, but his special dwelling place was in his Temple.) The belief that a god might actually be present in a holy place was widespread throughout antiquity. In most ancient temples, however, the deity was present in the cult image, or **"idol,"** kept in a sacred room. The sacred room in the Jerusalem Temple, on the other hand, was completely empty. Since the Jewish God was so holy, unlike all else that is, he explicitly forbade any images to be made of him.

No one could enter this holiest of rooms except the Jewish high priest, and he did so only once a year on the Day of Atonement (Yom Kippur), when he performed a sacrifice for the sins of the people. The Holy of Holies was thus the most sacred spot in the Temple, and the rest of the building complex was structured so as to emphasize the holiness that emanated from its center. Before the Holy of Holies was the sanctuary, into which only certain priests could go; around it was the court of the priests, which allowed only priests and their assistants, the Levites. Farther out was the court of the Israelites, into which only Jewish men could go to bring their offerings to the priests. Beyond that was the court of (Jewish) women, who were not allowed any nearer to the inner sanctum (Jewish men may have assembled there as well), and finally beyond that came the court of the Gentiles, where even non-Jews could congregate.

Thus, the idea of a temple and the activities of prayer and sacrifice that transpired there were not so different from what one could find in other religions in the empire. Apart from the details of the cultic ceremonies (which, of course, differed to some degree in all ancient religions), what made this Temple unlike others was the fact that, according to its adherents, it was the only one to be built to their God, who dwelt there in holiness apart from any sacred image.

The Synagogue

Despite the fact that Jews from around the world paid an annual tax to support the Temple, most could not worship there on a regular basis. Indeed, many could not afford to make a pilgrimage there, ever. For this reason, apparently, centuries before Jesus—scholars debate when, exactly— Jews in the Diaspora devised an alternative mode of worship, one that did not involve sacrifice of animals but focused instead on discussing the sacred traditions of the Torah and praying to the God of Israel. These activities took place in community, as Jews came together on the Sabbath in either a home or a separate meeting place, sometimes a freestanding building, usually under the leadership of the more highly educated and literate of their members. The Scriptures were read

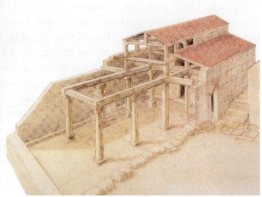

Figure 3.2 The remains of an ancient synagogue at Khirbat Shema, in Galilee, with an artist's cutaway drawing of what the synagogue would have looked like. This particular synagogue was first built about two centuries after the days of Jesus.

and discussed, and set prayers were said. These gatherings were called **"synagogues,"** from the Greek word for "gathering together," a term that eventually came to refer to the building in which the meetings took place.

By the time of Jesus, there were synagogues wherever there were communities of Jews in the empire, both in Palestine and abroad. In many respects these were not unlike the gathering places of like-minded individuals among non-Jews, where certain religious activities occurred and prayers were said. Greco-Roman "associations" were commonly organized, for example, for workers of the same trade in a locale, who might share a range of common interests. And it was not unusual to find other associations organized for the purpose of periodic social gatherings, where members would pool their funds to provide ample food and drink and, perhaps strange to the modern observer, provide, through a reserve, a proper burial for their deceased members.

Rarely, however, would such organizations, whether trade associations or funeral clubs, include men, women, and children; rarely would they meet together every week; and rarely would they devote themselves principally to the purposes of prayer and discussion of sacred traditions. To this extent, Jewish synagogues were distinctive.

FORMS OF EARLY JUDAISM

Even though Judaism as a whole had distinctive characteristics that set it off, in some respects, from other religions of the Greco-Roman world, it would be a mistake to think that all Jews agreed on every aspect of their religion. Quite the contrary, there were wide-ranging disagreements on fundamental issues, at least as sharp as the disagreements that one sees today in both Judaism (e.g., between the "orthodox" and "reformed") and Christianity (e.g., Roman Catholics and Southern Baptists). One way to highlight these differences is to give a quick overview of the political history of the Jewish people in their homeland, Palestine (modern-day Israel), and see how different forms of Judaism emerged from the crises that occurred.

POLITICAL CRISES IN PALESTINE AND THEIR RAMIFICATIONS

The ancient history of Palestine is long and complex. Here we will consider only the minute aspect of it that had a direct bearing on the context of the early Christian writings. In a nutshell, the political history of the land had not been happy for some 800 years; during this time it experienced periodic wars and virtually permanent foreign domination. In 721 B.C.E. the northern part of the land, the kingdom of Israel, was overthrown by the Assyrians; then, about a century and a half later, in 587–86 B.C.E., the southern kingdom of Judah was conquered by the Babylonians. Jerusalem was leveled, the Temple was destroyed, and the leaders of the people were taken into exile. Some fifty years later, the Babylonian Empire was overrun by the Persians, who brought an end to the forced exile and allowed the Judean leaders to return home. The Temple was rebuilt, and the priest in charge of the Temple, the high priest, was given jurisdiction as a local ruler of the people. This man was from an ancient family that traced its line back hundreds of years to a priest named **Zadok**. Ultimately, of course, the Persian king was the final authority over the land and its people.

This state of affairs continued for nearly two centuries, until the conquests of Alexander the Great, ruler of Macedonia (see box 2.2). Alexander overthrew the Persian Empire, conquering most of the lands around the Eastern Mediterranean as far as modern-day India. He brought Greek culture with him into the various regions he conquered, building Greek cities and schools and gymnasia (centers of Greek culture), encouraging the acceptance of Greek culture and religion, and promoting the use of the Greek language. Alexander died a young man in 323 B.C.E. The generals of his army divided up his realm, and Palestine fell under the rule of Ptolemy, the general in charge of Egypt. During all this time, the Jewish high priest remained the local ruler of the land of Judea. This did not change when the ruler of Syria wrested control of Palestine from the Ptolemaeans in 198 B.C.E.

It is hard to know how widespread or intense the antagonism toward foreign rule was throughout most of this period, given our sparse sources. No doubt many Jews resented the idea that their rulers were answerable to a foreign power. They were, after all, the chosen people of the one true God of Israel, who had agreed to protect and defend them in exchange for their devotion. Judea was the land that he had promised them, and for many Jews it must have been distressing, both politically and religiously, to know that ultimately someone else was in charge.

In any event, there is no doubt that the situation became greatly exacerbated under the Syrian monarchs. Over the century and a half or so since Alexander's death, Greek culture had become more and more prominent throughout the entire Mediterranean region. One Syrian ruler in particular, **Antiochus Epiphanes**, decided to bring greater cultural unity to his empire by requiring his subjects to adopt aspects of Greek civilization. Some of the Jews living in Palestine welcomed these innovations. Indeed, some men were enthused enough to undergo surgery to remove the marks of their circumcision, allowing them to exercise in the Jerusalem gymnasium without being recognized as Jewish. Others, however, found this process of **"Hellenization,"** or imposition of Greek culture, absolutely offensive to their religion. In response to their protests, Antiochus tightened the screws even further, making it illegal for Jews to circumcise their baby boys and to maintain their Jewish identity, converting the Jewish Temple into a pagan sanctuary, and requiring Jews to sacrifice to the pagan gods.

A revolt broke out, started by a family of Jewish priests known to history both as the **Maccabeans**, based on the name given to one of its powerful leaders, **Judas Maccabeus** ("the Hammerer"), and also as the **Hasmoneans**, based on the name of a distant ancestor. The Maccabean revolt began as a small guerrilla skirmish in 167 B.C.E.; soon much of the country was in armed rebellion against its Syrian overlords. In less than twenty-five years, the Maccabeans had successfully driven the Syrian army out of the land and assumed full and total control of its governance, creating the first sovereign Jewish state in over four centuries. They rededicated the Temple (one of their first acts, in 164 B.C.E., commemorated still in the Hanukkah celebration) and appointed a high priest as supreme ruler of the land. To the dismay of many Jews in Palestine, however, the high priest was not from the ancient line of Zadok but from the Hasmonean family.

The Hasmoneans ruled the land as an autonomous state for some eighty years, until 63 B.C.E., when the Roman general Pompey conquered it. The Romans allowed the high priest to remain in office, using him as an administrative liaison with

ANOTHER GLIMPSE INTO THE PAST

BOX 3.2 Flavius Josephus

Our best source of information about first-century Palestine is a man named Flavius **Josephus** (37–100 C.E.). Josephus is an unusually valuable historian: he actually lived in Palestine in the first century, knew most of its leading figures, and experienced firsthand not just its dominant culture but also its political and military crises.

Born to an aristocratic priestly family, as a relatively young man Josephus ben Matthias was appointed to head the Jewish troops in Galilee at the outset of the Jewish War against Rome (66 C.E.). As he later tells us in his autobiography, when his troops were surrounded by the Roman legions at the town of Jotaphatha, rather than surrender, they agreed to a suicide pact: they were to draw lots to determine who would kill whom, with the final two then to commit suicide.

As it happened, one of the final two lots (by a trick or chance) fell to Josephus; but when all the others were dead, he convinced his surviving colleague to turn themselves in to the Romans. Brought before the conquering general Vespasian, Josephus then had the good sense to utter a "prophecy" that he, Vespasian, would become the Roman emperor. As it turns out, the prophecy became a reality: Nero committed suicide, and eventually Vespasian was declared emperor by his troops.

And he never forgot that Josephus had predicted it. During the war, **Vespasian**, and then his son and successor in the field, **Titus**, used Josephus as an interpreter, urging the Jews inside the walls of Jerusalem to surrender. The Jews refused and were eventually destroyed in the onslaught of 70 C.E., when the walls of the city were breached, the Temple demolished, and the opposition slaughtered. Josephus was then taken back to Rome, set free, and appointed by Vespasian to be a kind of court historian.

He adopted Vespasian's family name (Flavius) and spent the next twenty-five years or so writing books about the Jewish people, including a six-volume work on the Jewish Wars (which he obviously knew about firsthand) and a twenty-volume history of the Jewish people called the *Antiquities of the Jews* (from Adam and Eve up to his own time).

These works betray the clear slant of their author: Josephus, for example, wanted to show the Romans that Jews were loyal to the empire and to show the Jews that they could not resist the might of Rome. His political agenda notwithstanding, Josephus's books are extremely useful for historians wanting to know about the life, customs, society, leading figures, politics, and culture of first-century Palestine, written by a competent scholar who was actually there at the time.

---

the local Jewish leadership, but there was no doubt who controlled the land. Eventually, in 40 B.C.E., Rome appointed a king to rule the Jews of Palestine, **Herod the Great**, renowned both for his ruthless exercise of power and for his magnificent building projects, which served not only to beautify the cities but also to elevate the status of Judea and employ massive numbers of workers. Many Jews, however, castigated Herod as an opportunistic collaborator with the Romans, a traitorous half-Jew at best. The latter charge was based in part on his lineage: his family was not from Judea, but from the neighboring country of Idumea and had converted to Judaism some fifty years before his birth.

During the days of Jesus, after Herod's death, Galilee, the northern region of the land, was ruled by Herod's son **Antipas**, and starting when Jesus was a boy, Judea, the southern region, was governed by Roman administrators known as prefects. **Pontius Pilate** was prefect during the whole of Jesus' ministry and for some years after his death. His headquarters were in Caesarea, but he came to the capital city Jerusalem, with troops, whenever the need arose.

The point of this brief sketch is not to indicate what children learned in their fifth-grade history classes in Nazareth; indeed, there is no way for us to know whether a boy like Jesus would ever have

Figure 3.3   Silver coin from Antioch with a portrait of Antiochus Epiphanes and the inscription: "King Antiochus, a god made manifest."

even heard of such important figures from the remote past as Alexander the Great or Ptolemy. Rather, the historical events leading up to his time are significant for understanding Jesus' life because they had social and intellectual ramifications for all Palestinian Jews. It was in response to the social, political, and religious crises of the Maccabean period that the Jewish sects of Jesus' day (e.g., the Pharisees, Sadducees, and Essenes) were formed, and it was Rome's domination that led to nonviolent and violent Jewish uprisings before, during, and after Jesus' time. For many Jews, any foreign domination of the Promised Land was both politically and religiously unacceptable. Moreover, it was the overall sense of inequity and the experience of suffering during these times that first inspired and then popularized the ideology of resistance known as apocalypticism, a worldview that was shared by a number of Jews in first-century Palestine.

THE FORMATION OF JEWISH SECTS

It was during the rule of the Hasmoneans, and evidently in large measure in reaction to it, that various Jewish sects emerged. The Jewish historian Josephus mentions four of these groups; the New Testament refers to three. In one way or another, all of them play a significant role in our understanding of the life of the historical Jesus.

I should emphasize at the outset that most Jews in Palestine did not belong to any of these groups. We know this much from Josephus, who indicates that the largest sect, the **Pharisees**, claimed 6,000 members and that the **Essenes** claimed 4,000. The **Sadducees** probably had far fewer. These numbers should be considered in light of the overall Jewish population in the world at the time; the best estimates put the number at something like 4 million.

What matters for our purposes here, however, is not the size of these groups, for they were influential despite their small numbers, but the ways in which they understood what it meant to be Jewish, especially in light of the political crises that they had to face. Members of all the sects, of course, would have subscribed to the basic principles of the religion, as sketched earlier in this chapter: each believed in the one true God, the creator of all things, who was revealed in the Hebrew Scriptures, who had chosen the people of Israel, and who had promised to protect and defend them in exchange for their committed devotion to him

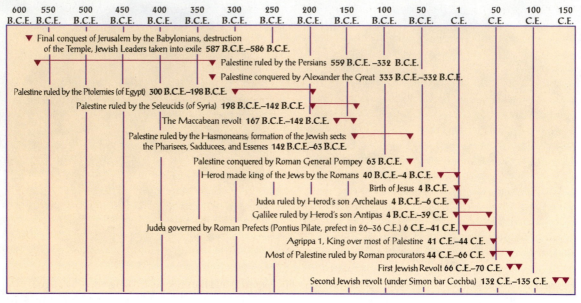

Figure 3.4 Time Line of Key Events in the History of Palestine.

through following his laws. The groups differed in significant ways, however, in their understanding of what obedience to God's laws required and in how they responded to the rule of a foreign power and to the presence of a high priest from a line other than Zadok's.

Pharisees

The Pharisees represent probably the best-known and least understood Jewish sect. Because of the way they are attacked in parts of the New Testament, especially in Matthew, Christians through the ages have wrongly considered the Pharisees' chief attribute to be hypocrisy. (Pharisees were not required to take a hypocritic oath.)

It appears that this sect began during the Maccabean period as a group of devout Jews intent above all else on keeping the entire will of God. Rather than accepting the culture and religion of the Greeks, these Jews insisted on knowing and obeying the Law of their own God to the fullest extent possible. One of the difficulties with the Law of Moses, however, is that in many places it is ambiguous. For example, Jews are told in the Ten

Commandments to keep the Sabbath day holy, but nowhere does the Torah indicate precisely how this is to be done. Pharisees devised rules and regulations to assist them in keeping this and all the other laws of Moses. These rules eventually formed a body of tradition, which, to stay with our example, indicated what a person could and could not do on the Sabbath day in order to keep it holy, or set apart from all other days. Thus, for example, when it was eventually determined that a faithful Jew should not go on a long journey on the Sabbath, it had to be decided what a "long" journey was, and consequently what distance a Jew could travel on this day without violating its holiness. Likewise, a worker who believed that he or she should not labor on the Sabbath had to know what constituted "work" and what therefore could and could not be done.

Or a second example: the Law of Moses commands Jewish farmers to give one-tenth of their crops, that is, a tithe, to the **priests** and **Levites** (for example, Num 18:20–21). Priests performed sacrifices in the temple, and Levites were their assistants. Since they themselves were not allowed to farm, the tithes they received represented their financial support for serving God. What should a person do, however, who purchased food from a farmer not knowing whether the food had been properly tithed? To be on the safe side, some Pharisees maintained that they should tithe the food they *purchased*, as well as the food they grew. This way they could be certain that God's law was being followed. And if it got followed twice in this case, so much the better—especially for God's priests and Levites!

The rules and regulations that developed among the Pharisees came to have a status of their own and were known in some circles as the **"oral" Law**, which was set alongside the "written" Law of Moses. It appears that the Pharisees generally believed that anyone who kept the oral law would be almost certain to keep the written law as a consequence. The intent was not to be legalistic but to be obedient to what God had commanded.

The Pharisees may have been a relatively closed society in Jesus' day, to the extent that they stayed together as a group, eating meals and having fellowship only with one another, that is, with those who were like-minded in seeing the need to maintain a high level of obedience before God. They did not have close ties with those who were less stringent in maintaining purity before God and avoided, therefore, eating meals with common people.

It is important to recognize that the Pharisees were not the "power players" in Palestine in Jesus' day. That is to say, they appear to have had some popular appeal but no real political clout. In some ways they are best seen as a kind of separatist group; they wanted to maintain their own purity and did so in relative (not complete) isolation from other Jews. Many scholars think that the term "Pharisee" itself originally came from a Persian word that means "separated ones." Eventually, however, some decades after Jesus' execution, the Pharisees did become powerful in the political sense. This was after the Jewish War against the Romans, which culminated in the destruction of Jerusalem and the Temple in the year 70 C.E. With this calamity, the other groups passed from the scene for a variety of reasons, and the descendents of the Pharisees were given greater authority by the Roman overlords. The oral tradition also continued to grow and to be invested with greater authority. It was eventually written down around the year 200 C.E. and is today known as the **Mishnah**, the heart of the Jewish sacred collection of texts, the **Talmud**.

The Pharisees are important for understanding the historical Jesus, in part because he set his message over against theirs. As we will see, Jesus did not think that scrupulous and detailed adherence to the laws of Torah was the most important aspect of a Jew's relationship with God, especially as these laws were interpreted by the Pharisees.

Sadducees

It is difficult to reconstruct exactly what the Sadducees stood for because not a single literary work survives from the pen of a Sadducee, in contrast to the Pharisees, who are represented to some extent by the later traditions of the Talmud; by Josephus, who was a Pharisee; and by the one Pharisee who left us writings before the destruction of the Temple (after he had converted to Christianity), the apostle Paul. To understand the Sadducees, however, we must turn to what is said *about* them in other sources, such as Josephus and the New Testament.

During Jesus' own day, the Sadducees were evidently the real power players in Palestine. They appear to have been, by and large, members of the Jewish aristocracy in Jerusalem who were closely connected with the Jewish priesthood in charge of the Temple cult. Most of the Sadducees were themselves priests (although not all priests were Sadducees). As members of the aristocracy, granted some limited power by their Roman overlords, Sadducees appear to have been conciliatory toward the civil authorities, that is, cooperative with the Roman governor. The local Jewish council, commonly called the Sanhedrin, which was occasionally called together to decide local affairs, was evidently made up principally of Sadducees. With their close connection with the Temple, Sadducees emphasized the need for Jews to be properly involved in the cultic worship of God as prescribed in the Torah. Indeed, it appears that the Torah itself, that is, the five books of Moses, was the only authoritative text that the Sadducees accepted. In any event, we know that they did not accept the oral traditions formulated by the Pharisees. Less concerned with the regulation of daily affairs, such as eating, travel, and work, the Sadducees focused their religious attention on the sacrifices in the Temple and expended their political energy on working out their relations with the Romans so that these sacrifices could continue.

It may have been their rejection of all written authority outside the five books of Moses that led the Sadducees to reject several doctrines that later became characteristic of other groups of Jews. They denied, for example, the existence of angels and disavowed the notion of the future resurrection of the dead. Their views of the afterlife may well have conformed, essentially, with those of most non-Jews throughout the empire: either the "soul" perishes with the body, or it continues on in a kind of shadowy netherworld, regardless of the quality of its life here on earth.

The Sadducees are of importance for understanding the historical Jesus, in part because he roused their anger by predicting that God would soon destroy the locus of their social and religious authority, their beloved Temple. In response, some of their prominent members urged Pontius Pilate to have him executed.

Essenes

The Essenes are the one Jewish sect not mentioned in the New Testament. Ironically, they are also the group about which we are best informed. This is because the famous **Dead Sea Scrolls** were evidently produced by a group of Essenes who lived in a community east of Jerusalem in the wilderness area near the Western shore of the Dead Sea, in a place that is today called **Qumran**. Although the term "Essene" never occurs in the scrolls, we know from at least one ancient authority, the Roman writer Pliny the Elder, that a community of Essenes was located in this area; moreover, the social arrangements and theological views described in the Dead Sea Scrolls correspond to what we know about the Essenes from these other accounts. Most scholars are reasonably certain, therefore, that the scrolls represent a library used by this sect or, at least, by the part of it living near Qumran.

The discovery of the Dead Sea Scrolls was completely serendipitous. In 1947, a shepherd boy searching for a lost goat in the barren wilderness near the northwest shore of the Dead Sea happened to toss a stone into a cave and heard it strike something. Entering the cave, he discovered an ancient earthenware jar that contained a number of old scrolls. The books were recovered by bedouin shepherds. When news of the discovery reached antiquities dealers, biblical scholars learned of the find, and a search was conducted both to find more scrolls in the surrounding caves and to retrieve those that had already been found by the bedouin, who cut some of them up to sell one piece at a time.

Some of the caves in the region yielded entire scrolls; others contained thousands of tiny scraps that are virtually impossible to piece back together, since so many of the pieces are missing. Imagine trying to do an immense jigsaw puzzle, or rather dozens of immense jigsaw puzzles, not knowing what the end product of any of them should look like, when most of the pieces are lost and those that remain are all mixed together! All in all hundreds of documents are represented, many of them only in fragments the size of postage stamps, others, perhaps a couple of dozen, in scrolls of sufficient length to give us a full idea of their contents.

Most of the scrolls are written in Hebrew, but some are in Aramaic. Different kinds of literature are represented here. There are at least partial copies of every book of the Jewish Bible, with the exception of the book of Esther, and some of them are fairly complete. These are extremely valuable because of their age; they are nearly a thousand years older than the oldest copies of the Hebrew Scriptures that we previously had. We can therefore check to see whether Jewish scribes over the intervening centuries reliably copied their texts. The short answer is that, for the most part, they did. There are also commentaries on some of the biblical books, written principally to show that the predictions of the ancient prophets had come to be fulfilled in the experiences of the Essene believers and in the history of their community. In addition, there are books that contain psalms and hymns composed by members of the community, prophecies that indicate future events that were believed to be ready to transpire in the authors' own day, and rules for the members of the community to follow in their lives together.

Figure 3.5 One of the most important of the Dead Sea Scrolls, a Hebrew copy of the book of Isaiah.

Sifting through all these books, scholars have been able to reconstruct the life and beliefs of the Essenes in considerable detail. It appears that their community at Qumran was started during the early Maccabean period, perhaps around 150 B.C.E., by pious Jews who were convinced that the Hasmoneans had usurped their authority by appointing a non-Zadokite as high priest. Believing that the Jews of Jerusalem had gone astray, this group of Essenes chose to start their own community in which they could keep the Mosaic law rigorously and maintain their own ritual purity in the wilderness. They did so fully expecting the apocalypse of the end of time to be imminent. When it came, there would be a final battle between the forces of good and evil,

between the children of light and the children of darkness. The battle would climax with the triumph of God and the entry of his children into the blessed kingdom.

Some of the scrolls indicate that this kingdom would be ruled by two messiahs, one a king and the other a priest. The priestly messiah would lead the faithful in their worship of God in a purified temple, where sacrifices could again be made in accordance with God's will. In the meantime, the true people of God needed to be removed from the impurities of this world, including the impurities prevalent in the Jewish Temple and among the rest of the Jewish people. These Essenes therefore started their own monastic-like community, with strict rules for admission and membership. A two-year initiation was required, after which, if approved, a member was to donate all his possessions to the community fund and share the common meal with all the other members. Rigorous guidelines dictated the life of the community. Members had fixed hours for work and rest and for their meals, there were required times of fasting, and strict penalties were imposed for unseemly behavior such as interrupting one another, talking at meals, and laughing at inappropriate times.

It appears that when the Jewish war of 66–73 C.E. began the Essenes at Qumran hid some of their sacred writings before joining in the struggle. It may well be that they saw this as the final battle, preliminary to the end of time when God would establish his kingdom and send its messiahs.

The Essenes are important for understanding the historical Jesus, in part because Jesus appears to have shared many of their apocalyptic views, even though he did not belong to their sect. Like them, he believed that the end of time was near and that people had to prepare for the coming onslaught.

The "Fourth Philosophy"

When Josephus writes about Judaism for a Roman audience, he describes each of the sects that we have discussed as a "philosophy," by which he means a group with a distinctive and rational outlook on the world. He never gives a name to the fourth sect that he discusses but simply calls it the **"Fourth Philosophy."** The tenets of this philosophy, however, are clear, and they were manifested in several different groups that we know about from various ancient sources. Each of these groups in its own way supported active resistance to Israel's foreign domination.

The view that characterized these sundry groups was that Israel had a right to its own land, a right that had been granted by God himself. Anyone who usurped that right, and anyone who backed the usurper, was to be opposed, by violent means if necessary. Among those who took this line in the middle of the first century were the **Sicarii**, a group whose name comes from the Latin

word for "dagger." These "daggermen" planned and carried out assassinations and kidnappings of high-ranking Jewish officials who were thought to be in league with the Roman authorities. Another group that subscribed to this philosophy, somewhat later in the century, were the Zealots. These were Jews who were "zealous" for the Law and who urged armed rebellion to take back the land God had promised his people. More specifically, based on what we find in Josephus, Zealots were Galilean Jews who fled to Jerusalem during the Jewish revolt around the year 67 C.E., overthrew the priestly aristocracy in the city in a bloody coup, and urged the violent opposition to the Roman legions that ultimately led to the destruction of Jerusalem and the burning of the Temple in 70 C.E.

Such groups are important for understanding the historical Jesus, in part because he, too, thought that the Romans were to be overthrown. But it was not to be by armed resistance.

THE JEWISH CONTEXT FOR THE TRADITIONS ABOUT JESUS

Despite the wide-ranging differences among Jews in the first century, they did appear to share certain things in common, as discussed earlier in this chapter. They all agreed that there was one true God, the God of Israel, who had made a covenant with his people and given them his law. This law was to be obeyed for Israel to stay within its special relationship with God, who was to be worshiped through prayer and sacrifices.

I should stress, however, that even in its distinctiveness, Judaism was not altogether unlike other religions of the empire. As we have seen, for example, even some pagans could accept the notion of monotheism. They also accepted that the gods had made special provisions for certain people (for example, the state gods of Rome), that they had given certain commandments (such as how to worship them), and that they were to be honored in certain places (temples) in certain ways, including prescribed prayers and sacrifices. Thus Judaism should be seen as one of the Greco-Roman religions, distinct and yet similar to the others, just as all religions of that world were distinct and yet similar to one another.

There is one further similarity between Judaism and the pagan religions of its environment, a similarity of particular importance to the traditions about Jesus that circulated throughout this world. Just as Judaism shared with other religions the notion that there were other divine beings of lesser majesty and power than the one true God, so, too, it maintained that these other divine beings sometimes appeared to people in human form. There are records of such appearances in the Jewish Scriptures, as when angels came and spoke to humans, imparting a divine revelation or performing a spectacular miracle. Moreover, there are accounts in Judaism of human beings who appeared to be far more than human. For example, Moses was said in the Hebrew Scriptures to have performed miracles through the power of God (e.g., sending the plagues against Egypt), the prophet named Elisha

reportedly healed the blind and multiplied loaves for the hungry, and Elijah overwhelmed his opponents through the power of God, miraculously supplied food and drink to those in need, and even raised the dead.

Outside the Hebrew Scriptures we know of Jews who were thought to stand in a special relation with God. These Jewish holy men, sometimes called the sons of God, reportedly could heal the sick and calm the storm. Some Jews believed that God spoke directly and intimately to them. The later rabbis sometimes told stories of such holy men, some of whom lived near the time of Jesus, also in Galilee. For example, Hanina ben Dosa and Honi the "circle-drawer" were famous among the rabbis for their memorable teachings and miraculous deeds (see box 3.3). Thus the stories about Jesus, the miracle-working Son of God, would have made sense not only to pagans, who were familiar with accounts of divine men, but to Jews as well, whether in Palestine or the Diaspora.

ANOTHER GLIMPSE INTO THE PAST

BOX 3.3   Other Jewish Miracle-Working Sons of God

Jesus was not the only one thought to be a miracle-working son of God, even within Judaism in his own day. His two most famous peers were probably **Honi the "circle-drawer"** and **Hanina ben Dosa**, both of whom are known through the writings of later Jewish rabbis. Honi was a Galilean teacher who died about one hundred years before Jesus. He was given his nickname because of a tradition that he prayed to God for much-needed rain and drew a circle around himself on the ground, declaring that he would not leave it until God granted his request. Lucky for him, God complied. Later sources indicate that Honi was a revered teacher and a miracle worker, who called himself the son of God. Like Jesus, he was martyred outside the walls of Jerusalem around the time of Passover. To punish the Jews who had brought about his death, God sent a powerful windstorm that devastated their crops.

Hanina ben Dosa (= son of Dosa) was a rabbi in Galilee in the middle of the first century C.E., just after

the time of Jesus. He was famous as a righteous and powerful worker of miracles, who (like Honi) could intervene with God to make the rain fall, who had the power to heal the sick, and who could confront demons and force them to do his bidding. Like Jesus, he was reputedly called the Son of God by a voice coming from the heavens.

Both these miracle-working sons of God are portrayed somewhat differently from Jesus, of course (most of their miracles, for example, were achieved through prayer, rather than through their own power), but they are also different in significant ways from each other (Jesus and Hanina, for example, are both portrayed as exorcists, whereas Honi is not). What is most interesting, however, is that anyone who called Jesus a miracle-working Jewish rabbi, the Son of God, would have been easily understood: other righteous Jews, both before Jesus and afterward, were portrayed similarly.

AT A GLANCE

BOX 3.4 The World of Early Judaism

1. Even though Judaism was widely diverse (e.g., in such groups as the Pharisees, Sadducees, and Essenes), it had several distinctive characteristics:

  a. Jews were to worship just one God, the God of Israel.

  b. This God had chosen Jews to be his special people.

  c. Jews were to respond to their election by God by obeying his will, as expressed in the Law.

  d. God could be worshiped by sacrifices made in the Temple in Jerusalem and by prayer and the study of the sacred traditions of Israel in synagogues located throughout the ancient world.

2. The political crises involving the Maccabean Revolt and the conquests by Rome led to the formation of several Jewish sects.

3. Chief among these sects were the Pharisees, the Sadducees, the Essenes, and the "Fourth Philosophy."

TAKE A STAND

1. Pretend you are a Jew living in the Roman Empire, and you are trying to convince your pagan neighbor to give up his worship of the Roman and local gods and become a Jew. Make your case!

2. Consider the various kinds of Judaism in the first century. In your opinion, is it better to talk about ancient Judaism or ancient Judaisms? Back up your opinion! Now suppose you want to argue the opposite side. What is the best case that you can make?

SUGGESTIONS FOR FURTHER READING

Anthologies of Texts

Cartlidge, David R., and David L. Dungan, eds. *Documents for the Study of the Gospels.* 2d ed. Philadelphia: Fortress, 1994. Presents a valuable selection of ancient literary texts that are closely parallel to the New Testament Gospels, including portions of Philostratus's *Life of Apollonius.*

Charlesworth, James H., ed. *The Old Testament Pseudepigrapha.* 2 vols. Garden City, N.Y.: Doubleday, 1983, 1985. The most complete collection of noncanonical writings of early Judaism from before and around the time of the New Testament, with full and informative introductions.

Vermes, Geza, ed. *The Dead Sea Scrolls in English.* rev. ed. Baltimore: Penguin Books, 2004. The most accessible collection and translation of the Dead Sea Scrolls available in English, with a clear introduction.

Studies of Early Judaism

Barclay, John M. G. *Jews in the Mediterranean Diaspora: From Alexander to Trajan (323 B.C.E.–117 C.E.).* Edinburgh: T&T Clark, 1996. An insightful study of Jews living outside Palestine from the time of Alexander the Great through the early Roman Empire.

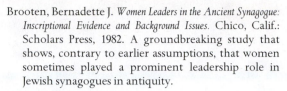

Brooten, Bernadette J. *Women Leaders in the Ancient Synagogue: Inscriptional Evidence and Background Issues.* Chico, Calif.: Scholars Press, 1982. A groundbreaking study that shows, contrary to earlier assumptions, that women sometimes played a prominent leadership role in Jewish synagogues in antiquity.

Cohen, Shaye. *From the Maccabees to the Mishnah.* 2d ed. Philadelphia: Westminster Press, 2006. Perhaps the best place for beginning students to turn for a clear overview of early Judaism.

Collins, John, and Daniel Harlowe, *Eerdmans Dictionary of Early Judaism.* Grand Rapids, Mich.: Eerdmans, 2010. A major reference work that provides 13 essays on major aspects of early Judaism and over 500 encyclopedia-length entries on everything of relevance in the field. An important research tool.

Kraft, Robert, and George Nicklesburg, eds. *Early Judaism and Its Modern Interpreters.* Philadelphia: Fortress; Atlanta:

Scholars, 1986. A collection of significant essays on major aspects of early Judaism, for more advanced students.

Magness, Jodi. *Stone and Dung, Oil and Spit: Jewish Daily Life in the Time of Jesus.* Grand Rapids, Mich.: Eerdmans, 2010. An intriguing account of the social realities of Jews in their everyday life at the time of the beginning of the Christian movement, by one of the world's premier archaeologists of Palestine.

Sanders, E. P. *Judaism: Practice and Belief, 63* B.C.E.*–66* C.E. London: SCM Press; Philadelphia: Trinity Press International, 1992. A full, detailed, and authoritative account of what it meant to be a Jew immediately before and during the time of the New Testament.

Vanderkam, James. *An Introduction to Early Judaism.* Grand Rapids, Mich.: Eerdmans, 2000. A highly informative and competent introduction to Judaism from the time of the New Testament, by one of the world's leading scholars in the field.

 ## KEY TERMS

Antiochus Epiphanes	Herod the Great	Maccabeans	Septuagint
Antipas	Holy of Holies	Mishnah	Sicarii
covenant	Honi the	oral Law	synagogue
Dead Sea Scrolls	"circle-drawer"	Palestine	Talmud
Diaspora	idol	Pentateuch	Temple, Jewish
Essenes	Josephus	Pharisees	Titus, emperor
Fourth Philosophy	Judaism	Pontius Pilate	Torah
Hanina ben Dosa	Judas Maccabeus	priests, Jewish	Vespasian, emperor
Hasmoneans	Law, Jewish	Qumran	Zadok
Hellenization	Levites	Sadducees	

Ancient Manuscripts of the New Testament

INTRODUCTION

We do not have the originals of any of the books of the New Testament. What we have are copies made later—in most cases many centuries later. All these copies have mistakes in them, whether accidental slips of the pen (many thousands of them) or intentional alterations made by scribes who wanted to change what the text actually said (these are fewer in number). Scholars involved in textual criticism examine all the surviving manuscripts to try to reconstruct what the biblical authors originally wrote and to see how scribes modified the author's words over the centuries of transmission. There are numerous places in the New Testament where scholars continue to debate what the original Greek wording may have been; there are some places where we may never know.

Included here are some of the most important and interesting surviving manuscripts of the New Testament, including some of the very oldest ones available.

Figure 1. P[52], a fragment of the Gospel of John (18:31–33, 37–38) discovered in a trash heap in the sands of Egypt. This credit card–sized scrap is the earliest surviving manuscript of the New Testament, dating from around 125–150 C.E. Both the front and back are pictured here.

Figure 2. This is one of the oldest surviving manuscripts of the letters of Paul, a valuable papyrus copy dating to about 200 C.E. (some 150 years after the books were themselves written) called P[46]. Contained here is the first part of the letter of Hebrews (which many scribes believed was written by Paul).

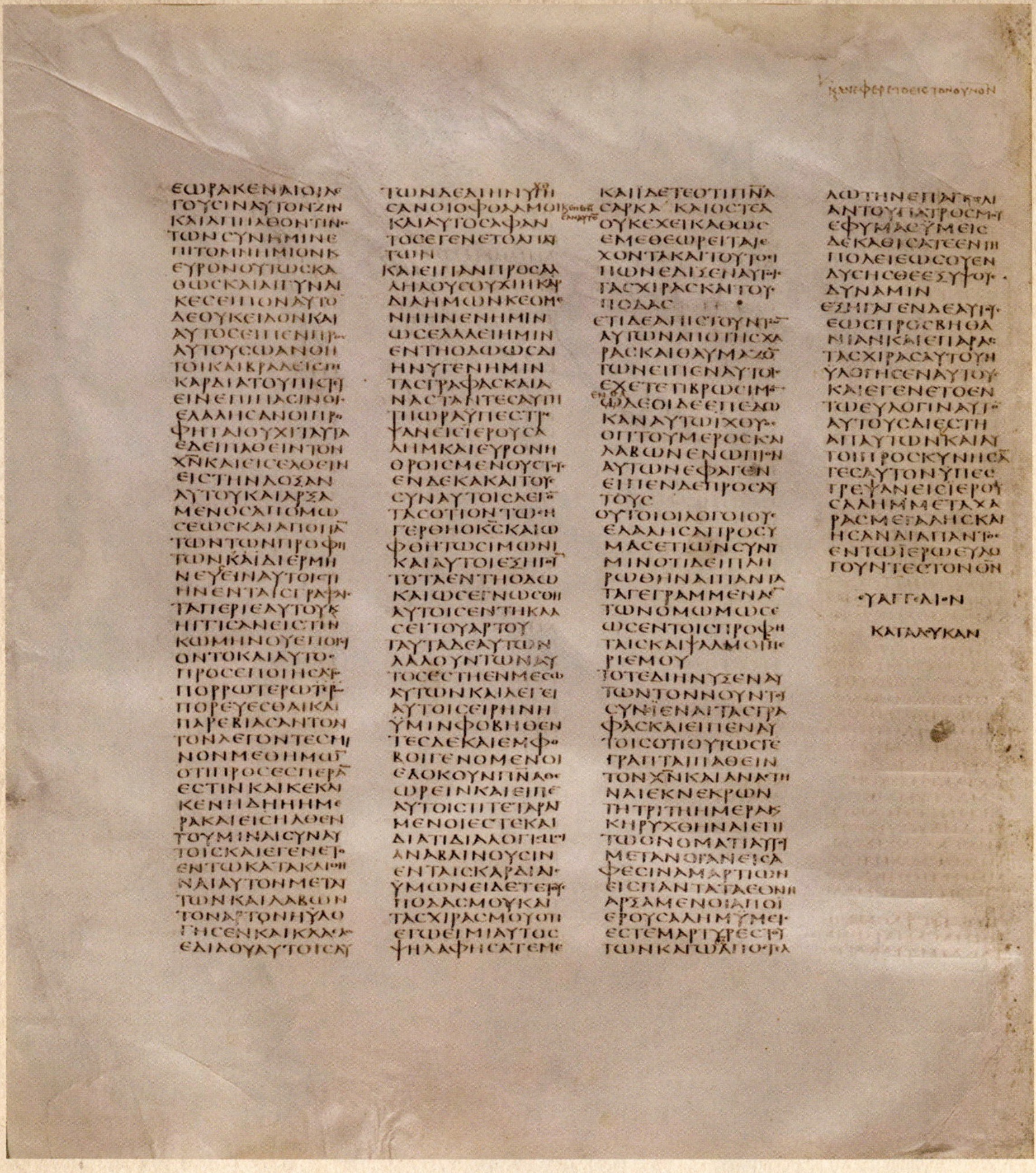

Figure 3. This is one of the most famous manuscripts of the Bible, called Codex Sinaiticus because it was discovered in the library of the monastery of St. Catherine on Mount Sinai in the nineteenth century by the famous manuscript scholar Constantine von Tischendorf. It dates from the mid-fourth century and is written on parchment, with four columns to a page. Shown here is the conclusion of the Gospel according to Luke.

Figure 4. The first chapter of the book of Hebrews in one of the oldest and best surviving manuscripts of the New Testament, Codex Vaticanus. Note the marginal note between the first and second columns. A corrector to the text had erased a word in verse 3 and substituted another word in its place; some centuries later, a second corrector came along, erased the correction, reinserted the original word, and wrote a note in the margin (between columns one and two) to castigate the first corrector. The note reads, "Fool and knave, leave the old reading, don't change it!"

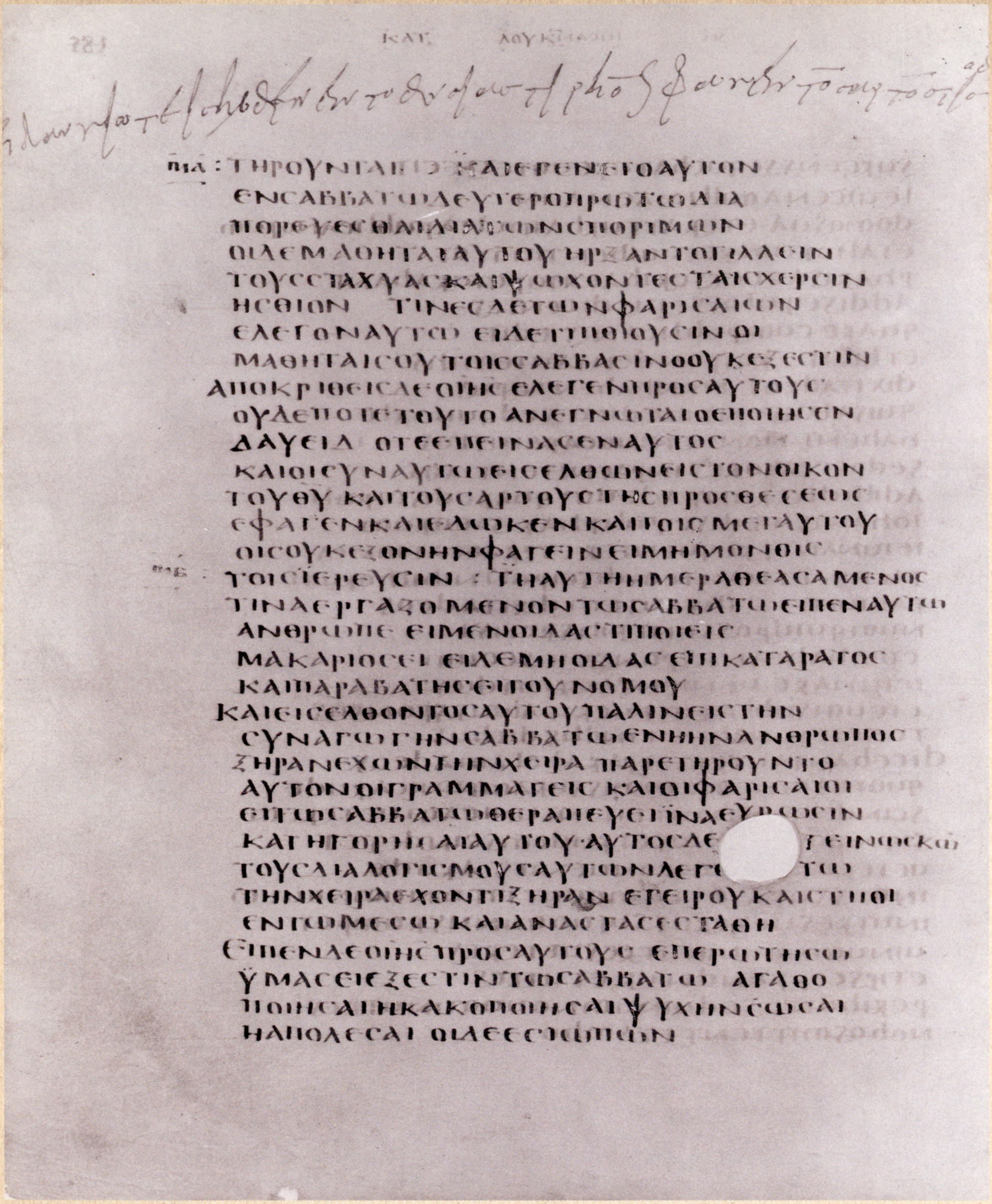

Figure 5. This is the famous manuscript D, called Codex Bezae, which dates to around the year 400. It is written with Latin on one side of the page and Greek on the other (only the Greek is shown here, from a passage of Luke 5). This manuscript differs in significant ways from most of our other early surviving witnesses. Notice the hole near the bottom of the page on the right and the scribbled note written at the top.

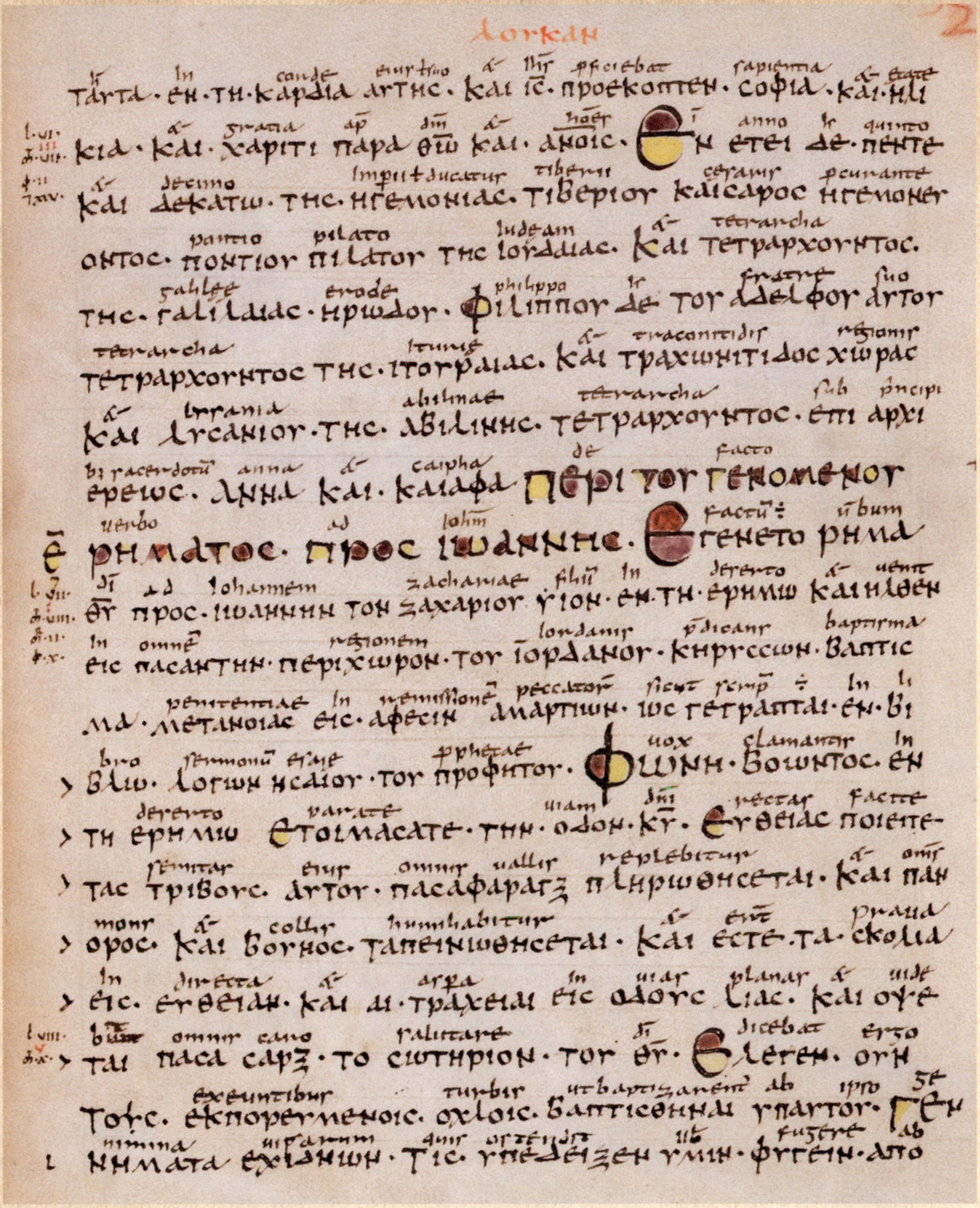

Figure 6. This interesting manuscript, called Codex Sangallensis, is from the ninth century. It is written in Greek. Each word had a Latin translation written above for the assistance of Latin-reading Christians who needed help understanding the Greek. Pictured is a passage of Luke 2–3.

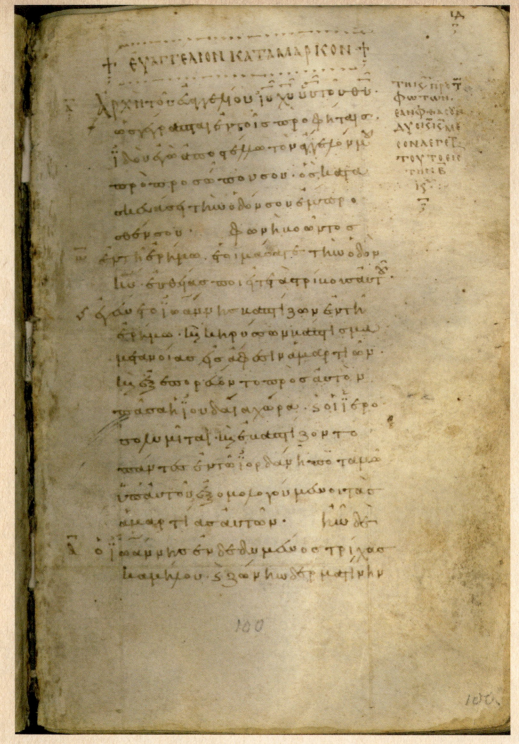

Figure 7. This is a parchment manuscript (MS 461) dated to 835 C.E.; it is noteworthy as the first dated manuscript to contain a minuscule style of writing, comparable in some ways to what we think of as cursive writing (as opposed to writing in block letters). Pictured here is the beginning of the Gospel of Mark.

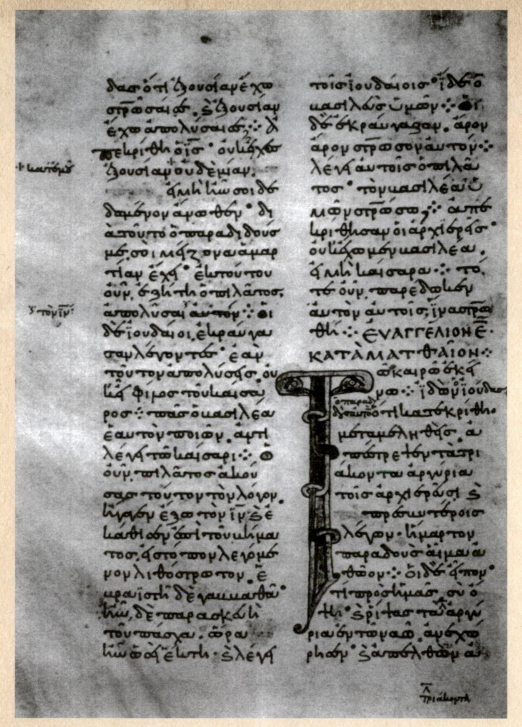

Figure 8. This visually interesting manuscript is a lectionary text; rather than giving the books of the New Testament in their entirety, it contains the readings from Scripture used in Christian worship services. Notice the elaborate artwork, especially the Greek *tau* (which looks like a **T**) in the right column, decorated with birds and vines. This text is from the late tenth century and contains portions of John 19 (the left column and most of the right) and Matthew 27 (the bottom of the right column).

4

The Traditions of Jesus in Their Greco-Roman Context

WHAT TO EXPECT

People who read the New Testament Gospels today generally assume that these books tell stories about Jesus simply as they happened. But is that true? None of these writers claims to be an eyewitness. And they wrote their accounts decades after the fact in a different language (Greek) from the one Jesus spoke (Aramaic).

Where did these writers get their stories? Did they simply drop out of the sky? Were they passed down by stenographers who followed Jesus and recorded everything he said and did? Did they come from notes taken by his disciples on their journeys? From somewhere else? Moreover, who were these authors? And what kind of books did they write?

We have already touched on one of the ironies involved in the historical study of the New Testament. If we choose to begin our study not with the earliest New Testament author, Paul, but with the person on whom his religion is in some sense based, Jesus, then we are compelled to begin by examining books that were written after Paul. Indeed, some of these books were among the last New Testament books to be produced. To reach the beginning, we have to start near the end.

At the same time, even though the **Gospels** themselves were written relatively late, they preserve traditions about Jesus that existed much earlier, many of them circulating among Christians long before Paul wrote his letters. Now that we have discussed several important aspects of the Greco-Roman environment within which the Christian religion was born and grew, we can examine the traditions themselves, as embodied near the end of the first century in the Gospels of Matthew, Mark, Luke, and John. How did these various authors acquire their traditions about Jesus?

ORAL TRADITIONS BEHIND THE GOSPELS

For the moment, we will leave aside the question of who these authors were (see "Some Additional Reflections" at the end of the chapter), except to point out that all the New Testament Gospels are anonymous: their authors did not sign their names. Our principal concern at present involves a different issue, namely, how and where these anonymous authors acquired their stories about Jesus. Here we are in the fortunate position of having some definite information, for one of these authors deals directly with this matter. Luke (we do not know his real name) begins his Gospel by mentioning earlier written accounts of Jesus' life and by indicating that both he and his predecessors acquired their information from Christians who had told stories about him (Luke 1:1–4). That is to say, these writings ultimately were based on oral traditions, stories that had circulated among Christians from the time Jesus died to the moment the Gospel writers put pen to paper. How much of an interval, exactly, was this?

No one knows for certain when Jesus died, but scholars agree that it was sometime around 30 C.E. In addition, most historians think that Mark was the first of our Gospels to be written, sometime between the mid-60s and the early 70s. Matthew and Luke were probably produced some ten or fifteen years later, perhaps around 80 or 85. John was written perhaps ten years after that, in 90 or 95. These are necessarily rough estimates, but almost all scholars agree within a few years.

Perhaps the most striking thing about these dates for the historian is the long interval between Jesus' death and the earliest accounts of his life. Our first written narratives of Jesus (i.e., the Gospels) appear to date from thirty-five to sixty-five years after the fact. This may not seem like a long time, but think about it in modern terms. For the shortest interval (the gap between Jesus and Mark), this would be like having the first written record of Richard Nixon's presidency appear today. For the longest interval (between Jesus and John), it would be like having stories about a famous preacher

from the early years of World War II show up in print for the first time this week. We should not assume that the Gospel accounts are necessarily unreliable simply because they are late, but the dates should give us pause. What was happening over these thirty, forty, fifty, or sixty years between Jesus' death and the writing of the Gospels?

Without a doubt, the most important thing that was happening for early Christianity was the spread of the religion from its inauspicious beginnings as a tiny sect of Jesus' Jewish followers in Jerusalem—the Gospels indicate that there were eleven men and several women who remained faithful to him after his crucifixion, say, a total of fifteen or twenty people altogether—to its status as a world religion enthusiastically supported by Christian believers in major urban areas throughout the Roman Empire. Missionaries like Paul actively propagated the faith, converting Jews and Gentiles to faith in Christ as the Son of God, who was crucified for the sins of the world and then raised by God from the dead.

By the end of the first century, this tiny group of Jesus' disciples had so multiplied that there were believing communities in cities of Judea, Samaria, and Galilee, probably in the region East of Jordan; in Syria, Cilicia, and Asia Minor; in Macedonia and Achaia (modern-day Greece); in Italy; and possibly in Spain. By this time Christian churches may have sprung up in the southern Mediterranean, probably in Egypt and possibly in North Africa.

To be sure, the Christians did not take the world by storm. Roman officials in the provinces appear to have taken little notice of the Christians until the second century; strikingly, there is not a single reference to Jesus or his followers in pagan literature of any kind during the first century of the Common Era. Nonetheless, the Christian religion quietly and persistently spread, not converting

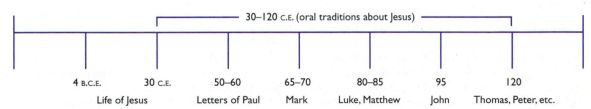

Figure 4.1 Time Line of the Early Christian Movement.

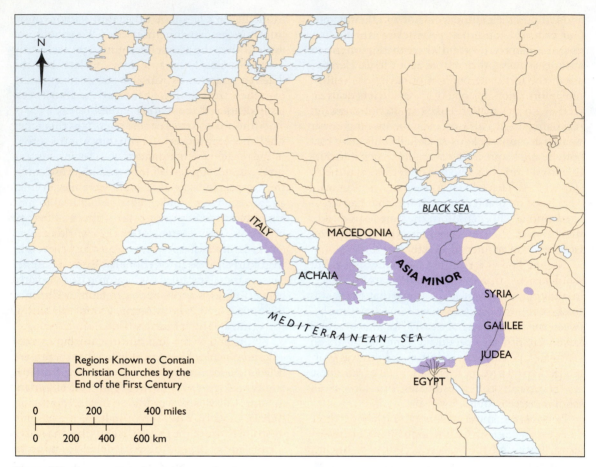

Regions Known to Contain
Christian Churches by the
End of the First Century

Figure 4.2 Christian Churches in Existence by 100 C.E.

millions of people, but almost certainly converting thousands, in numerous locations throughout the entire Mediterranean.

What did Christians tell people in order to convert them? Our evidence here is frustratingly sparse: examples of missionary sermons in the book of Acts and some intimations of Paul's preaching in his own letters (e.g., 1 Thess 1:9–10). We cannot tell how representative these are. Moreover, there are good reasons for thinking that most of the Christian mission was conducted not through public preaching, say on a crowded street corner, but privately, as individuals who had come to believe that Jesus was the Son of God told others about their newfound faith and tried to convince them to adopt it as well.

Since, in the Greco-Roman world, religion was a way of securing the favor of the gods, we are probably not too far afield to think that if faith in Jesus were known to produce beneficial, or even miraculous, results, then people might be persuaded to convert. If a Christian testified, for example, that praying to Jesus, or through Jesus to God, had healed her daughter, or that a believer in Jesus had cast out an evil spirit, or that the God of Jesus had miraculously provided food for a starving family, this might spark interest in her neighbor or coworker. Those with an interest in Jesus would want to learn more about him. Who was he? When did he live? What did he do? How did he die? The Christian, in turn, would be both compelled and gratified to tell stories about Jesus to anyone who was interested.

Such opportunities to tell stories about Jesus must have presented themselves throughout major urban areas of the Mediterranean for decades prior to the writing of the Gospels. Otherwise there is no way to account for the spread of the religion in an age that did not enjoy the benefits of tele-communication. When people had heard enough (however much that might have been), they might have decided to believe in Jesus. This would have involved, among other things, adopting aspects of Jesus' own religion, which for non-Jews meant accepting the Jewish God and abandoning their own gods, since Jews maintained that this One alone was the true God. Once the converts did so, they could join the Christian community by being baptized and receiving some rudimentary instruction.

We do not know exactly what the leaders would have told new converts, but we can imagine that they would have imparted some of the essentials of the faith: information about the one true God, his creation, and his son Jesus. To some extent, this would have involved telling yet other stories about who Jesus was, about how he came into the world, about what he taught, what he did, why he suffered, and how he died. Stories about Jesus were thus being told throughout the Mediterranean for decades, both to win people to faith and to edify those who had been brought in. They were told in evangelism, in instruction, and probably in services of worship. The stories would have, necessarily, been passed on by word of mouth, since, as we've seen, the Gospels had not yet been written. But who told the stories?

Unfortunately, we do not know the precise identity of those who were telling the stories about Jesus. Was every story told by one of the apostles? Impossible. The mission went on for years and years and years all over the map. Were the stories told by other eyewitnesses? Equally impossible. They must have been told, then, for the most part, by people who had not been there to see them happen, who had heard them from other people, who also had not been there to see them happen. The stories were passed on by word of mouth from one convert to the next. They were told in different countries, in Egypt, Judea, Galilee, Syria, and Cilicia, throughout Asia Minor, Macedonia, Achaia, Italy, and Spain. They were told in different contexts, for different reasons, at different times. They

were told in a language other than Jesus' own (he spoke Aramaic, while most of the converts spoke Greek), often by people who were not Jews, almost always by people who were not eyewitnesses and had never met an eyewitness.

Let me illustrate the process with a hypothetical example. Suppose I am a Greek-speaking worshiper of the goddess Artemis from Ephesus. I listen to a stranger passing through town, who tells of the wonders of Jesus, of his miracles and supernatural wisdom. I become intrigued. When I hear that this wandering stranger has performed miracles in Jesus' name— my neighbor's son was ill, but two days after the stranger prayed over him, he became well—I decide to inquire further. He tells of how Jesus performed great miracles and of how, even though wrongly accused by the Romans for sedition and crucified, he was raised by God from the dead. Based on everything I've heard, I decide to forego my devotion to Artemis. I put my faith in Jesus, get baptized, and join the local community.

I take a trip for business to nearby Smyrna. While there, I tell friends about my new faith and the stories I've learned about my new Lord. Three of them join me in becoming Christian. They begin to discuss these things with their neighbors and friends. Mostly they are rejected, but they acquire several converts, enough to come together once a week for worship, to discuss their faith, and to tell more stories. These new converts tell their own families the stories, converting some of them, who then take the word yet further afield.

And so it goes. As the new converts tell the stories, the religion grows, and most of the people telling the stories are not eyewitnesses. Indeed they have never laid eyes on an eyewitness or anyone else who has.

This example does not imply that if we had accounts based on eyewitnesses, they would necessarily be accurate. Even the testimonies of eyewitnesses can, and often do, conflict. But the scenario I have painted does help to explain why there are so many differences in the stories about Jesus that have survived from the early years of Christianity. These stories were circulated year after year after year, primarily by people who had believed their entire lives that the gods were sometimes present on earth, who knew of miracle workers who had appeared to benefit the human race, who had

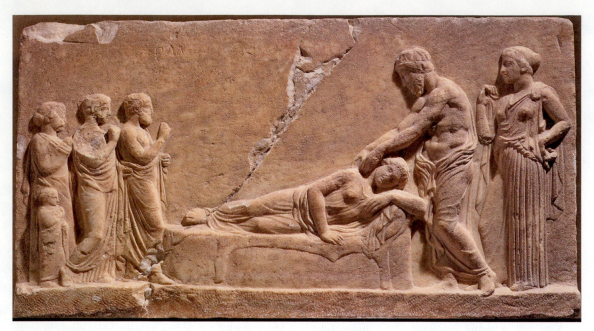

Figure 4.3 Stories of the power of the gods to heal the sick were widespread in the Greco-Roman world. Here we see a relief from the temple of the healing god Asclepius in the city of Piraeus, showing the god and his female assistant (on the right) curing a sleeping patient.

themselves heard fantastic stories about this Jewish holy man Jesus, and who were trying to convert others to their faith or to edify those who had already been converted. Furthermore, nearly all these storytellers had no independent knowledge of what really happened. It takes little imagination to realize what happened to the stories.

You are probably familiar with the old birthday party game "telephone." A group of kids sits in a circle, the first tells a brief story to the one sitting next to her, who tells it to the next, and to the next, and so on, until it comes back full circle to the one who started it. Invariably, the story has changed so much in the process of retelling that everyone gets a good laugh. (If it didn't work this way, who would play the game?!) Imagine this same activity taking place, not in a solitary living room with ten kids on one afternoon, but over the expanse of the Roman Empire (some 2,500 miles across), with thousands of participants—from different backgrounds, with different concerns, and in different contexts—some of whom

have to translate the stories into different languages (see box 4.1).

The situation, in fact, was even more complicated than that. People in the Christian communities that sprang up around the Mediterranean, like people just about everywhere, encountered severe difficulties in living their daily lives and thus sought help and direction from on high. The traditions about Jesus were part of the bedrock of these communities; his actions were a model that Christians tried to follow; his words were teachings they obeyed. Given this context, is it conceivable that Christians could have made up a story that proved useful in a particular situation? Creating a story is not far removed from changing one, and presumably people would have good reasons for doing both.

Christians would not have to be deceitful or malicious to invent a story about something that Jesus said or did; they would not even have to be conscious of doing so. All sorts of stories about people are made up without ill intent, and sometimes stories are told about persons that we know

ANOTHER GLIMPSE INTO THE PAST

BOX 4.1   Orality and Literacy in the Ancient World

Nearly everyone we come in contact with can read and write on at least an elementary level; most can read the sports page, for instance. Recent studies have shown, however, that things have not always been this way, that widespread literacy is a purely modern phenomenon. Preindustrial societies had neither the incentive nor the means to provide mass education in literacy for their children. They had no real incentive because the means of production didn't require that everyone read, and they couldn't afford the expense of providing the necessary training in any case. Such societies were far more dependent on the spoken word than the written.

Even ancient Greece and Rome were largely oral cultures, despite the unreflective assumption held even among some scholars that these societies, which produced so many literary classics, must have been largely literate. We now know that most people in the Greco-Roman world could not read, let alone write. Estimates of the level of literacy vary, but several important studies have concluded that in the best of times (e.g., Athens in the days of Socrates), only 10 to 15 percent of the population (the vast majority of them males) could read and write at an elementary level. Moreover, in this world even literary texts were oral phenomena: books were made to be read out loud, often in public, so that a person usually "read" a book by hearing it read by someone else.

Interestingly, even as these societies developed a dependence on texts—for example, by using writ-

ten tax receipts, contracts, and wills—they did not promote literacy for the masses. Instead, those who were literate began to hire out their services to those who were not.

Until recently it has been commonly thought (again, even among scholars) that oral cultures could be counted on to preserve their traditions reliably, that people in such societies were diligent in remembering what they heard and could reproduce it accurately when asked about it. This, however, is another myth that has been exploded by recent studies of literacy. We have now come to see that people in oral cultures typically do not share the modern concern for preserving traditions intact, and do not repeat them exactly the same way every time. On the contrary, the concern for verbal accuracy has been instilled in us by the phenomenon of mass literacy itself; since anyone now can check to see if a fact has been remembered correctly (by looking it up), we have developed a sense that traditions ought to remain invariable and unchanged. In most oral societies, however, traditions are understood to be malleable; that is, they are *supposed* to be changed and made relevant to the new situations in which they are cited.

The importance of these new studies should be obvious as we begin to reflect on the fate of the traditions about Jesus as they spread by word of mouth throughout the largely illiterate Greco-Roman world.

are not historically accurate: ask any well-known person who is widely talked about—a politician, religious leader, or university professor.

The Nature of the Gospel Traditions

It does not appear that the authors of the early Gospels were eyewitnesses to the events that they narrate. But they must have gotten their stories from somewhere. Indeed, one of them acknowledges that he has heard stories about Jesus and read

earlier accounts (Luke 1:1–4). It appears that in addition to preserving genuine historical recollections about what Jesus actually said and did, these authors also narrated stories that had been modified, or even invented, in the process of retelling.

The notion that the Gospels contain at least some stories that had been changed over the years is not pure speculation; in fact, we have hard evidence of this preserved in the Gospels themselves (we will examine some of this evidence in a moment). We also have reason to think that early Christians were not particularly concerned that stories about Jesus were being changed. Odd as it may seem to us, most believers appear to have been less concerned than we are about what we would call the facts of history. Even though we as twenty-first-century persons tend to think that something cannot be true unless it happened, ancient Christians, along with a lot of other ancient people, did not think this way. For them, something could be true whether or not it happened. What mattered more than historical fact was what we might call religious or moral truth.

On one level, even modern people consider "moral truth" to be more important than historical fact. That is, they will occasionally concede that something can be true even if it didn't happen. Consider, for example, a story that every second-grader in the country has heard, the story of George Washington and the cherry tree. As a young lad, George takes the axe to the tree in his father's front yard. When his father comes home and asks, "Who cut down my cherry tree?" George confesses, "I cannot tell a lie. I did it."

Historians know that this never happened. In fact, the Christian minister who made up the story (known as "Parson Weems") later admitted to it. Why then do we tell the story? For one thing, the story stresses one of the ultimate values that we claim as a country. We use the story to teach children that our country is rooted in integrity. Who was George Washington? He was the father of our nation. What kind of man was he? He was an honest man, a man of integrity! Really? How honest was he? Well, one time when he was a boy. . . . The point of the story? This country is founded on honesty. *It* cannot tell a lie. In other words, the story serves as a piece of national propaganda. I'm reasonably sure, at least, that it's not a story told to schoolchildren in Tehran.

The account of George Washington and the cherry tree is told for at least one other reason as well, related not so much to national image as to personal ethics. We tell this story to children because we want them to know that they should not lie under any circumstances. Even if they've done something bad, something harmful, they should not try to deceive others about it. It is better to come clean and deal with the consequences than to distort the truth and make things worse. So we tell the story, not because it really happened, but because in some sense we think it is true.

The stories about Jesus in the early church may have been similar. To be sure, many of them are accounts of things that really did happen (part of our task will be figuring out which ones did). Others are historical reminiscences that have been changed, sometimes a little, sometimes a lot, in the retelling. Others were made up by Christians, possibly well-meaning Christians, at some point prior to the writing of the Gospels (see box 4.2). But they all are meant to convey the truth, as the storyteller saw it, about Jesus.

A Piece of Evidence

That stories about Jesus were changed (or made up) in the process of retelling is not just a wild idea dreamed up by university professors with too much time on their hands. In fact there is good evidence for it, evidence that can be found in the stories themselves as they have come down to us in the Gospels. In numerous instances different Gospels tell the same story, but the stories differ in significant ways. Sometimes these differences represent simple shifts in emphasis. At other times, however, they represent irreconcilable conflicts. What is striking is that whether the changes are reconcilable or not, they often point to an attempt by some early Christian storyteller to convey an important idea about Jesus. Here we will look at just one example; dozens could easily be cited, all of them suggesting that many early Christians were willing to change a historical fact in order to make a theological point.

The illustration I have chosen concerns a small detail with profound implications—the day and time of Jesus' death. All four Gospels of the New Testament indicate that Jesus was crucified sometime during Passover week, in Jerusalem, on orders of the Roman governor, Pontius Pilate. But there is a key discrepancy in the accounts. To understand it, you will need some background information.

In the days of Jesus, **Passover** was the most important Jewish festival. It commemorated the exodus of the children of Israel from their bondage in Egypt. The Hebrew Scriptures narrate the commemorative event itself (Exod 7–12). According to

ANOTHER EARLY CHRISTIAN TEXT

BOX 4.2   The *Infancy Gospel of Thomas*

The only stories in the New Testament about Jesus prior to his baptism as an adult are the accounts of his birth in Matthew and Luke and the episode in Luke in which he stays behind as a twelve-year-old in Jerusalem after his parents return home from the Passover feast. Early Christians were curious, however, about what Jesus might have done during the "missing years" for which we have no record. Driving their curiosity was a question that some people still ask today: if Jesus was a miracle-working Son of God as an adult, what was he like as a kid?

To answer the question, Christians made up stories about Jesus' childhood. Some of these came to be written down in what are now referred to as the **"Infancy Gospels"** (since they record events from Jesus' very early childhood onward). Even though these are all legendary accounts, some of them were written quite early. Probably the earliest is one called the *Infancy Gospel of Thomas*. This is a narrative of Jesus' life between the ages of five and twelve.

It is an intriguing account, in part because it portrays the young Jesus as not only powerful but also a bit mischievous. When he is found to have made some clay sparrows in the mud near a riverbank on the Sabbath and is accused of violating the Sabbath law, he claps his hands, brings the birds to life, and sends them off chirping. ("I made clay sparrows?? *What* clay sparrows?!") When a child irritates him, Jesus speaks a word and he immediately dies. When a teacher is angry at him for not cooperating and smacks him on the head, Jesus withers him on the spot.

Eventually Jesus starts using his powers for the good—raising from the dead those he has zapped and proving remarkably handy around the house and carpenter shop (if his dad miscuts a board, Jesus is there to fix it miraculously).

It is hard to know whether this book was meant as a serious account or as an entertaining fictional narrative devised by Christians with good imaginations. But it's not hard to understand why the book never became part of the New Testament, given its portrayal of the mischievous boy Jesus.

the ancient accounts, God raised up Moses to deliver his people and through him brought ten plagues on the land of Egypt to convince the Pharaoh to set his people free. The tenth plague was by far the worst: the death of every first-born human and animal in the land. In preparation for the onslaught, God instructed Moses to have every family of the Israelites sacrifice a lamb and spread its blood on the lintels and doorposts of their houses. In that way, when the angel of death came to bring destruction, he would see the blood on the doors of the Israelites and "pass over" them to go to the homes of the Egyptians.

The children of Israel were told to eat a quick meal in preparation for their escape. There was not time even to allow the bread to rise; they were therefore to eat it unleavened. The Israelites did as they were told; the angel of death came and went. The Pharaoh pleaded with the children of Israel to leave, they fled to the Red Sea, where they made their final escape through the parted waters.

The Israelites were instructed through Moses to commemorate this event annually. Hundreds of years later, in the days of Jesus, the Passover celebration brought large numbers of pilgrims to Jerusalem, where they would participate in sacrifices in the Temple and eat a sacred meal of symbolic foods, including a lamb, bitter herbs to recall their bitter hardship in Egypt, unleavened bread, and several cups of wine. The sequence of events was typically as follows. Lambs would be brought to the Temple, or purchased there, for sacrifice with the assistance of a priest. They would then be prepared for the Passover meal by being skinned, drained of their blood, and possibly butchered. Each person or family who brought a lamb would then take it home and prepare the meal. That evening was the

Passover feast, which inaugurated the weeklong celebration called the Feast of Unleavened Bread.

As you may know, in Jewish reckoning, a new day begins when it gets dark (that is why the Jewish Sabbath begins on Friday evening). So the lambs would be prepared for the Passover meal on the afternoon of the day before the meal would actually be eaten. When it got dark, the new day started, and the meal could begin.

This now takes us to the dating of Jesus' execution. The Gospel of Mark, probably our earliest account, clearly indicates when Jesus was put on trial. On the preceding day, according to Mark 14:12, the disciples ask Jesus where he would have them "prepare" the Passover. This is said to happen on the day when the priests "sacrifice the passover lamb," or the day of Preparation for the Passover (the afternoon before the Passover meal). Jesus gives them their instructions, and they make the preparations. That evening—the start of the next day for them—they celebrate the meal together (14:17–25).

At this special occasion, Jesus takes the symbolic foods of the meal and endows them with additional meaning, saying, "This is my body . . . this is my blood of the covenant" (14:22–24). Afterward, he goes with his disciples to (the Garden of) Gethsemane, where he is betrayed by Judas Iscariot and arrested (14:32, 43). He is immediately put on trial before the Jewish Council, the Sanhedrin (14:53). He spends the night in jail; early in the morning the Sanhedrin delivers him over to Pilate (15:1). After a short trial, Pilate condemns him to death. He is led off to be crucified and is nailed to the cross at 9:00 a.m. (15:25). Thus, in the Gospel of Mark, Jesus is executed the day after the Preparation of the Passover, that is, on the morning after the Passover meal had been eaten.

Our latest canonical account of this event is in the Gospel of John. Many of the details here are similar to Mark: the same persons are involved, and many of the same stories are told. There are differences, however, and some of them are significant. (See box 4.3.) What is particularly striking, and significant for our investigation here, is that we are told exactly when the trial comes to an end with Pilate's verdict: "Now it was the day of Preparation for the Passover, and it was about 12:00 noon" (John 19:14). Jesus is immediately sent off to be crucified (19:16).

The day of Preparation for the Passover? How could this be? That is the day before the Passover meal was eaten, the day the priests began to sacrifice the lambs at noon. But in Mark, Jesus had his

---

WHAT DO YOU THINK?

BOX 4.3 Mark and John on the Time of Jesus' Death

Mark

The Jewish Passover meal takes place on a Thursday evening.

Jesus' Last Supper is a Passover meal; it occurs on a Thursday, the evening after the Passover lambs are slaughtered.

After the supper, Jesus is arrested. He spends the night in jail and is tried by Pilate in the morning.

Jesus is crucified at 9:00 a.m., the morning after the Passover meal was eaten.

John

The Jewish Passover meal takes place on a Friday evening.

Jesus' Last Supper is not a Passover meal; it occurs on a Thursday, the evening before the Passover lambs are slaughtered.

After the supper, Jesus is arrested. He spends the night in jail and is tried by Pilate in the morning.

Jesus is crucified after noon, the day before the Passover meal was eaten.

disciples prepare the Passover meal on that day, and then he ate the meal with them in the evening after it became dark, only to be arrested afterward.

If you read John's account carefully, you will notice other indications that Jesus is said to be executed on a different day than he is in Mark. John 18:28, for example, gives the reason that the Jewish leaders refuse to enter into Pilate's place of residence for Jesus' trial. It is because they do not want to become ritually defiled, and thereby prevented from eating the Passover meal that evening (recall, according to Mark, they had already eaten the meal the night before!). This difference in dating explains another interesting feature of John's Gospel. In this account Jesus never instructs his disciples to prepare for the Passover, and he evidently does not eat a Passover meal during his last evening with them (he does not, for example, take the symbolic foods and say, "This is my body" and "This is my blood"). The reason for these differences should by now be clear: in John's Gospel, Jesus was already in his tomb by the time of this meal.

We seem to be left with a difference that is difficult to reconcile. Both Mark and John indicate the day and hour of Jesus' death, but they disagree. In John's account, Jesus is executed sometime after noon on the day on which preparations were being made to eat the Passover meal. In Mark's account, he is killed the following day, the morning after the Passover meal had been eaten, sometime around 9:00 a.m. If we grant that there is a difference, how do we explain it?

Some scholars have argued that John's account is more accurate historically, since it coincides better with Jewish sources that describe how criminal trials were to be conducted by the Sanhedrin. If these scholars are right, then Mark or one of his sources may have changed the day on which Jesus was killed in order to promote the idea that Jesus himself had instituted the Lord's Supper during the Passover meal. This is possible, but may not be the best explanation. The Jewish sources that describe the procedures of the Sanhedrin were written nearly 200 years after this event and thus are probably not our best guide.

If we concede that the later account (John's) is on general principle less likely to be accurate, since so many more years and so many more storytellers would have intervened between the account

and the events it narrates, an intriguing possibility arises to explain why John, or his source, may have changed the detail concerning Jesus' death. John is the only Gospel in which Jesus is actually identified as "the lamb of God who takes away the sins of the world." Indeed, he is called this at the very start of the Gospel, by his forerunner, John the Baptist (1:29; cf. 1:36). In the Fourth Gospel, Jesus' death represents the salvation of God, just as the sacrifice of the lamb represented salvation for the ancient Israelites during the first Passover. Perhaps John (or his source) made a change in the day and hour of Jesus' death precisely to reinforce this theological point. In this Gospel, Jesus dies on the same day as the Passover lamb, at the same hour (just after noon)—to show that Jesus really is the lamb of God.

Conclusion: The Early Traditions about Jesus

This analysis gives just one example of how historical facts may have been changed to convey theological "truths." We could easily examine other examples pertaining to such key events in the Gospels as Jesus' birth, his baptism, his miracles, his teachings, and his resurrection. The main point is that the stories that Christians told and retold about Jesus were not meant to be objective history lessons for students interested in key events of Roman imperial times. They were meant to convince people that Jesus was the miracle-working Son of God whose death brought salvation to the world and to edify and instruct those who already believed. Sometimes the stories were modified to express a theological truth. For the early Christians who passed along the stories we now have in the Gospels, it was sometimes legitimate and necessary to change a historical fact in order to make a theological point. Moreover, these are the stories that the Gospel writers inherited.

This conclusion has some profound implications for our investigation of the Gospels. The first concerns the Gospels as pieces of early Christian literature. Just as the Gospel writers inherited stories that try to make a point, they themselves have attempted to produce coherent accounts of Jesus' life and death to make certain points. Each Gospel author may have had his own points to make, and these may not have been the same in every case. Mark's point may not have been John's point in his story of Jesus' crucifixion. It is important then—indeed, absolutely crucial—that we allow each author to have his own say, rather than assume that they are all trying to say the same thing. We need to study each account for its own emphases.

The second implication concerns the Gospels as historical sources for what happened during the life of Jesus. If the Gospels have differences in historical detail, and each Gospel preserves traditions that have been changed, then it is impossible for the historian simply to take these stories at face value and uncritically assume that they provide historically accurate information. We will therefore need to develop some criteria for deciding which features of the Gospels represent Christianizations of the tradition and which represent the life of Jesus as it can be historically reconstructed.

Over the course of the next several chapters, we will devote our attention to the first aspect of our study, the literary emphasis of each Gospel. Once we understand in greater detail where the Gospels came from and what each one has to say, we will

then be equipped to address the second issue, asking broader historical questions in an attempt to establish what actually happened in the life of Jesus.

THE GOSPELS AS BIOGRAPHIES OF JESUS

Now that we know where the Gospel writers got their stories about Jesus, what can we say about the books they wrote? What kind of writings are they?

Scholars have come to recognize that the Gospels are not completely unlike other kinds of literature from the Greco-Roman world, but are like **"ancient biographies"** of other important people. This does not mean that the Gospels are like *modern* biographies. Modern biographies are usually based on extensive research and archival work by their authors, who examine hundreds of sources to put together an accurate chronological sketch of a person's life and who are interested particularly in providing explanations of why they said and acted the way they did (often explaining their personality traits on the basis of the formative influences on their early lives).

AT A GLANCE

BOX 4.4 The Traditions of Jesus

1. Jesus died around 30 C.E.; the Gospels were written thirty-five to sixty-five years later, between 65 and 95 C.E.

2. The authors of the New Testament Gospels are anonymous; they did not claim to be eyewitnesses to the events they narrate.

3. The authors of the Gospels inherited their accounts of Jesus from oral traditions that had been in circulation during the intervening decades.

4. Stories passed on by word of mouth tend to change over time, sometimes significantly.

5. There is evidence that the Gospels contain stories changed in the long process of retelling, for example, when different Gospels tell the same story in different, even irreconcilable, ways.

6. From a literary perspective, each account should thus be studied on its own terms. We should not assume that all the accounts have the same message.

7. Moreover, from a historical perspective, differences in our sources require us to devise methods for determining what really happened in the life of Jesus.

8. The Gospels are ancient biographies of Jesus.

9. As such, they are based on several oral and written sources, which were used to provide chronological accounts of Jesus' life that portrayed his personal character, starting with the opening scenes of the narrative.

But ancient biographies were different. There were not as many sources to consult, as a rule, and no "data retrieval systems" to assist authors in compiling data. Ancient biographies were, to be sure, usually based on oral and written sources. But unlike modern biographers, ancient ones often showed a preference for the oral (since unlike written sources, oral ones can be questioned!). Moreover, ancient biographies were less concerned with relating historical events than with showing the *character* of the main figure through his or her words, deeds, and interactions.

Perhaps most important, ancient biographies did not try to show how a person's character developed over time because most ancient people believed that a person's character was relatively constant through his or her life. Instead, ancient biographies showed how a person's character was manifest in his or her daily life—starting from childhood. Since personality traits were thought of as constant, an ancient biography would often portray the main figure's character at the very outset of the narrative.

Knowing this about ancient biographies is useful because if the Gospels are that kind of writing, we can expect them to share these same features: the Gospels then will be narrative descriptions of what Jesus said and did, based on oral and written sources. In them Jesus' character will be portrayed as constant throughout his life, and one does not need to wait long to find out what that character is. It will be evident at the very outset of the narrative.

SOME ADDITIONAL REFLECTIONS: THE AUTHORS OF THE GOSPELS

Some Christians of the second century, some decades after most of the New Testament books had been written, claimed that their favorite Gospels had been penned by two of Jesus' disciples—Matthew, the tax collector, and John, the beloved disciple—and by two friends of the apostles—Mark, the secretary of Peter, and Luke, the traveling companion of Paul. But it is difficult to accept this tradition, for several reasons.

First of all, none of these Gospels makes any such claim about itself. All four authors chose to

keep their identities anonymous. Would they have done so if they had been eyewitnesses? This certainly would have been possible, but one would at least have expected an eyewitness or a friend of an eyewitness to authenticate his account by appealing to personal knowledge, for example, by narrating the stories in the first person singular ("On the day that Jesus and I went up to Jerusalem . . .").

Moreover, we know something about the backgrounds of the people who accompanied Jesus during most of his ministry. The disciples appear to have been uneducated peasants from Galilee. Both Simon Peter and John the son of Zebedee, for example, are said to have been peasant fishermen (Mark 1:16–20) who were "uneducated," that is, literally, unable to read and write (Acts 4:13). Now it is true that the Gospels do not represent the most elegant literature from antiquity, but their authors were highly educated; they write, for the most part, correct Greek. Could two of them have been disciples?

Again, it is possible. Jesus and his apostles, however, appear to have spoken Aramaic, the common language of the Jews in Palestine. Whether they could also have spoken Greek as a second language is something that scholars have long debated, but at the very least it is clear that Greek was not their native tongue. The authors of the Gospels, on the other hand, are absolutely fluent in Greek. Did the apostles go back to school after Jesus died, overcome years of illiteracy by learning how to read and write at a relatively high level, become skilled in foreign composition, and then later pen the Gospels? Most scholars consider it somewhat unlikely.

Perhaps an even more important aspect of the authorship of the Gospels is the evidence that they appear to preserve stories that were in circulation for a long period. This observation certainly applies to narratives for which no eyewitnesses were evidently present. For example, if Pilate and Jesus were alone at the trial, as indicated in John 18:28–19:16, and Jesus was immediately executed, who told the Fourth Evangelist what Jesus actually said? An early Christian must have come up with words that seemed appropriate to the occasion. The same principle applies to the other accounts of the Gospels as well. All of them appear to have circulated by word of mouth among Christian converts throughout the Mediterranean world.

One of our four authors, Luke, explicitly tells us that he used oral and written sources for his narrative (Luke 1:1–4), and he claims that some of these sources were drawn ultimately from eyewitnesses. This circumstance raises another interesting question. Is it likely that authors who extensively used earlier sources for their accounts were themselves eyewitnesses? Suppose, for example, that Matthew actually was a disciple who accompanied Jesus and witnessed the things he said and did. Why then would he take almost all his stories, sometimes word for word, from another written account (as we will see in Chapter 6)?

In short, it appears that the Gospels have inherited traditions from both written and oral sources, as Luke himself acknowledges, and that these sources drew from traditions that had been circulating for years, decades even, among Christian communities throughout the Mediterranean world.

TAKE A STAND

1. You're talking to a friend about religion, and she tells you that in her opinion, the stories about Jesus that were in oral circulation before the Gospels were written down must have been highly accurate and factual because there were still eyewitnesses around who could verify what really happened in Jesus' life. Do you agree or disagree? State your reasons.

2. Another friend tells you that the Gospels are historically accurate and do not have any "changed" traditions in them; that is, everything the Gospels say about the life and teachings of Jesus happened exactly the way they say it did. Moreover, in his opinion, this can be demonstrated, since the Gospels were written by eyewitnesses who were concerned to get the story straight (and historically accurate). How do you respond?

3. You read an article on the Internet that claims that the Gospels were written by Matthew, the tax collector-disciple of Jesus; John the beloved disciple; Mark the secretary of Peter; and Luke the companion of Paul. What is your view, and why?

SUGGESTIONS FOR FURTHER READING

Aune, David. *The New Testament in Its Literary Environment.* Philadelphia: Westminster, 1987. A superb introduction to the genres of the New Testament writings in relation to other literature of the Greco-Roman world.

Burridge, Richard. *What Are the Gospels? A Comparison with Greco-Roman Biography.* 2d ed. Cambridge: Cambridge University Press, 2004. A thorough study that emphatically argues that the Gospels are best understood as a kind of ancient biography.

Dibelius, Martin. *From Tradition to Gospel.* Trans. B. L. Woolf. New York: Scribner, 1934. This groundbreaking study deals with the character of the traditions about Jesus in circulation orally prior to being written down in the Gospels.

Gerhardsson, Birger. *Manuscript and Memory: Oral Tradition and Written Transmission in Rabbinic Judaism and Early Christianity.* Lund, Sweden: Gleerup, 1961. One of the most influential studies to maintain, contrary to the present chapter, that the traditions about Jesus in the New Testament Gospels were not changed, for the most part, in the process of being retold; for advanced students.

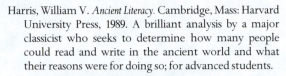

Harris, William V. *Ancient Literacy*. Cambridge, Mass: Harvard University Press, 1989. A brilliant analysis by a major classicist who seeks to determine how many people could read and write in the ancient world and what their reasons were for doing so; for advanced students.

Hezser, Catherine. *Jewish Literacy in Roman Palestine*. Tübingen, Germany: Mohr Siebeck, 2001. The most thorough and scholarly treatment of every aspect of reading and writing in Palestine at the time of the beginning of Christianity; for advanced students.

McKnight, Edgar V. *What Is Form Criticism?* Eugene, Ore.: Wipf and Stock, 1997. A basic introduction to the study of how oral traditions about Jesus were modified and formed prior to the writing of the Gospels.

Macmullen, Ramsey. *Christianizing the Roman Empire* A.D. *100–400*. New Haven, Conn.: Yale University Press, 1984. A concise and insightful account of the spread of Christianity through the Roman world, including discussion on how Christians engaged in their mission and the reasons for their success.

Ong, W. J. *Orality and Literacy*. 2d ed. London: Routledge, 2002. An intriguing discussion of the social and psychological differences between oral and written cultures (between cultures in which traditions are typically heard and those in which they are typically read); for more advanced students.

 KEY TERMS

| ancient biographies Gospels | Passover | *Infany Gospel of Thomas* | **Infancy Gospels** |

5

Jesus, the Suffering Son of God
THE GOSPEL ACCORDING TO MARK

WHAT TO EXPECT

If the early Christian Gospels were ancient religious biographies of Jesus, how should that affect their interpretation? Should we take them to be historically accurate accounts? Pure fictions? Something in between?

We begin exploring such questions by taking the Gospel of Mark as our first example. Mark is the shortest and probably the earliest surviving account of Jesus' life. In this chapter we will be especially concerned with the author's overarching message, seeing how, in a series of scenes, he establishes Jesus' character as the messiah sent from God in fulfillment of the Jewish Scriptures, the Son of God chosen by God to fulfill his mission on earth.

To this point of our study we have seen important aspects of the Greco-Roman environment of the New Testament, especially early Judaism, and we have considered both the oral traditions that lie behind the Gospels and the "genre" (i.e., kind of literature) that these books are: ancient biographies of Jesus. We are nearly ready to plunge into our study of the Gospel texts themselves. But before we do so, we need to consider an important aspect of how the Gospels are related to one another.

THE SYNOPTIC PROBLEM

Matthew, Mark, and Luke are very much like each other and (as we will see) very different from John. These first three Gospels are *so* much alike—telling many of the same stories, frequently in the same sequence, often in the same words—that they can be placed side by side in columns and carefully compared with one another. For this reason they are called the **"Synoptic" Gospels** (from the Latin word for "seen together"). How does one explain the fact that these Gospels agree so extensively, and yet also disagree a lot? The technical term for this question is **"The Synoptic Problem."**

Since the early days of Christianity, it has been recognized that the best solution to the Synoptic Problem is that the authors of these Gospels all copied from the same written sources, sometimes keeping the wording of their sources intact and sometimes changing the wording as they saw fit. Since the late nineteenth century, scholars have

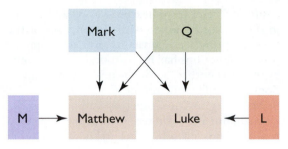

Figure 5.1   The Four-Source Hypothesis.

widely thought that it is possible to speak of *four* sources for these books.

1. First, it is usually understood that Mark was the first Gospel written and that Matthew and Luke borrowed many of their stories, often word for word, from Mark. This view is called **"Markan Priority"** (since Mark was written prior to the other Gospels).

2. Second, Matthew and Luke have a number of passages in common that are not found in Mark (e.g., the Lord's Prayer and the Beatitudes). It does not appear that one of these authors derived his stories from the other. They both, therefore, must have used some other source that is no longer available. Scholars call this source **"Q"** (short for "Quelle," the German word for "source"). Q, then, is the material found in both Matthew and Luke that is *not* found in Mark. Most of this material consists of Jesus' sayings.

3. Third, Matthew has some stories not found in either of the other Gospels (e.g., the visit of the wise men). These stories must have come from some other source that scholars call **"M"** (= Matthew's special source). M may well have been several different sources, written or oral.

4. Finally, Luke also has stories found nowhere else (e.g., the parable of the Good Samaritan). These must have come from yet another source, commonly labeled **"L"** (Luke's special source). L may well have been several different sources, written or oral.

And so we have the **four-source hypothesis** as the most popular explanation for the Synoptic Problem. Since this solution maintains that Mark was our first Gospel to be written, we can begin our examination of these books there.

 MARK, OUR EARLIEST GOSPEL

We do not know who the author of the Gospel of Mark was, only that he was a Greek-speaking Christian, presumably living outside Palestine, who had heard a number of stories about Jesus. Mark (as I will continue to call him since we do not know his real name) penned an extended account of Jesus' life beginning with his appearance as an adult to be baptized by John and ending with the report of his resurrection. In addition to stories that he had heard, Mark may also have used some written sources for portions of his narrative. If so, these sources no longer survive.

An introductory textbook such as this cannot provide an exhaustive analysis of Mark (or the other Gospels). My purpose here is simply to provide some guidance for your own interpretation of the book by supplying you with important keys for unlocking its meaning. My working assumption, throughout our discussions, is that you have already familiarized yourself with the contents of the book by reading it carefully all the way through a couple of times.

There are a number of ways we could approach this investigation. Indeed, we will be taking different approaches to each of the Gospels that we examine. We will study Mark, however, in light of the issues discussed in the previous chapter. Let's assume that we are informed readers of this text, conversant with the genre and knowledgeable about the world within which it was written. Knowing that Mark is a kind of Greco-Roman biography about Jesus, we can ask, who was Jesus, according to this literary portrayal, and what did he do? And how is this message conveyed through the shape of the narrative?

 THE BEGINNING OF THE GOSPEL: JESUS THE MESSIAH, THE SON OF GOD WHO FULFILLS SCRIPTURE

One of the first things that strikes the informed reader of Mark's Gospel is how thoroughly its traditions are rooted in a Jewish worldview. The book begins, as do many other ancient biographies, by naming its subject: "The Beginning of the Gospel of Jesus Christ" (1:1). Readers living in the Greco-Roman world would not recognize **"Christ"** as a name; for most of them it was not even a meaningful title. The word comes from the verb "anoint" and typically referred to someone who had just had a rubdown (with oil). "Christ" *was* a title in Jewish circles, however, as the Greek equivalent of the Hebrew word **"messiah."** Mark, then, is a book about Jesus the messiah.

We now know that Jews in the first century could have meant a range of things by the title messiah (see box 5.1). Many of these meanings, however, can be subsumed under two major rubrics (which are not necessarily mutually exclusive). For some Jews, the messiah was the future king of Israel, who would deliver God's people from their oppressors and establish a sovereign state in Israel through God's power. For others, he was a cosmic deliverer from heaven, who would engage in supernatural warfare with the enemies of the Jews and bring a divine victory over their oppressors. Both notions had been around for some time by the first century; both, obviously, were designations of grandeur and power.

Mark begins his Gospel by calling Jesus the messiah. But as we will see—and as everyone who read the book probably already knew—Jesus did not conform to either of the general conceptions of this title. He neither overthrew the Romans in battle nor arrived on the clouds of heaven in judgment. Instead, he was unceremoniously executed for treason against the state. What in the world could it mean to call *him* the messiah? This is one of the puzzles that Mark's Gospel will attempt to solve.

The Jewishness of the Gospel becomes yet more evident in the verses that follow. First there is a tantalizing statement that the story, or at least the

ANOTHER GLIMPSE INTO THE PAST

BOX 5.1 The Jewish Messiah

The term "messiah" comes from a Hebrew word that means "anointed one," the exact equivalent of the Greek term *christos* (thus "messiah" and "Christ" mean the same thing). In the Hebrew Bible the term is applied to the Jewish king, who was anointed with oil at his inauguration ceremony as a symbolic expression of God's favor; he thus was called "the Lord's anointed" (see 1 Sam 10:1; Ps 2:2).

The term came to refer to a future deliverer of Israel only after the Babylonians overthrew the nation of Judea in 587 B.C.E. and removed the Jewish king from the throne. From that time on, there was no anointed one (messiah) to rule for several centuries (until the Hasmonean rulers, starting in the mid-second century B.C.E.). But some Jews recalled a tradition in which God had told David, his favorite king, that he would always have a descendant on the throne (2 Sam 7:14–16). This is probably the origin of the idea that there would be a future messiah to fulfill God's promises, a future king like David who would rule the people of God once again as a sovereign nation in the Promised Land.

By the time of the New Testament, different Jews had different understandings of what this future ruler would be like. Some expected a warrior-king like David, others a more supernatural cosmic judge of the earth, and still others (such as the community that produced the Dead Sea Scrolls) a priestly ruler who would provide the authoritative interpretations of God's law for his people. All these figures are designated "messiah" in the ancient Jewish sources.

In no source prior to the writing of the New Testament, however, is there any reference to a future messiah who is to suffer and die for the sins of the people. This notion appears to be a Christian creation, as we will see more fully in Chapter 17. It may represent a combination of the belief in a future messianic deliverer with the notion that the one who is truly righteous suffers, a notion expressed in such biblical passages as Psalms 22 and 69 and Isaiah 53. Surprisingly for many Christian readers, the term "messiah" never occurs in these passages.

first part of it, is a fulfillment of an ancient prophecy recorded in the Jewish Scriptures (it is quoted, of course, in the Greek translation, the Septuagint; 1:2–3; see box 3.1). Then there is the appearance of a prophet, John the Baptist, proclaiming a Jewish rite of baptism for the forgiveness of sins. John's dress and diet (1:6) are reminiscent of another Jewish prophet, Elijah, also described in the Jewish Scriptures (cf. 2 Kings 1:8). This John not only practices baptism, he also preaches of one who is to come who is mightier than he. Mightier than a prophet of God? Who could be mightier than a prophet?

Jesus himself then appears, coming from the northern part of the land, from the region of Galilee and the village of Nazareth. He is baptized by John, and upon emerging from the waters, he sees the heavens split open and the Spirit of God descend upon him like a dove. He then hears a voice call out from heaven: "You are my beloved Son, in you I am well pleased" (1:11). The proclamation appears to have serious implications: Jesus is immediately thrust out into the wilderness to confront the forces of evil (he is "tempted by Satan," 1:13). He returns, victorious through the power of God ("the angels" have "ministered to him" 1:13), and begins to make his proclamation that God's kingdom is soon to appear (1:14–15).

Here, then, is a Gospel that begins by describing the forerunner of Jesus, the **Son of God**, and the miraculous proclamation of his own Sonship. Up to this point, a Gentile reader may have recognized the Jewish character of the account, but the designation "Son of God" would no doubt have struck a familiar chord. When Jesus was proclaimed the Son of God (by God himself no less), most readers in the Greco-Roman world would probably have taken this to mean that he was like other sons of God—divinely inspired teachers or rulers whose miraculous deeds benefited the human race. But given the Jewishness of the rest of the beginning, perhaps we should inquire what a Jewish reader would make of the title Son of God.

Even within Jewish circles there were thought to be special persons endowed with divine power to do miracles and to deliver inspired teachings (see Chapter 2). Two of them we know by name Hanina ben Dosa and Honi the "circle-drawer" (see box 3.3). These men, living roughly at the time of Jesus, were understood to have a particularly

Figure 5.2 Portrayal of Jesus' Baptism by John and the Descent of the Dove, from a Vault Mosaic in Ravenna, Italy.

intimate relationship with God and, as a result, were thought to have been endowed with special powers. Accounts of their fantastic deeds and marvelous teachings are recorded in later Jewish sources. What made these persons special was their unique relationship with the one God of Israel. The notion that mere mortals could have such a relationship was itself quite ancient, as shown by the Jewish Scriptures themselves, where an individual was sometimes called "the son of God." The king of Israel, for example, was thought to mediate between God and humans and so stand in a special relationship with God as a child does to a parent. Even kings with dubious public records were sometimes called "the son of God" (e.g., 2 Sam 7:14; Ps 2:7–9). And others receive the title as well: occasionally the entire nation of Israel, through whom God worked his will on earth (Hos 11:1), and sometimes God's heavenly servants, beings that we might call angels (Job 1:6; 2:1). In all these instances in Jewish circles, "the son of God" referred to someone who had a particularly intimate relationship with God, who was chosen by God to perform a task, and who thereby mediated God's will to people on earth. Sometimes these sons of God were associated with the miraculous.

What, then, does Mark mean by beginning his account with the declaration, by God himself, that Jesus (this one who was to be executed as a criminal) is his son? We can begin our quest for an answer by examining key incidents in the Gospel's opening chapter, recalling that ancient biographies tended to set the character of their subjects in the early scenes.

JESUS THE AUTHORITATIVE SON OF GOD

The reader is immediately struck by the way in which Jesus is portrayed as supremely authoritative. At the outset of his ministry, he sees fishermen plying their trade. He calls to them, and without further ado they leave their boats and family and hapless coworkers to follow him (1:16–20). Jesus is an authoritative leader; when he speaks, people obey.

Jesus enters the synagogue to teach and astonishes those who hear. Mark tells us why: "He taught them as one who had authority, and not as the scribes" (1:22). Jesus is an authoritative teacher; when he gives instruction, people hang onto his every word.

He immediately encounters a man possessed by an unclean spirit, who recognizes him as "the Holy One of God" (1:24). Jesus rebukes the spirit and by his word alone drives it out from the man. Those who witness the deed declare its significance: "With authority he commands even the unclean spirits, and they obey him" (1:27). Not only does he drive out evil spirits who embody opposition to God, he also heals the sick, both relatives of his followers (1:29–31) and unknown townsfolk (1:32–34). Soon he is seen healing all who come, both the ill and the possessed. Jesus is an authoritative healer; when he commands the forces of evil, they listen and obey.

This portrayal of Jesus as an authoritative Son of God sets the stage for the rest of the Gospel. Throughout his public ministry, Jesus goes about doing good, healing the sick, casting out demons, even raising the dead (5:1–43). His fame spreads far and wide as rumors of his fantastic abilities reach the villages and towns of Galilee (1:28; 1:32–34; and 1:45). Moreover, he attracts the crowds by his inspired and challenging teaching, especially when he tells parables, brief stories of everyday, mundane affairs that he endows with deep

ANOTHER GLIMPSE INTO THE PAST

BOX 5.2 Son of God and Son of Man

The way that most people understand the terms "Son of God" and "Son of Man" today is probably at odds with how they would have been understood by many Jews in the first century. In our way of thinking, a "son of God" would be a god (or God) and a "son of man" would be a man. Thus, "Son of God" refers to Jesus' divinity and "Son of Man" to his humanity. But this is just the opposite of what the terms meant for many first-century Jews, for whom "son of God" commonly referred to a human (e.g., King Solomon; cf. 2 Sam 7:14) and "son of man" to someone divine (cf. Dan 7:13–14).

In the New Testament Gospels, Jesus uses the term "son of man" in three different ways. On some occasions he uses it simply as a circumlocu-tion for himself; that is, rather than referring directly to himself, Jesus sometimes speaks obliquely of "the son of man" (e.g., Matt 8:20). In a related way, he sometimes uses it to speak of his impending suffering (Mark 8:31). Finally, he occasionally uses the term with reference to a cosmic figure who is coming to bring the judgment of God at the end of time (Mark 8:38), a judgment that Mark's Gospel expects to be imminent (9:1; 13:30). For Mark himself, of course, the passages that speak of the coming Son of Man refer to Jesus, the one who is returning soon as the judge of the earth. As we will see later, scholars debate which, if any, of these three uses of the term can be ascribed to the historical Jesus.

spiritual significance. Interestingly, most of those who hear his words do not understand what they mean (4:10–13).

Given the incredible following that Jesus amasses, the amazing teachings that he delivers, and the miraculous deeds that he performs, one would think that he would become immediately and widely acknowledged for who he is, a man specially endowed by God, the Son of God who provides divine assistance for those in need. Ironically, as the careful reader of the Gospel begins to realize, nothing of the sort is destined to happen. Jesus, this authoritative Son of God, is almost universally misunderstood by those with whom he comes in closest contact. Even worse, despite his clear concern to help others and to deliver the good news of God, he becomes hated and opposed by the religious leaders of his people. Both of these characteristics are major aspects of Mark's portrayal of Jesus. He is the opposed and misunderstood Son of God.

JESUS THE OPPOSED SON OF GOD

A good deal of Mark's Gospel shows that despite Jesus' fantastic deeds, the leaders of his people oppose him from the outset, and their antagonism escalates until the very end, when it results in the catastrophe of his execution. Despite this hostility between Jesus and the leaders of Israel, Mark does not portray Jesus as standing in opposition to the religion of Judaism (at least as Mark sees it). Recall that Jesus is said to be the Son of the Jewish God, the Jewish messiah, come in fulfillment of the Jewish Scriptures and preceded by a Jewish prophet. He teaches in the Jewish synagogue and works among the Jewish people. Later we will find him teaching in the Temple, discussing fine points of the Jewish Law with Jewish scholars, and observing the Jewish Passover. Indeed, even though Jesus' understanding of the Law will come to be challenged, Mark maintains that he was himself faithful to the Law. Consider the account of the leper in one of the opening stories (1:40–44). After Jesus heals the man, he instructs him to show himself to a Jewish priest and to make an offering on behalf of his cleansing "as Moses commanded" (1:44). Jesus is scarcely bent on subverting the Jewish religion.

Why, then, do the Jewish leaders—the scribes and Pharisees in Galilee and the chief priests in Jerusalem—oppose him? Do they not recognize who he is? In fact, they do not recognize him, as we will see momentarily. Even more seriously, they are gravely offended by the things that he says and does. This is evident in the accounts recorded in 2:1–3:6, a group of conflict stories that show a crescendo in the tension between Jesus and the Jewish leaders, the scribes and Pharisees. At first these leaders merely question his actions (2:7); they then take offense at some of his associations (2:16) and his activities (2:18), then protest the actions of his followers (2:24), and finally take serious exception to his own actions and decide to find a way to put him to death (3:6).

In particular, these authorities take umbrage at Jesus' refusal to follow their own practices of purity. He eats with the unrighteous and with sinners, those thought to be unclean and to pollute the pure. For Jesus, these are the ones who need his help (2:15–17). Nor does he follow the Pharisees' prescriptions for keeping the seventh day holy (2:23–3:6); he puts human needs above the requirement to rest on the Sabbath. In Jesus' view, the Sabbath was made for the sake of humans and not humans for the Sabbath; it is therefore legitimate to prepare food or heal a person in need on this day (2:27; 3:4). From the Pharisees' perspective (as portrayed by Mark), these are not honest disagreements over matters of policy. They are dangerous perversions of their religion, and Jesus needs to be silenced. The Pharisees immediately take counsel with their sworn enemies the Herodians and decide to have him killed (3:6).

After these opening stories of conflict, Jewish authorities are constantly on the attack. In virtually every instance they are the ones who initiate the dispute, even though Mark consistently portrays Jesus as getting the better of them in dialogue (see esp. 11:27–12:40). In the end, however, the chief priests triumph, convincing the Roman governor that Jesus has to die. Why, ultimately, do they do so? The short answer is that they find Jesus threatening because of his popularity and find his words against their Temple cult offensive, as shown in his violent and disruptive actions in the Temple itself (11:18). But in the larger picture painted by Mark's Gospel, the Jewish authorities do not seek Jesus'

Figure 5.3 Palestine in New Testament Times.

death merely because they are jealous or because they disagree with him over legal, theological, or cultic matters. They oppose him because he is God's unique representative on earth—God's authoritative Son—and they, the leaders of Israel, cannot understand who he is or what he says. In this, however, they are not alone, for virtually no one else in Mark's narrative can understand who he is either.

JESUS THE MISUNDERSTOOD SON OF GOD

One way to establish misunderstanding as a Markan theme is to read carefully through the first half of the Gospel and ask, who realizes that Jesus is the Son of God? The answer may come as a bit of a surprise. Clearly God knows that Jesus is his Son, because he himself declares it at the baptism (1:11). And since this declaration comes directly to Jesus ("You are my beloved Son"), the reader can assume that he knows it as well. In addition, the evil demons recognize Jesus as the Son of God; on several instances they scream it out when they encounter him (3:11, cf. 1:24). Who else knows? Only two other persons: the author of the Gospel, who recounts these various tales, and you, the one who reads them.

Through the first half of this Gospel, no one else recognizes Jesus' identity, including even those who are closest to him. Early on, when he comes to his hometown, his family tries to snatch him from the public eye because they think that he has gone crazy (3:21). Jesus' own townspeople neither understand nor trust him. When he teaches in their synagogue, they take offense at his words and wonder how he has the ability to do such miraculous deeds, since he is a mere carpenter whose (unremarkable) family they know (6:1–6). The Jewish scholars think they know the source of his power. Refusing to acknowledge the divine authority behind Jesus' words and deeds—how could one so profane come from God (2:7)?—they claim that he is possessed by Beelzebul, the prince of the demons, and so does miracles through the power of the Devil (3:22).

Perhaps most striking of all, Jesus' own disciples fail to understand who he is, even though he has specially chosen them to follow him (3:13–19)

and given them private instruction (e.g., 4:10–20). When they watch him calm a violent storm at sea with a word, their question is genuine: "Who then is this, that even wind and sea obey him?" (4:41). When they later behold Jesus walking upon the water, they continue to be mystified: "For they did not understand . . . but their hearts were hardened" (6:51–52). When, later still, Jesus warns them "to beware of the leaven of the scribes and Pharisees" (8:15), they mistake his meaning, thinking he is angry because they have forgotten to bring bread, even though they had seen him miraculously feed thousands of hungry people on two different occasions. Now Jesus expresses his own exasperation: "Do you not yet understand?" (8:21). No, they do not. But they will begin to have an inkling, right here at the midpoint of the Gospel.

JESUS THE ACKNOWLEDGED SON OF GOD

One of the keys to understanding Mark's portrayal of Jesus lies in the sequence of stories that begins immediately after Jesus' exasperated question of 8:21. The sequence begins with perhaps the most significant healing story of the Gospel, an account that Mark appears to have invested with special symbolic meaning. This is a story of a blind man who gradually regains his sight (8:22–26).

It is striking that the healing takes place in stages. Indeed, it is the only miracle in the Gospel that Jesus does not perform immediately and effortlessly. When he is asked to heal the blind man, he takes him by the hand, leads him out of the village, spits on his eyes, and asks if he can see. The man replies that he can, but only vaguely: people appear like walking trees. Jesus then lays his hands upon his eyes and looks intently at him, and the man begins to see clearly.

A perceptive reader will recognize the symbolism of the account in light of its immediate context. In the very next story, the disciples themselves, who until now have been blind to Jesus' identity (cf. 8:21), gradually begin to see who he is, in stages. It starts with a question from Jesus: "Who do people say that I am?" (8:27). The disciples reply that some think he is John the Baptist, others Elijah, and yet others a prophet raised from the dead. He then turns the question on them: "But who do you say

ANOTHER GLIMPSE INTO THE PAST

BOX 5.3   The Messianic Secret in Mark

After Peter's confession, Jesus instructs his disciples not to tell anyone who he is. Interestingly, Jesus attempts to keep his identity a secret on a number of other occasions in Mark's Gospel as well. When he casts out demons, he refuses to let them speak "because they knew him" (1:34; cf. 3:12). When he heals a leper, he commands him to "say nothing to any one" (1:43). When he raises a young girl from the dead, he strictly orders "that no one should know this" (5:43). Indeed, before his discussion with the disciples at the end of Chapter 8, he never speaks openly to anyone about his identity. And there, when someone finally recognizes that he is the messiah, he commands silence.

How does one explain this ironic feature of Mark's Gospel, that Jesus is the Son of God, the messiah, but that he does not want anyone to know? This puzzle has been called the **"messianic secret"** since the early twentieth century, when a German scholar named William Wrede propounded a now famous solution—that the historical Jesus himself never urged secrecy at all because he did not actually see himself as the mes-

siah. After his death, however, Jesus' followers began to proclaim that he *had been* the messiah. How could it be that Jesus was thought to be the messiah when he had made no such claim about himself? Wrede's explanation was that the early Christian community invented the idea that Jesus tried to keep his identity under wraps. They then fabricated the stories of Jesus' commands to silence to show that a messianic Jesus did not proclaim himself to be the messiah.

Whether or not Wrede was right, it is worth asking how the messianic secret functions literarily in the context of Mark's story of Jesus. Here Jesus is clearly the messiah (cf. 1:1), but just as clearly he is not the great king or cosmic warrior that many Jews may have anticipated. Why then the commands to silence? One explanation is that Jesus in Mark's Gospel does not want people to have the wrong idea about him, for example, by thinking that he is the kind of messiah they have anticipated. For Mark, the title "messiah" does not signify earthly grandeur and power but just the opposite. As messiah, Jesus was the Son of God who had to suffer and die.

that I am?" (8:29). Peter, as spokesperson for the group, replies, "You are the Christ."

This is a climactic moment in the narrative. Up to this point, Jesus has been misunderstood by everyone, by family, neighbors, religious leaders, and followers, and now, halfway through the account, someone finally realizes who he is, at least in part. (The reader knows that Peter's confession is correct to some extent, since for Mark Jesus is the messiah: recall how he identifies him in the very first verse of the narrative as "Jesus the Christ.") Rather than rejecting or repudiating Peter's confession, Jesus orders the disciples not to spread the word: "And he sternly ordered them not to tell anyone about him" (8:30; see box 5.3).

Still, Peter's identification of Jesus as the messiah is correct *only* in part. That is to say, Peter has begun to see who Jesus is, but still perceives him only dimly. The reader knows this because of what

happens next. Jesus begins to teach that he "must suffer many things, and be rejected by the elders and the chief priests and the scribes, and be killed, and after three days rise from the dead" (8:31). Jesus is the messiah, but he is the messiah who has to suffer and die. And this makes no sense to Peter. He takes Jesus aside and begins to rebuke him.

But why would Peter reject Jesus' message of his approaching **"Passion"** (a term that comes from the Greek word for "suffering")? Evidently he understands the role of the messiah quite differently from the way Jesus (and Mark) does. The author never delineates Peter's view for us, but perhaps it is not so difficult to figure out. If Peter uses the term "messiah" in the way most other first-century Jews did, then he understands Jesus to be the future deliverer of Israel, a man of grandeur and power who will usher in God's kingdom in a mighty way (whether as a warrior-king or as a cosmic judge of the earth; see box 5.1). But for Mark, this is only a partial truth, a dim perception of who Jesus is. For him, Jesus is the messiah who must suffer and die to bring about salvation for the world.

Peter's failure to perceive this truth forces Jesus to turn the rebuke back on him: "Get behind me Satan! For you are setting your mind not on divine things but on human things" (8:33). The idea that the messiah had to suffer may have appeared totally anomalous to most Jews of the first century, including Jesus' own disciples, but in Mark's view, to understand Jesus in any other way is to succumb to the temptations of the devil. Thus Peter has begun to see, but not yet clearly; he is like a blind man who has partially recovered his sight. Perhaps this is better than being totally blind, but in another sense it is worse because partial perception can lead to misperception: people seem to be trees, and Jesus appears to be the messiah of popular expectation. For Mark, however, Jesus is the suffering Son of God.

JESUS THE SUFFERING SON OF GOD

Throughout the early portions of Mark's Gospel, the reader is given several indications that Jesus will have to die (e.g., 2:20; 3:6). After Peter's confession, however, Jesus begins to be quite explicit about it. Even though he is the Christ, the Son of God—or rather because he is—he must suffer death. Three times Jesus predicts his own impending Passion in Jerusalem: he is to be rejected by the Jewish leaders, killed, and then raised from the dead. Strikingly, after each of these "Passion predictions" Mark has placed stories to show that the disciples never do understand what Jesus is talking about.

We have already seen the first prediction in 8:31. When Jesus declares that he must be rejected and killed, Peter, who has just declared Jesus to be the messiah, not understanding fully what this means, takes him aside to rebuke him (8:32). Jesus turns the rebuke back on him and begins to teach that suffering is to be not only his lot but that of his followers as well: "Whoever would come after me must take up the cross and follow me." Being a disciple means affliction and pain, not power and prestige; it means giving up one's life in order to gain the

world. Those who reject these words will have no part of Christ at the end of the age (8:34–38).

The next prediction occurs a chapter later, after Jesus' hidden glory is revealed on the Mount of Transfiguration to three of the disciples, who even then fail to understand what they have seen (9:2–13; especially vv. 6, 10). In nearly the same terms as before, Jesus predicts his coming death, and Mark states that the disciples do not know what he means (9:30–31). Immediately afterward, they begin to argue over who is the greatest among them (9:33–34). Jesus again tells them that being his disciple means a life of lowly servitude rather than grand eminence.

The final prediction occurs in the chapter that follows (10:33–34). In this instance, the details are somewhat more graphic, but the response of the disciples is remarkably similar. James and John, two of his closest followers, request positions of prominence when Jesus enters into his glorious kingdom. Jesus has to tell them, yet again, that following him means certain death, and that if they want to be great, they must become the slaves of all. This, in fact, is what he has done himself: "For the Son of Man came not to be served, but to serve, and to give his life a ransom for many" (10:45).

From this point on, the narrative marches inexorably toward Jesus' death, as Mark recounts the familiar stories of the "Passion narrative." Jesus triumphally enters Jerusalem to shouts of acclamation from the crowds, who appear to accept the disciples' notion of what it means for Jesus to be the messiah (11:1–10). He enters the Temple and drives out those who are in business there, incurring yet further opposition from the Jewish leadership (11:15–19). He teaches in the Temple and engages in disputes with his opponents among the leaders, who try to trap him and stir up the crowds against him (11:28–12:40). He launches into a lengthy description of the imminent destruction of the Temple, when the end of time comes and the cosmic judge, the Son of Man, appears to bring judgment to the earth and salvation to the followers of Jesus (13:1–36). He assures his hearers that this apocalyptic drama will unfold soon, within their own generation (13:30).

Finally we reach the account of the Passion itself. Jesus is anointed with oil by an unknown woman, evidently the only person in the entire narrative who knows what is about to happen to him (14:1–9; she may, however, simply be performing a kind deed that Jesus himself explains as a preparation for his burial). He celebrates his Last Supper with his disciples (14:12–26) and then goes out with them to (the Garden of) Gethsemane to pray that he not be required to suffer his imminent ordeal (14:26–42). God, however, is silent. Jesus is arrested (14:43–52) and put on trial before the Jewish Council, the Sanhedrin, where he is confronted with witnesses who accuse him of opposing the Temple (14:53–65). The false witnesses on the inside are matched by the false disciples on the outside: while Jesus is being tried, Peter, as predicted, denies him three times (14:66–72).

Jesus is finally questioned directly by the high priest concerning his identity: "Are you the Christ, the Son of the Blessed One?" The reader, of course, already knows the answer: Jesus is the messiah, the Son of God, but not in any way that these Jewish authorities would recognize. Jesus now confesses to his identity and again predicts that the Son of Man, the cosmic judge from heaven, will soon arrive on the clouds of heaven (14:61–62; see box 5.4). The Sanhedrin charges him with blasphemy and finds him worthy of death (see box 5.4). The next morning they deliver him over to Pilate, who tries him on the charge of claiming to be King of the Jews (15:1–15). When Jesus refuses to answer his accusers, Pilate condemns him to execution for treason against Rome. Pilate gives the Jewish crowds the option of releasing Jesus or a Jewish insurgent, Barabbas (15:6–15). They prefer Barabbas. Jesus is flogged, mocked, and beaten. They take him off and crucify him at 9:00 a.m. (15:25).

ANOTHER GLIMPSE INTO THE PAST

Box 5.4 The Charge of Blasphemy according to Mark

Jesus' trial before the Jewish Sanhedrin in Mark is as poignant as it is difficult to understand. The high priest asks Jesus, "Are you the Messiah, the Son of the Blessed One?" Jesus replies, "I am; and you will see the Son of Man seated at the right hand of the Power and coming with the clouds of heaven" (14:61–62). The high priest immediately cries out "Blasphemy," and the entire Sanhedrin concurs. But what was the blasphemy?

It was not blasphemous to claim to be the messiah. Other persons before Jesus had done so, and others would later. Nearly a century after Jesus' death, one of the leading rabbis of the day (Rabbi Akiba) proclaimed a Jewish general (Simon bar Kosiba) to be the long-awaited messiah, and no charges of blasphemy were brought against him. If the messiah were the future deliverer of Israel, then a person claiming to be the messiah was simply claiming to be the next king.

Nor was it blasphemous to call oneself the Son of God. Recall, other people were also called this, both in the Jewish Scriptures and during Jesus' own day. Nor, finally, was it blasphemous to predict that the Son of Man was soon to arrive on the clouds of heaven. This, in fact, was prophesied in the book of Daniel, and there were a number of Jewish preachers who proclaimed that his much-awaited appearance would soon come.

So what was Jesus' blasphemy? From a historical point of view, Jesus does not appear to have committed one in Mark's narrative. But it is possible that Mark *thought* that Jesus' committed one, at least in the eyes of the Jewish high priest. Remember that Mark understood Jesus to be the Son of Man (see box 5.2). Perhaps Mark projected his own Christian understanding of Jesus back onto the high priest, so that in the narrative, when Jesus spoke about the Son of Man being seated on the throne next to God, the high priest "realized" (as the author of Mark himself believed) that Jesus was referring to himself. If so, then the high priest (in Mark's narrative, not in real life) would have understood that Jesus was claiming to be divine in some sense. This claim would be a blasphemy. Perhaps this is why the high priest in Mark finds Jesus' words blasphemous, even though technically speaking, no blasphemy had occurred.

JESUS THE CRUCIFIED SON OF GOD

It is clear from Mark's Gospel that Jesus' disciples never do come to understand who he is. As we have seen, he is betrayed to the Jewish authorities by one of them, Judas Iscariot. On the night of his arrest, he is denied three times by another, his closest disciple, Peter. All the others scatter, unwilling to stand up for him in the hour of his distress. Perhaps Mark wants his readers to understand that the disciples were shocked when their hopes concerning Jesus as messiah were thoroughly dashed: Jesus did not bring victory over the Romans or restore the kingdom to Israel. For Mark, of course, these hopes were misplaced. Jesus was the Son of God, but he was the Son of God who had to suffer. Until the very end, when Jesus was actually crucified, there is nobody in the Gospel who fully understands this.

Mark's narrative may even intimate that at the end Jesus himself was in doubt. In Gethsemane he prays three times not to have to undergo his fate, suggesting perhaps that he thinks there could be another way. When he finally succumbs to his destiny, he appears yet more uncertain, and with good reason. Deserted by his own followers, condemned by his own leaders, rejected by his own people, he is publically humiliated, beaten, spat upon, flogged. He is nailed to the cross, and even there he is mocked by passersby, Jewish leaders, and the two criminals who are crucified along with him. He suffers throughout this entire ordeal in silence, until the very end, when he cries out the words of Scripture: "My God, My God, why have you forsaken me?" (15:34; cf. Ps 22:2). He then utters a loud cry and dies.

Is this a genuine question of the dying Jesus? Does he truly feel forsaken in the end even by God? Does he not fully understand the reason for his death? These are questions on which readers of the account may disagree. On one point, however, there can be no disagreement. Even though no one else in the Gospel appears to know the significance of Jesus' death, the reader knows. Mark reveals it by narrating two events that transpire immediately after Jesus breathes his last: the curtain in the Temple is torn in half from top to bottom (15:38), and the Roman centurion confesses Jesus to be the Son of God (15:39).

Without posing the historical question of what really happened to the curtain in the Temple (there is no reference in any non-Christian source to its being torn or damaged in any way), one might ask how the reader is supposed to understand Mark's claim that it was ripped asunder. Recall: most ancient Jews ascribed a particular holiness to the Temple as the one place in which sacrifices could be offered up to God. This was a sacred place to be revered and respected. The most sacred area within the holy Temple was the Holy of Holies, the square room in whose darkness God's very presence was thought to dwell. This room was so holy that no one could enter, except on one day of the year, the Day of Atonement (Yom Kippur), when the Jewish high priest could go behind the thick curtain into the presence of God to perform a sacrifice to atone for the sins of the people.

Mark indicates that when Jesus died, the curtain separating this holiest of places from the outside world was torn in half. The event appears to signify, for Mark, that God is no longer removed from his people; his holiness is now available to all. No longer do his people need to rely on the Jewish high priest and his sacrifice for their sins on the Day of Atonement. The ultimate sacrifice has been made, voiding the necessity of all others. Jesus, the Son of God, has "given his life as a ransom for many" (10:45). People now have direct access to God, who comes to them in the death of Jesus.

The second event cited by Mark is equally significant. No one throughout the Gospel has fully understood that Jesus is the Son of God who has to suffer. Until now. Strikingly, it is not one of Jesus' family or followers who understands. It is the Roman centurion who has presided over his crucifixion. This pagan soldier, seeing Jesus die, proclaims, "Surely this man was God's Son" (15:39). This brings the recognition of Jesus' true identity full circle. It was proclaimed at his baptism at the beginning of the Gospel (from heaven); it is now proclaimed at his crucifixion at the end (on earth). Moreover, it is significant who makes the proclamation: a pagan soldier, one who had not been Jesus' follower. This in itself may intimate what will happen to the proclamation of Jesus through the years until the time when Mark pens his account. The proclamation will not find fertile soil among Jews, either those

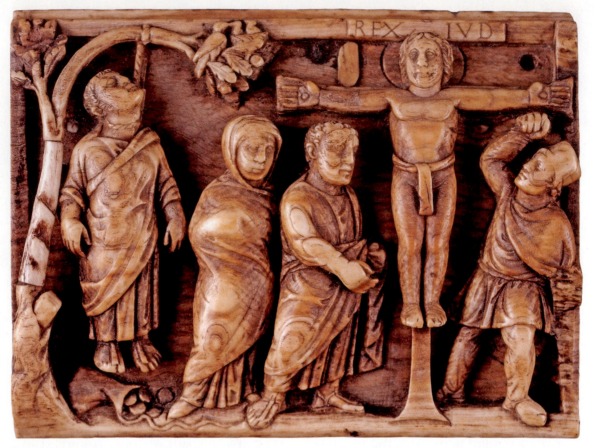

Figure 5.4 One of the earliest surviving portrayals of Jesus' crucifixion, from a miniature ivory panel of the fourth century.

who had known Jesus or those who had not. It will be embraced principally by those outside Judaism, by Gentiles as represented by this Roman centurion. Jesus is the Son of God, rejected by his own people but acknowledged by the Gentiles, and it is this confession of the suffering and death of the Son of God, Mark reveals, that has brought salvation to the world. This, however, is not the end of the story.

JESUS THE VINDICATED SON OF GOD

One of the most fascinating aspects of Mark's Gospel is the way in which he chose to conclude it. Jesus is buried by a respected leader among the Jews, Joseph of Arimathea (indicating, perhaps, that not all Jews, or even all prominent Jews, were bound to reject him; 15:42–47, cf. 12:28–34). Two women see where he is placed. The next day is the Sabbath. Early in the morning on the day after Sabbath, Mary Magdalene, Mary the mother of James, and Salome come to provide a more decent burial for the body, but they discover that the stone before the tomb has been rolled away. Going inside, they find a young man in a white robe who tells them that Jesus has risen. He instructs them to tell the disciples and Peter that Jesus is going ahead of them to Galilee and that they are to go there to see him (16:1–7). Then comes the breath-taking conclusion. The women flee the tomb and tell nobody anything, "for they were afraid" (16:8). That's where the book ends.

ANOTHER EARLY CHRISTIAN TEXT

BOX 5.5 The *Gospel of Thomas*

We have seen that the Gospel of Mark understands that the death of Jesus is what brings salvation. This view was shared by the other authors of the New Testament, including the other Gospel writers and the apostle Paul. But interestingly enough, it was not a view shared by *everyone* who considered themselves Christian in the ancient world.

Among the writings discovered near Nag Hammadi (see p. 4) was a Gospel allegedly written by Jesus' disciple (and brother?) Judas Thomas. This Gospel does not narrate Jesus' death and resurrection—in fact, it tells no stories of any kind. Instead, it is a collection of Jesus' sayings, 114 of them altogether. Some scholars have thought that this was the kind of Gospel that Q was—principally Jesus' teachings (see p. 61). But why would someone write a Gospel that didn't describe what Jesus did? Did the author assume that his readers already believed in Jesus' death and resurrection?

No, probably not. In this author's view, it was not Jesus' death, but his teachings that bring eternal life. Many of the sayings of this Gospel are mysterious and strange. And for this author, it is only when you interpret them correctly that you can have eternal life. This is clear from the outset of the book, which begins as follows:

> These are the secret teachings of the living Jesus. And Didymus Judas Thomas wrote them down. Anyone who finds the interpretation of these sayings will not taste death!

It appears that this is a Gospel written by and for Christian Gnostics—a group of early Christians who believed that this world we live in is evil and needs to be escaped; salvation comes to those who learn the divine secrets of how the world came to be, how we came to be here, and how we can escape. In this Gospel, it is the secret teachings of Jesus that can bring this kind of deliverance from the evil of this world. Anyone who correctly understands these teachings will never die but live forever. Rarely has an author placed so much importance on his book and so much pressure on his readers to interpret it correctly!

Christian readers from time immemorial have been shocked and dismayed by this conclusion. How could it end without the disciples hearing that Jesus has been raised? How could they remain in their ignorance? Surely the women must have told someone. In the early church, some copyists of this Gospel were so put off by the ending that they added one of their own, appending twelve additional verses that describe some of Jesus' appearances to his disciples. Modern scholars are unified, however, in recognizing this ending as secondary. Some have proposed, in its stead, that we assume that the final page of the Gospel somehow got lost.

These various explanations for Mark's ending, however, may be unnecessary. Mark devoted considerable effort to demonstrating that the disciples never could understand what Jesus meant when he talked about dying and rising again. They never do understand, to the very end. Mark's readers, how-

ever, understand. In fact, they understand a lot of things—about who Jesus really is, about how he was thoroughly misunderstood, about how his message was to go to the Gentiles, and about what it means for those who believe in him to be his disciples.

CONCLUSION: MARK AND HIS READERS

Can we decide who the original readers of this Gospel probably were? It is impossible, of course, to learn very much about them. Our only evidence comes from the Gospel itself, and conclusions drawn on these slim grounds will necessarily be tentative. But there are a few intimations both about the first readers and about Mark's overarching concerns for them, and I will conclude this discussion by considering them.

ANOTHER GLIMPSE INTO THE PAST

BOX 5.6 The Abrupt Ending of the Gospel of Mark

The Gospel of Mark is unique among the Gospels in ending abruptly: after his resurrection, Jesus is never said to appear to his disciples (or to anyone else) in this account. The story goes like this:

On the third day after Jesus was crucified, dead, and buried, several women followers come to the tomb to anoint his body, only to find the stone rolled away from the tomb and a young man—but not Jesus—inside. The young man instructs the women to go tell the disciples to travel to Galilee where they will see Jesus, raised from the dead. But the women flee the tomb and "did not say anything to anyone, for they were afraid" (Mark 16:8). And that's where the Gospel of Mark ends!

The ending comes as a surprise to many readers, who think that the women surely must have told *somebody!* After all, word of the resurrection did get out. And the other Gospels go on to tell the stories of Jesus' appearances to his disciples after the resur-

rection. How could Mark's Gospel end *here*, with the women not telling anyone?

Ancient scribes were also surprised by this abrupt ending, and so they did what scribes sometimes did: they added an ending that was more in keeping with their beliefs and with the other Gospels. The additional twelve verses that were added describe what, in the scribes' opinion, must have happened next: the women tell the disciples what they had seen and heard, and the disciples travel to Galilee and meet with Jesus, who gives them their final instructions before ascending to heaven.

This new ending does give a kind of closure to the account, but it is not original. It cannot be found in our oldest and best manuscripts of Mark, and its style of writings and vocabulary are not consistent with the rest of the Gospel otherwise. It was added by scribes who simply did not want the book to end where it did.

The first readers of this Gospel appear to have been the Christians of Mark's community, most of whom would have been illiterate, and thus "read" the Gospel by hearing it read (see box 4.1). They evidently resided outside Palestine and had Greek as their primary language. There are clues in the Gospel that most of them had converted to Christianity from pagan religions, not from Judaism, the most striking of which comes in 7:3–4, where Mark has to explain the Pharisaic custom of washing hands before eating for ceremonial cleansing. Presumably, if his audience were Jewish, they would already know this custom, and Mark would not have to explain it. What is even more intriguing is the fact that Mark appears to misunderstand the practice: he claims that it was followed by "all the Jews." We know from ancient Jewish writings that this is simply not true. For this reason, many scholars have concluded that Mark himself was not Jewish.

Many of Mark's traditions, however, are concerned with showing the Jewishness of Jesus and appear to presuppose strictly Jewish beliefs and practices. How can we explain this? Many of the oral traditions found in this Gospel must go back to the earliest Jewish followers of Jesus, who embodied their own beliefs and concerns in them. As the stories were passed along, their Jewish character was preserved. Mark and many people in his congregation (*some* of them Jewish?) converted to faith in Jesus, which necessarily involved converting to Jesus' religion, Judaism. They, too, came to worship the Jewish God and saw in Jesus the Jewish messiah, whose death brought about salvation not only for Jews but for the whole world.

It may be that this community continued to experience open conflict with a local Jewish synagogue that actively rejected these Christian claims about Jesus. And it may be that this conflict at times turned ugly. This would explain why Mark emphasizes that Jewish leaders, especially Pharisees, failed to understand Jesus and that following him involves a high cost. For Mark, following Jesus is not a ticket to glory, it is the path to suffering; being a disciple does not bring exaltation but humiliation and pain.

Mark stresses, however, that the suffering would not last forever. In fact, it would not last long. Just as Jesus was vindicated, so, too, will be his faithful followers. And the end was near (9:1). This may have been suggested to Mark by current events: many scholars believe that the Gospel was written during the early stages of the Jewish War against Rome (66–70 C.E.), at the conclusion of which the Temple itself was destroyed. Does this war mark the beginning of the end, predicted by Jesus as certain to occur during the lifetime of some of his disciples (see 8:38–9:1 and all of Chapter 13)? Indeed, for the Markan community, the Son of Man was at the gate, ready to make his appearance. Those who were ashamed of Jesus' words would be put to shame when the Son of Man arrived; those who accepted his words and became his followers would then enter into glory. Just as Mark's Jesus may not have fully understood the meaning of his own crucifixion, so, too, the Christian community currently experiencing suffering may not fathom its full meaning. But ultimately their pain will lead to redemption. This is just one of the paradoxical claims of Mark's Gospel.

Mark's story of Jesus is replete with such paradoxes: the glorious messiah is one who suffers an ignominious death; exaltation comes in pain, salvation through crucifixion; to gain one's life, one must lose it; the greatest are the most humble; the most powerful are the slaves; prosperity is not a blessing but a hindrance; leaving one's home or field or family brings a hundredfold homes and fields and families; the first will be last, and the last first. These lessons provide hope for a community that is in the throes of suffering, experiencing the social disruptions of persecution. They make particular sense for a community that knows that its messiah, the Son of God, was rejected and mocked and killed, only to be vindicated by God, who raised him from the dead.

AT A GLANCE

BOX 5.7 The Gospel of Mark

1. Mark was written in Greek, around 65–70 C.E.

2. Its anonymous author was a Greek-speaking Christian, probably living outside Palestine, who had heard numerous stories about Jesus before writing his account for his Christian community.

3. The Gospel begins with Jesus as an adult, and at the outset it reveals his character as the Son of God who leads, teaches, heals, and casts out demons with authority, but who is nonetheless opposed by Jewish religious leaders.

4. The Gospel stresses that Jesus' character and destiny were misunderstood by virtually everyone with whom he came in contact.

5. For Mark, Jesus was not to come in power to overthrow the forces of evil aligned against God and his people. He came to suffer and die at the hands of these forces.

6. But Mark indicates that God had the last say. After Jesus' suffering and death in Jerusalem, God raised him from the dead, and an angelic messenger announced that he would meet his followers in Galilee.

TAKE A STAND

1. The professor teaching this course has asked you and a classmate to debate the following resolution in front of the class: Resolved: the Gospel of Mark portrays Jesus as God. Choose one side of the resolution and argue (vehemently!) for it.

2. Your roommate tells you that since Mark is the earliest of our Gospels, it is historically accurate. Just for the sake of an argument, you decide to disagree (whether you do or not). Make your case!

3. Your brother tells you that our earliest Gospels do not have any theological interests, but are simply interested in giving the facts of Jesus' life. Thinking for the moment just of our first Gospel, Mark, do you agree with him or not? State your reasons.

SUGGESTIONS FOR FURTHER READING

Hooker, Morna. *The Message of Mark*. 2d ed. London: Epworth, 2007. A very nice overview of the most significant features of Mark's Gospel; ideal for beginning students.

Kingsbury, Jack D. *The Christology of Mark's Gospel*. Philadelphia: Fortress, 1983. A useful discussion of Mark's view of Jesus from a literary-critical perspective that looks for clues to the meaning of the text in the flow of the narrative.

Harrington, Daniel J. *What Are They Saying about Mark?* New York: Paulist, 2005. An excellent overview of modern scholarship on Mark, for beginning students.

Nickle, Keith. *The Synoptic Gospels: Conflict and Consensus*. 2d ed. Atlanta: Westminster John Knox, 2001. One of the best introductory discussions of the background and message of the three Synoptic Gospels.

Perkins, Pheme. *Introduction to the Synoptic Gospels*. Grand Rapids, Mich.: Eerdmans, 2009. An overview of the major historical and literary issues involved with studying Matthew, Mark, and Luke; good for beginning students.

Rhodes, David, Joanna Dewey, and Donald Michie, *Mark as Story*. 2d ed. Philadelphia: Fortress, 1999. A brief but insightful discussion of how Mark's Gospel can be understood as a narrative through the application of sophisticated literary techniques.

Stein, Robert. *The Synoptic Problem: An Introduction*. Grand Rapids, Mich.: Baker Book House, 1994. A good book-length treatment of the range of issues involved in the Synoptic Problem; for beginning students.

Telford, William. *Mark* (T & T Study Guides). London: T & T Clark, 2004. A discussion of all the significant features of the Gospel of Mark, its contents, literary character, and historical problems; a full and useful overview for beginning students.

Wrede, William. *The Messianic Secret*. Trans. J. C. G. Greig. Cambridge: Clarke, 1971. The classic study of Mark's literary technique and theological agenda; for advanced students.

KEY TERMS

Christ	L	messianic secret	Son of Man
four-source	M	Passion	Synoptic Gospels
hypothesis	Markan Priority	Q source	Synoptic Problem
genre	messiah	Son of God	

Jesus, the Jewish Messiah
THE GOSPEL ACCORDING TO MATTHEW

WHAT TO EXPECT

People used to think that Mark was a condensed account of Matthew's Gospel—a kind of *Reader's Digest* version. Scholars today, however, think just the opposite, that Matthew used Mark as one of its sources. How can that help us understand what Matthew wanted to emphasize in his account?

In this chapter we will use a "redactional" method to study Matthew, seeing how he "edited" Mark by adding, omitting, and changing stories and considering how these changes reveal something about Matthew's vested interests. In particular, we will see Matthew's overarching emphases by looking at two of the most famous and interesting parts of his Gospel, which are not found in Mark: the stories of Jesus' birth in Bethlehem and the famous three-chapter sermon called the "Sermon on the Mount."

The Gospel of Matthew was one of the most highly treasured accounts of Jesus' life among the early Christians. This may explain why it was given pride of place as the first Gospel in the New Testament canon. Its popularity continues unabated today, in no small measure because it preserves such cherished and revered teachings of Jesus as the memorable sayings of the **Sermon on the Mount**, including the **Beatitudes**, the **Golden Rule**, and the **Lord's Prayer**—teachings that have inspired Christian readers through the ages and convinced them of Jesus' genius as a teacher of religious principles.

We can begin our discussion of Matthew by reflecting on several of the points that we have already learned. We do not know the name of its author: the title found in our English versions ("The Gospel according to Matthew") was added long after the document's original composition. Since he produced his Gospel in Greek, presumably for a Greek-speaking community, he was probably located somewhere outside Palestine (since most early Christians in Palestine would have spoken **Aramaic** as their native tongue). To construct his narrative about Jesus, he made use of a variety of sources available to him, both written documents and oral reports that he had heard, possibly from Christian evangelists and teachers within his own community. Among his written sources were Mark's Gospel and the collection of traditions that scholars designate as Q. If Mark was produced around 65 or 70 C.E., then Matthew was obviously written later, but it is difficult to know how much later. Most scholars are content to date the book sometime during the latter part of the first century, possibly, as a rough guess, around 80 or 85 C.E.

Matthew, as I will continue to call the author for the sake of convenience, chose to follow his predecessor Mark by bringing together stories about Jesus into a connected narrative of his words and deeds culminating in his death and resurrection. An ancient reader would have recognized the book as a kind of Greco-Roman biography and so would have entertained certain expectations about what to find in it. Such a reader would have expected the book to describe Jesus' life according to some kind of chronology, highlighting those sayings, actions, and experiences that revealed his essential character. Moreover, he or she would have expected this portrayal to be established by the events described at the very outset.

As was the case with Mark, we will by no stretch of the imagination cover everything of interest and importance in this Gospel. One of the most recent scholarly commentaries on Matthew fills three volumes, the first of which alone runs nearly 800 pages! Here we will discuss the entire book in a fraction of that space, and so merely scratch the surface. But if you scratch a surface in the right places, you can at least get an idea of what lies beneath.

A REDACTIONAL APPROACH TO MATTHEW

When we studied the Gospel of Mark, we used a method that we might call **"literary-historical"**— that is, we tried to understand it in light of the way its *literary* genre (Greco-Roman biography) worked in its own *historical* context. We could obviously study Matthew the same way, since it, too, is a biography of Jesus. But I have decided to introduce a different approach for Matthew, to show that there is more than one way to study a text.

Since it appears (based on the four-source hypothesis) that one of Matthew's sources was Mark, we can compare Matthew carefully to see how he has added stories to Mark, omitted stories from Mark, and modified the stories that he borrowed from Mark. That is to say, we can see how Matthew *edited* one of his sources (since we have both Matthew and Mark, his source). The assumption of this kind of study is that Matthew would have edited—that is, changed—Mark only if he wanted to express things differently. By looking at the differences—by seeing what Matthew added, omitted, or modified—we can see what Matthew may have wanted to emphasize in his portrayal of Jesus.

Another name for an editor is a **"redactor."** This approach to Matthew (which could obviously be used for Luke as well) is therefore called **"redaction criticism."** Given the importance of beginnings for Greco-Roman biographies, we can start a redactional study of Matthew at the beginning, by considering his opening chapters in relation to Mark.

 THE IMPORTANCE OF BEGINNINGS: JESUS THE JEWISH MESSIAH IN FULFILLMENT OF THE JEWISH SCRIPTURES

Matthew follows his predecessor Mark in beginning his Gospel by identifying Jesus as the Christ. He will therefore have a similar task of explaining how Jesus could be the glorious and powerful messiah of the Jews when he was known to have experienced a public humiliation and ignominious death by crucifixion. Far from shrinking from the task, Matthew approaches it head on, in the very opening verse, by emphasizing Jesus' credentials as the messiah: he was "the son of David, the son of Abraham." As Matthew's readers would realize full well, Abraham was thought to be the father of the Jews. And David was their greatest king, whose descendant was to resume his rule, enthroned in Jerusalem and reigning over a sovereign state of Israel as God's anointed. This son of David would be the messiah.

Thus Matthew begins his Gospel by indicating that Jesus was a Jew (from Abraham) in the line of the ancient kings (from David). One is immediately impressed by a distinctive feature of this narrative: Jesus is portrayed as thoroughly and ineluctably

Jewish. He was Jewish in Mark's Gospel as well, of course, but here the emphasis is yet stronger. Matthew's narrative will show that Jesus was the ultimate fulfillment of the hopes of the Jews.

The Genealogy of Jesus the Messiah

The Jewish identity of Jesus is confirmed by what follows. Unlike Mark, Matthew provides a genealogy of Jesus, tracing his family line all the way back to the father of the Jews, Abraham himself. Genealogies are not among the most popular reading for students of the Bible today, but this one is remarkable for a number of reasons. It is structured around several key persons in the history of the nation Israel, many of whom are well known from stories preserved in the Jewish Scriptures (e.g., Abraham, Isaac, Jacob; David, Solomon, Rehoboam; Ahaz, Hezekiah, Manasseh). The text consistently, almost monotonously, traces fathers and sons first from Abraham (v. 2) to King David (v. 6), then from David to the deportation to Babylon (v. 12), and then from the deportation to Jacob, the father of Joseph (v. 16). At this point, however, a problem arises: it turns out that the genealogy is of Joseph, the husband of Mary, the woman to whom Jesus is born. According to Matthew, however, Joseph is not Jesus' father, for in this Gospel (unlike Mark, which says not a word about Jesus' birth) Jesus' mother is a virgin. For this reason, Matthew is forced to shift from his description of father and son relationships when he comes to the conclusion of his genealogy at the end of verse 16: "Matthan was the father of Jacob, and Jacob was the father of Joseph, the husband of Mary, of whom was born Jesus, called the Christ."

But what would be the point of tracing Jesus' bloodline back to David and Abraham, when in fact he is not connected to this line? His only link to it is through Joseph, a man who is not his father.

To be sure, the matter is perplexing, even though the basic point that the author is trying to make is relatively clear. He is trying to show that Jesus has Jewish roots and, more specifically, that he can legitimately claim to be of the line of David, as would be necessary for the "son of David," the messiah. Thus, even though the genealogy may appear irrelevant at first glance, in that Jesus doesn't belong to the bloodline that it delineates,

it is clearly meant to make a statement about him; because Joseph was in some sense Jesus' "father" (through adoption?), Jesus is related through him to the greats of Israel's past.

Yet more striking is verse 17, which summarizes the genealogy in such a way as to show its real motivation. There were fourteen generations between Abraham and David, fourteen between David and the deportation to Babylon, and fourteen between the deportation to Babylon and the messiah, Jesus. This coincidence is amazing. Between the father of the Jews and the greatest king of the Jews were fourteen generations, as there were between the greatest king of the Jews and the greatest catastrophe of the Jews (the destruction of their nation by the Babylonians) and between the greatest catastrophe of the Jews and the ultimate deliverer of the Jews, the messiah.

The genealogy suggests—indeed, it almost demonstrates—that the entire course of Israel's history has proceeded according to divine providence. Moreover, this history has culminated in Jesus. At every fourteenth generation, something cataclysmic happens in Israel's history: their greatest king, their worst disaster, and now their ultimate salvation. Jesus' birth fourteen generations removed from the Babylonian deportation shows that in him God was going to do something significant, something unprecedented for his people Israel.

But is this sequence of fourteen-fourteen-fourteen actually viable? It is not difficult to find out: nearly two-thirds of the names in the genealogy are known to us from the Jewish Scriptures, Matthew's own source for the generations from Abraham to the deportation to Babylon. Unfortunately, when the sequence is checked against this source, there do appear to be some problems. The most glaring one comes in verse 8, where Joram is said to be the father of Uzziah; for we know from 1 Chron 3:10–12 that Joram was not Uzziah's father, but his great-great-grandfather. (Read the 1 Chronicles passage for yourself, but bear in mind that Uzziah is called Azariah in this book, as can be seen by comparing 2 Kings 14:21 with 2 Chron 26:1.) Why, then, would Matthew say that he was his father?

The answer should be obvious. If Matthew were to include all the generations between Joram and Uzziah (his father Amaziah, grandfather Joash, and great-grandfather Ahaziah), he would no longer be able to claim that there were fourteen generations between David and the deportation to Babylon! This would disrupt the entire notion that at every fourteen generations a cataclysmic event happens in the history of the people. And this, in turn, would compromise his implicit claim that because of when he was born, Jesus must be someone special and significant in the divine plan for Israel (see box 6.1).

Thus the genealogy cannot be historically right. But at this stage, we are less interested in pursuing the question of what really happened in the life of the historical Jesus than in seeing how Matthew meant to portray him. Matthew begins right

off the bat by informing us, through a genealogy that is not found in his predecessor, Mark, that Jesus was intimately connected with the history of the people of Israel. Indeed, the connection of Jesus with the Jewish people will be a key theme of the Gospel. Jesus will be portrayed in no uncertain terms as the Jewish messiah, come to the Jewish people in fulfillment of their greatest hopes. As the Jewish Savior sent from the Jewish God, he will embrace the Jewish Law and require his followers to do so as well. He will nonetheless come to be rejected by the Jewish leaders, who will mislead most of the Jewish people into rejecting him.

Obviously this portrayal of Jesus is not contradictory to Mark's, since most of Mark's stories have

WHAT DO YOU THINK?

BOX 6.1   Matthew's Scheme of Fourteen

Since Matthew apparently had to manipulate Jesus' genealogy in order to have something of major significance happen every fourteen generations, for example, by leaving out some of the names, we are justified in wondering whether the number fourteen was of particular importance to him. (You'll notice, incidentally, that the final sequence contains only thirteen names, even though Matthew claims that it contains fourteen!) Is there something significant about the number fourteen itself?

Over the years, interpreters of Matthew have puzzled over this question and put forth a variety of theories to account for it. Let me mention two of the more interesting ones.

First, in ancient Israel, as in a number of other ancient societies in which numbers had symbolic significance, the number seven was of supreme importance as a symbol of perfection or divinity (we'll see a lot of sevens when we come to study the Book of Revelation). The ancients divided the week into seven days, probably because they believed that there were seven planets. For some ancient Jews there were seven stages in a person's life and seven parts to the human soul; there were seven heavens, seven compartments of hell, and seven divisions of Paradise; there were seven classes of angels and seven attributes of God;

and so on. Consider the words of the famous first-century Jewish philosopher Philo: "I doubt whether anyone could adequately celebrate the properties of the number seven, for they are beyond words" (*On the Creation of the World,* 30).

If seven is a perfect number, a number associated with the divine, what then is fourteen? *Twice* seven! In cultures for which numbers matter, it would have been a doubly perfect number. Did Matthew set up Jesus' genealogy to show the divine perfection of his descent?

A second theory ties the genealogy yet more closely into Matthew's own portrayal of Jesus. Ancient languages typically used the letters of the alphabet to represent numerals, so that one could add up the letters in a name and come up with a numerical value. As we have already seen, Matthew emphasizes Jesus' messianic character as a descendant of King David. In Hebrew, David's name is spelled with three letters, equivalent to our letters *D, V,* and *D* (ancient Hebrew did not use vowels). Interestingly enough, the *D* in Hebrew is worth 4 and the *V* is worth 6, so the numerical value of David's name is fourteen. Has Matthew emphasized the number fourteen in Jesus' genealogy in order to stress his Davidic roots as the messiah of the Jews?

made it into Matthew, but the focus of attention, and therefore the basic portrayal of Jesus, is somewhat different. Here the center of attention is located even more squarely on the nature of Jesus' relationship to Judaism.

The Birth of the Messiah

This strong focus on Jesus' Jewish roots is confirmed in the birth narrative that follows (chaps. 1 and 2). (Recall: there is no account of Jesus' birth in Mark.) What is perhaps most striking about Matthew's account is that it all happens according to divine plan. The Holy Spirit is responsible for Mary's pregnancy, and an angel from heaven allays Joseph's fears. This conception fulfills a prophecy of the Hebrew Scriptures (1:23). Indeed, so does every other event in the narrative: Jesus' birth in Bethlehem (2:6), the family's flight to Egypt (2:14), Herod's slaughter of the innocent children of Bethlehem (2:18), and the family's decision to relocate in Nazareth (2:23). These stories occur only in Matthew.

Matthew's emphasis on Jesus' fulfilling of the Scripture occurs not only in his birth narrative, but throughout the entire book. On eleven separate occasions (including those just mentioned), Matthew uses a phrase that scholars have sometimes labeled a **"fulfillment citation."** The formulas of these citations vary somewhat, but they typically run something like this: "this occurred in order to fulfill what was spoken of by the prophet." In each instance, Matthew then cites the passage of Scripture that he has in mind, showing that Jesus is the long expected messiah of the Jews. These fulfillment citations are not found in Mark, and among all four New Testament Gospels they occur only in Matthew. Even more than his predecessor, then, Matthew explicitly and emphatically stresses that Jesus is the fulfillment of the Jewish Scriptures.

Jesus fulfills the Scripture in two different ways for Matthew, the first of which is easy to grasp. The Hebrew prophets occasionally made predictions about the future messiah. According to Matthew, Jesus fulfills these predictions. For example, Jesus is born in Bethlehem because this is what was predicted by the prophet Micah (2:6), and his mother is a virgin because this is what predicted by the prophet Isaiah (1:23).

The second way in which Jesus fulfills the Scripture is a little more complicated. Matthew portrays certain key events in the Jewish Bible as foreshadowings of what would happen when the messiah came. The meaning of these ancient events was not complete until that which was foreshadowed came into existence. When it did, the event was "fullfilled," that is, "filled full of meaning." In the birth narrative, for example, Matthew indicates that Jesus' family flees to Egypt to escape the wrath of Herod "in order to fulfill what was spoken by the Lord through the prophet, saying, 'Out of Egypt I have called my son'" (2:15). The quotation is from Hos 11:1 and originally referred to the exodus of the children of Israel from their bondage in Egypt. For Matthew, Jesus fills this event with meaning. The salvation available to the children of Israel was partial, looking forward to a future time when it would be made complete. With Jesus the messiah, that has now taken place.

Understanding this second way in which Jesus fulfills the Scripture for Matthew helps to explain certain aspects of the opening chapters of Matthew's Gospel (chaps. 1–5) that have long intrigued scholars. Think about the following events in rough outline, and ask yourself how they might have resonated with a first-century Jew who was intimately familiar with the Jewish Scriptures. A male child is miraculously born to Jewish parents, but a fierce tyrant in the land (Herod) is set to destroy him. The child is supernaturally protected from harm in Egypt. Then he leaves Egypt and is said to pass through the waters (of baptism). He goes into the wilderness to be tested for a long period. Afterward he goes up on a mountain and delivers God's Law to those who have been following him.

Sound familiar? It would to most of Matthew's Jewish readers. Matthew has shaped these opening stories of Jesus to show that Jesus' life is a fulfillment of the stories of Moses (read Exodus 1–20). The parallels are too obvious to ignore: Herod is like the Egyptian pharoah, Jesus' baptism is like the crossing of the Red Sea, the forty days of testing are like the forty years the children of Israel wandered in the wilderness, and the Sermon on the Mount is like the Law of Moses delivered on Mount Sinai. These parallels tell us something significant about Matthew's portrayal of Jesus. Certainly he agrees

BOX 6.2   The Women in Matthew's Genealogy

One of the most intriguing features of Matthew's genealogy is its explicit reference to women among Jesus' ancestors. Women hardly ever appear in other ancient Jewish genealogies, which invariably traced a person's lineage from father to son (or vice-versa) all the way back through the family line (see, e.g., 1 Chronicles 1–9). But not only does Matthew end this genealogy by naming Mary, Jesus' mother, he also includes four other women: Tamar (v. 3), Rahab (v. 5), Ruth (v. 5), and the "wife of Uriah," that is, Bathsheba (v. 6). Stories about all four of these women are found in the Jewish Scriptures (Tamar: Genesis 38; Rahab: Joshua 2, 6; Ruth: Ruth 1–4; and Bathsheba: 2 Samuel 11–12). But why does Matthew mention them here? Among the numerous theories proposed over the years, two are particularly intriguing.

1. All four of the women appear to have been Gentiles, that is, non-Israelites (Tamar and Rahab were both Canaanites; Ruth was a Moabite; and Bathsheba was married to Uriah, a Hittite). Could it be that Matthew mentions them to show that God's plan of salvation had always encompassed not only Jews but also Gentiles (cf., for example, his story of the Magi)? This is an attractive theory, but it has one particular shortcoming: it doesn't explain how these four women are connected with the final one mentioned, Mary, who was *not* a Gentile. And so, perhaps a second explanation is to be preferred:

2. All four women were involved with sexual activities that were viewed as scandalous by outsiders but that furthered the purposes of God. Tamar, for example, tricked her father-in-law into having sex with her by disguising herself as a prostitute; Rahab was a prostitute who lived in Jericho (and who, according to Matthew, later became the mother-in-law of Ruth); Ruth seduced her kinsman Boaz, who then proposed marriage to her (they became the grandparents of King David); and Bathsheba committed adultery with David and ended up marrying him (and fathering his child Solomon) after he arranged to have her husband killed. Why would allusions to such stories strike Matthew as appropriate for his genealogy of Jesus? Could it have to do with Mary, the mother of Jesus, herself? Recall: she, too, was thought to have engaged in illicit sexual activity (she became pregnant out of wedlock). Even Joseph was suspicious and decided to dissolve their relationship in secret! Matthew, however, saw the matter differently: once again God used a potential sex scandal to further his plans, having Jesus miraculously born from a woman who was still a virgin.

---

with Mark that Jesus is the suffering Son of God, the messiah, but here Jesus is also the new Moses, come to set his people free from their bondage (to sin 1:21) and give them the new Law, his teachings.

We have seen that among first-century Jews there was not just one set of expectations concerning their future deliverer. Many hoped for a future king like David, who would lead his people to military victory over their oppressors and establish Israel as a sovereign state in the Promised Land. Others anticipated the appearance of a cosmic figure on the clouds of heaven, coming in judgment to the earth. Still others looked forward to an authoritative priest who would guide the community through divinely inspired interpretations of the Mosaic Law. One other form that the future deliverer sometimes took is of particular relevance for understanding Matthew's portrayal of Jesus. Some Jews hoped that a prophet like Moses would appear, who not only brought salvation from the hated oppressors of Israel, the Egyptians who had enslaved them for 400 years, but also disclosed the Law of God to his people. Indeed, according to the ancient traditions, Moses himself had said that there would be another prophet like him who would arise among his people (Deut 18:15–19). The hope for a messianic figure like Moses, one chosen by God to bring salvation and new direction, was very much alive among some Jews in the first century.

Unlike some later Christians who insisted that a person had to choose between Moses and Jesus, Matthew maintains that the choice is instead between Moses without Jesus and Moses with Jesus. For him, false religion involves rejecting Jesus, precisely because Jesus is a new Moses. This new Moses does not replace the old one, however. Quite the contrary, he is the true and final interpreter of what the earlier Moses recorded in his Law. Jesus also gives the divine Law in this Gospel, but for Matthew this law does not stand at odds with the Law of Moses; it is a fulfillment of that Law (5:17). Followers of Jesus must follow the Law of Moses, not abandon it; moreover, they must follow it by understanding it in the way prescribed by the new Moses, Jesus the messiah.

Just as Moses was a prophet who was confronted and rejected by those who refused to recognize his leadership, like all the prophets in the Jewish Scriptures, according to Matthew, so, too, Jesus in Matthew is constantly opposed by the leaders of his own people. We have already seen this basic motif of Jesus' rejection in Mark. In many respects, Matthew emphasizes the antagonism even more, and Jesus engages in a far more active counterattack, accusing his opponents of placing a higher value on their own traditions than on the law of God, attacking their wicked motives, and above all charging them with hypocrisy, that is, knowing and teaching the right thing to do but failing to do it.

The Rejected King of the Jews

We do not have to wait long to find Matthew portraying the Jewish leaders as hypocrites, who know the truth but do not follow it. They are presented this way at the outset of the Gospel, while Jesus is still an infant.

The story of the visit of the Magi (2:1–12), found only in Matthew, is one of the most interesting tales of the New Testament. Here we are less interested in the historical problems that the story raises (e.g., how *can* a star stand over a particular house?) than in the point of the story in Matthew's Gospel. Ancient readers would have recognized the Magi as astrologers from the East (perhaps Assyria), who

could read the course of human events from the movements of the stars. These wise men are pagans, of course, whose astral observations have led them to recognize that a spectacular event has transpired on earth, the birth of a child who will be king.

The text never explains why Assyrian scholars would be interested in the birth of a foreign king. Perhaps their worship of him indicates that they understand him to be far greater than a mere mortal, king or otherwise. The reader of this account already realizes this, of course, since the child is said to have no human father. What the Magi evidently do not know is where the child is to be born. The star takes them to Jerusalem, the holy city of the Jews, the capital of Judea. There they make their inquiries. Herod, the reigning king of the Jews, hears of their presence and is naturally distraught. Israel has room for only one king, and he himself sits on the throne. He has a reason of his own, then, to locate the child: not to worship him but to destroy him.

Herod calls in the Jewish chief priests and the scholars trained in the Scriptures for counsel, and here we find the key irony of the account. The Jewish leaders know perfectly well where the messiah is to be born: Bethlehem of Judea. They can even quote the Scriptures in support and do so before Herod, who informs the wise men.

Who, then, goes to worship Jesus? Not those who knew where he was to be born, not the Jewish chief priests or the Jewish Scripture scholars or the Jewish king. They stay away. It is the Gentiles, the non-Jews who originally did not have the Scriptures but who learn the truth from those who do, who go to worship the king of the Jews. The Jewish authorities, on the other hand, as represented by Herod their king, plot to kill the child.

This story functions in Matthew's Gospel to set the stage for what will happen subsequently. Jesus fulfills the Scripture and urges his followers to do so as well; he is nonetheless rejected by the leaders of his own people, who plot his death. There are others, however, who will come and worship him. If you study Matthew's Gospel carefully, you will find this particular Matthean theme played out not only in stories that Matthew has added to his Markan framework but also in the changes that he has made to stories he inherited from Mark.

THE PORTRAYAL OF JESUS IN MATTHEW: THE SERMON ON THE MOUNT AS A SPRINGBOARD

Since we are applying a redactional method of analysis to Matthew's Gospel, rather than a literary-historical one, we will not follow the procedure used with Mark of tracing the development of the narrative and showing how the unfolding of the plot gives an indication of the identity of its main character. If we had sufficient time and space, of course, we could proceed through the entire Gospel as we have started, asking how the author has added to, subtracted from, and otherwise changed the one source that we are reasonably certain that he had, the Gospel of Mark. I have opted instead simply to analyze portions of the Sermon on the Mount, one of the most memorable portions of Matthew's narrative, for by examining several of its key passages, we can uncover themes that recur throughout the rest of the Gospel.

Jesus: The New Moses and the New Law

The Sermon on the Mount (chaps. 5–7) is the first of five major blocks of Jesus' teaching in Matthew (the others: chap. 10, Jesus' instructions to the apostles; chap. 13, the parables of the kingdom; chap. 18, other teachings on the kingdom and on the church; chaps. 23–27, the "woes" against the scribes and Pharisees and the apocalyptic discourse describing the end of time). We have seen that Matthew appears to portray Jesus as a new Moses. Some scholars have suggested that this collection of his teachings into five major blocks of material is meant to recall the five books of the Law of Moses.

As I have already indicated, a good deal of the material in the Sermon on the Mount comes from Q. Since these Q passages are scattered throughout Luke's Gospel, rather than gathered together in one place, it appears that the Sermon on the Mount may be Matthew's own creation. By taking materials dispersed throughout his sources, Matthew has formed them into one finely crafted collection of Jesus' important teachings.

One of the overarching messages of the sermon is the connection between Jesus and Moses. If the Law of Moses was meant to provide divine guidance for

Figure 6.1   A portrayal of Mary, Jesus, an angel (upper left side), and the three Magi bringing gifts, from an ancient ivory produced in the Coptic church of Egypt. Interestingly enough, Matthew, the only Gospel to narrate the story, does not indicate that there were three Magi—only that there were three gifts.

Jews as the children of Israel, the teachings of Jesus are meant to provide guidance for his followers as children of the kingdom of heaven (see the summary statement at the end of the sermon, 7:24–28). As I have already intimated, this does not mean that Jesus' followers are to choose between Moses and Jesus; they are to follow Moses by following Jesus. For Matthew, Jesus provides the true understanding of the Jewish Law, and his followers must keep it.

The sermon is thus largely about life in the kingdom of heaven, which according to the statement in 4:17 (immediately before the sermon) was the main emphasis of Jesus' teaching: "Repent, for the kingdom of heaven has come near." This kingdom of heaven does not refer to the place people go when they die. Rather, it refers to God's presence on earth, a kingdom that he will bring at the end of this age by overthrowing the forces of evil. When God does this, the weak and oppressed will be exalted, and the high and mighty will be abased. This appears to be the point of the beginning of the sermon, the Beatitudes (the descriptions of those who are blessed) found in 5:3–10:

> Blessed are the poor in spirit, for theirs is the kingdom of heaven. Blessed are those who mourn, for they will be comforted. Blessed are the meek, for they will inherit the earth. Blessed are those who hunger and thirst for righteousness, for they will be filled. Blessed are the merciful, for they will receive mercy. Blessed are the pure in heart, for they will see God. Blessed are the peacemakers, for they will be called children of God. Blessed are those who are persecuted for righteousness' sake, for theirs is the kingdom of heaven.

How are we to interpret these Beatitudes? Given the fact that John the Baptist sets the stage for Jesus' teaching by proclaiming that the end (that is, the kingdom) is near and that Jesus himself proclaims that "the kingdom of heaven is at hand" (4:17), it seems probable that they refer to the coming kingdom. Even so, scholars have long debated the precise function of these words. Is Jesus setting up the requirements for entrance into the kingdom? Is he saying that people need to become poor in spirit, for example, in order to receive the kingdom? While this is possible, Jesus does not appear to be issuing commands so much as making statements of fact. It would be hard, for example, to think that he was telling people that if they didn't mourn they wouldn't be allowed into the kingdom. Perhaps, then, we should see the Beatitudes as assurances to those who are presently lowly and oppressed, weak and suffering, for when the kingdom of heaven comes, they will receive their reward. Those who now mourn will be comforted, those who now hunger for justice will be

granted it, and those who are now persecuted for doing what is right will be vindicated.

Taking Jesus' words in this way, however, creates another problem of interpretation. Do the Beatitudes suggest that everyone experiencing problems will be exalted in the coming kingdom? Or are they instead directed just to those who were following Jesus, the ones to whom Jesus was actually speaking (5:1–2)? This issue cannot be resolved until we examine more fully what it means, for Matthew, to follow Jesus.

Jesus and the Law

Contrary to what many Christians have thought throughout the ages, for Matthew following Jesus does not mean abandoning the Jewish Law and joining a new religion that is opposed to it. Even in Matthew's day some Christians appear to have thought that this is what Jesus had in mind—that he sought to overturn the Law of Moses in his preaching about the way of God. For Matthew, however, nothing could be further from the truth. The keynote of the sermon is struck soon after the Beatitudes in this statement, found only in Matthew's Gospel:

> Do not think that I have come to abolish the law or the prophets; I have come not to abolish but to fulfill. For truly I tell you, until heaven and earth pass away, not one letter, not one stroke of a letter will pass from the law until all is fulfilled. Therefore, whoever breaks one of the least of these commandments, and teaches others to do the same, will be called least in the kingdom of heaven; but whoever does them and teaches them will be called great in the kingdom of heaven. For I tell you, unless your righteousness exceeds that of the scribes and the Pharisees, you will never enter the kingdom of heaven. (5:17–20)

In Matthew, Jesus is not opposed to the Law of Moses. He himself fulfills it, as seen in the important events in his birth, life, and death, events that are said to be fulfillments of the prophecy of Scripture. Moreover, Jesus in Matthew also requires his followers to fulfill the Law, in fact, to fulfill it even better than the Jewish leaders, the scribes and the Pharisees. Matthew indicates what he means in the very next passage, the famous **"Antitheses"** (5:21–48).

Jesus' Followers and the Law

An "antithesis" is a contrary statement. In the six antitheses recorded in the Sermon on the Mount, Jesus states a Jewish Law and then sets his interpretation of that Law over and against it. I should emphasize that Matthew does not portray Jesus as contradicting the Law; for example, he does not say, "You have heard it said, 'You shall not commit murder,' but I say to you that you should." Instead, Jesus urges his followers to adhere to the Law, but, to do so more rigorously than even the religious leaders of Israel. The contrasts of the antitheses, then, are between the way the Law is commonly interpreted and the way Jesus interprets it. In all these antitheses Jesus goes to the heart of the law in question, to its root intention as it were, and insists that his followers adhere to that, rather than the letter of the Law as strictly interpreted.

For example, the Law says not to murder (5:21). This law functions to preserve the harmony of the community. The root of disharmony (which leads to murder) is anger against another. Therefore, if one wants to fulfill the Law by obeying its root intention, he or she must not even become angry with another. The Law also says not to commit adultery (5:27), that is, not to take the wife of another. This law preserves ownership rights, since in ancient Israel, as in many ancient societies, the wife was seen as the property of her husband (e.g., see the Tenth Commandment, where wives are grouped together with houses, slaves, oxen, and donkeys as the property of one's neighbor that is not to be coveted; Exod 20:17). The root of adultery, in this view, is a man's passionate desire for another man's wife. Therefore, those who want to keep the Law completely should not passionately desire a person who belongs to another.

The Law says to take an eye for an eye, a tooth for a tooth (Matt 5:38). This law serves to guarantee justice in the community, so that if a neighbor knocks out your tooth, you cannot lop off his head in exchange. Contrary to the way in which this law is commonly understood today, it was originally meant to be merciful, not vindictive; the penalty should fit and not exceed the crime. Since, however, the root of this law is the principle of mercy, Jesus draws the radical conclusion: instead of inflicting a penalty on another, his followers should prefer to suffer wrong. Therefore, someone who is struck on one cheek should turn the other to be struck as well.

As can be seen from these examples, far from absolving his followers of the responsibility to keep the Law, Matthew's Jesus intensifies the Law, requiring his followers to keep not just its letter but its very spirit. This intensification of the Law, however, raises a number of questions. One in particular has occurred to many readers over the years: can Jesus be serious? Is he really saying that no one who becomes angry, or who lusts, or who returns a blow can enter into the kingdom?

Readers of Matthew have frequently tried to get around this problem by softening Matthew's rigorous statements by importing views not presented in the text itself. For example, it is commonly suggested that Jesus means to set up an ideal standard that no one could possibly achieve to force people to realize that they are utter sinners in need of divine grace for salvation. The point of Jesus' words, then, would be that people cannot keep God's Law even if they want to. The problem with this interpretation is that Jesus in Matthew does not suggest that it is impossible to control your anger or lust, any more than the author of the Torah suggests that it is impossible to control your coveting.

At the same time, Matthew is not simply giving a detailed list of what Jesus' followers must do and not do in order to enter into the kingdom. On the contrary, his point seems to be that overly scrupulous attention to the detail of the Law is not what really matters to God. Even scribes and Pharisees can adhere to laws once they are narrowly enough prescribed, for example, by not murdering and not committing adultery and not eating forbidden foods. God wants more than this kind of strict obedience to the letter of the Law.

The Fulfillment of the Law

What then is the real purpose of the Law? We get a hint of Matthew's answer already in the Sermon on the Mount, in Jesus' famous expression of the golden rule. We know of other ancient teachers who formulated similar guidelines of behavior (see box 6.3), but Jesus' particular formulation is important: "In everything do to others as you would have them do to you; for this is the law and the prophets" (7:12). The final phrase of the saying is the key; the entire Law with all of its commandments can be summarized in this simple principle, that you treat others as you want them to treat you.

For Jesus in Matthew, the true interpretation of the Law does not require nuanced descriptions of how precisely to follow each of its commandments; it involves loving others as much as one's self. This principle can be found in other passages of Matthew's Gospel, most strikingly in 22:35–40, where in response to a question from a "lawyer" (i.e., an expert in the Jewish Law) Jesus summarizes the entire Torah in terms of two of its requirements: that "you shall love the Lord your God with all your heart, and with all your soul, and with all your mind" (Deut 6:5) and that "you love your neighbor as yourself" (Lev 19:18). Mark has this story as well, but Matthew tacks a different ending onto it: "On these two commandments hang all the Law and the Prophets" (22:40). For Matthew, the entire Law is thus at its very core a commandment to love: to love God with one's entire being and to love one's neighbor as one's self. This is the real intent of the Law, and the followers of Jesus must adhere to it in order to enter into the kingdom of heaven.

Another question naturally emerges from Jesus' insistence that his followers keep the Law. The laws that we have examined so far, for example, in the antitheses and the golden rule, would not have been seen as distinctively Jewish by many people in the ancient world. Most other people in Roman antiquity would have agreed that you should not commit murder or take your neighbor's wife or mete out unfair punishment. What about the laws

ANOTHER GLIMPSE INTO THE PAST

BOX 6.3   The Golden Rule

The most familiar form of the golden rule is "Do unto others as you would have them do unto you." Many people think that Jesus was the first to propound this ethical principle, but in fact, it was given in a variety of forms by moral philosophers from the ancient world. In most of these formulations, it is expressed negatively (stating what should *not* be done) rather than positively.

The rule was found, for example, among the ancient Greeks many centuries before Jesus. One of the characters described by the Greek historian Herodotus (fifth century B.C.E.) said, "I will not myself do that which I consider to be blameworthy in my neighbor," and the Greek orator Isocrates (fourth century B.C.E.) said, "You should be such in your dealings with others as you expect me to be in my dealings with you." The saying was present in Eastern cultures as well, most famously on the lips of Confucius (sixth century B.C.E.): "Do not do to others what you would not want others to do to you."

Nearer to Jesus' time, the golden rule was endorsed (in various forms of wording) in a number of Jewish writings. For example, in the apocryphal book of Tobit, we read, "And what you hate, do not do to anyone," and in an ancient Jewish interpretation of the book of Leviticus we find "Do not do to him (your neighbor) what you yourself hate."

Perhaps the best known expression of the rule in Jewish circles, however, comes from the most revered rabbi of Jesus' day, the famous Rabbi Hillel. A pagan approached the rabbi and promised him that he would convert to Judaism if Hillel could recite the entire Torah to him while standing on one leg. Hillel's terse reply sounds remarkably like the statement of Jesus in Matt 7:12: "What is hateful to you do not do to your neighbor; that is the whole Torah, while the rest is commentary. Go and learn it."

Jesus, in short, was not the only teacher of his day who taught the golden rule or who thought that the essence of the Law of Moses could be summed up in the commandment to love.

of Scripture, however, that were widely recognized as making Jews a separate people from non-Jews, for example, the laws that required Jews to circumcise their baby boys, to keep the Sabbath day holy, and to observe certain dietary restrictions? We know from other evidence that by the time Matthew wrote his Gospel, these laws were not being followed by many Gentile Christians. Indeed, as we will see when we come to the letters of Paul (which were written before Matthew and the other Gospels), there were many Christians, including Paul himself, who insisted that Gentile believers should not keep these laws. What, then, about Matthew? Does he think that Jesus radicalized these laws as well as the others? Does Matthew's Jesus expect his followers to keep them?

Matthew never addresses head on the question of keeping such distinctively Jewish laws. Several points, however, can be raised. The first is that Jesus never disavows any of these Scriptural laws in Matthew or instructs his followers not to keep them. Moreover, in a number of passages not found in

Mark, Jesus appears to affirm aspects of traditional Jewish piety. For instance, he castigates the hypocritical ways that the Pharisees give alms, pray, and fast, but he restates the importance of engaging in these practices themselves (6:1–18; see also 23:23).

Similar emphases are found in the changes Matthew made in stories taken from Mark. For example, in Mark's apocalyptic discourse, Jesus speaks of the coming disaster and tells his disciples to "pray that it not be in winter" (because it would then be harder to escape; Mark 13:18). Interestingly, Matthew takes over this verse but adds the words "or during the Sabbath" (Matt 24:20). Why? Apparently because, for Matthew, extensive travel on the Sabbath was forbidden to Jesus' followers as those who kept the Law.

All these examples would make it appear that Jesus in Matthew is not intent on requiring his followers to abandon traditional forms of Jewish piety as rooted in the Torah. He simply assumes, for the most part, that they will practice them as they practice the entire Law (5:17–20).

ANOTHER EARLY CHRISTIAN TEXT

BOX 6.4 The *Gospel of the Nazareans*

Matthew is often called the "most Jewish" of the Gospels because of its emphases on the Jewishness of Jesus and on the need for his followers to keep the Law. In the second century, some decades after Matthew was written, there was a group of Jewish believers in Jesus who considered themselves his truest followers because they continued to keep the Jewish Law (e.g., observing Sabbath and keeping kosher) and insisted that the Law was essential for salvation. In taking this view, they stood against other Christians who appealed to the apostle Paul in saying that Christians no longer keep the Law (cf. Gal 2:16). But these Jewish Christians—who were sometimes called **Nazareans**—did not accept the authority of Paul. And remember, this was before there was a canon of the New Testament that could be appealed to in order to settle disputes.

These Nazareans had a Gospel that they revered, which supported their Jewish perspective. It

is known today as the *Gospel of the Nazareans*, and even though we no longer have it in its entirety, we do have quotations from it by early church writers. It appears in fact that the *Gospel of the Nazareans* was either a translation of Matthew into Aramaic (the language of Palestine that Jesus himself spoke) or an original Aramaic composition very similar to Matthew. But because these Nazareans did not believe that Jesus had been born of a virgin (they thought he was the natural son of Joseph and Mary, whom God had chosen to be his messiah to die for the sins of the world), their Gospel did not have what are now Matthew 1–2, the passages that narrate Jesus' miraculous coming into the world.

The Nazareans eventually died out. But if their views had become more widely accepted, possibly the New Testament would not contain our Greek Gospel of Matthew but a shorter version in Aramaic!

JESUS REJECTED BY THE JEWISH LEADERS

When Jesus' strong affirmation of the Torah of Moses is set over against his strong opposition to the Jewish leadership, perhaps the most striking aspect of Matthew's Gospel emerges. On the one hand, Jesus is portrayed as altogether Jewish. He is the Jewish messiah sent by the Jewish God to the Jewish people in fulfillment of the Jewish Scriptures. He is also the new Moses who gives the true interpretation of the Mosaic Law. On the other hand, he violently opposes Judaism as it is configured in this Gospel among the Jewish leadership. Somewhat paradoxically, then, in this Gospel Jesus commands his followers to adhere to the Jewish religion as it should be (i.e., as he himself interprets it), while urging them to reject the Jewish authorities, who are portrayed as evil hypocrites, opposed to God and his people.

The hypocrisy of the Jewish leaders was hinted at in the story of the Magi, which we have already considered. It is also found in the Sermon on the Mount, where the "hypocrites" pray, give alms, and fast simply in order to be seen and revered as holy, not out of true devotion to God (6:1–8). These, of course, are stories unique to Matthew. The same emphasis can be seen in stories that Matthew has taken over from Mark. You can see this for yourself by comparing, for instance, the stories of Matthew 12 with those of Mark 2:1–3:6.

A crescendo builds in Jesus' controversies with his opponents, reaching a climax in chapters 21–23, where Jesus himself takes the offensive. As in Mark, he "cleanses the Temple" (Matt 21:12–13), rousing the ire of the authorities. But in Matthew they become particularly incensed when they see him heal the blind and the lame and when they hear young children proclaim him the Son of David (21:14–15, only in Matthew). Jesus responds to their indignation by quoting the Psalms: "Out of the mouths of infants and nursing babes you have prepared praise for yourself" (21:16). Despite having witnessed his miracles, the Jewish leaders refuse to believe.

More than that, they attack Jesus by disputing his authority (21:23). In response, Jesus tells a parable (unique to Matthew) of a father with two sons, one of whom said that he would do his father's bidding and yet did not, the other of whom said that he would not but then did (21:28–32). Jesus likens his opponents to those who agree to do what their father (God) requires but fail to do so. He ends by claiming that the most despised of sinners—tax collectors and prostitutes—will enter into the kingdom of heaven ahead of them (21:32).

His assault continues in the parables that follow and reaches its climax in chapter 23, which contains the "Seven Woes" against the Pharisees. Here Jesus condemns his enemies, the "scribes and Pharisees," in no uncertain terms: they are concerned only with praise and admiration, not with doing what is right before God; they are hypocrites, blind guides concerned with minutia instead of with what really matters; they are whitewashed tombs, clean on the outside but full of rot and corruption within; they are a brood of vipers, murderers of the righteous prophets of God, false leaders who shed innocent blood.

Jesus' Passion in Matthew

According to Matthew, the Jewish authorities are fully responsible for the blood of Jesus as well. Many of the stories of Matthew's passion narrative are taken over from Mark, and a detailed study of the ways in which they have been changed can pay rich dividends. Many of the changes work to emphasize both Jesus' innocence and the corresponding guilt of the Jewish leaders who demand his death. As in Mark, for example, Pilate offers to release a prisoner to the Jewish crowds in honor of the Passover feast. In Matthew's account, however, he more clearly prefers to release Jesus rather than the notorious Barabbas (27:15–18). In part, Pilate acts on advice from his wife, who tells him that she has suffered a bad dream about Jesus, whom she knows to be innocent (27:19, found only in Matthew). The "chief priests and elders," however, stir up the crowds to demand Barabbas instead. Pilate insists that Jesus does not deserve punishment, since he has done nothing wrong (27:22), but the people become persistent and demand his crucifixion (27:23).

Then comes a well-known and ill-fated account, found only in Matthew. Pilate calls for water

Figure 6.2 A miniature portrayal of several scenes from Jesus' passion in Matthew's Gospel: Pilate washing his hands, Jesus carrying his cross, Peter making his denials, and the rooster crowing.

and washes his hands of the blood of Jesus, proclaiming, "I am innocent of this man's blood; see to it yourselves" (27:24). The entire crowd responds in words that have served hateful purposes ever since: "His blood be on us and our children" (27:25). Here the Jews gathered in Jerusalem claim responsibility for Jesus' unjust execution. Over the centuries, this verse has been used for all kinds of malicious acts of anti-Semitism—as if Jews who were not present at the scene could possibly be held responsible for the actions of those who were.

Matthew, however, does not himself portray all Jews as wicked opponents of God, as "Christ-killers" (an anti-Semitic slogan derived largely from this passage). Quite the contrary. As we

have seen, Jesus himself is a Jew in this Gospel, as are all his disciples. He is the Jewish messiah descended from David, the new Moses who urges his followers to fulfill the Jewish Law. Nowhere in the Gospel does Jesus condemn Jews for being Jews. Whenever Jesus lambastes specific opponents in Matthew, they are in every instance Jewish *leaders* (Pharisees, scribes, chief priests, and so on). Even in Jesus' trial before Pilate, where Matthew appears to lay the blame of miscarried justice on all the Jewish people who are present, the real culprits are the "chief priests and elders," who stir up the crowds to say what they do (v. 19). Thus, the problem for Matthew is never the Jews or the Jewish religion per se; it is

ANOTHER EARLY CHRISTIAN TEXT

BOX 6.5 The *Gospel of Peter*

We have seen that the New Testament Gospels are anonymous, but there were other Gospels written about Jesus that claimed to be written by his own apostles, even though today they are recognized as forgeries. One of the most intriguing is a Gospel allegedly written by Simon Peter, which was discovered in 1887, buried in the tomb of a monk.

Only a fragmentary portion of the *Gospel of Peter* was found in this tomb; this is the portion of the Gospel that describes Jesus' trial before Pilate, crucifixion, and resurrection. It is like the Synoptic Gospels in many ways, especially Matthew. Here, for example, there is also a scene of Pilate washing his hands to proclaim his innocence in Jesus' death and a posting of the guard to watch over Jesus' tomb (passages otherwise found only in Matthew).

But there are interesting differences as well. In the *Gospel of Peter*, when Jesus is crucified he is said to have remained silent "as if he had no pain." Is it possible that this pseudonymous author understood Jesus to be completely divine and not human, so he couldn't really suffer? And another difference: in this Gospel it is the Jews, rather than the Romans, who

are completely at fault for Jesus' death, and they are said to have regretted very much what they did afterward. Is this Gospel even more anti-Jewish than those in the New Testament?

The most interesting part of this Gospel is near the end. In the New Testament, when Jesus rises from the dead, no one sees it happen. But they do in the *Gospel of Peter*. As the guards watch, two angels descend from heaven, the stone before Jesus' tomb rolls away by itself, and they enter. Then there emerge *three* men, two of whose heads reach the sky and another, whom they support (i.e., Jesus), whose head reaches above the sky. Following them there emerges the cross itself. A voice comes from heaven, "Have you preached to those who are sleeping (i.e., the dead)?" And the cross replies, "Yes."

This is a terrific narrative: a giant Jesus and a walking-talking cross! Some early Christians believed this book really was written by Peter and revered it as sacred Scripture. Imagine how different the New Testament would have been had it finally been included in the canon.

---

the Jewish authorities. This Gospel consistently affirms Judaism, at least Judaism as it was interpreted by Matthew's Jesus.

MATTHEW AND HIS READERS

On the basis of the portrayal of Jesus in this Gospel, we can hypothesize some things about the context of the author and his audience. Matthew's insistence that Jesus continued to adhere to traditional forms of Jewish piety and that he advanced the true interpretation of the Law of Moses suggests that the author himself and some, perhaps most, of his audience were themselves Jewish (see box 6.6). Would non-Jews be this interested in seeing Jesus as a thoroughly Jewish teacher intent on keeping

the Law who insisted that his disciples followed suit? For Jewish Christians, however, this emphasis seems fairly natural. Moreover, believing in Jesus did not require abandoning the ancestral traditions that stem from Moses. On the contrary, Jesus showed how to understand these traditions and commanded his followers to obey them.

At the same time, there must have also been a good number of Gentiles in Matthew's congregation. This would explain Jesus' claim that many outsiders would enter into the kingdom ahead of Jews (8:8–10), and also the "Great Commission," which urged missionary work principally among "the Gentiles" (28:19–20). In short, Matthew's congregation appears to be mixed, comprising both Jews and Gentiles. Many scholars have thought that it makes sense to locate it somewhere near

BOX 6.6 Was Matthew a Jew?

Some scholars have come to doubt that Matthew was a Jew despite the heavy emphasis on Jesus' own Jewishness in this Gospel. One of the more intriguing pieces of evidence that is sometimes cited involves Matthew's interpretation of passages drawn from the Hebrew Bible, especially Zech 9:9, as quoted in Matt 21:5: "Look your king is coming to you, humble, and mounted on a donkey, and on a colt, the foal of a donkey."

Anyone who has studied the Jewish Scriptures extensively recognizes the literary form of this passage. Throughout the Psalms and other books of poetry, Hebrew authors employed a kind of parallelism in which a second line of a couplet simply repeated the ideas of the first line using different words. Here the parallelism is between the "donkey" of the first line and the "colt, the foal of a donkey" in the second.

Matthew, however, appears to have misunderstood the parallelism or at least to have understood it in a highly unusual way. For he seems to have thought that the prophet was speaking of two differ-

ent animals, one of them a donkey and the other a colt. So, when Jesus prepares to ride into Jerusalem, his followers actually acquire two animals for him, which he straddles for the trip into town (21:5–7; contrast Mark 11:7)! Some scholars have argued that no educated Jew would have made this kind of mistake about the Zechariah passage (none of the other Gospel writers, it might be pointed out, does so), so this author could not have been Jewish.

Most other scholars, however, have not been convinced, in part because we know all sorts of educated authors from the ancient world (as well as the modern one) who seem to misread texts. They include ancient Jewish interpreters of their own Hebrew Scriptures, some of whom produce interpretations that are no more bizarre than Matthew's interpretation of Zechariah (including some late rabbinic sources, which also indicate that Zechariah was referring to two animals!). On these grounds, at least, the identity of Matthew has to be left as an open question.

Palestine in a major urban area (where Jews and Gentiles might congregate in large numbers), for instance, in Antioch of Syria, where the second-century authors who first quote the book of Matthew happen to have resided.

Perhaps the best way to explain Matthew's extensive criticism of the Jewish authorities is to say that his own community continued to experience opposition from non-Christian Jews, especially influential scribes and rabbis of the local synagogue(s), who accused them of abandoning Moses and the Law, of becoming apostate from the Jewish religion through their ill-advised faith in Jesus.

Matthew, an anonymous Jewish leader of the Christian community (assuming that his strong literary skills, indicative of a higher education, gave him a place of prominence there), penned a Gospel narrative to show that Jesus was in fact the Jewish

messiah, who like Moses gave the law of God to his people. More precisely, he was the prophet like Moses who gave the Jewish people the true interpretation of Moses' Law, and beyond that he was a Savior who died for the sins of his people (1:21) and was vindicated by God by being raised from the dead. Moreover, Matthew went out of his way to affirm more strongly than his predecessors Mark and Q that Jesus did not annul the ancient Law of Moses but fulfilled it himself and insisted that all his followers, both Jews and Gentiles, do so as well. This they could do by holding on to Jesus' teachings and by following the principle at the heart of the Torah, given long ago to Jesus' forerunner Moses: to love God with their entire being and their neighbor as much as themselves, "for on these two commandments hang all the Law and the Prophets."

AT A GLANCE

BOX 6.7   The Gospel of Matthew

1. Matthew's Gospel was written in Greek, around 80–85 C.E.

2. Its author left his identity anonymous; he must have been a Greek-speaking Christian, probably from outside Palestine.

3. Among his sources were Mark, Q, and M.

4. By studying his additions, omissions, and alterations of Mark (i.e., by doing redaction criticism), we can get a sense of some of his major emphases.

5. In the genealogy and birth stories (not found in Mark), he stresses Jesus' Jewishness, as the Jewish messiah sent from the Jewish God to the Jewish people in fulfillment of the Jewish Law.

6. In other passages, such as the Sermon on the Mount (also not found in Mark), Matthew's Jesus stresses that his followers must also adhere to the Jewish Law.

7. Matthew, in fact, portrays Jesus as the new Moses, who provides the correct interpretation of the Mosaic Law and expects his followers to keep it.

8. Jesus, however, is rejected by the Jewish leaders, who are lambasted severely for their failure to keep the Law in the way God desires.

TAKE A STAND

1. Suppose you want to show your roommate—who tends not to believe anything you say about the New Testament—that redaction criticism can be a useful way of highlighting the key emphases of the Gospel of Matthew. Make your case!

2. You are talking to a person who identifies herself as a "messianic Jew"—that is, someone who tries to keep the Jewish law, but understands Jesus is the messiah. She argues that if you take the Gospel of Matthew seriously, you, too, will see that it is necessary to continue to keep the Law (kosher foods, Sabbath observance, festivals, and the like). Do you agree or not? State your reasons.

3. Debate the following resolution, arguing either the affirmative side in favor of it or the negative side against it: Resolved: The Gospel of Matthew is anti-Semitic.

4. Pretend you are a first-century Christian who is trying to convince your Jewish neighbor that Jesus really is the messiah, and the only text you have available to you is the Gospel of Matthew. Make your case!

SUGGESTIONS FOR FURTHER READING

Allison, Dale C. *The New Moses: A Matthew Typology.* Minneapolis: Fortress, 1993. An interesting examination of Matthew's portrayal of Jesus as a new Moses.

Brown, Raymond. *The Birth of the Messiah: A Commentary on the Infancy Narratives in Matthew and Luke.* 2d ed. Garden City, N.Y.: Doubleday, 1993. A massive and exhaustive discussion of the birth narratives of Matthew and Luke, suitable for those who want to know simply everything about every detail.

Carter, Warren. *What Are They Saying about Matthew's Sermon on the Mount?* New York: Paulist, 1994. The best introductory sketch of the scholarly debates concerning the formation and meaning of Matthew's Sermon on the Mount.

Edwards, Richard A. *Matthew's Story of Jesus.* Philadelphia: Fortress, 1985. A nice introductory overview of the major themes of Matthew's Gospel for beginning students.

Nickle, Keith. *The Synoptic Gospels: Conflict and Consensus.* 2d ed. Atlanta: Westminster John Knox, 2001. A fine introduction to the major themes of Matthew's Gospel.

Perkins, Pheme. *Introduction to the Synoptic Gospels.* Grand Rapids, Mich.: Eerdmans, 2009. An overview of the major historical and literary issues involved with studying Matthew, Mark, and Luke; good for beginning students.

Riches, John K. *Matthew* (T &T Study Guides). London: T & T Clark, 2004. A discussion of all the significant features of the Gospel of Matthew, its contents, literary character, and historical problems; a full and useful overview for beginning students.

Senior, Donald. *What Are They Saying about Matthew?* 2d ed. New York: Paulist, 1995. An overview of scholarly views of Matthew's Gospel, excellent for beginning students.

 KEY TERMS

Antitheses	**Golden Rule**	**literary-historical**	**redaction criticism**
Aramaic	*Gospel of the*	**method**	**redactor**
Beatitudes	*Nazareans*	**Lord's Prayer**	**Sermon on the Mount**
fulfillment citation	*Gospel of Peter*	**Nazareans**	

Jesus, the Rejected Prophet
THE GOSPEL ACCORDING TO LUKE

WHAT TO EXPECT

There is obviously more than one way to study a Gospel. In this chapter we learn a new method that is in some ways similar to redaction criticism. The "comparative method" looks at similarities and differences between one text and one or more others without being concerned over whether they were used as its sources.

We will then apply the comparative method to the Gospel of Luke, seeing how it is both like and unlike Matthew and Mark, the two Gospels we have already studied at some length. As we will see, Luke is particularly concerned to explain how salvation moved from the Jewish people to non-Jews, the Gentiles. And yet he does so by portraying Jesus as a prophet, comparable in many ways to the prophets of the Old Testament.

I have had two overarching goals in our study of the early Christian Gospels to this point. The first has been to explain different methods that scholars have used in their investigation of these texts; the second has been to apply these methods to uncover the distinctive emphases of each Gospel. My underlying assumption has been that the results of our investigation are no more compelling than the methods that we use to attain them. That is to say, while it is important to know what a text means, it is also important to recognize how we know (or think we know) what it means. Moreover, it is useful not only to understand what our methods involve in theory but also to see how they work in practice.

Thus we applied the literary-historical method to discuss the Gospel of Mark and the redactional method to study Matthew. These particular Gospels do not have to be examined in these particular ways. We could just as easily have used a literary-historical method to study Matthew and, at least theoretically, a redactional method to study Mark (although the latter would have proved somewhat difficult since we do not have direct access to any of Mark's sources).

A third way to study a Gospel text (or any other text, for that matter) might be called the "**comparative method.**" Like the redactional method, this involves comparing two texts carefully with one another. But in this case it does not matter whether one document had been used as the source for another (so that we will not be looking at what has been added, omitted, or altered in a source); instead, two documents are simply *compared* with one another to see how they are alike and how they are different. The idea behind the method is that if you can find key differences in the way two authors describe the same event, those differences may be useful for illuminating the emphasis of each author.

As it turns out, this is an interesting method to use with Luke, in that this Gospel is very much like Matthew and Mark in some ways, but is also different. The differences are particularly interesting because they can reveal some of the major aspects of Luke's understanding of Jesus.

A COMPARATIVE OVERVIEW OF THE GOSPEL

We have already learned several basic points about Luke's Gospel in relation to Matthew and Mark. Like them, Luke is a kind of Greco-Roman biography of Jesus. It, too, is anonymous and appears to have been written by a Greek-speaking Christian somewhere outside Palestine. The author evidently penned his account somewhat later than the Gospel of Mark, perhaps at about the same time as the Gospel of Matthew. In the second century, the book came to be attributed to Luke, the traveling companion of the apostle Paul (we will consider the merits of this attribution in the following chapter).

Perhaps the most obvious difference between this Gospel and all others from antiquity (not just Matthew and Mark) is that it is the first of a two-volume set. The unknown author provided a continuation of the story in volume two, the Acts of the Apostles. The Gospel of Luke provides a sketch of the life and death of Jesus, and the book of Acts narrates the birth and life of the Christian church that emerged afterward. The author appears to have meant these books to be read together. For the purposes of our comparative study, however, we will restrict ourselves in this chapter to an analysis of Luke, reserving an investigation of Acts for a later chapter.

THE PREFACE TO LUKE'S GOSPEL

Given the importance that I have attached to the ways in which each of the other Gospels has begun, we do well to start our comparative study of Luke by considering his introduction. Unlike Mark and Matthew, Luke begins with a formal preface, found in the opening four verses of his account. Readers who are conversant with a wide range of Greco-Roman literature will have no difficulty understanding the significance of this beginning, for it is quite similar to other prefaces of the period, particularly among works by Greek historians. By beginning his Gospel with a standard "historiographic" preface, written in a much better style of Greek than anything found in Mark or Matthew, Luke alerts his reader both to his own abilities as a writer and to the scope of his work. His book is to be taken as a serious piece of historical writing, at least according to ancient readers' expectations of "history."

Historiographic prefaces in Greco-Roman literature typically indicate that the author has done extensive research of the historical topics under discussion. They commonly refer to the sources that were at his disposal, and they not infrequently suggest that the final product of the author's labors, the volume being read, is far superior to anything previously written on the subject. Sometimes the preface includes the name of the person to whom the work is being dedicated.

All these features are found in Luke 1:1–4. The author (whom I will continue to call Luke for convenience) indicates that he has had several predecessors in writing a narrative of the life of Jesus (v. 1) and that these narratives are ultimately based on stories that have been passed down by "eyewitnesses and ministers of the word" (v. 2). In other words, the author concedes that his Gospel is based on oral traditions that were circulating among Christian congregations of the first century and that he has made use of other written sources. As we have seen, two of these earlier "narratives of the things which have been accomplished among us" are the Gospel of Mark and the document scholars call Q. Some readers have been struck by the tone of Luke's reference to these predecessors. He claims that his narrative, evidently in contrast with theirs, will be orderly (1:3) and that he is writing so that

Figure 7.1 Like many modern-day readers, ancient Christians conflated the accounts of Jesus' birth from Matthew and Luke into a single narrative. This can be seen, for example, in this depiction of the birth narratives from a panel on a sixth-century ivory throne of Archbishop Maximianus, which shows the angel coming to Joseph in his sleep (found only in Matthew) *and* Mary and Joseph's journey to Bethlehem (found only in Luke).

his reader will now learn the "truth concerning the things about which you have been instructed" (1:4). An intriguing comment this: is Luke making a negative, if implicit, evaluation of Mark's Gospel?

Luke dedicates his work to someone he calls "most excellent **Theophilus**." Unfortunately, he never tells us who this is. Luke does, however, use the title "most excellent" on three other occasions, each of them in reference to a governor of a Roman province (in the second volume of his work; Acts 23:26; 24:3; 26:25). On these grounds, some scholars have thought that Luke's two volumes were written for a Roman administrative official. If this is correct, one might wonder why a Christian would give a non-Christian governor books on the life of Jesus and the beginnings of the Christian church. According to one point of view, he did so to show someone in power that Jesus and the religion he founded are in no way to be seen as a threat to the social order and that there is therefore no reason to persecute Christians, since neither they nor their founder have ever opposed the empire or done anything to merit opposition.

Not everyone accepts this view, for reasons that I will explain shortly. But if it were true, it would help to make sense of several aspects of Luke's portrayal of Jesus. He shows a special concern, for example, to relate the history of Jesus to the broader historical events transpiring within the empire (e.g., 2:1–2; 3:1–2). Moreover, his narrative goes to some lengths to show that Jesus was executed by the state only because Pilate's hand was forced by the leaders of the Jews. In this Gospel, Pilate declares on three different occasions that he finds no guilt in Jesus (23:4, 14–15, 22), and after Jesus dies, the centurion responsible for his execution also proclaims that he was innocent (23:47). Could this Gospel, then, along with its sequel, Acts, have been written as an "apology," that is, an informed defense of Christianity in the face of official opposition of the state (see box 7.1)?

Even though this view can account for some of the features of Luke's narrative, it cannot explain a large number of others, including most of its prominent themes (as we shall see). Moreover, if Luke's overarching purpose was to curry the favor of Roman officials, it is odd that he did not portray them in a more favorable light. Pilate, for example, is depicted as a weak administrator who bows to pressure from his own subjects, a portrayal that, in fact, does not square well with the public record of his governorship. Other officials are portrayed in yet less favorable terms in the book of Acts. Most problematic of all, it is nearly impossible to imagine any tangible historical context within which

ANOTHER GLIMPSE INTO THE PAST

BOX 7.1 Apologetic Literature in Early Christianity

Formally speaking, an **apology** is a reasoned defense of a person's actions. In the ancient world, there was a genre of literature called "apology" in which an author would mount either a self-defense or a defense of a social group in the face of accusations. Probably the most famous example is the *Apology of Socrates,* Plato's account of the legal defense that the philosopher Socrates made before the Athenian court that condemned him to death.

From the time prior to Christianity, we know of several Jewish apologies; these were treatises penned by Jews justifying their customs and explaining their ways to hostile outsiders. This literary form was later picked up by some of the more educated Christians in the second century. When Christianity came to be persecuted as a religion, its more literate members had to show why this mistreatment was altogether unjustified and to explain that the Christian faith was intellectually defensible and socially and politically innocuous.

Scholars who maintain that Luke and Acts are apologetic literature use the term in this formal sense. In their opinion, these books were written by a highly educated Christian who wanted to show that the life of Jesus was exemplary, as was the Christian church that emerged in his wake, and that both Jesus and his followers were deserving of better treatment from the hands of the government.

a Christian would write two such large volumes (together, they take up approximately one-fourth of the entire New Testament) and deliver them over to a Roman official with any real expectation that he would read them, let alone be influenced by them.

It is much more likely that these books, along with all the other Gospels, were "in-house" literature, written by Christians for Christians, rather than evangelistic or propagandistic texts. Who in the outside world would bother to read them? Who on the inside would be foolish enough to think they would? It is worth noting that the first reference to any outsider having any clue as to what was in these books does not come for nearly a hundred years after the production of Luke-Acts (the reference is in the work of an anti-Christian writer named Celsus).

If Luke's Theophilus is not a Roman administrator, who might he be? The name was fairly common in Greek antiquity. Literally translated, it means either "lover of God" or "beloved of God." For this reason, some scholars have plausibly argued that Luke's addressee is a code name for the Christians (the "beloved of God") to whom he writes. Just as other historians prefaced their works by dedicating them to a patron who had provided material support or to some other person deemed worthy of honor, so Luke may have dedicated his work to his fellow believers, who were worthy of the greatest accolades as those whom God loves, or "Theophilus." If this view of the matter is correct, then the apologetic aspects of the narrative would be directed not to outsiders but to those within the church. Luke's aim may have been to show the Christians themselves that their movement has been nonviolent and socially respectable from the very beginning, thus perhaps providing them with answers they needed when confronted by the objections of outsiders.

LUKE'S BIRTH NARRATIVE IN COMPARATIVE PERSPECTIVE

The two lengthy chapters that begin Luke's account contain stories relating the births of Jesus and his predecessor, John the Baptist. By beginning with a birth narrative, Luke has an obvious point of contact with Matthew. Mark, you will recall, begins with Jesus as an adult.

There are some very broad and basic similarities between the birth narratives of Matthew and of Luke. In both, for example, Jesus is born in the city of Bethlehem to a virgin named Mary, who is betrothed to a man named Joseph. For most readers, however,

ANOTHER EARLY CHRISTIAN TEXT

BOX 7.2   The Proto-Gospel of James

As we have seen, even though only four Gospels made it into the final canon of the New Testament, many others were written, read, and cherished in early Christianity. None was more widely known and appreciated than the book called the Proto-Gospel of James. This account is called a Proto-Gospel because it deals with the events leading up to the birth narratives of Matthew and Luke. In large part, it is designed to answer the question many Christians have wondered about over the years. Why is it that Mary was chosen to be the one who would bear the Son of God? This question intrigued Christians down through the Middle Ages, when adoration of Mary was widespread; as a result, this Proto-Gospel of James was often more important for Christian thinking than even some of the canonical Gospels.

The Gospel claims to be written by James, the "brother" of Jesus—someone who would well know about his personal family life. But in this account James is not actually a (half-)brother of Jesus. He is the son of Joseph from a previous marriage. Joseph is portrayed here as an elderly widower who becomes acquainted with Mary only at the end of his life (this is why he is always an old man in medieval paintings of Jesus' birth). And who was Mary?

In this account Mary herself is miraculously born by the intervention of God, who allows a pious but barren couple, the very wealthy Jew, Joachim, and his wife, Anna, to conceive. Mary is not only brought into the world miraculously, she is raised miraculously. Most of her young life is spent in the Jewish Temple, being raised by priests and daily fed by an angel of God. When she reaches the marriageable age of fourteen, God reveals that she is to be given to the wealthy builder Joseph, who, of course, never lays a finger on her. When she becomes pregnant, the priests in the Temple understandably think that either she has gone astray or that she has broken her vows and had sex with Joseph. But a divine miracle shows it is not true.

Yet more marvelous—this is a very interesting story—after Mary gives birth to Jesus in a cave outside Bethlehem, a Hebrew midwife comes to give her an internal postpartum inspection and finds, to her amazement, that Mary's hymen is still intact. Mary not only conceived as a virgin, she has given birth as a virgin—completely unviolated physically. This is the beginning of the later Catholic doctrine of Mary's "perpetual virginity." According to official Catholic doctrine, Mary never did have sex. This is why, then, the "brothers" of Jesus, such as James, are not related by blood to Jesus; they are not even half-brothers, because they come from Joseph, whereas Jesus came from the virgin Mary.

---

what is far more striking are the differences between these accounts. Indeed, none of the specific stories of Luke's narrative occurs in Matthew, just as none of Matthew's appears here. You can see this easily by making a list of everything that happens in Luke and a separate list of everything that happens in Matthew and comparing the lists. In one of them you will find the shepherds, in the other the Magi; one describes the journey to Bethlehem, the other the flight to Egypt; one records an angel's words to Mary, the other the angelic words to Joseph; and so forth. These are two discrete narratives, and the Christmas story recounted by Christians every December is a conflation of the two.

From a comparative perspective, perhaps the most important feature of these infancy nar-

ratives is not simply that they differ from one another but that they do so in ways that are extremely hard to reconcile. These differences give us an excellent opportunity to apply the comparative method of analysis.

An Illustration of the Comparative Method: Joseph and Mary's Hometown

One of the telling differences between the two accounts has to do with the question of Mary and Joseph's hometown. Most people simply assume that the couple lived in Nazareth. In the familiar story of Luke's Gospel, Mary and Joseph leave town for a trip to register for the census in Bethlehem. Mary happens to give birth there (2:1–7), and the couple then returns home just over a month later (2:39; following the law spelled out in Leviticus 12).

Before examining this account in greater detail, we should recall what Matthew says about the same event. Matthew gives no indication at all that Joseph and Mary made a trip from Galilee in order to register for a census. On the contrary, Matthew intimates that Joseph and Mary originally came from Bethlehem. This is suggested, first of all, by the story of the wise men (found only in Matthew), who arrive to worship Jesus after making a long journey in which they followed the star that appeared in the heavens to indicate his birth. They find Jesus in Bethlehem in a "house" (not a stable or a cave; Matt 2:11). Unless one had reason to think otherwise—and Matthew gives readers no reason for doing so—one would assume that the house is where Jesus and his family normally live.

Consider next what Herod does in Matthew's account when he learns from the Magi the time at which they had first seen the star. Based on this information, he sends forth his troops to slaughter every boy in Bethlehem who is two years and under (2:16). In other words, the "slaughter of the innocents" did not occur immediately after Jesus' birth, but some months, or perhaps a year and some months, later: otherwise, Herod would have been quite safe to slaughter only the newborns.

According to Matthew's account, Joseph and Mary are still in Bethlehem at this time, presumably because that is simply where they live.

Perhaps most telling of all, some time after they had fled to Egypt to escape Herod's wrath, Joseph learns in a dream that he can now return home. But where does he plan to go? The answer is quite clear. He intends to return to the place whence they came, the town of Bethelehem. Only when he learns that the ruler of Judea is Archelaus, a potentate worse than his father Herod, does he realize that they can't return there. For this reason Joseph decides to relocate his family in Galilee, in the town of Nazareth (2:22–23). Thus in Matthew's account, Joseph and Mary appear to have originally lived in Bethlehem, but they relocated to Nazareth when Jesus was a boy and raised him there.

In the Gospel of Luke Jesus is also born in Bethlehem and raised in Nazareth, but the way this comes about is altogether different (see box 7.3). In this account Joseph takes his betrothed Mary from their hometown Nazareth to Bethlehem for a worldwide census ordered by Caesar Augustus, while Quirinius was governor of Syria (2:1–5). Mary goes into labor while in town, so Jesus' birthplace is Bethlehem. After about a month (Luke 2:22–23, 39; see Lev 12:4–6), the family returns to their home in Nazareth, where Jesus is raised

WHAT DO YOU THINK?

BOX 7.3   Historical Problems with Luke's Birth Narrative

In addition to the difficulties raised by a detailed comparison of the two birth narratives found in the New Testament, serious historical problems are raised by the familiar stories found in Luke alone. Contrary to what Luke indicates, historians have long known from several ancient inscriptions, the Roman historian Tacitus, and the Jewish historian Josephus that **Quirinius** was not the governor of Syria until 6 C.E., fully ten years after Herod the Great died. If Jesus was born during the reign of Herod, then Quirinius was not the Syrian governor.

We also have no record of a worldwide census under Augustus or under any emperor at any time.

Moreover, a census in which everyone was to return to his or her ancestral home would have been more than a bureaucratic nightmare; it would have been well nigh impossible. In Luke, Joseph is said to return to Bethlehem because his ancestor David came from there—but David lived a thousand years before Joseph. Can it be possible that everyone in the empire was to return to the place his or her ancestors lived a thousand years earlier? If such a census were required in our day, where would you go? Imagine the massive migrations involved. Then imagine that no other ancient author considered it important enough to mention, even in passing!

BOX 7.4   The Virginal Conception in Matthew and Luke

Both Matthew and Luke make it quite clear that Jesus' mother conceived as a virgin, but they appear to understand the significance of Jesus' virginal conception differently. In Matthew, Jesus' birth is said to fulfill the prediction of the Hebrew prophet Isaiah, who foretold that "a virgin shall conceive and bear a son" (1:23). Luke neither quotes this Isaiah passage nor indicates that Jesus' birth fulfills Scripture. What the event means for Luke is suggested in the story of the Annunciation (1:28–38, a passage found only in Luke), where the angel Gabriel assures Mary that her son "will be great, and will be called the Son of the Most High, and the Lord God will give to him the throne of his ancestor David." Mary is disturbed by this pronouncement: how can she bear a son if she has never had sexual relations (1:34)? The angel's reply is striking: "The Holy Spirit will come upon you,

and the power of the Most High will overshadow you; therefore the child to be born will be holy; he will be called Son of God" (1:35).

Why, then, is Jesus conceived of a virgin in Luke? Evidently, because Jesus really is God's son ("therefore . . . he will be called the Son of God"). In other words, his father is not a human but God himself.

As we will see later, Luke is generally thought to have been writing to a Christian community that was largely Gentile. It may be that he has molded his portrayal of Jesus for these converts from other Greco-Roman religions. He presents the story of Jesus' birth in a way that would make sense to a pagan reader who was conversant with tales of other divine beings who walked the face of the earth, and other heroes and demigods who were born of the union of a mortal with a god.

(2:39–40). As you might realize, the family's direct return north in Luke does not seem to allow time for Matthew's wise men to visit them in their home in Bethlehem a year or so later, or for their subsequent flight to Egypt.

Of course, it might be possible to reconcile these two narratives if we worked hard enough at it, and certainly Matthew and Luke do not explicitly contradict each other. But the two narratives are quite different from one another, and interestingly, the differences are highlighted by their one overarching similarity (see box 7.4). Both authors indicate that Jesus was born in Bethlehem but raised in Nazareth, even though this happens in strikingly different ways in their two narratives. (For other accounts of Jesus as a child, see box 4.2.)

The Salvation of the Gentiles: Luke's Orientation to the Whole World

We spent some time examining Matthew's genealogy of Jesus (actually, his genealogy of Joseph, the husband of Jesus' mother). Luke too has a genealogy (3:23–38). One of the most obvious differences

between them is that they are, in fact, different genealogies! Both of them do trace Jesus' lineage through Joseph, even though in neither Gospel is Joseph Jesus' father, and in both of them Joseph is a descendant of King David. What is striking, however, is that Joseph's ties to David are traced through different lines in the two accounts. In Matthew, Joseph is a direct descendant (from father to son) of David's son Solomon; in Luke he is descended through a different line, from David's other son Nathan. The discrepancy can best be seen by moving backward through the genealogy, beginning from Joseph. Who was Joseph's father? Was it Jacob (as in Matthew) or Heli (as in Luke)? Was his paternal grandfather Matthan or Matthat? Was his paternal great-grandfather Eleazar or Levi? His great-great-grandfather Eliud or Melchi? And so forth. One of the fascinating aspects of scholarship is to see how readers have attempted to explain these differences over the years. Some have claimed, for instance, that one of the genealogies is Joseph's and the other is Mary's. The problem, of course, is that both of them explicitly trace the ancestry of Joseph (Matt 1:16; Luke 3:23).

A second difference is perhaps even more obvious to a first-time reader of Luke. Unlike Matthew's genealogy, Luke's does not occur where you might expect, in the narrative of Jesus' birth, but after his baptism (3:23–38). Why would Luke wait until Jesus is a grown man of "about thirty" to describe his genealogy (3:23)? Possibly the best way to answer this question is to consider an important connection between Jesus' baptism and his genealogy in Luke. Both passages conclude by showing that Jesus is the Son of God. The baptism ends with the declaration from heaven that Jesus is God's own son (3:22). The genealogy ends by implicitly making the same declaration but in a radically different way. Here Jesus' lineage is traced not just to David or to Abraham or even to Adam, the first human being. The genealogy goes all the way back to God, the "father" of Adam—making Jesus the Son of God by direct descent!

The third significant difference between these two genealogies is closely related. Luke's genealogy does not so much stress Jesus' Jewishness, as one descended from the father of the Jews, or his messiahship, as the Son of David. Jesus' human lineage goes far beyond both of these figures who are so important for the history of Judaism, back to the man responsible for the human race itself, Adam. Thus, if Matthew's genealogy was important in showing that Jesus belonged to the Jews, Luke's is important in showing that he belongs to all people, both Jews and Gentiles.

Here we have an important indication that for Luke the message of salvation that begins in the heart of Judaism is a message for all the nations of earth. In fact, as we will see, Luke devotes virtually his entire second volume to showing how this message came to be rejected by Jews, and so went forth to the Gentiles. Indeed, a careful reader of Luke's work does not need to wait for volume two to get this message. It is embodied here in the Gospel itself, as the comparative method of analysis can clearly demonstrate.

FROM JEW TO GENTILE: LUKE'S PORTRAYAL OF JESUS THE REJECTED PROPHET

We have already seen that both Mark and Matthew establish essential aspects of their portrayals of Jesus by the way they describe the beginning of his public ministry. Mark, for example, uses his early narratives to show that Jesus was an authoritative leader, teacher, and healer; Matthew uses his to portray Jesus as the new Moses bringing the authoritative interpretation of God's Law. In Luke, Jesus' ministry begins with a sermon in the synagogue that infuriates his fellow Jews, who then make an attempt on his life. It is not an auspicious beginning.

In order to begin Jesus' ministry in this way, Luke narrates a story that does not occur until nearly halfway through both Mark's and Matthew's account of the ministry (Mark 6:1–6; Matt 13:53–58; Luke 4:16–30). This is the famous narrative of Jesus' sermon in his hometown of Nazareth, a story that is much longer and more detailed in Luke than in the other Gospels and that, as the opening account, sets the stage for Luke's overall portrayal of Jesus. As a visitor to the synagogue, in Luke, Jesus is given the opportunity to read and comment on the Scripture. He reads from the book of Isaiah, in which the prophet claims to be anointed with the spirit of God in order "to bring good news to the poor . . . to proclaim release to the captives and recovery of sight to the blind, to let the oppressed go free, to proclaim the year of the Lord's favor" (4:18–19).

After reading the Scripture, Jesus sits and begins to proclaim that the predictions of the prophet have now come to fulfillment—by implication, in him. Those in the synagogue are incredulous; they know, after all, who Jesus is (or think they do; they call him "Joseph's son" in v. 22). Jesus understands their reaction: they want him to prove himself by doing miracles for them like he has done in Capernaum. This may strike the reader as a somewhat peculiar request, since in this Gospel, unlike Mark and Matthew, Jesus has not yet gone to Capernaum or done any miracles.

In any event, Jesus responds by launching into an extended sermon, not found in the other Gospels, in which he recounts two familiar stories from the Jewish Scriptures about prophets who were sent by God, not to Jews but to Gentiles. He tells how Elijah was sent to assist a widow in the city of Zarephath during an extended drought and how Elisha was sent to heal not the lepers of Israel but Naaman, the leper king of Syria (4:25–27). In both instances God sent his prophet, not to help his people the Israelites, but to pronounce

Figure 7.2 Picture of Saint Luke from a tenth-century manuscript of the Gospels. Notice the five books of Moses resting on his lap and the Old Testament prophets that he lifts up—graphic portrayals of Luke's view that the life and death of Jesus were a fulfillment of the Law and the prophets (see Luke 24:26–27).

judgment against them for having turned against him. These prophets ministered to Gentiles outside the people of God.

These are the stories that Jesus uses to explain how he fulfills the prophecy of Isaiah. His message is clear: he, too, is a **prophet** of God who will not receive a warm welcome among his own people in Israel, who like their ancestors have rejected God along with his prophets. Because of this rejection, Jesus' message will be taken to the Gentiles.

Jesus' sermon is not a smashing success; in fact, it is very nearly a smashing failure. The Jews in the synagogue rise up in anger and try to throw him off a cliff. Jesus escapes, leaves town, and takes his message elsewhere (4:28–30). For Luke, this reaction marks the beginning of the fulfillment of the sermon that Jesus has just preached. The prophet

of God is opposed by his own people, and they will eventually call for his death. As a prophet, he knows that this is to happen. Indeed, it has all been predicted in the Jewish Scriptures. Rejecting him, the people have rejected the God that he represents. This compels the prophet to take his message elsewhere. Eventually, the message will go not simply to another city of Israel, but to another people, indeed to all other peoples, the nations of the earth.

LUKE'S DISTINCTIVE EMPHASES THROUGHOUT HIS GOSPEL

The passages that we have examined from the outset of Luke's narrative intimate many of the key themes that you will find throughout the rest of the Gospel, themes related to Luke's understanding of Jesus and to the way his salvation affects the entire world. As we will see, many of these themes continue to play a significant role in the second volume of Luke's work, the Acts of the Apostles.

Jesus the Prophet

Our comparative analysis has begun to show that Luke understood Jesus to be a prophet sent by God to his people. For ancient Jews, a prophet was not a crystal-ball gazer, a person who made inspired predictions about events far in the future. He was a spokesperson for God, a messenger sent from God to his people. Often the message was quite straightforward, involving a call to the people of God to mend their ways and return to God by living in accordance with his will. Throughout the Hebrew Scriptures, of course, prophets make predictions; usually (but not always) these are dire. If the people of God do not repent and begin to live in accordance with God's Law, he will punish them through plague, famine, or military disaster. Prophets tend to see into the future only insofar as it affects those who reject or accept their message.

Jesus as a Prophet in Life. Mark and Matthew, of course, also understand Jesus to be a prophet. In both Gospels he speaks God's word and predicts the coming destruction of Jerusalem and his own death at the hands of his enemies. But Luke places an even greater emphasis on Jesus' prophetic role as the spokesperson for God who comes to be rejected by his own people. This emphasis can be seen not only in the inaugural story of Jesus' ministry, the sermon in Nazareth, but also in a number of other stories that occur in Luke but in neither of the other Gospels.

In fact, the prophetic character of Jesus is seen even before the rejection scene in Nazareth, for in this Gospel Jesus is born as a prophet. Scholars have long noted that the birth narrative of Luke 2 appears to be closely modeled on the account of the birth of the prophet Samuel, as narrated in the Jewish Scriptures (1 Sam 1–2). In both instances, a devout Jewish woman miraculously conceives, to the joy and amazement of her family, and she responds in song, praising the God of Israel, who exalts those who are humble and humbles those who are exalted (compare the song of Hannah in 1 Sam 2:1–10 with the "Magnificat" of Mary in Luke 1:46–55). Anyone conversant with the Jewish Scriptures would recognize these allusions and conclude that Jesus is born like a prophet.

Moreover, when Jesus begins his public ministry, he explicitly claims to be anointed as a prophet who will proclaim God's message to his people. Recall his opening sermon in Nazareth, the fullest text of which is found in Luke. And not only does Jesus preach as a prophet in this Gospel, he also does miracles as a prophet. Among our surviving Gospels, Luke alone relates the story in which Jesus raises the only son of a widow from Nain from the dead (7:11–17). The story is clearly reminiscent of a miracle of the prophet Elijah, who in the Jewish Scriptures raises the only son of the widow from Zerephath from the dead (1 Kings 17:17–24). The similarity of the events is not lost on Jesus' companions. When they see what he has done, they proclaim "A great prophet has arisen among us" (7:16).

Jesus as a Prophet in Death. Not only is Luke's Jesus born as a prophet, and not only does he preach as a prophet and heal as a prophet, he also is said to die as a prophet. There was a long-standing tradition among Jews that their greatest prophets, both those about whom stories were told in the Scriptures (e.g., Elijah and Elisha) and those who penned scriptural books themselves (e.g., Jeremiah, Ezekiel, and Amos), were violently opposed and sometimes even martyred by their own people. In Luke's account, Jesus places himself in this prophetic line.

In a passage that is again unique to Luke, Jesus laments for Jerusalem, anticipating that he will suffer there the fate of a prophet:

> Listen, I am casting out demons and performing cures today and tomorrow, and on the third day I finish my work. Yet today, tomorrow, and the next day I must be on my way, because it is impossible for a prophet to be killed outside of Jerusalem. Jerusalem, Jerusalem, the city that kills the prophets and stones those who are sent to it! How often have I desired to gather your children together as a hen gathers her brood under her wings, but you were not willing. (13:32–34)

Jesus' knowledge that he must die as a prophet may explain some of the unique features of Luke's Passion narrative. These features can be highlighted by comparing Luke's account with the one we have studied so far in the greatest depth, Mark's.

In Mark's Passion narrative, as we have seen, Jesus appears somewhat uncertain of the need for his own death up until the very end. He does, of course, predict that he is soon to die and at one point he even explains why it is necessary ("as a ransom for many"; 10:45), but when the moment arrives, he appears torn with uncertainty (see Chapter 5). There is no trace of uncertainty, however, in Luke's account. Here Jesus the prophet knows full well that he has to die and shows no misgivings or doubts, as can be seen by making a detailed comparison of the two accounts of what Jesus does prior to his arrest in the Garden of Gethsemane (Mark 14:32–42; Luke 22:39–46; see box 7.5).

The same contrast appears in the accounts of Jesus' crucifixion. We have seen that in Mark's Gospel Jesus is silent throughout the entire proceeding. (Is he in total shock?) His only words come at the very end, after everyone (his disciples, the Jewish leaders, the crowds, the Roman authorities, the passersby, and even the two other criminals on their crosses) has either betrayed, denied, condemned, mocked, or forsaken him. Then he cries out, "My God, my God, why have you forsaken me?" and dies.

Luke paints a very different portrayal of Jesus in the throes of death. For one thing, Jesus is not silent on the way to crucifixion. Instead, when he sees a group of women weeping for him, he turns and says to them, "Daughters of Jerusalem, do not weep for me, but weep for yourselves and for your children"

BOX 7.5   Jesus' Bloody Sweat in Luke

One of the most striking things about Luke's account of Jesus' Passion is that Jesus does not appear to experience any deep anguish over his coming fate. This becomes clear in a comparative study of what Jesus does prior to his betrayal and arrest (Luke 22:39–46; Mark 14:32–42). In Mark's account, Jesus is said to become "distressed and agitated" (14:33). Luke's version says nothing of the sort. In Mark, Jesus tells his disciples that his soul is sorrowful unto death (14:34), words not found in Luke. In Mark, Jesus leaves his disciples and falls to his face on the ground to pray (14:35). In Luke, he simply takes to his knees. In Mark, Jesus prays fervently three times for God to "remove this cup from me" (14:36, 39, 41). In Luke, he asks only once, and prefaces his prayer with "if you are willing." Thus in comparison with Mark, Luke's Jesus does not appear to be in gut-wrenching distress over his coming fate. But consider the famous verses found in the middle of the scene, Luke 22:43–44, where an angel from heaven comes to give Jesus much needed support and where his sweat is said to have become "like great drops of blood falling to the ground"? Don't these verses show Luke's Jesus in profound agony?

They do indeed. But the question is whether these verses were originally written by Luke or were added by later scribes who felt somewhat uneasy over the fact that Jesus in this version does not seem distraught by his coming fate. If you are using the New Revised Standard Version (or any of a number of other modern translations as well), you will notice that the verses are placed in double brackets. These show that the translators are fairly confident that the verses did not originally form part of Luke's Gospel but were added by well-meaning scribes at a later time. One reason for thinking so is the fact that these verses about Jesus' bloody sweat are absent from our oldest and many of our best **manuscripts** of the New Testament.

If these manuscripts are *right* and the verses were *not* original to Luke, then for this Gospel, without exception, Jesus remains calm and in control of his destiny, assured of God's ongoing concern and able to face his fate with confidence and equanimity.

(23:28). Jesus does not appear to be distraught about what is happening to him; he is more concerned for the fate of these women. This note of confidence and concern for others is played out in the rest of the narrative. While being nailed to the cross, rather than being silent, Jesus asks forgiveness for those who are wrongfully treating him: "Father forgive them, for they do not know what they are doing" (23:34). While on the cross, Jesus engages in an intelligent conversation with one of the criminals crucified beside him. Here (unlike in Mark) only one of the criminals mocks Jesus; the other tells his companion to hold his tongue, since Jesus has done nothing to deserve his fate. He then turns to Jesus and asks, "Jesus, remember me when you come into your kingdom" (23:42). Jesus' reply is stunningly confident: "Truly I tell you, today you will be with me in Paradise."

Jesus is soon to die, but as a prophet he knows that he has to die, and he knows what will happen to him once he does: he will awaken in paradise.

And this criminal who has professed faith in him will awaken beside him. Most striking of all is the way in which the scene ends. Whereas in Mark Jesus appears to die in despair, forsaken not only by friends, companions, and fellow Jews, but even by God himself—in Luke's Gospel he dies in full assurance of God's special care and favor. Here he does not cry out in anguish, "My God, my God, why have you forsaken me?" Instead, he offers up a final prayer, indicative of his full confidence in God's love and providential care: "Father, into your hands I commend my spirit" (23:46).

These differences are significant and should not be downplayed, as if Mark and Luke were portraying Jesus in precisely the same way. When modern readers act as if they were, for example, by thinking that Jesus said all of these things on the cross, some of them recorded by Mark and others by Luke, they take neither account seriously, but rather create their own account, in which Jesus is portrayed as all things at one and the same time. But Mark has one way of portraying Jesus and Luke another, and readers who combine their two portraits form a different Gospel, one that is neither Mark nor Luke.

In Mark Jesus is in real agony at the end. In Luke he dies in calm assurance. Each author wanted to emphasize something significant about Jesus' death. We have already seen Mark's emphasis. Luke's is somewhat different. Luke emphasizes that Jesus died as a righteous, blameless martyr of God. As a prophet he knew that this had to happen.

Jesus' Death in Luke

One other important aspect of Luke's portrayal of Jesus in his death emerges when we consider the events that transpire at the close of the scene. As we saw in Mark's Gospel, the view that Jesus' death was an atoning sacrifice was suggested by the tear-ing of the curtain in the Temple immediately after he expired and the confession of the centurion that "this man was the Son of God." Oddly, Luke includes both events but narrates them in ways that differ significantly from the accounts in Mark (and in Matthew).

In Luke's Gospel the curtain is torn in half, not after Jesus breaths his last, but earlier, when darkness comes upon the land as the light of the sun fails (due to an eclipse? 23:45). Scholars have long debated the significance of this difference, but most think that for Luke the tearing of the curtain does not show that Jesus' death brings access to God, since here, it is torn before he dies, but rather that God has entered into judgment with his people as symbolized by this destruction within the Temple. In this Gospel, Jesus himself proclaims to his enemies among the Jewish authorities that "this is your hour and the power of darkness" (22:53). The torn curtain accompanies

Figure 7.3   The Last Supper, as portrayed in a sixth-century manuscript called the "Rossano Gospels."

WHAT DO YOU THINK?

BOX 7.6   The Institution of the Lord's Supper in Luke

We have already seen that some of the ancient manuscripts of the New Testament differ from one another in significant ways (see box 7.5). One of the places that this matters is in Luke's account of the Last Supper (22:14–23). One peculiarity of this passage is that in some manuscripts, including those on which most of our English translations are based, Jesus does more than give his disciples the bread and the cup of wine, as he does in Mark. In these manuscripts, and most translations, he gives his disciples the cup, and then the bread, and then the cup again.

Of still greater interest is what Jesus actually says in these verses. In verse 19, he speaks of his body "which is given for you," and in verse 20 he calls the (second) cup the "the new covenant in my blood." Nowhere else in Luke's Gospel does Jesus claim that

his death is a sacrifice that brings salvation. In fact, Luke is missing all such claims that are present in both Mark and Matthew (e.g., Mark 10:45; Matt 20:28). What, then, are we to make of these particular verses, which do make such a claim?

Some of our ancient manuscripts do not include this portion of the passage. Indeed, the early Christian writers who quote Luke's account of the Last Supper did not know that the verses exist. Thus, they may well have been added to this Gospel later by well-meaning scribes who wanted to stress the view that salvation came through Jesus' broken body and shed blood. This finding is significant, for apart from these verses, Luke nowhere expresses Mark's view that Jesus' death was a sacrifice that brought an atonement for sin.

the eerie darkness over the land as a sign of God's judgment upon his people, who have rejected his gift of "light to those who sit in darkness and in the shadow of death" (1:79).

Moreover, in Luke the centurion does not make a profession of faith in the Son of God who had to die ("Truly this man was God's Son," Mark 15:39; Matt 27:54); here his words coincide with Luke's own understanding of Jesus' death: "Certainly this man was innocent" (Luke 23:47). For Luke, Jesus dies the death of a righteous martyr who has suffered from miscarried justice; his death will be vindicated by God at the resurrection. What both of these differences suggest is that Luke does not share Mark's view that Jesus' death brought about atonement for sin. An earlier statement in Mark corroborates his perspective; Jesus' own comment that "the Son of Man came not to be served, but to serve, and to give his life a ransom for many" (10:45; Matt 20:28). It is striking and significant that this saying is not found in Luke.

Jesus, then, must die because he is a prophet who comes to be rejected by God's people. His death does not appear to bring salvation in and of itself, and yet the death of Jesus must relate to

salvation for Luke. But how? This is a puzzle we will take up further when we study the second volume of his work, the Acts of the Apostles. For now I can point out that the salvation that Jesus preaches in Luke is similar to the salvation preached by the prophets of the Hebrew Scriptures. The people of God need to repent of their sins and return to God. When they do so, he will forgive them and grant them salvation. For Luke, the biggest sin of all was killing God's prophet. As we will see in our study of Acts, when people realize what they have done in this grotesque miscarriage of justice, they are driven to their knees in repentance. And when they turn to God in recognition of their guilt, he responds by forgiving their sins. Thus, what brings a right relationship with God for Luke is not Jesus' death per se but the repentance that his death prompts.

The Gentile Mission

We have already seen that Luke places considerable emphasis on Jesus' significance for the Gentile as well as the Jew. This emphasis is not unique, of course. Mark himself may have been a Gentile, and almost certainly a large portion of his audience was. Matthew also appears to have written to a mixed congregation of Jews and Gentiles, even though he was himself probably Jewish. For both authors, salvation in Jesus comes to all people. Even more than in Matthew and Mark, however, this is a special emphasis in Luke, as we have seen already in his genealogy. For Luke, salvation comes to the Jewish people in fulfillment of the Jewish Scriptures, but since they reject it, the message goes to the Gentiles. This too, as we will see in our study of Acts, happens in fulfillment of the Scriptures.

One of the unmistakable indications that Luke is especially concerned for the Gentile mission is the fact that he is the only Gospel writer who includes a sequel recounting the spread of the religion throughout the empire, particularly among non-Jews. This concern is also found elsewhere in the Gospel. As we have seen, after Jesus' death the disciples are not told to go to Galilee (contrast 24:6, 49 with the instructions to the women in Mark 16:7). They remain in Jerusalem, where they encounter the resurrected Jesus (contrast Luke 24 with Matt 27:10, 16–20). On this occasion, Jesus explains that everything that happened to him was in fulfillment of the Scriptures; indeed, so is the Gentile mission that is yet to take place, for "repentance and forgiveness of sins is to be proclaimed in his name to all nations [same word as 'Gentiles'], beginning from Jerusalem" (24:47).

The Divine Plan

Thus the Gentile mission was all part of God's plan, in place, according to Luke, since time immemorial. As we will see, the spread of the Christian church in the book of Acts occurs under the powerful direction of the Holy Spirit. This is the reason it proves so successful: since God is behind it, it cannot be stopped. The divine plan is at work in the Gospel as well, where Luke places a careful emphasis on terms like the "will" and the "plan" of God (e.g., see 4:43; 13:33; 22:37; 24:7, 26, 44).

The Delay of the End of Time

Luke's idea of the divine plan relates to one other distinctive aspect of his Gospel. In Mark and Matthew, as we saw, Jesus predicts the imminent end of the world. In Luke all of these predictions about the end are worded differently. In Luke, Jesus does not envisage the end of the age happening immediately. How could he? First the Christian church had to be spread among the Gentiles, and this would take time.

Consider the differences between the apocalyptic predictions of Mark and those of Luke. In Mark 9:1, Jesus claims that some of his disciples will not taste death "until they see that the kingdom of God has come with power." Luke has the same story, but here the disciples are told simply that some of them will not taste death until "they see the kingdom of God" (9:27; note that they are not promised to see its "coming in power," i.e., with the coming of the Son of Man). For Luke, the disciples already see the kingdom of God because for him, the kingdom of God is already present in Jesus' ministry. This becomes clear in several stories found only in Luke: the kingdom of God is said to have "come near" in the ministry of Jesus' disciples (10:9, 11), it is said to have already "come to you" in Jesus' own ministry (11:20), and it is said already to be "among you" in the person of Jesus himself (17:21). To be sure, even in Luke there is to be a final cataclysmic end to history at the end of this age (21:7–32), but this will not come during the disciples' lifetime.

Luke's emphasis on the delay of the end also explains the difference in Jesus' reply when interrogated by the high priest. Whereas in Mark Jesus stated that the high priest would "see the Son of Man seated at the right hand of the Power, and coming with the clouds of heaven" (14:62), in Luke his response is simply that "from now on the Son of Man will be seated at the right hand of the power of God" (22:69). Luke appears to know full well that this high priest would not live to see the Son of Man coming in his glory to bring the end of the age; in his version of the story, Jesus never predicts that he will.

Other differences in Luke's account point in the same direction. For example, only in Luke is Jesus said to have delivered the parable of the pounds, precisely in order to disabuse those who thought that "the kingdom of God was to appear immediately" (19:11–27; contrast the parable of the talents in Matt 25:14–30). One final Lukan emphasis also relates closely to the delay of the end: Jesus' social concerns.

The Social Implications of the Gospel

Throughout the history of religion, people committed to the belief that the end is near have occasionally withdrawn from society and shown little concern for its ongoing problems. Why commit oneself to fighting poverty and oppression if the world is going to end next week? In Luke's Gospel, Jesus knows that the end is *not* imminent, and this may explain one other way in which his Gospel stands out as unique. More than either of the other Synoptics, Luke emphasizes Jesus' concern for the social ills of his day.

Luke contains many of the beatitudes found in Matthew, but they are worded differently, and the differences clearly illustrate Luke's social agenda. Whereas Jesus in Matthew says, "Blessed are the poor in spirit" (5:3), in Luke he says, "Blessed are you who are poor" (6:20). Luke's concern here is for literal, material poverty. Whereas Matthew's Jesus says, "Blessed are those who hunger and thirst for righteousness" (5:6), in Luke he says, "Blessed are you who are hungry now" (6:21). Moreover, in Luke Jesus not only blesses the poor and oppressed; he also castigates the rich and the oppressor: "Woe to you who are rich. . . . Woe to you who are full now. . . . Woe to you who are laughing now" (6:24–26).

Luke's social agenda is also evident in the attention that Jesus pays to women among his followers here. As we will later see, the negative attitudes toward women that exist today were rooted early in Western culture. From a feminist perspective, things were much worse at the beginning of the Christian era than they are now. In Luke's Gospel, on the other hand, Jesus associates with women, has women among his followers, and urges his women followers to abandon their traditional roles as caretakers so they can heed his words as his disciples (e.g., see 8:1–3 and 10:38–42, stories unique to Luke).

CONCLUSION: LUKE IN COMPARATIVE PERSPECTIVE

We are in a position now to wrap up our reflections on the Gospel according to Luke. Here, as in Matthew and Mark, we have a kind of Greco-Roman biography in which the things Jesus says, does, and experiences reveal who he is to the attentive reader. Had we chosen, we could have examined this Gospel without recourse to these other biographies of Jesus, following the literary-historical method that we used to study Mark. Alternatively, we could

---

AT A GLANCE

BOX 7.7   The Gospel of Luke

1. Luke was written around 80–85 C.E., by a Greek-speaking Christian, probably outside Palestine.

2. Among his sources were Mark, Q, and L.

3. He dedicates his book to an otherwise unknown person, "Theophilus." Theophilus may have been a Roman administrative official, or the name may be symbolic, referring to the Christian audience as those "Beloved of God."

4. A comparative method of analysis, which considers the similarities and differences of Luke with other Gospels, reveals several distinctive themes.

5. Luke is concerned to show that the salvation of God was rejected by and large by the Jewish people and so was sent to the non-Jews, the Gentiles.

6. The narrative explains this movement of God's salvation from Jew to Gentile by portraying Jesus as a Jewish prophet, rejected by his own people. Jesus is born as a prophet, preaches as a prophet, heals as a prophet, and dies as a prophet.

7. In this Gospel, everything that happens to Jesus is according to the divine plan. So, too, is the spread of the Gospel to the Gentiles. Since the whole world needed to be saved, the end was not to come immediately upon Jesus' departure from this world.

have analyzed it strictly in light of how the author modified his sources, as we did for Matthew. Instead we explored this text in light of similar biographies of Jesus, irrespective of whether Luke used any of them as sources. Has this approach proved useful?

Our comparative analysis has shown that Luke has a number of distinctive emphases. Luke stresses that the salvation that came in Jesus was first directed to the heart of Judaism, but Jesus as a Jewish prophet was rejected by his own people. The message was then to be sent into the whole world for the salvation of all people, Jew and Gentile, a message of forgiveness of sins to all who would repent. The worldwide mission envisioned by Jesus was planned from time immemorial by God himself and would be completed before the end of the age could come. Since the end was not to be imminent in Jesus' own day, the mission involved not only preaching the news of God's salvation but also working to right the ills of society in a world beset by poverty and oppression.

We might ask what these distinctive emphases can tell us about the author of this book and his audience. The question might be premature, however, for the Gospel of Luke is the first volume of a two-volume work, which ultimately must be read as a unit if we are to understand the full message of its author (see Chapter 11).

TAKE A STAND

1. It is Christmas time, you are home for the break, and one of your friends invites you to her church's Christmas pageant. Afterward you begin to talk about what the New Testament says about the events leading up to Jesus' birth, and you tell her that, in your opinion, Matthew and Luke tell completely different stories that cannot be reconciled. She is shocked and in disbelief and wants you to prove it. Do your best.

2. Suppose you wanted to argue that the portrayal of Jesus in Luke's Gospel is fundamentally different from the portrayal in Mark. How would you make your case?

3. Your teacher has given you an assignment: you are to map out the ways that Luke emphasizes that Jesus is a Jewish prophet. You do not have to write a full paper for this assignment, just an outline of the argument you would use. Make the outline (but include relevant verse references).

SUGGESTIONS FOR FURTHER READING

Brown, Raymond. *The Birth of the Messiah: A Commentary on the Infancy Narratives in Matthew and Luke.* Garden City, N.Y.: Doubleday, 1977. A massive and exhaustive discussion of the birth narratives of Matthew and Luke, suitable for those who want to know simply everything about every detail.

Brown, Raymond. *The Death of the Messiah: From Gethsemane to the Grave.* 2 vols. London: Doubleday, 1994. A detailed and thorough discussion of the Passion narratives of the four Gospels, in all their aspects and for all their verses.

Cadbury, H. J. *The Making of Luke-Acts.* 2d ed. London: SPCK, 1968. A classic study that shows how the author of Luke and Acts used the traditions and sources at his disposal to produce a unified narrative; for advanced students.

Conzelmann, Hans. *The Theology of St. Luke.* New York: Harper & Row, 1960. This classic study of Luke from a redaction-critical perspective argues that Luke modified the traditions he received particularly in light of the delay of the end of time; for advanced students only.

Juel, Donald. *Luke-Acts: The Promise of History.* Atlanta: John Knox, 1983. A clearly written discussion of the background of Luke-Acts and its overarching themes; ideal for beginning students.

Maddox, R. *The Purpose of Luke-Acts.* Edinburgh: T & T Clark, 1982. An intelligent and incisive discussion of the prominent themes and major emphases of Luke and Acts.

Nickle, Keith. *The Synoptic Gospels: Conflict and Consensus.* Rev. and expanded ed. Philadelphia: Westminster John Knox, 2001. One of the best introductory discussions of the background and message of the three Synoptic Gospels.

Perkins, Pheme. *Introduction to the Synoptic Gospels.* Grand Rapids, Mich.: Eerdmans, 2009. An overview of the major historical and literary issues involved with studying Matthew, Mark, and Luke; good for beginning students.

Powell, M. A. *What Are They Saying about Luke?* New York: Paulist, 1989. An excellent survey of modern scholarly views of Luke's Gospel; for beginning students.

Tuckett, Christopher M. *Luke* (T & T Clark Study Guides). London: T & T Clark, 2004. A discussion of all the significant features of the Gospel of Mark, its contents, literary character, and historical problems; a full and useful overview for beginning students.

 ## KEY TERMS

| apology | manuscripts | Quirinius | Theophilus |
| comparative method | prophet | | |

8

CHAPTER

Jesus, the Man Sent from Heaven
THE GOSPEL ACCORDING TO JOHN

WHAT TO EXPECT

The Gospel of John is unique among our Gospels. Whereas Matthew, Mark, and Luke tell many of the same stories, sometimes in exactly the same way, John has a large number of unique stories and a very different portrayal of Jesus. In this Gospel Jesus is portrayed less as a human messiah and more as a divine being come to earth to reveal the truth that is necessary for salvation. For this reason, from the earliest of times, John has been thought of as the "most spiritual" of the Gospels.

In our examinations of Matthew, Mark, Luke, and Acts, we apply a different method of study to each book. What would happen if we applied *all four* methods to the same book? That's what we will find out in this chapter on the Gospel of John, one of the most popular books of the New Testament and the most distinctive of our canonical Gospels.

The Gospel of John has always been one of the most popular and beloved books of the New Testament. It is here that Jesus makes some of his most familiar and yet extraordinary declarations about himself, where he says that he is "the bread of life," "the light of the world," "the good shepherd who lays down his life for his sheep," and "the way, the truth, and the life." This is the Gospel that identifies Jesus as the Word of God "through whom all things were made." It is here that he makes the astonishing claim that "before Abraham was, I am," where he confesses that "I and the Father are one," and where he tells Nicodemus that "you must be born again." And it is in this Gospel that Jesus performs many of his most memorable acts: turning the water into wine, raising his friend Lazarus from the dead, and washing his disciples' feet.

These sayings and deeds, and indeed many more, are found only in the Fourth Gospel, making it a source of perpetual fascination for scholars of the New Testament. Why are such stories found in John but nowhere else? Why is Jesus portrayed so differently here than in the other Gospels? Why, for example, does he talk so much about his own identity in John but scarcely at all in the Synoptic Gospels? And why does this Gospel identify Jesus as God's equal, when none of the earlier Gospels does?

These questions will be at the forefront of our investigation in this chapter. Before beginning our study, however, I should say a word about how we will proceed. Historians are responsible not only for interpreting their ancient sources but also for justifying these interpretations. This is why I have deliberately introduced and utilized different methods: the literary-historical method for Mark, the redactional method for Matthew, the comparative method for Luke, and the thematic method for Acts (see Chapter 11). As I have indicated, there is no reason for historians to restrict themselves to any one of these approaches: each could be applied to any one of these books.

To illustrate this point, we will apply all four methods to the Gospel of John. This exercise will show how a variety of approaches can enrich the process of interpretation.

THE GOSPEL OF JOHN FROM A LITERARY-HISTORICAL PERSPECTIVE

Despite its wide-ranging differences from the Synoptics, the Gospel of John clearly belongs in the same Greco-Roman genre. It, too, would be perceived by an ancient reader as a biography of a religious leader: it is a prose narrative that portrays an individual's life within a chronological framework, focusing on his inspired teachings and miraculous deeds and leading up to his death and divine vindication.

As was the case with the other Gospels, the portrayal of Jesus is established at the very outset of the narrative by the introductory passage known as the **"Johannine Prologue"** (1:1–18). This prologue, however, is quite unlike anything we have seen in our study of the Gospels to this stage. Rather than introducing the main character of the book by name, it provides a kind of mystical reflection on the "Word" of God, a being from eternity past who was with God and yet was God (v. 1), who created the universe (v. 3), who provided life and light to all humans (vv. 4–5), and who entered into the world that he had made, only to be rejected by his own people (vv. 9–11). John the Baptist testified to this Word (vv. 6–8), but only a few received it; those who did so became children of God, having received a gift far greater even than that bestowed by the servant of God, Moses himself (vv. 12–14, 16–18).

It is not until the end of the prologue that we learn who this "Word" of God was. When the Word became a human being, his name was Jesus Christ (v. 17). Up to this point, that is, through the first eighteen verses of the book, the ancient reader may not have realized that he or she was reading an introduction to a biography. Rather, the prologue appears to be a philosophical or mystical meditation. Beginning with 1:19, however, the book takes on a biographical tone that continues to the very end.

What can we make of the prologue, then, from the literary-historical perspective? Since ancient biographies typically established the character traits of the protagonist at the outset of the narrative, it is perhaps best to assume that an ancient reader, once he or she realized that this book is a biography of Jesus, would be inclined to read the rest of the story in light of what is stated about him in the mystical reflection at the outset. This is no biography of a mere mortal. Its subject is one who was with God in eternity past, who was himself divine, who created the universe, who was God's self-revelation to the world, who came to earth to bring light out of darkness and truth out of error. He is a divine being who became human to dwell here and reveal the truth about God. This Gospel will present a view of Jesus that is far and away the most exalted among our New Testament narratives.

A more complete literary-historical analysis would examine some of the critical incidents that occur early on in the narrative and perhaps focus on key events that transpire throughout. Here I would like simply to introduce the possibilities of this method for the Fourth Gospel, rather than utilize it at length, and so will summarize the major developments of the plot and indicate something about how the narrative itself is structured.

After the prologue, the Gospel is readily divided into two major blocks of material. The first twelve chapters narrate events in Jesus' public ministry, which appears to extend over a two- or three-year period (since there are three different Passover feasts mentioned). This section begins with John the Baptist and several of his disciples, who recognize Jesus as one who was specially sent from God. Most of this first section (chaps. 1–12) is devoted to recording Jesus' own declarations of who he is (the one sent from heaven to reveal God) and the miraculous **"signs"** that he does to demonstrate that what he says about himself is true. Altogether, Jesus performs seven such signs (in chaps. 2, 4, 5, 6, 9, and 11), most of them directly tied to his proclamations (see box 8.1). Thus, for example, he multiplies the loaves of bread and claims that he is the "bread of life" (6:22–40); he gives sight to the blind and says that he is "the light of the world" (9:1–12); and he raises the dead and calls himself "the resurrection and the life" (11:17–44).

Also included in these stories of Jesus' public ministry are several discourses not directly tied to the signs. In these speeches Jesus explains his identity at greater length, for instance, to Nicodemus in chapter 3 and to the Samaritan woman at the well in chapter 4. Closely connected to these self-revelations are stories of Jesus' rejection by his enemies, "the Jews" (see box 8.2), and his denunciatory responses in which he castigates those who fail to recognize him as the one sent from God (see chaps. 5, 8, and 10).

The plot of the Fourth Gospel unfolds, then, like this. Jesus proclaims that he is the one sent from heaven to reveal the truth about God, and he does signs to demonstrate that he is who he says he is. Some people he encounters accept his message, but most, especially the Jewish leaders, reject it. He condemns their failure to believe, and at the end of the first section, in chapter 12, decides to do no more work among them. From this point on, Jesus removes himself from the public eye, delivering no more self-proclamations to Jewish outsiders and performing no more signs to establish his identity.

Indeed, starting with chapter 13, there is not much time left before Jesus is to return to his heavenly home. Whereas the first twelve chapters stretch over two or three years, chapters 13–19 take place within a single twenty-four-hour period. These chapters begin by recounting the events and discussions at Jesus' final meal with his disciples. After he washes his disciples' feet (13:1–20) and announces that he will soon be betrayed (13:21–30), he launches into his longest discourse of the Gospel, commonly known as the "Farewell Discourse." Here Jesus states that he is soon to leave the disciples to return to the Father; they are not to be dismayed, however, for he will send them another comforter, the Holy Spirit, who will assist and instruct them. When Jesus leaves, his disciples will be hated by nonbelievers in the world, but they are to continue doing his commandments, confident of his presence among them in the Spirit.

This speech consumes more than three chapters. In chapter 17, Jesus offers a final prayer to his Father for his disciples, that they may remain faithful even after he has gone. The rest of the book, chapters 18–21, presents Jesus' Passion and resurrection in stories more or less similar to those found in the Synoptics. As he predicted, Jesus

ANOTHER GLIMPSE INTO THE PAST

BOX 8.1 Jesus' Signs in the Fourth Gospel

The following are the seven miraculous signs that Jesus performs in the Fourth Gospel:

 - Turning water into wine (2:1–11)
 - Healing the Capernaum official's son (4:46–54)
 - Healing the paralytic by the pool of Bethzatha (5:2–9)
 - Feeding the 5,000 (6:1–14)
 - Walking on water (6:16–21)

 - Healing the man born blind (9:1–12)
 - Raising Lazarus from the dead (11:1–44)

Jesus performs no other public miracles in John, but notice the statement near the end of the book: "Now Jesus did many other signs in the presence of his disciples, which are not written in this book. But these are written so that you may come to believe that Jesus is the Messiah, the son of God, and that through believing you may have life in his name" (20:30–31).

BOX 8.2 "The Jews" in the Fourth Gospel

You will notice in reading through the Fourth Gospel that the phrase "the Jews" is almost always used as a negative term of abuse. The Jews are portrayed as the enemies of Jesus who are consequently opposed to God and aligned with the Devil and the forces of evil (see especially 8:31–59). Vitriolic statements of this kind may sound anti-Semitic to our ears—as indeed, they should: hateful acts of violence have been perpetrated over the years by those who have taken such charges as divine sanctions for oppression and persecution. But we will also see that our modern notion of anti-Semitism may not be appropriate for understanding the meaning of such comments in the early Christian literature.

Despite these harsh statements about Jews in the Gospel of John, even here Jesus and his followers are portrayed as Jews who subscribe to the authority of Moses and participate in the Jewish cult and the Jewish festivals. If Jesus and his followers are Jews, how can all Jews be lumped together and branded as the enemies of God? Perhaps it is enough to note that "the Jews" is a technical term of disapprobation throughout this narrative; thus, when I refer to John's own comments, I will place the term in quotation marks.

is betrayed by his own disciple Judas; he is interrogated by the high priest, denied by his disciple Peter, and put on trial before the Roman governor Pilate. At the instigation of his enemies among the Jews, he is condemned to crucifixion. He dies and is buried by Joseph of Arimathea, but on the first day of the week, he is raised from the dead. Chapters 20–21 narrate various appearances to his followers, whom he convinces that he is both alive and divine.

THE GOSPEL OF JOHN FROM A REDACTIONAL PERSPECTIVE

As we have seen in our earlier discussions, redaction criticism works to understand how an author has utilized his or her sources. Scholars have successfully used this method with the Gospels of Matthew and Luke, where they have posited two sources with reasonable certainty (Mark and Q). The rationale for using this method is somewhat more tenuous in the case of the Fourth Gospel, since this author's sources are more difficult to reconstruct. Still, John must have derived his stories about Jesus from somewhere (since he evidently didn't make them all up).

One perennial question is whether John had access to and made use of the Synoptic Gospels.

The question is somewhat thorny, and we cannot delve into all its complexities here. Instead, I will simply indicate why many scholars continue to be persuaded that he did not utilize the Synoptics.

As we have seen, the principal grounds for assuming that one document served as a source for another are their wide-ranging similarities; when they tell the same stories and do so in the same way, they must be literarily related to one another. Thus Matthew, Mark, and Luke must have sources in common because they agree with one another on a number of occasions, often word for word. This is not the case for the Fourth Gospel. Most of John's stories outside the Passion narrative are found only in John, whereas most of the stories in the Synoptics are not found in John. If this author had used the Synoptics as sources, why would he have omitted so many of their stories? Or—to put the burden of proof in its proper place—why should someone think that John used the Synoptics as sources when they do not have extensive verbatim agreements, even in the stories that they happen to share?

When thinking about the relationship of the New Testament writings to one another, we must constantly bear in mind that in the ancient world books were not published as they are today. In the modern world, books are mass-produced and sold all over the world, with the distribution of copies taking weeks at the most. In the ancient world, books were copied one at a time, and distribution was haphazard at best. In-house literature was not advertised, and circulation was random and un controlled. Suppose, for example, that the Gospel of Luke was produced in Asia Minor; Christians in Alexandria may not have heard about it until years later. Or if Matthew was produced in Syria, the Christians of Corinth may not have known of it for decades. Thus there is no guarantee that simply because John was penned some ten or fifteen years after the Synoptics, its author would have known them. On the contrary, given the sizable differences between them, it appears unlikely that he did.

How then can we account for the similar stories that John and the Synoptics tell on occasion? The simplest explanation is that they would have been independently drawn from the oral traditions circulating about Jesus. In different regions of the world, both where there were written accounts about Jesus and where there were not, some of the same stories would naturally have been told. The story of Jesus' Passion is one example. It appears that Christians in many places told of how Jesus was betrayed by one of his own disciples, denied by another, and abandoned by all the rest and of how he was confronted by the Jewish religious leaders, turned over to Pontius Pilate, and crucified for claiming to be the king of the Jews. The similarities between John and the Synoptics in such stories may simply derive from related oral traditions in circulation in their respective communities.

Evidence of Sources in John

Just because John does not appear to have used the Synoptic Gospels as sources, however, does not mean that he did not use other written documents. Indeed, scholars have typically pointed to three pieces of evidence to suggest that he did.

Differences in Writing Style. Every author has a distinctive style of writing. When you are familiar enough with the way someone writes, you are able to recognize his or her work when you see it. For example, if someone were to insert a page of James Joyce into a story by Mark Twain, a careful reader would immediately recognize the difference. Apart

from the change of subject matter, the style itself would be a dead giveaway.

Nothing quite so radical occurs with the changes of style in the Fourth Gospel, but there are passages that appear to come from different writers. We have already looked briefly, for example, at the prologue. Scholars have long recognized the poetic character of this passage, which makes it quite unlike the rest of the narrative. Indeed, it appears to be almost hymnic in quality, as if it were composed to be sung in praise of Christ. Notice, for instance, how the various statements about "the Word" are linked together by key terms, so that the end of one statement corresponds to the beginning of the next. This pattern is even easier to see when the passage is read in the original Greek, as a literal translation can show: "In the beginning was the Word, and the Word was with God, and God was the Word . . . in him was life, and the life was the light of humans, and the light shines in the darkness, and the darkness has not extinguished it."

Interestingly, this careful poetic pattern is broken up in the two places where the subject matter shifts away from the Word to a discussion of John the Baptist (vv. 6–8, 15). It may be that the original hymn did not include these verses. You will notice that when they are taken out, the passage flows quite smoothly without a break.

Is it possible that this hymn was written by someone other than the author of the Fourth Gospel, who borrowed it for the beginning of his biographical account of Jesus? Most scholars find this view entirely plausible. Recall that the central theme of the prologue, that Jesus is the Word made flesh, occurs nowhere else in the entire Gospel. This may indicate that whoever composed these opening verses did not produce the rest of the narrative. Thus we may be dealing with different authors.

Repetitions. There are several passages in this Gospel that appear redundant, where similar accounts are repeated in slightly different words. These passages may derive from different sources. For example, chapters 14 and 16 (parts of the Farewell Discourse) are remarkably alike in their key themes. In both chapters Jesus says that he is leaving the world but that the disciples should not grieve because the Holy Spirit will come in his stead; the disciples will be hated by the world, but

ANOTHER GLIMPSE INTO THE PAST

BOX 8.3   Jesus and the Woman Taken in Adultery

How significant are the changes that scribes made to the copies of the New Testament? The most famous story of Jesus from the New Testament was probably not originally found in the Gospels, but was added by later scribes.

This is the account of Jesus and the woman taken in adultery—a story found in virtually every Hollywood film about Jesus. The story is found only in some manuscripts of the Gospel of John. According to the account, the Jewish authorities drag a woman before Jesus and tell him that she has been caught in the act of adultery. The Law of Moses commands them to stone her to death, but what does Jesus say?

The authorities are setting a trap for him: if he says, "Yes, go ahead and stone her," then he is violating his own teachings of love and forgiveness. But if he says, "No, forgive her," then he is violating the Law of Moses. So what is he to do?

Jesus always seems to find a way out of these traps. In this case, he stoops down and begins to write on the ground, and then he looks up and says, "Let the one without sin among you be the first to cast a stone at her." He stoops down to write again, and one by one, the Jewish authorities begin to leave, presumably feeling guilty for their own sins. Jesus finally looks up and sees the woman standing alone. He asks her "Where have they gone? Is there no one left here to condemn you? She replies, "No Lord, no one." He then says, "Neither do I condemn you. Go your way and sin no more."

It is a terrific story, powerful, and moving. Unfortunately, it was not originally part of the Gospel of John—or of any other Gospel. It is not found in our earliest and best manuscripts of John, and its vocabulary and writing style are significantly different from the rest of the Gospel. It does not start showing up regularly in Greek manuscripts until about the ninth century, some 800 years after John was first written.

Scholars agree, then: this was a story that was added to the Gospel by a later scribe. It became so popular that other scribes copied it time and again until it became one of the most popular accounts of Jesus from the Middle Ages down until today, even though it was not originally part of the Bible.

they will be instructed and encouraged by the Spirit present among them. Why would this message be given twice in the same speech? It may have been repeated for emphasis, but the repetition seems less emphatic than simply redundant. Another explanation might be that the author had access to two different accounts of Jesus' last words to his disciples, which were similar in their general themes but somewhat different in their wording. When he composed his Gospel, he included them both.

The Presence of Literary Seams. The two preceding arguments for sources in John may not seem all that persuasive by themselves. The third kind of evidence, however, should give us pause. Inconsistencies in John's narrative, sometimes called literary seams, provide the strongest evidence that the author of John used several written sources when producing his account.

Authors who compose their books by splicing several sources together don't always neatly cover up their handiwork but sometimes leave **literary seams**. The Fourth Evangelist was not a sloppy literary seamster, but he did leave a few traces of his work, which become evident as you study his final product with care. Here are several illustrations.

1. In chapter 2, Jesus performs his "first sign" (2:11) in Cana of Galilee by changing the water into wine. In chapter 4, he does his "second sign" (4:54) after returning to Galilee from Judea, healing the Capernaum official's son. The problem emerges when you read what happens between the first and second signs, for John 2:23 indicates that while Jesus was in Jerusalem many people believed in him "because they saw the signs that he was doing." How can this be? How can he do the first sign, and then other signs, and then the second sign? This is

an example of a literary seam; in a moment I will explain how it indicates that the author used sources.

2. In John 2:23, Jesus is in Jerusalem, the capital of Judea. While there, he engages in a discussion with Nicodemus that lasts until 3:21. Then the text says, "After this Jesus and his disciples went into the land of Judea" (3:22). But they are already *in* the land of Judea, in fact, in its capital. Here, then is another literary seam. (Some modern translations have gotten around this problem by mistranslating verse 22 to say that they went into the "*countryside* of Judea," but this is not the meaning of the Greek word for "land.")

3. In John 5:1, Jesus goes to Jerusalem, where he spends the entire chapter healing and teaching. The author's comment after this discourse, however, is somewhat puzzling: "After this, Jesus went to the other side of the Sea of Galilee" (6:1). How could he go to the other side of the sea if he is not already on one of its sides? In fact, he is nowhere near the Sea of Galilee; he is in Jerusalem of Judea.

4. At Jesus' last meal with his disciples, Peter asks, "Lord, where are you going?" (13:36). A few verses later, Thomas says to Jesus, "Lord, we do not know where you are going" (14:5). Oddly enough, several minutes later, Jesus states, "But now I am going to him who sent me; yet none of you asks me, 'Where are you going?'" (16:5)!

5. At the end of chapter 14, after delivering a speech of nearly a chapter and a half, Jesus says to his disciples, "Rise, let us be on our way" (14:31). The reader might expect them to get

up and go, but instead Jesus launches into another discourse: "I am the true vine, and my Father is the vinegrower . . ." (15:1). This discourse is not just a few words spoken on the way out the door. The speech goes on for all of chapter 15, all of chapter 16, and leads into the prayer that takes up all of chapter 17. Jesus and the disciples do not leave until 18:1. Why would Jesus say, "Rise, let us go," and then not leave for three chapters?

Readers have devised various ways of explaining these kinds of literary problems over the years, but the simplest explanation is probably that the author decided to weave different written sources into his narrative. To show how this theory works, we can consider the Farewell Discourse. Recall the various problems in this portion of the Gospel: there appears to be a repetition of material between chapters 14 and 16, and there are at least two literary "seams" here, one involving the question of where Jesus is going (13:36; 14:5; 16:5) and the other involving Jesus' injunction for them all to get up and leave (14:31; 18:1).

The theory of sources can solve these problems. Suppose for the sake of argument that the author had two different accounts (A and B) of what happened at Jesus' last meal with his disciples. Suppose further that account A told the stories that are now located in chapters 13, 14, and 18, and account B told the stories found in chapters 15, 16, and 17 (see fig. 8.1). If the author of the Fourth Gospel had taken the two accounts and spliced them together, inserting account B into account A, between what is now the end of chapter 14 and the beginning of

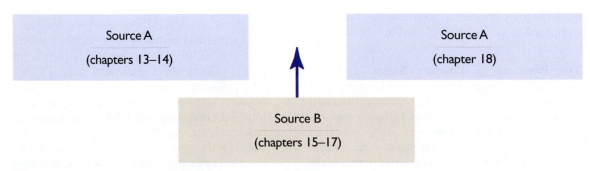

Source A

(chapters 13–14)

Source A

(chapter 18)

Source B

(chapters 15–17)

Figure 8.1 Sources in the Farewell Discourse.

chapter 18, this would explain all the problems we have discussed. There is a repetition between chapters 14 and 16 because the author used two accounts of the same event and joined them together. Moreover, Jesus states that "no one asks me, 'Where are you going?'" because in account B, (chaps. 15–17) no one *had* asked him where he was going; the questions of Peter and Thomas were originally found in the other account (A). Finally, in account A Jesus had said, "Arise, let us go," and he and his disciples immediately got up and went. In the final version of John they do not get up and go for three chapters because account B was interposed between two verses (14:31 and 18:1) that stood together in account A.

Character of the Sources in John

Thus the theory of written sources behind the Fourth Gospel explains many of the literary problems of the narrative. These sources obviously no longer survive, but we can make some inferences about them.

The Signs Source. Some of the seams that we have observed appear to suggest that the author incorporated a source that described the signs of Jesus, written to persuade people that he was the messiah, the Son of God. There are seven signs in the Gospel; it is possible that these were all original to the source. You may recall that seven is the perfect number, the number of God; is it an accident that there were seven signs?

The source may have described the signs that Jesus did in sequence and enumerated each one ("This is the first sign that Jesus did," "This is the second sign," and so on). If so, the evangelist kept the first two enumerations (2:11 and 4:54) but for some unknown reason eliminated the others. Keeping the first two, however, left a seam in his narrative, since Jesus does other signs between them (2:23).

The **signs source** may well have concluded after its most impressive sign, the raising of Lazarus, with the words that are now found in 20:30–31: "Now Jesus did many other signs in the presence of his disciples, which are not written in this book. But these are written so that you may come to believe that Jesus is the Messiah, the Son of God, and that through believing you may have life in his name." The book of signs, then, would have been some kind of missionary tractate designed to convince Jews of Jesus' identity through his miraculous

WHAT DO YOU THINK?

BOX 8.4 The Death of the Beloved Disciple in the Johannine Community

John 21:21–3 preserves an interesting conversation between the resurrected Jesus and Peter. When Peter asks him about the unnamed "beloved disciple," Jesus responds, "If it is my will that he remain until I come, what is that to you? Follow me." The author goes on to explain that some people misunderstood Jesus' words as a promise that this disciple would not die before Jesus returned from heaven at the end of the age, but that, in fact, Jesus had not explicitly said this. Why would the author of this story want to correct this misunderstanding?

In the opinion of some scholars, it was because some members of the Johannine community had expected that their beloved leader, this unnamed disciple, would not die before the coming of the end. When he did, they were thrown into confusion. Had the Lord gone back on his promise? This author constructs the story to explain that Jesus never had said "that he would not die" (21:23). If this interpretation is correct, then the Gospel would have been published in its final form, with the addition of chapter 21, only after the death of the beloved disciple, and probably after the martyrdom of Peter as well (see 21:18–19).

deeds. At some point the events it describes would have been combined with sayings of Jesus that related closely to the things he did. Thus, in John, Jesus not only feeds the 5,000 but also claims to be the bread of life; he not only heals the blind but also claims to be the light of the world; he not only raises the dead but also claims to be the resurrection and the life.

Discourse Sources. Jesus' lengthy speeches in this Gospel appear to have come from a source; indeed, as we have seen, there must have been more than one of them. This, at least, is the best explanation for the literary problems in the Fare well Discourse (chaps. 13–17). The other sayings may derive from the same or similar sources.

Passion Source. Most scholars are persuaded that John's Passion narrative (chaps. 18–20) derives from a source that was similar in many ways to the narrative that is found in Mark. It is difficult to know, however, whether the source was written or oral.

Other Sources. We have already seen that the prologue to the Gospel appears to have been derived from a source, possibly an early Christian hymn to Christ. Something similar can be said of the last chapter, in which Jesus makes a final appearance to several of his disciples after his resurrection (he had already appeared to them in chapter 20). An earlier edition of the Gospel appears to have ended with the words I have just quoted from 20:30–31, which certainly sound like the ending of a book. The final chapter was added later to record one other incident of significance to the author (see box 8.3). It is here that Jesus indicates that Peter will be martyred for his faith and where he is mistakenly understood to say that the unnamed "beloved disciple" will not die prior to his own return.

THE GOSPEL OF JOHN FROM A THEMATIC PERSPECTIVE

Whereas the literary-historical approach to the Gospels focuses on the conventions of the biographical genre, and so determines how a book

portrays its main character through the unfolding of the plot as he interacts with those around him, and the redactional method considers how an author modified his sources, the thematic approach isolates prominent themes at key points of the narrative and traces their presence throughout, more or less overlooking questions of plot and character interaction. If we were to examine John from a strictly thematic point of view, we might look at some of the salient motifs established at the outset in the prologue and in some of the speeches of the main character.

From a thematic point of view, it is interesting to note that although the prologue identifies Jesus as the Word of God who has become human, he is never explicitly called this anywhere else in the Gospel. Nonetheless, certain other aspects of the prologue's description recur throughout the narrative. For example, just as the Word is said to be "in the beginning" with God, so Jesus later speaks of possessing the glory of the Father "before the world was made" (17:5); just as the Word is said to be "God," so Jesus says "I and the Father are one" (10:30); just as in the Word "was life," so Jesus claims to be "the resurrection and the life" (11:25); just as this life is said to be the "light that enlightens all people," so Jesus says that he is "the light of the world" (9:5); just as the Word is said to have come from heaven into this world, so Jesus maintains that he has been "sent" from God (e.g., 17:21, 25); and just as the Word is said to be rejected by his own people, so Jesus is rejected by "the Jews" (chap. 12), and later unjustly executed (chap. 19).

A full analysis, of course, would look at each of these themes at length. It would also consider other ideas found elsewhere, for example, in Jesus' discourses. These include (a) his first public speech in chapter 3, where he indicates to Nicodemus that only through a birth from "above" can one enter into the kingdom of God and that only the one who comes from above (i.e., he himself, Jesus) can reveal what is necessary for this heavenly birth; (b) his final public speech in chapter 12, where he proclaims that those who have seen him have seen the Father who sent him, whereas those who reject him have rejected God; and (c) his prayer in chapter 17, which more or less functions as his final speech in the presence of his disciples, where

ANOTHER EARLY CHRISTIAN TEXT

BOX 8.5 The *Gospel of Judas*

The *Gospel of Judas* (Iscariot) is the most recent Gospel to be discovered, and its publication created a huge public stir. It is an account of Jesus' life—especially the secret teachings he delivered to his disciples—told from the perspective of Judas Iscariot, his betrayer. What is most striking about this Gospel is that here Judas is not portrayed as the villain of the story, but as its hero. He alone among the disciples understands who Jesus is and does what he wants.

Like many of the Gospels discovered earlier at Nag Hammadi, in 1947 (see p. 4), the *Gospel of Judas* is a "gnostic" Gospel—that is, it is written by someone who believed that secret "knowledge" provides the means to escape this evil material world, which was the creation not of the one true God but of a lesser, ignorant, deity. Like other gnostic Gospels, the *Gospel of Judas* contains secret teachings that Jesus delivers to his insiders. But here Jesus gives his revelation principally to Judas, who alone can

understand what he is trying to say. The other disciples misunderstand their teacher, thinking that Jesus represents the God who created this world. Jesus finds this idea risible—in fact, he laughs at the disciples' misunderstanding on four different occasions. Judas understands, though, that Jesus is from another realm, above the creator God, and that he needs to return there once he has completed his mission here on earth. Judas' superiority to all the other disciples is proclaimed by Jesus himself: "You will exceed all of them, for you will sacrifice the man that clothes me."

In other words, Jesus, like his true followers, is only temporarily in the material realm, in a body. He is soon to escape and return to the spiritual realm whence he came. And it is Judas who will make it happen. So, unlike the Gospel of John, where Judas is called a "devil" (6:70–71), in this newly discovered Gospel Judas is Jesus' closest confidant, who does only what is asked of him.

he affirms that he has come from God and is now soon to return to him.

THE GOSPEL OF JOHN FROM A COMPARATIVE PERSPECTIVE

One of the most striking features of the Fourth Gospel is the way in which some of the distinctively Johannine themes stand in such stark contrast to those in the other early Christian writings that we have examined so far. Even to the casual reader, the Fourth Gospel may seem somewhat different from the other three within the canon. Nowhere in the other Gospels is Jesus said to be the Word of God, the creator of the universe, the equal of God, or the one sent from heaven and soon to return. Nowhere else does Jesus claim that to see him is to see the Father, that to hear him is to hear the Father, and that to reject him is to reject the Father. Exactly how different is the Fourth Gospel from the

others? The comparative approach seeks to answer this question.

Comparison of Contents

Despite the important and significant differences among the Synoptic Gospels, they are much more similar to one another than any one of them is to John. Suppose we were to list the most significant accounts of the Synoptics. In two of them Jesus is said to be born in Bethlehem, to a virgin named Mary. In all three, his public ministry begins with his baptism by John, followed by a period of temptation in the wilderness by the Devil. When he returns, he begins to proclaim the coming kingdom of God. This proclamation is typically made through parables; in fact, according to Mark's Gospel (4:33–34), this is the only way that Jesus taught the crowds. In addition to teaching, of course, Jesus also performs miracles. In Mark, his first miracle involves the exorcism of a demon. Throughout the first part

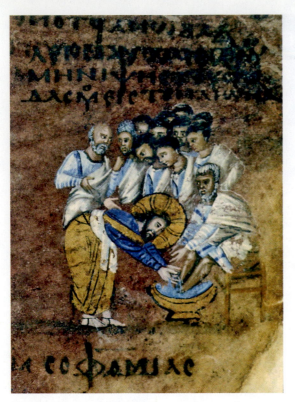

Figure 8.2 Portrayal of Jesus washing the disciples' feet, one of the stories of the Fourth Gospel that does not occur in the Synoptics, from the sixth-century manuscript, the "Rossano Gospels."

of his ministry, then, Jesus engages in exorcisms (and other miracles) and teaching, principally in parables. Halfway through these Gospels, he goes up onto a high mountain and is transfigured before his disciples; it is there that he reveals to them his glory. Otherwise, it remains hidden. Indeed, he does not speak openly of his identity in these books (even in Matthew, where it is occasionally recognized), and he commands the demons and others who know of it to keep silent. At the end, he has a last meal with his disciples, in which he institutes the Lord's Supper, distributing the bread ("This is my body . . . ") and then the cup ("This is the cup of the new covenant in my blood . . . "). He afterward goes out to pray in the Garden of Gethsemane, where he asks God to allow him to forgo his coming Passion. He is then arrested by the au-

thorities and made to stand trial before the Jewish authorities of the Sanhedrin, who find him guilty of blasphemy before delivering him over to the Romans for trial and execution.

These stories make up the backbone of the Synoptic accounts of Jesus. What most casual readers of the New Testament do not realize is that none of them is found in John.

Read the text carefully for yourself. There is no word about Jesus' birth in Bethlehem here or about his mother being a virgin (in John, as in Mark, Jesus appears for the first time as an adult). Jesus is not explicitly said to be baptized by John. He does not go into the wilderness to be tempted by the Devil. He does not proclaim the kingdom of God that is coming and he never tells a parable. Jesus never casts out a demon in this Gospel. He does not go up onto the Mount of Transfiguration to reveal his glory to his disciples in a private setting, nor does he make any effort to keep his identity secret or command others to silence. Jesus does not institute the Lord's Supper in this Gospel, nor does he go to Gethsemane to pray to be released from his fate. In this Gospel, he is not put on trial before the Sanhedrin or found guilty of committing blasphemy.

If John does not have these stories about Jesus, what stories does he have? The majority of John's stories are unique to John; they are found nowhere else. To be sure, many of the same characters appear in this Gospel: Jesus, some of his family, his male disciples, several female followers, John the Baptist, the Jewish leaders, Caiaphas, Pontius Pilate, and Barabbas. Moreover, some of the same (or similar) stories are found in John and the Synoptics, including, for example, the feeding of the 5,000, the walking on the water, and many of the events of the Passion narrative: Jesus' anointing, his entry into Jerusalem, his betrayal and arrest, the denial by Peter, the Roman trial, and the crucifixion. But most of the events of the Synoptics, except for the Passion narrative, are not found in John, just as, by and large, the words and deeds recorded in John occur only in John. Only here, for example, do we hear of some of Jesus' most impressive miracles: the turning of water into wine (chap. 2), the healing of the lame man by the pool of Bethzatha (chap. 5), the restoration of sight to the man born blind (chap. 9), and the raising of Lazarus from the dead (chap. 11). Only here do we get the long discourses, including the dialogues with Nicodemus in chapter 3, with the Samaritan woman in chapter 4, with his opponents among the Jews in chapters 5 and 8, with his disciples in chapters 13–17. Just in terms of content, then, John is quite different from the Synoptics.

Comparison of Emphases

The differences between John and the Synoptics are perhaps even more striking in stories that they have in common. You can see the differences yourself simply by taking any story of the Synoptics that is also told in John and comparing the two accounts carefully (as we did for the time of Jesus' death in Chapter 4). A thorough and detailed study of this phenomenon throughout the entire Gospel would reveal several fundamental differences. Here we will look at two differences that affect a large number of the stories of Jesus' deeds and words.

First, the deeds. Jesus does not do as many miracles in John as he does in the Synoptics, but the ones he does are, for the most part, far more spectacular. Indeed, unlike in the Synoptics, Jesus does nothing to hide his abilities; he performs miracles openly in order to demonstrate who he is. To illustrate the point, we can compare two stories that have several striking resemblances: the Synoptic account of the raising of Jairus's daughter (Mark 5:21–43) and John's account of the raising of Lazarus (John 11:1–44). Read them for yourself. In both, a person is ill and a relative goes to Jesus for help. Jesus is delayed from coming right away, so that by the time he arrives the person has already died and is being mourned. Jesus speaks of the person as "sleeping" (a euphemism for death). Those present think that he has come too late and that now he can do nothing, but Jesus approaches the one who has died, speaks some words, and raises the person from the dead. Both accounts end with Jesus' instructions to care for the person's well-being.

Although the two stories are similar in kind, they differ in the details of how the miracle is portrayed. First of all, in the story in Mark, Jesus is delayed inadvertently; he has an encounter with someone in the crowd, and, in the meantime, the young girl dies. In John's Gospel, on the other hand, Jesus intentionally stays away until Lazarus dies (v. 6). Why would he want Lazarus

to die? The text of Jesus' words tells us in no uncertain terms: "Lazarus is dead; and for your sake I am glad that I was not there, so that you may believe" (v. 15). In John's Gospel, Lazarus has to die so that Jesus can raise him from the dead and convince others of who he is. As Jesus himself puts it: "This illness . . . is for the glory of God, so that the Son of God may be glorified by means of it" (v. 4).

There is another significant difference between the accounts. In Mark, Jesus heals the girl in private, taking only her parents and three of his disciples with him. In John, Jesus makes the healing a public spectacle, with crowds looking on. We have already discussed why Mark may have wanted to portray Jesus as performing his miracles in secret, but why the publicity in John? A complete study of John would show why: unlike the Synoptics, the Fourth Gospel uses Jesus' miracles to convince people of who he is. Indeed, as Jesus states in this Gospel, "Unless you see signs and wonders, you will not believe" (4:48).

It is striking that in the Synoptic Gospels Jesus refuses to do miracles in order to prove his identity. When the scribes and Pharisees approach him and ask him to do a "sign" (Matt 11:38), he bluntly refuses, maligning them as sinful and adulterous for wanting a sign when his own preaching, superior to that of Jonah and Solomon (both of whom converted the disbelieving by their proclamations), should suffice. A similar lesson is conveyed through the Synoptic story of Jesus' temptation in the wilderness (drawn from Q; Matt 4:1–11, Luke 4:1–13). As you will recall, at one point Jesus is

Figure 8.3 Portrayal of Jesus raising Lazarus, while his sister Mary pleads for Jesus to help, from the lid of a small fifth-century silver ornamental box.

tempted to jump off the pinnacle of the Temple. A thoughtful reader may wonder why this would be alluring. One can understand why fasting for forty days might make Jesus tempted to turn stones into bread, but why would anyone be tempted to jump off a ten-story precipice? The text itself provides an explanation: if Jesus jumps, the angels of God will swoop down and catch him before he hits bottom. One must assume that the crowds of faithful Jews down below would see this supernatural intervention on Jesus' behalf—this is in the Jerusalem Temple—and so become convinced of who he was. Thus, in the Synoptic temptation narrative, when Jesus is tempted to prove his identity by doing a miracle, he resists the temptation as satanic.

Neither of these stories—the request for a sign or the account of the temptation—is found in the Fourth Gospel. For in this Gospel, far from spurning the use of miracles to reveal his identity, Jesus performs them for precisely this purpose. Thus, the Fourth Gospel does not actually call Jesus' spectacular deeds "miracles," which is a Greek word that means something like "demonstration of power" (and is related to our English word "dynamite"); instead it calls them "signs," for they are signs of who Jesus is.

What, then, is the function of the miraculous deeds in the Fourth Gospel? Unlike in the Synoptics, they are done publicly in order to convince people of Jesus' identity so that they may come to believe in him. This purpose is made plain by the words of the Fourth Evangelist himself, in his concluding comment on the significance of Jesus' great deeds: "Jesus did many other signs in the presence of his disciples, which are not written in this book. But these are written so that you may come to believe that Jesus is the Messiah, the Son of God, and that through believing you may have life in his name" (20:30–31).

John's unique understanding of Jesus' miracles is matched by his distinctive portrayal of Jesus' teachings. In the Synoptic Gospels, you will have noticed that Jesus scarcely ever speaks about himself. There his message is about the coming kingdom of God and about what people must do to prepare for it. His regular mode of instruction is the parable. In John, however, Jesus does not speak in parables, nor does he proclaim the imminent appearance of the kingdom. He instead focuses his

words on identifying himself as the one sent from God (see box 8.6).

In the Fourth Gospel, Jesus has come down from the Father and is soon to return to him. His message alone can bring eternal life. He himself is equal with God. He existed before he came into the world. He reveals God's glory. Only those who receive his message can partake of the world that is above, only they are in the light, and only they can enter into the truth. Jesus himself is the only way to God: "I am the way, and the truth, and the life. No one comes to the Father except through me" (14:6).

Whereas Jesus scarcely ever talks about himself in the Synoptics, that is virtually all he talks about in John, and there is a close relationship here between what he says and what he does. He says that he is the one sent from God to bring life to the world, and he does signs to show that what he says is true.

In short, John is markedly different from the Synoptics in both content and emphasis and with respect to both Jesus' words and his deeds.

THE AUTHOR OF THE FOURTH GOSPEL

Like Mark, Matthew, Luke, and Acts, the Gospel of John was written anonymously. Since the second century, however, it has been customarily attributed to John the son of Zebedee, commonly thought to be the mysterious "beloved disciple."

The idea that one of Jesus' own followers authored the book has traditionally been based on a couple of comments made in the text itself: (*a*) the reference to an eyewitness who beheld the water and blood coming from Jesus' side at his crucifixion (19:35) and (*b*) the allusion to the beloved disciple as the one who bore witness and wrote about these things (21:24).

There are serious questions, however, about whether these verses should be taken to indicate that the beloved disciple authored the Gospel. For example, 19:35 says nothing about who actually wrote down the traditions, but only indicates that the disciple who witnessed Jesus' death spoke the truth ("He who saw this has testified so that you also may believe. His testimony is true, and

ANOTHER GLIMPSE INTO THE PAST

BOX 8.6   Jesus and the "I Am" Sayings in John

Readers have often noticed that Jesus speaks about himself far more in John than in the Synoptics. Jesus refers to himself using the phrase "I am" only two times in both Mark and Luke (Mark 6:50, 14:62; Luke 22:27, 24:39), and only five times in Matthew (11:29; 14:27; 18:20; 27:43; 28:20). Contrast this with the Gospel of John, where Jesus uses the verb to refer to himself a total of forty-six times! Among Jesus' important self-identifications in this Gospel are seven **"I am" sayings** in which he speaks of himself symbolically: "I am the bread of life" (6:35, 51), "I am the light of the world" (8:12), "I am the gate" (for the sheep; 10:7, 9), "I am the good shepherd" (10:11, 14), "I am the resurrection and the life" (11:25), "I am the way, the truth, and the life" (14:6), and "I am the true vine" (15:1). All of these images show that Jesus is uniquely important as the way to God and eternal life.

In several other places in the Fourth Gospel Jesus simply says of himself "I am." The most striking oc-currence is in 8:58. Jesus' opponents have objected to his reference to the father of the Jews, Abraham; in order to show that he is himself greater than Abraham, Jesus replies, "Very truly I tell you, before Abraham was, I am" (cf. 8:24, 28; 13:19). It appears that Jesus is not simply claiming to be very old here (Abraham lived some 1,800 years earlier); by calling himself "I am" he may actually be taking the name of God. In the Jewish Scriptures, when Moses is sent by God to assist the Israelites, he asks God his name. God replies "I am who I am. . . . Thus you shall say to the Israelites, 'I am has sent me to you'" (Exod 3:14).

If God's name as revealed to Moses was "I am," and Jesus in John calls himself "I am," is he claiming to be God? His hearers appear to understand it in this way. They immediately pick up stones to execute him for blasphemy.

---

he knows that he tells the truth"). Furthermore, 21:24 indicates that, whoever this disciple may have been, it was someone other than the author of the final form of the book. Notice how the verse differentiates between the "disciple who is testifying to these things and has written them" and the author who is describing them: "we [i.e., someone other than the disciple himself] know that his testimony is true."

Some of the traditions of this Gospel, then, may ultimately go back to the preaching of one of the original followers of Jesus, but that is not the same thing as saying that he himself wrote the Gospel. Could this unnamed disciple have been John, the son of Zebedee? One of the puzzling features of this Gospel is that John is never mentioned by name here. Those who think that he wrote the Gospel claim that he made no explicit reference to himself out of modesty. Not surprisingly, those who think he did not write it argue just the opposite, that he is not named because he was an insignificant figure in Jesus' story for the members of this community.

Indeed, the evidence could probably be read either way. For what it is worth, the book of Acts suggests that John, the son of Zebedee, was uneducated and unable to read and write (the literal meaning of the Greek phrase "uneducated and ordinary"; Acts 4:13).

In any event, it should be clear from our analysis that the Fourth Gospel was probably not the literary product of a single author. Obviously, one person was responsible for the final product, but that person, whoever he or she was, constructed the Gospel out of a number of preexisting sources that had circulated within the community over a period of years. The author appears to have been a native speaker of Greek living outside Palestine. Since some of the traditions presuppose a Palestinian origin (given the Aramaic words), it may be that the community relocated to a Greek-speaking area and acquired a large number of converts there at some point of its history. Whether the author accompanied the community from the beginning or was a relative latecomer is an issue that can probably never be resolved.

WHAT DO YOU THINK?

BOX 8.7 John's De-Apocalypticized Gospel

We have already seen that Luke's Gospel tones down the apocalyptic character of Jesus' proclamation, as it is found, for example, in the Gospel of Mark. In John's Gospel, the apocalyptic message is toned down even more. For John, eternal life is not a future event. As the author puts it early on in the narrative, using the present tense: "Whoever believes in the Son has eternal life" (3:36). Eternal life in this Gospel does not come at the end of time, when the Son of Man arrives on the clouds of heaven and brings in the kingdom. Eternal life is here and now, for all who believe in Jesus. That is why Jesus does not deliver an "apocalyptic discourse" in this Gospel (cf. Mark 13) or speak about the coming Son of Man or the imminent kingdom of God. The kingdom of God is entered by those who have faith in Jesus, in the present (cf. 3:3).

That a person's standing before God is determined not by the future resurrection, but the present relationship with Jesus, is illustrated by John's account of the dialogue between Jesus and Martha in the story of Lazarus. Jesus informs Martha that her brother will rise again (11:23). She thinks he is referring to the resurrection at the end of time, and agrees with him

(11:24), but he corrects her. He is referring to possibilities in the present, not the future. "I am the resurrection and the life. Those who believe in me, even though they die, will live, and everyone who lives and believes in me will never die" (11:25–26).

Jewish apocalyptists maintained a dualistic view of the world, in which this age belonged to the forces of evil whereas the age to come belonged to God. In John's Gospel this dualism does not have a temporal dimension (this age and the future age) but a spatial one (this world and the world that is above). Those who are from the world that is above belong to God, those from below belong to the Devil. How does one belong to the world that is above? By believing in the one who has come from that world, Jesus (3:31). Thus, in this Gospel Jesus' proclamation is no longer an apocalyptic appeal to repent in the face of a coming judgment; it is an appeal to believe in the one sent from heaven so as to have eternal life in the here and now. John, in short, presents a de-apocalypticized version of Jesus' teaching. (For a remnant of the older apocalyptic view, found even here, see 5:28–29.)

AT A GLANCE

BOX 8.8 The Gospel of John

1. The Gospel of John was the last canonical Gospel to be written, probably around 90–95 C.E.

2. It is traditionally ascribed to John the son of Zebedee, but there are reasons to doubt that ascription. It was written in Greek, probably outside of Palestine.

3. John is distinctive among the four Gospels: few of John's accounts of Jesus' words and deeds are in the Synoptics and few of the Synoptic accounts are in John.

4. John also has different emphases: Jesus' speeches focus on his divine origin and identity; and his miraculous deeds are "signs" meant to prove that what he says about himself is true.

5. John utilized a number of sources for constructing his account: a signs source (for Jesus' miracles), one or more discourse sources (for Jesus' long speeches), and a Passion narrative, roughly similar to those lying behind the Synoptics.

TAKE A STAND

1. Suppose you wanted to show a friend that John's Gospel must have been based on a number of sources, but the Synoptic Gospels were not among them. Make your case.

2. Argue for or against the following proposition: The portrayal of Jesus in the Gospel of John is fundamentally different from his portrayal in the Synoptics.

3. A friend is trying to convince you that the historical Jesus believed he was God, and she quotes several passages from the Gospel of John to prove it (e.g., 8:58; 10:30). What do you think? Do these verses demonstrate that the historical Jesus thought of himself as God?

SUGGESTIONS FOR FURTHER READING

Anderson, Paul N. *The Riddles of the Fourth Gospel: An Introduction.* 2d ed. Philadelphia: Fortress, 2001. A full coverage of all the historical and literary problems posed by the Gospel of John; good for beginning students.

Ashton, John. *Understanding the Fourth Gospel.* 2d ed. New York: Oxford University Press, 2009. A massive treatment of the major problems and critical issues of the Gospel of John, for advanced students.

Brown, Raymond. *The Community of the Beloved Disciple.* New York: Paulist, 1979. A superb and influential study that uses a socio-historical method to uncover the history of the community behind the Fourth Gospel.

Culpepper, Alan. *The Anatomy of the Fourth Gospel: A Study in Literary Design.* Philadelphia: Fortress, 1983. A study of John from a literary perspective, in which the history of the tradition is bypassed in order to understand the Gospel as a whole as it has come down to us; for somewhat more advanced students.

Kysar, Robert. *John the Maverick Gospel.* 3d ed. Atlanta: Westminster John Knox, 2007. All in all, probably the best introduction to the unique features of John's Gospel; for beginning students.

Martyn, J. Louis. *History and Theology in the Fourth Gospel.* 3d ed. Nashville: Abingdon, 2003. A fascinating and highly influential study of the social history that led to the development of John's traditions of Jesus.

Sloyan, Gerard S. *What Are They Saying about John?* 2d ed. New York: Paulist, 2006. A very nice introductory sketch of the modern scholarly debates concerning major aspects of John's Gospel.

Smith, D. Moody. *John among the Gospels: The Relationship in Twentieth-Century Research.* 2d ed. Minneapolis: Fortress, 2001. A very clear discussion of the relationship of John and the Synoptics, as seen by scholars of the twentieth century.

Smith, D. Moody. *The Theology of the Gospel of John.* Cambridge: Cambridge University Press, 1994. A clearly written and incisive discussion of the major themes of the Fourth Gospel; for beginning students.

KEY TERMS

Gospel of Judas	Johannine Prologue	signs	signs source
"I am" sayings	literary seams		

9

The Historical Jesus

WHAT TO EXPECT

It is one thing to study the Gospels as pieces of literature, to see what their authors thought about the meaning and importance of Jesus; that has been our approach to the Gospels so far. It is another thing to ask what the Gospels can tell us about the man Jesus himself—what he actually said, did, and experienced. That is the question we will be addressing in the present chapter.

The chapter starts by considering other sources for Jesus' life and death outside the New Testament. It then moves to consider our best historical sources, the New Testament Gospels. Even these pose problems for historians: they were written decades after the facts, by people who were not eyewitnesses, in a different language from Jesus', based on stories that had been circulating by word of mouth for decades and that had been changed and occasionally made up.

Still, by using methods devised by historians, we can study the Gospels to see what Jesus was really like, what he really said and did. The second part of the chapter will show that Jesus is best understood as a Jewish apocalypticist, who preached the need to repent in view of the coming judgment and the Kingdom of God, which was expected to arrive very soon.

Up to this point in our study we have examined the early Christian Gospels as discrete pieces of literature, uncovering their unique portrayals of Jesus through a variety of methods: literary-historical, redactional, comparative, and socio-historical. At every stage, we have been interested in learning how an author, and the sources he used, understood and portrayed the life of Jesus.

But at no point have we moved beyond these literary concerns to ask about what actually happened during the life of Jesus, to find out what he really said, did, and experienced. We are now in a position to explore these other, purely historical issues. Apart from what certain Christian authors said about Jesus long after the fact, what can we know about the man himself, about the actual life of the historical Jesus?

PROBLEMS WITH SOURCES

The only way that we can know what a person from the past said and did is by examining sources from the period that provide us with information. Most of our sources for the past are literary, that is, they are texts written by authors who refer to the person's words and deeds. But sources of this kind are not always reliable. Even eyewitness accounts are often contradictory, and contemporary observers not infrequently get the facts wrong. Moreover, most historical sources, for the distant past at least, do not derive from eyewitnesses but from later authors reporting the rumors and traditions they have heard.

For these reasons, historians have to devise criteria for determining which sources can be trusted and which ones cannot. Most historians would agree that for reconstructing a past event, the ideal situation would be to have sources that (*a*) are numerous, so they can be compared to one another; (*b*) derive from a time near the event itself, so that they are less likely to have been based on hearsay or legend; (*c*) were produced independently of one another, so that their authors were not in collusion; (*d*) do not contradict one another, so that one or more of them is not necessarily in error; (*e*) are internally consistent, suggesting a basic concern for reliability; and (*f*) are not biased toward the subject matter, so that their authors have not skewed their accounts to serve their own purposes.

Are the New Testament Gospels—our principal sources for reconstructing the life of Jesus—these kinds of sources? Before pursuing the question, let me emphasize that I am not passing judgment on the worth of these books, trying to undermine their authority for those who believe in them, or asking whether they are important as religious or theological documents. I am instead asking the question of the historian: are these books reliable for reconstructing what Jesus actually said and did?

As a first step toward an answer, we can ask whether any of the Gospel accounts can be corroborated by other ancient sources that describe the life and teachings of the historical Jesus.

As it turns out—this may surprise you—we do not have sources outside the New Testament that can assist us much in knowing what Jesus really said, did, and experienced. We have no birth records for Jesus, or accounts of his trial and death, or references at all to his words and deeds among any of the many writings that survive from his own day. Oddly enough his name is never even *mentioned* by any Roman pagan until about the year 115 C.E.—that is, some eighty-five years after his death. Even then we are given only a brief reference in the Roman historian **Tacitus**, who does at least indicate that Jesus was executed by Pontius Pilate. Not even Jewish sources of the first century mention him, with one exception: the Jewish historian Josephus, who gives a basic sketch of Jesus' life in his twenty-volume work called the *Antiquities of the Jews* (see box 3.2). As you will see in box 9.3, this brief statement is enough to let us know that Josephus at least knew about Jesus, but it does not really help us to decide what Jesus was really like.

Of course, as we have seen on several occasions, there were other Christian Gospels written about Jesus, which theoretically may shed some light on his life (see boxes 4.2, 5.5, 6.4, 6.5, and 8.5). But virtually all these Gospels were written long after Jesus died and are filled with legendary materials.

One might think that the letters of Paul or the other writings of the New Testament would provide us with valuable information about Jesus' life. Unfortunately, there are not many references to Jesus' words and deeds in Paul or any of these other authors (who were more interested in his death and resurrection than his life).

For all these reasons, we are more or less restricted to our four earliest surviving accounts of Jesus' life—Matthew, Mark, Luke, and John—if we want to discover what he actually said, did, and experienced. It's a great advantage, of course, to have four different sources of Jesus' life—that's far more than we have for most people from antiquity! The problem is that these books were not written to provide objective biographical information about Jesus. They were *Gospels*, that is, proclamations of the good news that Jesus brings salvation to the world. The books were written decades after the events they narrate, by people who were not eyewitnesses, who are telling the tales in a different language from Jesus', based on oral traditions that the authors themselves had heard and that had circulated by word of mouth decade after decade before being written down. These traditions were modified when they were told and

WHAT DO YOU THINK?

BOX 9.1 Did Jesus Exist?

Scholars are widely convinced that some of the stories about Jesus in the New Testament are not historically accurate, but have been changed or even "made up" by his followers in the years after his death. But is it possible that Jesus himself was made up? That he never existed? That he was "invented" by later Jews who wanted to create a savior figure who never actually lived?

That is the view set forth in a number of recent books—most of them not written by scholars but by sensationalists wanting to cause a stir—and on a number of Internet websites. The authors of these claims point out that Jesus is not mentioned in any non-Christian sources of the first century except Josephus; moreover, they claim that even the comments about Jesus in Josephus were not original, but were inserted into his writings by later Christians. Furthermore, since Jesus is so much like other "divine men" (see pp. 15–18 for example), he may well have been fabricated by fervent Jewish religious persons who wanted someone to worship like the pagan sons of God.

There are insurmountable problems with this view, however, as scholars have long known (see the book *Did Jesus Exist?* by Ehrman in For Further Reading). For one thing, even though there are no references to the historical Jesus in early Roman sources, the references to him in Christian sources are all over the place, in surviving authors and in sources behind the Gospels: Paul, Mark, Q, M, L, John's Signs Source and Discourse Sources, the Gospel of Peter, the Gospel of Thomas—all of them independent of one another. No one person or group *could* have made up Jesus. He was talked about all over the map. Moreover, the traditions can easily be traced back to a year or so after the traditional date of Jesus' death: some of them contain Aramaic words, which reveal that they date from the earliest years of Palestinian Aramaic-speaking Christianity. It is especially striking, as well, that one of our surviving authors, Paul, indicates that he personally knew Jesus' own brother James and his closest disciple Peter (Gal. 1:18–2:10). If Jesus never existed, you would think that his brother and best friend would know about it!

For these reasons—and many others—scholars have virtually no doubts whatsoever: whatever one wants to say about Jesus, it is clear at least that he existed.

retold, and modified further when written down (see Chapter 4). How can these Gospels be used—not to tell us what the authors *thought* about Jesus (the task we pursued in the preceding chapters), but to find out what actually happened in his life?

 USING OUR SOURCES

Some Rules of Thumb

There are in fact some basic methodological principles that can be used to determine what probably happened during the life of Jesus, using our surviving sources. These principles include the following:

1. The earlier the better. Sources closest in time to Jesus' life obviously are nearer to the facts

than those written much later. This is not to say that late sources (e.g., the Gospels of John and *Thomas*) cannot contain historically reliable information. But generally speaking, earlier sources have had less time to be modified and embellished. And so, early sources such as Mark and Q (as it is reconstructed) are most valuable.

2. The more the better. If there is a tradition about Jesus found in two or more sources independently of one another, then it is more likely to go back to Jesus than a tradition found in only one source. The criterion works only when the sources are *not* dependent on each other: for example, when Mark and John and Paul, none of whom knew the others' work, independently indicate that Jesus preached mainly to Jews, or that he had brothers, or that

he was crucified—then chances are improved that these traditions are historical. (Note: a story found in Matthew, Mark, and Luke is *not* multiply attested, since Matthew and Luke would have gotten it from Mark.)

3. The more it works against a bias the better. All sources, of course, are biased. But if there is a tradition found in a source that seems to work *against* the Christian perspective of the source itself, then you can be pretty sure that the author of that source did not *make up* the story. If he had, he would have made it coincide with his own bias. And so, when the Gospels speak of Jesus being baptized—would Christians (who thought that the spiritually superior person always baptized the spiritually inferior one) have made it up? It seems unlikely. Or when they say that Jesus came from Nazareth (a little one-horse hamlet that no one had heard of), why would they have invented *that*? Sometimes this rule is described as **"the criterion of dissimilarity"**: if a tradition of Jesus is dissimilar to what Christians telling the stories would have wanted to say about him (e.g., that he was baptized, or that he came from Nazareth, or that one of his closest followers betrayed him), then it is probably authentic.

4. The more contextually credible the better. If there are traditions about Jesus that cannot fit into a first-century Palestinian Jewish context, they are probably not authentic. If, for example, there is a clever saying of Jesus that works as a pun in Greek (the language of the Gospels) but not in Aramaic (the language he really spoke), then it is probably not something he actually said.

When these rules are applied carefully to the traditions of Jesus, it becomes clear that he was a Jew like many other Jews of his day, who worshiped the God of the Jews and followed his Law. But as we have already seen, there were lots of different kinds of Jews in the first century (you may want to review Chapter 3 at this point). What kind was Jesus?

In order to make sense of our earliest and best preserved traditions about Jesus, it is important to make a brief detour to consider a form of Judaism that was prevalent in Jesus' day, a form of Juda-

ism that scholars have labeled "apocalyptic," from the word "unveiling" or "revealing." Many Jews of Jesus' day believed that God had revealed the truth that he was soon to overthrow the mysterious forces of evil (e.g., the Devil and his demons) in a mighty show of power. What more fully was this world view of apocalypticism, and how can it help explain what Jesus said and did?

JEWISH APOCALYPTICISM

We know about Jewish **apocalypticism** from a number of sources, including the Dead Sea Scrolls (written from around the time of Jesus) and other writings from the time. Apocalypticists were concerned with the question of why the people of God were suffering (e.g., through foreign oppression), and they called into question the view that had held sway for many centuries: that people suffered because they had done something wrong and God was punishing them. If that older explanation were correct, why is it that when people repent and return to God they *still* suffer? Moreover, how can one explain that the righteous suffer—often even more than the wicked—sometimes for doing what is *right*?

Jewish apocalypticists maintained that God's people were suffering not because God was punishing them for evil, but because there were evil forces in the world who were opposed to God and his people and were bent on harming and destroying all those who sided with God. But, according to this view, God was still sovereign over the world, and he would soon vindicate his name and his people by bringing an end to the suffering and the evil forces who were causing it. He would then bring in his new Kingdom on earth, in which good, peace, and justice would prevail forever.

More specifically, Jewish apocalypticists as a whole subscribed to four major tenets: dualism, pessimism, vindication, and imminence.

Dualism

Jewish apocalypticists were dualists. They maintained that there were two fundamental components to all of reality: the forces of good and the forces of evil. The forces of good were headed by God himself, the forces of evil by his superhuman

BOX 9.2   The Apostles as Guarantors of the Truth?

Some people have maintained that the Gospels must be historically accurate because the apostles of Jesus would surely have not allowed false information to circulate concerning Jesus while they were still alive and active in the Christian communities and able to verify the accounts that were being told of him.

On the surface this view seems plausible—but not when you start thinking about how stories of Jesus were orally transmitted and then written down over the decades. When the Gospels were written, some thirty-five to sixty-five years after Jesus' death, most of the disciples would have already died. The Gospels were written in other lands, by people who didn't know the disciples. Moreover, even before that the twelve apostles could not be everywhere at once. The stories, however, were circulating in cities, towns, and villages all over the Mediterranean. As a result, it would have been impossible for the apostles to serve as "watchdogs" to make sure traditions were never invented or changed.

There is only one way to know whether stories about Jesus were ever made up or modified. That's by looking at all the stories, comparing them with one another, and deciding for yourself. In fact, no one really thinks that stories were never made up: consider the story of Jesus emerging from his tomb tall as a skyscraper, with the cross walking behind him, in one of our earliest Gospels, the *Gospel of Peter*. Or the stories of Jesus as a mischievous young boy in the *Infancy Gospel of Thomas*. *Someone* was making up stories! And that stories were often changed is equally easy to prove. Simply compare the same story told by any two Gospel writers of the New Testament in detail, and in almost every instance you will find differences, great and small.

The apostles no doubt did tell the stories of Jesus' life as they remembered them. But these came to be modified and embellished over time, and other stories came to be made up. The task of the historian is to determine which of the surviving stories are historically accurate and which are not.

---

enemy, sometimes called Satan, Beelzebub, or the Devil. On the side of God were the good angels; on the side of the Devil were the demons. On the side of God were righteousness and life; on the side of the Devil were sin and death. These forces were cosmic powers to which human beings were subject and with which they had to be aligned. No one was in neutral territory. People stood either with God or with Satan, in the light or in darkness, in the truth or in error.

This apocalyptic dualism had clear historical implications in that all of history could be divided into two ages: the present age and the age to come. The present age was the age of sin and evil. The powers of darkness were in the ascendancy, and those who sided with God were made to suffer by those in control of this world. Sin, disease, famine, violence, and death were rampant. For some unknown reason, God had relinquished control of this age to the powers of evil—and things were getting worse.

At the end of this age, however, God would reassert himself, intervening in history and destroying the forces of evil. After a cataclysmic break in which all that was opposed to God would be annihilated, God would bring in a new age. In this new age, there would be no more suffering or pain; there would be no more hatred, despair, war, disease, or death. God would be the ruler of all, in a kingdom that would never end.

Pessimism

Even though, in the long run, everything would work out for those who sided with God, in the short term things did not look good. Jewish apocalypticists maintained that those who sided with God were going to suffer in this age, and there was nothing they could do to stop it. The forces of evil were going to grow in power as they attempted to wrest sovereignty over this world away from God.

BOX 9.3   The Testimony of Flavius Josephus

Probably the most controversial passage in all of Josephus's writings is his description of Jesus in book 18 of *The Antiquities of the Jews.*

> At this time there appeared Jesus, a wise man, if indeed one should call him a man. For he was a doer of startling deeds, a teacher of people who receive the truth with pleasure. And he gained a following both among many Jews and among many of Greek origin. He was the Messiah. And when Pilate, because of an accusation made by the leading men among us, condemned him to the cross, those who had loved him previously did not cease to do so. For he appeared to them on the third day, living again, just as the divine prophets had spoken of these and countless other wondrous things about him. And up until this very day the tribe of Christians, named after him, has not died out. (*Ant.* 18. 3. 3)

This testimony to Jesus has long puzzled scholars. Why would Josephus, a devout Jew who never became a Christian, profess faith in Jesus by suggesting that he was something more than a man, calling him the messiah (rather than merely saying that others *thought* he was), and claiming that he was raised from the dead in fulfillment of prophecy?

Many scholars have recognized that the problem can be solved by looking at how, and by whom, Josephus's writings were transmitted over the centuries. For in fact they were not preserved by Jews, many of whom considered him to be a traitor because of his conduct during and after the war with Rome (see box 3.2). Rather, it was Christians who copied Josephus's writings through the ages. Is it possible that this reference to Jesus has been beefed up a bit by a Christian scribe who wanted to make Josephus appear more appreciative of the "true faith"?

If we take out the Christianized portions of the passage, what we are left with, according to one of the most convincing recent studies, is the following:

> At this time there appeared Jesus, a wise man. For he was a doer of startling deeds, a teacher of people who receive the truth with pleasure. And he gained a following both among many Jews and among many of Greek origin. And when Pilate, because of an accusation made by the leading men among us, condemned him to the cross, those who had loved him previously did not cease to do so. And up until this very day the tribe of Christians, named after him, has not died out. (Meier 1991, 61)

There was no thought of being able to improve the human condition through mass education or advanced technology. The righteous could not make their lives better because the forces of evil were in control, and those who sided with God were opposed by those who were much stronger than they. Things would get worse and worse until the very end, when, quite literally, all hell would break loose.

Vindication

At the end, when the suffering of God's people was at its height, God would finally intervene on their behalf and vindicate his name. In the apocalyptic perspective, God was not only the creator of this world but also its redeemer. His vindication would be universal; it would affect the entire world, not simply the Jewish nation. Jewish apocalypticists maintained that the entire creation had become corrupt because of the presence of sin and the power of Satan. This universal corruption required a universal redemption; God would destroy all that is evil and create a new heaven and a new earth, one in which the forces of evil would have no place.

Different apocalypticists had different views concerning how God would bring about this new creation, even though they all claimed to have received the details in a revelation from God. In some apocalyptic scenarios, God was to send a human messiah to lead the troops of the children of light into battle against the forces of evil. In others, God was to send a kind of cosmic judge of the earth, sometimes also called the messiah or the Son of Man, to bring about a cataclysmic overthrow of the demonic powers that oppressed the children of light.

This final vindication would involve a day of judgment for all people. Those who had aligned themselves with the powers of evil would face the Almighty Judge and render an account of what they had done; those who had remained faithful to the true God would be rewarded and brought into his eternal kingdom. Moreover, this judgment applied not only to people who happened to be living at the time of the end. One could not side with the powers of evil, oppress the people of God, die prosperous and contented, and get away with it. God would allow no one to escape. He was going to raise all people bodily from the dead to receive their reward or punishment: eternal bliss for those who had taken his side, eternal torment for everyone else.

Imminence

According to Jewish apocalypticists, this vindication of God was going to happen very soon. Standing in the tradition of the prophets of the Hebrew Bible, apocalypticists maintained that God had revealed to them the course of history and that the end was almost here. Those who were evil had to repent before it was too late. Those who were good, who were suffering as a result, were to hold on, for it would not be long before God would intervene by sending a savior, possibly on the clouds of heaven, to pass judgment on the people of the earth and bring the good kingdom to those who had remained faithful to his Law. Indeed, the end was right around the corner. In the words of one first-century Jewish apocalypticist: "Truly I tell you, there are some standing here who will not taste death until they see that the kingdom of God has come with power." These, in fact, are the words of Jesus (Mark 9:1). Or as he says elsewhere, "Truly I tell you, this generation will not pass away before all these things have taken place" (Mark 13:30).

JESUS IN HIS APOCALYPTIC CONTEXT

Some of the earliest traditions about Jesus portray him as a Jewish apocalypticist who responded to the political and social crises of his day, including the domination of his nation by a foreign power,

by proclaiming that his generation was living at the end of the age, and that God would soon intervene on behalf of his people. He would send a cosmic judge, the Son of Man, who would destroy the forces of evil and set up God's kingdom. In preparation for his coming, the people of Israel needed to repent and turn to God, trusting him as a kindly parent and loving one another as his special children. Those who refused to accept this message would be liable to the punishment of God.

Is this ancient portrayal of Jesus, which is embodied in a number of our oldest traditions, historically accurate? Was Jesus a Jewish apocalypticist?

This is one of the most hotly debated questions among New Testament researchers today. Even so, the majority of critical scholars who have studied the question carefully over the past hundred years have been convinced that this is precisely what Jesus was. The reasons have to do with our surviving sources. The earliest traditions about Jesus portray Jesus consistently as proclaiming an apocalyptic message. This is the case of Q (e.g., Luke 17:24, 26–27, 30; cf. Matt 24:27; 37–39); Mark (8:38–9:1; 13:24–27, 30), M (Matt 13:40–43), and L (Luke 21:34–36). These sources are all independent of one another. Moreover, some of these traditions pass the "criterion of dissimilarity." And all of them are contextually credible, given the circumstance that we know of other Jews making a similar proclamation in Jesus' day.

Apart from these particular passages that are found in our earliest sources, one especially compelling reason for thinking that Jesus must have been an apocalypticist is an argument that I sometimes call "the beginning and end as keys to the middle." The argument is a bit involved, but it focuses on what we know with relative certainly about both the beginning of Jesus' public ministry and its aftermath, and it makes best sense that Jesus himself is the connecting link between that beginning and that end.

THE BEGINNING AND END AS KEYS TO THE MIDDLE

There is little doubt about how Jesus began his ministry: he was baptized by John. The story is independently attested by multiple sources; Mark, Q, and John all begin with Jesus' associating with the Baptist. Also, it is not a story the early Christians would have been inclined to invent, since it was commonly understood that the one doing the baptizing was spiritually superior to the one being baptized (i.e., the story passes the criterion of dissimilarity). Moreover, the event is contextually credible. John appears to have been one of the "prophets" who arose during the first century of the Common Era in Palestine. Somewhat like first-century Jewish prophets called Theudas and the Egyptian (see box 9.9), he predicted that God was about to destroy his enemies and reward his people, as he had done in the days of old. And like them, he was destroyed by the ruling officials.

John the Baptist appears to have preached a message of coming destruction and salvation. Mark portrays him as a prophet in the wilderness who proclaims the fulfillment of the prophecy of Isaiah that God would again bring his people from the wilderness into the Promised Land (Mark 1:2–8). When this happened the first time, according to the Hebrew Scriptures, it meant destruction for the nations already inhabiting the land. In preparation for this imminent event, John baptized those who repented of their sins, that is, those who were ready to enter into this coming kingdom. The Q source gives further information, for

WHAT DO YOU THINK?

BOX 9.4   Explaining Away the Apocalyptic Traditions:
Seeking the Lost

Since one cannot very well deny that our earliest surviving sources portray Jesus as an apocalypticist, one interesting approach taken by scholars who do not see him this way is to claim that he was portrayed differently in the earliest *non*-surviving sources. One of the most popular proposals along this line involves the Q source, which, as I've pointed out, we no longer have (see p. 61). This has not stopped scholars from telling us all sorts of things about it— not only what its precise contents were (and, more important, what they were not) but also what the communities that produced it were like and what had happened in their social lives together. Not bad for a nonexistent source!

This is an important issue precisely because of the undeniable fact that if Q was the source for the materials in common between Matthew and Luke that are not found in Mark, then it was loaded with apocalyptic traditions. If one does not want to portray Jesus as an apocalypticist, how can one get around this problem? By arguing that Q in fact came out in multiple editions.

According to this line, the *original* edition of Q did not have the apocalyptic traditions about Jesus. These were only added later, when the document was edited by Christians who were a bit obsessed with the imminent end of the age. Thus, according

to this theory, Q as we have it (well, even though we don't have it), may be an apocalyptic document. But in fact it provides evidence of a nonapocalyptic Jesus.

This proposal is principally held by scholars who maintain that Jesus was a witty and compelling teacher, but not an apocalyptic preacher of the coming end of the age. And it's easy to see the drawing power of the theory: in the earliest edition of this nonexistent source, Jesus is said to have delivered a lot of terrific one-liners, but uttered not a word about a coming Son of Man, sent from heaven in judgment.

Still, the proposal is enormously problematic. To reconstruct what we think was in Q is hypothetical enough. But at least in doing so we have some hard evidence, since we do have traditions that are repeated verbatim in Matthew and Luke (but not found in Mark), and we have to account for them in *some* way. But to go further and insist that we know what was *not* in the source—for example, all its apocalyptic sayings—really goes far beyond what we can know, however appealing such "knowledge" might be. And remember: these sayings *are* found in the only two documents that provide us our only solid evidence for the contents of Q!

What evidence, however, exists to *disprove* this particular theory of Q? Well, strictly speaking, none. The document doesn't exist!

here John preaches a clear message of apocalyptic judgment to the crowds that have come out to see him: "Who warned you to flee from the wrath to come? Bear fruits worthy of repentance. . . . Even now the ax is lying at the root of the trees; every tree therefore that does not bear good fruit is cut down and thrown into the fire" (Luke 3:7–9). Judgment is imminent (the ax is at the root of the tree) and it will not be a pretty sight. In preparation, Jews can no longer rely on having a covenantal relationship with God: "Do not begin to say to yourselves, 'We have Abraham as our ancestor'; for I tell you, God is able from these stones to raise up children to Abraham" (Luke 3:8). Instead, they must repent and turn to God anew by doing the things he requires of them.

Jesus went out into the wilderness to be baptized by this prophet. But why did he go? Since nobody compelled him, he must have gone to John, instead of to someone else, because he agreed with John's message. Jesus did not join the Pharisees, who emphasized the scrupulous observance of the Torah, or align himself with the Sadducees, who focused on the worship of God through the Temple cult. He did not associate with the Essenes, who formed monastic communities to maintain their own ritual purity, or subscribe to the teachings of the "fourth philosophy," which advocated a violent rejection of Roman domination. He associated with an apocalyptic prophet in the wilderness who anticipated the imminent end of the age.

That was how Jesus began. Is it possible, however, that he changed his views during the course of his ministry and began to focus on something other than what John preached? This is certainly possible, but it would not explain why so many

WHAT DO YOU THINK?

BOX 9.5 Explaining Away the Apocalyptic Traditions: Getting a Date

One of the most prominent scholars engaged in the study of the historical Jesus is a witty and indomitable historian named John Dominic Crossan, whose books on Jesus have become best sellers. Crossan does not think Jesus was an apocalypticist. What does he do with the fact that our earliest sources, Q, Mark, M, and L, portray Jesus as an apocalypticist? He denies that these are our earliest sources.

Crossan engages in a detailed analysis to argue that *other* sources not found in the New Testament are earlier than the sources that are. These others include such documents as the "Egerton Gospel," a fragmentary text from the second century that contains four stories about Jesus; the *Gospel of the Hebrews*, which, as we have seen, no longer survives, but is quoted a bit by some church fathers in the late second to the early fifth centuries; and parts of the *Gospel of Peter*, which survives again only in fragments. Such sources, Crossan claims, provide more reliable access to Jesus than the New Testament Gospels, which everyone, including Crossan, dates to the first century.

Again, one can see the appeal of such an argument for someone who denies that Jesus was an apocalypticist. For if in fact the *Gospel of the Hebrews*, to pick one example, is older than the Gospel of Mark, even though it's never mentioned or even *alluded* to until 190 C.E. or so (and is seen by nearly everyone else, therefore, as a second-century production), then Mark's apocalyptic Jesus could well be a later creation formed from the nonapocalyptic Jesus of the *Gospel of the Hebrews*!

But this strikes most scholars as a case of special pleading. Most recognize clear and certain reasons for dating the New Testament Gospels to the first century. But giving yet earlier dates to noncanonical Gospels that are, in most cases, not quoted or even mentioned by early Christian writers until many, many decades later seems to be overly speculative and driven by an ultimate objective of claiming that Jesus was not an apocalypticist even though our earliest sources indicate that he was.

apocalyptic sayings are found on Jesus' own lips in the earliest sources for his life. Even more seriously, it would not explain what clearly emerged in the aftermath of his ministry. I have argued that we are relatively certain about how Jesus' ministry began; we are even more certain about what happened in its wake. After Jesus' death, those who believed in him established communities of followers throughout the Mediterranean. We have a good idea of what these Christians believed because some of them have left us writings. These earliest writings are imbued with apocalyptic thinking. The earliest Christians were Jews who believed that they were living at the end of the age and that Jesus himself was to return from heaven as a cosmic judge of the earth to punish those who opposed God and to reward the faithful (e.g., see 1 Thess 4:13–18; 1 Cor 15:51–57, writings from the earliest Christian author, Paul). The church that emerged in Jesus' wake was apocalyptic.

Thus, Jesus' ministry began with his association with John the Baptist, an apocalyptic prophet, and ended with the establishment of the Christian church, a community of apocalyptic Jews who be-

lieved in him. The fact that Jesus' ministry began apocalyptically and ended apocalyptically gives us the key to interpreting what happened in between. The only connection between the apocalyptic John and the apocalyptic Christian church was Jesus himself. How could both the beginning and the end be apocalyptic if the middle was not as well? Jesus himself must have been a Jewish apocalypticist.

To call Jesus an apocalypticist does not mean that Jesus was saying and doing exactly what every other Jewish apocalypticist was saying and doing. We are still interested in learning specifically what Jesus taught and did during his life. Knowing that his overall message was apocalyptic, however, can help us understand other aspects of the tradition about him that can be established as authentic. For our purposes here, I can give only a brief sketch of his deeds and teachings.

THE APOCALYPTIC DEEDS OF JESUS

The Crucifixion

The most certain element of the tradition about Jesus is that he was crucified on the orders of the Roman prefect of Judea, Pontius Pilate. The crucifixion is independently attested in a wide array of sources and is not the sort of thing that believers would want to make up about the person proclaimed to be the powerful Son of God (see box 5.2). Why, historically, was Jesus crucified? This is the question that every reconstruction of the life of Jesus has to answer, and some of the answers proffered over the years have been none too plausible. If, for example, Jesus had simply been a great moral teacher, a gentle rabbi who did nothing more than urge his devoted followers to love God and one another, or an itinerant philosopher who urged them to abandon their possessions and live a simple life, depending on no one but God (see box 9.6), then he would scarcely have been seen as a threat to the Romans and nailed to a cross. Great moral teachers were not crucified—unless their teachings were considered subversive. Nor were charismatic leaders with large followings—unless their followers were thought to be dangerous.

Figure 9.1 Jesus, the Good Shepherd. This is one of the earliest paintings of Jesus to survive from antiquity (from about two centuries after Jesus' death), from the catacomb of San Callisto in Rome.

WHAT DO YOU THINK?

BOX 9.6　Was Jesus a Cynic Philosopher?

A number of recent American scholars have proposed that Jesus should be understood not as a Jewish apocalypticist but as a kind of Jewish **Cynic philosopher**. The term "cynic" in this context does not carry the same connotations that it does for us when we say that someone is "cynical." When referring to the Greco-Roman world, it denotes a particular philosophical position that was advocated by a number of well-known public characters.

The term "cynic" actually means "dog." It was a designation given to a certain group of philosophers by their opponents, who claimed that they lived like wild mongrels. In some respects, the designation was apt, for Cynics urged people to abandon the trappings of society and live "according to nature." For them, the most important things in life were those over which people could have some control, such as their attitudes toward others, their likes and dislikes, and their opinions. Other things outside of their control were of no importance. Followers of the cynics were therefore admonished not to burden themselves with material possessions, such as nice houses or fine clothes, or to worry about how to earn money or what to eat. To this extent, the Cynics were closely aligned in their views to the Stoic philosophers. They differed, however, in the degree of their social respectability. Cynics rejected most constraints imposed by society, even society's ethical mores, so as to live "naturally." The Cynics who practiced what they preached had virtually no possessions, often lived on the streets, rarely bathed, begged for a living, performed private bodily functions in public places, and spent their days haranguing people to adopt their philosophical views. They were especially renowned for abusing people on street corners and in marketplaces, where they cas-

tigated those who thought that the meaning of life could be found in wealth or in any of the other trappings of society.

Scholars who think that Jesus was a Jewish teacher who embraced Cynic values point out that many of his teachings sound remarkably similar to what we hear from the Cynics. Jesus' followers were to abandon all their possessions (Matt 6:19–21; Mark 11:21–22); they were not to be concerned about what to wear or what to eat (Matt 6:25–33); they were to live with the bare essentials and accept whatever was given to them by others (Mark 6:6–13; Luke 10:1–12); they were to condemn those who rejected their message (Luke 10:1–12); and they were to expect to be misunderstood and mistreated (Matt 5:11–12). Was not Jesus, then, a Jewish Cynic?

Other scholars believe that this is taking matters too far. All of our ancient sources portray Jesus as quoting the Hebrew Scriptures to support his perspective, but never does he quote any of the Greek or Roman philosophers or urge his followers to adhere to their teachings. Moreover, the message of his teaching is not, ultimately, about living in accordance with nature. It is about the God of Israel, the true interpretation of his law, and the coming judgment against those who are unrepentant. Thus, while it is true that Jesus' followers were told not to concern themselves with wealth and the trappings of society, these teachings were not rooted in a concern for promoting self-sufficiency in a harsh and capricious world. Rather, his followers were not to be tied to the concerns of this age because it was passing away and a new age was soon to come. Jesus may have appeared to an outsider to be similar in some ways to an itinerant Cynic philosopher, but his message was in fact quite different.

The subversive teachers from Jesus' day were labeled as prophets, people who proclaimed the imminent downfall of the social order and the advent of a new kingdom to replace the corrupt ruling powers. According to the traditions recorded in the New Testament and Josephus, John the Baptist was imprisoned and executed because of his preaching; according to the Gospels he directed his words against Herod Antipas, appointed to rule over the Promised Land. Jesus was to fare no better. Those who prophesied the triumph of God were liable to the judgment of Rome.

In the case of Jesus, however, it is not altogether clear that Rome initiated the proceedings. It appears that Jesus' message was directed not only against the Roman powers but also against the Jewish leadership of Jerusalem that supported them, as seen in another tradition that can be established beyond reasonable doubt as authentic.

The Temple Incident

We know with relative certainty that Jesus predicted that the Temple was soon to be destroyed by God. Predictions of this sort are contextually credible, given what we have learned about other prophets in the days of Jesus. Jesus' own predictions are independently attested in a wide range of sources (cf. Mark 13:1; 14:58; John 2:19; Acts 6:14). Moreover, it is virtually certain that some days before his death Jesus entered the Temple, overturned some of the tables that were set up inside, and generally caused a disturbance.

The account is multiply attested (Mark 11 and John 2), and it is consistent with the predictions scattered throughout the tradition about the coming destruction of the Temple. Therefore, it is unlikely that Christians invented the story in order to show their own opposition to the Temple, as some scholars have claimed. It is possible, however, that Christians modified the tradition in some ways, as they modified most of the stories that they retold over the years. In the earliest surviving account, Jesus displays a superhuman show of strength, shutting down the entire Temple cult by an act of his will (Mark 11:16). But the Temple complex was immense, and there would have been armed guards present to prevent any major disturbances. Mark's account, then, may represent an exaggeration of the effect of Jesus' actions.

It is hard to know whether Jesus' words during this episode should be accepted as authentic. He quotes the prophets Isaiah and Jeremiah to indicate that the Temple cult has become corrupt, calling it "a den of thieves." Indeed, it is possible that Jesus, like the Essenes, believed that the worship of God in the Temple had gotten out of hand and that the Sadducees in control had abused their power and privileges to their own end. But it is also possible that Jesus' actions are to be taken as a kind of enacted parable, comparable to the symbolic actions performed by a number of the prophets in the Hebrew Scriptures (see box 9.7). By overturning the tables and causing a disturbance, Jesus could

WHAT DO YOU THINK?

BOX 9.7 The Temple Incident as an Enacted Parable

Parables are simple stories that are invested with deeper spiritual meaning. An **enacted parable** is a simple action that carries a symbolic, spiritual significance. In the Hebrew Bible, prophets were sometimes told by God to perform a symbolic action to accompany their message. For some interesting examples, read Jer 13:1–14; 19:1–15; and 32:1–44, and Ezek 4:1–17. One of the most dramatic occurs in Isa 20:1–6 (one of the first recorded instances of streaking in human history).

Is it possible that Jesus' actions in the Temple were enacted parables meant to symbolize something far greater than themselves? It is indeed possible that by overturning the tables and disrupting a small part of the Temple operation, Jesus was making a symbolic gesture to indicate what was to happen in the coming destruction. Such an action would fit well with the predictions of the Temple's destruction by Jesus throughout the early (and late) traditions.

Jesus was by no means the first Jewish prophet to attack the Temple. Some 600 years earlier the prophet Jeremiah pronounced a judgment that was quite similar (Jer 7:1–15; 26:1–15) and received a comparable response from the leaders in charge of the place (see Jer 26:8, 11). This may be one additional piece of evidence to suggest that Jesus saw himself principally as a prophetic spokesperson of God urging the people of Israel to repent in light of the coming judgment.

have been projecting what was to happen when his words against the Temple came to fruition, foreshadowing the destruction of the Temple that he anticipated was soon to come.

But how did Jesus' prediction that the Temple would be destroyed fit into his broader apocalyptic message? Two possible answers suggest themselves. It may be that he believed that in the new age there would be a new Temple, totally sanctified for the worship of God. This was the view of the apocalyptically minded Essenes. Or it may be that Jesus believed there would be no need for a temple at all in the kingdom that was coming, since there would no longer be any evil or sin, and therefore no need for the cultic sacrifice of animals to bring atonement. In either case, the implication of Jesus' actions is clear: for Jesus, the Temple cult and the officials in charge of it were a temporary measure at best and a corruption of God's plan at worst. They would soon be done away with when the kingdom arrived.

This message did not escape the notice of those in charge of the Temple, the chief priests who also had jurisdiction over the local affairs of the people in Jerusalem. These priests, principally Sadducees, were the chief liaison with the Roman officials, in particular, the Roman prefect Pilate. For these reasons, the most plausible scenario for explaining Jesus' death is that Jesus' apocalyptic message, including its enactment in the Temple, angered some of the chief priests on the scene. These priests recognized how explosive the situation could become during the Passover feast, given the tendency of the celebration to become a silent protest that might erupt into something much worse. The Sadducean priests conferred with one another, had Jesus arrested, and questioned him for his words against the Temple. Knowing that they could not execute Jesus themselves, perhaps because the Romans did not allow the Jewish authorities to execute criminals (the matter is debated among historians), they delivered him over to Pilate, who had no qualms at all about disposing of yet one more troublemaker who might cause a major disturbance.

Jesus' Associations

One other aspect of Jesus' public ministry can be spoken of with confidence by the historian, and here again an apocalyptic context provides some important insights. With whom did Jesus associate? There is little doubt that he had twelve followers whom he chose as his special disciples; the Gospels of Mark (3:16) and John (6:67) and the apostle Paul (1 Cor 15:5) all mention "the Twelve." Curiously, even though the Synoptics give different names for some of these followers (Mark 3:13–19; Matt 10:1–4; and Luke 6:12–16), all three Gospels know that there were twelve of them. But why twelve? Why not eight? Or fourteen?

The number twelve makes sense from an apocalyptic perspective. The present age was coming to an end; God was bringing in his new kingdom for his people. Those who repented and did what God wanted them to do, as revealed in the teachings of Jesus, would enter into that kingdom. This new people of God would arise out of the old. Just as Israel had started out as twelve tribes headed by twelve patriarchs (according to the book of Genesis), so the new people of God would emerge from old Israel with twelve leaders at their head: "Truly I tell you, at the renewal of all things, when the Son of Man is seated on the throne of his glory, you who have followed me will also sit on twelve thrones, judging the twelve tribes of Israel" (Matt 19:28; from Q). Thus the disciples represented the new people of God, those who had repented in anticipation of the kingdom that would come soon, on the day of judgment. This appears to be why Jesus chose twelve of them.

We know that Jesus also associated with two other groups of people, whom early sources designate as "tax collectors" and "sinners." We can accept this tradition as authentic because references to these groups are scattered throughout our sources (e.g., see Mark 2:15; Luke 7:34 [Q]; Luke 15:1–2 [L]); moreover, this is probably not the sort of tradition that a follower of Jesus would be inclined to make up. "Tax collectors" refers to local Jews employed by regional tax corporations to collect the revenues to be paid to Rome. These persons were unpopular in first-century Palestine because they supported Roman rule and sometimes grew rich through their association with the imperial government. For these reasons, tax collectors had a bad reputation among many of the Jewish subjects of Rome; they were not the sort of people that pious religious leaders were supposed to befriend. "Sinners" does not necessarily refer to prostitutes,

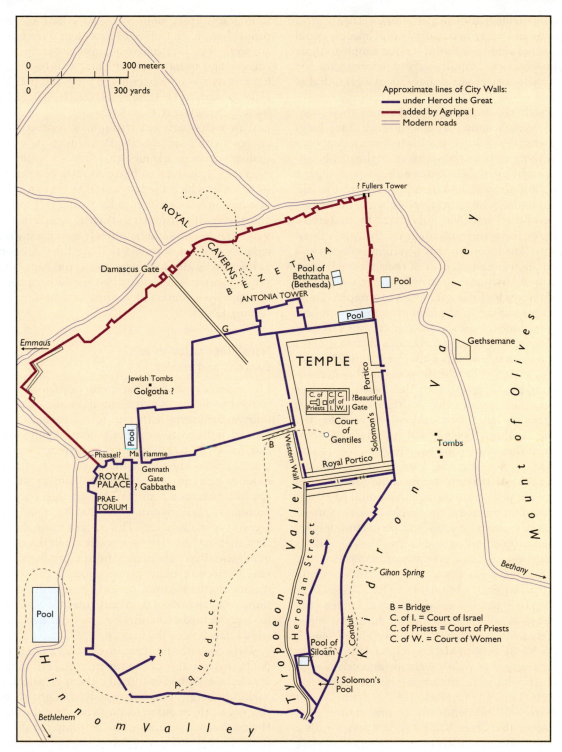

Figure 9.2 Jerusalem in the First Century C.E.

as is sometimes thought, although certainly prostitutes and other habitually "sinful" people could be included in their ranks. It refers simply to those who were not scrupulous about observing the law of God. Jesus appears to have spent a good deal of his time with such folk.

From an apocalyptic perspective, these associations make sense. We have numerous teachings of Jesus in which he proclaims that the kingdom is coming not to those who are righteous but to those who are sinful. We have already seen that he does not associate in a friendly way with the religious leaders who scrupulously observe the regulations of the Torah, faithfully attend to the Temple cult, or focus their attention on their own ritual purity. The kingdom that is coming is open to all who are willing to repent of their misdeeds, even the most lowly; they need only turn to God in love and receive his loving acceptance in return. Those who are willing to abandon everything to follow the teachings of Jesus, to turn from their evil ways and love God above all else and their neighbors as themselves—whether they are from the lower social classes, like the impoverished fishermen among the disciples, from the scandalous upper classes, like some of the wealthier tax collectors, or from the ranks of the religious outcasts, like the sinners—all such people will enter into the kingdom of God that is soon to arrive.

Finally, it is clear that Jesus was widely known to have associated with women and ministered to them in public, even though this would have been unusual for a first-century rabbi. Still, the importance of women for Jesus' ministry is multiply attested in our earliest traditions. Mark, L (Luke's special source), and even Thomas, for example, indicate that Jesus was accompanied by women in his travels (Mark 15:40–41; Luke 8:1–3; *Gosp. Thom.* 114). Mark and L also indicate that women provided Jesus with financial support during his ministry, evidently serving as his patrons (Mark 15:40–41; Luke 8:1–3). In both Mark and John, Jesus is said to have engaged in public dialogue and debate with women who were not among his immediate followers (John 4:1–42; Mark 7:24–30). Both Gospels also record, independently of one another, the tradition that Jesus had physical contact with a woman who anointed him with oil in public (Mark 14:3–9; John 12:1–8). Moreover, in all four of the canonical Gospels, women are said to have accompanied Jesus from Galilee to Jerusalem during the last week of his life, to have been present at his crucifixion, and to have been the first to believe that Jesus' body was no longer in the tomb (Matt 27:55; 28:1–10; Mark 15:40–41; 16:1–8; Luke 23:49, 55; 24:10; John 19:25; 20:1–2; cf. *Gosp. Pet.* 50–57).

This widely attested tradition is contextually credible within an apocalyptic context. If, as we shall see, Jesus proclaimed that God was going to intervene in history to bring about a reversal of fortunes in which the last would be first and the first last, in which the humble would be exalted and the exalted humbled, then it would make sense that Jesus would have freely associated with women, who were generally looked down upon as inferior by the men who made the rules and ran the society—and that they would have been particularly intrigued by his proclamation of the coming Kingdom.

Jesus' Reputation as an Exorcist and Healer

I have already stressed that it is impossible for the historian who sticks to the canons of historical inquiry to demonstrate that miracles have been performed in the past—whether by Jesus, Apollonius, Hanina ben Dosa, Muhammad, or anyone else (see box 9.8). To acknowledge that a miracle occurred requires belief in a supernatural realm to which the historian, as a historian, has no direct access (although a historian may feel that he or she has access to it as a believer). This does *not* mean, however, that the historian cannot talk about the *reports* of miracles that have been handed down from the past. These are a matter of public record, and when it comes to the historical Jesus, of course, there are numerous such reports. In particular, he is said to have performed exorcisms (i.e., cast out demons) and to have healed the sick.

To begin with the exorcisms, there can be little doubt that whether or not supernatural evil spirits invade human bodies to make them do vile and harmful things, Jesus was widely thought to be able to cast them out, restoring a person to health. His exorcisms are among the best-attested deeds of the Gospel traditions, with individual accounts scattered throughout the first part of Mark (e.g.,

BOX 9.8   Jesus the Miracle Worker

When considering Jesus' deeds, one is naturally struck by all the miracles he is said to have done in the Gospels. From start to end his life is miraculous, with miracles occurring on nearly every page of the Gospels—as Jesus heals the sick, stills the storm, multiplies the loaves, walks on water, casts out demons, and raises the dead. What is the historian, who wants to know what Jesus *really* did, to make of these reports?

Unfortunately, the historian is put into a bind by the stories of the miracles. The problem does not involve the philosophical issue of whether miracles can happen (some people say yes, some say no—but whatever they say, there is still a problem). Instead, the problem involves the nature of history and historical evidence. By their very nature, historians can only establish what *probably* happened in the past. We can never *prove* the past, we can only show what probably happened. But what are miracles? They are

events that are *so* improbable that they defy the odds completely, contradicting all the known workings of nature to such an extent that . . . that we call them *miracles*!

And so the "historical" **problem of miracles**: since miracles are by definition the most improbable of occurrences, and since historians, by the very nature of their trade, can only establish what probably happened in the past, they can never say (by definition) that a miracle probably happened—whether it's a miracle by Jesus, Apollonius of Tyana, Muhammad, or anyone else!

What historians *can* say, of course, is that certain people (like the three I just mentioned) were widely *thought* to have done miracles. When it comes to verifying the Gospel reports of the supernatural, that is about as far as the historian, whether a believer or not, can go. Jesus was widely believed to be someone who defied nature through his miraculous deeds.

1:21–28; 5:1–20; 7:24–30), in M (e.g., Matt 9:32–34; this may be Q), and in L (e.g., Luke 13:10–14). Moreover, the theme that Jesus could and did cast out demons is documented in multiply attested forms throughout the sayings materials, for example, Mark, Q, and L (Mark 3:22; Matt 12:27–28; Luke 11:15, 19–20; 13:32). Such traditions cannot pass the criterion of dissimilarity, of course, since Christians who thought that Jesus had overcome the powers of evil might well have wanted to tell stories to show that he did. But they are contextually credible, to the extent that we know of other persons, both pagan and Jewish, who were said to have had power over demons, including, for example, the great pagan holy man, Apollonius of Tyana, who lived a bit later in the first century (see also Mark 9:38).

It is interesting to observe that the controversy over Jesus was not about whether or not he had this ability but whether he had this power from God or the Devil. As reported in our earliest surviving Gospel:

> And the scribes who came down from Jerusalem were saying that "He has Beelzebul, and by the ruler of the demons he casts out demons." (Mark 3:22)

Jesus' response to the charge is telling, especially in the version preserved in the Q source:

> If I cast demons out by Beelzebul, by whom do your sons cast them out? . . . But if I cast demons out by the spirit of God, behold the Kingdom of God is come upon you. Or how is anyone able to enter into the house of a strong man and steal his property, if he does not first bind the strong man? Only then he can plunder his house. (Matt 12:27–30; cf. Luke 11:19–23)

Note that everyone—Jesus and his opponents together—admits not only that Jesus can cast out demons, but that other Jewish exorcists can do so as well. Moreover, for Jesus, casting out demons signified the conquest over the forces of evil (the "strong man," in this case, would represent the main power opposed to God, Satan). And most importantly, Jesus' exorcisms are interpreted apocalyptically. They show that the Kingdom of God was at the doorstep. Strikingly, this apocalyptic view is the earliest understanding of the widespread tradition that Jesus could cast out demons.

Much the same can be said about Jesus' reputation as a healer. On numerous layers of our traditions Jesus is said to have healed those with various ailments—fever, leprosy, paralysis, hemorrhaging, lameness, blindness, and so on—and even to have raised some who had already died (see Mark 5:35–43 and John 11:38–44). Whatever you think about the philosophical possibility of miracles of healing, it's clear that Jesus was widely reputed to have done them. I might add that he was also known to have performed other miracles not associated with healing physical ailments, although dealing still with the "natural" world—for example, multiplying the loaves, walking on water, stilling the storm. Such miracles too are attested in multiple sources. Like the exorcisms, they cannot, of course, pass the criterion of dissimilarity.

They are contextually credible to the extent that there were other persons from the ancient world—lots of them, in fact—who were said to have done some fairly miraculous things, either through prayer (as in the case of Hanina ben Dosa and Honi the "circle-drawer") or directly because of their own holiness (e.g., Apollonius of Tyana). It may be worth noting that many of the healing and nature miracles of Jesus in fact are closely related to miracles described in the Hebrew Bible of other Jewish prophets, and invariably, Jesus comes off looking even better than his prophetic predecessors. The prophet Elijah, for example, had to engage in some real personal theatrics to raise a child from the dead (1 Kings 17:17–24); Jesus could do it with just a word (Mark 5:35–43). Elijah's successor, Elisha, allegedly fed 100 people with just twenty barley loaves (2 Kings 4:42–44); Jesus fed over 5,000 (not counting the women and children!) with just five (Mark 6:30–44). Elisha was able to make an axhead float on the water (2 Kings 6:1–7); Jesus could *himself* walk on the water (Mark 6:45–52).

Interestingly enough, our earliest sources did not understand these activities to be signs that Jesus was himself God. They were the sorts of things that Jewish prophets did. Jesus simply did them better than anyone else. Moreover, the earliest traditions again assign an apocalyptic meaning to these acts. In the coming Kingdom of God there would be no more disease or death. Jesus healed the sick and raised the dead. In a small way, then, the Kingdom was already becoming manifest. And there was not much time to wait before the end finally arrived. According to an account in Q, when John the Baptist wanted to know whether to expect another one to come or whether Jesus was himself the final prophet before the end, Jesus reportedly replied:

> Tell John the things you have seen and heard: the blind are regaining their sight, the lame are starting to walk, the lepers are being cleansed, the deaf are starting to hear, the dead are being raised, and the poor are hearing the good news! (Luke 7:22; Matt 11:4–5)

The end has come, and the Son of Man is soon to appear in the climactic act of history, after which there will never again be any who are blind, lame, leprous, deaf, or poor. Jesus represented the final prophet before the end, who was already overcoming the forces of evil in the world.

In Sum: The Deeds of Jesus

Although historians cannot demonstrate that Jesus performed miracles, they have been able to establish with some degree of certainty a few basic facts about Jesus' life: he was baptized, he associated with tax collectors and sinners, he chose twelve disciples to be his closest companions, he caused a disturbance in the Temple near the end of his life, this disturbance eventuated in his crucifixion at the hands of the Roman prefect Pontius Pilate, and in the wake of his death his followers established vibrant Christian communities. What is striking is that all of these pieces of information add up to a consistent portrayal of Jesus. Jesus was an apocalyptic prophet who anticipated the imminent end of the age, an end that would involve the destruction of Israel, including the Temple and its cult, prior to the establishment of God's kingdom on earth. As we turn now to consider more specifically some of the teachings of Jesus, we can fill out this basic apocalyptic message.

THE APOCALYPTIC TEACHINGS OF JESUS

Scholars have been unable to establish a solid consensus on what the historical Jesus said. Certainly, we cannot uncritically assume that he said many of the things recorded in such Gospels as *Thomas* or even John. As we have seen, a number of these teachings are not independently attested, and most of them appear to conform to the perspectives on Jesus that developed within the communities that preserved them. Thus, although Jesus makes many self-identifications in John's Gospel—"I am the bread of life," "I am the light of the world," "I am the way, the truth, and the life, no one comes to the Father but through me," "I and the Father are one"—none of these is independently attested in any other early source and all of them coincide with the Christology that developed within the Johannine community. Indeed, one interesting piece of evidence that the author of the Fourth Gospel modified his traditions of Jesus' sayings in conformity with his own views is that it is nearly impossible to know who is doing the talking in this narrative, unless we are explicitly told. For John

the Baptist, Jesus himself, and the narrator of the story all speak in almost exactly the same way, suggesting that there is only one voice here, that of the Gospel writer.

Is it not possible, however, that the apocalyptic sayings of Jesus were also modified in accordance with the views of the early Christians, who, after all, were apocalypticists? This indeed is a possibility, and one that should be carefully considered, but remember that we have already established *on other grounds* that Jesus was an apocalypticist. It is very hard to explain the basic orientation of his ministry otherwise, given the fact that it began with his decision to associate with the apocalypticist John the Baptist and was followed by the establishment of apocalyptic communities of his followers. Moreover, the deeds and experiences of Jesus that we can establish beyond reasonable doubt are consistent with his identity as an apocalypticist.

Given this orientation, it is not surprising that a large proportion of Jesus' sayings in our earliest sources are teachings about the imminent arrival of the Son of Man, the appearance of the Kingdom of God, the coming day of judgment, and the need to repent and live in preparation for that day, the

Figure 9.3 Ancient portrayal of Jesus teaching the apostles, from the catacomb of Domitilla in Rome.

climax of history as we know it. While we cannot assume that every saying in the Gospels that has any tint of apocalypticism in it is authentic, many of the apocalyptic sayings must have come from Jesus himself. Mark's summary of Jesus' teaching appears to be reasonably accurate (Mark 1:15): "The time has been fulfilled, the kingdom of God is near; repent and believe in this good news!" For Jesus, the time of this age was all but complete; the bottom of the sand clock was nearly filled. This age was near its end and the new Kingdom was almost here. People needed to prepare by turning to God and accepting this good news.

Here we cannot consider all the sayings that can be established as authentically from Jesus, but we will explore several of the more characteristic ones. Jesus taught that God's kingdom was soon to arrive on earth. Given Jesus' social context and the apocalyptic character of his ministry, we can assume that he had in mind an actual kingdom—which people could "enter," in which there would be human rulers and paradisial banqueting (see Matt 19:28; Luke 13: 23–29). This kingdom would replace the corrupt powers that were presently in control, a kingdom perhaps headed by God's special anointed one, his messiah. This kingdom was going to come in a powerful way (Mark 9:1); people must watch for it and be prepared, for no one could know when exactly it would come and it would strike unexpectedly (Mark 13:32–35; Luke 21:34–36). But Jesus did know that it was to arrive soon—at least within the lifetime of some of his disciples (Mark 9:1; 13:30).

It appears that Jesus expected the kingdom to be brought by one whom he called the Son of Man. Scholars have engaged in long and acrimonious debates about how to understand this designation. Is it a title for a figure that Jews would generally understand, for instance, a reference to the figure mentioned in Dan 7:13–14? Is it a general description of "a human-like being"? Is it a self-reference, a circumlocution for the pronoun "I"? Moreover, did Jesus actually use the term? Or did the Christians come up with it and attribute it to Jesus? If Jesus did use it, did he actually refer to himself as the Son of Man?

The details of this debate cannot concern us here, but I can indicate what seems to me to be the best way to resolve it. Some of Jesus' sayings men-

tion the Son of Man coming in judgment on the earth (e.g., Mark 8:38; 13:26–27; 14:62; Luke 12:8); these appear to presuppose a knowledge of the passage in Daniel where "one like a son of man" comes and is given the kingdoms of earth. We know of other Jewish apocalypticists who anticipated a cosmic judge of this type, sometimes called the "Son of Man" (see box 9.9). Jesus himself seems to have expected the imminent appearance of such a cosmic judge. In some sayings, such as the ones cited earlier (especially Mark 8:38 and 14:62), he does not identify himself as this figure but seems, at least on the surface, to be speaking of somebody else. If Christians were to make up a saying of Jesus about the Son of Man, however, they would probably not leave it ambiguous as to whether he was referring to himself. As we have seen, therefore, on the grounds of dissimilarity (again, hotly debated) such sayings are probably authentic. Jesus anticipates the coming of a cosmic judge from heaven who will bring in God's kingdom.

When he comes, there will be cosmic signs and a universal destruction. The messengers of God will gather together those who have been chosen for the kingdom (Mark 13:24–27). On the day of judgment, some people will be accepted into the kingdom, and others cast out. The judge will be like a fisherman who sorts through his fish, taking only the best and disposing of all the others (Matt 13:47–50; *Gosp. Thom.* 8).

This judgment will bring about a total reversal of the social order. Those in positions of power and prestige will be removed, and the oppressed and afflicted will be exalted. It is the forces of evil who are currently in charge of this planet, and those who side with them are the ones in power. Those who side with God, however, are the persecuted and downtrodden, who are dominated by the cosmic powers opposed to God. Thus, when God reasserts his control over this planet, all of this will be reversed: "The first shall be last and the last first" (Mark 10:30), and "all those who exalt themselves will be humbled, and those who humble themselves will be exalted" (Luke 14:11; 18:14[Q]). This was not simply a hopeful pipe dream; Jesus expected it actually to happen.

The coming of the Son of Man is not good news for those in power. They would be better served to relinquish their power—to become like children

ANOTHER GLIMPSE INTO THE PAST

BOX 9.9 Another Apocalyptic Jesus

As we have seen, Jesus of Nazareth was not the only apocalyptic prophet who proclaimed the imminent judgment of God, which would befall not just the Jewish enemies (the Romans), but some of the Jews themselves. In addition to the "Egyptian," and the prophet named "Theudas," Josephus tells us of yet another apocalyptic figure from the first century, who lived about thirty years after the death of Jesus of Nazareth. Oddly enough, this other prophet was also named Jesus (not an unusual name at the time).

According to Josephus (*Jewish Wars,* Book 6), **Jesus, the son of Ananias**, appeared in Jerusalem during an annual feast and began to cry aloud, "A voice from the east, a voice from the west, a voice from the four winds, a voice against Jerusalem and the holy house [i.e., the Temple] . . . a voice against the whole people." The local authorities found this purveyor of doom a nuisance and had him beaten, but that did not stop him. He continued to proclaim loudly, in public, "Woe, woe to Jerusalem." The Roman procurator then had him arrested and flogged within an inch of his life. But deciding that he was literally crazy, the procurator had him released.

For another seven years this Jesus continued to proclaim that the destruction of Jerusalem was coming, until the city was laid siege in the late 60s and he himself was killed by a stone catapulted over the walls by the Romans.

In any event, Jesus of Nazareth was not the only Jewish prophet to proclaim the coming destruction of the city, nor the only one to be opposed by the local Jewish leadership, nor the only one to be arrested and punished by the Roman governor. He was not even the only one like this to be named Jesus!

(Mark 10:13–15), to give away their wealth and become poor (Mark 10:23–30), to yield their positions of prestige and become slaves (Mark 10:42–44). Not even the official leaders of the Jewish people would escape, for everyone who lords it over another would be liable. Indeed, the very locus of power for the influential Sadducees, the Temple of God itself, would be destroyed on judgment day: "There will be not one stone left upon another that will not be destroyed" (Mark 13:2).

On the other hand, those who currently suffer, the oppressed and downtrodden, would be rewarded. This promise is expressed in Jesus' Beatitudes, found in Q: "Blessed are you who are poor, for yours is the kingdom of Heaven [meaning that they will be made rich when it arrives]; Blessed are you who hunger now, for you shall be satisfied [when the Kingdom comes]; Blessed are you who weep now, for you shall rejoice; Blessed are you who are hated by others, and reviled . . . for your reward will be great" (Luke 6:20–23; see *Gosp. Thom.* 54, 68–69).

Because there is to be such a dramatic reversal when the Son of Man brings the kingdom, a person should be willing to sacrifice everything in order to enter into it. A person's passion to obtain the kingdom should be like that of a merchant in search of pearls; when he finds one that is perfect, he sells everything that he has to buy it (Matt 13:45–46; *Gosp. Thom.* 76). People should not, for this reason, be tied to this world or the alluring treasures that it has to offer; instead, they should focus on the kingdom that is coming (Matt 6:19, 33; *Gosp. Thom.* 63).

At the same time, we should not think that Jesus was maintaining that everyone who happened to be poor or hungry or mistreated would enter into God's kingdom. He expected that people first had to repent and adhere to his teachings (see Mark 1:15; 2:17; Luke 15:7). This is what his own disciples had done; they left everything to follow him. As a result, they were promised special places of prominence in the coming kingdom. Similarly, Jesus' association with tax collectors and sinners should not be taken to mean that he approved of any kind of lifestyle. To be sure, he did not insist that his followers keep the detailed traditions of the Pharisees: he appears to have believed that what mattered was at the heart of the Torah, the command for people

BOX 9.10 Judas and the Roasting Chicken

When trying to determine which stories in the Gospels are historically accurate, we need to look not only at the Gospels of the New Testament, but at all the surviving ancient narratives that discuss Jesus' life. In many instances, however, the accounts are quite obviously legendary, written for the entertainment, edification, or even instruction of their readers. One example occurs in a fourth- or fifth-century document known as the *Gospel of Nicodemus* (also called the *Acts of Pilate*). In one of the most interesting manuscripts of this Gospel, we find a tale about what happened to **Judas Iscariot** after he betrayed Jesus. Filled with remorse for what he has done, Judas returns home to find some rope with which

to hang himself. When he comes into the kitchen, he finds his wife roasting a chicken on a spit over a charcoal fire. To her horror, he announces his plan to commit suicide. She asks why he would want to do such a thing, and he indicates that it is because he has betrayed the Lord to his death, but that Jesus will surely rise from the dead, and then he, Judas, will be in *real* trouble. His wife assures him: Jesus cannot rise from the dead any more than this chicken on the spit can come back to life.

But as soon as she utters these words, the dead chicken rises up, spreads its wings, and crows three times. A terrified Judas runs out to grab some rope and end his life.

to love God with their entire being and to love their neighbors as themselves (Mark 12:28–31, where he quotes Deut 6:4 and Lev 19:18; see *Gosp. Thom.* 25). Occasionally, in his view, the overly scrupulous attention to the details of the Torah could, perhaps ironically, lead to a violation of these basic principles (Mark 7:1–13). The Sabbath, for example, was created for the sake of humans, not humans for the Sabbath. Human need, therefore, had priority over the punctilious observation of rules for keeping the Sabbath (Mark 2:27–28). For Jesus, then, keeping the Torah was indeed important; this happened, however, not when Jews followed the carefully formulated rulings of the Pharisees but when they repented of their bad behavior and turned to God with their entire being and manifested their love for him in their just and loving treatment of their neighbors.

These examples make it clear that the guidelines for living that Jesus gave, that is, his ethics, were grounded in his apocalyptic worldview. They are probably misunderstood, therefore, when they are taken as principles for a healthy society. Jesus did teach that people should love one another, but not because he wanted to help them lead happy and productive lives or because he knew

that if love were not at the root of their dealings with one another society might fall apart. He was not a teacher of ethics concerned with how people should get along in the future. For Jesus, the end was coming soon, within his own generation. The motivation for ethical behavior, then, sprang from the imminent arrival of the kingdom, to be brought by the Son of Man in judgment.

Those who began to implement the ideals of the kingdom, where there would be no sin, hatred, or evil, had in a sense begun to experience the rule of God here and now. This rule of God would find its climax in the powerful appearance of the Son of Man. The followers of Jesus who had begun to live the life of the kingdom by loving God and their neighbors as themselves were merely a small prelude; they were like a tiny mustard seed in comparison with the great mustard bush that represented the coming kingdom (Mark 4:30–31; *Gosp. Thom.* 20). Indeed, they were not many in number, since the words of Jesus for the most part fell on deaf ears. But when these words came to those who were chosen for the kingdom, they were like vibrant seed falling on rich soil; they bore fruit of far greater worth and magnitude than one could imagine (Mark 4:1–9; *Gosp. Thom.* 9). For this reason, those who heard the good news of the kingdom were not only to prepare themselves but also to proclaim the message of Jesus to others. As the Gospels express it, no one puts a lamp under a bushel but on a light stand, so that all might see the light and recognize the truth

that has now been made clear, the truth of God's coming kingdom (Mark 4:21–22; *Gosp. Thom.* 33).

It is difficult to know what Jesus thought about his own role in this imminent Kingdom of God. On occasion he speaks as if he expected to enter into

---

WHAT DO YOU THINK?

BOX 9.11   Jesus and "Family Values"

One of the hardest things for modern people who are interested in Jesus to realize is that he lived in a completely different culture from ours, with a foreign set of cultural values and norms—so much so that people commonly claim that he did not mean (or rather could not have meant) what he said. Nowhere is this more clear than in the area known today as "family values."

Since the modern sense of family values seems to be so good and wholesome, it is only natural for people to assume that Jesus too must have taught them. But did he? It is striking that in our earliest traditions, Jesus does *not* seem to place a high priority on the family. Consider the words preserved in Q: "If anyone comes to me and does not hate his own father and mother and wife and children and brothers and sisters and even his own life, he is not able to be my disciple" (Luke 14:26; Matt 10:37). A person must *hate* his or her family? The same word is used, strikingly, in the saying independently preserved in the *Gospel of Thomas*: "The one who does not hate his father and mother will not be worthy to be my disciple" (*Gosp. Thom.* 55). If we understand "hate" here to mean something like "despise in comparison to" or "have nothing to do with," then the saying makes sense. Parents, siblings, spouses, and even one's own children were to be of no importance in comparison with the coming kingdom.

This may help explain Jesus' reaction to his own family. For there are clear signs not only that Jesus' family rejected his message during his public ministry, but that he in turn spurned them publicly (independently attested in Mark 3:31–34 and *Gosp. Thom.* 99).

And Jesus clearly saw the familial rifts that would be created when someone became committed to his message of the coming Kingdom of God:

You think that I have come to bring peace on earth; not peace, I tell you, but division. For from now on there will be five people in one house, divided among themselves: three against two and two against three; a father will be divided against his son and a son against his father, a mother against her daughter and a daughter against her mother; a mother-in-law against her daughter-in-law and a daughter-in-law against her mother-in-law. (Luke 12:51–53; Matt 10:34–46; independently attested in *Gosp. Thom.* 16)

And family tensions would be heightened immediately before the end of the age, when "a brother will betray his brother to death, and a father his child, and children will rise up against their parents and kill them" (Mark 13:12).

These "antifamily" traditions are too widely attested in our sources to be ignored (they are found in Mark, Q, and *Thomas*, for example) and suggest that Jesus did not support what we today might think of as family values. But why not? Could it be that Jesus was not ultimately interested in establishing a good society and doing what was necessary to maintain it? Remember: for him the end was coming soon, and the present social order was being called radically into question. What mattered were not strong family ties and the social institutions of this world. What mattered was the new thing that was coming, the future kingdom. And it was impossible to promote this teaching while trying to retain the present social structure. That would be like trying to put new wine into old wineskins or trying to sew a new piece of cloth to an old garment. As any winemaster or seamstress could tell you, it just won't work. The wineskins would burst and the garment would tear. New wine and new cloth require new wineskins and new garments. The old is passing away and the new is almost here (Mark 2:18–22; *Gosp. Thom.* 47).

the kingdom himself, and he seems to have anticipated that this was to be soon (e.g., Mark 14:25). As we have seen, the disciples were to be leaders in this new kingdom, but who would lead them? Would it still be Jesus? Would he be the ultimate leader of this new Kingdom of God on earth, the one whom God appoints as king? If this is what Jesus thought—and, of course, it is impossible to know what anyone thinks, especially someone who lived 2,000 years ago, whom we know only through such fragmentary sources—then he may have considered himself to be the future messiah—but only in this apocalyptic sense.

THE APOCALYPTIC DEATH OF JESUS

As we have seen, several aspects of the Gospel Passion narratives appear to be historically accurate. Jesus offended members of the Sadducees by his apocalyptic actions in the Temple just prior to the Passover feast. They decided to have him taken out of the way. Perhaps they were afraid that his followers would swell as the feast progressed and that the gathering might lead to a riot, or perhaps they simply found his views offensive and considered his attack on the Temple of God blasphemous. In either case, they appear to have arranged with one of his own disciples to betray him. Jesus was arrested and questioned by a Jewish Sanhedrin called for the occasion, possibly headed up by the high priest Caiaphas. He was then delivered over to the Roman prefect Pontius Pilate, who condemned him to be crucified. The time between his arrest and his crucifixion may have been no more than twelve hours; he was sent off to his execution before anyone knew what was happening.

What else can we know about Jesus' last days? Here we will look at some of the more intriguing questions that have occurred to scholars over the years. One of these is, why was Jesus in Jerusalem in the first place? The theologian might say that Jesus went to Jerusalem to die for the sins of the world; this view, however, is based on Gospel sayings of Jesus that cannot pass the criterion of dissimilarity (e.g., his three Passion predictions in Mark). In making judgments about why this itinerant

Figure 9.4 A portrayal of Jesus' triumphal entry, found on the famous sarcophagus of a Christian named Junius Bassus.

teacher from Galilee went to Jerusalem, we should stick to our historical criteria.

It is possible that Jesus simply wanted to celebrate the Passover in Jerusalem, as did so many thousands of other Jews every year. But Jesus' actions there appear to have been well thought out. When he arrived, he entered the Temple and caused a disturbance. Afterward he evidently spent several days in and out of the Temple, teaching his message of the coming kingdom. Given Jesus' understanding that this kingdom was imminent and the urgency with which he taught others that they needed to repent in preparation for it, we should perhaps conclude that he had come to Jerusalem to bring his message to the center of Israel itself, to the Temple in the holy city, where faithful Jews from around the world would be gathered to worship the God who saved them from their oppressors in the past and who was expected to do so once more. Jesus came to the Temple to tell his people how this salvation would occur and to urge them to prepare for it by repenting of their sins and accepting his teachings. He proclaimed that judgment was coming and that it would involve a massive destruction, including the destruction of the Temple.

Did Jesus realize that he was about to be arrested and executed? Again, there is simply no way to know for certain what Jesus thought. It is not hard to imagine, however, that anyone with any knowledge at all of how prophets of doom were generally received, both in ancient times and more recently, might anticipate receiving similar treatment. Moreover, Jesus would probably have known that the leaders in Jerusalem did not take kindly to his message, and he certainly would have known about their civil power. According to the traditions, of course, Jesus knew that his time had come on the night of his arrest. There are a number of difficulties with accepting the accounts of the Last Supper as historically accurate, especially when Jesus indicates that his death will be for the forgiveness of sins, a clearly Christian notion that cannot pass the criterion of dissimilarity. Still, we have two independent accounts of the event (Mark 14:22–26 and 1 Cor 11:23–26), the earliest of which was written in the mid-50s by Paul, who claims to have received the tradition from others. Did he learn it from someone who was present at the event, or from a Christian who knew someone who was there? In any case, the basic notion that at his last meal Jesus explained that he would not last long in the face of his powerful opposition is not at all implausible.

Why did Judas betray Jesus, and what did he betray? These again are extraordinarily difficult questions to answer. That Judas did betray Jesus is almost certain; it is multiply attested and is not a tradition that a Christian would have likely invented. Why he did so, however, will always remain a mystery. Some of our accounts intimate that he did it simply for the money (Matt 26:14–15; cf. John 12:4–6). This is possibly the case, but the "thirty pieces of silver" is a reference to a fulfillment of a prophecy in the Hebrew Bible (Zech 11:12) and may not be historically accurate.

What appears certain is that Jesus was eventually handed over to the Roman authorities, who tried him on the charge that he called himself king of the Jews. That this was the legal case against him is multiply attested in independent sources. Moreover, as has often been noted, in the early Gospels the designation of Jesus as king

of the Jews is found only in the crowd's acclamation (not the disciples'!) at his entry into Jerusalem and in the accounts of his trial (Mark 15, Matthew 27, Luke 23, John 18–19); nowhere do his disciples actually call him this. Since the early Christians did not generally favor, or even use, the designation "king of the Jews" for Jesus, they probably would not have made it up as the official charge against him. This must, therefore, be a historically accurate tradition.

Claiming to be king of the Jews was a political charge that amounted to insurrection or treason against the state. That is why Jesus was executed by the Romans under Pontius Pilate, not by the Jewish authorities, who may not have been granted the power of capital punishment in any case. That the Romans actually did the deed is attested by a wide range of sources, including even Josephus and Tacitus.

But why did the Roman authorities execute Jesus if it was the Jewish authorities who had him arrested in the first place? We know that Jesus must have offended powerful members of the Sadducees by his action in the Temple. Through the high priest **Caiaphas**, the chief authority over local affairs, these leaders arranged to have Jesus arrested. Once he was taken, he was brought in for questioning. We cannot know for certain how the interrogation proceeded; none of Jesus' disciples was present, and our earliest account, Mark's, is historically problematic (see box 5.4). Perhaps we can best regard it as a fact-finding interrogation. The Sanhedrin evidently decided to have Jesus taken out of the way. Using the information (given by Judas?) that he had been called the messiah, they sent Jesus before the prefect Pilate. We do not know exactly what happened at this trial. Possibly Pilate was as eager to be rid of a potential troublemaker during these turbulent times as the chief priests were.

When Pilate chose to have someone executed, he could do so on the spur of the moment. There was no imperial legal code that had to be followed, no requirements for a trial by jury, no need to call witnesses or to establish guilt beyond reasonable doubt, no need for anything that we ourselves might consider due process. Roman governors were given virtually free rein to do whatever was required to keep the peace and collect the tribute. Pilate is known to history as a ruthless administrator, insensitive to the needs and concerns of the people he governed, willing to exercise brutal force whenever it served Rome's best interests. So, perhaps on the basis of a brief hearing in which he asked a question or two, Pilate decided to have Jesus executed. It was probably one of several items on a crowded morning agenda; it may have taken only a couple of minutes. Two other persons were charged with sedition the same morning. All three were taken outside the city gates to be crucified.

According to the Gospel traditions, Jesus was first flogged. It is hard to say whether this is a Christian addition to show how much Jesus suffered or a historical account. In any event, he and the others would have been taken by soldiers outside the city gates and forced to carry their crossbeams to the upright stakes kept at the site of execution. The uprights were reused, possibly every day. There the condemned would have been nailed to the crossbeams, or possibly to the uprights themselves, through the wrists and possibly the ankles. There may have been a small ledge attached to the upright on which they could sit to rest.

The death itself would have been slow and painful. Crucifixion was reserved for the worst offenders of the lowest classes: slaves, common thieves, and insurrectionists. It was a death by suffocation. As the body hung on the cross, the lung cavity would distend beyond the point at which one could breathe. To relieve the pain on the chest, one had to raise the body up, either by pulling on the stakes through the wrists or by pushing on those through the feet, or both. Death came only when the victim lacked the strength to continue. Sometimes it took days.

In Jesus' case, death came within several hours, in the late afternoon, on a Friday during Passover week. He was taken from his cross and given a quick burial sometime before sunset on the day before Sabbath.

AT A GLANCE

BOX 9.12 Jesus the Apocalyptic Prophet

1. The earliest surviving traditions about Jesus portray him as an apocalypticist. Many of these traditions pass our historical criteria.

2. That Jesus was an apocalypticist also makes sense of the facts that

   a. He began his ministry by being baptized by John the Baptist (an apocalyptic prophet).

   b. The early Christian church (which was also apocalyptic) appeared in his aftermath.

3. The historically reliable traditions of Jesus' deeds make sense in an apocalyptic context: his crucifixion, cleansing of the Temple, choice of twelve disciples, association with outcasts, and reputation as miracle worker.

4. The teachings of Jesus that pass our criteria are apocalyptic as well:

   a. The Son of Man was to appear from heaven, coming in judgment on the earth.

   b. Those who sided with Jesus and accepted his teachings, reforming their lives as he proclaimed, would be saved in this judgment.

   c. Those who did not would be destroyed.

   d. This judgment of God was imminent, to happen within his disciples' lifetimes.

5. We know more about the last days and death of Jesus than about any other period of his life. He was betrayed by one of his own followers to the Sadducaic leaders in Jerusalem, handed over to the Roman governor Pontius Pilate (in town to keep the peace during Passover), condemned after a brief trial, and crucified outside the city walls on a Friday morning during the festival.

TAKE A STAND

1. Your roommate tells you that, in his opinion, you don't need to know anything about first-century Judaism to understand the historical Jesus and his message. You are in a cantankerous mood and decide to argue against him. Make the strongest case you can.

2. Suppose you wanted to argue *against* the idea that Jesus was an apocalypticist. What are the best arguments you can think of? What is your personal opinion: do you think he was or not? And why?

3. Choose any three incidents from Jesus' life or teaching in the New Testament Gospels, and using the "Rules of Thumb" for mounting a historical argument (pp. 130–31), show why, in your opinion, they must represent historically accurate information.

 ## SUGGESTIONS FOR FURTHER READING

Allison, Dale, *Constructing Jesus: Memory, Imagination, and History*. Grand Rapids, Mich.: Baker, 2010. A sophisticated account of how Jesus was "remembered" in the early church and how these "memories" relate to the life of the historical Jesus itself, insofar as that can actually be reconstructed; for advanced students.

Allison, Dale C. *Jesus of Nazareth: Millenarian Prophet*. Minneapolis: Fortress, 1998. A detailed discussion of the criteria used to reconstruct the life of Jesus, which makes a compelling case that Jesus is to be understood as an apocalyptic prophet; for advanced students.

Beilby, James, ed. *The Historical Jesus: Five Views*. Nottingham, UK: Intervarsity Press, 2009. Five prominent scholars present their views of Jesus, ranging from the very conservative evangelical to the mythicist (the view that claims Jesus never existed). A terrific introduction to the range of scholarly opinion.

Crossan, John Dominic. *Jesus: A Revolutionary Biography*. San Francisco: Harper San Francisco, 1994. An intriguing and moving portrayal of Jesus as one who was not an apocalypticist, by one of the leading scholars in this field; a national best seller.

Crossan, John Dominic. *The Historical Jesus: The Life of a Mediterranean Jewish Peasant*. San Francisco: Harper San Francisco, 1991. A large, controversial, and widely read study of the historical Jesus, which argues that Jesus is best understood as a kind of Jewish Cynic, based on

a rigorous application of the method of independent (multiple) attestation.

Ehrman, Bart D. *Did Jesus Exist? The Historical Case for Jesus of Nazareth*. San Francisco: HarperOne, 2012. Directed against those who claim that Jesus never existed, but was made up by Jews in imitation of pagan "divine men," this book shows why there is little doubt that Jesus actually lived (and that we can say some things about him as a historical figure).

Ehrman, Bart D. *Jesus: Apocalyptic Prophet of the New Millennium*. New York: Oxford University Press, 1999. A fuller treatment of the issues and views set forth in the present chapter; for popular audiences.

Evans, Craig, and Bruce Chilton, eds. *Studying the Historical Jesus: Evaluations of the Current Stage of Research*. Leiden: Brill, 1994. Essays on important aspects of the historical Jesus; some of these essays take exception to the view of Jesus as an apocalypticist, preferring instead to see him as a kind of first-century Jewish Cynic; for more advanced students.

Fredriksen, Paula. *Jesus of Nazareth, King of the Jews: A Jewish Life and the Emergence of Christianity*. New York: Knopf, 1999. A fresh and intriguing look at the life of Jesus, which, among other things, takes seriously the evidence outside the Synoptic Gospels.

(continued)

SUGGESTIONS FOR FURTHER READING *(continued)*

Green, Joel, et al., eds. *Dictionary of Jesus and the Gospels.* Downers Grove, Ill.: Intervarsity Press, 1994. A Bible dictionary with in-depth articles on a wide range of topics pertaining to the historical Jesus and the Gospels, written by prominent evangelical Christian scholars who, by and large, represent different perspectives from those presented in this chapter.

Harrington, Daniel. *Historical Dictionary of Jesus.* Lanham, Md.: Scarecrow Press, 2010. A prominent New Testament scholar presents short dictionary-length entries on some 400 topics, covering just about everything the beginning student will want to know about the historical Jesus.

Horsley, Richard A. *Jesus and the Spiral of Violence: Popular Jewish Resistance in Roman Palestine.* Minneapolis: Fortress, 1993. An intriguing alternative view, which sees Jesus principally as an advocate of nonviolent social revolution against the imperialistic policies of Rome.

Meier, John. *A Marginal Jew: Rethinking the Historical Jesus.* Vols. 1–4. New York: Doubleday, 1991, 1994, 2001, 2009. Written at an introductory level, but filled with erudite documentation in the endnotes, this is one of the finest treatments of the historical Jesus of the twentieth century.

Sanders, E. P. *The Historical Figure of Jesus.* London: Penguin, 1993. All in all, perhaps the best single-volume sketch of the historical Jesus for beginning students.

Schweitzer, Albert. *Quest of the Historical Jesus.* Trans. W. Montgomery. New York: Macmillan, 1968. The classic study of the major attempts to write a biography of Jesus up to the first part of the twentieth century, and one of the first and perhaps the most important attempt to portray Jesus as a Jewish apocalypticist.

Tatum, W. Barnes. *In Quest of Jesus: A Guidebook.* Atlanta: Westminster John Knox, 1982. An excellent introduction that includes discussions of the problems involved in establishing historically reliable traditions in the Gospels and the criteria that can be used to do so.

Vermes, Geza. *The Authentic Gospel of Jesus.* London: Penguin, 2003. An authoritative account of the message of Jesus by one of the leading experts in the field in modern times.

Wright, N. T. *Jesus and the Victory of God.* Minneapolis: Fortress, 1996. A full examination of the Jesus of history by a traditional British scholar; for more advanced students.

KEY TERMS

apocalypticism	dissimilarity,	Jesus the son of	miracles, problem of
Caiaphas	criterion of	Ananias	Tacitus
Cynic philosophy	enacted parable	Judas Iscariot	

10

CHAPTER

From Jesus to the Gospels

WHAT TO EXPECT

We have seen that Jesus taught an apocalyptic message—that God was soon to intervene in the course of history and overthrow the evil forces of this world in a cataclysmic act of judgment to be brought by the Son of Man. But Christians believed that it was Jesus himself who was the key to God's judgment of the world, that he himself was the Son of Man. Eventually they came to believe that he was much more than that, that he was in some sense divine—even God himself. How did Christianity become a religion based on the death and resurrection of Jesus, if that is not what Jesus himself actually taught?

We began our study of the New Testament with the oral traditions about Jesus that were in circulation in the early Christian churches and saw how the stories that eventually made it into the Gospels were modified and sometimes, perhaps, created by Christians who narrated them in order to convert others to faith and to educate, encourage, and admonish those who had already been converted. We moved from there to a study of our earliest written accounts of Jesus—books that were not the first to be produced by Christians (the letters of Paul were earlier) but were the first to portray the most important figure of early Christianity, Jesus himself. We initially examined these works as literary documents, trying to uncover their distinctive portrayals of Jesus. We then moved behind these portrayals to reconstruct the life of the man himself by applying a variety of historical criteria to uncover what Jesus actually said and did.

We have now come full circle back to where we began. This is an ideal stage for us to pause and re-examine the original point of entry into our study in light of what we have learned en route. Here we will discuss with somewhat greater sophistication (and brevity) the development of the traditions about Jesus that circulated in the early decades of the Christian movement.

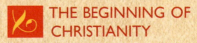 THE BEGINNING OF CHRISTIANITY

Hypothetically speaking, every religious and philosophical movement has a point of origin. When did Christianity begin? There are several possibilities.

We might say that it began with Jesus' ministry. Obviously, without the words and deeds of Jesus, there would have been no religion based on him. At the same time, Christianity has traditionally been much more than a religion that espouses Jesus' teachings. Indeed, if Jesus was the apocalyptic prophet that he appears to have been, then the Christianity that emerged after his death represents a somewhat different religion from the one he himself proclaimed. In the simplest terms, Christianity is a religion rooted in a belief in the death of Jesus for sin and in his resurrection from the dead. This, however, does not appear to have been the religion that Jesus preached to the Jews of Galilee and Judea. To use a formulation that scholars have tossed about for years, Christianity is not so much the religion of Jesus (the religion that he himself proclaimed) as the religion about Jesus (the religion that is based on his death and resurrection).

Should we say, then, that Christianity began with Jesus' death? This, too, may contain some element of truth, but it also is somewhat problematic. If Jesus had died and no one had come to believe that he had been raised from the dead, then his death would perhaps have been seen as yet another tragic incident in a long history of tragedies experienced by the Jewish people, as the death of yet another prophet of God, another holy man dedicated to proclaiming God's will to his people. But it would not have been recognized as an act of God for the salvation of the world, and a new religion would probably not have emerged as a result.

Did Christianity begin with Jesus' resurrection? Historians would have difficulty making this judgment, since it would require them to accept certain theological claims about the miraculous working of God (see box 9.8). Yet even if historians were able to speak of the resurrection as a historically probable event, it could not, in and of itself, be considered the beginning of Christianity, for Christianity is not the resurrection of Jesus but the *belief* in the resurrection of Jesus. Historians, of course, have no difficulty speaking about the belief in Jesus' resurrection, since this is a matter of public record. It is a historical fact that some of Jesus' followers came to believe that he had been raised from the dead soon after his execution. We know some of these believers by name; one of them, the apostle Paul, claims quite plainly to have seen Jesus alive after his death.

Thus, for the historian, Christianity begins after the death of Jesus, not with the resurrection itself, but with the belief in the resurrection.

JESUS' RESURRECTION FROM AN APOCALYPTIC PERSPECTIVE

How did belief in Jesus' resurrection eventually lead to the Gospels we have studied? Or to put the question somewhat differently, how does one understand the movement from Jesus, the Jewish prophet who proclaimed the imminent judgment of the world through the coming Son of Man, to the Christians who believed in him, who maintained that Jesus himself was the divine man whose death and resurrection represented God's ultimate act of salvation? To answer this question, we must look at who the first believers in Jesus' resurrection actually were.

The Gospels provide somewhat different accounts about who discovered Jesus' empty tomb and about whom they encountered, what they learned, and how they reacted once they did so. But all four canonical Gospels agree that the empty tomb was discovered by a woman or a group of women, who were the first of Jesus' followers to realize that he had been raised (see box 10.1). Interestingly, the earliest author to discuss Jesus' resurrection, the apostle Paul, does not mention the circumstance that Jesus' tomb was empty, nor does he name any women among those who first believed in Jesus' resurrection (1 Cor 15:3–8). On one important point, however, Paul does stand in agreement with the early Gospel accounts: those who initially came to understand that God had raised Jesus from the dead were some of Jesus' closest followers, who had associated with him during his lifetime.

It is probably safe to say that all these followers had accepted Jesus' basic apocalyptic message while he was still alive. Otherwise they would not have followed him. Thus, the first persons to believe in Jesus' resurrection would have been apocalyptically minded Jews. For them, Jesus' resurrection was not a miracle that some other holy person had performed on his behalf. Jesus' followers believed that God had raised Jesus from the dead. Moreover,

WHAT DO YOU THINK?

BOX 10.1   The Women and the Empty Tomb

One of the striking features of the stories of Jesus' resurrection is that in none of the Gospels is the empty tomb discovered by Jesus' male disciples or by the Jewish male leaders or by men at all. It is discovered by women: Mary Magdalene and another Mary, according to Matthew (28:1); Mary Magdalene, Mary the mother of James, and Solome, according to Mark (16:1); Mary Magdalene, Joanna, Mary the mother of James, and other women left unnamed, according to Luke (24:10); just Mary Magdalene, according to John (20:1); and Mary Magdalene and some of her women friends, according to the *Gospel of Peter* (50–51).

In view of these traditions, it may seem odd that when the apostle Paul offers "evidence" of the resurrection in 1 Cor 15:3–8, he mentions not the empty tomb (discovered by women), but the appearance of the resurrected Christ—and not to women (despite other early Gospel traditions), but only to men.

Why does Paul not refer to the empty tomb or to the women?

Some feminist historians interested in the question have made an excellent case that the Gospels record a primitive and historically reliable tradition that in fact it was women, **Mary Magdalene** chief among them, who discovered Jesus' empty tomb, and that, as a result, they were the first witnesses to his resurrection. Christianity, then, was in some sense started

by women. The tradition is, after all, multiply attested and it passes the criterion of dissimilarity—since men telling the stories about Jesus would scarcely have made up a tradition that it was women who first realized that Jesus had been raised.

Some feminist scholars, however, have made a contrary suggestion. Noting that Paul wrote long before the Gospels and that he betrays no knowledge of an empty tomb tradition (only of traditions involving the appearances of Jesus), they ask whether it is possible that Christians in Paul's churches had never heard that the tomb was discovered empty on Easter morning. If so, once they came to learn of it, they would no doubt try to explain why neither Paul nor anyone else had ever told them. And so, this theory goes, they explained their previous ignorance by indicating that it was *women* who found the empty tomb, women who were too giddy or terrified to tell anyone (cf. Mark 16:8) or whose reports were not believed, since they were merely the idle talk of silly women (cf. Luke 24:11).

If this theory is right, then the Gospel accounts of women discovering the empty tomb would not function to elevate the status of women but to denigrate them. For now women would not be the earliest witnesses to the resurrection but, rather, obstacles to the spread of the gospel.

---

he had not been raised for a brief period of time, only to die a second time. Jesus had been raised from the dead never to die again. What conclusions would be drawn by these Jewish apocalypticists, the earliest Christians?

We have already seen that apocalypticists believed that at the end of this age, the powers of evil would be destroyed. These powers included the Devil, his demons, and the cosmic forces aligned with them, the forces of sin and death. When these powers were destroyed, there would be a resurrection of the dead, in which the good would receive an eternal reward and the evil would face eternal punishment. Many Jewish apocalypticists, like Jesus himself, believed that this end would be

brought by one specially chosen by God and sent from heaven as a cosmic judge of the earth. Given this basic apocalyptic scenario, there is little doubt as to how the first persons who believed in Jesus' resurrection would have interpreted the event. Since the resurrection of the dead was to come at the end of the age and since somebody had now been raised (as they believed), then the end must have already begun. It had begun with the resurrection of a particular person, the great teacher and holy man Jesus, who had overcome death, the greatest of the cosmic powers aligned against God. Thus, Jesus was the personal agent through whom God had decided to defeat the forces of evil. He had been exalted to heaven, where he now lived until he would return to finish God's work. For this reason, people were to repent and await his second coming.

Sometime after Jesus' resurrection—it is impossible to say how soon (since our sources were written decades later)—these earliest apocalyptic believers began to say things about Jesus that reflected their belief in who he was now that he had been raised. These early reflections on Jesus' significance strongly influenced the beliefs that came to be discussed, developed, and modified for centuries to follow, principally among people who were not apocalyptic Jews to begin with. For example, the earliest Christians believed that Jesus had been exalted to heaven; that is, God had bestowed a unique position upon him. Even during his lifetime, they knew, Jesus had addressed God as Father and taught his disciples that they should trust God as a kindly parent. Those who came to believe in his resurrection realized that he must have had a relationship with God that was truly unique. In a distinctive way, for them, he was *the* Son of God.

Moreover, these Christians knew that Jesus had spent a good deal of time talking about one who was soon to come from heaven in judgment over the earth. For them, Jesus himself was now exalted to heaven; clearly, he must be the judge about whom he had spoken. Therefore, in their view, Jesus was soon to return in judgment as the Son of Man.

Jesus also spoke of the Kingdom of God that was to arrive with the coming of the Son of Man. As we have seen, he may have thought that he would be given a position of prominence in that kingdom. For these early Christians, that was precisely what would happen: Jesus would reign over the kingdom that was soon to appear. For them, he was the king to come, the king of the Jews, the messiah (see box 10.2).

Jesus also taught that in some sense this kingdom had already been inaugurated. He therefore taught his followers to implement the values of the kingdom and adopt its ways in the here and now by loving one another as themselves. Those who believed in his resurrection maintained that the kingdom proclaimed by Jesus had indeed already

WHAT DO YOU THINK?

BOX 10.2   Jesus, the Messiah, and the Resurrection

Over the years, many people have assumed that first-century Jews who came to believe that Jesus had been raised from the dead would naturally conclude that he was the messiah. This is probably an erroneous assumption, for to our knowledge there were no Jews prior to Christianity who believed that the future messiah was to die for sins and then be raised from the dead.

Why, then, did the earliest Christians use Jesus' resurrection to prove that Jesus was the messiah? Perhaps the ones who first insisted on Jesus' messiahship after his resurrection were those who already thought that he was the messiah before he died. The scenario may have been something like this. Before Jesus was crucified, some of his followers came to think he was the messiah. This belief, however, was radically disconfirmed by what happened to him when he came to Jerusalem. He was summarily ex-

ecuted for sedition against the state, thereby shattering the hopes of his followers that he could be the future deliverer of his people. But these hopes took on a new life, so to say, when some of Jesus' followers came to believe that he had been raised from the dead. This belief compelled them to reassert their earlier convictions with even greater vigor: since God had vindicated Jesus, he must be the one they had said he was.

Even so, he clearly was not the messiah anyone had expected. The earliest Christian believers were therefore compelled to insist that the messiah, contrary to general expectation, was to die and be raised from the dead, and they began to search their Scriptures for divine proof. Thus began the distinctively Christian notion of a suffering messiah, who died for the sins of the world and was vindicated by God in a glorious resurrection.

begun. As the exalted one, he was already its ruler. He was, in fact exalted above all of creation; for believers, Jesus was the Lord of all that is, in heaven and on earth.

These new and important ways of understanding Jesus came to prominence quickly and naturally. Within several years after his death he was proclaimed in small communities scattered throughout the Eastern Mediterranean as the unique Son of God, the coming Son of Man, the Jewish messiah, and the Lord of all. Christians who understood Jesus in these ways naturally told stories about him that reflected their understanding. For example, when they mentioned Jesus' teaching about the Son of Man, they sometimes changed what he said so that instead of speaking about this other one to come, he was said to be speaking of himself, using the first person singular: "Whoever acknowledges me before others, I will acknowledge before my Father who is in heaven" (Matt 10:32; contrast Mark 8:38). Likewise, when Jesus spoke about himself, they sometimes changed words given in the first person singular ("I") to the title "Son of Man." Thus Matthew's form of Jesus' question to his disciples is, "Who do people say that the Son of Man is?" (Matt 16:13; contrast Mark 8:27).

JESUS' DEATH, ACCORDING TO THE SCRIPTURES

As we have seen, the earliest Christians had an obvious problem when they tried to convince their fellow Jews that Jesus was the one upon whom God had shown his special favor. For non-Christian Jews who were anticipating a messiah figure were not looking for anyone remotely like Jesus. To be sure, the Jewish messianic expectations reflected in the surviving sources are quite disparate. But they all had one thing in common: they all expected the messiah to be a powerful figure who would command the respect of friend and foe alike and lead the Jewish people into a new world that overcame the injustices of the old (see box 5.1). Jesus, on the other hand, was a relatively obscure teacher who was crucified for sedition against the empire. How could a convicted criminal be God's messiah? Jesus never overthrew the state; he was mocked, beaten, and executed by the state. For most Jews,

to call Jesus the messiah, let alone Lord of the universe, was preposterous, even blasphemous. To our knowledge, prior to the advent of Christianity, there were no Jews who believed that the messiah to come would suffer and die for the sins of the world and then return again in glory.

Christians today, of course, believe that this is precisely what the messiah was supposed to do. The reason they think so, however, is that the earliest Christians came to believe that the Jewish Bible anticipated the coming of a suffering messiah (see box 10.2). Recall: these earliest Christians were Jews who believed that God spoke to them through their sacred writings. For them, the Scriptures were not simply the records of past events; they were the words of God, directed to them, in their own situation. Not only the earliest Christians, but most Jews that we know about from this period understood the Scriptures in a personal way, as a revelation of meaning for their own times. Thus, even though the Hebrew Bible never specifically speaks of the messiah as one who is to suffer, there are passages, in the Psalms, for example, that speak of a righteous man who suffers at the hands of God's enemies and who comes to be vindicated by God. Originally, these **"Psalms of Lament"** may have been written by Jews who were undergoing particularly difficult times of oppression and who found relief in airing their complaints against the evil persons who attacked them and expressing their hopes that God would intervene on their behalf (e.g., see Psalms 22, 35, and 69). Christians who read such Psalms, however, saw in them not the expressions of oppressed, righteous Jews from the distant past but the embodiments of the pain, suffering, and ultimate vindication of the one truly righteous Jew who had recently been unjustly condemned and executed.

As they reflected on what had happened to Jesus, these Jewish Christians saw in his suffering and death a fulfillment of the words of the righteous sufferer described in the Psalms. In turn, these words shaped the ways Christians understood and described the events of Jesus' own Passion. They took the words of Psalm 22, for example, as expressive of the events surrounding Jesus' execution:

"My God, my God, why have you forsaken me" (v. 1); "All who see me mock at me, they make mouths at me, they shake their heads" (v. 7); "I am poured out like water, and all my bones are out of joint . . . my mouth is dried up like a potsherd, and my tongue sticks to my jaws" (vv. 14–15); "A company of evildoers encircles me. My hands and feet have shriveled; I can count all my bones—they stare and gloat over me; they divide my garments among them, and for my clothing they cast lots." (vv. 16–18)

For the early Christians, the sufferings of the righteous Jesus were foreshadowed by the sufferings of the righteous Jew of the Psalms. His sufferings were therefore no mere miscarriage of justice; they were the plan of God.

Other portions of Scripture explained why this suffering was God's plan. Again, these were passages that did not mention the messiah, but Christians nonetheless took them to refer to Jesus, whom they believed to be the messiah. Most important were passages found in the writings of the prophet Isaiah, who also speaks of the suffering of God's righteous one, whom he calls the "Servant of the Lord." According to the **"Songs of the Suffering Servant,"** as scholars have labeled four different passages in Isaiah, the most important

of which is Isa 52:13–53:12, this servant of God was one who suffered a heinous and shameful fate: he was despised and rejected (53:3); he was wounded and bruised (53:4–5); he was oppressed and afflicted; he suffered in silence and was eventually killed (53:7–8). This is one who suffered and died to atone for the sins of the people (53:4–5).

The interpretation of the original meaning of this passage is difficult, but the widely held view among scholars is that it was originally speaking of the suffering of the nation of Israel during the Babylonian captivity (see Isa 49:3). We have no indication that any Jew, prior to Christianity, ever took the passage as a reference to the future Jewish messiah. You may notice in reading it that the author refers to the Servant's suffering as already having taken place in the past (although his vindication is in the future). Christians, however, understood Jesus' own suffering in light of this and similar passages. For them, these ancient words described well what Jesus went through. Moreover, for them, Jesus clearly was the chosen one, given his resurrection and exaltation (see box 10.2). Their conclusion: God's messiah had to suffer as a sacrifice for the sins of the world. (see box 10.3)

The crucifixion, then, was turned from a stumbling block for Jews into a foundation stone for Christians (see 1 Cor 1:23). In reflecting upon their Scriptures, the earliest Jewish Christians concluded that Jesus was meant to suffer and die. His death was no mere miscarriage of justice; it was the eternal plan of God. Jesus faithfully carried out his mission, bringing salvation to the world. God therefore exalted him to heaven, making him the Lord of all and setting in motion the sequence of events that would lead to his return in fiery judgment on the earth.

Figure 10.1 Jesus was buried by Joseph of Arimathea in a tomb hewn in the rock, with a stone that rolled before the door (see Matt 27:60)—possibly much like this one. (Note the round rolling stone to the left of the entrance of the tomb.)

THE EMERGENCE OF DIFFERENT UNDERSTANDINGS OF JESUS

Not all the Christian communities that sprang up around the Mediterranean were completely unified in the ways they understood their belief in Jesus as the one who had died for the sins of the world. We have seen numerous differences that emerged among these groups, particularly as the religion spread from the small group of apocalyptically minded Jews who followed Jesus in Galilee

WHAT DO YOU THINK?

BOX 10.3 Vicarious Suffering in Jewish Martyrologies and Other Greco-Roman Literature

The idea that someone would suffer and die in order to save others, a notion called "**vicarious suffering**," was not invented by the Christians. Prior to Christianity the notion is found, for example, in a number of stories of Jewish martyrs. Is it possible that these tales affected the ways Christians narrated their stories about Jesus?

In the account of the Maccabean revolt known as 1 Maccabees, we find a Jewish warrior named Eleazar who single-handedly attacks an elephant thought to be bearing the king of Syria, the enemy of God. Eleazar ends up beneath the beast, crushed for his efforts. In the words of the author, "So he gave his life to save his people" (1 Macc 6:44).

A later account of martyrs from the Maccabean period, known as 4 Maccabees, describes in graphic detail the tortures that faithful Jews underwent because they refused to forsake the Law of Moses. The author claims that God accepted their deaths as a sacrifice on behalf of the people of Israel: "Because of them our enemies did not rule over our nation, the tyrant was punished, and the homeland purified—they having become, as it were, a ransom for the sin of our nation. And through the blood of those devout ones and their death as an atoning sacrifice, divine

Providence preserved Israel that previously had been mistreated" (4 Macc 17:20–22). In these writings, the death of the faithful martyr brings salvation to others.

Literary portrayals of vicarious suffering can be found in ancient pagan literature as well. One of the most interesting instances occurs in the moving play of Euripides entitled *Alcestis*. Alcestis is the beautiful wife of Admetus. He is fated to die at a young age, but the god Apollo, who had earlier befriended him, has worked out a special arrangement with the Fates: someone else can voluntarily die in his stead. Admetus tries in vain to persuade his parents to undertake the task as a familial duty. As a last resort, Alcestis agrees to perform the deed. After her death, Admetus is understandably stricken by grief, although, perversely enough, he is more upset that people will think badly of him than that he has actually made his wife sacrifice her own life for his. But he is comforted by the god Heracles, who goes down into Hades in order to rescue Alcestis from the throes of death and brings her back alive to her stricken husband. Euripides' story is thus about a person who voluntarily dies in someone else's stead and is then honored by a god who conquers death by raising the victim back to life. Sound familiar?

and Jerusalem to other regions and different types of people. This variety can be seen, on its most basic level, in the ways that different believers in the first decades of Christianity would have understood the descriptions of Jesus that we have already examined.

The term "Son of Man," for example, might have made sense to Jews familiar with the prediction of Dan 7:13–14 that "one like a son of man" was to come on the clouds of heaven. For such an audience, the identification of Jesus as the Son of Man would have meant that he was destined to be the cosmic judge of the earth. A pagan audience, on the other hand, would have had to be told about the book of Daniel, or, as sometimes happened, they would have tried to understand the

phrase as best they could, perhaps by taking it to mean that since Jesus was the son of a man, he was a real human being. This is the way many Christians today understand the term, even though it probably would not have meant this either to Jesus or to his apocalyptically minded followers.

The term "Son of God" would have meant something quite different to Jews, who could have taken it as a reference to the king of Israel (as in 2 Sam 7:14 and Psalm 2), than to Gentiles, for whom it would probably mean a divine man. The term "messiah" may have made no sense at all to Gentiles who were not familiar with its special significance in Jewish circles. Literally it would have designated someone who had been anointed or oiled (e.g., an athlete after a hard workout)—

scarcely a term of reverence for a religious leader, let alone for the Savior of the world!

Even communities that agreed on the basic meaning of these various titles may have disagreed on their significance as applied to Jesus. Take, for instance, the title Son of God. If, in the general sense, the title refers to Jesus' unique standing before God, the question naturally arises, when did Jesus receive this special status? Some early communities appear to have thought that he attained it at his resurrection when he was "begotten" by God as his son. This belief is reflected, for example, in the old traditions preserved in Acts 13:33–34 and Rom 1:3–4. Other communities, perhaps somewhat later, came to think that Jesus must have been God's special son not only after his death but also during his entire ministry. For these believers, Jesus became the Son of God at his baptism, when a voice from heaven proclaimed, "You are my son, today

I have begotten you," as the story is preserved in some manuscripts of Luke and among some Jewish Christians. Others came to think that Jesus must have been the Son of God not only for his ministry but for his entire life. Thus, in some of the later Gospels, we have accounts that show that Jesus had no human father, so that he literally was the Son of God (e.g., see Luke 1:35). Still other Christians came to believe that Jesus must have been the Son of God not simply from his birth but from eternity past. By the end of the first century, Christians in some circles had already proclaimed that Jesus was himself divine, that he existed prior to his birth, that he created the world and all that is in it, and that he came into the world on a divine mission as God himself. This is a far cry from the humble beginnings of Jesus as an apocalyptic prophet. Perhaps these beginnings can be likened to a mustard seed, the smallest of all seeds. . . .

Figure 10.2 Portrayal of Hercules (Heracles, with the club, middle) leading Alcestes (left) back to life from the god of the underworld, Pluto (seated), after she had voluntarily died in the place of her husband. The scene is found on a pagan sarcophagus of the second century C.E. (see box 10.3).

The various notions of who Jesus was, and the diverse interpretations of the significance of what he had said and done, came to be embodied in the various written accounts of his life. This, in my judgment, is a certainty. Otherwise, there is no way to explain the radically different portrayals of Jesus that we find, for instance, in the Gospels of Mark, John, *Thomas*, and *Peter*. It was only later, when Christians decided to collect several of these Gospels into a canon of Scripture that the differences came to be smoothed over. From that time on, Matthew, Mark, Luke, and John were all acclaimed as authoritative and interpreted in light of one another. Their placement in the Christian canon thus led to a homogenization, rather than illumination, of their distinctive emphases.

AT A GLANCE

BOX 10.4   From Jesus to the Gospels

1. Christianity is best understood as beginning not with the teachings of Jesus per se, or with his death or resurrection, but with the *belief* in his resurrection.

2. Once his followers came to believe he had been raised from the dead, and so had been shown unique favor by God, they reconsidered his teachings.

3. They began to claim that he himself was the Son of Man he had anticipated; that he was not simply close to God, but was the unique Son of God; and that he was not simply their leader and master, but was the Lord of the world.

4. They also reflected on the meaning of his death in light of their Scriptures, finding passages that referred to the death of God's righteous one and taking them to refer to Jesus.

5. These Christians then developed the idea, unknown to Judaism, that the messiah was one who must suffer and die.

6. Different Christian communities developed various understandings of who Jesus was and what he had done.

7. Some, but by no means all, of these different understandings are still reflected in our earliest Gospels, those of the New Testament. These Gospels may appear to represent the *same* understanding of Jesus, but to some extent, this is only because they have been placed side by side within a canon of Scripture.

TAKE A STAND

1. Make a careful and detailed comparison of the stories of Jesus' resurrection in Matthew 28, Mark 16, Luke 24, and John 20–21, noting all the major similarities and differences. How do you account for all the differences? Are there any differences that strike you as flat-out contradictions? If not, explain the passages that might *seem* to contain discrepancies.

2. You have just attended an evangelistic meeting in which the keynote speaker has argued that historians can prove that Jesus was physically raised from the dead. Do you agree that the resurrection is subject to historical "proof"? If so, explain why. If not, explain why not.

3. Some scholars have argued that Christianity is not so much the religion *of* Jesus (that is, the religion that Jesus had) as the religion *about* Jesus (that is, the religion based on the belief in his death and resurrection). Do you agree or not? State your reasons. And then answer the related question: Was Jesus a Christian?

 ## SUGGESTIONS FOR FURTHER READING

Bousset, Wilhelm. *Kurios Christos: A History of the Belief in Christ from the Beginnings of Christianity to Irenaeus.* Trans. John E. Steely. New York: Abingdon, 1970. A classic study that tries to show how the view of Jesus as the Lord developed very early in Christianity among Gentiles living in a polytheistic environment where there were numerous other competing "Lords."

Brown, Raymond. *The Death of the Messiah: From Gethsemane to the Grave.* 2 vols. London: Doubleday, 1994. A massive and exhaustive discussion of the Passion narratives of the Four Gospels; among other things, Brown discusses how the Jewish Scriptures influenced early Christian reflections on Jesus' death and resurrection.

Brown, Raymond E. *An Introduction to New Testament Christology.* New York: Paulist Press, 1994. A basic and solid overview of the varieties of ways the earliest Christians understood and portrayed Jesus, as represented within the writings of the New Testament.

Dunn, James D. G. *Christology in the Making: A New Testament Inquiry into the Origins of the Doctrine of the Incarnation.* 2d ed. Grand Rapids, Mich.: Eerdmans, 1996. A systematic attempt to understand how Christians developed their exalted views of Jesus through the New Testament period.

Fredriksen, Paula. *From Jesus to Christ: The Origins of the New Testament Images of Jesus.* New Haven, Conn.: Yale University Press, 1988. An important study of the earliest Christian views of Jesus and the ways they developed as Christianity moved away from its Jewish roots.

Fuller, Reginald. *Foundations of New Testament Christology.* London: James Clark, 2002. A classic study that explores the use of christological titles in the New Testament (e.g., Son of Man, Son of God, Messiah, Lord) to learn how early Christians developed their thinking about Jesus.

Hengel, Martin. *Between Jesus and Paul: Studies in the Earliest History of Christianity.* Trans. J. Bowden. Eugene, Ore.: Wipf and Stock, 2003. A collection of interesting and provocative essays that show the continuities between the apostle Paul's views and those that he inherited from the tradition before him, going back to Jesus; for more advanced students.

Hurtado, Larry. *One God, One Lord: Early Christian Devotion and Ancient Jewish Monotheism.* 2d ed. London: T & T Clark, 2003. A valuable study that argues that the source of conflict between early Christians and non-Christian Jews was not, strictly speaking, over whether Jesus could be thought of as divine but whether he was to be worshiped.

Kraemer, Ross, and Mary Rose D'Angelo, eds. *Women and Christian Origins.* New York: Oxford University Press, 1999. An excellent collection of essays dealing with major aspects of women and gender in the New Testament, early Christianity, early Judaism, and the broader Greco-Roman world.

 ## KEY TERMS

| Mary Magdalene | Psalms of Lament | Songs of the Suffering Servant | vicarious suffering |

The Material World of Jesus and the Gospels

Since most of our information about Jesus, the Gospels, and early Christianity comes from literary texts, it is not surprising that these have been the focus of attention for most New Testament scholars. Another field of inquiry, however, can also assist us in understanding the early Christian movement. Archaeologists try to discover and examine the material remains of ancient peoples and cultures, rather than literary remains; they are concerned not so much with interpreting written texts as with finding cultural artifacts that can help explain what it was like to live in a certain time and place. And occasionally the material remains of a culture—its public buildings, private houses, furniture, dishes and containers, utensils, tools, playthings, coins, objects of worship, and so on—can help explain (and sometimes cast doubt on) what is said in literary texts.

This brief insert contains some of the most striking archaeological discoveries that can help us further understand Jesus and the Gospels. Many of them illuminate the Greco-Roman and Jewish world in which Jesus and the evangelists lived; others have some direct bearing on the Gospel stories.

It should be emphasized that the material remains from antiquity do not provide us with direct, unmediated *facts*. Archaeological discoveries, like written texts, require interpretation. But considering material remains is another way of coming to the past and understanding it. The best history uses both material and literary remains to reconstruct the past.

Archaeological discoveries have been especially useful in providing indirect confirmation of persons, places, and events mentioned in the Gospels. Equally significant are discoveries that provide us with a sense of daily life, commerce, political events, and religious practices in the historical world of Jesus and his followers.

STATUES AND BUSTS

Modern Christians sometimes wonder what Jesus, the divine man they worship, actually looked like. People in the Roman Empire who considered their emperors divine men (see box 2.4 and pp. 15–18) did not have to wonder about *their* appearances: Statues and busts of the emperors could be found in public places throughout the empire. Figures 1 and 2 are examples of two of the most important emperors for the New Testament writings.

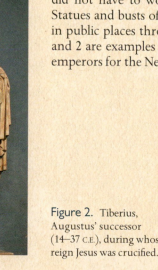

Figure 1. Caesar Augustus, the first emperor, during whose reign (27 B.C.E.–14 C.E.) Jesus was born.

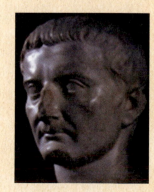

Figure 2. Tiberius, Augustus' successor (14–37 C.E.), during whose reign Jesus was crucified.

✗⊘ INSCRIPTIONS

Some of the most significant archaeological finds have been inscriptions—texts not written on paper (or papyrus or parchment), but cut into hard surfaces such as tombstones, potsherds, and, especially, monuments and walls (e.g., walls of temples, synagogues, public buildings). In an age in which literary texts were not in wide circulation, and in which most people could not read in any event, public inscriptions were a common form of mass communication, a public way to announce laws, proclaim major triumphs or successes, dedicate buildings, express gratitude for divine or human favor, push state or city propaganda, make public one's own accomplishments, and so on.

For parts of the Roman world, inscriptions are our best source of information about the culture and religion of a people (where, for example, no literary texts survive). On occasion, inscriptions confirm what we already knew, or suspected, from literary sources.

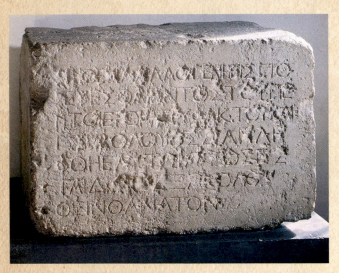

Figure 3. This inscription was discovered in the Temple in Jerusalem and confirms what Josephus says about the sanctity of the Temple. Josephus had indicated that Gentiles could enter within the walls but could not pass into the "Court of the Israelites," reserved only for Jews. This inscription, written in Greek, was mounted at one of the entry ways into the inner court and provided the following warning:

> "No foreigner may enter the forecourt beyond the barrier rail around the sanctuary; Anyone who is caught will have himself to blame for his own death."

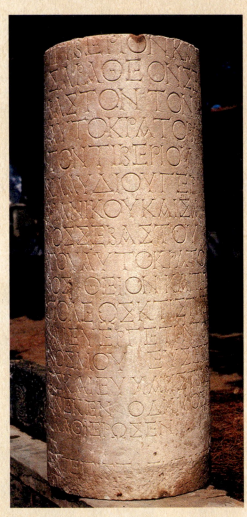

Figure 4. This commemorative inscription, written on a column, is comparable to what one could find throughout the empire. It was produced in the city of Sardis, in Asia Minor, indicating the honors that the city had voted to bestow on the emperor Tiberius.

☯ TEMPLES

Prominent among the buildings in public spaces throughout the Roman Empire were temples of the gods who were worshiped—whether local deities of the city or region or the great gods known to us today in Greek and Roman mythology. Temples were of a wide range of size and design: some were small simple structures, others were enormous, elaborate, and fantastically expensive.

Temples throughout the empire, however, tended to share common features. A temple was thought to be the house of a god, whose image was kept in an inner room. Temples were places to worship the god (or gods—since some temples were dedicated to more than one) through prayers, hymns, incense, and animal sacrifice. Altars tended to be outside the temple building itself, in the open air, where animals could be slaughtered and certain portions burned for the god(s). The rest of the animal was then cooked and eaten by the worshipers—either at home or in a dining facility connected with the temple. These sacrifices were special occasions that could be looked forward to as a time for a good meal and good drink with family and friends.

Most ancient temples are now in ruins, but often the ruins reveal just how spectacular they must have been in their day.

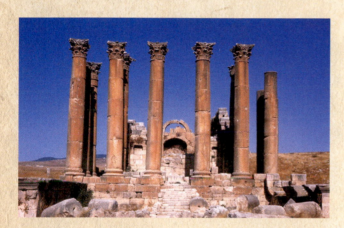

Figure 5. Greek temple to the goddess Artemis in Jerash (modern-day Jordan).

Figure 6. Temple to Zeus in Athens.

QUMRAN AND THE DEAD SEA SCROLLS

One of the most significant archaeological discoveries of modern times was completely accidental, made not by professional archaeologists but by bedouin living in the wilderness of Judea. In 1947, a shepherd boy happened to climb into a cave in an area just west of the Dead Sea and found there some earthenware jars that contained some very old scrolls. As it turns out, this was just the beginning of the story of discovery: as word got out that a cache of ancient documents had been uncovered, other bedouin (interested in the money such finds could bring) and professional scholars (interested in what such finds could reveal) searched the caves in the surrounding area. Archaeologists also excavated a nearby ruin.

Of the hundreds of caves nearby, eleven contained the remains of ancient texts. Some of the texts—including those discovered in a jar by the shepherd boy—were magnificent scrolls, extremely well preserved; others, especially those uncovered in the fourth cave, were in sad shape—thousands of small fragments from scrolls that had been eaten away over the years by the elements.

The Dead Sea Scrolls provide invaluable information for ancient historians, because they contain texts of the Hebrew Bible 1,000 years earlier than our previous oldest copies and writings from the Jewish sect of the Essenes, who evidently lived nearby in the settlement now called Qumran (after the name of a wadi beside it).

For more information about the Dead Sea Scrolls and their importance to the study of the New Testament and the historical Jesus, see pages 40–42.

Figure 7. Some of the caves, in the wilderness west of the Dead Sea near the Qumran community, in which the Dead Sea Scrolls were found.

Figure 8. Two of the scrolls discovered at Qumran, the Psalm Scroll (containing Psalms from the Hebrew Bible along with other, noncanonical Psalms), discovered in Cave 11 (left), and the Copper Scroll (a highly unusual scroll, actually made of rolled up copper, which describes places where buried treasure can be found), discovered in Cave 3 (right).

CAPERNAUM

One of the most significant places in the Gospels is Capernaum, where Jesus chose to establish his base of operation for his preaching ministry after leaving his home village of Nazareth (see Matt 4:13). Nazareth was a tiny village of perhaps 200 to 400 Jewish peasants. Capernaum was a step up from there: it had public buildings (including a synagogue), a larger population (600 to 1,500, according to the best recent estimates; see Reed), and easy access, via the Sea of Galilee, to other areas.

Since the nineteenth century, archaeologists have made important findings in Capernaum. The synagogue that has been excavated is from the fourth or fifth century, but it may stand on the site of an earlier structure in which Jesus is said to have preached in Mark 1:21. Moreover, in the 1960s, Italian archaeologists claimed to have uncovered the very house in which Simon Peter lived and Jesus stayed, underneath a church built in the fifth century to memorialize the spot.

Archaeology of the town itself has turned up no evidence of any "pagan" influence and no suggestion of much wealth. The houses were built on the foundations of basalt boulders common to the area and were made chiefly of stones with thatched roofs and dirt floors. This was principally a Jewish fishing village on the shores of the Sea of Galilee, possibly chosen by Jesus as the center of his ministry because of the easy access to other parts of the region by water.

Figure 9. Remains of some of the houses in Capernaum built on basalt rock.

Figure 10. The Capernaum synagogue, probably of the fourth or fifth century and possibly built on the spot of an earlier synagogue from the days of Jesus.

ON THE SEA OF GALILEE

A remarkable discovery was made in 1986 by two amateur archaeologists living on the Kibbutz Ginnosar on the northwest side of the Sea of Galilee. There had been a severe drought in the region for nearly two years, and the water from the Sea of Galilee was slowly evaporating, allowing them to explore on foot parts of the sea that had previously been underwater. One day, to their surprise, among the sundry coins and nails they turned up, they saw the oval outline of a boat buried in the mud.

After making some inquiries, they realized the boat must have been buried for some time. When they contacted a professional, he determined from the top exposed portion of the boat that it was in fact very ancient.

A sophisticated rescue operation was put into place, and the boat was retrieved from the mud, transported to a specially made holding facility, and studied carefully by experts.

The boat is now known to date to the first century, possibly to the time when Jesus and his disciples themselves were taking boats—the same kind of boats—across the Sea of Galilee. The spot of the discovery: just four miles or so from Capernaum, where Jesus centered his ministry.

Figure 11. The "Galilean Boat" discovered in 1986. It is 26 1/2 feet long, 7 1/2 feet wide, and 4 1/2 feet high. The boat had a mast (which did not survive), so it could have been either sailed or rowed (with four rowers). It was used for a long time—it had been repaired several times in antiquity—probably for fishing, but possibly also for transportation of goods and passengers.

FIGURES FROM THE LIFE OF JESUS

Rarely does archaeology provide specific verification of historical events known through our early Christian literary records. But three important discoveries have provided confirmation for historical figures otherwise known only from such literary sources as the Gospels and Josephus.

Figure 12. In 1962, Italian archaeologists uncovered this fragmentary stone from Caesarea. The stone had been reused in the fourth-century rebuilding of the theater there. The stone's fragmentary inscription reads "this Tiberium, Pontius Pilate, prefect of Judea, did. . . ." It was evidently set up at the request of Pilate to name himself as the one responsible for constructing a building in honor of the emperor Tiberius. This is the only material remains to name Pilate, the governor of Judea who condemned Jesus to death.

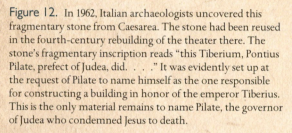

Figure 13. According to the Gospels, a man named Caiaphas was the high priest presiding in Jerusalem when Jesus was arrested. In 1990, construction workers in Jerusalem accidentally uncovered the burial chamber of Caiaphas's family. Inside the tomb was this ossuary, a stone container regularly used to store bones of a deceased person. Among the skeletal remains inside were evidently those of Caiaphas himself. On the side of the box, remarkably, is scribbled an Aramaic inscription "Yehosef bar Caiapha."

THE CRUCIFIXION

Crucifixion is mentioned in a wide range of ancient sources, and there are occasional references to the various ways Romans (who did not invent the practice; it was used by the Persians much earlier) performed the deed. But there are no explicit descriptions of how it was done. Until fairly recently there was not a single piece of archaeological evidence to explain the practice.

In 1968, however, a significant archaeological discovery was made in a suburb of Jerusalem: an ossuary with the skeletal remains of a man named Yehochanan (John) who had been crucified.

Yehochanan had been nailed to an upright beam of wood through the ankle, but the nail hit a knot in the wood and bent, making it difficult to be removed after his death. And so a chunk of the wood was broken off, and Yehocanan was buried with wood and nail still attached to the ankle bone.

The discovery of his remains caused quite a sensation, and experts who have examined them have drawn some important historical findings. Yehochanan, who would have been 5 feet 5 inches tall and probably in his mid-twenties, was nailed through the ankle on to the side of the upright beam; his arms were evidently tied rather than nailed.

It seems doubtful, however, that this was the normal mode of crucifixion—the early traditions about Jesus, written by first-century persons who presumably understood the practice quite well, presuppose that he was nailed in both wrists (hands) and feet (see John 20:25).

Figure 14. Remains of the crucified Yehochanan: the ankle bone with stake still in place.

Luke's Second Volume

THE BOOK OF ACTS

WHAT TO EXPECT

In this chapter we consider the second volume of Luke's two-volume work, the book of Acts (the first volume was the Gospel). Acts provides a historical sketch of the spread of the Christian Gospel by Jesus' apostles, especially the apostle Paul, a latecomer to the group, who converted to follow Jesus only after being a Christian persecutor.

Nearly a fourth of the book contains speeches given by Paul and other apostles—speeches to potential converts, to the converted, to governmental officials. How did Luke know what the apostles said on these occasions? Did someone take notes?

As we'll see, ancient historians typically *made up* the speeches of their main characters. As a result, by examining the speeches of an ancient narrative, you can get some insight into what the real author of the speeches (in this case, Luke) wanted to emphasize. That is what we will do in this chapter by introducing a new kind of analysis, the *thematic method*.

For people interested in knowing what happened to Jesus' followers after his death and resurrection, the Acts of the apostles has always been the first place to turn. This is our earliest account of the Christian church, an account that speaks of massive conversions to the faith, of miraculous deeds performed by the apostles, of opposition and persecution by nonbelievers, of the inner workings of the apostolic band and their interactions with significant newcomers like Paul, and, above all, of the dramatic spread of the Christian church from its inauspicious beginnings among the few followers of Jesus in Jerusalem to the heart of the empire, the city of Rome.

We have already seen that the book of Acts is the second volume of a two-volume work, as it was written by the same author who produced the Gospel of Luke (see Chapter 7). But it is not the same kind of book as that first volume. The Gospel of Luke portrays the life of Jesus, the rejected Jewish prophet, from his miraculous conception to his miraculous resurrection. The portrayal is comparable in many ways to the Gospels of Mark and Matthew and is best classified, in terms of genre, as a Greco-Roman biography. The book of Acts, however, is quite different. Here there is no solitary figure as a main character; instead, the book sketches the history of Christianity from the time of Jesus' resurrection to the Roman house arrest of the apostle Paul.

THE GENRE OF ACTS AND ITS SIGNIFICANCE

Some scholars have argued that since the two volumes were written as a set, they must be classified together, in the same genre. The books are structured quite differently, however. The book of Acts is concerned with the historical development of the Christian church. Moreover, the narrative is set within a chronological framework that begins with the origin of the movement. In these respects the Acts of the Apostles is closely related to other histories produced in antiquity.

Unlike biographies, **ancient histories** have a number of leading characters, sometimes, as in Josephus, a large number of them. Like biographies, however, they tend to utilize a wide range of subgenres, such as travel narratives, anecdotes, private letters, dialogues, and public speeches. On the whole, histories from Greco-Roman antiquity were creative literary exercises rather than simple regurgitations of names and dates; historians were necessarily inventive in the ways they collected and conveyed the information that they set forth.

All histories, however, whether from the ancient world or the modern, cannot be seen, ultimately, as objective accounts of what happened in the past. Because so many things happen in the course of history (actually, billions of things, every minute of every day), historians are compelled to pick and choose what to mention and what to describe as significant. They do so according to their own values, beliefs, and priorities. Thus, we can almost always assume that a historian has narrated events in a way that encapsulates his or her understanding of the meaning of those events.

This aspect of limited objectivity is particularly obvious in the case of historians living in antiquity. Theirs was a world of few written records but abundant oral tradition. Indeed, many ancient historians expressed a preference for hearing an account from an oral source rather than finding it in a written record. This approach stands somewhat at odds with the modern distrust of "mere hearsay," but there is some logic behind it: unlike written documents, oral sources can be interrogated to clarify ambiguities. Still, one can imagine the difficulties of determining what really happened on the basis of oral accounts. Moreover, when it came to the written record, ancient historians obviously had no access to modern techniques of data retrieval. For these reasons, they generally had little concern for, and less chance of, getting everything "right," at least in terms of the high level of historical accuracy expected by modern readers.

Nowhere can this be seen more clearly than in the case of sayings and speeches that are recorded in the ancient histories. On average, speeches take up nearly a quarter of the entire narrative in a typical Greco-Roman history. What is striking is that ancient historians who reflected on the art of their craft, like the Greek historian Thucydides (fifth century B.C.E.), admitted that speeches could never be reconstructed as they were really given: no one took notes or memorized long oratories on the spot. Historians quite consciously made up the speeches found in their accounts themselves, composing discourses that seemed to fit both the character of the speaker and the occasion.

What can we say then, in general terms, about the significance of the genre of Acts and the relationship of the book to the Gospel of Luke? When we read the book of Acts as an ancient history, we should expect to find a narration of events that the author considers significant for understanding the early Christian movement. Furthermore, if we are interested in reading his book as an ancient reader would, we should not evaluate it strictly in terms of factual accuracy. In addition, we should be looking for themes and points of view that parallel those found in volume one, the Gospel of Luke. Finally, since this book is also a chronologically arranged narrative, even though of a different kind from the Gospel, we might expect our ancient author to set the tone for the rest of the account at the very outset.

THE THEMATIC APPROACH TO ACTS

For each of the Gospels examined so far, I have explained and used a different method of analysis: a literary-historical method with Mark, a redactional method with Matthew, a comparative method with Luke, and a combination of these methods with John. Theoretically, each of these methods could be used with the book of Acts as well, even though it is the only general history preserved within the New Testament. Here, however, we will explore the possibilities of yet a fourth approach, one that might be labeled the "**thematic method**."

Every author has major ideas that he or she tries to communicate in writing. A thematic approach attempts to isolate these ideas, or themes, and through them to understand the author's over-arching emphases. Themes can be isolated in a number of ways—as we will see, the other methods can be useful in this regard—but the focus of attention is not on how the narrative plot unfolds (as in the literary-historical method) or on how the work compares and contrasts with another (as in the redactional and comparative). The focus is on the themes of the book and the ways they are developed throughout the work.

As with all methods, the thematic approach is best explained by showing it at work. In this introduction to Acts, we will focus on two portions of the narrative that provide special promise for understanding Luke's main emphases: the opening scene, which relates the work back to what has already transpired in the Gospel of Luke and anticipates what will take place in the narrative to follow, and the speeches of the main characters, which are scattered throughout the text and appear to represent compositions of the author himself.

FROM GOSPEL TO ACTS: THE OPENING TRANSITION

The first and most obvious thing to notice in the opening verses of Acts is that, like the Gospel of Luke, this book is dedicated to "Theophilus" (see p. 97), who is reminded of the basic content of the first volume of the work, namely, "all that Jesus did and taught from the beginning until the day when he was taken up to heaven" (1:1–2). This kind of opening summary statement was common in multivolume works of history in antiquity, as a transition from what had already been discussed. The dedication to Theophilus and the accurate summary of the first volume, as well as the similar themes and consistent writing style of Luke and Acts, have convinced virtually all scholars that the same author produced these two books.

The story of Acts begins with Jesus' appearances over a course of forty days after his resurrection. During this time, he convinces his former disciples that he has come back to life, and he teaches them about the kingdom (v. 3). In keeping with Luke's emphasis in volume one on Jerusalem as the place to which salvation came, the disciples are told to remain in Jerusalem until they receive the power of the Holy Spirit (v. 4; contrast the resurrection narratives of Mark and Matthew). In Acts the message of God's redemption goes forth from the holy city because it is rejected there. Just as Jesus the prophet was rejected by his own people in Jerusalem, so, too, his apostles will be rejected in Jerusalem. The spreading of the message was anticipated in the sermon of Jesus in Luke 4: because Jews will reject the message, it will be taken outside, to the Gentiles. The book of Acts is largely about this movement of the gospel from Jew to Gentile, from Jerusalem to the ends of the earth.

This theme is announced in these opening verses. The disciples inquire whether this is the time that the Kingdom will be brought to Israel (v. 6). They expect that now is the time in which their apocalyptic hopes will be realized, when God will intervene in history and establish his glorious kingdom for his people. We saw in the Gospel that Luke rejected the idea that the end was to come during the lifetime of Jesus' disciples. Here as well, Jesus tells his disciples not to be concerned about when the end will come. Instead, they are to work in the present to spread the gospel through the power of the Holy Spirit:

> It is not for you to know the times or periods that the Father has set by his own authority. But you will receive power when the Holy Spirit has come upon

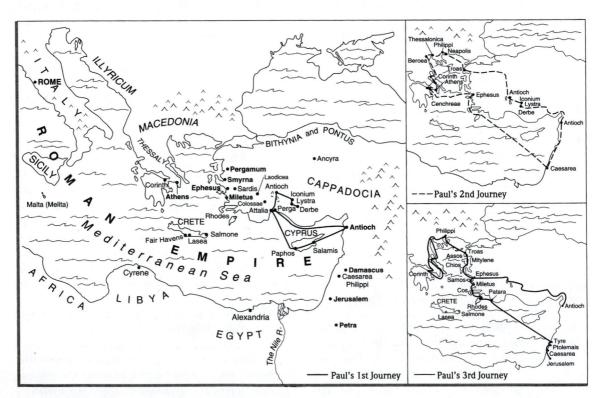

you; and you will be my witnesses in Jerusalem, and in all Judea and Samaria, and to the ends of the earth. (1:7–8)

This injunction to engage in the Christian mission foreshadows what is to take place throughout the rest of the book; indeed, the spread of the church provides the organizing motif for the entire narrative. In broad terms, it happens as follows. As anticipated, the Holy Spirit comes upon the apostles in the next chapter, on the day of Pentecost. The Spirit works miracles on their behalf and empowers them to proclaim the gospel of Christ. Thousands upon thousands of Jews convert as a result (chaps. 3–7), but opposition arises among the Jewish leadership, as it did in the case of Jesus himself in the Gospel. Christians scatter from the city, taking the gospel with them, first to Judea and Samaria (chap. 8). The most significant convert in these early years is a former opponent of the church, Saul, also known as Paul (chap. 9).

Largely, although not exclusively, through Paul's work, the gospel is taken outside Palestine and spreads throughout several of the provinces of the empire. Over the course of three missionary journeys (see fig. 11.1), Paul establishes churches in major cities in Cilicia, Asia Minor, Macedonia, and Achaia (which roughly correspond to modern-day Turkey and Greece; chaps. 13–20).

Eventually, he makes a fateful journey to Jerusalem (chap. 21), where he is arrested by Jewish leaders, put on trial, allowed to make several speeches in his own defense, and finally sent to stand before Caesar in Rome (chaps. 22–27). The book ends with Paul under house arrest in Rome, preaching the good news to all who will hear (chap. 28). This appears to fulfill Luke's anticipation that the gospel would go to the "ends of the earth," for the message of Christ has now spread far and wide, and is proclaimed in the very heart of the empire, in the capital city itself.

The geographic spread of the Christian church is not Luke's only concern in Acts. In some ways,

Figure 11.1 Paul's Missionary Journeys according to the Book of Acts.

Luke is even more dedicated to showing how the gospel came to cross ethnic boundaries. Indeed, he goes to great lengths to explain, and justify, how the Christian gospel ceased being a message only to Jews. To be sure, the earliest converts were Jews, as were Jesus himself and his closest disciples, but many Jews rejected this gospel. According to Luke, God therefore opened up the faith to the non-Jew. This first happens in chapter 8 with the conversion of a number of Samaritans, people who lived in Samaria who were considered to be "half-Jews" by many who lived in Judea. Soon thereafter, the apostle Peter learns through a vision that God means for the Gentiles also to hear and accept the message of salvation in Christ (chaps. 10–11). Much of the rest of the book shows how the gospel meets continual opposition among Jews in every province to which it goes but finds ready acceptance among Gentiles, especially those associated with the Jewish synagogues. The main character involved in spreading this gospel is Paul.

This emphasis on the Gentile mission of the church naturally raises some pressing questions. If the message of salvation that came to the Jews goes to the Gentiles, do these Gentiles first have to become Jews? To put the matter somewhat differently, if (as Luke's Gospel itself indicates) Jesus was a Jew, sent from the Jewish God as a Jewish prophet to the Jewish people, in fulfillment of the Jewish Scriptures, then isn't this religion Jewish? Surely for a person to become a follower of Jesus, he or she must first adopt Judaism. The author of Acts does not think so. As we will see, he devotes a good portion of his history to explaining why.

But if Gentiles coming into the church do not need to become Jewish, then hasn't the religion itself ceased being Jewish? And haven't its representatives, such as Paul, made an irreparable break with their Jewish past? Again, the author of Acts does not think so. And again, he devotes a good portion of his account to explaining why.

Before examining these explanations in the themes set forth in the speeches in Acts, we should complete our investigation of the opening passage. It ends with Jesus physically ascending into heaven. Two men in white robes suddenly appear to the apostles as they watch him depart. They tell the apostles not to stand by gaping into heaven, for just as Jesus departed from them, so he will return (vv. 10–11).

These words of comfort to the apostles may suggest that for Luke, even though the end of the age was not to come in the lifetime of Jesus' disciples, it was still destined to come soon. Indeed, Luke may have anticipated that it would come in his own lifetime; Jesus had yet to return on the clouds of heaven in judgment to set up his kingdom on earth. For Luke himself the end still is at hand, and the gospel needs to be proclaimed with yet greater urgency, as Jew and Gentile join together in their faith in the Christ of God.

Thus we can see many of the major themes of Luke's Gospel repeated at the outset of Acts, and we can anticipate their recurrence throughout the narrative (see box 11.1). These themes include the focus on Jerusalem, the proclamation of the gospel beginning with the Jews but moving to the Gentiles, the necessary delay of the end while this worldwide proclamation takes place, and, perhaps most important, the divine guidance of the Christian mission by the Holy Spirit. For Luke, it is God who directs the movement of the Christian church from start to end.

We can see how a number of these themes recur in the speeches delivered by the main characters of the book, speeches that reflect what "Luke," the author of the account, himself wrote and placed on their lips.

THEMES IN THE SPEECHES IN ACTS

As with most ancient histories, speeches figure prominently in the book of Acts. Indeed, they take up nearly one-quarter of the entire narrative, about average for histories of the period. To isolate some of the important Lukan themes in the book, we will examine several examples of different kinds of speeches.

One of the ways to classify the speeches in Acts is to consider the different kinds of audiences to which they are delivered, on the assumption that speakers will stress different things in different contexts. Some of the speeches are delivered by Christian leaders to other Christians as a means of instruction or exhortation, others are addressed by Christians

BOX 11.1   Luke's Artistry as a Storyteller I

Readers of the New Testament have long noticed many clear similarities between what happens to Jesus in the Gospel of Luke and to Christian believers in the book of Acts. These parallels show that Luke was no mere chronicler of events, set on providing an objective account of the early years of the Christian movement. He compiled this history with a clear purpose, part of which was to show that the hand of God was behind the mission of the church as much as it was behind the mission of Jesus. Thus, for example, at the beginning of Jesus' ministry in Luke, he is baptized and receives the Holy Spirit; when new believers are baptized in the book of Acts, they also receive the Spirit. The Spirit empowers Jesus to do miracles and to preach in Luke; so, too, it empowers the apostles to do miracles and to preach in Acts. In Luke, Jesus heals the sick, casts out demons, and raises the dead; in Acts, the apostles heal the sick, cast out demons, and raise the dead. The Jewish authorities in Jerusalem confront Jesus in Luke; the same authorities confront the apostles in Acts. Jesus is imprisoned, condemned, and executed in Luke; some of his followers are imprisoned, condemned, and executed in Acts.

These parallels are not simply interesting coincidences. One author has produced both books, and he uses the parallel accounts to make a major point: the apostles continue to do Jesus' work and thereby prolong his mission through the power of the same Spirit. Thus they engage in similar activities, experience similar receptions, and suffer similar fates.

---

to potential converts in the context of evangelism, and yet others are given by Christians to legal or religious authorities, as apologies (see box 7.1).

Speeches to Christian Believers

Peter's Opening Speech. The first speech in the book is delivered by Peter, right at the outset of the narrative. After seeing Jesus ascend into heaven, the eleven disciples return to Jerusalem and devote themselves to prayer with Jesus' female followers and family. The first concrete action that the group takes is to elect a new member of "the Twelve" to replace Judas Iscariot, who after betraying Jesus suffered an ignominious death (see box 11.3). Peter arises and delivers a speech on how they ought to proceed in their new circumstances (1:15–22). The speech anticipates many of the central themes of the book, including the important issue of how this new religious movement relates to its Jewish roots. Before delving into Peter's view of this relationship (at least, as Luke portrays it), we should consider the broader context.

To most Jews in the book of Acts, the Christian claims about Jesus are altogether unacceptable, and throughout the narrative the principal instigators of persecution against the Christians are Jews. From a historical perspective, this opposition is understandable. Christians claimed that Jesus was the messiah, but the messiah, in the expectations of most Jews, was to be a figure of power and grandeur who brought in the millennial age of peace. Jesus, on the other hand, was a crucified criminal. In the opinion of most Jews (both historically and in the narrative of Acts), those who proclaim Jesus as the messiah have not only lost touch with their Jewish roots, they have also violated the clear teaching of Scripture.

Luke has a different perspective. We have already seen that some of Luke's predecessors and contemporaries (e.g., Mark and Matthew) claimed that Jesus was the fulfillment of the Jewish Scriptures. Luke takes this view a step further. The entire Christian movement *after* Jesus is a fulfillment of Scripture as well. This theme is played out in the narrative of Acts and is anticipated already by the opening words of Peter's first speech. Peter argues that the death of Judas, and the need to replace him with someone else, was predicted by David in the Psalms.

BOX 11.2 Luke's Artistry as a Storyteller 2

Luke's literary artistry is not limited to creating parallels between the Gospel and Acts (see box 11.1). Just as interesting are the parallels between the main characters in the narrative of Acts itself, particularly between Peter, the main character of chapters 1–12, and Paul, the main character of chapters 13–28.

Several examples of these parallels stand out. Both Peter and Paul preach sermons to Jewish crowds, and what they have to say is in many respects remarkably similar (e.g., see the speeches in chaps. 3 and 13). Both perform amazing miracles; both, for example, cure the sick without having any direct contact with them. Thus Peter's shadow can bring healing (5:15), as can Paul's handkerchiefs (19:12). Both are violently opposed by leaders among the Jews but vindicated

by God; they are imprisoned for their proclamation yet delivered from their chains by divine intervention (12:1–11; 16:19–34). Perhaps most important of all, both become absolutely convinced, on the grounds of divine revelation and the success of their proclamation, that God has decided to admit Gentiles into the church without their first becoming Jews (chaps. 10–11, 15).

These parallels reinforce our earlier impression that throughout this narrative Luke is intent on showing that God is at work in the Christian mission. Those who are faithful to God give similar speeches with similar results; they perform similar miracles, receive similar revelations, and experience similar fates. Luke's artistry, then, serves a clear thematic purpose.

Peter cites two Psalm texts to support his view (1:20). Since he is addressing a friendly audience, he evidently does not need to provide a rationale for the way he interprets these passages. But if you read these quotations in their original contexts (Psalm 69 and Psalm 109), you will probably find it hard to understand how anyone could think that they predict what was going to happen hundreds of years later to one of the messiah's followers. In Luke's account, however, Peter interprets them in precisely this way. This in itself can tell us something about what was happening at the time of Luke, the author of Peter's speech. In Luke's own day, Christians were evidently combing the Jewish Scriptures to find indications of what had been fulfilled in their midst, not only in the life of Jesus but also in the life of their own communities. From Luke's perspective, the history of Christianity fulfills the Scriptures.

This basic approach to the Jewish Scriptures was not unique to early Christianity. In any event, since Luke understood not only Jesus but also the entire Christian movement to be a fulfillment of the Jewish Scriptures, he did not see it as standing in opposition to Judaism. Rather, it was in direct con-

tinuity with it. Why, then, would Christianity be rejected by leaders among the Jews? Luke's reader is left to infer that those who opposed Jesus' followers were necessarily opposed to their own religion and, as a consequence, to their own God. This is a strong statement, even if made only by implication.

Perhaps more obviously, as a corollary, Luke's view that Christianity is a fulfillment of Scripture indicates that God himself was behind the Christian movement. This indeed is perhaps the overarching theme of the entire narrative. This movement comes from God (see especially 5:33–39). God's involvement is clearly seen in one other way in this early scene, although not directly in Peter's speech itself. How do the disciples elect a new member to join the Twelve? They pray and cast lots. This was an ancient method of determining the divine will for an action. A jar containing two or more stones or bones was shaken until one of them fell out. Since the process could not be rigged, the lot that fell was understood to be God's choice. Evidently, the procedure worked to Luke's satisfaction: Matthias becomes the twelfth apostle.

This takes us back to Peter's speech and the final theme for us to consider. The speech is meant to

BOX 11.3 The Death of Judas

Only two passages of the New Testament describe the death of Judas: Acts 1:18–19 and Matt 27:3–10. It is interesting to compare their similarities and differences. In Matthew, Judas tries to return the thirty pieces of silver that he has been paid to betray Jesus. When the priests refuse to take them, he throws them down in the Temple and goes out and hangs himself. The priests are unable to use the silver for the Temple treasury, since it is "blood money," that is, money tainted with the blood of Jesus' execution, so they decide to use it to purchase a piece of property as a place to bury strangers. From that time on, since the place was bought with blood money, it was appropriately called the "Field of Blood."

In Acts Judas's death is again associated with the Field of Blood but for an entirely different reason. In Peter's speech we learn that Judas himself purchased the field, after which he died a bloody death. He does not appear to have hanged himself, however; Peter says that he fell headlong and burst in the middle so that his intestines "gushed out." It is hard to know what Luke, the author of Peter's speech, has in mind

as the cause of death (was it a suicide? did Judas fall on a sword? did he jump off a cliff? did he spontaneously swell up and burst?). In any event, Luke clearly thinks the Field of Blood obtained its name from Judas's blood being spilled on it.

These two accounts are difficult to reconcile, but in some respects it is their similarities that are of greatest interest. Why do they both connect the name of this Field of Blood with the death of Judas? Is it possible that there actually was a field in Jerusalem made up of red clay and called the Field of Blood because of its color? A slight piece of evidence for this conclusion derives from Matthew, who indicates that it was a "potter's field" (27:10), that is, a field from which clay was extracted for pottery. It is difficult to decide whether Judas actually killed himself there, whether he was at some point its owner, or whether his blood money was used to purchase it. At the least, we can say that later Christians came to associate this clay lot with the disciple who had betrayed his master and then experienced an ignominious death.

persuade the believers to engage in a particular course of action. This is a typical feature of speeches to believers in this book, but what is curious in the context of the wider narrative is the particular course of action that Peter urges. Peter persuades the assembly to elect a new member of the Twelve to be a witness of Jesus' resurrection. This is to be a person who had accompanied the other disciples throughout the whole of Jesus' ministry, from his baptism by John to his ascension (1:21–22). The first requirement is itself somewhat odd, in that Jesus does not call his disciples until well after his baptism in Luke (see Luke 5); in any event, the new member of the apostolic band was to have been with Jesus from the outset of his ministry.

What is more perplexing is that the speech intimates that the election of this new apostle is crucial for the propagation of the Christian gospel that is to take place in the subsequent narrative. In fact,

this is not the case at all. After Matthias is elected to be an apostle, he is never mentioned again in the book of Acts. Why, then, does Luke compose a speech urging his election? To put the question into a broader context, I should point out that Matthias is not the only apostle who fails to appear in the rest of the narrative. Most of the Twelve do not. Why would a book entitled "The Acts of the Apostles" not discuss the acts of the apostles?

As already seen, the titles of our New Testament books were not original but were added by later Christian scribes. In this case, at least, the title is not at all apt. For the book is not about the deeds of the apostles per se but about the spread of the Christian religion through the labors of only a few of them, and about the reactions that it provoked among those who refused to accept it. Indeed, there are only two main characters in the book (along with numerous minor characters), one of whom, the chief protagonist for most of the narrative, is Paul, who was not one of the Twelve.

Why is it so important for Luke to begin his account with the election of a twelfth apostle, if neither he nor most of his companions figure prominently in the narrative, whereas one who is not among their number ends up being the central character? Perhaps the answer relates to another of Luke's prominent themes: the notion of continuity in early Christianity. We have already seen one form of continuity in our discussion of Luke's Gospel, namely, the continuity between Jesus and Judaism; we have uncovered a second form in our study of Acts to this point, the continuity between Judaism and Christianity. But there is yet a third form at work in Luke's narrative—a continuity between Jesus and his church. This continuity is assured by the Twelve, who start out as Jesus' original disciples and provide the transition as the leaders of the Christian community in Jerusalem. The thematic point for Luke is that Christianity is not something that begins, strictly speaking, after Jesus' death. It is something that is intimately connected

with his life. Those who were closest to Jesus in his lifetime were responsible for the original dissemination of this religion after his death.

Indeed, even though the twelve apostles rarely appear individually (with the chief exception of Peter and the partial exception of John), they play a prominent role in the founding of the church at the outset of the narrative. They are present en masse when Peter preaches his first evangelistic sermon, converting several thousand Jews (2:14); they are the teachers of the newfound community of faith, a community unified around their instruction (2:42); they perform miracles, convincing others to believe (2:43; 5:12); they edify believers by testifying to the resurrection of Jesus (4:33); and they organize and run that early community, distributing funds that are raised and taking care of those in need (4:35–36). Moreover, they make all the key decisions affecting the church throughout the world. This final theme comes to prominence in the series of speeches delivered to believers assembled for the famous Jerusalem Council in chapter 15, another critical juncture of the narrative.

Figure 11.2 Peter, Jesus, and Paul, the three most important characters of Luke-Acts, from a catacomb painting in Rome.

The Speeches at the Jerusalem Council. The narrative backdrop of these speeches is as follows. After Paul is converted by a vision of Jesus on the road to Damascus (chap. 9), the apostle Peter learns through a vision and an encounter with a group of believing Gentiles that God makes no distinction between Jew and Gentile, that Gentiles can belong to the people of God without first becoming Jews (chaps. 10–11). Soon thereafter, Paul and his companion Barnabas are set apart by the church in Antioch as missionaries to other lands; they engage in an evangelistic campaign (Paul's "first missionary journey"), chiefly in Asia Minor. Some Jews convert, but many others resist; Paul comes to be opposed, sometimes with violence, by leaders of the Jewish synagogues (chaps. 13–14). This Jewish opposition in turn forces Paul and Barnabas to proclaim their faith to the Gentiles, many of whom come to faith.

When they arrive back in Antioch, Paul and Barnabas are confronted by Christians from Judea who insist that Gentile men must be circumcised to experience salvation. This leads to a major controversy. Paul, Barnabas, and several others are appointed to go to Jerusalem to discuss the matter with the apostles. At this conference, Peter and James, the brother of Jesus, give their opinions in speeches delivered to the assembled body of believers.

Many of the themes that we have already isolated in Acts can be found here as well (15:7–21): God has been totally in charge of the Christian mission, including the conversion of the Gentiles (vv. 7–8); he makes no distinction between Jew and Gentile in that all are saved on equal grounds (vv. 9–11); and the salvation of the Gentiles represents a fulfillment of Scripture (vv. 15–19). Once the apostles, along with the other leaders of the Jerusalem church, have heard these speeches, they are unified in their judgment and write a letter to the Gentile churches explaining their decision. The net result is that not just the Jerusalem church but all the churches in the empire (e.g., those founded by Paul and Barnabas) stand under the leadership of the apostles, the original eyewitnesses of Jesus, who are themselves totally unified in their teaching.

In Sum: Speeches to Believers in Acts. What can we say in conclusion about the important themes found in the speeches of Christians to other believers in Acts? Above all, they tell us something about Luke's view of the nature of the early Christian church. Strictly speaking, the church for Luke is not a new thing. On the one hand, it represents the fulfillment of the Jewish Scriptures; on the other hand, it stands in direct continuity with Jesus through the twelve apostles. These apostles may not have been directly involved in the spread of this religion after the opening scenes of the narrative— it is chiefly Paul, who is not one of their number, who takes the gospel abroad—but they are the ones who bear ultimate responsibility for this mission. They began the process in Jerusalem and continue to guide and direct the church along the paths ordained by God. Moreover, these apostles are in complete agreement on every important issue confronting the church. The church begins with a golden age of peace and unity under the leadership of the apostles.

Evangelistic Speeches: Peter's Speech on the Day of Pentecost

We can now turn to consider several of the speeches delivered by Christians to potential converts. Each speech, of course, has unique elements of its own, but certain basic themes recur throughout them all. Our thematic approach will isolate these recurring motifs in the first evangelistic speech of the narrative, the one delivered by Peter on the Day of Pentecost in chapter 2 (see also the speeches in 3:12–26; 4:8–12, 23–30; 7:1–53; and 13:16–41).

The Pentecost speech immediately follows the coming of the Holy Spirit, an event predicted by Jesus in both Luke and Acts. After the election of Matthias, the followers of Jesus are gathered together in one place when they suddenly hear a sound like strong wind and see tongues like fire alighting on one another's heads. They begin to speak in foreign languages that none of them has previously learned. A large number of Jews from around the world has gathered in Jerusalem for the feast of Pentecost (the annual Jewish agricultural feast that took place fifty days after Passover). Crowds descend upon the spirit-filled apostles and their colleagues; the foreigners are shocked to hear "Galileans" speaking to them in their own native languages. Some of the bystanders begin to mock the apostolic band as a group of drunk and rowdy revelers.

Figure 11.3 The remains of the theater in Ephesus, where, according to Acts 19, a riot nearly erupted over the preaching of Paul, whose message threatened the local pagan idol-making industry.

This development provides Peter with an occasion to make a speech and an audience to hear it. He declares that what has happened is nothing less than a fulfillment of the plan of God as foretold by the prophet Joel:

In the last days it will be, God declares, that I will pour out my Spirit upon all flesh, and your sons and your daughters shall prophesy, and your young men shall see visions, and your old men shall dream dreams. (2:17, quoting Joel 2:28)

Peter is particularly emphatic that the Spirit that has come among the believers has been sent by none other than Jesus. The sermon quickly shifts to who Jesus is and to the way in which he can affect a person's standing before God (2:22–36). Here we come to one of the most interesting aspects of the theology of Luke, the author of the speech. Jesus is portrayed here as a mighty man who did fantastic miracles, who was lawlessly executed by evil people but vindicated by God, who raised him from the dead in fulfillment of the Scriptures. After this brief narration of Jesus' story, Peter moves quickly to the climax of his speech: "God has made him both Lord and Messiah, this Jesus whom you crucified" (v. 36).

The point is quite clear. Jesus was the innocent victim of miscarried justice and the people who hear the sermon are themselves to blame, but God reversed their evil action by raising Jesus. The message has its desired effect: cut to the quick, the crowds ask what they should do, that is, how they might make amends for their evil deed. Peter gives an immediate response: they must repent of their sins and be baptized in the name of Jesus. Those who do so will find forgiveness (vv. 38–39).

As you can see, the way Peter describes Jesus and the salvation he brings corresponds with the views that we found in the Gospel according to Luke. Jesus' death does not bring an atonement (contrast Mark's Gospel). It is a miscarriage of justice. Nor does Jesus' resurrection, in itself, bring salvation. It instead demonstrates Jesus' vindication by God. How then do Jesus' death and resurrection affect a person's standing before God, according to this evangelistic speech in Acts? When people recognize how maliciously Jesus was treated, they realize their own guilt before God—even if they were not present at Jesus' trial. They have committed sins, and the death of Jesus is a symbol of the worst sin imaginable, the execution of the prophet chosen by God. The news of Jesus' death and vindication drives people to their knees in repentance. When they turn from their sins and join the community of Christian believers (through baptism), they are forgiven and granted salvation.

Thus salvation for Luke does not come through the death of Jesus per se; it comes through repentance and the forgiveness of sins. This theme is played out in all the missionary sermons of Acts. As the Christian preachers emphasize time and again, Jews have a history of disobedience to God, a history that has climaxed in their execution of God's Son Jesus. They must realize how wrong they have been and turn to God to make it right.

Most of the Jews in the book continue to manifest an attitude of disobedience, from Luke's perspective. They not only resist the message of salvation, they actively reject it by opposing the Christian mission and persecuting the Christian missionaries. The persecution begins in Jerusalem but continues everywhere the message is proclaimed. It leads to the first martyrdom in early Christianity, that of Stephen, following a lengthy missionary speech (chaps. 7–8). Before long, the opposition is headed by Saul of Tarsus (Paul), who participates in Stephen's death but, as we have seen, soon converts to Christianity and becomes its leading missionary.

Paul's conversion does nothing to abate the Jewish opposition to the faith. If anything, it intensifies it. In virtually every city and town that he enters, after experiencing some initial success among Jews in the synagogues, Paul is violently opposed by Jewish authorities, who drive him out. After making three missionary journeys to Asia Minor, Macedonia, and Achaia, he makes a final fateful trip to Jerusalem (compare Jesus in the Gospel). There he is arrested by the authorities at the instigation of the unbelieving Jews and forced to stand trial, on a number of occasions, for his faith.

Paul's arrest and trials take up a substantial portion of the narrative in Acts (chaps. 21–28; compara-

ble to the space devoted to Jesus' last days in Luke). Much of this final third of the book is devoted to speeches in which Paul defends himself against accusations by Jewish leaders that he has violated the Torah and is a menace to the Empire. By considering some of the themes of these **"apologetic" speeches**, we will see yet further aspects of Luke's overall conception of the early Christian church.

Apologetic Speeches: Paul's Final Appeal to Jews in Rome

Before we examine the themes of the apologetic speeches, we should review the basic narrative. Paul is arrested in Jerusalem while making an offering in the Temple, which was meant to show that he was in no way opposed to the Law of Moses (chap. 21). He is taken into Roman custody and allowed to make a defense to the Jewish crowds (chap. 22). He is then made to stand trial before the Jewish Sanhedrin (chap. 23). When the Roman tribune learns of a plot to assassinate him, he has him removed to Caesarea to await trial before the governor Felix (chap. 23). He there makes his defense, but Felix, hoping for a bribe, leaves him in prison for two years (chap. 24). Felix is replaced as governor by Porcius Festus, who also puts Paul on trial. Rather than heeding Paul's plea of innocence, Festus chooses to ingratiate himself with the Jewish leaders by offering to let Paul stand trial before them in Jerusalem. Realizing the slim odds of a fair hearing there, Paul demands his rights as a Roman citizen to stand before the emperor himself (chap. 25). Before departing for Rome, Paul has an opportunity to speak before the visiting king of the Jews, Herod Agrippa II (chap. 26).

Every time Paul defends himself in these chapters, the ruling authorities have ample opportunity to recognize his innocence. But either because of a desire for a bribe (Felix), or as a favor to the Jewish leaders (Festus), or because of Paul's appeal to Caesar (Festus and Agrippa), nothing is done to release him. He is instead sent to Rome to stand trial before Caesar. On the way, he experiences a number of harrowing adventures at sea, including shipwreck (chap. 27). He miraculously survives, however, and makes it to Rome, where the book ends with him under house arrest for two years. As he awaits trial, he preaches to all

Figure 11.4 Portrayal of one of Jesus' apostles, preaching the Gospel, with scroll in hand, from a fifth-century ivory panel now in the Louvre (Paris).

to release me, because there was no reason for the death penalty in my case. But when the Jews objected, I was compelled to appeal to the emperor—even though I had no charge to bring against my nation. For this reason therefore I have asked to see you and speak with you, since it is for the sake of the hope of Israel that I am bound with this chain. (28:17–20)

Here are sounded the characteristic themes of Paul's apology: (*a*) he has done nothing against the Jewish people or Jewish customs, but on the contrary continues to subscribe in every way to the religion of Judaism; (*b*) he was found to be innocent by the Roman authorities; and (*c*) his current problems are entirely the fault of recalcitrant Jewish leaders. The final theme we have already seen throughout the book of Acts. What might we say about the other two?

Just as Jesus is portrayed as fully Jewish in the Gospel of Luke (see, for example, the early emphasis on the Temple and Jerusalem), and the earliest Christian movement is portrayed as fully Jewish in the opening chapters of Acts (where Christians spend their days in the Temple), so Paul is shown to be devoted to his ancestral traditions even after his conversion. He is a Jewish Christian who does nothing at any time contrary to the Law of Moses. To be sure, he is accused of violating the Law—when he is arrested in chapter 21, he is charged with bringing Gentiles into an area of the Temple reserved for Jews—but Luke goes out of his way to show that the charge is categorically false. Paul's companions in the Temple were Jews. They were fulfilling their sacred vows as prescribed in the Torah. Paul himself was there to pay for these vows and to perform a sacrifice of cleansing. Thus Paul is portrayed here as incontrovertibly Jewish.

This portrayal of Paul is consistent throughout the entire narrative of Acts. Never does Paul renounce his faith in the God of Israel, never does he violate any of the dictates of Torah, never does he spurn Jewish customs or practices. His sole "faults" are his decisions to believe in Jesus and to take his message to the Gentiles. For Paul himself, however, neither his newfound faith nor his Gentile mission compromise his Jewish religion; quite the contrary, they represent fulfillments of Judaism.

who would hear and defends himself against all charges (chap. 28).

As was the case with the speeches to believers and to potential converts, each of the apologetic speeches in Acts has its own orientation and emphasis. Here again, a number of themes recur throughout. One of the shortest speeches of the entire book is delivered to the local Jewish leaders in Rome, who appear before Paul in the final chapter:

Brothers, though I had done nothing against our people or the customs of our ancestors, yet I was arrested in Jerusalem and handed over to the Romans. When they had examined me, the Romans wanted

ANOTHER EARLY CHRISTIAN TEXT

BOX 11.4 The Acts of John

The Acts of the Apostles is the only narrative account of the apostles' (postresurrection) activities in the New Testament, but there were numerous accounts written later. These "apocryphal" (i.e., noncanonical) Acts are highly legendary descriptions of the adventures and escapades of individual apostles who take the Gospel throughout the world. And so we have a range of Acts: of Peter, of Paul, of Andrew, and so on. Among the most famous of the apocryphal Acts is one about his close disciple, John, the son of Zebedee.

This is an account filled with John's miraculous deeds. John is a man of wondrous powers, who can even raise people from the dead to the amazement of the crowds, who regularly convert when they observe his unique abilities. In one of the strangest tales of the account, however, John does not work miracles to convert others, but to provide himself with a good night's sleep. The story involves a large number of pestiferous bed bugs.

John and his companions have come to a country inn to spend the night, but upon lying down, John discovers to his dismay that the bed is infested with nasty bugs. He needs his rest, and so orders the critters to leave him in peace. His companions find this amusing, until they get up the next morning to see a large throng of bedbugs waiting at the door. John wakes up and tells the bugs they can return now to their home, and they obediently do so.

Here is an apostle who not only has power over life and death, but even over the nasty little creatures of the world that can make one's life miserable and ruin one's beauty rest. (For another apocryphal Acts, see the *Acts of Thecla* discussed in box 18.4.)

Throughout his speeches in Acts, Paul stresses that his new faith is rooted in Jesus' resurrection from the dead (the "hope of Israel," 28:20). Moreover, he insists that belief in the resurrection is the cornerstone of the Jewish religion. For him, failure to believe in Jesus' resurrection results from a failure to believe that God raises the dead. And failure to believe that God raises the dead is to doubt the Scriptures and deny the central affirmation of Judaism. For this reason, according to Paul's speeches, faith in Jesus' resurrection is an affirmation of Judaism, not a rejection of it.

This does not mean that Paul (as portrayed by Luke) maintained that Gentiles have to become Jews in order to belong to the people of God. In fact, Gentiles are allowed to remain Gentiles and are not compelled to practice circumcision or to keep kosher food laws. For Luke this is far from a rejection of Judaism; throughout this book, Jews like Paul remain Jewish, even after coming to faith in Christ.

Thus, part of Paul's defense in Acts is to show that he has not compromised his Judaism one iota by becoming a believer in Jesus. The other part relates to his standing before the Roman Empire. His opponents claim that he is a dangerous person who must be destroyed. As you might expect, Luke has a different opinion. Indeed, his narrative shows that Paul was innocent of any wrongdoing, just as Jesus was in the Gospel. As Paul himself proclaims in his apologetic speeches, he has violated no laws and caused no problems for the ruling authorities. Problems erupt only because those who hear Paul's proclamation oppose him and create disturbances. As we have seen, in most instances it is Jews who are at fault (interestingly, Luke never portrays these rabble-rousers as being punished; for him, it is only the innocent who suffer!). On occasion there are pagans to blame (e.g., see the riot in Ephesus in chap. 17). In no case is Paul himself responsible for any wrongdoing, as even the governors before whom he appears attest. Nonetheless, just as Pilate condemned Jesus to death after declaring him innocent, so the Roman administrators of Acts treat Paul as if he is guilty, knowing full well that he is not.

In one sense, as a prominent spokesperson of the emerging Christian church, Paul represents

AT A GLANCE

BOX 11.5 The Book of Acts

1. The book of Acts is the second of a two-volume work by the author of Luke. It, too, is dedicated to an otherwise unknown "Theophilus."

2. These books have been traditionally ascribed to Luke, the traveling companion of Paul; there are, however, reasons to suspect this tradition.

3. Like the Gospel of Luke, the book was written around 80–85 C.E.

4. A thematic approach to the book reveals several prominent themes:

   a. The Jewish origins of Christianity, its fulfillment of the Jewish Scriptures, and its continuity with Judaism.

   b. The portrayal of Jesus as a Jewish prophet, rejected by his own people.

   c. The consequent movement of the religion from the Jews to the Gentiles and a concomitant geographic shift from the holy city of Jerusalem to the ends of the earth.

   d. The proclamation to Jew and Gentile alike of salvation through the repentance of sins and the forgiveness of God, with Gentiles who accept this offer of salvation not needing to adopt the ways of Judaism.

   e. The delay of the time of the end to make this Christian mission a possibility.

   f. The "rightness" of this religion in both the divine sense (it came from God in fulfillment of the Scriptures) and the human one (it did nothing to violate Jewish custom or imperial law).

   g. The complete unity and harmony of the church as guided by the apostles, who agree on every issue and resolve every problem through the direction of the Spirit.

   h. Ultimately, the hand of God directing the course of Christian history behind the scenes, from Jesus' own life and death to the life and ministry of the apostles he left behind.

---

the entire Christian movement for Luke. Here is one who remained faithful to his Jewish roots and in full compliance with the laws of the state. The narrative of his trials and defenses shows that the disturbances that erupted during the early years of the Christian movement could not be laid on the Christians themselves. They are innocent of all wrongdoing, whether judged by the Torah or by rulers of the empire.

CONCLUSION: THE AUTHOR AND HIS THEMES IN CONTEXT

Discerning the distinctive emphases of the narrative as we have can tell us something about the author and about his audience.

A good place to begin is with some of the observations we made in our discussion of the first volume, the Gospel of Luke. We might ask, for example, why the author of Luke modified Mark's account of Jesus' demeanor in the face of death. Jesus in Luke is portrayed as a kind of ideal martyr for the faith. Throughout the book of Acts as well, Christian leaders face opposition boldly, refusing to bow to the unreasonable demands of those who oppose them. It is possible that these narratives were meant to bolster the confidence and courage of Luke's readers, who themselves confronted hostility in the world around them.

Why does Luke emphasize that the end was not supposed to have come in the lifetime of Jesus' disciples? Obviously because it had not come, and perhaps many or most of Jesus' disciples were already dead. For Luke, however, this clearly was according to plan. The divine purpose of the Christian church was to spread the gospel through the lands of the Gentiles. This, of course, requires time; time itself, therefore, could not come to a screeching halt. By the time Luke was writing, however, the gospel had already been preached to the "ends of the earth," for the book of Acts concludes in Rome, in the heart of the empire, where the gospel was brought by Paul. What more needed to be done before the end? Perhaps nothing, for Luke. He and his congregation may have expected to be the last generation before the end.

Luke could provide no absolute assurance of this, however, so he emphasizes to his readers that their ultimate concern should not be with the future but with the present. Thus they should act on the social implications of Jesus' message in the Gospel (by helping the poor and the oppressed) and continue spreading the good news in Acts. This author wants to stress that the delay of the end cannot be used to nullify the truth of the Christian message. It is likely that some nonbelievers in the author's locality were using the delay precisely to this end, by pointing out that Jesus' failure to return in judgment was a sure sign that the Christians had been wrong all along. In opposition to such a view, Luke stresses that God did not mean for the end to come right away. More important, he indicates that despite the delay of the end, there is good reason to believe that God was and still is behind the Christian mission. Otherwise, from Luke's perspective, it would be impossible to explain the miraculous success of the Christian mission throughout the world. The hand of God was behind this mission, and there was nothing that any human could ever do to stop it.

Finally, we should look at two of Luke's themes that might appear at first glance to be at odds with one another: his emphasis on the Jewish roots of Christianity and his concern for the Gentile mission. Why would Luke focus on Jesus' fulfillment of the Jewish Scriptures if he was writing for Gentiles who did not have to become Jews to be Jesus' followers? Why would he stress that Christianity itself was predicted in Jewish texts, if most of the converts to the religion were not Jewish? Why, in short, would Luke situate this increasingly Gentile movement so squarely in the context of Judaism?

One possible answer to these questions lies outside our investigation of the books per se, in the world in which they were written and read. Even into the late second century of the Common Era, when Christianity had become a distinct religion,

separated from Judaism, the intellectual defenders of Christianity—the "apologists," as they were known (see box 7.1)—continued to stress the claims made by Luke, that Christianity was not something new but something old, older even than the Jewish prophets, as old as the author of the Torah and Moses himself. They stressed this claim because of a common notion shared by most persons of the ancient world (whether pagan, Jewish, or Christian) that anything new—an idea, a philosophy, a religion—was automatically suspect. Unlike in the modern age, where creative ideas and new technologies are widely recognized as good (the newer the better!), in the ancient world older was better. There was a strong regard for antiquity in antiquity. This was particularly the case when it came to religion. If a religion was new, it could scarcely be true.

Christians in the Roman world were confronted with a basic problem. Everyone knew that Jesus was crucified under Pontius Pilate when Tiberius was emperor. Even by the second century, Jesus was considered "recent." If something recent is automatically suspect, then a religion based on Jesus is in peril. To deal with this problem, the second-century apologists appealed to the Jewish roots of the religion, as already stressed, for example, by the Gospel of Luke and (perhaps for a different reason) by the Gospel of Matthew. According to these later authors, Christianity was not a new thing but an old thing. It was predicted by the prophets and anticipated by Moses. As the apologists pointed out, Moses wrote 800 years before the greatest Greek philosopher, Plato, and 400 years before the oldest Greek poets, Homer and Hesiod. If Jesus was predicted by the Jewish prophets and Moses, then the religion he established is very old indeed.

It is at least possible that Luke, a Gentile living in a largely pagan environment, wanted to stress the Jewish roots of Christianity for precisely such reasons. The religion founded on Jesus is ancient; it is a fulfillment of the Jewish Scriptures. It is, in fact the true expression of faith in the God of Israel, whose people, the Jews, have long disobeyed him and who have now done so once too often. Now they have rejected the great prophet of God, God's own Son, whose message of salvation has as a consequence gone forth to the Gentiles.

TAKE A STAND

1. Suppose you are talking with a friend about the historical reliability of the New Testament, and he wants to claim that we have the very words of Peter, Paul, and other apostles in the Book of Acts. Feeling in an argumentative mood, you want to claim (whether you believe it or not) that all speeches in Acts were in fact produced by Luke himself and are not the words actually spoken by the apostles. Make your case.

2. You decide to write a paper arguing that one of the major themes of the book of Acts is that Gentiles do not have to become Jews in order to be true followers of Jesus. Make an outline of your paper.

3. Pick either side of the following resolution and argue your position. Resolved: The Book of Acts was written by Luke, the traveling companion of Paul.

SUGGESTIONS FOR FURTHER READING

In addition to the works listed at the end of Chapter 7, see the following studies:

Hengel, Martin. *Acts and the History of Earliest Christianity.* Trans. J. Bowden. Eugene, Ore.: Wipf and Stock, 2003. A detailed study, for advanced students, that argues (in contrast to the present chapter) that the book of Acts for the most part presents a historically reliable account.

Keck, Leander E., and J. Louis Martyn, eds. *Studies in Luke-Acts.* Nashville: Abingdon, 1966. A superb collection of significant essays on Luke and Acts. Especially important is P. Vielhauer, "Paulinisms of Acts," pp. 35–50, a classic study that mounts convincing arguments that the portrayal of Paul in Acts does not coincide with Paul's portrayal of himself.

Parsons, Mikeal Carl, and Richard I. Pervo. *Rethinking the Unity of Luke and Acts.* Minneapolis: Fortress, 1993. An interesting study by two prominent New Testament literary critics who reopen the question of whether Luke-Acts should be read as a single work.

Powell, M. A. *What Are They Saying about Acts?* New York: Paulist, 1991. An overview of modern scholarship on the book of Acts, for beginning students.

Reardon, B. P., ed. *Collected Ancient Greek Novels.* Berkeley: University of California Press, 1989. A very nice collection of all the ancient Greek novels, useful for comparison with the book of Acts for those who think that Acts contains novelistic features.

KEY TERMS

ancient histories   apologetic speeches   thematic method

Paul the Apostle

THE MAN AND HIS MISSION

WHAT TO EXPECT

Next to Jesus himself, the apostle Paul was arguably the most important person in early Christianity. Nearly half the New Testament books, for example, claim to be written by him.

In this chapter we begin our study of Paul's life and writings. In particular, we will consider the difficulties of knowing what Paul taught—including knowing which of the books written in his name are actually his.

The chapter then gives a brief overview of Paul's life, as we can reconstruct it from both the book of Acts (in which he is one of the main characters) and his own letters. It was an interesting life: before becoming a great Christian missionary and theologian, Paul was an arch-enemy of the Christian church. His conversion to follow Jesus played a significant role for the fate of Christianity, since Paul's ideas and teachings about Jesus affected the beliefs of Christians for all time.

The importance of the apostle Paul in the Christian movement was not universally recognized in his own day. Indeed, Paul appears to have been a highly controversial figure among his contemporaries. From his own letters it is clear that he had at least as many enemies as friends. Nonetheless, for the entire history of Christianity from the first century to our own, no figure except Jesus has proved to be more important.

Consider the New Testament itself. Thirteen of its twenty-seven books claim to be written by Paul. One other book, the Epistle to the Hebrews, was accepted into the canon only after Christians came to believe that Paul had written it, even though it makes no such claim for itself. Yet another book, the Acts of the Apostles, sketches a history of early Christianity with Paul as the principal character. Thus, well over half the books of the New Testament, fifteen out of twenty-seven, are directly or indirectly related to Paul.

Consider next the spread of Christianity after its inauspicious beginnings among a handful of Jesus' followers in Jerusalem. By the beginning of the second century the religion had grown into an interconnected network of believing communities scattered throughout major urban areas of the empire. Paul was instrumental in this Christian mission. He did not, of course, accomplish it single-handedly. As he himself admits, at the outset he was violently and actively hostile to the spreading Christian church. But in one of the most dramatic turnabouts in history, Paul converted to the faith that he had previously persecuted and became one of its leading spokespersons, preaching the gospel in cities and towns of Syria, Cilicia, Asia Minor, Macedonia, and Achaia (modern-day Syria, Turkey, and Greece), which were significant areas of growth for Christianity in its first few decades.

As important as his role in the geographic spread of the faith—in some respects, far more important—was Paul's contribution to its spread across ethnic lines. More than anyone else that we know about from earliest Christianity, Paul emphasized that faith in Jesus as the messiah who died for sins and was raised from the dead was not to be restricted to those who were Jews. The salvation brought by Christ was available to everyone, Jew or Gentile, on an equal basis.

This may not sound like a radical claim in our day, when very few people who believe in Jesus are Jewish and when it would seem nonsensical to argue that a person must convert to Judaism before becoming a Christian, but people like Paul had to argue the point vehemently in antiquity. For Paul, even though faith in Jesus was in complete conformity with the plan of the Jewish God as found in the Jewish Scriptures, it was a faith for all persons, Jews and Gentiles alike.

At first, Paul probably stood in the minority on this issue. To most of the earliest followers of Jesus, who were born and raised Jewish, it was Paul's claim that a person did not have to be a Jew to be counted among the people of God that would have made no sense. These early Christians maintained that Jesus was the Jewish messiah sent by the Jewish God to the Jewish people in fulfillment of the Jewish Scriptures. Jesus himself had followed Jewish customs, gathered Jewish disciples, and interpreted the Jewish Law. The religion he founded was Jewish. People who wanted to follow Jesus had to become Jews first. This seemed fairly obvious to most early Christians. But not to Paul. The kind of Christianity that he advocated was open to both Jews and Gentiles and was rooted in the belief that Jesus had died and been raised for the salvation of the world, not just of Israel.

Before we can begin to examine Paul's views in greater depth, we need to engage in two preliminary tasks. First, we must explore the methodological difficulties that this kind of study involves. Second, we must set our investigation into a somewhat broader context by considering some of the major aspects of Paul's own life, insofar as these can be deduced from his surviving writings.

ANOTHER GLIMPSE INTO THE PAST

BOX 12.1   The Pauline Corpus

Undisputed Pauline Epistles (almost certainly authentic)
Romans
1 Corinthians
2 Corinthians
Galatians
Philippians
1 Thessalonians
Philemon

Deutero-Pauline Epistles (possibly pseudonymous)
Ephesians
Colossians
2 Thessalonians

Pastoral Epistles (probably pseudonymous)
1 Timothy
2 Timothy
Titus

THE STUDY OF PAUL: METHODOLOGICAL DIFFICULTIES

The problems of reconstructing the life and teachings of the historical Paul are in some ways analogous to the problems of reconstructing the life and teachings of the historical Jesus, in that they relate to the character of our sources. But there is one significant difference: Jesus left us no writings, whereas Paul did. Indeed, thirteen letters in the New Testament are penned in Paul's name. A major problem involved in studying these letters, however, is that scholars have good reasons for thinking that some of them were not written by Paul, but by later members of his churches writing in his name.

The Problem of Pauline Pseudepigrapha

The fact that some ancient authors would falsely attribute their writings to a famous person (like Paul) comes as no shock to historians. Writings under a false name (what we today call "forgery," see pp. 264–69) are known to scholars as **"pseudepigrapha."** We know of numerous pseudepigrapha produced by pagan, Jewish, and Christian writers of the ancient world. Indeed, let-

ters allegedly written by Paul continued to be produced in the second and later centuries. Among those that still survive are a third letter to the Corinthians (see box 17.1), a letter addressed to the church in the town of Laodicea (cf. Col 4:16), and an exchange of correspondence between Paul and the famous Greek philosopher **Seneca** (see box 12.2). The question of why authors in antiquity would forge documents in someone else's name is intriguing, and we will take it up later in Chapter 17.

Is it conceivable, however, that some of the letters that made it into the New Testament are this kind of literature, pseudonymous writings in the name of Paul? For most scholars, this is not only conceivable but almost certain; they have, as a consequence, grouped the letters attributed to Paul into three categories (see box 12.1). (In Chapter 17, I will discuss the arguments that have proved persuasive to most historians and allow you to weigh their merits for yourself.)

First there are the three **Pastoral epistles**. These are the letters allegedly written to the pastors Timothy (1 and 2 Timothy) and Titus, which provide instruction on how these companions of Paul should engage in their pastoral duties in their churches. For a variety of reasons, most critical scholars are persuaded that these letters were written not by Paul but by a later member of one of his

---

ANOTHER EARLY CHRISTIAN TEXT

BOX 12.2 The Correspondence of Paul and Seneca

One of the most interesting Pauline pseudepigrapha is the set of correspondence forged by a third-century Christian in the names of Paul and Seneca, the famous philosopher and mentor of the emperor Nero. Written some 200 years after both parties were dead (both of them killed, according to tradition, by order of Nero), these fourteen letters were meant to show that Paul's significance as an author was recognized by one of the greatest philosophical minds of his day. In the second letter that "Seneca" addresses to Paul, he claims to be particularly impressed with Paul's writings and

expresses his desire to make them known to the emperor himself:

> I have arranged some scrolls [of your letters] and have brought them into a definite order corresponding to their several divisions. Also I have decided to read them to the emperor. If only fate ordains it favourably that he show some interest, then perhaps you too will be present; otherwise I shall fix a day for you at another time when together we may examine this work. And if only it could be done safely, I would not read this writing to him before meeting you. You may then be certain that you are not being overlooked. Farewell, most beloved Paul.

churches, who wanted to appeal to Paul's authority in dealing with a situation that had arisen after his death. As we will see, the arguments revolve around whether the writing style, vocabulary, and theology of these letters coincide with what we find in the letters that we are reasonably certain Paul wrote and whether Paul's own historical context can make sense of the issues that the letters address (see Chapter 17).

Next, there are the three epistles of Ephesians, Colossians, and 2 Thessalonians, called the **"Deutero-Pauline" epistles** because each of them is thought by many scholars to have been written by a "second Paul," a later author (or rather three later authors) who was heavily influenced by Paul's teachings (the term "Deutero-" means "second"). Scholars continue to debate the authorship of these books. Most continue to think that Paul did not write Ephesians and probably not Colossians; the case for 2 Thessalonians has proved somewhat more difficult to resolve (see Chapter 17).

Finally, there are seven letters that virtually all scholars agree were written by Paul himself: Romans, 1 and 2 Corinthians, Galatians, Philippians, 1 Thessalonians, and Philemon. These **"undisputed" Pauline epistles** are similar in terms of writing style, vocabulary, and theology. In addition, the issues that they address can plausibly be situated in the early Christian movement of the 40s and 50s of the Common Era, when Paul was active as an apostle and missionary.

The significance of this threefold classification of the Pauline epistles should be obvious. If scholars are right that the Pastorals and the Deutero-Paulines stem from authors living after Paul rather than from Paul himself, then despite the importance of these letters for understanding how Pauline Christianity developed in later years, they cannot be used as certain guides to what Paul himself taught. For methodological reasons, a study of Paul has to restrict itself to letters that we can be confident he wrote, namely, the seven undisputed epistles.

The Problem of Acts

What, however, about the book of Acts, Luke's account of the history of the early church, which features Paul as one of its chief protagonists? For a historically accurate account of what Paul said and did, can we rely on Luke's narrative?

Different scholars will answer this question differently. Some trust the book of Acts with no qualms, others take its accounts with a grain of salt, and still others discount the narrative altogether (that is, they discount its historical credibility for establishing what Paul said and did, not necessarily its importance as a piece of literature). My own position is that the book of Acts is about as reliable for Paul as the Gospel of Luke is for Jesus. Just as Luke modified aspects of Jesus' words to reflect his own theological point of view, for instance, with respect to when the end was to arrive, and similarly changed some of the traditions concerning his actions, for instance, with respect to what occurred during his Passion, so, too, in the book of Acts Paul's words and deeds have been modified in accordance with Luke's own perspective. Thus, Acts can tell us a great deal about how Luke understood Paul, but less about what Paul himself actually said and did.

In our discussion of Acts I have already indicated why I do not think that the book was written by one of Paul's traveling companions. Even if it were, we would still have to ask whether its portrayal of Paul is historically accurate, for even eyewitnesses have their own perspectives. In any event, in evaluating the reliability of Acts, we are fortunate that Paul and Luke sometimes both describe the same event and indicate Paul's teachings on the same issues, making it possible to see whether they stand in basic agreement.

Events of Paul's Life. In virtually every instance in which the book of Acts can be compared with Paul's letters in terms of biographical detail, differences emerge. Sometimes these differences involve minor disagreements concerning where Paul was at a certain time and with whom. As one example, the book of Acts states that when Paul went to Athens, he left Timothy and Silas behind in Berea (Acts 17:10–15) and did not meet up with them again until after he left Athens and arrived in Corinth (18:5). In 1 Thessalonians Paul himself narrates the same sequence of events and indicates just as clearly that he was not in Athens alone but that Timothy was with him (and possibly Silas as well). It was from Athens that he sent

Timothy back to Thessalonica in order to see how the church was doing there (1 Thess 3:1–3).

Although this discrepancy concerns a minor detail, it shows something about the historical reliability of Acts. The narrative coincides with what Paul himself indicates about some matters (he did establish the church in Thesssalonica and then leave from there for Athens), but it stands at odds with him on some of the specifics.

Other differences are of greater importance. For example, Paul is quite emphatic in the epistle to the Galatians that after he had his vision of Jesus and came to believe in him, he did *not* go to Jerusalem to consult with the apostles (1:15–18). This is an important issue for him because he wants to prove to the Galatians that his gospel message did not come from Jesus' followers in Jerusalem (the original disciples and the church around them) but from Jesus himself. His point is that he has not corrupted a message that he received from someone else; his gospel came straight from God, with no human intervention. The book of Acts, of course, provides its own narrative of Paul's conversion. In this account, however, Paul does exactly what he claims not to have done in Galatians: after leaving Damascus some days after his conversion, he goes directly to Jerusalem and meets with the apostles (Acts 9:10–30).

It is possible, of course, that Paul himself has altered the real course of events to show that he couldn't have received his gospel message from other apostles because he never consulted with them. If he did stretch the truth on this matter, however, his statement of Galatians—"In what I am writing to you, before God, I do not lie"— takes on new poignancy, for his lie in this case would have been bald-faced. More likely the discrepancy derives from Luke, whose own agenda affected the way he told the tale. For him, as we have seen, it was important to show that Paul stood in close continuity with the views of the original followers of Jesus because all the apostles were unified in their perspectives. Thus, he portrays Paul as consulting with the Jerusalem apostles and representing the same faith that they proclaimed.

Paul's Teaching. Paul's teachings in Acts differ in significant ways from what he says in his own letters. Here we look at just one important example.

Almost all of Paul's evangelistic sermons mentioned in Acts are addressed to Jewish audiences. This itself should strike us as odd given Paul's repeated claim that his mission was to the Gentiles. In any event, the most famous exception is his speech to a group of philosophers on the Areopagus in Athens (chap. 17). In the **Areopagus speech,** Paul explains that the Jewish God is in fact the God of all, pagan and Jew alike, even though the pagans have been ignorant of him. Paul's understanding of pagan polytheism is reasonably clear here: pagans have simply not known that there is only one God, the creator of all, and thus cannot be held accountable for failing to worship him. Since they have been ignorant of the true God, rather than willfully disobedient to him, he has overlooked their false religions until now. With the coming of Jesus, however, he is calling all people to repent in preparation for the coming judgment (Acts 17:23–31).

This perspective contrasts sharply with the views about pagan idolatry that Paul sets forth in his own letters. In the letter to the Romans, for example, Paul claims that pagan idolaters are *not* ignorant of the one true God, that all along they have known of his existence and power by seeing the things that he has made. Here the worship of idols is said to be a willful act of disobedience. Pagans have rejected their knowledge of the one true God, the maker of all, and chosen of their own free will to worship the creation rather than the creator. As a result of their rejection of God, he has punished them in his wrath (Rom 1:18–32).

These passages appear to be at odds with one another on a number of points. Do pagans know that there is only one God? (Acts: no; Romans: yes.) Have they acted in ignorance or disobedience? (Acts: ignorance; Romans: disobedience.) Does God overlook their error or punish it? (Acts: overlooks; Romans: punishes.)

Some scholars think that the two passages can be reconciled by considering the different audiences that are being addressed. In Acts Paul is trying to win converts, and so he doesn't want to be offensive, whereas in Romans he is addressing the converted, so he doesn't mind saying what he really thinks. To be sure, it is possible that Paul would say the opposite of what he believed in order to convert people or tell a white lie intended to bring about a greater good; but another explanation is that Luke, rather than Paul, is the author of the speech on the Areopagus, just as he is the author of all the other speeches in his account, as we saw in Chapter 11. This explanation goes a long way toward showing why so many of the speeches in Acts sound similar to one another, regardless of who the speaker is— Paul sounding like Peter, for example, and Peter like Paul (compare the speeches of Acts 2 and 13). Rather than embodying Paul's view of the pagan religions, then, the Areopagus speech may embody Luke's view and thus represent the kind of evangelistic address that he imagines would have been appropriate to the occasion.

What then are we left with? The book of Acts appears to contain a number of discrepancies with the writings of Paul himself, with respect both to the events of his life and to the nature of his teachings. If this is so, then it cannot be accepted uncritically as a historically accurate portrayal of Paul, any more than the Gospel of Luke can be accepted uncritically as a historically accurate portrayal of Jesus. To gain a historical understanding of Paul, however, we are at least able to proceed on the basis of his own writings, for we have seven other New Testament books that derive from his pen. Our study of Paul and his teachings will therefore rely principally on the undisputed Pauline epistles. Even the use of these letters, however, is not without its problems.

The Occasional Nature of Paul's Letters

Letters were a common form of written communication in the ancient world, and people wrote a number of different kinds, as can be seen in the thousands of samples that have survived from antiquity. Some letters were collected and published by famous authors like Cicero, Seneca, and Pliny the Younger. Others were written by private and otherwise unknown individuals and discarded by their recipients, only to be discovered in modern times by archaeologists who make a living out of digging through ancient trash heaps buried in the sands of Egypt.

In the modern world, different kinds of letters require different kinds of writing conventions. A cover letter that you send with your résumé to a prospective employer will look very different from a letter that you send home from school or a note

that you dash off to a boyfriend or girlfriend. Likewise, in the ancient world, private letters to friends differed from open letters to be read by everyone; letters of recommendation differed from literary letters discussing important topics for educated audiences; and public letters persuading a community to engage in a certain course of action differed from private letters to governmental officials that petitioned for a particular cause.

Private letters in the ancient world, unlike modern ones, generally began by identifying the person writing the letter, either by name or, in rare cases, by some other descriptive term (see 3 John 1). This identification was followed by an indication, usually by name, of the person being addressed. Normally the author included some form of greeting and well-wishing at the outset, perhaps a prayer on the recipients' behalf and an expression of thankfulness to the gods for them. In interpreting ancient letters, these introductory conventions cannot be taken too literally as expressing the author's real feelings, any more than modern conventions (as, for example, when I addressed the IRS agent in charge of my income tax audit as "Dear" Mr. Sanders).

After these introductory items would come the body of the letter, in which the subject of the letter and the author's concerns were expressed. Finally, the letter might conclude with some words of encouragement or consolation or admonition, an expression of hope of being able to see one another face to face, greetings to others in the family or community, a farewell, and sometimes a final prayer and well-wishing (see box 12.3).

In studying the writings of Paul, it is most important to recognize that, like most letters from antiquity, Paul's are **"occasional."** They are not essays written on set themes or systematic treatises that discuss important issues of theology. They are actual communications to particular individuals and communities, sent through the ancient equivalent of the mail. With all but one exception, Paul wrote these letters to address problems that arose in the Christian communities he established. In every case, they are occasioned by situations that he felt compelled to address as an apostle of Christ.

The circumstantial nature of these writings means that we have to know their *context* in order

ANOTHER GLIMPSE INTO THE PAST

BOX 12.3 A Letter from Greco-Roman Egypt

Private letters in the Greco-Roman world were written for many of the same reasons they are written today. Consider the following letter that a young man, Aurelius Dius, sent to his father, Aurelius Horion. Away at school, he wrote to assure his father that he was doing his homework and living responsibly. One might wonder why he greets so many people back home, many of whom he calls "mother" and "father," evidently out of love and respect. Is the boy homesick? The letter comes from Egypt and was written some time during the third century of the Common Era.

Aurelius Dius, to Aurelius Horion, my sweetest father. Many greetings! I say a prayer to the gods of this region every day for you. Do not be worried about our studies, father. We are working hard and getting plenty of sleep, so that everything will go well with us. Greet my mother Tamiae and my sisters Tnepherous and Philous; also greet my brother Patermouthis and my sister Thermouthis; greet also my brother Heracleis and my brother Kollouchis; and greet my father Melanus and my mother Timpesouris and her son. Greetings to all of you from Gaia, and from my father Horion and Thermouthis.

I pray that you enjoy good health, father. (*Oxyrhynchus Papyri* 10, no. 1296, author's translation)

to make sense of what they say. And so, for the study of Paul's letters, as well as for all the New Testament epistles, we will be following a **"contextual method"** of investigation. The need for this method is rooted in a theoretical view of language shared by many scholars, that knowing a document's historical context is absolutely vital for its interpretation. According to this view, words convey meaning only within a context; thus, when you change the context of words, you change what they mean.

This is because, as we have seen, words and phrases do not have any inherent meaning but mean what they do only in relationship to other words and phrases, so that words and phrases can be made to mean a wide variety of things (practically anything, according to some theorists). Let me illustrate the point through a brief example. Suppose you were to hear the phrase "I love this course." It would obviously mean something altogether different on the lips of your roommate when he is about to break 80 on the eighteenth hole at the public golf course than it would coming from your precocious younger sister at her first posh restaurant in the midst of the second course of a five-course meal. And it would mean something quite different still if spoken by your buddy at his favorite race-car track or by the woman sit-

ting behind you in your New Testament class after hearing yet another scintillating lecture.

You might think, however, that the phrase in all these cases means basically the same thing. Somebody appreciates something called a "course." But suppose you are in the middle of the most boring lecture by your most boring professor, wondering why you are there instead of outside catching some rays, when you hear a guy in the back row whisper the same words, "I *love* this course," and then snicker? You know full well what the words mean; they mean just the opposite of what they meant for the woman in the scintillating lecture. Thus, words mean what they do only in light of their context. If you change the context, you change what the words mean. This is true of all words in every language.

One practical implication of this insight is that if we are to understand a person's words, we have to understand the context within which they are spoken. This principle applies not only to oral communication but written communication as well. With ancient literature, however, only in rare instances do we have solid evidence for the historical context within which words were spoken or written. Thus, we have to work hard at reconstructing the situation that lies behind a text if we want to understand the context within which it was produced. Only then can we use these contexts to help us interpret the texts.

Unfortunately, in many instances the only way we can know about the precise historical context of a writing is through clues provided by the writing itself. Doesn't this procedure, then, involve a kind of circular reasoning: to interpret a writing, we have to understand the context, but we cannot understand the context until we interpret the writing?

The procedure probably is circular on some level, but it does not have to be completely so, for some ways of understanding the context within which a writing is produced will make better sense of the writing than others. Consider this analogy. Have you ever listened to someone talk on the phone and, on the basis of what he or she said, figured out what the other person was saying as well? What you did was to reconstruct the words you did not hear on the basis of the words that you did, and understood the words you heard in light of those you did not. To put it differently, you reconstructed the context of what you heard and made sense of the words in light of it. Now in some cases you may be wrong, but if you listen carefully enough, and if the speaker gives you enough to go on (and does not simply grunt in agreement every now and then), you can in many instances understand the full conversation based on your reconstruction of the words coming from the other end of the line.

Something like this happens when we apply the contextual method to a New Testament writing. On the basis of the conversation that we do hear, we try to reconstruct the conversation that we do not, and thereby come to a better understanding of what the author is trying to say. For some of the books of the New Testament, including the Pauline epistles, this method can prove to be quite enlightening. To be sure, there are some serious limitations to this approach, some of which have been overlooked by scholars for whom it is the method of choice. But the nature of these limitations cannot be fully appreciated in the abstract; they will make sense as we apply the method to specific texts, such as the Pauline epistles.

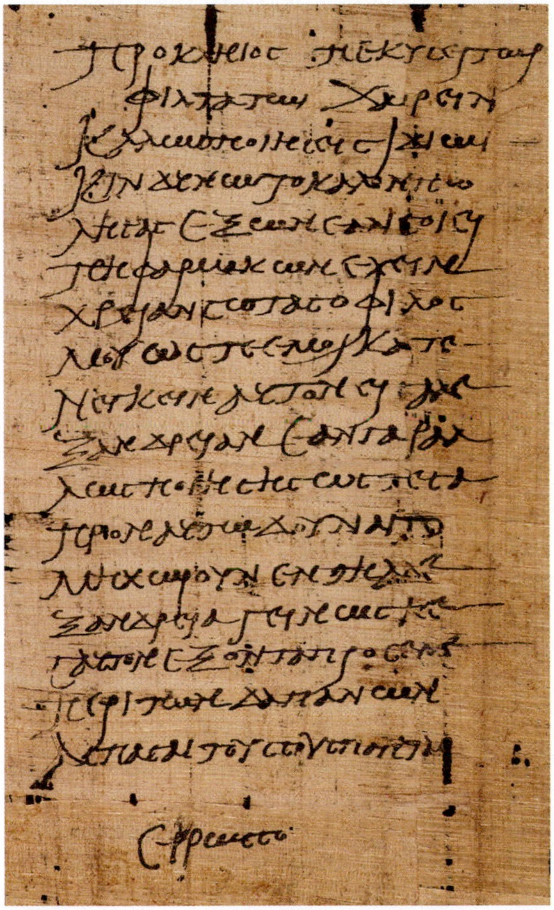

Figure 12.1 Example of a papyrus letter from antiquity; letters tended (like this one) to be much shorter than those of the New Testament. This particular specimen is from a person in Alexandria to a physician, requesting that he provide a friend with the suitable, and effective, medication he needs.

THE LIFE OF PAUL

Paul's letters are chiefly concerned with problems that have arisen in his churches, not with events that transpired in his life. On occasion, however, Paul has reason to mention his past, for instance, when he is trying to establish his credentials as a true apostle of Christ. It appears from such self-references as Gal 1:11–2:14 and Phil 3:4–10 that Paul visualized his past in three stages: his life as a Pharisee prior to faith in Christ, his conversion experience itself, and his activities as an apostle afterward.

Paul the Pharisee

We can say very little for certain about Paul prior to his conversion. He does tell us that he was a Jew born to Jewish parents and that he was zealous for the Law, adhering strictly to the traditions endorsed by the Pharisees (Gal 1:13–14; Phil 3:4–6). He does not tell us when he was born, where he was raised, or how he was educated. The book of Acts, however, does provide some information along these lines. There Paul is said to have been from the Greek city of **Tarsus** (21:39) in Cilicia, in the southeastern part of Asia Minor, and to have been educated in Jerusalem under the renowned rabbi **Gamaliel** (22:3). Since Paul himself makes neither claim, a historian might suspect Luke of attempting to provide superior credentials for his protagonist. Tarsus was the location of a famous school of Greek rhetoric, that is, a school of higher learning

Figure 12.2 A page of P⁴⁶, the earliest surviving manuscript of Paul's letters, from around the year 200 C.E.

reserved for the social and intellectual elite, something like an Ivy League university. Jerusalem, of course, was the center of all Jewish life, and Gamaliel was one of its most revered teachers.

Paul's own letters give little indication of the extent of his formal education. Simply his ability to read and write shows that he was better educated than most people of his day; recent studies indicate that some 85–90 percent of the population in the empire could do neither. Moreover, Paul writes on a fairly sophisticated level, showing that he must have had at least some formal training in rhetoric, the main focus of higher education at the time. He is certainly not one of the highest of the literary elite, but he just as certainly had some advanced schooling. It is not altogether implausible, then, that he grew up in a place like Tarsus, if not Tarsus itself. In any event, Paul's native tongue was almost without question Greek, and he gives no indication at all of knowing Aramaic, the language more widely used in Palestine. This is probably an indication that Luke is right in situating him in the Jewish Diaspora.

Although Paul gives no indication that he studied in Jerusalem, he clearly did study the Jewish Scriptures extensively, perhaps in some kind of formal setting (comparable, perhaps, to a later rabbinic school?). He appears to be able to quote the Scriptures extensively from memory and to have meditated and reflected on their meaning at a fairly deep level. He knows these Scriptures in their Greek translation, the Septuagint (see box 3.1). Since his letters are all addressed to Greek-speaking Christians, it is difficult to know whether he quoted the text in this way in order to accommodate his readers or whether this was the only form of the text that he knew. That is to say, it is hard to know whether or not he could also read the Scriptures in their original Hebrew.

What is certain is that prior to becoming a believer in Jesus, Paul was an avid Pharisee (Phil 3:5). In fact, Paul's letters are the only writings to survive from the pen of a Pharisee, or former Pharisee, prior to the destruction of the Temple in 70 C.E. Paul claims that he rigorously followed the "traditions of the fathers" (Gal 1:14). These are usually understood to be the Pharisaic traditions (sometimes called "oral laws") that were in circulation in Paul's youth, nearly two centuries before they, or ones like them, were written down in the Mishnah. We get a picture, then, of a devout and intelligent Jewish young man totally committed to understanding and practicing his religion according to the strictest standards available.

As a Pharisee, Paul's religion would have centered on the Law of God, the Torah of Moses, the greatest gift of God to Israel, the exact and thorough adherence to which was the ultimate goal of devotion. Looking back on his early life, Paul could later claim that he had been "blameless" with respect to the righteousness that the Law demands (Phil 3:6). It is hard to know exactly what he meant by that. Did he mean that he never violated a solitary commandment of God? This seems unlikely given his insistence elsewhere that no one has kept the Law in all its particulars (e.g., Rom 3:10–18), a view that he claimed is taught by the Law itself (Rom 3:19–20). Did he mean that he did his best to keep the Law, so he could not be faulted for effort? This interpretation seems more likely. But he may also have meant that he was blameless because the Law itself makes provision for those who sin, in the sacrifices that it requires. These sacrifices were explicitly given for those who inadvertently broke the Law, as a way to restore them to a right standing before God. If Paul did his utmost to keep the Law and performed the required sacrifices for his sins when he failed (perhaps on pilgrimages to Jerusalem), he may well have considered himself "blameless" with respect to the righteousness that the Law demands. In that case, not even the Law could blame him, since he had done what it requires.

Paul's view of himself before the Law is but one of the many issues that have perplexed his interpreters through the years. Somewhat less perplexing is the general view of the world that he must have had as a devoted Pharisee. As we have seen, one of the salient features of the Pharisees, which distinguished them from the Sadducees, for example, was their fervent expectation of a future resurrection of the dead. It appears that Pharisees of the first century, along with other groups such as the Essenes, were by and large Jewish apocalypticists, who anticipated the intervention of God in the world and the destruction of the forces of evil that oppose him. At the end of the age, which would be imminent, God would send a deliverer

for his people, who would set up God's kingdom on earth; the dead would be raised, and all would face judgment. Paul almost certainly held these views prior to his conversion to Christianity.

What else can we say about the life of this upright Jewish Pharisee? The one aspect of his former life that Paul himself chose to emphasize in his autobiographical statements in Galatians 1 and Philippians 3 is that it was precisely as a law-abiding, zealous Jew that he persecuted the followers of Jesus. Far from adhering to the gospel, he violently opposed it, setting himself on destroying the church, and he interpreted this opposition as part of his devotion to the one true God.

Why was Paul so opposed to Jesus' followers, and how exactly did he go about persecuting them? Unfortunately, Paul never tells us, but we can make some intelligent guesses, especially with regard to the reasons for his opposition. We have already seen how the Christian proclamation of Jesus as the messiah would have struck most Jews as ludicrous. Various Jews had different expectations of what the messiah would be like. He might be a warrior-king who would establish Israel as a sovereign state, an inspired priest who would rule God's people through his authoritative interpretation of God's Law, or a cosmic judge who would come to destroy the forces of evil. Each of these expectations, however, involved a messiah who would be glorious and powerful. Jesus, on the other hand, was known to have been nothing more than an itinerant preacher with a small following who was opposed by the Jewish leaders and executed by the Romans for sedition against the state. For most faithful Jews, to call him God's messiah was an affront to God.

For Paul, there appears to have been an additional problem, related to the precise manner of Jesus' execution. Jesus was crucified; that is, he was killed by being attached to a stake of wood. Paul, well versed in the Scriptures, recognized what this meant for Jesus' standing before God, for the Torah states, "Cursed is anyone who hangs on a tree" (Deut 21:23, quoted in Gal 3:13). Far from being the Christ of God, the one who enjoyed divine favor, Jesus was the cursed of God, the one who incurred divine wrath. For Paul the Pharisee, to call him the messiah was probably blasphemous.

This problem would have given Paul sufficient grounds for persecuting the Christian church.

How exactly he went about doing so cannot be known. According to the book of Acts, he received authorization from the high priest in Jerusalem to capture and imprison Christians. Paul himself says nothing of the sort, and the fact that churches in Judea had never seen him before he visited them as a Christian argues against it (see Gal 1:22). At the same time, whatever he did to the Christians as a Jewish persecutor, and on whatever authority, he apparently gained some notoriety for it. He later acknowledges his reputation among the Christian churches as a sworn enemy (Gal 1:13, 23).

All this changed, of course, when the greatest persecutor of the church became its greatest proponent. The turning point in Paul's life came with his encounter with the risen Jesus. Both Acts and Paul intimate that this happened when Paul was a relatively young man.

Paul's Conversion and Its Implications

It is difficult for historians to evaluate what actually happened to make Paul "turn around," the literal meaning of "convert." Both Acts and Paul attribute his **conversion** to the direct intervention of God, and this kind of supernatural act, by its very nature, is outside the purview of the historian (see box 9.8). The historian can, of course, talk about a person's descriptions of divine acts, since narratives of this kind are a matter of the public record. So we will restrict ourselves to what Paul claims to have happened at his conversion and consider how he understood its significance. But even here there are problems. Some of these are easily disposed of, because they relate less to Paul than to widespread misperceptions about him by modern readers, as found, for example, in historical novels about his life that can be picked up in used bookstores. In some of these accounts, the pre-Christian Paul is a guilt-ridden legalist who felt bound to follow a set of picayune laws that were impossible to keep and whose remorse over his own failings drove him both to insist with increasing vehemence that the Law had to be followed at all costs and to hate those who experienced a personal freedom like the one that Christ reputedly brought. In this version of his life, Paul saw the light when he realized that the solution to his guilt was not to intensify his efforts but to find forgiveness of his sins in Christ, who died to

set him free from the Law. Paul, in this view, converted from a religion of guilt to a religion of love, and so became Jesus' faithful follower, bringing the good news of release from sins to those burdened with guilt complexes like his own.

It is with good reason that accounts like this are found in the fiction section of a bookstore. Paul himself does not indicate that he experienced a profound sense of guilt over his inability to keep God's commandments before becoming a Christian, even though after becoming a Christian he came to recognize that God's Law was nearly impossible to keep (see Rom 7:14–24). Prior to his faith in Christ, however, he considered himself to be blameless before the Law (Phil 3:4–6). Thus, he did not convert because he was burdened by a Law that he knew he could not keep. In some sense, this popular view of Paul derives more from a kind of implicit anti-Semitism—the Jews are burdened with an impossible Law and don't do a good job in keeping it—than from Paul himself.

Why, then, did Paul convert, and what did his conversion mean? The book of Acts provides a detailed account of the event, or, rather, it provides three accounts (chaps. 9, 22, and 26) that mention details not found in Paul (e.g., that he was on the "road to Damascus" and that he was "blinded by the light"). These accounts, however, are difficult to reconcile with one another (see box 12.4). Even Paul's own references to the event are somewhat problematic because he is remembering the event long afterward and is reflecting on it in light of his later experiences.

The first thing to observe about Paul's conversion is that he traces it back to an encounter with the resurrected Jesus. In 1 Cor 15:8–11 he names himself as the last person to have seen Jesus raised from the dead and marks this as the beginning of his change from persecutor to apostle. He appears to be referring to the same event in Gal 1:16, where he indicates that at a predetermined point in time, God "was pleased to reveal his Son to me." When Paul experienced this revelation from God, he became convinced, then and there, according to his later perspective, that he was to preach the good news of Christ to the Gentiles.

Whatever Paul experienced at this moment, he interpreted it as an actual appearance of Jesus himself. We don't know how long this was after

WHAT DO YOU THINK?

BOX 12.4   Paul on the Road to Damascus

The book of Acts narrates the events of Paul's conversion on the **road to Damascus** on three separate occasions. The event itself is narrated in 9:1–19; Paul later recounts it to a hostile Jewish crowd after his arrest in 22:6–16 and then again to King Agrippa in 26:12–18. When you compare these accounts carefully, you will find a number of apparent discrepancies, including the following more obvious ones:

❖ When Jesus appears to Paul in chapter 9, Paul's companions "heard the voice but saw no one" (9:7). But when Paul recounts the tale in chapter 22, he claims that they "saw the light but did not hear the voice" (22:9).

❖ In chapter 9 Paul's companions are left standing while he is knocked to the ground by the vision (v. 7). But according to chapter 26, they all fall to the ground (26:12).

❖ In the first account Paul is instructed to go into Damascus to receive instruction from a disciple of Jesus named Ananias. In the last account he is not sent to Ananias but is instructed by Jesus himself (26:16–18).

These may seem like minor details, but why are the accounts at odds with one another at all?

Jesus' death (several months? several years?) or how Paul, when he saw whatever he saw, knew it to be Jesus, but there is no doubt that he believed that he saw Jesus' real but glorified body raised from the dead. Indeed, as we will see later, one of the reasons that he believed Christians would eventually experience a bodily resurrection from the dead is that he "knew" that Jesus did. For him, Jesus was the "first-fruit" of those who would be raised (1 Cor 15:20).

Did this experience, then, lead Paul to reject his Judaism in favor of a religion for the Gentiles? Was this a conversion to a completely different and contrary set of beliefs? What exactly did his vision of the resurrected Jesus mean for Paul? As we have seen, Paul was probably an apocalyptic Jew prior to coming to believe in Jesus. If it is true that we can understand something new only in light of what we already know, we can ask how Paul would have understood this "new" event of Jesus' resurrection in light of his "old" worldview of Jewish apocalypticism. We can approach the question by considering two related matters: aspects of Paul's worldview that would have been confirmed by an encounter with a man raised from the dead and aspects that would have been reformulated in light of the experience.

The Confirmation of Paul's Views in Light of Jesus' Resurrection. Apocalypticists maintained that at the end of the age God would intervene in history to overthrow the forces of evil and establish his good reign on earth, and that at that time the dead would be raised to face judgment. What would an apocalyptic Jew conclude if he or she came to believe that God had now raised someone? Clearly, for such a person, the end had already begun.

Paul drew exactly this conclusion. As we will see in greater detail later, he believed that he was living in the end of time and that he would be alive when Jesus returned from heaven (see 1 Thess 4:13–18 and 1 Cor 15:51–57). Thus, he speaks of Jesus as the **"first-fruit of the resurrection,"** evoking an agricultural image that refers to the celebration that comes at the conclusion of the first day of the harvest. On the following day, the workers go to the fields and continue their labor. Jesus was the first-fruit of the resurrection in the sense that all the others would also soon be gathered in.

Other agricultural metaphors were common in Jewish apocalyptic circles. The end of the age would be like a great harvest, in which the fruit was gathered and the chaff was destroyed. As an apocalyptic Jew, Paul probably already believed that at the end of the age God would intervene to reward the faithful and punish the sinner and overthrow the forces of evil that plague this world, the demonic rulers and the wicked powers of sin and death. Jesus' resurrection must have confirmed these views, for one of the reasons that there will be a resurrection at the end of time is that death is God's enemy, and when it is destroyed, there will be no more dying and no more death. Those who have died will therefore return to life.

For Paul, Jesus has already returned to life, which means that God has begun to defeat the power of death in him. This much Paul "knows," for if Jesus died but is dead no longer, as Paul believes (because he has seen him alive after his death), then he has conquered this most dread of God's enemies. The cosmic destruction of the forces of evil has therefore begun.

The Reformulation of Paul's Views in Light of Jesus' Resurrection. Whereas some of Paul's views were confirmed by his belief in Jesus' resurrection, others had to be reconsidered.

1. *Paul's View of Jesus.* First and foremost, of course, was Paul's understanding of Jesus himself. Rather than being the cursed of God (Paul's original view), Jesus must be the one specially blessed by God, for he was the one God raised from the dead to conquer the cosmic forces of sin and death. Jesus, the conqueror, was thus indeed the messiah, the one appointed by God as Lord. Moreover, he was currently in heaven, awaiting the moment of his return in glory when he would finish the deed that he had begun.

   Once Paul came to believe that Jesus was raised from the dead, the crucifixion itself must have begun to make better sense. Paul appears to have turned to the Jewish Scriptures to understand how Jesus' death was according to the plan of God, evidently knowing that it had to be, since the resurrection showed that Jesus experienced God's special blessing. From the Scriptures, of course, Paul knew of the suffering of the Righteous One of God, whom God ultimately vindicated. Since Jesus was the one whom God vindicated, for Paul he must have been that righteous one who suffered, not as a punishment for his own actions, but for the sake of others. That is to say, even though Jesus was cursed by dying on

the cross, the curse could not have been deserved since he was God's righteous one. He must, then, have borne the curse that was meant for others. As the righteous servant of God, Jesus took the punishment that others deserved and bore it on the cross. God vindicated this faithful act by raising him from the dead.

By raising Jesus, God showed that his death was meaningful rather than meaningless. It was meaningful because it served as a sacrifice for the sins of others (see box 10.3). More than that, it was a death that actually conquered the cosmic power of sin. Paul "knew" that Jesus conquered sin because he had obviously conquered death. Otherwise he would have remained dead. In Jesus himself, then, God had worked to conquer the evil forces that until now had been in control of this world.

This new belief in Jesus raised an obvious problem for Paul, the upright Jewish Pharisee whose upbringing and commitments were centered on the Jewish Law. If salvation from sins and the defeat of the powers of sin and death came through Jesus, what was the role of the Law of God, God's greatest gift to his people?

2. *Paul's View of the Law.* Paul's understanding of the Law in light of his faith in Christ is extremely complicated. Some scholars have wondered, given the variety of things Paul says about the Law, whether he ever managed to construct an entirely consistent view. At the very least, it seems clear that Paul came to believe that a person could not be put into a right standing before God by keeping the Law; only faith in Christ could do this. Moreover, he maintained that this view was not contrary to the Law but, perhaps ironically, was precisely what the Law itself taught (Rom 3:31). As we will see, he devotes most of the letter to the Romans to making these points.

   It appears that after his conversion Paul began to think that the Jewish Law, even though in itself an obviously good thing (see Rom 7:12), had led to some bad consequences. The problem for Paul, however, was not the Law per se, but the people to whom it was given.

   Those who had received the good Law of God, according to Paul, had come to misuse it. Rather than seeing the Law as a guide for their actions as the covenant people of God, they began keeping the Law as a way to establish a right standing before God, as if by keeping its various injunctions, they could earn God's favor (e.g., Rom 4:4–5; 10:2–4). It is not clear whether Paul thought that Jews *intentionally* used the Law in this way. Moreover, Paul does not appear to have held this view of the Law prior to his conversion, but only afterward. Indeed, this view is found in virtually no other Jewish writing from the ancient world.

In any event, after his conversion Paul came to think that his fellow Jews had attempted to use the Law to bring about a right standing before God. For him this was a misuse of the Law. Instead of making people right before God, the Law shows that everyone is alienated from God: "For no human being will be justified in God's sight by deeds prescribed by the law, for through the law comes the knowledge of sin" (Rom 3:20).

What Paul means by this statement is debated among scholars. On the one hand, he is almost certainly thinking about the repeated insistence in the Jewish Scriptures themselves that God's people have fallen short of his righteous demands (Rom 3:10–20). In addition, he may have been reflecting on the sacrificial system that is provided by the Torah as a way of dealing with human sins (although Paul never mentions it directly), for why would God require sacrifices for sin if people didn't need them? Whatever Paul's precise logic was, it appears certain that as a Christian, he came to believe that the Law points to the problem of human sinfulness against God, on the one hand, but does not provide the power necessary to overcome that sinfulness, on the other. (Why the divinely ordained sacrifices are not sufficient to overcome sin is an issue that he never addresses.) The problem for Paul the Christian apocalypticist is that humans are enslaved by powers opposed to God, specifically the cosmic powers of sin and death, and the Law can do nothing to bring about their release. Since the problem is enslavement to an alien force, people cannot be liberated simply by renewing their efforts to keep the Law of God. It

is Christ alone who brings liberation, for Paul, in that he alone has broken the power of death, as proved by his resurrection. Christ has also, therefore, conquered the power of sin.

The Law, then, cannot bring about a right standing before God for those who observe it. Since everyone is enslaved to sin, they are all alienated from God. Only the one who has defeated sin can bring deliverance from sin.

3. *Paul's View of Jews and Gentiles.* As an apocalyptic Jew prior to his conversion, Paul probably believed that at the end of time God would intervene not only on behalf of his people Israel but on behalf of the entire world, since everyone was enslaved to the cosmic forces that opposed God. In other words, Paul would have been particularly attuned to the Jewish Scriptures that spoke of all the nations coming to worship the true God, after turning from their vain devotion to pagan idols and acknowledging that the God of Israel was the one true God (e.g., in Isaiah 40–66). Once he had decided that the death of Jesus, rather than the Law, was the way to a right relationship with God, he came to believe that the other nations would become God's people not through converting to the Law but through converting to Christ.

In reading the Scriptures, Paul recognized that God had made more than one covenant with the Jewish patriarchs. The first covenant was not with Moses (see Exodus 19–20) but with the father of the Jews, Abraham (see Genesis 17). God promised Abraham that he would be a blessing for all nations, not just Israel (Gen 12:3). Abraham believed God's promise and was rewarded with a right standing before God, or, as Paul calls it, "righteousness." In Paul's view, this promise was fulfilled in Jesus, not only for the Jew who later inherited the covenant given to Moses but also for the Gentile who trusted that God had fulfilled his promise in the person of Jesus. In other words, the original covenant was for all people, not just the Jews, and it was bestowed before and apart from the Law of Moses, which was given specifically to the Jews. Gentiles, therefore, did not have to follow this Law in order to be heirs of the original covenant.

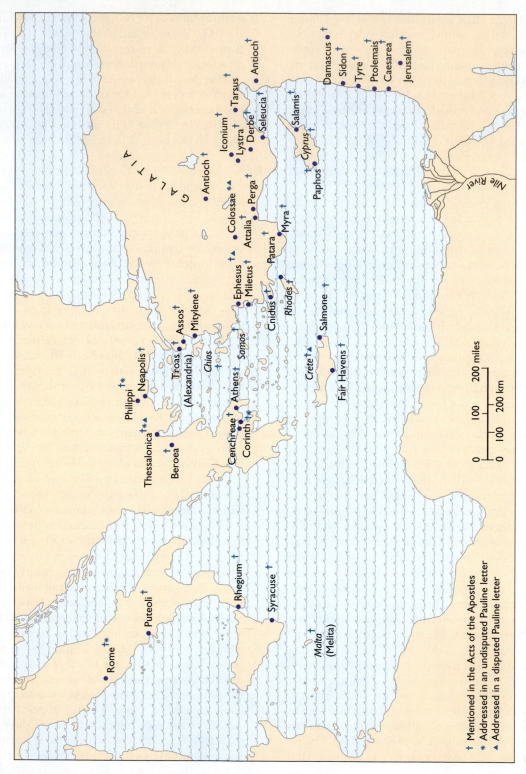

GALATIA

Antioch

Iconium †
Lystra †
Tarsus †
Derbe †
Seleucia †
Salamis †
Cyprus
Paphos †
Perga †
Attalia †
Colossae *▲
Ephesus †▲
Miletus †
Patara †
Myra †
Cnidus †
Rhodes †
Salmone †
Crete †▲
Fair Havens †

Damascus ●
Sidon †
Tyre †
Ptolemais †
Caesarea ●
Jerusalem †

Nile River

Assos †
Mitylene †
Troas †
(Alexandria)
Chios
Samos †
Athens †
Cenchreae †
Corinth †*
Neapolis †
Philippi †*
Thessalonica †*▲
Beroea †

Rome †*
Puteoli ●
Rhegium †
Syracuse †
Malta
(Melita)

0   100   200 miles
0   100   200 km

† Mentioned in the Acts of the Apostles
* Addressed in an undisputed Pauline letter
▲ Addressed in a disputed Pauline letter

Figure 12.3 Places associated with Paul in the New Testament.

ANOTHER GLIMPSE INTO THE PAST

BOX 12.5   What Did Paul Look Like?

We have no pictures of Jesus or of any of his apostles from their own time, or for at least two centuries after their deaths. But we do have a description of what Paul looked like from the document known as the *Acts of Paul and Thecla* (see chap. 22). This, too, is not from a contemporary source, but from a hundred years after Paul passed off the scene, and it appears not to be based on anything like a historically accurate account. But it is interesting—in part because it shows Paul as anything but a handsome, winsome figure! He is said to have been

a man short in stature, with a bald head, bowed legs, in good condition, eyebrows that met, a fairly large nose, and full of grace. At times he seemed human, at other times he looked like an angel.

Ancient discussions of physical characteristics suggest that this is the description of someone who is weak, sensual, a bit lazy, not overly intelligent, and a shade cunning. At the same time, the author stresses that Paul had an angelic air about him. Possibly he is trying to tell us that even though his physical appearance was pathetic, Paul's spiritual power was superhuman.

In short, Paul came to believe, on the basis of his experience of the resurrected Jesus, that all people, both Jews and Gentiles, could have a right standing with God through Christ. Faith in Jesus' death and resurrection was the only way to achieve this standing. The Law was not an alternative way because the Law brings the knowledge of sin but not the power to conquer it. Christ conquered sin, however, and whoever believes in him and accepts his work on the cross will participate in his victory.

Our brief exploration of Paul's theology here has given some indication of how his conversion affected his understanding of Christ, the Law, salvation, faith, and the relationship between Jews and Gentiles. This background will help you in your own reading of Paul's letters. As you will see, the letters, themselves, for the most part, presuppose these points of view rather than describe them. Except for a few places that can be tough going, these Pauline epistles are not heavy-duty theological treatises.

Paul the Apostle

After his conversion, Paul spent several years in Arabia and Damascus (Gal 1:17). He doesn't tell us what he did there. After a brief trip to Jerusalem, he then went into Syria and Cilicia and eventually

became involved with the church of Antioch. It is not altogether clear when he began his missionary activities farther west, in Asia Minor, Macedonia, and Achaia, but in one of his final surviving letters, he claims that he was actively involved in spreading the gospel all the way from Jerusalem to Illyricum, north of modern-day Greece (Rom 15:19).

Throughout his career as a preacher of the gospel, Paul saw himself as the "apostle to the Gentiles." By this he meant that he had been appointed by God to bring the good news of salvation through faith in Christ to those who were not Jews. Paul's normal practice appears to have been to establish a Christian community in cities that had previously been untouched by a Christian presence (we will explore his methods in the next chapter). After staying with the new church for some time and providing it with some rudimentary instruction, he would move on to another city and start from scratch. In his wake, evidently, other Christian missionaries would commonly arrive. These sometimes presented a different version of the gospel from the one Paul preached. Some of Paul's letters warn against such people. Moreover, problems frequently arose within the congregations themselves, problems of disunity, immorality, confusion over Paul's teachings, or opposition from outsiders who took exception to this new faith.

Figure 12.4 We sometimes forget that ancient travelers going on foot would often have had a rough go of it. These are the famous "Cilician Gates" in the Taurus mountains, the gorge—sixty feet across at its widest point—through which Paul would have had to pass in order to travel north from Tarsus into Asia Minor.

When Paul learned of such problems, he fired off a letter to warn, admonish, encourage, instruct, or congratulate the church. As we will see, in some instances he was himself the problem.

The letters that we have from Paul's hand represent only some of this correspondence. We can probably assume that there were dozens of other letters that for one reason or another have been lost. Paul mentions one of them in 1 Cor 5:9. The authentic letters that have survived are all included within the New Testament. In the chapters that follow, we will examine these letters, beginning with a relatively detailed assessment of the earliest one, 1 Thessalonians. In this first instance, we will be looking for information concerning Paul's modus operandi as an apostle, to learn (*a*) how Paul went about establishing a church and communicating with it after he had left, (*b*) the nature of his mes-

sage when he worked to convert people to faith in Christ and when he wrote to resolve problems that had arisen in his absence, and (*c*) the actual constituency of his churches and the character of their interactions with one another and with the world around them. Having thus set the stage, we will move on in the following chapters to examine five of the other letters, 1 and 2 Corinthians, Galatians, Philippians, and Philemon. There we will apply the contextual method to reconstruct each situation that Paul addresses and assess his response to the problems that he perceives. Finally, an entire chapter will be devoted to the letter to the Romans, the most influential of Paul's writings. There we will explore further some of the important ideas of this apostle, a figure of paramount importance in the history of Christianity down to our own day.

AT A GLANCE

BOX 12.6   Paul and His Mission

1. Paul was a central figure in the spread of Christianity, especially among the Gentiles, whom he insisted (contrary to the claims of others) did not need to become Jewish in order to follow Jesus.

2. There are difficulties in trying to reconstruct Paul's life and teachings:
   a. Some of the letters written in his name are probably pseudonymous.
   b. The book of Acts is not always historically reliable in recounting his life and preaching.
   c. The letters he wrote were occasional, that is, written to address specific situations that had arisen in his churches, not general treatises systematically laying out his thought.

3. Paul had been a highly religious Pharisee who persecuted the Christians before becoming convinced, on the basis of a visionary experience, that God had raised Jesus from the dead.

4. Belief in Jesus' resurrection confirmed Paul's basic apocalyptic view of the world. He came to believe that God had already begun to intervene in history to overthrow the cosmic forces of evil.

5. This belief radically affected Paul's understanding of Jesus (he is the way of salvation), the Jewish Law (it is not important for a person's standing before God), and the relationship of Jew and Gentile (they are equal before God).

6. Once he came to these convictions, Paul began a missionary campaign to convert others—principally Gentiles—to faith in Jesus, in major urban areas of the northern Mediterranean, especially Asia Minor, Macedonia, and Achaia.

TAKE A STAND

1. You are talking with your roommate about the New Testament, and she says that it is quite easy to know what the apostle Paul did and said, since we have an account of his life in the book of Acts and thirteen of his letters. You like to disagree with everything your roommate says and so decide to argue the opposite side, that these sources are in fact problematic for knowing about Paul's life and teachings. Make your case.

2. Resolved: Paul's religion was radically different from that of Jesus. Argue both sides of this resolution. Where do you stand, so far?

3. A lot of people think that what matters about Jesus is his ethical teaching, not his death and resurrection. Pretend you are the apostle Paul and write a response to that view.

SUGGESTIONS FOR FURTHER READING

In addition to the books mentioned here, see the suggestions for reading in Chapters 13–16.

Aune, David. *The New Testament in Its Literary Environment*. Philadelphia: Westminster, 1987. Includes a superb discussion of the practices of letter-writing in Greco-Roman antiquity as the social context for Paul's epistles.

Bassler, Jouette. *Navigating Paul: An Introduction to Key Theological Concepts*. Philadelphia: Westminster John Knox, 2006. A highly useful discussion of some of the major theological themes in the Pauline letters, written in clear and compelling terms.

(continued)

SUGGESTIONS FOR FURTHER READING *(continued)*

Beker, J. Christiaan. *Paul the Apostle: The Triumph of God in Life and Thought.* Philadelphia: Fortress, 1980. A sophisticated and astute discussion of the apocalyptic character of Paul's theology and its various forms of expression in different situations that the apostle confronted; for advanced students.

Bruce, F. F. *Apostle of the Heart Set Free.* Grand Rapids, Mich.: Eerdmans, 2000. A full study of Paul's life and teachings by a major evangelical Christian scholar.

Crossan, John Dominic, and Jonathan Reed. *In Search of Paul: How Jesus' Apostle Opposed Rome's Empire with God's Kingdom.* San Francisco: HarperOne, 2005. A controversial discussion of Paul that focuses on his cultural, political, and historical situation and message more than on his theology, written by a prominent scholar of the historical Jesus (Crossan) and an archaeologist (Reed).

Dunn, James D. *The Theology of Paul the Apostle.* 2d ed. Grand Rapids, Mich.: Eerdmans, 2006. A clear and full overview of the major theological views of Paul, by a leading British New Testament scholar.

Ehrman, Bart. *Forged: Writing in the Name of God. Why the Bible's Authors Are Not Who We Think They Are.* San Francisco: HarperOne, 2011. A discussion of all the "pseudepigrapha" of the New Testament, including those attributed to Paul, which argues that it is best to understand these as ancient forgeries; for beginning students.

Hawthorne, Gerald, and Ralph Martin. *Dictionary of Paul and His Letters.* Downers Grove, Ill.: Intervarsity, 1993. A Bible dictionary that contains over 200 articles on various topics related to the life and writings of Paul, written by prominent evangelical scholars who on several major issues take a different perspective from the one presented here (such as the authorship of the Deutero-Pauline and Pastoral epistles).

Horrell, David. *Introduction to the Study of Paul.* 2d ed. London: T & T Clark, 2006. A comprehensive discussion of all the important aspects of Paul's life, letters, and teaching that shows the different views of important scholars and why they hold them.

Meeks, Wayne. *The First Urban Christians. The Social World of the Apostle Paul.* New Haven, Conn.: Yale University Press, 1983. An impressive and highly influential study that explores the Pauline epistles from a sociohistorical rather than theological perspective; for more advanced students.

Meeks, Wayne, and John Fitzgerald eds. *The Writings of St. Paul.* 2d ed. New York: Norton, 2007. A very useful annotated edition of Paul's letters that includes a number of classic essays on various aspects of Paul's thought and significance.

Roetzel, Calvin. *The Letters of Paul: Conversations in Context.* 4th ed. Atlanta: Westminster John Knox, 2011. Perhaps the best introductory discussion of each of the Pauline epistles.

Roetzel, Calvin. *Paul: The Man and the Myth.* Minneapolis: Fortress, 1999. An introductory-level discussion of the life and teachings of Paul by a significant Pauline scholar.

Sanders, E. P. *Paul and Palestinian Judaism.* Philadelphia: Fortress, 1977. An enormously influential and erudite study that situates Paul in the context of early Judaism; for advanced students.

Sanders, E. P. *Paul: A Very Short Introduction.* New York: Oxford University Press, 2001. The title says it all! The book is for the early beginner and is written by one of the most learned and influential Pauline scholars of modern times.

Segal, Alan. *Paul the Convert: The Apostolate and Apostasy of Saul the Pharisee.* New Haven, Conn.: Yale University Press, 1990. A very interesting study by a Jewish scholar who examines the importance of Paul's conversion for his theology and practice.

 KEY TERMS

Areopagus speech	first-fruit of the	Pastoral epistles	Tarsus
contextual method	resurrection	pseudepigrapha	undisputed Pauline
conversion	Gamaliel	road to Damascus	epistles
Deutero-Pauline	occasional	Seneca	
epistles			

Paul and His Apostolic Mission

1 THESSALONIANS AS A TEST CASE

WHAT TO EXPECT

Given the central importance of Paul, not just for the New Testament itself but for the spread of Christianity in its early decades, it would be interesting to see how he worked, how he managed to convert people, where he met with them, what he said to them, how he persuaded them, what he did with them once they were converted, and so on. This chapter focuses on Paul's "modus operandi" by looking carefully at the very first of his surviving letters, 1 Thessalonians, the earliest piece of Christian literature that we have (written at least fifteen years before Mark, our earliest Gospel).

The chapter not only considers how Paul went about converting the Thessalonians from their pagan beliefs to faith in Christ but also discusses the problems that arose in the church after Paul left, compelling him to write a letter to deal with them.

First Thessalonians is a particularly good place to begin a study of Paul's letters. Scholars are almost unanimous in thinking that it was the first of his surviving works to be written, which also means that it is the oldest book of the New Testament and consequently the earliest surviving Christian writing of any kind. It is usually dated to about the year 49 C.E., that is, some twenty years after Jesus' death. It is written to a congregation for which Paul has real affection and in which no major problems have arisen, at least in comparison with what we will find in the letters to the Corinthians and the Galatians. As a consequence, Paul spends most of the letter renewing his bonds of friendship with the congregation, largely by re-

counting aspects of their past relationship. Since he has just recently left the community, memories of this relationship are still fresh.

Given the nature of the letter, we can learn a good deal about how Paul established this church and about what the people who composed it were like. We can also learn about the difficulties they experienced when they converted, the problems that emerged in their community soon thereafter, and the approach that Paul took to dealing with these problems. To be sure, we are not provided with as much information as we would like about such things; Paul after all was not writing to us, but to people who were already intimately familiar with him (and who knew their own situation!). Nonetheless, for historians who are interested in knowing how the Christian mission was conducted and how the Christian converts fared in their world, 1 Thessalonians provides ample food for thought.

We will examine this particular letter, therefore, not only to learn about its immediate occasion (i.e., the reasons that Paul wrote it) and to uncover its principal themes, but also to find clues about various social and historical aspects of Paul's apostolic mission to the Gentiles. This kind of **sociohistorical method of investigation** will then set the stage for our study of the other Pauline letters.

THE FOUNDING OF THE CHURCH IN THESSALONICA

Thessalonica was a major port city, the capital of the Roman province of **Macedonia**, where the Roman governor kept his residence, and one of the principal targets chosen by Paul for his mission in the region. This choice appears to be consistent with Paul's missionary strategy otherwise. As far as we can tell, he generally chose to stay in relatively large urban areas where he would have the greatest opportunity to meet and address potential converts.

How then did Paul go about converting people to faith in Christ? That is, how did a Christian missionary like Paul, after arriving in a new city where he had no contacts, actually go about meeting people and talking to them about religion in an effort to convert them? First Thessalonians provides some interesting insights concerning Paul's missionary tactics, that is, his apostolic modus operandi.

Paul's Modus Operandi

One might imagine that when Paul arrived in town as a complete stranger, he would simply stand on a crowded street corner and preach to those passing by, hoping to win converts by his sincerity and charisma and by the appeal of his message. As we will see, there was a precedent for this kind of proselytizing activity among some of the philosophers in the Greco-Roman world, but Paul gives no indication that this is how he proceeded.

Nor does the book of Acts. In Acts, Paul invariably makes new contacts by going to the local synagogue, where as a traveling Jew he would be quite welcome, and using the worship service there as an occasion to speak of his belief in Jesus as the messiah come in fulfillment of the Scriptures. This tactic seems reasonable, and Acts is quite explicit in saying that this is how Paul did evangelize the people of Thessalonica, winning converts among the Jews and the "devout Gentiles" who joined them in their worship of the God of Israel (Acts 17:2–4). Luke sometimes calls this latter group "[God]-fearers," by which he seems to mean non-Jews who have abandoned their idolatry to worship the Jewish God, without, however, keeping every aspect of the Torah, including circumcision if they were men. According to Acts, Paul converted a number of such people in Thessalonica over a period of three weeks, after which a group of antagonistic Jews rose up to run him out of town (17:2–10).

This portrayal in Acts, however, stands in sharp contrast with Paul's own reminiscences of his Thessalonian mission. Curiously, Paul says nothing about the Jewish synagogue in his letter; indeed, he never mentions the presence of any Jews, either among his Christian converts or among their opponents in town. On the contrary, he indicates that the Christians that he brought to the faith were former pagans, whom he himself converted from worshiping "dead idols to serve the living and true God" (i.e., the Jewish God, whom Paul himself continues to worship through Jesus; 1:9). These converts, in other words, were neither Jews nor God-fearers. How then do we explain the account in Acts 17? It may be that Luke knew in general that Paul had preached in Thessalonica but did not know how he had proceeded or whom he had converted.

If Paul did not preach from the street corner or work through the synagogue, how did he go about making contacts and, eventually, converts? In the course of his letter, Paul reflects on the time he had spent among the Thessalonians, recalling with great pride how he and his Christian companions had worked "night and day so that we might not burden any of you while we proclaimed to you the gospel of God" (2:9). Recent scholars have realized that Paul literally means that he had been working full time and had used his place of business as a point of contact with people to proclaim the gospel. Paul preached while on the job.

Paul's emphasis on the burdens of his toil (2:9) makes it reasonably clear that his job involved some kind of manual labor. The book of Acts indicates that he worked with leather goods (18:3). Sometimes this is interpreted to mean that he was a tentmaker, although the term used can refer to a number of occupations involving animal skins. Paul himself doesn't indicate the precise nature of his employment (presumably the Thessalonians would already know). What he does indicate is that he was not alone in his labors but was accompanied in Thessalonica by two others, Timothy and Silvanus. The three arrived in town in active pursuit of converts; they all, evidently, engaged in the same form of manual labor, and all preached their faith to those with whom they came in contact.

Before we try to imagine how this mission took place, we should review the historical context. In our earlier discussion of Greco-Roman religions, we saw that none of the religions of the empire was exclusive; that is, none of them claimed that if you worshiped any one of the gods, it was inappropriate to worship others as well. Perhaps because of their inclusive character, none of these religions was missionary, none of them urged their devotees to pursue converts to participate in their cult and their cult alone. Thus, when Paul and his coworkers were trying to make converts, they were not modeling themselves on what representatives of other sacred cults in their day were doing.

On the other hand, some of the Greco-Roman philosophical schools were missionary, in that they had leading spokespersons actively engaged in winning converts to their way of looking at the world. In particular, **Stoic** and **Cynic** philosophers were involved in these kinds of activities. They tried to

Figure 13.1   A reconstructed model of a Roman insula, with shops on the lower level and living quarters above, similar to one that Paul may have worked and lived in while engaged in his missionary endeavors in such places as Thessalonica and Corinth.

convince people to change their notions about life and their ways of living to conform to the philosophical views that alone could bring personal well-being. More specifically, Stoic and Cynic philosophers urged people to give up their attachments to the things of this world and to make their overarching concerns those aspects of their lives that they themselves were able to control. The Stoic theory was that people who were ultimately committed to matters outside their control, such as wealth, health, careers, or lovers, were constantly in danger of forfeiting their well-being through the vicissitudes of bad fortune. What happens if you base your happiness on material goods or personal relationships, but then they are lost or destroyed? The solution to this problem is not to take measures to protect what you have, since this may not be within your power; it is, instead, to redirect your affections so your happiness is based on things that cannot be taken away, such as your freedom to think whatever you like, your honor, and your sense of duty. Since these are things that can never be lost, they should lie at the root of your personal well-being and so be the objects of your greatest concern.

Proselytizers for such philosophies could be found in a variety of urban settings throughout the empire. Cynics—who took the Stoic doctrine to an extreme by abandoning all social conventions, including decent clothing, lodging, bathing, and privacy for bodily functions (see box 9.6)—sometimes frequented crowded public places, where they urged their views on passersby, maligned those who turned away, and badgered people for money (since they rejected social convention, they could scarcely be expected to work for a living). More socially respectable philosophers were often connected with wealthy households, somewhat like scholars-in-residence, and had wealthy patrons who provided for their physical needs in exchange for services rendered toward the family's intellectual and spiritual needs. A few Greco-Roman philosophers believed in working for a living to keep from depending on the support of others for their needs and becoming subservient to the so-called "nicer things in life."

As far as we can tell, this final kind of philosopher was somewhat rare in the empire, but Paul and his companions may have been identified as such outsiders in Thessalonica. They were missionaries with

Figure 13.2 The remains of an insula in the city of Ostia, near Rome.

a particular worldview who were trying to convert others to their ideas; they worked hard to support themselves and refused to take funds from others (e.g., 1 Thess 2:9).

Perhaps their mission proceeded something like this. Paul and his two companions arrived in the city and as a first step rented out a room in a downtown insula. **Insula** were the ancient equivalents of modern apartment buildings, packed close together in urban areas. They had a ground floor containing rooms that faced the street for small businesses (grocers, potters, tailors, cobblers, metal workers, engravers, scribes, and so forth), while the upper two or three stories served as living quarters for the people who worked below and for anyone else who could afford the rent. Shops were places not only of commerce but of social interaction, as customers, friends, and neighbors would stop by to talk. Given the long workdays and the absence of weekends (Jews, of course, took the Sabbath off, and everyone else closed up for special religious celebrations), the workplace was much more an arena of social intercourse than most modern business establishments are today. Contacts could be made, plans could be laid, ideas could be discussed—all over the potter's wheel or the tailor's table or the cobbler's bench.

Did Paul and his companions set up a small business, a kind of Christian leather goods shop, in the cities they visited? If so, this would explain a good deal of what Paul recounts concerning his interaction with the Thessalonian Christians in the early days. He and his companions toiled night and day while preaching the gospel to them (2:9). Like philosophers in that world, they exhorted, encouraged, and pleaded with those who dropped by, urging them to change their lives and adhere to the Christian message (2:12). Like some of the

Figure 13.3 A shoemaker and cordmaker at work, from an ancient sarcophagus. These were manual laborers like Paul, who according to Acts 18:3 was a leatherworker.

Stoics, they refused to be a burden on any of their converts, choosing to work with their own hands rather than rely on the resources of others (2:9–10).

Paul's Message

Paul obviously could not launch into a heavy exposition of his theology with people who were just stopping by. This was not simply because of the setting but even more because of the nature of his typical encounter. Even though Paul was engaged in manual labor, he was not an ordinary "blue-collar" worker. He was highly educated, far more so than most of the people that he would meet during a workday, and his theological reflections would be enough to befuddle the average person on the street. Moreover, most people stopping by the shop were almost certainly pagans, worshipers of Greco-Roman deities, who believed that there were lots of gods, all of whom deserved devotion and cult.

How would Paul begin to talk about his gospel with people like this? We are again fortunate to have some indications in Paul's letter. The critical passage is 1:9–10, where Paul reminds his recent converts what he originally taught them:

> [To turn] to God from idols, to serve a living and true God, and to wait for his Son from heaven, whom he raised from the dead—Jesus, who rescues us from that wrath that is coming.

This appears to have been the core of Paul's proclamation to his potential converts. His first step was to have them realize that the many gods they worshiped were "dead" and "false" and that there was only one "living" and "true" God. In other words, before Paul could begin to talk about Jesus, he first had to win converts to the God of Israel, the one creator of heaven and earth, who chose his people and promised to bless all the nations of earth through them. Thus, Paul's proclamation began with an argument against the existence and reality of the deities worshiped in the local cults.

We have no way of knowing how Paul actually persuaded people that there was only one true God. Quite possibly he recounted tales of how this one God had proved himself in the past, for example, in the stories found in the Jewish Scriptures or

in tales of Jesus' followers, who were said to have done miracles. It is likely that these converts had at least heard of the Jewish God before, so Paul's initial task appears to have been to convince them that this was the only God worthy of their devotion and that their own gods had no power but were dead and lifeless. It may be that some of these people were already inclined to accept the belief in one God in view of the increasingly widespread notion even in non-Jewish circles that ultimately there was one deity in control of human affairs (see Chapter 2). If so, then Paul's success lay in his ability to convince them, somehow, that this one God was the God that he proclaimed to them.

Once Paul's listeners accepted the notion of the one true God, Paul pressed upon them his belief that Jesus was this one God's Son. Again, it is hard to know how he elaborated this view. There are reasons to doubt that he proceeded by describing Jesus' earthly life, narrating tales of what he said and did prior to his crucifixion, for even though he constantly reminds his Thessalonian audience of what he taught them, he says nary a word about Jesus' sayings or deeds (recall that none of our Gospels was yet in existence). What, then, did he teach them?

Later in the letter we learn that a central component of the converts' faith was the belief that Jesus died "for them" (5:10) and that he was raised from the dead (4:14). From this we can surmise that Paul taught his potential converts that Jesus was a person who was specially connected with the one true God (the "Son of God," as he calls him in 1:9), whose death and resurrection were necessary to put them into a right relation with God. What appears to have been the most important belief about Jesus to the Thessalonians, however, was that he was soon to return from heaven in judgment on the earth. The first reference to this belief is already here in 1:10, where Paul reminds his readers that he taught them to "wait for his Son from heaven—Jesus, who rescues us from the wrath that is coming." Further references to the notion of Jesus' return are found in every chapter of the letter (e.g., see 2:19; 3:13; 4:13–18; 5:1–11).

The Thessalonian congregation was also acquainted with the reason that Jesus was soon to return. On this point Paul is unequivocal: Jesus was coming for his followers to save them from God's wrath. Paul, in other words, had taught his

This appears to have been the burden of Paul's preaching. From beginning to end it was rooted in a worldview that Paul appears to have embraced as a Jewish apocalypticist even prior to his conversion. Thus, to some extent his preaching to the Thessalonians involved convincing them to accept such basic apocalyptic notions as the end of the age, the coming of God's judgment, the need for redemption, and the salvation of the godly. It is striking, in this connection, how much apocalyptic imagery Paul uses throughout the letter. Consider, for example, 5:1–11, where Paul indicates that the end will come suddenly, like a woman's labor pains, that it will come like a thief in the night, that the children of light will escape but not the children of darkness, and that the faithful need to be awake and sober. All of these images can be found in other Jewish apocalyptic texts as well. Moreover, many of Paul's allusive comments throughout the letter make sense only within a Jewish apocalyptic framework; among these are his reference to Satan, the great enemy of God and his people (2:18) and his assurance that suffering is necessary for God's people here at the end of time (3:3–4). Thus, in its simplest terms, Paul's proclamation was designed to transform the Thessalonian pagans into Jewish apocalypticists, who believed that Jesus was the key to the end of the world.

THE BEGINNINGS OF THE THESSALONIAN CHURCH: A SOCIOHISTORICAL PERSPECTIVE

To some extent, Paul succeeded in his mission. We have no idea how many people he and his companions converted, but there were clearly some. Here we will explore the nature of this group of converts from the perspective of a social historian, asking not so much what they came to believe but rather who they were and how they functioned as a social group.

It is nearly impossible to gauge what kind of people Paul's Gentile converts in Thessalonica were. If they were in regular contact with manual laborers like Paul and his companions in their insula, and if it would have been an excessive burden for them to provide financial support for

Figure 13.4 Statue of Artemis (the goddess Diana) from Ephesus. The almost grotesque portrayal of her many breasts emphasizes her role as a fertility goddess, one who gives life in abundance. For Paul, however, she (along with all other pagan deities) was nothing but a "dead idol" (see 1 Thess 1:8–10).

Thessalonian converts a strongly apocalyptic message. This world was soon to end, when the God who created it returned to judge it; those who sided with this God would be delivered , and those who did not would experience his wrath. Moreover, the way to side with this God, the creator and judge of all, was by believing in his Son, Jesus, who had died and been raised for the sins of the world and who would return soon for those who believe in him, to rescue them from the impending wrath.

the missionaries, then we might suppose that, for the most part, the converts were not among the wealthy and the social elite in town, although certainly some may have been drawn from among the upper classes. If this sketch is correct, then the Thessalonian Christians, as a social group, may have been roughly comparable to the people Paul was later to convert in the city of Corinth farther to the south, the majority of whom were not well educated, influential, or from among the upper social classes, according to 1 Cor 1:26 (presumably some were, or Paul would have not have said that "not many of you are").

It seems plausible that the people Paul converted began meeting together periodically, perhaps weekly, for fellowship and worship. This appears to have been the pattern of Paul's churches, as you will see from his other letters (e.g., 1 Cor 11:17–26; 16:1), and it would make sense of his decision to send a letter to "the church" rather than to individual converts. Most historians think that churches like this would have met in private homes, and so call them "house churches" (e.g., see Philemon 2). We have no hard evidence of actual church buildings being constructed by Christians for another two centuries (see box 20.5).

It appears that people in this kind of group experienced unusual cohesion as a social unit. There were, of course, other kinds of social groups in the Greco-Roman world that met periodically for worship and socializing. We are especially well informed about ancient **trade organizations** and **funeral societies**. The church in Thessalonica may have been roughly organized like one of these groups (see box 13.1). On the other hand, given its central commitment to a religious purpose, it may have had some close organizational affinities with the Jewish synagogue as well, although the Jewish community was probably much larger than the Christian group. It appears that some of the local converts became leaders in the Christian congregation and that they organized their meetings, distributed the funds they collected, and guided the thinking of the group about religious matters (5:12–13).

From a sociohistorical point of view, certain features of these converts' new religion provided strong bonds with the group. For one thing, they appear to have understood themselves as a closed

group. Not just anyone could come off the street to join; membership was restricted to those who accepted Paul's message of the apocalyptic judgment that was soon to come and the salvation that could be obtained only through faith in Jesus, who died and was raised from the dead. The Thessalonian church had a unified commitment to this teaching, and it made them distinct from everyone else that they came in contact with.

This distinctiveness was evidently known to outsiders as well. Throughout 1 Thessalonians Paul refers to the persecution that the community experienced from those who did not belong. As an apostle who proclaimed the gospel in the face of malicious opposition, Paul himself had suffered in some undisclosed way in the city of Philippi before arriving in Thessalonica (2:1–2). His statement is consistent with Luke's account of the founding of the Philippian church in Acts 16:19–40, although Paul does not corroborate any of Luke's details. In any event, he instructs his Thessalonian converts that they too should expect to suffer (3:3–4). He does not say why they should expect this, but perhaps it is because he believed that the forces of evil were out in full strength here at the end of time (cf. 2:18; 5:1–11). Moreover, he indicates that the Thessalonians had already experienced persecution from their compatriots, just as the earlier Christian communities had been persecuted by the non-Christian Judeans, who had always served as a thorn in the side of the church, in Paul's opinion, from the days of Jesus onward (2:14–16).

A shared experience of suffering can help to consolidate a social group that is already unified by a common set of beliefs and commitments. That is to say, suffering for the cause can function to emphasize and sharpen the boundaries that separate those who "live according to the truth" from those who "live in error." Moreover, the Christian believers in Thessalonica shared their insider status with similar groups of believers throughout their world. Thus Paul emphasizes that their faithfulness to the gospel had become well known to Christian communities throughout the provinces of Macedonia and Achaia (1:7–9) and that they were linked to the communities of Judea as well.

Paul never indicates directly why he mentions the churches of Judea, but he may have done so

ANOTHER GLIMPSE INTO THE PAST

BOX 13.1   Rules for a Private Association

Christian house churches may have appeared to outsiders to be like other kinds of **voluntary associations** found in the Greco-Roman world. Associations were privately organized small groups that met periodically to socialize and share a good meal together; they would often perform cultic acts of worship together; many of them were concerned with providing appropriate burial for their members (a kind of life-insurance arrangement that covered expenses hard to manage on an individual basis). The social activities of such groups were sometimes underwritten by one or more of their wealthier members who served as patrons for the body.

Voluntary associations had rules for membership, some of which we know from surviving inscriptions. To see the close connections of such societies with the early Christian communities, consider the following set of bylaws of a burial society in Lanuvium, Italy, a group that met at the temple of the divine man Antinoüs. These bylaws come to us from an inscription dated to 136 C.E. Note the concerns for good food and good wine, for order in the community, and for a decent burial once one departed this life. [A sesterce was a coin worth about one-quarter of an average worker's daily wage.]

> It was voted unanimously that whoever desires to enter this society shall pay an initiation fee of 100 sesterces and an amphora of good wine, and shall pay monthly dues of [2 sesterces]. . . . It was voted further that upon the decease of a paid-up member of our body there will be due him from the treasury 300 sesterces,

from which sum will be deducted a funeral fee of 50 sesterces to be distributed at the pyre [among those attending]; the obsequies, furthermore, will be performed on foot. . . .

> Masters of the dinners in the order of the membership list, appointed four at a time in turn, shall be required to provide an amphora of good wine each, and for as many members as the society has, a [loaf of] bread costing [1 sesterce], sardines to the number of four, a setting, and warm water with service.

> It was voted further that any member who has [served as chief officer] honestly shall [thereafter] receive a share and a half of everything as a mark of honor, so that other [chief officers] will also hope for the same by properly discharging their duties.

> It was voted further that if any member desires to make any complaint or bring up any business, he is to bring it up at a business meeting, so that we may banquet in peace and good cheer on festive days.

> It was voted further that any member . . . who speaks abusively of another or causes an uproar shall be fined 12 sesterces. Any member who uses any abusive or insolent language to a [chief officer] at a banquet shall be fined 20 sesterces.

> It was voted further that on the festive days of his term of office, each [chief officer] is to conduct worship with incense and wine and is to perform his other functions clothed in white, and that on the birthdays of [the goddess] Diana and [the divine] Antinoüs he is to provide oil for the society in the public bath before they banquet. (Taken from Naphtali Lewis and Meyer Rheinhold, *Roman Civilization*, 3rd ed. [New York: Columbia University Press, 1990] 2.186–88.)

because of his cherished notion that his message did not represent a new religion but the religion of the Jews come now to fulfillment in Jesus. Paul did not teach these converts that they had to become Jews, but he did teach them that the one true God whom they now worshiped was the God of Israel, who in fulfillment of his promises had sent his messiah to die for the sins of the world. This was Jesus, the Son of the Jewish God, who was now prepared to return to deliver his people from the wrath that was to come.

The group of believers in Thessalonica thus understood itself to be part of a much broader social and historical network of the faithful, a network stretching across broad tracks of land and reaching back into the misty ages of history. They were brothers and sisters (1:4) bonded together for a common purpose, standing against a common enemy, partaking of a common destiny—and connected with other communities of like purpose and destiny who all shared the history of the people of God, as recorded in the traditions of the Jewish Scriptures.

The exhortations and instructions that Paul gives serve further to unify the group as rules, guidelines, beliefs, and practices that they share in common. He gives them these instructions, of course, in response to situations that have arisen in the community.

THE CHURCH AT THESSALONICA AFTER PAUL'S DEPARTURE

First Thess 3:1 indicates that after Paul and his companions left Thessalonica, they journeyed to Athens, perhaps again to set up shop. After a while, feeling anxious about the young church, they sent **Timothy** back to check on the situation, and possibly to provide additional instruction and support. When Timothy rejoined his colleagues (either in Athens or in Corinth, which was evidently their next stop; Acts indicates the latter but Paul says nothing of it), he filled them in on the situation (3:6). First Thessalonians represents a kind of follow-up letter. Even though, technically speaking, it was coauthored by Paul, **Silvanus**, and Timothy (1:1), Paul himself was evidently the real author (e.g., see 2:18).

The most obvious piece of information that Timothy brought back to his colleagues was that the congregation was still strong and deeply grateful for the work they had done among them. The letter is remarkably personable, with professions of heartfelt gratitude and affection flowing from nearly every page, especially in the first three chapters.

Although Paul's epistles generally follow the form of most Greco-Roman letters (see Chapter 12), they are, as a rule, much longer and tend to have a shape of their own. They typically begin with a prescript that names the sender(s) and the addressees, followed by a prayer or blessing ("Grace to you and peace . . ."), and then an expression of thanksgiving to God for the congregation. In most of Paul's letters, the body of the letter, where the main business at hand is addressed, comes next, followed by closing admonitions and greetings to people in the congregation, some references to Paul's future travel plans, and a final blessing and farewell. In 1 Thessalonians, however, the majority of the letter is taken up by the thanksgiving (1:2–3:13). This is clearly a letter that Paul was happy to write, in contrast, say, to Galatians, where the thanksgiving is replaced by a reprimand!

The closest analogy to 1 Thessalonians from elsewhere in Greco-Roman antiquity is a kind of correspondence that modern scholars have labeled the **"friendship letter."** This is a letter sent to renew an acquaintance and to extend friendly good wishes, sometimes with a few requests or admonitions. Paul's letter also contains some requests and admonitions, based on the news that he has received from Timothy. The congregation has not experienced any major problems, but one important issue has arisen in the interim since Paul's departure. Paul writes to resolve the issue and to address other matters that are important for the ongoing life of the community.

Before considering the major issue that has arisen, we should examine another aspect of life in the Thessalonian church—the community's persecution. We do not know exactly what this persecution entailed. We do know that in a somewhat later period, some sixty years after 1 Thessalonians was written, Roman provincial authorities occasionally prosecuted Christian believers simply for being Christian. At least during the New Testament period, however, there was no official opposition to Christianity, in the sense of an established governmental policy or legislation outlawing the religion. People could be Christian or anything else as long as they didn't disturb the peace.

Christians sometimes did disturb the peace, however, and when they did, there could be reprisals. Paul himself indicates that over the course of his career he had been beaten with "rods," a standard form of Roman corporal punishment, on three occasions (2 Cor 11:25). Were the Christians of Thessalonica, the capital of the Roman province of Macedonia, being condemned to punishment by the governor who resided there?

In later times, the case against the Christians was taken up by governors at the instigation of the populace, who feared that this new religion was offensive to the Roman gods. Other non-Roman religions were generally not seen as offensive because they did not prohibit their adherents from participating in the state cult. Jews generally did not participate, of course, but they were granted an exemption because of the great antiquity of their traditions (recall: in that world, if something was old, it was venerable). Christianity, on the other hand, was not at all ancient; moreover, the Christians not only refused to worship the state gods, they also insisted that their God was the only true God and that all other gods were demonic. For the most part, this notion did not sit well with those who believed not only that the gods existed but also that they could terrorize those who refused to acknowledge them in their cults. Some decades after Paul, cities that experienced disaster would sometimes blame the false religion of the Christians; when that happened, Christian believers were well advised to keep a low profile.

Had something like this happened in Thessalonica? While it is possible that the governor of the province had sent out the troops at the instigation of the masses, Paul says nothing to indicate that the situation was so grave or dramatic. It could be, then, that the Christians were opposed not by the government but by other people (organized groups?) who found their religion offensive to their sense of right and duty—duty to the gods who bring peace and prosperity and duty to the state, which was the prime beneficiary of the gods' kindnesses. It commonly happens that closed, secret societies bring out the worst in their neighbors, and it may be that the Thessalonian Christians, with their bizarre teachings about the end of the world and the return of a divine man from heaven, along with their inflammatory rhetoric (for example, against other local cults), proved to be too much for others. These others could have included families and former friends of the converts, who knew enough to be suspicious but were not themselves inclined to join up. Perhaps they maligned the group or abused it in other ways (physical attacks? graffiti on the walls of its house church? organized protests?).

If something like this scenario is at all plausible, it would help explain some of the other things Paul says in this letter by way of exhortation. He begins the body of the letter (4:1–5:11) by urging his converts not to engage in sexual immorality. The meaning of his words is hotly debated by scholars. It may be that Paul simply wants the Thessalonian Christians to keep their image pure before the outside world, just in case they are suspected of vile ac-

tivities commonly attributed to secret societies in the ancient world (see box 13.2). After all, there is no reason to give outsiders additional grounds to malign your group when they already have all the grounds they need.

The same logic may underlie the exhortations in 4:9–12. The believers are urged to love one another, in what we might call the platonic sense, not to make waves in society ("mind your own affairs"), and to be good citizens ("work with your own hands"). These admonitions serve both to promote group cohesion and to project an acceptable image of the group to those who are outside.

The Major Issue in the Congregation

In 4:13 Paul finally comes to the one serious issue that the Thessalonians themselves have raised. Perhaps not surprisingly, given what we have seen about the character of Paul's message when he converted and instructed these people, it is a question pertaining to the events at the end of time. Paul had earlier instructed the Thessalonians about the imminent end of the world, which would bring sudden suffering to those who were not prepared, like the birthpangs of a woman in labor (see 5:1–3). He had warned them that they must be ready, for the day was coming soon and was almost upon them; they must be awake and sober lest it catch them unawares (5:4–9). His converts had presumably taken his teaching to heart; they were eagerly awaiting the return of Jesus to deliver them from the wrath that was coming. But Jesus hadn't returned and something troubling had happened: some of the members of the congregation had died.

These deaths caused a major disturbance among some of the survivors. The Thessalonians had thought that the end was going to come before they passed off the face of the earth. Had they been wrong? Even more troubling, had those who died missed their chance to enter into the heavenly kingdom when Jesus returned?

Paul writes to respond to their concern. You will notice that the response of 4:14–17 is bracketed by two exhortations to have hope and be comforted in light of what will happen when Jesus appears. At his return in glory those who have died will be the first to meet him; only then will those who are alive join up with them in the air "to be

BOX 13.2 Christians Maligned as Perverts and Criminals

There is no solid evidence to suggest that specific allegations of wrongdoing were being made against the church in Thessalonica at the time of Paul's writing, but we do know that other secret societies were widely viewed with suspicion and that certain standard kinds of slander were leveled against them. The logic of these slanders is plain: if people meet together in secret or under the cloak of darkness, they must have something to hide.

It is possible that Paul was aware of such charges and wanted the Thessalonian Christians to go out of their way to avoid them. Such a concern would make sense of his injunctions to maintain pure sexual conduct and to keep a good reputation among outsiders.

You might be amazed at the kinds of accusations that were later leveled against the Christians, that they were cannibals and perverts who killed babies and then ate them. Consider, for example, the comments of Fronto, the tutor of the emperor Marcus Aurelius and one of the most highly respected scholars of the mid-second century:

> They [the Christians] recognize each other by secret marks and signs; hardly have they met when they love each other, throughout the world uniting in the practice of a veritable religion of lusts. Indiscriminately they call each other brother and sister, thus turning even ordinary fornication into incest. . . . It is also reported that they worship the genitals of their pontiff and priest, adoring, it appears, the sex of their "father." . . . The notoriety of the stories told of the initiation of new recruits is matched by their ghastly horror. A young baby is covered over with flour, the object being to deceive the unwary. It is then served before the person to be admitted into their rites. The recruit is urged to inflict blows onto it—they appear to be harmless because of the covering of flour. Thus the baby is killed with wounds that remain unseen and concealed. It is the blood of this infant—I shudder to mention it—it is this blood that they lick with thirsty lips; these are the limbs they distribute eagerly; this is the victim by which they seal their covenant; it is by complicity in this crime that they are pledged to mutual silence; these are their rites, more foul than all sacrileges combined. . . . On a special day they gather for a feast with all their children, sisters, mothers—all sexes and all ages. There, flushed with the banquet after such feasting and drinking, they begin to burn with incestuous passions. They provoke a dog tied to the lampstand to leap and bound towards a scrap of food which they have tossed outside the reach of his chain. By this means the light is overturned and extinguished, and with it common knowledge of their actions; in the shameless dark with unspeakable lust they copulate in random unions, all equally being guilty of incest. (Minucius Felix, *Octavius* 9:2–6)

with the Lord forever" (4:17; this is the verse used by some modern evangelical Christians to support their belief in the "rapture"—a term that occurs neither here nor anywhere else in the New Testament). In other words, there will not simply be a resurrection of the dead for judgment at the end of time; there will also be a removal of the followers of Jesus, both dead and alive, from this world prior to the coming of the divine wrath. The Thessalonians are to be comforted by this scenario. Those who have already died have not at all lost out; rather, they will precede the living as they enter into the presence of the Lord at the end of time.

There are two further points of interest about this passage. First, it is clear that Paul expects that he and some of the Thessalonians will be alive when this apocalyptic drama comes to be played out. He contrasts "those who have died" with "we who are alive, who are left until the coming of the Lord" (v. 15; also see v. 17). He appears to have no idea that his words would be discussed after his death, let alone read and studied some nineteen centuries later. For him, the end of time was imminent.

Second, Paul's scenario presupposes a **three-storied universe**, in which the world consists of an "up" (where God is, and now Jesus), a "here" (where we are), and a "down" (where those who have died are). According to this scenario, Jesus was here with us; he died and so went down to the place of the dead; then God raised him up to where

BOX 13.3 The Thessalonians' Perplexity

The occasion of 1 Thessalonians raises some intriguing historical questions. Why were the Thessalonian Christians surprised that some of their members had died, and why didn't they know that at Jesus' return he would raise the dead to be with him forever? Had Paul simply neglected to tell them that part? Morever, why was Timothy unable to answer their question? Why did he have to return to ask Paul about it, leaving them in uncertainty for some weeks at the least? Didn't Timothy know what was supposed to happen at the end?

One possibility is that when Paul was with the Thessalonians, his own views were in a state of flux. If he himself didn't realize how long it would be before Jesus returned, he might not have discussed the matter with either the Thessalonians or his own close companions, Silvanus and Timothy.

he is. Soon he is going to come back down to earth on the clouds (i.e., from heaven above the sky) to raise up both those who are here and those who are down below, elevating them to the clouds to live with him forever.

This scenario is based on an ancient way of looking at the world where there actually was an up and a down in the universe. It stands in stark contrast, obviously, to our modern understanding of the earth as the third planet of a solar system formed around a minor star, just one of the billions of stars that make up our galaxy, which itself is just one of billions of galaxies in a universe—in other words, a universe in which there is no such thing as up and down, no "heaven" above our heads or "place of the dead" below. This is simply a reminder that Paul's world, and consequently his worldview, is not ours.

CONCLUSION: PAUL THE APOSTLE

It is clear that Paul's self-acclaimed title "apostle of the Gentiles" was no empty phrase. His converts, at least in Thessalonica, were former pagans, whom he contacted from his place of employment and convinced to abandon their traditional cults to worship the one true God, the creator of the world. Moreover, he and his colleagues couched their proclamation in apocalyptic terms: the creator of the world was also its judge, and his day of reckoning was imminent. Soon he was to send his Son, Jesus, who had died and had been raised from the dead and exalted to heaven and who would deliver his followers from the wrath that was soon to come.

Those who accepted this message formed a social group, a church, that met periodically in one of the member's home (or in several homes, depending on its size). The members of the group had unusually strong bonds of cohesion, reinforced by several factors: (*a*) the insider information they had as those who understood the course of history here at the end of time, (*b*) the mutual love and support that they showed one another, (*c*) the common front they projected in the face of external opposition from those who did not know the "truth," and (*d*) the rules that governed their lives together. Moreover, they understood themselves to stand in unity with other groups similarly organized throughout the provinces of Macedonia and Achaia and reaching all the way to Judea. These groups were unified by their common faith and common commitment to the God of Israel, who now in the end of time had fulfilled his promises to his people through Jesus, and through him to all peoples of the earth, both Jews and Gentiles.

Difficulties had arisen in this community, and Paul wrote a letter to help resolve them. In this the Thessalonians were probably like most of Paul's churches, communities that he established in major urban areas throughout the Mediterranean, each of which experienced problems that required the apostle's intervention and advice.

BOX 13.4 | Thessalonians

1. I Thessalonians is the earliest of Paul's epistles, and thus the earliest book of the New Testament and the earliest surviving Christian writing of any kind.

2. It can be used to provide clues concerning how Paul went about his missionary activities.

   a. He evidently did not preach on the street corner or stage evangelistic rallies, and he did not (contrary to the book of Acts) begin by preaching in a local synagogue.

   b. He instead started up a business in town and talked to his customers, convincing them about the Christian message.

   c. Virtually all of his converts were pagan. He needed to convince these people that the Jewish God was the only true God, that Jesus was his son who had died for their sins, and that God had raised him from the dead and was sending him back, soon, in judgment.

3. This kind of preaching activity made Paul appear like philosophers in the Greco-Roman world.

4. His converts formed closely knit communities that gathered together periodically for worship, and saw themselves as a group that stood over against outsiders.

5. After Paul left the Thessalonian church, problems arose—particularly concerning the fate of those who had already died prior to Jesus' return in judgment, which had been expected to be very soon.

6. Paul's letter addresses this and other problems, assuring the Thessalonians that they can retain their hope in the apocalyptic end of the world to be brought by Jesus and that those who had already died had not missed out on the benefits of the apocalyptic kingdom soon to arrive.

TAKE A STAND

1. Pretend you are the apostle Paul and that you have just arrived in a predominantly pagan city to convert as many people as you can to belief in Jesus. Write a speech to give to a group of pagans who have come to do business with you in your workshop.

2. Suppose you are an elderly Christian in the church of Thessalonica. Fifty years ago, as a young man, you came to believe in Jesus because you heard Paul proclaim that the end of the age was imminent and that Jesus was very soon to return to earth from heaven. That obviously never happened, and now—five decades later—your family and friends are making fun of you for your beliefs. How do you respond to them?

SUGGESTIONS FOR FURTHER READING

See also the general bibliography for Chapter 12.

Hock, Ronald. *The Social Context of Paul's Ministry: Tentmaking and Apostleship.* Philadelphia: Fortress, 1980. An interesting investigation of Paul's apostolic modus operandi in light of representatives of other philosophies in the Greco-Roman world, who worked to support themselves and used their workplace as a forum to propagate their views.

Malherbe, Abraham. *Paul and the Thessalonians: The Philosophic Tradition of Pastoral Care.* Eugene, Ore.: Wipf and Stock, 2011. An insightful study of Paul's interaction with the Thessalonians from a socio-historical perspective.

 KEY TERMS

Cynics	Macedonia	Stoics	Timothy
friendship letter	Silvanus	Thessalonica	trade organizations
funeral societies	sociohistorical	three-storied	voluntary
insula	method	universe	associations

CHAPTER

Paul and the Crises of His Churches

THE CORINTHIAN CORRESPONDENCE

WHAT TO EXPECT

One of the fascinating aspects of the study of the Pauline writings is that each of Paul's letters was addressed to deal with different situations. In this chapter we consider two of his undisputed epistles to see what problems had arisen in the churches that he addresses and how he deals with them (1 and 2 Corinthians). As it turns out, the problems are quite diverse.

Paul is compelled in these letters to address these issues one by one. In examining these writings, we will see how some aspects of Paul's proclamation remain constant—his regular conviction, for example, that Christ is God's salvation for this sinful world, which is soon to pass away. Other aspects of his message, however, vary from situation to situation as he tries to address the theological and practical problems that had arisen in his churches.

The thirteen New Testament epistles attributed to Paul are arranged roughly according to length, with the longest (Romans) coming first and the shortest (Philemon) last. As we have seen, this arrangement does not coincide with the actual sequence in which the letters were written; 1 Thessalonians is Paul's earliest surviving letter and Romans the latest. Of the five undisputed letters that remain, however, a case can be made that their canonical sequence also happens to be their chronological. For this reason, we can deal with each of these remaining letters in their canonical order: 1 and 2 Corinthians in this chapter and Galatians, Philippians, and Philemon in the next.

 I CORINTHIANS

Corinth was a large and prosperous city south of Thessalonica, in the Roman province of **Achaia**, of which it was the capital. Located on the isthmus dividing the northern and southern parts of modern-day Greece, it was a major center of trade and communication, served by two major ports within walking distance. The city was destroyed in 146 B.C.E. by the Romans but was refounded a century later as a Roman colony. In Paul's time, it was a cosmopolitan place, the home of a wide range of religious and philosophical movements.

Corinth is perhaps best remembered today for the image problem it suffered throughout much

some modern historians have suggested that its image was intentionally tarnished by the citizens of Athens, one of its nearby rivals and the intellectual center of ancient Greece. It was an Athenian, the comic poet Aristophanes, who invented the verb "Corinthianize," which meant to engage in sexually promiscuous activities. In any event, many people today know about the city only through the letter of 1 Corinthians, a document that has done little to enhance its reputation.

The congregation that Paul addresses appears to have been riddled with problems involving interpersonal conflicts and ethical improprieties. His letter indicates that some of its members were at each other's throats, claiming spiritual superiority over one another and trying to establish it through ecstatic acts during the course of their worship services. Different members of the community would speak prophecies and make proclamations in languages that no one else (including themselves) knew, trying to surpass one another in demonstrating their abilities to speak in divinely inspired tongues. This one-upmanship had evidently manifested itself outside the worship service as well. Some people had grown embittered enough to take others to court (over what, we are not told). In addition, the personal conduct of community members was not at all what Paul had in mind when he led them away from what he viewed as their degenerate pasts into the church of Christ. At their periodic community meals, some had been gorging themselves and getting drunk while others had been arriving late to find nothing to eat. Some of the men in the congregation had been frequenting prostitutes and didn't see why this should be a problem; one of them was sleeping with his stepmother. And this is the community that Paul addresses as the "saints who are in Corinth" (1:2). One wonders what the Corinthian sinners looked like.

Figure 14.1 Picture of an ancient philosopher leaning on his walking stick, from a wall painting of the first century B.C.E. Paul himself would have appeared to many people in his world as an itinerant philosopher.

The Beginnings of the Church

After leaving Thessalonica, Paul and his companions, Timothy and Silvanus, arrived in Corinth and began, again, to preach the gospel in an effort to win converts (2 Cor 1:19). Possibly they proceeded as they had in the capital of Macedonia, coming

of its checkered history, at least among those who advocated the ancient equivalent of "family values." Its economy was based not only on trade and industry but also on commercialized pleasures for the well-to-do. It is not certain that Corinth's loose reputation was altogether deserved, however;

into town, renting out a shop in an insula, setting up a business, and using the workplace as a forum to speak to those who stopped by. In this instance, the book of Acts provides some corroborating evidence. Luke indicates that Paul did, in fact, work in a kind of leather goods shop in Corinth, having made contact with a Jewish couple named **Aquila and Priscilla** who shared his profession in both senses of the term; they had the same career and the same faith in Jesus.

In other respects, however, the narrative of Acts contrasts with what Paul himself says about his sojourn in Corinth. For one thing, Luke indicates that Paul devoted himself chiefly to evangelizing the Jews in the local synagogue until he was dismissed with the left foot of fellowship. Even after leaving the synagogue, according to Luke, Paul principally converted Jews (18:4–11). Paul's own letter gives an entirely different impression. Most of his converts, as one would expect, given his claim to be the apostle to the Gentiles, appear to have been non-Jews. "You know that when you were pagans, you were enticed and led astray to idols that could not speak" (12:2). Here, as in Thessalonica, Paul and his companions worked primarily with Gentiles to convince them both that there was only one God worthy of devotion and worship (the God of Israel) and that Jesus was his Son.

The majority of Paul's converts were evidently from the lower classes, as he himself reminds them: "Not many of you were wise by human standards [highly educated], not many were powerful, [influential in the community], not many were of noble birth [in the upper classes]" (1:26). Recent scholars have observed, however, that at least some of the Corinthian converts must have been well educated, powerful, and well born, or else Paul would not have said that "not many" of them were. Indeed, if we assume that some members of the community came from the upper classes, we can make better sense of some of the problems that they experienced as a group. It would explain, for example, why some of those coming together for the communal meal (a potluck-to-share kind of thing) could come early and enjoy lots of food and good drink; these were comparatively wealthy Christians who didn't have to work long hours. Others, however, had to come late and had scarcely anything to eat; these were the poorer members, possibly slaves, who had to put in a full day's work. The presence of some upper-class Christians would also explain why some members of this community were perturbed that Paul would not allow them to support him, that is, to become his patrons and care for his financial needs so as to free him up to preach the gospel (9:7–18, cf. especially 2 Cor 12:13). One of the common ways for a philosopher to make a living in the Greco-Roman world was to be taken into a wealthy household to serve as a kind of scholar-in-residence in exchange for room, board, and other niceties (depending on the wealth of the patron). Paul had reasons for wanting none of this arrangement—he saw it as putting his gospel up for sale—but some of the influential members of the congregation found his attitude puzzling and even offensive, as will become yet clearer in 2 Corinthians.

Other problems in the congregation may also have been related to the different socioeconomic levels of its members. If we can assume that the upper classes in antiquity would have been relatively well educated, it may be that the "knowledge" of some of these people in the Corinthian church allowed them to see things differently from the lower classes and that this led to some differences of opinion in the community. For example, some members may have thought that eating meat offered to idols was a real and present danger, in view of the demonic character of the pagan gods (possibly a lower-class view), while others took such scruples as baseless superstition (possibly the view of some of the more highly educated). This is one of the major issues that Paul addresses in the letter (chaps. 8–10).

During their stay in Corinth, Paul and his companions appear to have converted a sizable number (dozens?) of pagans to the faith. The book of Acts indicates that they spent a year and a half there, in contrast to just three weeks in Thessalonica. Paul himself makes no clear statement concerning the length of his stay, but there are indications throughout his letter that the Christians in Corinth, or at least some of them, had a much more sophisticated understanding of the faith than those in Thessalonica—even if they had, from Paul's perspective, gotten it wrong at points. Indeed, unlike the Thessalonians, who understood their new religion at a fairly rudimentary level, some of the Corinthians had so much knowledge of their faith that they took Paul's gospel simply as a starting point and developed their views in vastly different directions.

The Message Paul Preached There

What can we say about the message that Paul originally preached to these people? Again, he evidently instructed them in the need to worship the one true God and to await his Son from heaven. As we will see, however, the second part of this message ("to await his Son") made significantly less impact on the converts in Corinth than on those in Thessalonica. It is difficult to know exactly what else he taught these people. It does appear, however, that Paul devoted little if any effort to narrating tales about what Jesus said and did during his public ministry (at a later stage, we will consider whether Paul himself knew very much about this ministry; remember, he was writing long before the Gospels were written). He does summarize a couple of sayings of Jesus, to the effect that Christians should not get divorced (7:10–11) but should pay their preacher (9:14), and he does narrate the incident of Jesus' institution of the Lord's Supper (11:24–28). But he says nary a word about Jesus' baptism, temptation, transfiguration, preaching of the coming kingdom of God, encounters with demons, appearance before Pontius Pilate, and so on—all of which would have been directly germane to the problems that the Corinthians appear to have experienced. What he does say, and say emphatically, is that the only thing he "knew" among the Corinthians was "Jesus Christ, and him crucified" (2:2).

In other words, Paul's principal message was about Jesus as the crucified Christ. It appears to be a message that the Corinthians, or at least a good portion of them, didn't "get," at least in Paul's opinion. We will see why momentarily. First, we should consider in some detail Paul's own brief recollection of what he taught the Corinthians about Jesus. In 15:1–2, he reminds his converts of "the

good news that I proclaimed to you, which you in turn received, in which also you stand, through which also you are being saved, if you hold firmly to the message that I proclaimed to you." He then summarizes this message:

> For I handed on to you as of first importance what I in turn had received: that Christ died for our sins in accordance with the scriptures, and that he was buried, and that he was raised on the third day in accordance with the scriptures, and that he appeared to Cephas and then to the twelve. (15:3–5)

Thus, of primary importance in Paul's preaching to the Corinthians was the message of Christ's death and resurrection. Jesus died, fulfilling the Jewish Scriptures, and there's proof: he was buried. Moreover, God raised him from the dead, fulfilling the Scriptures. Again there's proof: he was later seen alive. Paul had preached a similar message in Thessalonica, but with two differences, one in the message and the other in the way that it was received.

With regard to the message itself, we find subtle indications in 1 Thessalonians that Paul directly linked his gospel message with the Jewish religion, but never does he quote the Jewish Scriptures or assume that his followers are personally conversant with them. The situation is quite different with the Corinthians. From the outset, Paul had taught them that Jesus' death and resurrection were both anticipated in the Scriptures; moreover, throughout this letter he appeals to the Scriptures in order to make his points. Strikingly, when he does so he emphasizes that the Scriptures were not written only, or even especially, for Jews in times past, but even more particularly for Christians in the present (e.g., 1 Cor 9:9–10; 10:1–13). If the Thessalonians had insider knowledge, the Corinthians have even more; all of God's interactions with his people have been leading up to the present time. The Christian community is God's ultimate concern, and always has been.

This is heady stuff, and there is some indication that it had in fact gone to the heads of some of Paul's converts. This can be seen in a second difference between the Thessalonians and the Corinthians. The former group saw Jesus' resurrection as

Figure 14.2 One of the earliest visual representations of Jesus' crucifixion, from a cyprus panel door in the church of Saint Sabina in Rome, nearly 350 years after Paul's day. Earlier Christians were reluctant to portray the crucifixion (contrast Paul in 1 Cor 2:2).

the beginning of the major climax of history, when he would return and remove the Christians from this world before God's wrath destroys all his enemies. Some of the Corinthians, on the other hand, appear to have interpreted Jesus' resurrection in a more personal sense as his exaltation to glory that they themselves, as those who have participated in his victory, have come to share. Despite Paul's protests, some (or perhaps most?) of the Corinthians came to believe that they had already begun to enjoy the full benefits of salvation in the here and now, as members of Christ's resurrected and exalted body. In Paul's words (which must be taken

as a sarcastic echoing of their views, given everything else he says in this letter), "Already you have all you want! Already you have become rich! Quite apart from us you have become kings!" (4:8).

For Paul himself, the Corinthians' notion that they were already enjoying an exalted status couldn't be further from the truth. In his view, the forces of evil were to remain in power in this world until the end came and Christ returned. Until then, life would be a struggle full of pain and suffering, comparable to the pain and suffering experienced by the crucified Christ himself. Those who believed that they had already experienced a full and complete share of the blessings of eternity had simply deceived themselves, creating immense problems for the church and misconstruing the real meaning of the gospel.

The Subsequent History of the Community

There is nothing to indicate that the problems addressed in this epistle had come to a head during Paul's original stay in Corinth. Eventually, Paul and his companions left to proclaim their gospel elsewhere, leaving the Christians behind to continue the mission for themselves. Soon thereafter, an acquaintance of Paul named **Apollos** came to Corinth and proved instrumental in providing additional instruction to the Christians there. According to the book of Acts, Apollos was a skilled speaker (18:24–28), and it is clear from Paul's letter that he acquired a considerable following in the congregation (1:12; 3:4–6).

We are not certain of the precise course of Paul's journeys, but he evidently ended up in the city of Ephesus not long after leaving Corinth. Ephesus, another large urban area, was in the western portion of Asia Minor (modern-day Turkey). From there Paul wrote the letter of 1 Corinthians (see 16:8). Timothy and Silvanus had apparently departed from him already, for he wrote the letter not with them but with someone named **Sosthenes**, who is otherwise mentioned in the New Testament only in Acts 18:17 as the ruler of the Jewish synagogue in Corinth and a convert to Paul's gospel. Paul obviously wrote the letter of 1 Corinthians to deal with problems that had arisen in the congregation. He indicates that he has heard of these problems from two different sources, one oral and one written.

At the beginning of the letter, after the prescript (1:1–3) and thanksgiving (1:4–9; notice how much shorter it is than the one to the Thessalonians), Paul states that he has learned about the activities of the congregation from "Chloe's people" (1:11). We do not know who this **Chloe** was; the name occurs nowhere else in the letter or in the rest of the New

Figure 14.3 Paul evangelized the cities he visited by setting up a small business and discussing his gospel with clients. Shown here are the remains of some of the streetfront shops that can still be found in the ruins of Corinth.

Testament. We do know that it was the name of a woman, and the reference to her "people" is usually taken to mean her slaves or former slaves who had come to Ephesus, perhaps on her business, and had met with Paul to pass along some news. Since Chloe owned slaves who managed her business affairs, she must have been a wealthy woman in Corinth; whether she herself was a member of the Christian community is difficult to judge. In any event, her unnamed "people" must have been active in the congregation, given the inside information that they passed along to Paul.

The news was not good. The church was divided against itself, with different factions claiming different leaders, each of whom, from Paul's perspective, was seeking to usurp the claims of others by demonstrating their own spiritual superiority and claiming to represent the true faith as expounded by one or another famous authority (Paul, Cephas, Apollos, and Christ himself; 1:12). The conflicts had gotten nasty at times, with some of the members taking others to court over their differences (not their differences over inner church politics, of course, but over matters that the civil law courts could decide). Moreover, immorality was evidently rampant. Generally, this was not the happy community of the faithful that Paul had envisioned, especially compared to the model church of the Thessalonians.

The information from Paul's other source was equally troubling. It appears that he had received a letter from some of the Corinthians (probably not all of them; as we will see, not everyone felt beholden to him) in which they expressed their different opinions on some critical matters and sought Paul's judgment (e.g., see 7:1). The letter had been brought by three members of the church—**Stephanas, Fortunatus, and Achaicus**—who evidently had waited for Paul to pen a reply (16:15–18). The issues were of some moment; there were members of the congregation, just to take one example, who had been teaching that it was not right even for married couples to have sex. One can sense the urgency of their query.

Paul wrote 1 Corinthians to deal with the various problems and issues that had arisen. Giving fairly straightforward answers, he deals with each problem in turn. From Paul's perspective, however, one big problem evidently underlay all these specific problems.

Paul's Response to the Situation: The End as the Key to the Middle

Paul's perspective is best seen toward the conclusion of the letter. In good rhetorical style (i.e., following the instructions of those who taught rhetoric in his day), Paul provides at the end the key to what has come before. We saw earlier that Paul begins chapter 15 by summarizing the content of the gospel message that he preached to the Corinthians, the message of Christ's death and resurrection; he then draws out the implications of this message. Sometimes this chapter is misunderstood by modern readers as an attempt to prove that Jesus was raised from the dead, for example, by citing a group of "witnesses" in verses 5–8. In fact, Paul is not trying to demonstrate to the Corinthians something they don't believe; he is reminding them of something they already know (see vv. 1 and 3), that Jesus was raised bodily from the dead.

For Paul, Jesus' resurrected body was a glorified spiritual body, not like the paltry mortal flesh that we ourselves are stuck with, but just as important, it was an actual body that could be seen and recognized (15:5–8, 35–41). Paul's point is that the exalted existence that Jesus entered involved the total transformation of his body (15:42–49, 53–54). It was not some kind of ethereal existence in which his disembodied soul was elevated to the realm of divinity; his was a bodily resurrection (see box 14.1). The reason this matters becomes clear in the context of Paul's response. There were some in Corinth who were saying that there was no such thing as the resurrection of bodies from the dead (15:12).

Paul spends most of chapter 15 demonstrating that since Christ was raised bodily from the dead—and since he is the "first fruit" of the resurrection, as all the Corinthians came to believe when they accepted his gospel message—then there is going to be a future resurrection of the dead when Christians come to participate in Christ's exalted status, that is, when they themselves are raised in glorious immortal bodies (15:12–23, 50–55). It is then that Christian believers will enjoy the full benefits of their salvation. For Paul, the end has not come yet. Despite the claims of some, presumably some of

ANOTHER GLIMPSE INTO THE PAST

BOX 14.1   Possibilities of Existence in the Afterlife

Some interpreters have thought that Paul and his Corinthian opponents disagreed about the resurrection because they had fundamentally different understandings about the nature of human existence, both now and in the afterlife. Perhaps it would be useful to reflect on different ways that one might conceive of life after death.

Annihilation. One possibility is that a person who dies ceases to exist. This appears to have been a popular notion in the Greco-Roman world, as evidenced by a number of inscriptions on tombstones that bemoan the brevity of life which ends in nonexistence. One of the most widely used Latin inscriptions was so popular that it was normally abbreviated (like our own R.I.P. for "Rest in Peace") as N.F.N.S.N.C.: "I was not, I am not, I care not."

Disembodied Existence. Another possibility is that life after death is life apart from the body. In some strands of Greek thought influenced above all by Plato, the body itself was thought to be the bane of human existence because it brought pain, finitude, and death to the soul that lived within it. These people did not think of the soul as immaterial; it was thought to be a "substance," but a much more re-

fined substance than the clunker of a shell that we call the body. The catchy Greek phrase sometimes used to express the notion that the coarse material of the body is the prison or tomb for the more refined substance of the soul was "sōma—sēma," literally, "the body—a prison." For people who thought such things, the afterlife involved a liberation of the soul from its bodily entombment.

Bodily Resurrection. A third possibility is that the body is not inherently evil or problematic but has simply become subject to the ravages of evil and death. For many Jews, for example, the human body was created by God, as were all things, and so is inherently good. And what God has created, he will also redeem. Thus, the body will not ultimately perish but will live on in the afterlife. How can this be, given the indisputable fact that bodies eventually decay and disappear? In this view, God will transform the physical body into a spiritual body that will never experience the ravages of evil and death, a glorified body that will never get sick and never die. As a Jewish apocalypticist, Paul maintained this third view of the nature of human existence, whereas his opponents in Corinth, like many Christians after them down to our own day, appear to have subscribed to the second.

the most "spiritual" among the Corinthian leaders, Christians do not yet have the full benefits of salvation; they are not yet exalted to a heavenly status. Even the elect are living in a world of sin and evil, and they will continue to do so until the end comes.

This basic message underlies not just chapter 15 but all of 1 Corinthians. To some extent, each of the problems experienced by this congregation is related to the basic failure to recognize the limitations and dangers of Christian existence in the age before the end. The first problem that Paul attacks (in chaps. 1–4) is the divisions within the church that were caused, evidently, by leaders claiming to be spiritually superior to one another and to adhere to the teachings of various predecessors (Paul, Cephas, Apollos, or Christ; 1:12). One might expect Paul to

take a side in this argument, that is, to insist that the faction that had the good sense to line up with him was right. Instead, he insists that all the sides (even his) are in error. They are in error because they have elevated the status of individual leaders on the basis of their superior wisdom and superhuman power (1:18–25), perhaps thinking that these characteristics could be transferred from one person to the next in the act of baptism (as suggested, possibly, in 1:14–17). The leaders themselves, who are left unnamed, have apparently agreed on one major point, that wisdom and power indicate the superior standing of those who have already been exalted to enjoy the privileges and benefits of the exalted life in Christ.

For Paul, however, a high evaluation of wisdom and power represents a fundamental misunderstanding of the gospel. The gospel is not about human wisdom and human power, things that may be impressive and attractive by normal standards. Instead, and somewhat ironically, God works not through what appears to be wise and powerful but through what appears to be foolish and weak. What could be more (apparently) foolish and weak than the plan to save the world through a crucified man (1:18–25)? According to Paul's gospel, that is precisely what God has done, and by so doing, he has shown that human power and wisdom have no part to play in the salvation of the world. Paul goes on to note that the congregation as a whole, and he himself, are scarcely powerful and wise by normal standards (1:26–2:5). God does not work in human ways.

Paul points out that the very existence of several of the Corinthians' problems shows that the Corinthian believers have not been exalted to the heavenly heights. The "wise and powerful" leaders of the community, for example, have been unable to deal with the most rudimentary issues. They have not recognized how shameful it is for a man to sleep with his stepmother (5:1–3) or for others to visit prostitutes (6:15–20) or for others to rely on civil law courts instead of the "wise" judgment of those in the community (6:1–9). Moreover, by foolishly thinking that they are already exalted and ruling with Christ, these believers overlook the real and present dangers in their daily existence. They do not see that there are still evil forces in the world, which will infect the congregation if allowed to enter. They do not see, to take one of the most complicated of Paul's discussions, that if women fail to wear head coverings during church services, they are susceptible to the invasion of evil angels who might pollute the entire body of believers (11:10); nor do they realize that those who have been united with Christ can infect the entire body when they become united with a prostitute (6:15–20).

In addition, the Corinthians' sense of self-exaltation, in Paul's judgment, has made them ultimately unconcerned about how to treat one another in this sinful and fallen world. Many have engaged in uncontrolled acts of ecstasy in their services of worship, prophesying and speaking in tongues not to benefit others who are in attendance but, in Paul's view, simply to elevate themselves in the eyes of others (chaps. 12–14). From

their own vantage point, they may have understood their worship activities as signs of their participation in the heavenly resurrected existence that is theirs in Christ. But Paul believes these activities reveal something else. Those who engage in them have forgotten that the Spirit gives gifts to members of the congregation so they can benefit and serve others, not exalt themselves (especially chap. 12). Anyone who has all the gifts that can be given by the Spirit but who fails to love the brothers and sisters in Christ is still in total poverty. This is the message of 1 Corinthians 13, the famous **"love chapter,"** which is a favorite passage even today, especially at Christian weddings. The passage, however, does not speak of love in the abstract, and certainly not to modern notions of sentiment and sexual passion. Specifically it is about the use of spiritual gifts in the church. If the gifts are not used to benefit others, then they are of no use.

Paul's notion that Christian love is to guide ethical behavior in this evil age explains a number of positions that he takes in this letter. One prominent example is his position on **meat offered to idols**. In rough outline, the historical situation is reasonably clear. Meat that was sold at the pagan temples could be purchased at a discount. We are not altogether certain why. Possibly the meat was considered as already used, since it had been offered to a god, or possibly it was left over from a pagan festival. In any event, some of the Corinthian Christians (those who were less educated, in the lower classes?) thought that to eat such meat was tantamount to sharing in idolatry; they would not touch it on any condition. Others (more highly educated, in the upper classes?) claimed superior knowledge in this case, pointing out that idols had no real existence since there were no gods other than the one true God. Eating such meat could therefore do no harm and could actually save on much-needed resources.

Oddly enough, even though Paul agrees that the other gods don't exist, he disagrees that it is proper to eat the meat (chaps. 8–9). His reasoning is that those who see a Christian eating such meat may be encouraged to do so themselves, even while thinking that the gods do exist. They would be encouraged, that is, to do something that they themselves think is wrong, and this could harm their conscience (8:7–10). Rather than behaving in ways that might eventually hurt somebody, then, believers should do everything to help others, even if it involves avoiding something that in itself is not wrong (8:11–13).

Ultimately, this is an apocalyptic view. The need to love one another and to behave in ways that are most useful to them is directly related to the fact that evil still prevails in this world. Since Christians continue to live in an age dominated by the forces of evil, they are not yet exalted and are not altogether free to do whatever their superior knowledge permits them to do.

Paul's apocalyptic notions appear to affect his entire view of life in this world. In another example drawn from this letter, Paul maintains that married couples should not pretend that they already live as angels, "who neither marry nor are given in marriage" (to quote another famous person; see Mark 12:25). Sexual temptations are great in this age, and marriage is a legitimate way to overcome them in God's eyes. Spouses should

therefore grant one another their conjugal rights (7:1–6). Those who are able to withstand such temptations, however—like Paul himself, who says that he has the "gift" (7:7)—should not go to the trouble of becoming married in the first place. In Paul's view, his generation is living at the very end of time, and much work needs to be done before Christ returns. Those who are married are obligated to take time for their spouses and tend to their needs; those who are not can be fully committed to Christ (7:25–38). Thus, it is better to remain single, but if one cannot stand the heat, it is better to marry than to burn (7:8–9).

In Sum: Paul's Gospel Message to the Corinthians

While we have not been able to explore the Corinthians' questions and problems or Paul's responses in depth, we have seen what the big problem was

Figure 14.4 Painting of the Christian celebration of a ritual meal from the catacomb of Priscilla (see 1 Cor 11:23–26).

BOX 14.2 | 1 Corinthians

1. 1 Corinthians is written to the church located in Corinth, in the Roman province of Achaia, a city with a reputation for dubious morals in antiquity.

2. Paul had established the church by converting former pagans to faith in Jesus; most of his converts were poor and uneducated, but some came from the upper classes. The different socioeconomic levels of the Corinthian Christians may explain some of their problems (tensions over the community meals, for example).

3. After Paul left the community, a number of problems had arisen, involving disunity in the church,

immorality (of various kinds), and difficulties during worship services.

4. Paul deals with all these problems one by one in the letter, and at the end deals with the major problem of all: the Corinthians' failure to appreciate the true nature of the resurrection of believers, which was to be future and physical.

5. Understanding that the resurrection will be bodily was to affect the Corinthians' sense of what, in the meantime, they were to do with their bodies.

from Paul's perspective and how it manifested itself in so many ways in his Corinthian congregation. Overall, the message that Paul had for the Corinthians was not so different from the message that he had for the Thessalonians. Jesus was soon to return when God entered into judgment with this world. When he did so, his followers would experience a glorious salvation. Until then, however, believers were compelled to live in this world. Their exaltation was a future event, not a present reality, however much it was prefigured in their community, the church.

The church in Corinth appears not to have been a happy place. Paul saw a community that was divided against itself and that tolerated immoral and scandalous behavior while claiming (ironically, in Paul's eyes) to enjoy an exalted standing with Christ. One can sense Paul's exasperation and disbelief: You are living a heavenly existence? You??? Even more, one can sense his concern. This was a major church in his mission field, yet it had gone astray from the basic intent of his gospel message. He treated the Corinthians as friends (e.g., see the prescript and closing) but realized that he was at odds with a number of them on significant issues. As we are going to see, the situation did not much improve once they received his letter.

 ## 2 CORINTHIANS

One of the reasons that Paul's letters to the Corinthians are so fascinating is that they allow us to trace his relationship with the congregation over a period of time. In no other instance do we have undisputed letters addressed to the same community at different times (with the possible exception of the church in Philippi). Paul's relationship with the Corinthians continued to ebb and flow in light of events that transpired after the writing of 1 Corinthians. By the time he came to write 2 Corinthians, his tone had changed, although his tune had not.

The Unity of the Letter

Paul's tone changes even within his second letter, and rather severely. Indeed, many scholars are convinced that 2 Corinthians does not represent a solitary letter that Paul sat down one day and wrote but a combination of two or more letters that he penned at different times for different occasions. According to this theory, someone else, possibly a member of the Corinthian congregation itself, later edited these letters with "scissors and paste." The result was one longer letter, possibly designed for broader circulation among Paul's churches.

When you read through the letter carefully yourself, you may be struck by the change of tone that begins with chapter 10 and continues to the end. In chapters 1–9 Paul appears to be on very good terms with this congregation. He is overflowing with joy for them, almost as much as he was for the Thessalonians, even though he acknowledges that their relationship has been more than a little stormy in the past (see especially 2:1–11 and 7:5–12). He gives us some of the details. Some time before (but after the writing of 1 Corinthians) he had paid a second visit to Corinth (the first being when he converted them; 1:19). For some undisclosed reason, over some undisclosed issue, someone in the congregation publicly insulted him, and he departed in humiliation. He indicates that he had been one angry fellow when he left. Soon thereafter he wrote a harsh letter that caused him great pain, in which he upbraided the congregation severely for their conduct and views and threatened to come to them again in judgment. But now, just prior to the writing of 2 Corinthians itself (or at least prior to the writing of chaps. 1–9), the bearer of the painful letter, Titus, had returned and given him the good news that the Corinthians had repented of their poor judgment and behavior, disciplined the person who had caused Paul's pain, and committed themselves once more to Paul as their spiritual father in Christ (7:5–12).

Paul's reaction could not be more appreciative: "He [Titus] was consoled about you, as he told us of your longing, your mourning, your zeal for me, so that I rejoiced still more" (7:7). Thanks to this good news, Paul now bubbles with joy for their renewed relationship, despite the hardships that he himself continues to experience: "I often boast about you; I have great pride in you; I am filled with consolation; I am overjoyed in all our affliction" (7:4). Paul is writing this conciliatory letter to express his gratitude for their about-face (1:15–2:4) and to explain why he was not fickle when he changed his travel plans: he had chosen not to visit them a third time simply to avoid causing anyone any more pain (2:1–2).

But then, in chapters 10–13, everything seems to change, or rather, to revert. No longer is Paul joyful in this congregation that has returned to him. Now he is bitter and incensed that they have come to question his authority and to badmouth his person (10:2, 10–11). He threatens to come to them a "third" time in judgment, in which he will not be lenient (13:1–2), and he warns the congregation against those who oppose him, newcomers in their midst whom he sarcastically calls **"superapostles"** (11:5). He admits that these superapostles can perform miraculous deeds and spectacular signs, but he nonetheless sees them as false apostles, ministers of Satan who prey on the minds of the Corinthians (11:12–14) and lead them into all sorts of disorder and disobedience (12:19–21).

Is it possible that Paul could gush with joy over this congregation and at the same time threaten fierce retribution against it? Of course it is possible, but it doesn't seem likely. How, then, might we explain this change of tone?

One detail of this summary may have struck you: in chapters 10–13 Paul threatens to make a third visit in judgment against the congregation, whereas in chapters 1–9 he indicates that he had canceled his visit because he did not want to cause further pain. Indeed, he intimates that there was no longer any need to make it. The congregation received his angry and painful letter, and it had its desired effect (or Titus, the bearer of the letter, had this effect). They have come to grieve over how they mistreated him and have now returned to his good graces.

Based on the differences between the two parts of the letter, many scholars believe that chapters 10–13 represent a portion of the earlier "painful" letter mentioned in 2:4, that is, the letter that was written soon after Paul's public humiliation and before his reconciliation with the Corinthians, a reconciliation gratefully discussed in chapters 1–9. If so, then a later editor has combined the two letters by eliminating the closing of one of them (the "thankful" or **"conciliatory" letter** of chapters 1–9, which was written second) and the prescript of the other (the **"painful" letter** of chapters 10–13, written first). By doing so, the editor created one longer letter that embodies the ebb and flow of Paul's relationship with the Corinthians over a relatively long period of time. Some scholars go even further, and maintain that more than two letters are embodied here, based on the uneven flow of Paul's argument throughout chapters 1–9 (see box 14.4).

The History of Paul's Relationship with the Community

We can map out the history of Paul's interaction with the Corinthians in terms of a sequence of visits and letters. There is, of course, a good deal of information that we do not have; but what we do have, including the bits and pieces that come from 1 Corinthians, falls out along the following lines.

Paul's First Visit. This was when Paul and Silvanus and Timothy first arrived in Corinth, set up shop, preached the gospel, won a number of converts, and provided them with some rudimentary instruction before leaving for other areas ripe for mission (2 Cor 1:19).

Paul's First Letter. Paul evidently wrote a letter to the Corinthians that has been lost. He refers to it in 1 Cor 5:9. It appears to have dealt, at least in part, with ethical issues that had arisen in the community.

The Corinthians' First Letter to Paul. Some of the Corinthians, either in response to Paul's first letter or independently of it, wrote Paul to inquire further about ethical matters, for example, about whether Christians should have sex with their spouses (1 Cor 7:1).

Paul's Second Letter: 1 Corinthians. In response to the Corinthians' queries and in reaction to information that he received from "Chloe's people," Paul wrote 1 Corinthians from Ephesus. In it he announced his plans to travel through Macedonia south to Corinth, where he hoped to spend the winter (1 Cor 16:5–7). He apparently sent the letter back with Stephanas and his two companions, who were members of the Corinthian church (1 Cor 16:15–17).

Paul's Second Visit. In 2 Cor 2:1–4 Paul indicates that he does not want to make "another" painful visit; this suggests that his most recent visit had been painful. It appears, then, that after the writing of 1 Corinthians, Paul fulfilled his promise to come to Corinth for a second time. But he was not well received. Someone in the congregation did something to cause him pain and possibly public humiliation (2 Cor 2:5–11). He left, uttering dire threats that he would return in judgment against them (2 Cor 13:2).

ANOTHER EARLY CHRISTIAN TEXT

BOX 14.3 Paul's Third Letter to the Corinthians

A sample of a Pauline pseudepigraphon is the third letter that Paul allegedly wrote to the Christians of Corinth to oppose heretics who had arisen in their midst. As the following extract shows, the letter was in fact produced after Paul's death, to attack views that proto-orthodox Christians of the mid-second century considered heretical, including the docetic view that Jesus did not have a real fleshly body and the adoptionist view that his mother was not a virgin. Interestingly enough, these are issues that Paul himself never explicitly addresses in his authentic letters. Does the author wish he had?

Paul, the prisoner of Jesus Christ, to the brethren in Corinth—greeting! Since I am in many tribulations, I do not wonder that the teachings of the evil one are so quickly gaining ground. For my Lord Jesus Christ will quickly come, since he is rejected by those who falsify his words. For I delivered to you in the beginning what I received from the apostles who were before me, that . . . God, the almighty, who is righteous and would not repudiate his own creation, sent the Holy Spirit through fire into Mary the Galilean, who believed with all her heart, and she received the Holy Spirit in her womb that Jesus might enter into the world, in order that the evil one might be conquered through the same flesh by which he held sway, and convinced that he was not God. For by his own body, Jesus Christ saved all flesh. . . . *(3 Cor 1:1–4, 12–14)*

The Arrival of the Superapostles. Either prior to Paul's departure or soon thereafter, other apostles of Christ arrived in town, claiming to be true spokespersons of the gospel. These "superapostles" (as Paul calls them; 2 Cor 11:5) were of Jewish ancestry (11:22) and appear to have appealed precisely to that aspect of the Corinthians' views that Paul found most repugnant, their notion that life in Christ was already an exalted, glorified existence. For these superapostles it was; that was why they could do the spectacular deeds that established their credentials as apostles. Clearly they and Paul did not see eye to eye. At some point the attacks became personal: the

superapostles evidently maligned Paul for his clear lack of power and charismatic presence ("his bodily presence is weak and his speech contemptible," 10:10); he in turn claimed that they were ministers of Satan rather than apostles of Christ (11:13–15). Paul argued that his gospel message would be totally compromised if the Corinthians accepted the claims of his opponents (11:4).

Paul's Third Letter (the "Painful" Letter, Partly Embodied in 2 Corinthians 10–13). After his second visit, Paul wrote a letter in which he went on the attack against the superapostles. He continued to

WHAT DO YOU THINK?

BOX 14.4   The Partitioning of 2 Corinthians

A number of New Testament scholars believe that 2 Corinthians comprises not just two of Paul's letters but four or five of them, all edited together into one larger composition for distribution among the Pauline churches. Most of the **"partition theories,"** as they are called (since they partition the one letter into a number of others), maintain that chapters 1–9 are not a unity but are made up of several letters spliced together. Read the chapters for yourself and answer the following questions:

❖ Does the beginning of chapter 8 appear to shift abruptly to a new subject, away from the good news Titus has just brought Paul (about the reconciliatory attitude of the Corinthians) to Paul's decision to send Titus to collect money for the needy among the Christians? There is no transition to this new subject, and 8:1 sounds like the beginning of the body of a letter. Could it have been taken from a different writing?

❖ Do the words of 9:1 seem strange after what Paul has said in all of chapter 8? He has been talking for twenty-four verses about the collection for the saints, and then in 9:1 he begins to talk about it again as if it were a new subject that had not yet been broached. Could chapter 9 also, then, have come from a separate letter?

❖ Does the paragraph found in 6:14–7:1 seem odd in its context? The verse immediately preceding it (6:13) urges the Corinthians to be open to Paul, as does the verse immediately following it (7:2). But the paragraph itself is on an entirely different and unannounced topic: Christians should not associate with nonbelievers. Moreover, there are aspects of this passage that appear unlike anything Paul himself says anywhere else in his writings. Nowhere else, for example, does he call the Devil "Beliar" (v. 15). Has this passage come from some other piece of correpondence (possibly one that Paul didn't write) and been inserted in the midst of Paul's warm admonition to the Corinthians to think kindly of him?

If you answered yes to all three of these questions, then you agree with those scholars who see fragments of at least five letters in 2 Corinthians: (a) 1:1–6:13; 7:2–16 (part of the conciliatory letter); (b) 6:14–7:1 (part of a non-Pauline letter?); (c) 8:1–24 (a letter for the collection, to the Corinthians) (d) 9:1–15 (a letter for the collection, to some other church?); and (e) 10:1–13:13 (part of the painful letter).

insist that the life of the believer is not the glorified, exalted existence that Christ presently enjoys. Believers live in an age of evil and suffering, in which God's enemy Satan is still active and in control. Those who boast of their power and wisdom do not understand that the end has not yet come, that this is an age of weakness in which God's wisdom appears foolish. Apostles, in particular, suffer in this age, since they are the chief opponents of the cosmic powers of evil who are in charge (11:20–31). Even though apostles may have had a glimpse of the glory to come (12:1–4), they are still subject to pain and suffering, which keeps them from boasting of their own merits and forces them to rely totally on the grace of God for what they can accomplish (12:5–10). In light of these criteria, the superapostles are not apostles at all. Paul also used this letter to attack the person who had publicly humiliated him and to warn the congregation to deal with him prior to his arrival in judgment, for Paul himself would not be lenient when he came (13:1–2).

Part of this letter, principally the part that dealt with the superapostles, is found in what is now 2 Corinthians 10–13. The letter was sent with Paul's companion **Titus**, and it evidently had its desired effect. The Corinthians punished the one who had insulted Paul (2 Cor 2:5–11), repented of the pain they had caused him, and returned to his fold (2 Cor 7:5–12). Paul in the meantime canceled his plan to make another visit to the congregation (2 Cor 1:15–2:2).

Paul's Fourth Letter (the "Conciliatory" Letter, Partly Embodied in 2 Corinthians 1–9). After hearing the good news from Titus, Paul wrote a friendly letter to express his pleasure at the Corinthians' change of heart (2 Cor 2:5–11; 7:5–16). He also wanted to explain why he had not come for another visit, to assure them that he was not simply being fickle in making and revising his plans (1:15–2:4). Part of this letter (without, at least, its closing) is found in 2 Corinthians 1–9, or possibly only chapters 1–7, since some scholars think that chapters 8–9 are part of another letter or possibly even two letters (see box 14.4).

The Overarching Points of the Letter

After someone edited the two (or three or four or five) letters into the one book that we call 2 Corinthians, we lose sight of Paul's relationship with this congregation. Thus, we can never know whether all the problems were solved, or whether any more stormy incidents occurred. Nor can we determine whether the Corinthians decided to adopt Paul's point of view and reject the perspectives brought in by others from the outside.

Clearly, however, the basic message that Paul tried to convey in 1 Corinthians is very much in evidence in the collection of letters we are investigating here. Consider first the fragment of the painful letter (chaps. 10–13), written in part to address the claims of superiority made by the superapostles. Rather than simply attacking them on their own terms, for example, by arguing that he could do better miracles than they, Paul dismisses their very grounds for considering themselves apostles. This is reminiscent of the way he treated the leaders of the divisive factions in 1 Corinthians 1–4, where he denies that earthly wisdom and power are signs of the divine. For him, the credentials of an apostle are not the glorious acts that he or she can perform, as if this were an age of exaltation and splendor. The true apostle will suffer, much as Christ suffered. For the end has not yet come, and those who rely on spectacular acts of power must be suspected of collusion with the cosmic forces that are in charge of this age, namely, Satan and his vile servants (11:12–15).

This is why Paul goes to such lengths to "boast in his weaknesses" in this letter (12:5), principally by detailing all the ways that he has suffered as Christ's apostle (11:17–33). It may not seem like much to boast about—being beaten up regularly, living in constant danger and in fear for one's life—but for Paul these are signs that he is the true apostle of Christ, who himself suffered the ignominious fate of crucifixion. In particular, Paul claims that God has kept him weak so that he would be unable to boast about any work that he himself has performed. Anything good that comes of his ministry has necessarily been performed by God (12:6–10). The same cannot be said of the superapostles.

Paul's apocalyptic message stresses in the strongest terms that believers are not yet glorified with Christ. They live in a world of sin and evil and must contend with forces greater than themselves, until the end comes and Christ's followers are raised into immortal bodies to be exalted with him. For reasons that are ultimately unknown, the Corinthians came to agree with Paul on precisely this point. It is hard to imagine what changed their minds. Was Paul (or his representative Titus) simply too persuasive to refute? Were the superapostles discredited in some other way? We will never know.

We do know that after their reconciliation, Paul wrote another letter in which, along with his gratitude for the church's change of heart, he expressed in a somewhat more subdued fashion his basically apocalyptic view of life in this world. He begins the letter, now embodied in 2 Corinthians 1–9 (or 1–7), by stressing his own suffering and the grace of God that was manifest through it (1:3–11). This is to some extent the message of the entire epistle. The gospel is an invaluable treasure, even though

it has not been fully manifested in this age of pain and suffering. The body has not yet been glorified, and believers are not yet exalted. As a result, "we have this treasure in clay jars" (4:7). Believers themselves are lowly and their bodies of little worth, but the gospel message that they proclaim is a treasure for the ages. As Paul puts it later, in the body the believer groans, longing to be clothed with a heavenly, glorified body (5:1–10). The present age is therefore one of suffering and of longing for a better age to come.

With this longing, however, comes the assurance that in the future the hoped-for glory will become a reality for those who have been reconciled to God through Christ (5:16–21). Until this future reality makes itself known, life in this world is characterized by affliction and hardship. The suffering of the present age, however, is not enough to tarnish the hope of the true believer, for "this momentary affliction is preparing us for an eternal weight of glory beyond all measure" (4:17). This, above all else, is the apocalyptic message that Paul seeks to convey to his Corinthian converts.

AT A GLANCE

BOX 14.5 2 Corinthians

1. 2 Corinthians appears to embody at least two of Paul's letters (chaps. 1–9 and 10–13), and possibly as many as four or five.

2. At a later time, someone took these various letters and edited them together into one.

3. It is possible to trace the history of Paul's relationship with this community based on the different letters combined here.

4. After he wrote 1 Corinthians, Paul visited Corinth again and faced a public humiliation. Soon thereafter, other Christian apostles arrived in town advocating a view that Paul himself opposed, that Christians already could experience the full benefits of salvation in the here and now (without waiting for the future apocalyptic act of God).

5. Paul responded by writing an angry letter, which may be found (partially) in chapters 10–13, sent through a personal messenger, Titus.

6. This letter, or Titus, had the desired effect; the community changed its mind. Paul wrote a grateful, conciliatory letter in response, partly found now in chapters 1–9.

7. Many of the same apocalyptic themes of 1 Corinthians can be found in the fragments of letters now comprising 2 Corinthians.

TAKE A STAND

1. Suppose you are a Christian in the church of Corinth who disagrees with Paul. You think that it is OK to eat meat offered to idols, to have sex with prostitutes, to speak in tongues frequently in your church meetings, and to enjoy lots of food and drink at your church's weekly meals. In part you base your views on the belief that you have already begun to enjoy the benefits of Christ's resurrection in the here and now. Write a letter to Paul to explain why he is wrong about all these things.

2. Your best friend considers himself an expert on the New Testament and does not think for a second that 2 Corinthians comes from several letters that have been patched together. You decide to argue that it is. Make the best argument you can.

3. Pick three critical issues or problems that occurred in the Corinthian church and show how Paul's teaching on "love" could be called upon to deal with them.

SUGGESTIONS FOR FURTHER READING

In addition to the suggestions at the end of Chapter 12, see the following:

Martin, Dale. *The Corinthian Body*. New Haven: Yale University Press, 1999. An important sociohistorical study of Paul's letters to Corinth in light of ancient understandings of the "body"—both the individual body and the larger social body (such as the "church"); for advanced students.

Theissen, Gerd. *The Social Setting of Pauline Christianity: Essays on Corinth*. Eugene, Ore.: Wipf and Stock, 2004. A groundbreaking and highly influential set of essays that examines the letters to the Corinthians not from the theological but from a sociohistorical perspective; for advanced students.

KEY TERMS

Achaia
Apollos
Aquila and Priscilla
Chloe
conciliatory letter

Corinth
love chapter
meat offered to idols
painful letter

partition theories
Sosthenes
Stephanus, Fortunatus, and Achaicus

superapostles
Titus, Christian

Paul and the Crises of His Churches

GALATIANS, PHILIPPIANS, AND PHILEMON

WHAT TO EXPECT

Each church that Paul founded developed unique problems; the letters that he wrote tried to address these problems as he learned about them. We have already seen how Paul dealt with situations that had arisen in the churches of Thessalonia (in Achaia) and Corinth (in Macedonia). In this chapter we will consider his letters to the churches of Galatia and Philippi, as well as a personal letter that he sent to an individual named Philemon.

Here we will find a range of problems—from false teachers who proclaimed a version of Christianity that Paul found to be both outrageous and damnable to a sticky personal situation involving a runaway slave who had appealed to Paul for help. As with all of Paul's letters, understanding the occasion of the letters (their "context") will assist us in interpreting what he has to say.

ow that we have seen how Paul engaged in his missionary work in establishing churches, and observed how he addressed problems in the communities of Thessalonica and Corinth, we are in a position to consider three other undisputed letters: an intense and angry letter fired off to the church in the Asia Minor region of Galatia, a friendly and caring letter (or letters) sent to the Christians of the city of Philippi, and a personal letter sent to a convert named **Philemon** on behalf of a runaway slave named **Onesimus**.

 GALATIANS

With the letter to the Galatians, we enter into an entirely different set of issues from those evident so far in Paul's correspondence. On the one hand, there is no question concerning the unity of this epistle; it is just one letter, written completely at one time, to address one problem. But the problem itself was quite unlike anything that had arisen among the Thessalonians and the Corinthians. In brief, the occasion of the letter was as follows.

After Paul converted a number of Gentiles to faith in Christ in the region of Galatia, other missionaries arrived on the scene, insisting that believers must follow parts of the Jewish Law in order to be fully right before God. Specifically, the men in these congregations had to accept the Jewish rite of circumcision.

Paul was absolutely outraged at this proposal. Whereas other apostles to the Gentiles may have looked upon circumcision as merely unnecessary, a painful operation that Gentiles would have no reason to undergo unless they really wanted to, for Paul the matter was far more serious. For him, Gentiles who underwent circumcision showed a complete and absolute misunderstanding of the meaning of the gospel. In his view, for a Gentile to be circumcised was not simply a superfluous act; it was an affront to God and a rejection of the justification he has provided through Christ. Those who propose such a thing have perverted the gospel (1:7) and are cursed by God (1:8). Paul's anger in this letter is transparent at the outset. It is the only letter that he does not begin by thanking God for the congregation.

The Occasion and Purpose of the Epistle

Paul addresses the letter to "the churches of Galatia" (1:2). Unfortunately, we do not know, specifically, where the letter was sent. Before the Roman conquests, **Galatia** was a region in the north-central portion of Asia Minor (modern-day Turkey), a sparsely populated territory that was eventually linked by the Romans with the more populous region of the south, which included the cities of Lystra, Derbe, Iconium, and Pisidian Antioch. The Romans called this entire province Galatia, even though the name had earlier been used only to refer to its northern portion.

To what, then, is Paul referring when he speaks of the churches of Galatia? Does he mean churches throughout the entire Roman province, comparable to the churches of Achaia and Macedonia that he refers to elsewhere (e.g., 1 Thess 1:7)? Or is he referring only to churches in the northernmost region, the region inhabited by people who would, unlike the southerners, refer to themselves as Galatians (see Gal 3:1)? The problem is complicated by the fact that the book of Acts indicates that

Paul established churches in the southern region, in the cities that I have just named. Paul himself, however, never mentions these cities in Galatians or anywhere else. Moreover, he claims that he founded the Galatian churches in somewhat unusual circumstances: he had taken seriously ill and was nursed back to health by the Galatians (well, by some of them). In this context, he preached the gospel and converted them (4:13–17). He does not appear, then, to have established these churches as he passed through the region preaching in the local synagogues, as is recorded in Acts.

Although we do not know to which churches Paul sent the letter (but see figure 15.1), we do know that newcomers had arrived in Galatia preaching a gospel that Paul sees as standing at odds with his own, and the Galatian Christians appear to have been persuaded by them (1:6–9). We cannot be certain what these opponents actually preached. All we have is Paul's description of their message, and we have no guarantee that he knows, understands, or presents it accurately. It is clear, however, that he sees as the major point of contention the newcomers' insistence that (male) Gentile converts to Christianity have to be circumcised in order to be fully right before God (see e.g., 5:2–6). Paul interprets his opponents to mean that a person has to perform the works prescribed by the Jewish Law to have salvation. This message is totally unacceptable from his point of view. According to the gospel that he preaches—and this, as he points out, is the message that led the Galatians to faith in Christ in the first place—a person is **"justified"** (made right with God) not by doing the works of the Jewish Law, but by having faith in Christ (2:16). In Paul's view, the newcomers' message completely contradicts his own.

What else might these newcomers have taught? It is possible that they actually took the offensive against Paul himself (or at least that he thought they did) by questioning not only his views but also his authorization to proclaim them. This would explain the opening part of Paul's response, in which he vehemently denies that he has perverted the message of the gospel that he received from the apostles who came before him (e.g., Jesus' disciples in Jerusalem), because in fact his message didn't come originally from these apostles or from any human at all. It came from God, in a direct

Figure 15.1 The Roman Province of Galatia in the Midst of Asia Minor (modern-day Turkey). Some historians think that Paul wrote Galatians to churches in the southern part of the province, which are named in Acts as places of his missionary activities but which he himself never mentions (such as Derbe, Lystra, and Iconium). But since he actually *calls* his readers "Galatians"—an epithet that would apply only to the Celtic peoples of the northern part of the province—it appears that he addressed the letter to churches unknown to the author of Acts.

revelation. It is also possible that Paul's Galatian opponents insisted that their message was truer to the Scriptures than his; they may have argued that since the Jewish Bible portrays circumcision as the sign of the covenant, any man who wants to become a full member of this covenant must first be circumcised.

In basic outline, the message of Paul's Galatian opponents appears similar to that proclaimed by other early Christians. The implicit logic behind it may have been that God is totally consistent and does not "change the rules." This is the Jewish God who gave the Jewish Law, who sent the Jewish Jesus as the Jewish messiah to the Jewish people in fulfillment of the Jewish Scriptures. Those who want to enjoy the full benefits of salvation, according to this view, must obviously join the Jewish people by being circumcised if they are men and by practicing the Law whether they are men or women (see box 15.1).

Scholars dispute whether these newcomers were Jews from birth or Gentiles who had converted to Judaism. Gal 5:12 may suggest the latter: Paul hopes that when they perform the operation of circumcision on themselves, the knife slips. In either case, they were almost certainly believers in Jesus who taught others to adhere to some, or all, of the dictates of the Jewish Law. Paul finds this view offensive both to his person (since his authority is being questioned) and to his message (since his gospel is being compromised).

Paul's Response

Paul begins to make his case against his opponents already in the prescript of his letter; he is an apostle who has been "sent neither by human commission nor from human authorities, but through Jesus Christ and God the Father" (1:1). That is to say, he neither dreamed up his apostolic mission nor received it from any other human. He has been com-missioned by God himself. That this self-defense is occasioned by the Galatians' acceptance of a contrary message becomes clear as Paul moves into the body of the letter. Instead of thanking God for these churches, Paul begins with a rebuke: the Galatians have deserted God by adopting a gospel that differs from the one that Paul preached to them (1:6–9). Anyone who affirms a different gospel, however, stands under God's curse.

In this early stage of the letter, Paul does not indicate what this other gospel entails. He evidently can assume that the Galatians know perfectly well what he is referring to, even though we as outsiders do not find out until somewhat later. Rather than launching directly into a theological refutation, he begins his counterattack by raising the question of authorization. Quite apart from what his message is, what authority stands behind it? Did he invent his gospel message? Or did he receive it from someone else and then change some of its details? Paul insists that his message comes directly from a revelation of Christ. Consider the ominous implications: what if someone disagrees with it?

To establish his point, Paul devotes nearly two chapters to an autobiographical sketch of his earlier life. The sketch might seem odd to a reader who is familiar with Paul's general reluctance to

WHAT DO YOU THINK?

BOX 15.1 The Logic of the Opponents' Position in Galatia

Paul's Galatian opponents may well have appealed to the Jewish Scriptures to argue their position. For both Paul and his opponents, Gentiles had been allowed to enter into the covenant that God had made with the Jewish people. They, too, could stand in a unique relationship with this one who created the world and chose his people. But the Scriptures were quite clear concerning what this covenantal relationship had involved from the beginning, when God first established it with the father of the Jews, Abraham:

> God said to Abraham, "As for you, you shall keep my covenant, you and your offspring after you throughout their generations. This is my covenant which you shall keep, between me and you and your offspring after you:

Every male among you shall be circumcised . . . including the slave born in your house and the one bought with your money from any foreigner who is not of your offspring. So shall my covenant be in your flesh an everlasting covenant. Any uncircumcised male who is not circumcised in the flesh of his foreskin shall be cut off from his people; he has broken my covenant." (Gen 17:9–14)

Paul's opponents may simply have argued that while the covenant was now open to all who believed in Christ, God had not rescinded the rules of the covenant itself: it was an "everlasting" covenant, that is, one that would not be changed. Those who wished to belong to it must be circumcised, as God had said from the very beginning.

reminisce about his past, but the autobiography bears directly on the question at hand, the reliability of his gospel message. It shows that "the gospel that was proclaimed by me is not of human origin; for I did not receive it from a human source, nor was I taught it, but I received it through a revelation of Jesus Christ" (1:11–12).

To demonstrate his point, Paul recounts his conversion, in which he switched from being a persecutor of the church to being a preacher of its gospel. This conversion occurred through a direct act of God, who "was pleased to reveal his Son to me, so that I might proclaim him among the Gentiles" (1:15). Thus, the revelation of who Jesus really was, as opposed to who Paul had earlier thought he was, came directly from God and for a clear purpose: so Paul could take the message to the Gentiles, that is, to non-Jews like the Galatians.

This message was not given by the Jerusalem apostles or by anyone else: "I did not confer with any human being, nor did I go up to Jerusalem to those who were already apostles before me" (1:16–17; contrast Acts 9:19–30). Why is Paul so emphatic on this point? It may be that he suspects that his Galatian opponents have claimed that he modified the gospel that he originally learned from Jesus' earliest followers, the Jerusalem apostles. If so, then his autobiographical sketch shows that the claim is simply not true ("before God, I do not lie!" 1:20). On the other hand, he may know that his opponents have claimed superior authorization for themselves, by pointing to the Jerusalem apostles as the source of their own message. If so, then his sketch shows that whatever the source of his opponents' message, his own came straight from God.

To be sure, Paul does not deny that he has had some contact with the Jerusalem apostles. He admits that three years after his conversion (i.e., long after his views were set), he went to visit Cephas for fifteen days. He does not, however, indicate precisely why he went. Indeed, the term that he uses, which is sometimes simply translated "to visit" (Gal 1:18), can mean either that he went "to learn something" or "to convey some information." It may be that he went to keep **Cephas**, the chief apostle in Jerusalem at the time, apprised of his actions.

Some fourteen years later, Paul met with a larger group of apostles for a similar reason, to inform them of his missionary activities (2:1–10). It was his second trip to Jerusalem (in the book of Acts it happens to be his third), and it represented a critical moment for the Gentile mission. One does not get the sense from Paul that he made this second visit because he wanted to make sure that his gospel message was right, as if he could imagine it being wrong! (Remember, he claimed to have received it from God himself.) Instead, Paul went to convince the Jerusalem apostles that Gentiles were not required to follow the Jewish Law, including circumcision (the "sign of the covenant"), in order to be right with God, or "justified" (2:1–5). He met with the leaders privately to persuade them of his views (2:2), and he succeeded without qualification (2:7–10), even though others were present who argued the alternative perspective. Paul calls these other people "false believers" (2:4) and sees them as the predecessors of his opponents in Galatia.

The important point for Paul is that the Jerusalem apostles agreed with him rather than with his adversaries at the conference. Even though these apostles were committed to evangelizing Jews (2:7–9), they conceded that there was no need for Gentile converts to be circumcised. Emblematic of this decision was the fate of the Gentile Titus, who accompanied Paul to the conference and who was not compelled to be circumcised by those who took the opposing perspective (2:3–4). By securing this agreement with the Jerusalem apostles, Paul could rest assured that they would give his mission their full blessing and not try to undermine it. In his words, he knew that he "was not running, or had not run, in vain" (2:2).

Paul provides one other autobiographical detail to secure his point. After his meeting with the Jerusalem apostles, one of them, Cephas, came to spend time with him and his church in Antioch. At first, Cephas joined with Paul and the other Christians of Jewish background in sharing "table fellowship" with the Gentile believers ("he used to eat with the Gentiles"; 2:11–12). But when representatives of the apostle James, the brother of Jesus, arrived on the scene, Cephas withdrew from fellowship with the Gentiles, and the other Jewish-Christians joined with him (2:12–13). Paul saw this withdrawal as an act of hypocrisy and openly rebuked Cephas for it. In Paul's view, Cephas had compromised the earlier decision not to compel Gentiles to obey Jewish laws (2:14).

Scholars have different opinions concerning what this conflict was all about. It may be best to assume that eating with the Gentiles somehow required Cephas and his Jewish-Christian companions to violate kosher food laws. They may have thought that this was acceptable so long as they gave no offense to other believers, but when the representatives of James, that is, Jewish-Christians who perhaps continued to keep kosher, came to town, Cephas and his companions realized that they had to decide with whom they were going to eat. They chose not to give offense to their Jewish brothers and sisters and so ate with them.

For Paul, this was an absolute affront because it suggested that there was a distinction between Jew and Gentile before God, whereas the agreement that had been struck in Jerusalem maintained that there was not. Jew and Gentile were on an equal footing before God, and any attempt to suggest Jewish superiority was a compromise of the gospel.

We do not know the outcome of this confrontation, in part because we never hear Cephas's side of the argument. Paul's narration of the incident is important, though, because it introduces the issue that the letter is ultimately about: the relationship of Paul's gospel message to the Jewish Law (2:15).

At this stage, Paul begins to mount theoretical and scriptural arguments to show that the Jewish Law has no role in a person's right standing before God and that, as a consequence, his opponents in Galatia are in error not only for doubting his authorization but also for perverting his gospel. These arguments are somewhat intricate, so here I will simply summarize some of the salient points.

What Was the Basic Issue? Paul begins in 2:15–21 with a forceful expression of his views. Even as a good Jew himself, he has come to realize that a person's right standing ("justification") before God does not come through doing the works of the Jewish Law but through faith in Christ (2:16). If a person could be made right with God through the Law, then there would have been no reason for Christ to die (2:21).

Not only is this the right way to understand the Law, according to Paul, it is also the message that the Law itself teaches. Now that he has come to grasp this message of the Law, he can say that "through the Law I died to the Law" (2:19). This is a difficult saying, which might be paraphrased as follows: "Through the correct understanding of the Law that the Law itself has provided, I have given

BOX 15.2 Why Does Paul Appeal to the Law to Dispute This View of the Law?

One of the most striking things about Paul's response to the Galatians' situation is that he bases a good deal of his argument against his opponents' emphasis on the Law on a careful interpretation of the Jewish Scriptures themselves. This approach may seem ironic to an outside reader—Paul is citing the Jewish Law in order to show that the Law is to play no role in a person's standing before God! For Paul, however, this line of argument is completely sensible. He maintains that the Scriptures themselves teach that the Law was not given in order to bring about a right standing before God. From the very beginning, people have been made right with God by faith,

starting with the father of the Jews, Abraham himself, in Genesis, the first book of the Law. For Paul, the true children of Abraham are those who have faith, just as Abraham had faith—whether they are Jews who have the Law or Gentiles who don't (3:6–9).

It is also possible that Paul makes such a lengthy appeal to the teachings of the Torah to show that he himself is quite capable when it comes to interpreting the Jewish Scriptures. Not only was he raised Jewish and zealous for Jewish traditions prior to his conversion to Christ (1:13–14), he continues to explore the Jewish Scriptures and is second to none (including his opponents in Galatia) in his ability to interpret them.

up on the Law as a way of attaining a right standing before God." Once the Law is abandoned as a way to God, then, no one should pretend that it affects one's standing before God; to use Paul's image, it is wrong to "build up" the importance of the Law for salvation once its importance has already been "torn down" (2:18).

The matter is significant because the Galatians, former pagans who converted to faith in Christ, have begun to adopt the view that Paul opposes, namely, that doing works of the Law (in particular, circumcision) is important for one's standing before God. Paul is incensed and incredulous: "You foolish Galatians! Who bewitched you? . . . Did you receive the Spirit by doing the works of the law or by believing what you heard?" (3:1).

What Is the Problem with Gentiles Keeping the Law? Paul claims that those who do not live by faith but by the Law, that is, those who try to attain a right standing before God by keeping the Law, are subject to God's curse rather than his blessing, despite their motivation and desire. On the one hand, the Torah itself curses those who do not "obey all the things written in the book of the

law" (2:10). Paul does not explain why everyone is automatically put under this curse, but it may be because in his opinion no one ever does "obey all the things written in the law," as he indicates elsewhere (see Rom 3:9–20). Indeed, even though he does not explicitly mention this issue, Paul may be thinking that the Law itself demonstrates his point, since a good portion of the Torah is devoted to describing the sacrifices that have to be performed by all Jews, even the Jewish high priest, to atone for their sins when they inadvertently violate the Law. If one must obey all the things in the Law or suffer its curse, and the Law itself indicates that no one does so, where then does that leave us? Clearly everyone who tries to obey the Law stands under the curse that the Law itself pronounces.

Moreover, and this point is more clearly expressed in the passage, the Law cannot place someone in a right standing before God because the Scriptures indicate that a person will find life through having faith (Hab 2:6, quoted in 3:11). Carrying out the Law, though, is not a matter of trusting God (faith); it is a matter of doing something (work). If faith is the way to life, then doing the Law will not satisfy the requirement. Only

Figure 15.2 God giving the Law to Moses, from a panel of fifteenth-century bronze doors of the Baptistry in Florence, Italy, by Lorenzo Ghiberti. Unlike in this portrayal (and unlike in the book of Exodus itself), Paul claimed that the Law did not come directly from God but through angelic intermediaries, thereby lessening its divine character and eternal importance (Gal 3:19).

faith like the faith of Abraham, the father of all believers (not of Jews only), will put one in a right standing before God.

Why Then Did God Give the Law in the First Place? The question naturally arises, then, if practicing the Law does not put a person into a right standing before God, and it was never meant to do so, why was it ever given at all (3:19)? Paul's answer in 3:19–29 has caused interpreters difficulties over the years. Perhaps it is best to understand his comments to mean that the Law was given to provide instruction and guidance to the Jewish people, informing them of God's will and keeping them "in line" until God came to fulfill his promise to **Abraham** to "bless his offspring" (3:16). This fulfillment would come in Christ, who was himself the offspring of Abraham spoken of in the promise (3:16). Thus the Law served as a "disciplinarian" until the arrival of Christ; it is called a *paidagogos* (to use the Greek term), that is, one who made sure the children kept on the straight and narrow until they reached maturity. At no point, however, was the Law meant to put a person into a right standing before God. It couldn't do so because justification comes through faith, not action.

Who, Then, Are the True Descendants of Abraham? Paul understands that the Jews and Gentiles who have faith like that of Abraham are his true descendants, as opposed to unbelieving Jews who are simply his physical progeny. This perspective is especially clear in the allegory that Paul gives in 4:21–30. The allegory represents an original and intriguing interpretation of the story of Genesis 21. (You should read the story on your own before you examine again Paul's interpretation of it.) In Paul's view, Abraham's son Isaac, born of the promise, represents the Christian church (i.e., all those who believe in God's promise), while his son Ishmael, born of the flesh, represents Jews who do not believe in Christ. In other words, those who have faith in Christ are the legitimate heirs of God's promise. Unbelieving Jews, on the other hand, are children born into slavery (since Hagar, the mother of Ishmael, was a slave). Those who submit to the Jewish Law apart from faith in Christ submit to a yoke of slavery; they correspond to the son of the slave woman. Those who do have faith will never

submit to this yoke. An amazing interpretation this: Jews are not the children promised to Abraham, but Christians (whether Jews or Gentiles) are!

Doesn't This Teaching Lead to Lawlessness? Paul concludes this letter by addressing a problem that some might think is implicit in his teaching that all people, Jews and Gentiles, are made right with God through faith apart from performing the works of the Law. If the Law was given in order to provide direction and discipline to God's people, but Gentile believers don't have to keep it, aren't they liable to turn to wild and reckless behavior?

For Paul, nothing could be further from the truth. In perhaps one of the greatest ironies in his thinking, Paul indicates that Gentile believers in Christ, who are not obligated to keep the Law (and therefore must not be circumcised), are to be totally committed to one another in love because in so doing, they fulfill the Law! Indeed, for Paul, Christians must be enslaved to one another in love (5:13) precisely because "the whole law is summed up in a single commandment, 'You shall love your neighbor as yourself'" (5:14).

His argument raises a number of tantalizing questions. First, how can Paul tell his converts not to follow the Law (You must not be circumcised) and then require them to follow it (You must love one another so as to fulfill the Law)? Evidently—although this is not a point that he makes explicit in any of his writings—Paul thinks that there are different kinds of laws provided in the Jewish Scriptures (compare what we found with respect to the Gospel of Matthew in Chapter 6). There are some laws that are distinctive to being Jewish. These would include circumcision and kosher food laws. Paul insisted that his Gentile converts not keep these laws: indeed he claims here in Galatians that those who do so "have cut yourselves off from Christ; you have fallen from grace" (5:4). At the same time, he urges his converts to keep the principle that summarizes the entire Torah; they should love their neighbors as themselves. It is hard to escape the conclusion that Paul saw some laws as distinctively Jewish (Be circumcised) and others as applicable to all people (Love your neighbor).

Paul seems to imply in Galatians 3, however, that no one is able to keep all the laws (including, presumably, the law to love one's neighbor). How then can he insist that Christians fulfill the Law? Paul evidently believes that those who receive the Spirit of God through believing in Christ (3:1) are empowered by the Spirit to do what the Law commands. Indeed, their lives will bear fruit in ways that fulfill the law, and they will do those things that no law forbids (5:22–23). Those who do not have the Spirit, on the other hand, that is, those who are not believers, are necessarily ruled by their flesh and by nature engage in activities that are contrary to the Law and will of God (5:16–21). Such persons will never inherit the kingdom of God (5:21). Thus, perhaps ironically, those who have faith in Jesus, not those who are circumcised, are the ones who fulfill the righteous demands of God's Law.

In Sum: Paul and the Law

This question of the relationship of faith in Christ to the Jewish Law is one that continued to perplex Paul throughout his life. Indeed, it is one of the central questions that he had to address as an apostle of Christ, for he taught at one and the same time that Christ was the fulfillment of the Law and that believers did not have to perform the works of the Law—meaning, as we have seen, that they did not have to carry out those aspects of the Law that in outsiders' eyes made Jews Jewish. The question proved to be of ongoing importance because it re-

lated to larger ones that Paul's version of the gospel compelled him to address, including the questions of whether God had abandoned his people Israel by making faith in Christ the sole means of salvation and whether God had as a consequence proved himself to be unfaithful and untrustworthy by not staying true to his promise always to be the God of Israel. These are some of the issues that Paul would explore in the fuller, and somewhat less heated, exposition of his views of the gospel in his letter to the Romans (see Chapter 16).

 ## PHILIPPIANS

We do not know very much about the Christian community in **Philippi** because Paul does not provide as many explicit reminders of their past relationship as he does, for example, for the Thessalonians and Corinthians. There is some information provided in Acts 16; unfortunately, little of it can be corroborated from Paul's letter itself. Paul never mentions, for example, the principal characters of Luke's account, Lydia and the Philippian jailer.

The city of Philippi was in eastern Macedonia, northeast of Thessalonica, along one of the major trade routes through the region. Paul speaks in 1 Thessalonians of being shamefully treated in

AT A GLANCE

BOX 15.3   Galatians

1. The letter to the Galatians is written to a group of churches in the Roman province of Galatia, in Asia Minor.

2. Paul had established churches there, but after he left other missionaries arrived proclaiming a different version of the gospel.

3. These other missionaries insisted that Gentiles had to become circumcised and keep the Jewish Law in order to be fully right with God.

4. Paul's angry response begins with an autobiographical sketch designed to show that his

version of the gospel came directly from God through a vision of Christ, not through any human agency.

5. He then argues vehemently that salvation comes to Gentiles by faith in Christ alone, not by keeping the Jewish Law. Any Gentile who thinks Law observation is *necessary* has missed the point and may well miss out on salvation.

6. The letter concludes with ethical admonitions, showing that for Paul, the law-free gospel does not lead to lawless behavior.

Philippi prior to taking his mission to Thessalonica (1 Thess 2:1–2). We should probably assume that he is referring to his initial visit to the city when he founded the church there. In view of their rough treatment, Paul and his companions may not have spent much time there, perhaps only enough to make some converts, instruct them in the rudiments of the faith, and get out of town while the getting was good.

We have little information about the converts themselves. We can probably assume that the Philippian church, like the other congregations Paul established, consisted chiefly of converted pagans who had been taught to worship the one true God of Israel and to expect the return of his Son, Jesus. References to these teachings can be found throughout the epistle (e.g., 1:6, 10–11; 2:5–11; 3:20–21). Why, then, did Paul write it? The answer to this question is somewhat complicated, more complicated, for example, than in the case of Galatians, for it appears to many scholars that different parts of this letter presuppose different occasions. As was the case with 2 Corinthians, Philippians may represent a combination of two or more pieces of correspondence.

The Unity of the Letter

The first two chapters of Philippians sound very much like a friendship letter written by Paul to his converts. The occasion of the letter is reasonably evident (see especially 2:25–30). The Philippians had sent to Paul one of their stalwart members, a man named Epaphroditus, for some reason that is not disclosed (until chap. 4). While there ministering to Paul, **Epaphroditus** was taken ill; the Philippians had heard of his illness and grew concerned. Epaphroditus in turn learned of their concern and became distraught over the anxiety that he had caused. Fortunately, his health returned, and he was now set to make his journey back home to Philippi. Paul wrote this letter to keep the Philippians informed of his situation and to express his pleasure that all had turned out well.

Paul sent the letter from prison (1:7). We do not know where he was imprisoned or why, except that it was in connection with his preaching of the gospel. He uses the letter to comment on his adversity and to reassure his congregation that it has turned out for the good: as a result of his bonds,

others have become emboldened to preach (1:12–18). Paul uses his own situation to explain that suffering is the destiny of Christians in the present age (1:29–30)—a message comparable to that which he proclaimed in the Corinthian correspondence. He continues by providing some general words of admonition (as was common in friendship letters): the Philippians are to be unified, serving one another rather than themselves, and thereby following the example of Christ (2:1–11).

One of the most striking features of this letter comes after these general exhortations. For the friendly and joyful tone that characterizes the letter's first two chapters shifts almost without warning at the beginning of chapter 3. Indeed, if one didn't know that there were two more chapters left in the book, it would appear that the letter was drawing to a close at the end of chapter 2. Paul has explained his own situation, given some admonitions, stated the purpose of his writing, and provided his concluding exhortation: "Finally, brothers and sisters, rejoice in the Lord" (3:1). Why does he say "finally" but then change the subject completely and continue writing for another two chapters? Indeed, the words that follow are hard to understand in the immediate context: "To write the same things to you is not troublesome to me, and for you it is a safeguard" (3:1). Why would anyone find his exhortation to rejoice troubling? Paul immediately launches into a vitriolic attack on people who are his enemies, presumably in Philippi, people whom he calls "dogs," "evil workers," and "those who mutilate the flesh" (3:2). He then defends his own understanding of the gospel against these false teachers (3:3–11). A peaceful letter of friendship has now become a harsh letter of warning.

Moreover, the issue of unity within the Christian community takes on an additional twist in these chapters. We learn that there are two women in particular, **Euodia and Syntyche**, who are at odds with one another and causing something of a disturbance in the community (4:2–3). No longer does Paul deal in the abstract with the need for unity; now he actually puts some names on the problem. What is particularly interesting is that Epaphroditus is again mentioned in these closing chapters. If you didn't know better, though, you would think that he had just arrived, not that he had been with Paul already for an extended period of time (e.g., see 4:18, "I am fully satisfied, now that I have received from Epaphroditus the gifts you sent"). In any case, it is now clear why Epaphroditus has come and why Paul is penning this letter. The Philippians have sent him to bring a financial contribution, and Paul is writing a thank-you note.

The timing of his response is puzzling. If Epaphroditus has been with Paul for such a long period of time—long enough for him to become deathly ill, for the Philippians to get word of it, for him to learn that they were distressed, and for him then to recover—why is Paul only now writing to tell them that he has received the gift? Surely he was in communication with them before this (since they have heard that Epaphroditus arrived and that he later became deathly ill).

Scholars differ on how to evaluate the various pieces of this contextual puzzle. One solution is that there are two or possibly even three letters that have been edited together here, letters that come from different times and were written for different occasions. For simplicity's sake, I'll assume that there are two letters and explain how the theory works.

After Paul established the Philippian church, he left to pursue his apostolic work elsewhere. We don't know exactly where he was when he was writing this letter, or series of letters (Rome? Ephesus?), only that he was in jail. The Philippians learned of his needs and sent him a gift of money through the agency of one of their leading members, Epaphroditus. Paul thankfully received the gift and learned (from Epaphroditus himself?) about two major problems in the community: some false teachers had begun to stress the need to keep the Jewish Law (see 3:3–6), and two women in the congregation had argued over something in public (4:2–3). He wrote the Philippians a letter, partially embodied now in chapters 3–4, thanking them for the gift, warning against the false teachers, and urging Euodia and Syntyche to get along.

After Paul sent this letter, Epaphroditus became ill, the Philippians learned of it and became concerned, Epaphroditus heard of their concern and became distraught, and finally he recovered. In the course of the communication that was obviously going back and forth, Paul learned of the improved situation in Philippi. When Epaphroditus became well enough to travel, Paul sent another letter back

with him, a friendship letter explaining how things now fared with him and providing some renewed (but general) exhortations to the community to maintain their unity in Christ. Most of this letter is now found in Philippians 1–2. Some such scenario would explain why there are such differences between the first and second parts of the letter.

The Overarching Points of the Letter

Some of the issues that we have seen Paul address in other letters are found here as well. Throughout the Thessalonian and Corinthian correspondence, for example, we saw Paul emphasize that prior to the return of Christ in judgment, suffering was the lot of the Christian. This is part and parcel of his apocalyptic message, that even though the powers of evil have begun to be defeated through the cross of Christ, the end has not yet come. This continues to be an age under the dominion of the cosmic powers opposed to God, and those who stand against them will bear the brunt of their wrath. Christians will necessarily suffer, but all will be redeemed when Christ returns. This message continues to find expression here in Philippians, where Paul again portrays himself as one who suffers for the sake of Christ (e.g., 1:7, 17), where he again emphasizes that it is the call of the Christian to suffer (1:29), and where he again stresses that at Christ's return, all will be made right (3:20–21).

One other motif that holds the two parts of the letter together is the need for these Christians to maintain their unity by practicing self-giving love for one another. The message finds its most pointed expression in the request in chapter 4 for the two women Euodia and Syntyche to stop fighting, but it is expounded at greatest length in chapter 2. Here Paul recounts the actions of Christ on behalf of believers, in a passage that scholars have come to call the "Christ hymn" of Philippians (2:6–11; see box 15.4). This is one of the most poetic and beloved portions of all of Paul's letters; readers have long observed the striking cadences of the passage, its balanced rhythms and exalted views. It has all the marks of an early hymn sung in worship to Christ, and Paul quotes it in full because it makes an important point for his Philippian readers (cf. the prologue of the Fourth Gospel; see Chapter 8). Even though many of the

ANOTHER GLIMPSE INTO THE PAST

BOX 15.4 The Christ Hymn of Philippians

One of the first things any pagan author said about the early Christians was that they "sang hymns to Christ as if to a god" (Pliny the Younger's Letter X to Trajan). Many scholars believe that several of the earliest **Christ hymns** have been inserted by the authors of the New Testament in appropriate places of their writings (e.g., John 1:1–18). There are various ways to reconstruct the original form of the hymn that Paul appears to be citing in Phil 2:6–11. The following reconstruction shows how the hymn can be broken down into two major parts, each comprising three fairly equally balanced stanzas of three lines each; the first part indicates the progressive condescension (or self-humbling) of Christ, the second his subsequent exaltation by God.

The Condescension of Christ

Though he was in the form of God,
he did not regard equality with God
as something to be grasped.

But he emptied himself
taking the form of a slave
being born in human likeness.

And being found in human form,
he humbled himself,
and became obedient unto death.

The Exaltation of Christ

Therefore God also highly exalted him,
and gave him the name
that is above every name.

So that at the name of Jesus,
every knee should bend,
in heaven and on earth and under the earth.

And every tongue should confess
that Jesus Christ is Lord,
to the glory of God the Father.

---

details of the hymn are hotly disputed, its basic message is reasonably clear. Rather than striving to be equal with God, Christ humbled himself, becoming human and submitting to a death on the cross. God responded to this humble act of obedience by exalting Christ above everything else in creation, making him the Lord of all.

Paul does not cite this hymn simply because it is a powerful and moving expression of the work of Christ. Rather, he uses it because Christ's humble obedience provides a model of action for his followers, who should also lower themselves for the sake of others (2:1–4). Rather than seeking their own good and working for their own glory, Christians should seek the good and work for the glory of others. You will notice that Christ is not the only example of self-giving, sacrificial love in this chapter. Paul also claims that he himself is willing to be sacrificed for his Philippian converts (2:17),

that his companion Timothy seeks the interests of others rather than his own (2:19–24), and that their own Epaphroditus has risked everything for the sake of others (2:25–31). The Philippians are to follow these worthy examples, living in unity with one another through self-sacrificing love.

Whether this admonition had its desired effect or not is something we will probably never know. After this letter (or this sequence of letters), we hear nothing more from Paul of his relationship with his converts in Philippi.

PHILEMON

The letter to Philemon is a little gem hidden away in the inner recesses of the New Testament. Merely a single page in length, the size of an average Greco-Roman letter, it is the only undisputed

WHAT DO YOU THINK?

BOX 15.5   Was Paul Contemplating Suicide?

In an intriguing book that discusses suicide and martyrdom in the ancient world (*A Noble Death: Suicide and Martyrdom among Christians and Jews in Antiquity*. San Francisco: HarperSanFrancisco, 1992), Arthur Droge and James Tabor argue that the modern notion that suicide is a "sin" stems not from the Bible, but from the fifth-century Saint Augustine. Prior to Augustine, suicide per se was not condemned by pagans, Jews, and Christians. On the contrary, in certain circumstances it was even advocated as the right and noble thing to do. Indeed, several famous classical authors spoke of self-inflicted death as a "gain" over present inflictions that should be accepted joyfully. The protagonist of Sophocles's play *Antigone*, for example, says "if I am going to die before my time, I count it gain. For death is a gain to one whose life, like mine, is full of misery." She ends up, then, taking her own life. So, too, in a famous passage in Plato's *Apology*, Socrates, prior to ending his life by drinking hemlock, reflects that "the state of death is one of two things: either it is virtual nothingness . . . or it is a change and a migration of the soul from this place to another. And if it is uncon-

sciousness, like sleep in which sleeper does not even dream, death would be a wonderful gain."

It is striking that in Philippians, Paul indicates that for him "to live is Christ and to die is gain" (1:21). Is he contemplating suicide? Before making a snap decision that he could *not* have been (on the ground that suicide is a sin), it is important to remember that there were numerous instances of self-death that were "approved" in ancient texts: pagan (e.g., Socrates), Jewish (e.g., the martyrs discussed in the Maccabean literature), and Christian (e.g., early martyrs; and cf. Jesus himself, who is said in the Gospel of Mark to have "given his life" and in John to have "laid down his own life"). Even more important, we should notice how Paul himself talks about the possibilities of life and death in Philippians: "If it is to be life in the flesh, this would be a good work for me, and I do not know which *to choose* (the Greek here does not mean "prefer," as in some modern translations, but actually "choose"!), but I am constrained by the two things, having the desire to depart and be with Christ, for that is much better, but to remain in the flesh is more necessary for your sake" (1:22–24).

AT A GLANCE

BOX 15.6   Philippians

1. The letter is written to Christians whom Paul had converted in the city of Philippi, in eastern Macedonia. Paul wrote the letter from prison in an undisclosed location.

2. The letter, like 2 Corinthians, may be made up of two or more letters.

3. Paul wrote to thank the Philippian Christians for providing him with financial support, to express his joy at how well they were doing, to urge

them to maintain the unity of their congregation, and to put them at ease over their messenger Epaphroditus, who had taken ill but had recovered.

4. One of the key passages in the book, the "Christ hymn" of 2:5–11, may represent a pre-Pauline tradition (possibly a poem recited in praise of Christ?) that Paul inserted in an appropriate place in his letter.

epistle of Paul addressed to an individual. Rather than dealing with major crises that have arisen in the church, the letter concerns a single man, the runaway slave Onesimus, and his fate at the hands of his master, Philemon.

The Occasion and Purpose of the Letter

On first reading, there may be some confusion concerning the recipient of the letter, since it is addressed to three individuals and a church: "To Philemon our dear friend and co-worker, to Apphia our sister, to Archippus our fellow soldier, and to the church in your house" (v. 2). It is clear, however, that the letter is really addressed to a solitary individual because Paul speaks to a single person in the body of the letter ("you" singular in Greek, starting with v. 4 and continuing through v. 24). Evidently, the principal recipient is Philemon, since he is the first one to be named, just as Paul names himself first as the sender of the letter, prior to mentioning his "co-author," Timothy.

Our only clues about who Philemon was come from the letter itself. To begin with, he must have been a relatively wealthy Christian. He had a private home large enough to accommodate a church (i.e., a private gathering of Christians), and he owned slaves. Moreover, he evidently had valuable property that could be stolen, since Paul thinks that Onesimus may have run off with some of it, or else embezzled some of the funds entrusted to his charge (v. 18). Tradition holds that Philemon was a leader of the church in the town of **Colossae**, an identification possibly suggested by the fact that in verse 23 Paul conveys greetings from **Epaphras** who, according to Col 4:12, was a member of that church (although many scholars doubt that Colossians was actually written by Paul).

Wherever Philemon lived, he appears to have stood in Paul's debt, as Paul not so subtly reminds him: "I say nothing about your owing me even your own self" (v. 19). (By claiming to say nothing about it, of course, Paul says all that needs to be said!) For this reason, it appears likely that Philemon was one of Paul's converts. Apart from these things, we cannot say much about the man himself. As for the occasion of Paul's letter to Philemon, we know that Paul writes from prison (v. 1). Again, we don't know where he is or why he is being punished; it does

Figure 15.3 A bronze slave collar and a bronze slave plaque giving the name and address of the slave's owners. Slaves were often forced to wear such pieces of identification, much like dog tags today, with instructions to return them home if they ran away. This particular collar reads: "If captured, return me to Apronicanus, minister in the imperial palace, for I am a fugitive slave." It was discovered around the neck of a skeleton in Rome.

appear, though, that he anticipates being released (v. 22). While in prison, he met and converted Philemon's runaway slave Onesimus. When he speaks of Onesimus in verse 10 as one "whose father I have become," the Greek literally says "whom I begot"—the same phrase that Paul uses in 1 Cor 4:15 to refer to his converts in Corinth. The letter does not explicitly indicate whether Onesimus himself is imprisoned, for example, for having been caught in flight with some of his master's goods (v. 18), or whether he has come to visit Paul in jail as a friend of his master. The former option seems unlikely. The Roman Empire was a big place, and to think that Paul and the slave of one of his converts just happened to end up in the same jail cell, whether in a major urban center like Ephesus or in a small rural village, simply defies the imagination. On the other hand, if Onesimus was trying to get away from his master, why would he have gone straight to see one of his master's friends?

Recent studies of ancient Roman slavery law may provide an answer to this question. It was a legally recognized practice for a slave who had incurred his or her master's wrath to flee to one of the master's trusted associates to plea for his intervention and protection. The associate then served as a kind of official mediator, who would try to smooth out differences that had arisen through misunderstanding or even malfeasance. Malfeasance appears to be the issue here.

A possible scenario, then, would be something like the following. Philemon's slave Onesimus has done something wrong, possibly stealing from the household or incurring some other kind of financial loss for his master (v. 18). Rather than stand and face the consequences, he flees to Paul, the apostle who had converted his master to a new religion and who was therefore a known and respected authority for him. While visiting Paul, Onesimus himself becomes converted to faith in Christ, a conversion that proves convenient for the nasty little business at home: Paul can now urge Philemon to receive Onesimus back not only as a slave but as much more, as a brother in Christ (v. 16), one who has been "useful" to Paul and can now be "useful" to Philemon (v. 11). Here Paul is playing with words. Slaves were often given descriptive names, such as the Latin Fortunatus, which means "lucky," or Felix, which means "happy." The Greek name Onesimus means "useful."

In his mediatorial role, Paul urges Philemon not to punish his slave, who has now had a change of heart, and to charge the apostle himself with whatever debt he has incurred. Paul appears to know full well that Philemon will simply write off his loss, given the (spiritual) debt he owes him (vv. 18–19).

But is this all that Paul wants Philemon to do? Scholars have long debated the real meaning of his request, some thinking that Paul wants Philemon to **manumit** Onesimus (i.e., release him from his slavery), and others that he more specifically wants him to free him to engage in missionary work. Unfortunately, there is little in the text that suggests either possibility. Even verse 16, which urges Phi-

lemon to receive Onesimus "no longer as a slave but . . . [as] a beloved brother," is concerned with how he reacts to this errant member of his household; it does not tell him to change his status. (Consider an analogy: if I were to say to a female acquaintance, "I love you not as a woman but as a friend," this would not be to deny her gender!) It may be that the modern abhorrence of slavery has led interpreters to find in Paul a man ahead of his time, who also opposed the practice.

Yet Paul may be asking for something else. He emphasizes that Onesimus has been useful to him and states quite plainly that even though he would like to retain his services, he doesn't want to do so without the leave of his master (vv. 12–14). Moreover, at the end of his short letter, he asks Philemon to provide him with some kind of additional benefit in light of his own debt to Paul (the word "this" in v. 20 is not found in Greek; literally the text says, "Yes, provide me with a benefit"). What exactly is Paul looking for? Although Paul says not a word about Onesimus being set free, it appears that he would like to have him sent back. Perhaps Paul is asking Philemon to present him with a gift in the person of Onesimus, the slave.

Insights into Paul's Apostolic Ministry

The short letter to Philemon can provide us with some important insights into Paul's view of his apostolic ministry. One thing to observe is Paul's reciprocal relationship with his converts in this letter. In his other letters, he occasionally appears to be the all-knowing and all-powerful apostle, who makes his demands and expects people to follow them. On certain points that he feels strongly about, such as what his congregations believe about his apocalyptic message and how they treat the Jewish Law, he is altogether adamant. But on other issues he falls short of making demands. In the present instance, he expresses his desire as a request, although, to be sure, he phrases it in such a way that it would seem impossible for Philemon to turn him down. Even here, that is, while claiming not to assert his apostolic authority, Paul in fact appears to be doing so (cf. vv. 17–19).

A more important point to be gleaned from this letter relates specifically to its subject matter. It may come as a shock to modern readers that

Paul did not use this occasion to lambaste the evils of the institution of slavery. Not only does Paul fail to condemn slavery in general, but he does not denounce its practice among Christians in particular. He never commands his convert Philemon to manumit his brother in Christ, Onesimus, let alone set free all his other slaves. Was Paul not concerned for the plight of the oppressed?

Throughout his letters Paul shows a remarkable lack of concern for the social inequities of his world (a lack, that is, from a modern perspective). Despite his views that all people are equal in Christ—Jew and Gentile, slave and free, men and women (Gal 3:28)—Paul evidently did not see the need to implement this egalitarian ideal in the workings of society at large. He maintained that slaves should stay enslaved, that men should continue to dominate women, and that Christians as a whole should stay in whatever social roles they find themselves (see especially 1 Cor 7:17–24). But isn't this a bit short-sighted?

For us today it may indeed appear short-sighted, but for Paul it was based on the long view. For this evident lack of concern for a person's standing in society was related to his notion that the history of the world as we know it was soon going to come to a crashing halt when God entered into judgment with it. Soon the wrath of God would strike, annihilating the forces of evil and bringing in his kingdom, in which there would be no more pain or suffering or injustice or inequity. The equality that Paul sought was not one to be effected by social change; it was one to be brought by God himself, when he destroyed this evil age and set up his kingdom on earth. Little did Paul know that the faithful would still be around some nineteen centuries later to ponder his words.

AT A GLANCE

BOX 15.7 Philemon

1. Paul wrote the letter from prison, to a relatively wealthy Christian Philemon, about his runaway slave Onesimus, whom Paul had converted.

2. The letter is an intervention on Onesimus's behalf, urging Philemon not to punish him.

3. Paul may have wanted the letter to suggest that Philemon give him Onesimus for his own service.

TAKE A STAND

1. Pretend you are a Christian in the church of Galatia who thinks that Paul has gotten his gospel completely wrong, while the disciples of Jesus in Jerusalem—such as James and Cephas—have it right: to be a true follower of Jesus, the Jewish messiah, you have to follow the Jewish Law. Argue your case.

2. Pick any of the undisputed Pauline letters and show how knowing about its context can help you understand the positions that Paul takes in it.

SUGGESTIONS FOR FURTHER READING

See the suggestions at the end of Chapter 12.

 KEY TERMS

Abraham	Epaphras	justified	*paidagogos*
Cephas	Epaphroditus	manumission	Philemon
Christ hymn	Euodia and Syntyche	Onesimus	Philippi
Colossae	Galatia		

The Gospel according to Paul

THE LETTER TO THE ROMANS

WHAT TO EXPECT

The letter to the Romans is unique among Paul's writings, and is arguably the most important. It is the only letter Paul wrote to a church that he did not himself establish, and it is the only letter that does not try to solve the church's problems. Why would Paul write such a letter?

Anyone who can answer that question will have gained a significant insight into Romans. This chapter argues that Paul wanted to show the Roman Christians that his gospel message was on the up and up, hoping to convince them to provide some support (moral? financial?) for a missionary trip he planned to take farther west, to Spain. To make his case convincing, Paul had to explain carefully his understanding of the gospel of God, which brings salvation to all people, whether Jew or Gentile.

No book of the New Testament has proved to be more influential in the history of Christian thought than Paul's letter to the Romans. One of the most frequently quoted pieces of Christian literature during the early centuries of the church, it was awarded pride of place in the canon of Scripture as the first, and longest, of Paul's epistles. At the end of the fourth century it was instrumental in the conversion of Saint Augustine, a man whose own writings, based in large measure on his understanding of Romans, shaped the thinking of theologians throughout the Middle Ages. It stood at the center of the debates between Protestants and Catholics during the sixteenth-century Reformation, when Protestant leaders, such as Martin Luther, Philip Melanchton,

and John Calvin, saw it as the clearest exposition of Christian doctrine in the writings of the apostles. And the book continues to influence and inspire Christian readers in many lands and many languages today, theologians and laypeople alike, who cherish its words and puzzle over their meaning.

What, then, *is* this book that has inspired so much reflection and spawned so much controversy?

The short answer is that it is a letter by Paul to the Christian congregation in Rome. The historian who comes to the task of interpreting this letter cannot allow himself or herself to be so overawed by its historical significance as to lose sight of this simple fact. This was a letter that Paul wrote to a particular church. As with all his letters, this one had an occasion and was written for a reason.

THE OCCASION AND PURPOSE OF THE LETTER

In one important respect the letter to the Romans is unlike all of Paul's other letters: it is written to a congregation that Paul did not establish, in a city that he had never visited (see 1:10–15). Given what we have already seen about Paul's sense of his apostolic mission, this circumstance should give us pause. Paul's other letters were written to deal with problems that had arisen among those whom he had converted to faith in Christ. That clearly is not the case here.

Even more striking, Paul does not appear to be writing to resolve problems that he has heard about within the Roman church. The issues that he discusses appear to relate instead to his own preaching of the Christian gospel. This is clearly the case in chapters 1–11, but even his exhortations in chapters 12–15 are general in nature, not explicitly directed to problems specific to the Christians in Rome. Nowhere, for example, does Paul indicate that he has learned of their struggles and that he is writing to convey his apostolic advice (contrast all of his other letters). Possibly, then, he simply wants to expound some of his views and explain why he holds them. But why would he want to do so for a church that he has never seen?

There may be some clues concerning Paul's motivation at the beginning and end of the letter. At the outset he states that he is eager to visit the church to share his gospel with them (1:10–15). One might think, then, that Paul is preparing the Romans for his visit, giving them advance notice about what he is up to, but at the end of the letter a fuller agenda becomes more evident. In his closing, Paul indicates that he has completed the work that he has to do where he is—probably Achaia (in Corinth itself?), since according to 16:1 the person carrying the letter, **Phoebe**, is a deacon of the church in Cenchreae, Corinth's nearby port. Moreover, he says he is eager to extend his mission into the western regions, specifically Spain, and wants to visit Rome on the way:

> But now, with no further place for me in these regions, I desire, as I have for many years, to come to you when I go to Spain. For I do hope to see you on my journey and to be sent on by you, once I have enjoyed your company for a little while. (15:23–24)

In light of these comments, it appears that Paul is interested in more than simply meeting with the Roman Christians. He evidently wants them to provide support, moral and financial, for his westward mission; possibly he would like to use Rome as the base of his operation to the regions beyond. But why would he need to provide such a lengthy exposition of his views in order to get their support? Don't they already know who he is—the apostle to the Gentiles? And wouldn't they readily undertake to provide him with whatever assistance is needed?

Paul's lengthy discourse suggests either that the Romans have only a dim knowledge of who he is or, even more likely, that they have heard a great deal about him and that what they have heard has made them suspicious. If this is the case, or at least if Paul believes that it is, then presumably their suspicions would relate to the issues that Paul addresses throughout the letter, issues such as whether Gentiles and Jews can really be thought of as equal before God, and, if they can, (*a*) whether God has forsaken his promises that the Jews would be his special people and (*b*) whether Paul's "law-free gospel" to the Gentiles leads to lawless and immoral behavior (cf. Galatians).

The tone and style of this letter support the view that Paul wrote it to explain himself to a congregation whose assistance he was eager to receive. When reading through Romans carefully, one gets the sense that Paul is constantly having to defend himself and to justify his views by making careful and reasoned arguments (e.g., see 3:8; 6:1, 15; 7:1). Moreover, he makes this defense in a neatly crafted way, following a rhetorical style known in antiquity as the **"diatribe."** This involved advancing an argument by stating a thesis, having an imaginary opponent raise possible objections to it, and then providing answers to these objections. Consider the following rhetorical questions and answers:

> Then what advantage has the Jew? Or what is the value of circumcision? Much in every way. For in the first place the Jews were entrusted with the oracles of God. (3:1–2)

What then? Are we any better off? No, not at all; for we have already charged that all, both Jews and Greeks, are under the power of sin. (3:9)

What then are we to say? Should we continue in sin in order that grace may abound? By no means! How can we who died to sin go on living in it? (6:1–2)

Since the author both asks and answers the questions, the diatribe is remarkably effective in showing that he knows what he is talking about and that he is always right. By employing this style, Paul could effectively counter arguments that others had made against his teachings.

It should be noted that Paul's travel plans include not only the trip through Rome to Spain but an earlier jaunt to Jerusalem. Paul has collected funds for the poor Christians of Judea from his Gentile converts in Macedonia and Achaia (15:25–27) and appears uneasy over his upcoming trip to deliver them (15:30–32). He is openly fearful of "unbelievers" in Judea (presumably Jews who don't take kindly to his faith in Jesus) and apprehensive of his reception by the "saints" (presumably Jewish-Christians who have not warmed to his law-free gospel to the Gentiles). Some scholars have suspected that his letter to the Romans is a kind of trial run for presenting his views, an attempt to get his thoughts organized on paper before having to present them to a hostile audience in Judea.

There may be some truth in this, but chiefly the letter appears to be directed to the situation

Figure 16.1 Reconstruction of central city Rome, roughly as it would have looked soon after Paul's day.

that Paul expects to find where he addresses it, in Rome. He wants to use this church as his base of operation and knows (or thinks) that he has some opposition. He writes a letter to persuade this congregation of the truth of his version of the gospel. This gospel insists that Jews and Gentiles are on an equal footing before God: both are equally alienated from God and both can be made right with God only through Christ's death and resurrection. Moreover, the salvation that is offered in Christ comes to people apart from adherence to the Jewish Law, even though the Law itself bears witness to this faith as the only means of salvation. Indeed, Christ is the goal of this Law. Above all else, the gospel shows that God has not gone back on his promises to the Jews and has not rejected them as his people. In Christ, all the promises of God have come to fruition. Furthermore, the Romans can rest assured that this gospel does not lead to moral laxity: Paul is himself no moral reprobate, and he does not urge his converts to engage in wild and lawless activities.

THE THEME OF THE EPISTLE

Paul begins his letter to the Romans in his usual way, with a prescript naming and describing himself and his addressees, in which he anticipates the central concern of his letter, the meaning of his gospel (1:1–7). The prescript is followed by a thanksgiving to God for this congregation (1:8–15), in which he announces his plans to visit the congregation in order to share his gospel with them. Paul then gives a brief delineation of his gospel in two verses that scholars have long recognized as setting out the theme of the epistle:

> For I am not ashamed of the gospel; it is the power of God for salvation to everyone who has faith, to the Jew first and also to the Greek. For in it the righteousness of God is revealed through faith for faith; as it is written, 'The one who is righteous will live by faith.'" (1:16–17)

As he is occasionally wont to do, Paul has packed a great deal into these two verses. To help us understand the letter as a whole we should spend a few moments unpacking them.

1. *Paul is not ashamed of the gospel.* Paul may be writing the Romans to provide a relatively full and accurate account of the gospel message that he proclaims, perhaps in light of the partial and inaccurate report that he suspects they have already heard. He begins by assuring them that this message brings him no shame.

2. *Paul's gospel is God's powerful means of salvation.* The gospel that Paul preaches represents God's powerful act of salvation to the world; it is the way God has chosen to save those who are headed for destruction. The implication is clear: apart from this gospel, there would be no salvation.

3. *This salvation comes to those who have faith.* The English noun **"faith"** (*pistis*) and the verb **"believe"** (*pisteuein*) are translations of the same Greek root. For Paul faith (or believing) refers to a trusting acceptance of God's act of salvation. It does not refer simply to intellectual assent (as in "I believe you are right") but implies a wholehearted conviction and commitment. Throughout this letter Paul will insist that a person is put into a right relationship with God not by adhering to the dictates of the Jewish Law but by trusting God's act of salvation, that is, by believing in Christ's death and resurrection.

4. *Salvation comes first to the Jew and then to the Greek.* By "Greek" Paul simply means "Gentile" (since it stands in contrast to "Jew"). The salvation given in the gospel comes to both Jews and Gentiles. Jews received it first, since God is the God of the Jews who sent his Son to the Jewish people in fulfillment of the Jewish Scriptures (as Paul indicates both in Romans and throughout his writings), but it also comes to the Gentiles. Indeed, one of Paul's overarching points throughout this letter is that despite the advantages of the Jews (for example, having the Scriptures in which the promises of God are given), Jew and Gentile are on equal footing before God. All have sinned against God and all can be made right with God only by faith in Christ.

5. *The gospel reveals the righteousness of God.* Is it right that God should not give preference to his own people? Paul's gospel insists that God is unequivocally right in the way he brings about salvation; that is, he is **"righteous"** in the way that he makes all people, Jew and Gentile,

"right" with himself. This indeed is a major theme of Romans: God has not gone back on his promises and has not rejected his people the Jews. The death and resurrection of Jesus are the fulfillment of these promises, and faith in him is given first to Jews, and through them to the entire world.

6. *The Scriptures proclaim the gospel.* Paul claims that God has been perfectly fair and consistent ("righteous") in his treatment of the Jews and of all people because the Scriptures themselves teach that salvation is based completely on faith ("through faith for faith"), rather than on doing the works prescribed in the Jewish Law. Quoting the prophet Habakkuk, Paul emphasizes that a right standing before God, a standing that provides life, comes only through faith: "The one who is righteous will live by faith." To paraphrase: "the one who is made right with God through faith will find life."

Paul wants to emphasize that his gospel message is not something that he has made up himself. We saw in Galatians that he claimed to have received it through a revelation from God. We are going to see in Romans (as we saw in Galatians as well) that he also thinks that it is rooted in the Jewish Scriptures. In large measure, Romans is an extended argument that Paul's gospel of salvation, that is, his message of how a person, Jew or Gentile, comes into a right standing before God, derives from these sacred books.

PAULINE MODELS FOR SALVATION

Rather than launching into a passage-by-passage exposition of Romans, it may prove to be more useful for us to reflect in broader terms on what Paul has to say in this letter about his central theme, the gospel. (Remember: Paul is not speaking about a Gospel book that contains a record of Jesus' words and deeds but about his own gospel message.) Paul has a variety of things to say about it, and it is easy at places to become confused and wonder if Paul is being consistent with himself. In most instances (I'm not sure I can vouch for all of them), Paul is not inconsistent and is not himself confused. The

difficulty is that he discusses God's act of salvation in a number of different ways and sometimes does not clearly indicate which way he is thinking about. In other words, Paul has various modes of understanding, various conceptual models, of what it means to say that God brought about salvation through Jesus' death and resurrection.

There are at least two major models that Paul uses for understanding the importance of Christ's death in the letter to the Romans (see box 16.2). I will call these the **"judicial"** and the **"participationist" models** (these are not, of course, Paul's own terms). Paul does not see these as mutually exclusive of one another; on the contrary, he sometimes combines different conceptualities in one statement. For our immediate purposes, however, it will be useful to see how the models work in isolation from one another. Both models understand that human beings are somehow alienated from God and that Christ's death and resurrection somehow work to resolve that problem. The nature of the problem and the way Christ has solved it, however, are expressed differently in the two models.

The Judicial Model

Paul sometimes understands the human problem with respect to God and the divine solution to the problem in legal or judicial terms. In his mind there appears to be a rough analogy between the act of salvation and the human judicial process. The way it works, in simple terms, is as follows.

God is a lawmaker who has made laws for people to follow (all people, not just Jews); everyone, however, has broken these laws. God is also the judge before whom people appear as lawbreakers. The penalty for breaking God's laws is death, and everyone is found to be guilty as charged. This is the human problem. In Paul's words, "everyone has sinned" (i.e., broken God's laws, see Rom 3:23), and "the wages of sin is death" (i.e., death is the penalty for all who have sinned, Rom 6:23).

The divine solution to this problem is again conceived in judicial terms. Jesus is one who does not deserve the death sentence; he dies to pay the penalty for others. God shows that he is satisfied with this payment by raising Jesus from the dead (Rom 3:23–24; 4:24–25). Humans can avail themselves of

WHAT DO YOU THINK?

BOX 16.1   Two Different Ways of Salvation in Paul?

Some modern scholars have been struck by Paul's twofold insistence that (a) he himself continues to worship the Jewish God and (b) the Jewish Law can have no bearing on one's standing before God. How, ask these scholars, can he seriously propose (b) if he really means (a)? To our knowledge, all ancient Jews maintained that the Law was given by God precisely in order to show his people how to maintain their close, covenantal relationship with himself. How could someone abandon the Law—indeed, insist that the Law be abandoned—and yet still claim to follow this God?

One particularly interesting solution proposed in recent years is that we need to take seriously Paul's self-presentation as an apostle *to the Gentiles*. According to this view, Paul's letters were written not to Jews (whether Christian or non-Christian) but to Gentile followers of Jesus. It was to *these* people, and only to these people, that Paul maintained that adherence to the Law of the Jews would have no bearing on one's standing before God. Such people did not have to become Jews in order to enjoy a cove-

nantal relationship with God; for *them* it was Christ's death that brought them into this relationship. This does not mean, however, according to this view, that Jews were themselves to abandon the Law—or even, according to the most radical representations of this view, that they were to believe in Christ. Why would they need Christ if they were already standing in a covenantal relationship with God? There were, in short, two different paths of salvation: for Jews, salvation came through the Law; for Gentiles, it came through Christ. But since Paul's letters were addressed only to Gentiles, we learn there of only one of the two ways.

This is an intriguing and attractive hypothesis, argued at times with skill and erudition. But other interpreters of Paul have not been convinced. Perhaps the biggest problem is that Paul himself emphatically claims that everyone, Jew and Gentile, is equally guilty of sin before God, and that *all* (including Paul—a Jew himself!) are therefore justified equally—by faith in Christ and *not* by doing works of the Law (see especially Rom 3:9, 20, 23–26; Gal 2:15).

Christ's payment of their debt simply by trusting that God will find it acceptable. It is not a payment they have either earned or deserved; it is a beneficent act done on their behalf by someone else, an act that can be either accepted or rejected (3:27–28; 4:4–5). Those who accept it are then treated as if they are "not guilty" (even though they are in fact completely guilty) because someone else has accepted their punishment for them.

This, then, is the judicial model for understanding how salvation works. The problem is sin, which is understood to be a transgression of God's law; the solution is Christ's death and resurrection, which are to be received by faith. A person who has faith is restored to a right standing before God. Sometimes this way of looking at things is called Paul's doctrine of **justification by faith**. In this model the Jewish Law plays no role in salvation. Those who have broken the Law and incurred the sen-

tence of death cannot remove their guilt simply by obeying a number of other laws, just as a convicted embezzler will not be set free by pleading that he has obeyed all the traffic laws. The only way to be restored to a right standing before God (to be "justified") is through the death of Jesus, a payment of the penalty owed by others.

The Participationist Model

Most of us today have no trouble understanding how the act of salvation can be seen as analogous to a judicial process. The participationist model, however, is much harder to get our minds around. This is partly because it involves a way of thinking that is no longer prevalent in our culture. Under this second model, the human problem is still called sin, sin is still thought to lead to death, and Christ's death and resurrection still work to resolve the problem; but sin, death, and Jesus' death and resurrection all mean something *different* from what they mean under the judicial model.

Consider the following uses of the word "sin" in the book of Romans:

❖ Sin is in the world. (5:13)
❖ Sin rules people. (5:21; 6:12)
❖ People can serve sin. (6:6)
❖ People can be enslaved to sin. (6:17)
❖ People can die to sin. (6:11)
❖ People can be freed from sin. (6:18)

It should be reasonably clear that sin in these verses is not simply something that a person does, a disobedient action against God, a transgression of his laws. It is instead a kind of cosmic power, an evil force that compels people to live in alienation from God. The human problem under this model is that people are enslaved to this demonic power and are unable to break free from their bondage.

The power of sin is related to another power, the power of death. In the participationist model, death is not simply something that happens when a person stops breathing. It is a cosmic force that is intent on enslaving people; when it succeeds, it totally removes a person from the realm of God. Here again the situation is desperate; all people are subject to the overpowering force of death, and there is nothing that they can do to set themselves free.

As in the judicial model, the solution has to come from God himself, and it takes the form of

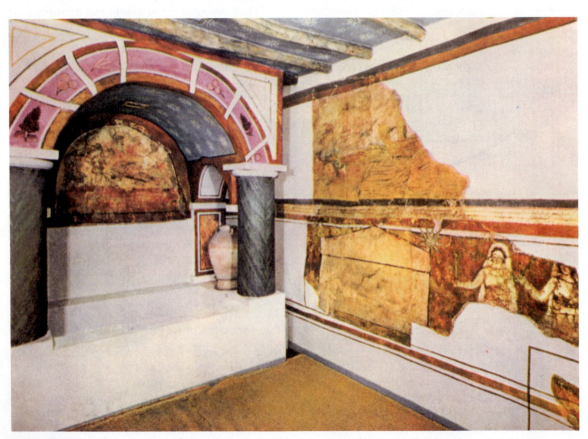

Figure 16.2 Baptism was an important Christian ritual for Paul's churches (see Rom 6:1–6), and it continued to be significant down through the centuries. Pictured here is the baptistry of the oldest surviving Christian church building (in the city of Dura, Syria), from about two centuries after Paul.

Jesus' death and resurrection. If the problem is enslavement to alien powers, then the solution must be liberation. Christ's death and resurrection provide freedom from the powers of sin and death that have subjugated the human race. How, then, does this liberation happen?

As an apocalypticist Paul knew that the cosmic force of sin was present in this world, but he came to believe that Christ's death had conquered the power of sin. He evidently came to believe this after he believed that Jesus had been raised from the dead. For Paul, Jesus' resurrection showed beyond any doubt that Jesus was no longer subject to the power of death, the most dreaded of all cosmic forces of evil. Jesus had conquered death through his resurrection; thus, reasoning backward, at Jesus' death he must have defeated the related powers (including the Devil and his agent, sin). Furthermore, Jesus' victory can lead to the salvation of others. That is to say, a person can participate with Christ in his victory (Rom 6:5–8): hence the name I have given this conceptual model. A person participates in this victory by being united with Christ in his death and resurrection. According to Paul, this happens when a person is baptized (Rom 6:3–4).

Baptism was a rite that had been practiced among the Christians from the earliest of times. In the early years of the religion, of course, no one was "born" a Christian; new members of the religion converted to it either from Judaism or from loyalty to one of the other cults. Those who converted were initiated into the church through the ritual of baptism. Baptism involved being immersed in water (later sources suggest that running water was to be preferred) while an officiant pronounced sacred words to indicate the significance of the act. For Paul the act was not simply significant as a symbolic statement that a person's sins had been cleansed or that he or she had entered into a new life; the act involved something that really happened. When people were baptized, they actually experienced a union with Christ and participated in the victory brought at his death (in the immersion under the water; see especially Rom 6:1–11).

Although Paul believed that a person who had been baptized had "died" with Christ, that is, had participated fully in Christ's victory over the power of sin, he evidently did not believe that such a person had yet been "raised" with Christ, that is, set completely free from the power of death. Paul knew full well that this had not yet occurred since people, even believers, continued to die! So he is quite emphatic that Christians have died with Christ but that they have not yet been raised with him (6:5, 8). They will be raised only when Christ returns and brings about the resurrection at the end of time. (You may recall that the major problem at Corinth was that some people believed that they had already been raised with Christ, and Paul had to insist that this was simply not so.) Until then, to be sure, Christians live in "newness of life" (Rom 6:4) because they are no longer subject to the power of sin. But their salvation is not

---

ANOTHER GLIMPSE INTO THE PAST

BOX 16.2 Judicial and Participationist Models of Salvation in Paul

The Judicial Model

Sin—human disobedience that brings a death penalty

Jesus' Death—payment of the penalty of sin

Appropriation—acceptance of the payment through faith, apart from works of the Law

The Participationist Model

Sin—a cosmic power that enslaves people

Jesus' Death—defeat of the power of sin

Appropriation—participation in Christ's victory through baptism yet complete, for the end has not yet come. Only when it does come will they "be united with him in a resurrection like his" (6:5).

Comparison and Contrast of the Two Models

The two **models of salvation** we have been looking at are ways of understanding something. They are not the thing itself. Paul's gospel is not "justification by faith" or "union with Christ." These are ways of reflecting on or thinking about his gospel. His gospel is God's act of salvation in Christ; the models are ways of conceptualizing how it worked.

The way salvation worked differed according to which model Paul had in mind. In both of them, the problem is "sin," but in one model, sin is an act of disobedience that a person commits, whereas in the other it is a cosmic force that works to enslave

people. In both models, the solution is provided by Christ's death and resurrection, but in one Christ's death pays the penalty for human disobedience, and in the other it breaks the cosmic power of sin. In both models a person has to appropriate the benefits of Christ's death, but in one this is done through faith, that is, a trusting acceptance of the payment, whereas in the other it occurs through baptism, a ritual participation in the victory.

As you read through Romans on your own, you can see that Paul does not neatly differentiate between these two models. Even though he uses the judicial model more consistently in chapters 1–4 and the participationist model in chapters 6–8 (to choose the clearest places), he does not ever think of them as conflicting with one another, and he regularly combines the two in the things he says. He would never have thought, for instance (so far

WHAT DO YOU THINK?

BOX 16.3 Jesus and Paul: Some of the Similarities

Some scholars consider Paul to be the "second founder" of Christianity. By that they mean that Paul's message differed significantly from that of Jesus, that whereas Jesus preached a message of repentance, urging people to return to God and keep his Law in view of the imminent day of judgment,

Paul preached the death and resurrection of Jesus for salvation. *Were* Jesus and Paul preaching the same message? In this box we consider some of their similarities; in the following box we consider some of their differences.

The Historical Jesus

Born and raised Jewish, and never saw self as departing from the truth of Judaism and the Jewish God

Proclaimed an apocalyptic form of Judaism

Expected the Son of Man to come from heaven in judgment during the lifetime of his own disciples

Dismissed the Pharisaic concern for scrupulous observance of the Law for a right standing with God

Taught the need for faith in God and saw the love of one's neighbor as the summing up of the Law

The Apostle Paul

Born and raised Jewish, and never saw self as departing from the truth of Judaism and the Jewish God

Proclaimed an apocalyptic faith in Christ

Expected Jesus to come from heaven in judgment during his (Paul's) own lifetime

Dismissed the need to observe the practices of the Jewish Law for a right standing with God

Taught the need for faith in Christ and saw the love of one's neighbor as the summing up of the Law

as we can tell), that someone could be baptized and so participate in Christ's death without also having faith and so trusting Christ's payment for sin. The two models go hand in hand; they are not so much confused as combined. Their coalescence is clear at a number of points in Paul's discussion. Why, for example, does Paul maintain that everyone is guilty before God? Because everyone has sinned, that is, committed acts of transgression (the judicial model, 3:23). Why has everyone sinned? Because everyone is enslaved to the power of sin (the participationist model, 3:9). Why is everyone enslaved to the power of sin? Because Adam committed an act of disobedience (judicial model), which allowed the power of sin to enter into the world (participationist model; 5:12). And so it goes.

Despite the fact that these two models neatly dovetail in Paul's own thought, it is often useful for readers to keep them conceptually distinct when reading through his letters, especially the letter to the Romans. Therefore, when you find Paul speaking of "sin" in any given verse, you should ask what he means by it. Is he referring to an act of transgression or a cosmic power? When he refers to

the effects of Christ's death and resurrection, is he thinking of a payment of a debt or liberation from bondage? In this connection, I should point out that these are not the only models that Paul uses to conceptualize what Christ has done for salvation (see box 16.5). They are, however, the two that appear most prominently throughout the book of Romans, as can be seen in the following section-by-section synopsis of the letter.

 ## THE FLOW OF PAUL'S ARGUMENT

❖ *The Human Dilemma: All Stand Condemned before God (1:18–3:20).* Paul's gospel follows a "bad news, good news" scheme that is designed to show the reader how desperate the situation is for all people, Gentiles and Jews. Gentiles have abandoned their knowledge of the one true God to worship idols, resulting in wild and rampant immorality (1:18–32). Jews are no better, for even though they have the Law and the sign of circumcision, they do

---

WHAT DO YOU THINK?

BOX 16.4   Jesus and Paul: Some of the Differences

The Historical Jesus	The Apostle Paul
The coming judge of the earth is the Son of Man.	The coming judge of the earth is Jesus himself.
To escape judgment, a person must keep the central teachings of the Law as Jesus himself interpreted them.	To escape judgment, a person must believe in the death and resurrection of Jesus, and not rely on observance of the Law.
Faith involves trusting God to bring his (future) kingdom to his people.	Faith involves believing in the (past) death and resurrection of Jesus.
Jesus' own importance lies in his proclamation of the coming of the end and in his correct interpretation of the Law.	Jesus' importance lies in his death and resurrection for sins.
The end of the age began in the lives of Jesus' followers, who accepted his teachings and began to implement them in their lives.	The end of the age began with the defeat of the power of sin at the cross of Jesus.

not practice the Law and so also stand condemned (2:1–29). Indeed, all people, Jews and Gentiles, have sinned against God (the judicial notion; 3:1–8), for all are under the power of sin (the participationist notion; 3:9). This view that Jew and Gentile are equally condemned before God does not at all represent a rejection of Judaism, however, for according to Paul it is the teaching of the Jewish Scriptures themselves (3:10–20).

❖ *The Divine Solution: Salvation through Christ's Death (3:21–31).* The Jewish Law gives the knowledge of sin but not the solution to sin. The solution comes in the fulfillment of this Law in the death of Jesus, a sacrifice for the sins of others to be received through faith. Performing the works of the Jewish Law does not contribute to this salvation through faith, so Jews have no grounds for boasting of

a special standing before God. Jews and Gentiles are on equal footing, all are made right with God through faith in the death of Jesus.

❖ *The Gospel Message Is Rooted in the Scripture (4:1–25).* The Father of the Jews, Abraham himself, shows that being made right with God comes through faith rather than by doing the works of the Law. Abraham was justified (made right with God) by trusting in God's promise before he was given the sign of circumcision (a "work" of the Law). His true descendants are those who continue to trust in God and in the fulfillment of his promises, which has now occurred in the death and resurrection of Jesus.

❖ *Christ's Death and Resurrection Bring Freedom from the Powers Opposed to God (5:1–8:39).* Those who believe in Christ have been made right with God and will be saved from the wrath of

ANOTHER GLIMPSE INTO THE PAST

BOX 16.5 Other Models of Salvation in Paul

In addition to the judicial and participationist models, Paul has other ways of conceptualizing God's act of salvation in Christ, even though he rarely explains how the analogies work in detail. Consider, for instance, the following.

❖ Sometimes Paul likens salvation to a reconciliation in which two people have had a falling out. A mediator (Christ), at a sacrifice to himself, intervenes and restores their relationship (e.g., see Rom 5:10 and 2 Cor 5:18–20).

❖ Paul often describes salvation as a **redemption**, in which a person's life is "purchased" by God through the price of Christ's blood, much as a slave might be purchased by gold (Rom 3:24; 8:23). Never does he explain, however, from whom or what the person is being purchased (the cosmic forces? the Devil? sin?).

❖ Paul sometimes portrays Christ's death as a sacrifice that, like the sacrifices of animals

in the Jewish Temple, was designed to bring atonement with God. This view embodies the ancient view that the blood of a sacrifice "covers over" the sins of the people: the technical term for this act of covering is "**expiation**" (Rom 3:25).

❖ At other times Paul compares salvation to a rescue from physical danger, in which a person is confronted with peril and certain death only to be saved by someone who heroically intervenes at the cost of his own life (see Rom 5:7–8).

These models are not all mutually exclusive; sometimes Paul applies several of them even within the same passage. Consider for yourself the theologically packed statement of Rom 3:21–26, where Paul uses the judicial, participationist, redemptive, and sacrificial models at one and the same time!

God that is coming upon this world (5:1–11). They will also be delivered from the reign of God's mortal enemy, death, which entered into the world through the disobedience of Adam, Christ's counterpart, but which has now been conquered by Christ's own act of obedience (5:12–21). Moreover, those who have been united with Christ in his death have participated in his victory over the power of sin; they can, therefore, and should, serve the new power that is over them in Christ, the divine power of righteousness (6:1–23). Before a person was united with Christ, he or she was compelled by the power of sin to violate the good Law that God had given, so that the Law led to condemnation rather than to salvation (7:1–25). But now the part of the self that was subject to sin, the flesh, has been put to death in Christ, so a person no longer needs to submit to its cravings and violate the Law (8:1–17). Those who have been united with Christ will eventually experience the complete salvation that will come when God redeems this fallen world (8:18–39).

❖ *The Gospel Message Is Consistent with God's Dealings with Israel and Represents a Fulfillment of His Promises (9:1–11:36).* Paul now deals with the major questions that have been simmering beneath the surface of the letter all along. If what he says is true, that God's act of salvation comes equally to Jew and Gentile alike, with no distinction, hasn't God gone back on his promises to Israel (9:6)? On the contrary, for Paul, God's decision to save Gentiles and Jews by faith is a fulfillment of his promises and is consistent with how he has always worked, as is evident from the Jewish Scriptures themselves. God has always chosen people not on the basis of their actions ("works") but on the basis of his own will (9:6–18). Indeed, the Jewish prophets indicate that God shows mercy on whom he chooses and that he had planned from ages past to make a people who were not his own (the Gentiles) into his own, whereas many of the Jews would be rejected (9:19–29). The

failing lies not in God but in the Jews who have not accepted Christ, for they have mistakenly supposed that God gave them the Law as a means for attaining a right standing before him, whereas the Law itself points to Christ (9:30–10:4). A right standing before God therefore comes exclusively through faith in Christ, and many of the Jews have been faithless (10:5–21). God himself, however, is faithful. He has remained true to his promises to the Jews, saving a remnant of them and using the salvation of the Gentiles to bring about his ultimate purpose, the salvation of all of Israel. Gentiles who have been added to the people of God must not therefore vaunt themselves against Jews; Israel is still the people of God's special calling, and he will once again bring them all to faith (11:1–36).

❖ *The Law-Free Gospel Does Not Lead to Lawless Behavior (12:1–15:13).* Those who believe in Christ give themselves to others in self-sacrificing love. Indeed, this is the new cultic act of worship that fulfills the old cultic acts of sacrifice (12:1–21). Believers in Christ are to be obedient to civil authorities (13:1–7), to follow the core of the Torah by loving others as themselves (13:8–10), to lead moral, upright lives in view of their coming salvation (13:11–14), and to refrain from passing judgment or doing things that offend others (14:1–15:6). Paul's law-free gospel, in other words, will not lead to lawless activities.

❖ *Close of the Letter (15:14–16:27).* Paul indicates his reasons for writing (15:14–21), discusses his travel plans (15:22–33), and sends greetings to a large number of persons in the congregation (16:1–27). Indeed, he greets so many people by name (twenty-eight altogether) that some scholars have questioned whether this final chapter originally belonged to the letter, since it was written to a congregation Paul had never visited. If the chapter is original to the book, it indicates that a number of people whom Paul had come to know in other contexts had moved to Rome or were known to be visiting there.

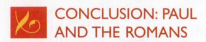

CONCLUSION: PAUL AND THE ROMANS

We do not know for certain whether Paul's plans to visit the congregation en route to Spain ever came to fruition. According to the book of Acts, Paul was arrested in Jerusalem before he could make the trip and was then, almost coincidentally, sent to Rome to stand trial before the Roman emperor for his alleged crimes (Acts 21–28). The author of Acts does not seem to know of any contact between Paul and the Christians living in Rome prior to his arrival; indeed, as customarily happens everywhere Paul goes in Acts, he ends up spending his days not with Christian believers but with recalcitrant Jewish leaders and, evidently, with anyone else who would come to hear him preach while under house arrest (Acts 28:16–31). There are later traditions that indi-

cate that Paul was eventually martyred in Rome; a member of the Roman church, writing sometime around 95 C.E., mentions Paul's death during the tyrannical persecution of the Christians during the reign of Nero (ca. 64 C.E.). This writing, traditionally attributed to the bishop of Rome, Clement, may indeed preserve a historical recollection.

Even though we cannot gauge whether Paul succeeded in his Western mission or, indeed, whether he ever gained a following among the Christians in Rome, we can say for certain that he succeeded in one respect. Romans is the most closely reasoned letter that survives from his pen, one that continues to intrigue scholars and to inspire believers. It lays out in the clearest terms he could muster important aspects of Paul's gospel, namely God's power that brings salvation for both Jew and Gentile.

AT A GLANCE

BOX 16.6 Romans

1. Unlike Paul's other surviving letters, Romans was written to a church he had not founded or even visited.

2. It was written evidently to secure the support of the Roman Christians for Paul's missionary endeavors further west, in Spain.

3. To receive their support, Paul had to correct some misperceptions about his gospel message. Thus he uses the letter to the Romans to explain his understanding of the gospel as God's act of salvation in Christ, for both Jew and Gentile, with no distinction.

4. A good portion of the letter deals with the implications of this gospel for understanding God's ongoing relationship with his chosen people Israel and the role of the Jewish Law, if in fact it does not contribute to salvation.

5. Paul has a variety of ways of conceptualizing his gospel message (these are best seen as complementary rather than contradictory), including

   a. a judicial model that expresses the act of salvation in legal terms.

   b. a participationist model that expresses the act of salvation in terms of union with Christ.

TAKE A STAND

1. Suppose you are a first-century Christian who does not appreciate the teachings of Paul. Among other things, you think that Paul's "law-free gospel" logically means that there can be no grounds for ethical behavior. Argue your case.

2. Summarize the forensic and participationist models of salvation in Paul and mount an argument that these two models are contradictory to one another in various ways. Now discuss: do you (actually) think that is true or not?

3. Your roommate has taken a class on the New Testament at another school and tells you that unlike Paul's other letters, there is no real "occasion" for the letter to the Romans. It is simply Paul laying out his views of the gospel. Do you agree with her? Give a lengthy argument for either position.

SUGGESTIONS FOR FURTHER READING

See also the suggestions at the end of Chapter 12.

Donfried, Karl P., ed. *The Romans Debate.* 2d ed. Peabody, Mass.: Hendrikson, 2005. A collection of significant essays by eminent New Testament scholars, who discuss (and disagree over) the occasion and purpose of Paul's letter to the Romans.

Gager, John G. *Reinventing Paul.* New York: Oxford University Press, 2000. An interesting and engaging study of Paul, which argues that Paul envisioned one way of salvation for Gentiles and another for Jews.

Gaston, Lloyd. *Paul and the Torah.* Eugene, Ore.: Wipf and Stock, 2006. A collection of significant essays by a leading proponent of the view that Paul's gospel of justification by faith in Christ apart from the works of the Law did *not* apply to Jews; for more advanced students.

Wedderburn, A. J. M. *The Reasons for Romans.* Edinburgh: T & T Clark, 2004. The most complete book-length discussion of the reasons that Paul wrote his letter to the Romans: it was to explain his law-free gospel to the predominantly Gentile Roman community in light of the tensions between Jews and Gentiles there and in view of his own imminent journey to Jerusalem.

KEY TERMS

baptism	faith	models of salvation	Phoebe
believe	judicial model	participationist	redemption
diatribe	justification by faith	model	righteous
expiation			

17

CHAPTER

In the Wake of the Apostle

THE DEUTERO-PAULINE AND PASTORAL EPISTLES

WHAT TO EXPECT

One of the most controversial issues in the study of the New Testament involves the authorship of its writings. We know of numerous ancient authors who forged books in the names of others, that is, who claimed to be someone famous in order to get a hearing for their views. Is it possible that any such pseudonymous books—forged writings—made it into the New Testament?

Scholars are reasonably sure that some of the letters of the New Testament written in Paul's name are pseudonymous. This chapter examines the six letters in question, the three Deutero-Pauline letters of Ephesians, Colossians, and 2 Thessalonians and the three Pastoral epistles of 1 and 2 Timothy and Titus, not only discussing their major themes but also showing why most critical scholars believe these books were not written by Paul, but by later authors claiming to be Paul, long after he was dead.

None of the New Testament writings that we have studied to this point can rightly be called pseudonymous. A pseudonymous writing, or "pseudepigraphon," to use the technical term (plural "pseudepigrapha"), is a book whose author writes under a false name, claiming to be someone other than he or she really is. None of the New Testament Gospels or the Johannine epistles or the book of Acts makes any such claim. As we have seen, these books were all written anonymously, only later to be attributed to persons named Matthew, Mark, Luke, and John.

We have found examples of pseudonymous writings outside the New Testament, however, in such works as the Gospels of Thomas and Peter.

Is it conceivable that any books of this sort came to be included in the New Testament canon? The consensus among critical scholars is a resounding yes. Before launching into a discussion of six such books—the three Deutero-Pauline epistles and the three Pastorals—I will set the stage a bit further by discussing the broader phenomenon of pseudonymity in the ancient world.

 PSEUDONYMITY IN THE ANCIENT WORLD

In the modern world, there are two kinds of pseudonymous writing. On the one hand, some authors assume a pen name simply to keep their

264

identity secret (sometimes, a transparent secret); this was the case when Samuel Clemens wrote as Mark Twain and when Marian Evans wrote as George Eliot. On the other hand, some authors deceptively claim to be someone famous. This happened, for example, some years ago when the so-called Hitler diaries turned up. These were forged to look like journals kept by Adolf Hitler through World War II. At first, the forger's craft fooled just about everyone, but before long experts determined beyond any doubt that the books were not authentic. They were then relegated to the trash heap of historical curiosities.

Thus, in the modern world, a **"forgery"** is a kind of pseudonymous writing in which an author falsely claims, for one reason or another, to be a famous person. Antecedents for this kind of pseudonymous writing can certainly be found in the ancient world. Indeed, forgery was a relatively common and widely recognized practice in antiquity. This was a world in which there were no copyright laws and, in fact, no legislation of any kind to guarantee literary ownership. Nor were means available for the mass production of literature; authors could not count on the worldwide dissemination of their books or assume that the kind and quality of their work would be widely known. Books were manufactured one at a time, by hand. New copies were ponderously and painstakingly made from old ones and disseminated slowly and sporadically at best. Libraries were rare, and most people could not read in any case. For most people, reading a book meant hearing someone else read it aloud.

We know that forgery was relatively widespread in this world because the ancients themselves say so. Authors throughout Greek and Roman antiquity make numerous references to the practice and issue frequent warnings against it. Some authors even mention books that were falsely written in their own names. One famous author from the second century C.E., the Roman physician Galen, went so far as to write a book explaining how his authentic writings could be distinguished from those forged by others. More commonly, literary people had to judge whether a book was authentic or not on the basis of its writing style and contents.

A number of factors motivated ancient authors to produce documents in someone else's name. For some forgers, there was the profit motive. If a new library began collecting old books and advertised its willingness to pay gold for original copies, an amazing number of "originals" could show up (sometimes of works that no one had ever heard of before!). At other times forgers produced writings in the name of an enemy in order to make him look bad. This happened, for example, to the infamous Greek philosopher Epicurus. One of his personal enemies, a man named Diotemus, wanted to impugn him for being completely immoral and so wrote fifty obscene letters in Epicurus's name and put them in circulation. These letters did nothing to help Epicurus's already dubious reputation. At yet other times a forger produced his work simply to see if he could get away with it, to pull the wool over the eyes of his readers—as sometimes happens even today.

But perhaps the most common reason to forge a writing in antiquity was to get a hearing for one's own views. Suppose that you as an amateur philosopher wanted to present your ideas to the world, not to make yourself rich or famous but simply because, in your judgment, the world needed to hear them. If you wrote in your own name (Mark Aristides, or whatever), no one would be much intrigued or feel compelled to read what you had to say. But if you signed your treatise "Plato," then it might have a chance.

Someone who wrote in the name of a famous person was therefore not necessarily driven by wicked intent. Sometimes the writer's motive was pure as the driven snow, at least in his or her opinion.

Ancient forgers used some fairly obvious and standard techniques to convince their readers that they were who they said they were. To begin with, the mere claim to be somebody carries a lot of weight with most readers, ancient and modern. If a book begins with the words "I Moses write to you these words" or "The vision which I, Abraham, had" or "Paul an apostle of Jesus Christ, to the saints who are in Ephesus," then most readers will simply assume that the alleged author is the actual author, barring the presence of something obvious in the text to discourage the assumption. The trick of the forger was to make sure that nothing of the sort could be found. Forgers, therefore, typically tried to imitate the writing style of the author they were claiming to be. Of course, some forgers made a more strenuous effort along these lines than others, and some were more gifted at it.

Such imitation was actually an art that was taught in the schools of higher learning as part of rhetorical training. Advanced students were regularly required to compose a speech on a set theme imitating the style of a great orator of the past.

Forgers typically added elements of verisimilitude to their works, that is, comments designed to make the writing appear to have come from the pen of its alleged author. In a forged epistle, for example, such comments might include off-the-cuff references to an event that the reader could be expected to recognize as having happened to the alleged author, personal requests of the recipient (why would anyone other than the real author ask his reader to do something for him?), or even an emphatic insistence that he himself really is the author, sometimes making it appear that the author "doth protest too much." One of the most interesting ploys along these lines is when a pseudonymous author insists that his readers not read books that have been written pseudonymously: who would suspect such an author to be a forger himself? An intriguing example occurs in a Christian book of the fourth century called the *Apostolic Constitutions,* a set of church instructions allegedly written by the apostles after Jesus' resurrection. The book admonishes its readers not to read books that falsely claim to be written by the apostles!

This final ploy can tell us something about the attitudes toward forgery among people in antiquity. Some modern scholars have argued that the practice was so widespread that nobody passed judgment on it; others have claimed that forgeries were so easily detected that everyone could see through them and simply accepted them as literary fictions. The ancient sources themselves suggest that both views are wrong. Forgers were commonly successful because people did not always see through them. When they did see through them, they were usually not amused. Indeed, despite its common occurrence, forgery was almost universally condemned by ancient authors.

Scholars in the ancient world went about detecting forgeries in much the same way that modern scholars do. They looked to see whether the ideas and writing style of a piece conformed with those used by the author in other writings, and they examined the text for any blatant anachronisms, that is, statements about things that could not have existed at the time the alleged author was

writing (like the letter reputedly from an early seventeenth-century new world colonist that mentions "the United States"). Arguments of this kind were used by some Christian scholars of the third century to show that Hebrews was not written by Paul or the Book of Revelation by John, the son of Zebedee. Modern scholars, as we will see, concur with these judgments. To be sure, neither of these books can be considered a forgery. Hebrews does not claim to be written by Paul (it is anonymous), and the John who wrote Revelation does not claim to be the son of Zebedee (it is therefore homonymous). Are there other books in the New Testament, though, that can be considered forgeries?

The question itself brings us up against a problem of terminology. Many scholars are loath to talk about New Testament "forgeries" because the term seems so loaded and suggestive of ill intent. Still, it is striking that few scholars object to using the term "forgery" for books, even Christian books, that occur outside the New Testament. This may suggest that the refusal to talk about New Testament forgeries is not based on historical grounds but on faith commitments (either of the scholars or of their audiences); that is, it represents a theological judgment that the canonical books need to be granted a special status. A historical introduction to these books should not, however, be so bashful.

In any event, as I suggested, the authors of forged documents may well have seen themselves as upright individuals who had good reasons for doing what they did. If they wrote in the name of some famous person, however, they were still producing a forged document. This is no less true for the canonical letter allegedly to Titus than for the noncanonical letter allegedly from Titus.

What now can we say about the Deutero-Pauline epistles of 2 Thessalonians, Colossians, and Ephesians? What are these letters about, and did Paul, their alleged author, really write them?

 ## THE DEUTERO-PAULINE EPISTLES

2 Thessalonians

We can begin with the letter whose authorship remains in greatest doubt, 2 Thessalonians. As was the case with 1 Thessalonians, this letter claims to be written by "Paul, Silvanus, and Timothy to

WHAT DO YOU THINK?

BOX 17.1   Is Forgery Too Negative a Term?

Many scholars prefer not to refer to early Christian writings produced by an unknown author in the name of a famous apostle as "forgeries." For these scholars, the term "forgery" is too negative and so should not be used. They prefer instead to call these works "pseudepigrapha."

It is understandable that scholars feel this way: some of these books, after all, are in the Bible. But calling them "pseudepigrapha" does not actually help matters much, except in that this term does not have negative connotations for most people, since they do not know what it means. But the term literally means "writings inscribed with a lie." That is not much of an improvement over the term "forgery," which is the word we normally use to refer to books whose authors lie about their identity instead of saying who they really are.

The ancient people who talked about forgery used negative terms for it as well. Most often books with false authorial claims were called "lies" (in Greek: *pseudoi*) and "bastards" (*notha*). The latter term had just as many negative connotations in antiquity as today. It referred to a book that did not really belong to the person claimed as its author. The book was, then, illegitimate, a bastard.

Some scholars have claimed that in the ancient world it was acceptable practice to write books in someone else's name. Recent research has shown that this view is not correct, as will be seen in box 17.3.

---

the church of the Thessalonians" (1:1). Whoever the actual author of the letter was, its occasion appears to be reasonably clear. It was written to a group of Christians who were undergoing intense suffering for their faith (1:4–6). We do not know how this suffering manifested itself—whether there was some kind of official governmental opposition to these people, or hostility from the local population, or something else. We do know that the author wrote to assure his readers that if they remained faithful, they would be rewarded when Christ returned in judgment from heaven. At this "parousia" of Jesus, those who opposed them and rejected their message would be punished with "eternal destruction," but the saints would enter into their glorious reward (1:7–12).

A second reason for the letter was that some members of this Christian community had come to believe that the end of time had already come upon them, that is, that the day of judgment was going to happen not in the indefinite future but right away (2:1–2). Some of those who thought this found confirmation in prophecies spoken by members of the congregation and, still more interesting, in a letter that was reputedly written by Paul (2:2). The author of 2 Thessalonians, claiming to be the real Paul, warns his readers not to be deceived. What-

ever an earlier forger may have asserted, the end had not yet come because there were certain events that had to transpire first (2:3).

The author describes these events in an apocalyptic scenario that sounds very much like what we find in the Apocalypse of John (see Chapter 21). A kind of antichrist figure is to be revealed on earth before Christ returns; this "lawless person" is ultimately "destined for destruction" (2:3). Exalting himself above every other "so-called god or object of worship," he will eventually take his seat in God's Temple in Jerusalem, "declaring himself to be God" (2:4). The author reminds his readers that he fully informed them of this scenario when he was with them (2:5); moreover, it has obviously not yet occurred, since no one has yet come forward to assume the grandiose role of this antichrist. Indeed, the author mysteriously indicates that there is some supernatural force restraining the lawless one for the time being, but once this force is removed, he will make his appearance, setting in motion the final confrontation between Christ and the forces of evil headed by Satan (2:6–12).

In large measure, then, this letter was written to assure this congregation of Christians that the end was not yet upon them. As "Paul" fully instructed them previously (2:5), Christ would not return until this apocalyptic scenario played itself out.

We discover in the final chapter of the book that the problem in the congregation was not simply one of establishing an appropriate timetable for upcoming events. Some members of this church were so persuaded that the end was absolutely imminent that they had quit their jobs and were simply waiting for it to happen (3:6–15). Their decision had grave social implications. Those who kept their jobs were having to feed those who hadn't, and this situation of apocalyptic freeloading was a source of tension in the congregation. In terms quite reminiscent of 1 Thessalonians, the author reminds his readers how he and his companions had lived among them, working for their own meals and refusing to be a burden on others (3:7–10). He insists that they do likewise (3:11–15).

The question is: Was this author actually Paul? It must be admitted that in places, at least, he *sounds* like Paul, for instance, in the prescript, which is very close to the opening of 1 Thessalonians, and in the recollection of Paul's toil among the Thessalonians when he was first with them. And a number of Pauline themes are sounded throughout the epistle: the necessity of suffering, the expectation of ultimate vindication, and the apocalyptic hope that stood at the core of Paul's gospel.

But do these similarities mean that Paul wrote the letter? The problem from a historian's point of view is that someone who had decided to imitate Paul would no doubt try to sound like Paul. If both Paul and an imitator of Paul could sound like Paul, how could we possibly know whether we are dealing with the apostle himself or one of his later followers?

There is, in fact, a way to resolve this kind of historical whodunit, and it involves looking at the other side of the coin, that is, at the parts of this letter that do not sound like Paul. These peculiar features provide the best indicators of whether the letter is authentic or was written by a member of one of Paul's churches after the apostle himself had passed from the scene. Such negative evidence is useful because we would expect an imitator to sound like Paul, but we would not expect Paul not to sound like Paul. It is, therefore, the differences from Paul that are most crucial for establishing whether Paul wrote this, or any other, disputed letter.

With respect to 2 Thessalonians, the most intriguing issue is one that I have already alluded to: the author writes to assure his readers that even though the end will be soon, it will not come right away. Other things must happen first. They should therefore hold on to their hopes and their jobs, for there is still time left. Does this sound like the same person who urged the readers of his first letter to stay alert so as not to be taken by surprise when Jesus returns (1 Thess 5:3, 6), since the end would come with no advance warning, "like a thief in the night" (1 Thess 5:2), bringing "sudden destruction" (1 Thess 5:3)? According to 2 Thessalonians there will be plenty of advance warning. That which is restraining the man of lawlessness will be removed, then the antichrist figure will reveal himself, exalt himself above all other objects of worship, establish his throne in the Jerusalem Temple, and declare himself to be God. Only then will Christ return. How is this like a thief in the night who comes when people least expect it?

These difficulties make it hard to see how Paul could have written both letters to the Thessalonians. One of the most interesting things about the second one is how it ends: "I, Paul, write this greeting with my own hand. This is the mark in every letter of mine; it is the way I write" (3:17). This means that "Paul" dictated the letter to a scribe but then added his own signature to it, as he did, for example, in Galatians (see Gal 6:11). What is peculiar is that he claims this to be his invariable practice, even though he does not appear to have ended most of his other letters this way, including, 1 Thessalonians! The words are hard to account for as Paul's, but they make perfect sense as the words of an imitator of Paul who wants his readers to be assured that despite the fact that they have received at least one letter that was forged in Paul's name (2:2), this is not another one.

We obviously don't know who actually wrote this letter if it wasn't Paul and can only speculate about when the real author was living. We can assume that he wrote sometime after Paul had died, possibly near the end of the first century, when writing letters in Paul's name became both more feasible and, from what we can tell, more popular. Moreover, we know that during the period some Christian groups were beginning to face increased hostilities within their social contexts and that some of them were turning to a renewed hope in the return of Christ in light of these conflicts.

Thus the author must have been a Christian from one of the churches that Paul established, who evidently had read 1 Thessalonians (hence, for example, the similar prescript). He wrote to help resolve the problems that Christians of his day were facing, choosing to do so in the name of Paul, the founder and hero of his church, one whose words would be heard and heeded. Writing as the apostle himself, he urged his readers to keep the faith and to maintain their hope but not to expect the end of the age in the immediate future. God's plan for the end was in the process of being implemented, but believers must not be too eager, living only for tomorrow and not tending to the needs of today. They must suffer boldly and wait faithfully for the day of judgment in which their longings would be fulfilled and their afflictions vindicated.

Colossians

As is the case with 2 Thessalonians, scholars continue to debate the authorship of Colossians, although here there is an entirely different set of problems to consider. There is no real problem, however, in understanding the ostensible occasion of the letter. "Paul" is in prison for preaching the gospel (4:3). While there, he has heard news of the church in Colossae (1:3), a small town in western Asia Minor not far from the larger cities of Hierapolis and Laodicea. "Paul" did not establish this church, but his coworker and companion Epaphras, a citizen of the place, did (1:7–8, 4:3). The news that "Paul" has learned about the Colossians is mixed. On the one hand, he is excited and pleased to learn that they have converted to faith in Christ and have committed themselves to his gospel through the work of Epaphras (1:7–8). On the other hand, he has learned that there are false teachers among them who are trying to lead them into a different kind of religious experience (2:4). He is writing to address the situation.

The author of the letter alludes to his opponents' notions but does not give a detailed description of them, on the assumption, we might suppose, that his readers already knew full well what he was talking about. He labels this new teaching a "philosophy and empty deceit" (2:8) and counters it by

indicating that believers have already experienced a "spiritual circumcision" (2:11). Moreover, he insists that since Christ has erased the requirements of the Jewish Law for believers through his death, they need not follow regulations concerning what to eat and concerning what special days to keep as religious festivals (2:13–17). These passages make it appear that the false teachers were advocating some form of Judaism, perhaps like the opponents of Paul in Galatia. But they also insisted on "self-abasement and the worship of angels," basing their appeal on special visions that they have had (2:18–19). This suggests that they advocated an ascetic lifestyle and possibly the ecstatic adoration of higher beings.

Scholars have debated the precise nature of this false teaching for many years. In general terms "Paul's" opponents were evidently promoting some kind of **Jewish mysticism**, comparable to that known from other ancient texts, in which people were encouraged to experience ecstatic visions of heaven and thereby be transported to the divine realm where they would find themselves filled with the joy and power of divinity. Such people were commonly ascetic, urging that bodily desires must be avoided if one wanted to escape the body and enjoy the pleasures of the spirit. If these persons were Jews, they may well have rooted their asceticism in the Jewish Scriptures and so, perhaps, urged their followers to keep kosher food laws, observe the Sabbath, and if they were males to be circumcised.

In response to these views, the author of Colossians insists that Christ himself is the fullest expression of the divine. In his words, Christ is the very "image of the invisible God, the firstborn of all creation" (1:15). There is little reason for Christian believers to worship angels when they can worship the one "in whom all the fullness of God was pleased to dwell" (1:19). Indeed, the other invisible beings are said to have been both created by and made subservient to Christ himself: "For in him all things in heaven and on earth were created, things visible and invisible, whether thrones or dominions or rulers or powers—all things have been created through him and for him" (1:16). Moreover, Christ alone is responsible for the ultimate benefits bestowed upon the believer. It is Christ who has reconciled all people to God (1:21–22;

BOX 17.2 The Resurrection of Believers in Paul and Colossians

If Paul did write Colossians, then his views about the time and significance of the resurrection of Christians changed, for here believers are said already to "have been raised with Christ" (3:1). Recall that 1 Corinthians was written in large measure against those who believed that Christians had already come to enjoy the blessings of the resurrected existence (see 1 Corinthians 15). The contrast in the verb tenses of Rom 6:4 and Col 2:12 (see italics) is also telling.

Rom 6:4

For if we have been united with him in a death like his, we will certainly *be united* with him in a resurrection like his. . . . But if we have died with Christ, we believe that we *will* also be *raised* with him.

Col 2:12

When you were buried with him in baptism, you *were also raised* with him through faith in the power of God, who raised him from the dead.

The question many interpreters have raised over the years is: Which is it? Have Christians already been raised or not?

2:13–15). When he did so, he destroyed everything that brought alienation, including the Law with all of its "legal demands" (2:14). What sense is there, then, in returning to the adherence to the Law? For this author, Christ destroyed the need to do so, and those who are in Christ can enjoy the full benefits of the divine (2:10, 14–19).

These benefits, which are conferred only through Christ, include an exalted status that is already available to the believer. This author maintains that there is no need for physical circumcision for those who have experienced the real, spiritual circumcision that comes through faith in Christ (2:9–10), or for ecstatic worship of angels for those who have already been raised up to the heavenly places in Christ (2:12; 3:1–3), or for human regulations of what to handle and what to eat, which give only the appearance of piety, for believers in Christ who have a full experience of the divine itself (2:20–23). Indeed, all that the Colossians have sought through their mystical experiences is already theirs in Christ, so long as they do not depart from the gospel message they have heard (2:23).

The Colossians are therefore to enjoy the full experience of the divine as those who have been raised to the heavenly places in Christ (3:1). This does not mean, however, that they can ne-

glect their physical lives in this world or behave as though their bodies no longer matter. Indeed, they must go on living in this world until Christ returns. This means maintaining moral and upright lives. Thus the author gives a number of moral exhortations concerning vices to avoid (fornication, passion, greed, and the like; 3:5–11) and virtues to embrace (compassion, kindness, humility, and the like; 3:12–17). In addition, he gives advice to different social groups within the congregation concerning their interactions with one another, addressing wives and husbands (3:18–19), children and fathers (3:20–21), slaves and masters (3:22–4:1).

The letter closes with some final instructions (4:2–6), greetings to members of the Colossian church, both from "Paul" and those with him (4:7–17), and his own signature and final benediction (4:18). But was this actually Paul's signature?

In a number of ways, this letter looks very much like those that Paul himself wrote. The prescript written in the names of both Paul and Timothy, the basic layout of the letter, and the closing all sound like Paul, and a number of important Pauline themes are sounded throughout: the importance of suffering in this world, Jesus' death as a reconciliation, and the participation of believers in

Jesus' death through baptism. Paul may well have written this letter.

There are, however, solid grounds for questioning Paul's authorship of this letter. One of the most compelling arguments depends on a detailed knowledge of Greek, for the writing style of Colossians differs markedly from that found in Paul's undisputed letters. Whereas Paul tends to write in short, succinct sentences, the author of Colossians has a more complex, involved style. The difference is not easily conveyed in English translation, in part because the long complicated Greek constructions have to be broken up into smaller sentences to avoid making them appear too convoluted. Col 1:3–8, for example, consists of just one sentence in Greek. The problem is not that this is bad or un-

acceptable Greek but that Paul wrote in a different style (just as Charles Dickens and William Faulkner both wrote correct English, but in very different ways). This kind of evidence has convinced a large number of linguistic specialists that Paul did not write the letter.

Other arguments can be more readily evaluated just from the English text. The most striking is one that you may have already surmised: this author believes that Christians have participated with Christ not only in his death but also in his resurrection. He is, in fact, quite emphatic on this critical point: believers have already been raised with Christ "in the heavenly places" to enjoy the full benefits of salvation (2:12; 3:1). Paul himself, however, is equally emphatic: even though Christians have "died" with

ANOTHER GLIMPSE INTO THE PAST

BOX 17.3 Forgeries, Philosophical Schools, and Secretaries

New Testament scholars often claim that when some unknown author wrote 1 Timothy, claiming to be Paul, or some other author wrote 2 Peter claiming to be Peter, their actions would not have been judged unacceptable or unethical in the ancient world. According to these scholars, it was common for followers of a philosopher or other teacher to write a treatise in his name, not claiming any credit for themselves, since all their ideas were given them by their master. To sign their own name would be arrogant. And so, out of humility, they signed their teacher's name.

This is an interesting idea. The problem is that there is virtually no evidence for it—even though scholars state the view all the time. If you ever hear a scholar say such a thing, ask him what his ancient evidence for it is. You will almost always find yourself faced with a tongue-tied scholar.

Most often it is said that this was a common practice in the Pythagorean schools of antiquity—that is, among the followers of the philosopher Pythagoras, years and centuries after his death. The evidence for the practice, however, is extremely thin—just one off-the-cuff comment by one philosopher, Iamblichus, living eight hundred years after Pythagoras had

died. There is nothing to suggest that this later philosopher was right that it was a widespread practice (if it was, why does no one else mention it?), and he says nothing about it being practiced in schools other than that of Pythagoras. There is nothing to suggest that the early Christians (living centuries before Iamblichus) had ever heard of any such thing.

It also should not be thought—as again many New Testament scholars have claimed—that the writings produced in someone else's name can be explained by claiming that a person's "secretary" actually wrote a book, putting his own stamp on it, or even just making it up himself in someone else's name. The evidence for secretaries doing anything besides taking dictation or maybe some simple copyediting is again very sparse, indeed, as the most recent studies have shown. Secretaries were not employed to write books for someone else. In fact, such a practice is almost never mentioned in any of our ancient sources. What was commonly practiced—and talked about and condemned—was forgery, writing a work while claiming to be a famous author, knowing full well you were someone else. (For further information on philosophical schools and secretaries, see the book *Forged* in Suggestions for Further Reading.)

Christ in their baptism, they have not yet been raised with him. And they will not be raised until the very end, when Christ returns (see box 17.2). Not only does Paul stress this point in his most explicit discussion of a baptized person's participation with Christ in his death in Romans 6, he also argues precisely this point against his opponents in Corinth, who claimed already to have experienced the resurrection and so to be ruling with Christ.

How is it that Paul in his undisputed letters can be so emphatic that believers have not yet experienced the resurrection with Christ, whereas the author of Colossians can be equally emphatic that they have? It is certainly possible that Paul changed his mind, either because he genuinely thought better of it later (although this seems unlikely given his vehemence on the point) or because when attacking a different heresy, he had to take a different approach, either consciously misrepresenting his views or forgetting what he had earlier said. It seems more plausible, however, that Paul went to his grave believing, and consistently insisting, that Christians had not yet been raised with Christ. If so, it is hard to accept that he wrote the letter to the Colossians.

Who wrote the letter if Paul did not? We will never know, but he must have been a member of one of Paul's churches who saw the apostle as an ultimate authority figure. This person wrote a fictitious letter to deal with a real problem that he had come to know about, possibly within his own congregation. If this is what happened, however, then the address to the "Colossians" is itself probably a fiction, for the town, and any church that happened to be there, was destroyed by an earthquake around the year 61 C.E. It may well be that this unknown author had access to one or more of Paul's other letters, including almost certainly the letter to Philemon, since the same names appear in the greetings of the two letters. Using these other letters as models, he penned an authoritative denunciation of a false philosophy that had begun to spread, putting this pseudonymous writing into circulation as an authentic letter of the apostle Paul.

Ephesians

While the arguments against the Pauline authorship of 2 Thessalonians and especially of Colossians have persuaded a number of scholars, with

the letter to the Ephesians the matter is even more clear-cut. The majority of critical scholars are convinced that Paul did not write this letter.

Before jumping to the question of authorship, we should begin once more with the ostensible situation lying behind the epistle. Unlike the other letters of the Pauline corpus, the occasion for Ephesians is notoriously difficult to determine. We do learn that "Paul" was writing from prison to Gentile Christians (3:1). There is some question, though, concerning where the epistle was sent and for what reason.

Most English translations indicate that the addressees are "the saints who are in Ephesus" (1:1), but the words "in Ephesus" are not found in the earliest and best Greek manuscripts of this letter. Most textual experts think that the words were not in the letter originally but were added by a scribe after it had already been in circulation for a time. If so, then Ephesians was written as a kind of "circular letter," designed to make the circuit of a number of Pauline churches, sent to "the saints who are faithful" but not to the saints of any particular location. Such a letter would have been copied in several of the places that it was received, including the city of Ephesus. It appears that the copyist in Ephesus decided to personalize the letter by adding the words "in Ephesus" to the addressees, so that when the Ephesian Christians read it they would think that it was written particularly to them. Then, both this scribe's copy of the letter and other copies that lacked the words "in Ephesus" were used by later copyists who reproduced the letter. This would explain why some of our surviving manuscripts have the words "in Ephesus" and others don't.

Originally, then, the letter may not have been sent to a particular congregation but to a number of congregations, for example, throughout Asia Minor. The overarching purpose of Ephesians is to remind its Gentile readers that even though they were formerly alienated from God and his people, Israel, they have now been made one through the work of Jesus—one with the Jews through Jesus' work of reconciliation and one with God through his work of redemption (2:1–22). More specifically, Jesus' death has torn down the barrier that previously divided Jew and Gentile, that is, the Jewish Law, so that both groups are now absolutely equal; Jews and Gentiles can live in harmony with

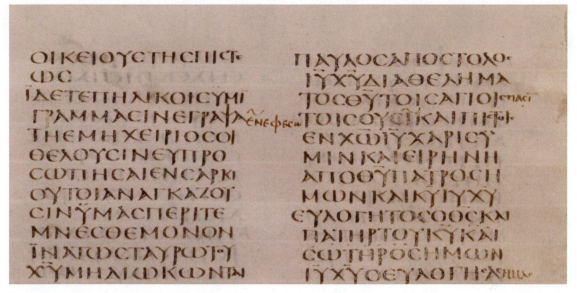

Figure 17.1 The first page of Ephesians in Codex Sinaiticus, the oldest complete manuscript of the New Testament. Notice that the first verse has been corrected in the margin between the columns. The letter was originally addressed "to the saints," but a later scribe made the address more specific by inserting the phrase "who are in Ephesus."

one another without the divisiveness of the Law (2:11–18). Moreover, Christ has united both Jew and Gentile with God (2:18–22). Believers have not only died with Christ, they have also been raised up with him to enjoy the benefits of a heavenly existence (2:1–10). Thus Jew and Gentile are unified with one another and with God. This is the "mystery" of the gospel that was concealed from earlier generations but has now been revealed to "Paul" and through him to the world (3:1–13).

The second half of the letter (chaps. 4–6) consists of exhortations to live in ways that manifest this unity. It is to be evident in the life of the church (4:1–16), in the distinctiveness of the believers from the rest of society (4:17–5:20), and in the social relations of fellow Christians, that is, in their roles as wives and husbands, children and fathers, slaves and masters (5:21–6:9). The letter closes with an exhortation to continue to fight against the forces of the devil that are trying to disrupt the life of the congregation (6:10–20) and then "Paul's" final closing statement and benediction (6:21–24).

Once again, however, we must ask the critical question: was this letter actually sent by Paul? Broadly speaking, Ephesians may sound like

something that Paul could have written. Allowance must be made, of course, for its character as a circular letter, in which the author addresses no specific problem, such as moral improprieties or false teachings, and therefore offers no specific resolutions. Some scholars have argued that Paul would not have written such a letter, but how could we know?

The real difficulty with Ephesians is not with its occasion or broad scope but with the details of what the author actually says and the way in which he says it (as was also the case with 2 Thessalonians and Colossians). Whereas the writing style of Colossians appears to be non-Pauline, the style of Ephesians is even more so. No one who reads this letter in Greek can help being struck by its incredibly long sentences when measured against Paul. In Greek, the opening thanksgiving of 1:3–14 (twelve verses) is one sentence. Again, this is not bad writing style; it simply isn't Paul's.

Some scholars have demonstrated this point in convincing terms (see the article on Ephesians by Victor Furnish in the *Anchor Bible Dictionary* II. 535–42). There are something like a hundred complete sentences in this book, nine of them over fifty

BOX 17.4   The Vocabulary of Salvation in Paul and Ephesians

One of the subtle contrasts between Ephesians and the undisputed Pauline epistles involves a technical difference in the language they use to describe salvation. In earlier chapters, we discussed Paul's view of salvation, that is, his general view of how a person enters into a restored relationship with God. Strictly speaking, however, Paul uses the actual term "salvation," and the verb "save," only in the future sense. For Paul, being saved refers to what will happen when Christ returns and delivers his followers from the wrath of God that will soon hit this world (e.g., see Rom 5:9–10; 1 Cor 3:15; 5:5). Odd as it might seem to many people today, Paul would have been puzzled by the question that you yourself may have been asked at some time: "Have you been saved?" His reply would have been, "Of course not," by which he would have meant that salvation, strictly speaking, is something that is going to happen at the parousia, not something that already has happened.

For the author of Ephesians, however, salvation is something that has already taken place. Just as Christians have already been raised up with Christ, they have also already been saved: "By grace you have been saved" (2:5). Could Paul have written this? Of course, he *could* have, but is it likely, given the way he regularly speaks elsewhere?

---

words in length. Contrast this with what you find in Paul's undisputed letters. Philippians and Galatians, for example, are roughly the same length as Ephesians; Philippians has 102 sentences, but only one of them is over fifty words, and Galatians has 181 sentences, with only one over fifty words. Or consider these portions of the longer undisputed letters: in the first four chapters of Romans there are 581 sentences, only three of which are over fifty words; in the first four chapters of 1 Corinthians, there are 621 sentences, with only one over fifty words. Paul tended to write in a succinct style. The author of Ephesians did not.

In addition, this author uses a total of 116 words that are not found in any of Paul's undisputed letters. To be sure, Paul uses unique words in all of his letters, depending on what he happens to be talking about, but 116 non-Pauline words seems inordinately high compared with what we find elsewhere. For example, the book of Philippians, a letter of comparable, but slightly shorter, length, has one of the highest number of unique words (in proportion to the total number of words) among Paul's undisputed epistles, but the total there is only 76.

When taken in combination with what the letter of Ephesians actually says, these differences in style and vocabulary suggest that someone other

than Paul wrote it, someone imitating the letters of Paul but without complete success. To examine the contents of Ephesians, we can look at one particular passage that is central to the overarching theme of the book and whose ideas appear to resemble those that Paul sets forth in some of his undisputed letters. Once we move beneath the surface, however, these resemblances begin to evaporate.

Ephesians 2:1–10 discusses the conversion of its Gentile readers from their earlier lives to the salvation they have experienced in Christ. There are a number of important Pauline themes here: a person's separation from God before being converted to Christ is spoken of as "death" (vv. 1–2), the devil is designated as "the ruler of the power of the air" (v. 2), the grace of God brings salvation through faith, not works (vv. 8–9), and the new existence leads to a moral life (v. 10). Surely this is Pauline material.

There are peculiarities here as well, however, as we can see when we dig deeper into the text. The first and most obvious problem concerns the status of the believer, which is described in a way that is strikingly similar to what we found in Colossians. Even though Paul's undisputed letters are quite emphatic that the resurrection of believers (even in a spiritual sense) has not yet happened, the author of Ephesians pronounces that "God . . . made us alive together with Christ . . . and raised us up with him and seated us with him in the heavenly places in Christ Jesus" (vv. 5–6). This view of the Christian believer is even more exalted than the one in Colossians; the words the author uses of the believer's status mirror those he uses of Christ himself:

> God put this power to work in Christ when he raised him from the dead and seated him at his right hand in the heavenly places, far above all rule and authority and power and dominion, and above every name that is named, not only in this age but also in the age to come. And he has put all things under his feet and made him the head over all things for the church. (vv. 20–22)

According to Ephesians 2, believers are seated with Christ in the heavenly places, above everything else. Can this be the same author who castigated the Corinthians for maintaining that they had already come to be exalted with Christ and were therefore already ruling with him?

Another interesting difference from Paul's own letters is the way the author of Eph 2:1–10 conceptualizes **"works."** In Paul's gospel, Gentiles are made right with God not by doing the works of the Law but through faith in Christ's death. Thus, when Paul speaks about works, he is referring to doing those aspects of the Law that make Jews distinctive as the people of Israel (e.g., circumcision

and kosher food laws). Ephesians, however, no longer refers to the Jewish Law, but speaks instead of "good deeds" (see 2:8–10). Interestingly, as we found in the previous chapter, the author of James countered a later version of Paul's gospel that insisted that faith without doing good deeds was adequate before God. It appears that the author of Ephesians understands "works" in this later, non-Pauline, sense.

Just as the notion of "works" appears to have lost its specifically Jewish content, so, too, does the author's own former life in which he engaged in these works. Paul himself spoke proudly of his former life as one in which he had kept the Jewish Law better than the zealous Pharisaic companions of his youth. In his own words, "with respect to the righteousness found in the Law, I was found to be blameless" (Phil 3:6). Paul's conversion was not away from a wild and promiscuous past to an upright and moral present; it was from one form of rigorous religiosity to another. What about the author of Ephesians? Evidently, he did not conceive of Paul's past in this way, for according to him "all of us once lived among them (i.e., the pagans) in the passions of our flesh, following the desires of flesh and senses" (2:3). It is true that Paul himself occasionally speaks of having been subject to the law of sin and of having done the things that he knew he ought not to have done (Romans 7), but in his undisputed letters the extent of his trans-

AT A GLANCE

BOX 17.5   The Deutero-Pauline Epistles

1. The Deutero-Pauline epistles are 2 Thessalonians, Ephesians, and Colossians. Critical scholars debate whether or not Paul wrote these books.

2. Thessalonians sounds like 1 Thessalonians in some ways, but its understanding of eschatology—particularly when the end will come (not right away, according to this book)—does not sound Pauline.

3. Colossians responds to a group of false teachers who promote a kind of Jewish mysticism; its writ-

ing style and theology seem quite different from Paul's—especially with respect to its understanding of the resurrection of believers (which it takes to be a past event).

4. Ephesians is a circular letter dealing with the relationship of Jew and Gentile in the church. Again, the vocabulary, writing style, and theology appear quite different from Paul's.

5. These letters may have been written by three different authors near the end of the first century.

gression involved such things as "coveting" (Rom 7:7–8), not the wild and dissolute lifestyle of the pagans that he sometimes maligned (e.g., see Rom 1:18–32). In terms of his lifestyle, Paul lived "blame-lessly." Not so the author of Ephesians.

Who, then, was this author and why did he write the letter? Once again, our historical curiosity is stymied by a lack of evidence. Clearly the author was a member of a church that was committed to Paul's understanding of the gospel, but he evidently lived at a later time, perhaps near the end of the first century, when some of Paul's views had developed in directions that Paul himself had not taken them, for example with respect to what it meant to be saved apart from works. This author may well have had access to other letters written under Paul's name. Scholars have long noted, for example, a number of similarities between Ephesians and Colossians, including their openings and closings, their views of being raised already with Christ, and their instructions to wives and husbands, children and fathers, slaves and masters.

Possibly, then, an unknown author concerned with tensions that had erupted between Gentiles and Jews in the churches that he knew (in Asia Minor?) wrote to reaffirm what he saw to be the core of Paul's message, that Christ brought about a unification of Jew and Gentile and a reconciliation of both with God, and that all members of the Christian church should respond to their new standing in Christ by embracing and promoting the unity provided from above.

THE PASTORAL EPISTLES

Up to this point I have tried to show why scholars continue to debate the authorship of the Deutero-Pauline epistles, but when we come to the Pastoral epistles, 1 and 2 Timothy and Titus, there is greater scholarly unanimity. These three letters are widely regarded by scholars as non-Pauline. In discussing the authorship of the Pauline epistles, we should constantly remember that we are not asking whether or not Christians in the first or second century would have forged documents in Paul's name. We know for a fact that some did: 2 Thessalonians alludes to a forged letter (2:2). More-

over, everyone agrees that some of the writings that survive in Paul's name are Christian forgeries (e.g., the correspondence between "Paul" and the philosopher Seneca and the apocalypse written by "Paul"). What we are asking, then, is whether any given document that claims to be written by Paul can sustain its claim.

Before addressing the issue of the authorship of the Pastoral epistles, we should note their ostensible occasion and overarching points, both as a group (since most scholars are reasonably certain that they all came from the same pen) and individually. These letters are grouped together as pastoral epistles because each claims to be written by Paul to a person he has appointed to lead one of his churches: **Timothy**, his young companion left to minister among the Christians in Ephesus, and Titus, his companion left on the island of Crete. Moreover, these epistles contain pastoral advice, that is, advice from the apostle to his appointed representatives concerning how they should tend their Christian flocks.

Each of these epistles presupposes a slightly different situation, but the overarching issues are the same. The problems involve (*a*) false teachers who are creating problems for the congregations and (*b*) the internal organization of the communities and their leaders. "Paul" urges his representatives to take charge, to run a tight ship, to keep everyone in line, and above all to silence those who promote ideas that conflict with the teachings that he himself has endorsed.

1 Timothy

1 Timothy presupposes that Paul and Timothy visited Ephesus on the way to Macedonia (1:3) and that Paul decided to leave Timothy behind to bring the false teachers under control (1:3–11), to bring order to the church (2:1–15), and to appoint moral and upright leaders to keep things running smoothly (3:1–13). Most of the letter consists of instructions concerning Christian living and social interaction, for instance on how Christians ought to pray, how they ought to behave toward the elderly, the widows, and their leaders, and what things they ought to avoid, namely, pointlessly ascetic lifestyles, material wealth, and heretics who corrupt the truth.

Figure 17.2 Picture of a woman presiding at a *refrigium,* a ritual meal held by families to commemorate the dead in early Christianity (in which the dead person was thought to be dining with the living on the commemoration of his or her death). The author of the Pastorals no doubt would have disapproved of a woman officiating at the meal.

The nature of the false teaching that the author disparages is somewhat difficult to discern. Some members of the congregation have evidently become enthralled with "myths and endless genealogies" (1:4). This phrase has struck a chord with modern interpreters familiar with various strands of Christian **Gnosticism**. You may recall that Gnostic Christians developed elaborate mythologies that traced the genealogies of divine beings all the way back to the one true God. Some strands of Gnosticism were deeply rooted in Judaism; the Jewish Scriptures themselves, especially the first chapters of Genesis, proved to be a limitless resource for speculation about how the world and the supernatural beings who rule it came into existence. It is striking in this connection that the

author of 1 Timothy goes on to attack those who want to be "teachers of the law" (1:7).

Most of the Gnostic groups that we know about were rigorously ascetic. Wanting to escape the material world, they chose to punish their bodies so as not to be enslaved by them, refraining from sexual relations and insisting on strict and uninteresting diets. The author of 1 Timothy correspondingly lambastes false teachers because they "forbid marriage and demand abstinence from foods" (4:3). Moreover, he concludes his letter with a final exhortation to "avoid the profane chatter and contradictions of what is falsely called knowledge" (6:20). The Greek word for "knowledge," is ***gnosis***; those who were Gnostics claimed to know what was not available to the general public, not even to their fellow

Christians. It seems altogether reasonable, then, to assume that this letter was directed against an early form of Christian Gnosticism.

The author does not attack the views of his opponents head-on but instead urges Timothy not to heed their words and, if possible, to bring them into submission (1:3). As we will see later, many of the instructions that the author gives to the leadership of the church may represent an effort to become organized in order to face these opponents with a unified front. In any event, the qualifications of those who are to be appointed leaders of the church, the bishops and deacons, whose duties are never spelled out, soon take center stage. For this author, only men are allowed to occupy these positions, and they are to be morally upright and strong personalities who can serve as models to the community and command respect in the world outside the church.

The tight organization of the church is important not only for addressing the problems posed by false teachers but also for monitoring the inner workings of the community itself. In particular, the author is concerned about the role women should play in the congregation (not much of one; see especially 1 Tim 2:11–15) and about the position and activities of "widows," who appear to be enrolled by the church and provided with some kind of material support in exchange for their pious deeds (5:4–16). The author evidently thinks that women in general and widows in particular have stirred up problems and are not to be trusted (e.g., 5:11–13; see Chapter 18).

2 Timothy

The second Pastoral epistle presupposes a somewhat different situation. It too is written by "Paul" to Timothy (1:1). Now, however, "Paul" is in prison in Rome (1:16–17; his location in 1 Timothy was not specified), and he is clearly expecting to be put to death soon (4:6–8), after a second judicial proceeding (the first one evidently did not go well; 4:17). He writes to Timothy not only to encourage him to continue his pastoral ministry and to root the false teachers out of his church but also to ask him to join him as soon as possible (4:21), bringing along some of his personal belongings (4:13).

In this letter we learn something more about Timothy himself. He is portrayed as a third-generation Christian, having been preceded in the faith by his mother Eunice and grandmother Lois (1:5). He was trained in the Scriptures from his childhood (3:15) and as an adult became a companion of "Paul," collaborating with him in his mission to some of the cities of Asia Minor (3:10–11). He was ordained to Christian ministry through the ritual of laying on of hands (1:6; 4:1–5). As the author's faithful representative in Ephesus (one of the few anywhere, evidently, see 1:16–17; 4:10–18), Timothy is charged with overcoming those who lead the saints astray with their idle talk and corrupt lives (2:16–18, 23–26; 3:1–9; 4:3–5).

There is even less evidence concerning the nature of the false teaching here than in 1 Timothy. Two of the opponents are specifically said to have claimed that "the resurrection has already taken place" (2:17), a claim that sounds familiar from other Pauline writings we have examined. But mostly the author attacks his opponents with general slander, providing no specifics concerning what they actually said. Thus, the opponents are called

> lovers of themselves, lovers of money, boasters, arrogant, abusive, disobedient to their parents, ungrateful, unholy, inhuman, implacable, slanderers, profligates, brutes, haters of good, treacherous, reckless, swollen with conceit, lovers of pleasure rather than lovers of God, holding to the outward form of godliness but denying its power. (3:2–5)

They may well have been all these things and more, but the passage provides no clue about what they actually taught or stood for. Timothy, in any event, is to oppose them with all his strength, and to continue the ministry that "Paul" has assigned to him until he comes to see the apostle in his bondage in Rome.

Titus

The book of Titus is far more like the first Pastoral epistle than the second. Indeed, the letter seems something like a *Readers' Digest* version of 1 Timothy, with its list of qualifications for church leaders and its moral instructions for members of the congregation in their relations with one another.

The presupposed situation is that "Paul" has left his trusted comrade Titus on the island of

Crete as an apostolic representative to the church there (1:4–5). In particular, Titus was supposed to appoint elders, or bishops, in the churches of every town (1:5–9). "Paul" is now writing in order to urge Titus to correct the false teachings promoted by Jewish-Christian believers, which appear to involve both complicated "mythologies" that confuse the faithful (1:10–16) and "genealogies and quarrels about the law" (3:9). As in 1 Timothy, the false teaching may therefore involve Gnostic speculation. Titus is not to argue with these people; he is to warn them twice to change their views and afterward simply ignore them, "since you know that such a person is perverted and sinful, being self-condemned" (3:11). The errant parties themselves, needless to say, probably thought otherwise.

A good portion of the epistle contains the apostle's sage advice to various social groups within the congregation: older men (2:2), older women (2:3), younger women (2:4–5), younger men (2:6–8), and slaves (2:9–10). Near the end, the advice becomes more general in nature, involving basic admonitions to engage in moral behavior in light of the new life for those who have been saved (3:1–7, especially v. 5). The letter concludes with several greetings and a request for Titus to join the apostle in the city of Nicopolis, where he plans to spend the winter (3:12). There were several cities of this name in Asia Minor and elsewhere in the empire; it is not clear to which of these the author refers.

THE HISTORICAL SITUATION AND AUTHORSHIP OF THE PASTORAL EPISTLES

Most scholars are reasonably convinced that all three Pastoral epistles were written by the same author. With 1 Timothy and Titus there can be little doubt. The writing style, subject matter, and specific content are altogether similar. If they were not written by the same person, we would have to suppose that one of them was used by an imitator as the model for the other, but there appears to be no reason to think that this is what happened. The question of 2 Timothy has proved somewhat more complicated since its content is different. Yet even

here the vocabulary and writing style are closely aligned with the other two. The salutation of the letter matches that of 1 Timothy: "To Timothy, my . . . child . . . : Grace, mercy, and peace from God the Father and Christ Jesus our Lord" (1 Tim 1:2; 2 Tim 1:2). No other Pauline letter has the same wording. Moreover, many of the same concerns are clearly to the fore in both letters, especially the concern for the administration of the church and the weeding out of false teachers.

Assuming, then, that all three letters come from the same hand (even granting 2 Timothy's different occasion and content), was that hand the apostle Paul's? By pursuing this question, we can learn a good deal about these epistles, particularly about the historical situation that they presuppose. Here I will set forth the arguments that have struck most scholars as decisive in showing that Paul did not write them.

At the outset, we should consider the unusual vocabulary used throughout these letters. Before adducing the data themselves, let me first explain their significance. Suppose (to imagine a relatively bizarre situation) that someone were to uncover a letter allegedly written by Paul that urged its readers to attend mass every Saturday night, to go to confession once a week, and to say three Hail Marys for every unintentional sin they committed. What would you make of such a letter? Some of its words would indicate Christian practices and beliefs that developed long after Paul had died (e.g., mass, Hail Marys). Others were used by Paul, but not in the same way (e.g., confession). With the passage of time, significant words in any language are invested with new meanings and new words are created, which is why Shakespearean English sounds so strange to many people today and why our language would have struck Shakespeare as peculiar. The vocabulary of this hypothetical letter alone would show you that the apostle Paul did not write it.

With the Pastoral epistles, of course, we find nothing so blatant, but we do find an inordinate number of non-Pauline words, most of which do occur in later Christians writings. Sophisticated studies of the Greek text of these books have come up with the following data (see the works cited in the suggestions for further reading): apart from personal names, there are 848 different words found in the Pastorals; of these, 306 occur nowhere else in the Pauline corpus of the New Testament (even including the Deutero-Paulines). This means that over one-third of the vocabulary is not Pauline. Strikingly, over two-thirds of these non-Pauline words are used by Christian authors of the second century. Thus, it appears that the vocabulary represented in these letters is more developed than what we find in the other letters attributed to Paul.

Moreover, some of the words that Paul does use in his own letters take on different meanings in the Pastorals. As brief examples, Paul's word for "having a right standing before God" (literally, "righteous") now means "being a moral individual" (i.e., "upright"; Titus 1:8) and the term "faith," which for Paul refers to a trusting acceptance of the death of Christ for salvation, now refers to the body of teaching that makes up the Christian religion (e.g., Titus 1:13).

Of course, the argument from vocabulary can never be decisive in itself. Everybody uses different words on different occasions, and the Christian vocabulary of Paul himself must have developed over time. The magnitude of these differences must give us pause, however, particularly since they coincide with other features of the letters that suggest they were written after Paul had passed off the scene. To begin with, there is the nature of the problems that the letters address. If the major form of false teaching being attacked was some kind of Christian Gnosticism, then one might ask when this kind of religion can be historically documented. In fact, the first Christian Gnostics that we know by name lived in the early to mid-second century. To be sure, the second-century Gnostics may have had some predecessors near the end of the first century, but there

Figure 17.3 Even though the author of the Pastoral epistles, and many of his male contemporaries, believed that women should not be involved with business outside the home, many women had to work in order to survive in the ancient Roman world, as seen in this funerary monument portraying two women working in a poultry/butcher shop.

is almost no evidence to suggest that they were spouting "myths and endless genealogies" that sanctioned strictly ascetic lifestyles or that they were otherwise plaguing the Christian congregations during the lifetime of Paul himself. Not even Paul's adversaries in Corinth were this advanced.

Of even greater importance for showing that these three letters were written long after Paul's day is the church structure that the letters presuppose, a structure that is not presupposed in any of Paul's undisputed letters, but which came to be found throughout Christianity by the end of the first century and the beginning of the second. To make sense of this argument, we need to recall what we have learned about the nature of Paul's own churches, when he was writing letters to them in the 50s of the Common Era.

The one Pauline community whose inner workings we know in some detail, thanks to the apostle's extended correspondence with it, is the church in Corinth. This was a troubled church, rife with inner turmoil, filled with what Paul considered to be personal immorality, and subject to what he regarded to be false teaching. How did Paul deal with the problems, or rather, to whom in the church did he appeal when he decided to deal with them? If you'll recall he wrote to the entire church, pleading with them to adhere to his advice. Why didn't he address his concerns to the person in charge, the elder or overseer who could make decisions and run a tighter ship? Quite simply because there was no such person there.

Paul's churches were **"charismatic" communities**, that is, congregations of people who believed that they had been endowed with God's Spirit and so had been given "gifts" (Greek *charismata*) to enable them to minister to one another as teachers, prophets, evangelists, healers, almsgivers, tongues-speakers, tongues-interpreters, and so on. There was nobody ultimately in charge, except the apostle (who wasn't on the scene), because everyone had received an equal endowment of the Spirit, and so no one could lord it over anyone else. At least that is how Paul thought the church ought to be (see 1 Corinthians 12–14).

What happens, however, when everyone feels Spirit-led but not everyone agrees on where the Spirit leads? In such a situation, who is to say that one person's teaching is of the Spirit and another's is not? Who is to decide how the church funds should be used? Who is to reprimand a brother or sister involved in dubious personal activities? At the start, Paul evidently did not find these issues of local leadership pressing, since he believed that the end was soon to arrive and that the Spirit was simply a sort of down-payment of what was to come, a kind of interim guide to how life would be in the kingdom. But what happens when the end does not arrive and there is no one person or group of persons to take charge? Presumably, as in the church in Corinth, what happens is a fair bit of chaos.

The developments within the Pauline communities appear to have taken place in response to this chaos. With the passing of time, Paul's churches developed a kind of hierarchy of authority in which church leaders emerged and began to take control of the congregations. To a limited extent, this development began in the later years of Paul's ministry: in the letter to the Philippians, for example, he mentions "overseers and deacons" as among his recipients (1:1). But Paul assigns no special roles to these persons nor does he assume that they can deal directly with the issues that he addresses.

Some fifty years or so after Paul had died, however, these offices had developed considerably in Christian circles. Each Christian locality had a clear-cut leader called a **"bishop"** (the Greek word is *episkopos,* literally meaning "overseer," as in Phil 1:1), under whom served **"presbyters"** (Greek for "elders"), who appear to have tended to the spiritual needs of the communities, and "deacons" (Greek for "ministers"), who may have focused on their material needs. Above all, the bishops were to root out all traces of heretical teaching.

With the passing of time, then, a church hierarchy developed out of the loosely organized, charismatic churches established by Paul and presumably by other missionaries like him. Where do the Pastoral epistles stand in this line of development? In these letters "Paul" writes to his officially designated representatives, ordained by the laying on of hands, instructing them to appoint bishops and deacons who are suitable for the governance of the church and to pass along to them the true teaching that the apostle himself has provided. The clerical structure of these letters appears far removed from what we find in the letters of Paul, but it is closely aligned with what we find in Christian authors of the second century.

The conclusion seems inevitable: based on the vocabulary, the nature of the problems addressed, and, most important, the presupposed church structure of these letters, the Pastoral epistles appear not to have been written by Paul in the 50s or 60s of the Common Era, but sometime later, possibly near the end of the first century, by an otherwise unknown member of one of Paul's churches who was intent on addressing the problems of his own day by assuming the authority of Paul, the great apostle of the Gentiles.

AT A GLANCE

BOX: 17.6 The Pastoral Epistles

1. 1 and 2 Timothy and Titus are called Pastoral epistles because they are ostensibly written by Paul to two of his younger colleagues who were pastors of churches, giving them pastoral advice about how to deal with problems in their communities—Timothy as the pastor of Ephesus and Titus as the pastor of Crete.

2. Most critical scholars think that Paul did not write them—based on their vocabulary, which differs significantly from Paul's, and, especially, on the different historical situation they presuppose.

3. The letters principally address

   a. False teachers who have created problems, possibly tied in some way to Gnostics.

   b. The internal organization of the communities, for example, the problem of women playing significant roles in the church.

4. The letters were evidently all written by the same author, living near the end of the first century, who decided to deal with the problems of his own day by claiming the authority of Paul.

TAKE A STAND

1. You have a friend who thinks that all thirteen books written in Paul's name in the New Testament must actually have been written by Paul. You decide to show him why scholars have argued that Paul did not write the Pastoral epistles. Make your argument.

2. Your roommate tells you that the letter to the Ephesians encapsulates Paul's thought better than any other book of the New Testament. You, on the other hand, think that its message differs in significant ways from Paul's teaching (whether you think this or not, pretend you do). What are the best arguments in your favor?

3. You're talking to two friends about the New Testament. One of them says that the New Testament cannot contain forgeries because the ancient church fathers who compiled the canon would not have accepted any such deceptions into it. The other says that if there are forgeries in the New Testament, they ought to be removed from it. How do you respond to each friend?

SUGGESTIONS FOR FURTHER READING

Beker, J. Christiaan. *The Heirs of Paul: Paul's Legacy in the New Testament and in the Church Today.* Grand Rapids, Mich.: Eerdmans, 1996. A clear assessment of the theology of the Deutero-Pauline and Pastoral epistles, especially in light of the views embodied in the undisputed Paulines.

Donelson, L. R. *Pseudepigraphy and Ethical Argument in the Pastoral Epistles.* Tübingen: Mohr/Siebeck, 1986. A study that sets the Pastoral epistles in the context of ancient practices of pseudepigraphy and that establishes their theological and ethical points of view.

Ehrman, Bart. *Forged: Writing in the Name of God. Why the Bible's Authors Are Not Who We Think They Are.* San Francisco: HarperOne, 2011. A discussion of all the "pseudepigrapha" of the New Testament, including the Deutero-Pauline and Pastoral epistles, which explains why it is best to understand these as ancient forgeries; for beginning students.

Harrison, P. N. *The Problem of the Pastoral Epistles.* Oxford: Humphrey Milford, 1921. A classic study that provides an authoritative demonstration that Paul did not write the Pastoral epistles in their present form.

Lincoln, Andrew, and A. J. M. Wedderburn. *The Theology of the Later Pauline Letters.* Cambridge: Cambridge University Press, 1993. A clear overview of the major themes of Colossians and Ephesians.

McDonald, Dennis. *The Legend and the Apostle: The Battle for Paul in Story and Canon.* Philadelphia: Westminster John Knox, 1983. An intriguing and controversial book that claims that the Pastoral epistles were written to oppose the kinds of views of Paul, highly supportive of women, found in such books as the Acts of Thecla.

MacDonald, M. Y. *The Pauline Churches: A Socio-historical Study of Institutionalization in the Pauline and Deutero-Pauline Writings.* Cambridge: Cambridge University Press, 1988. A study that uses a social-science approach to help explain various aspects of the institutionalization of churches associated with Paul, especially as evidenced in Ephesians, Colossians, and the Pastoral epistles; for more advanced students.

Pervo, Richard. *The Making of Paul: Constructions of the Apostle in Early Christianity.* Philadelphia: Fortress, 2010. An interesting and important sketch of how Paul was understood by Christian authors after his day, including the authors of the Deutero-Pauline and Pauline epistles.

Roetzel, Calvin. *The Letters of Paul: Conversations in Context.* 4th ed. Atlanta: Westminster John Knox, 2011. Perhaps the best introductory discussion of each of the Pauline epistles, including the Deutero-Paulines and Pastorals.

Young, Frances. *The Theology of the Pastoral Epistles.* Cambridge: Cambridge University Press, 1994. A clear overview of the major themes of the Pastoral epistles.

KEY TERMS

bishop	forgery	Mysticism, Jewish	Timothy
charismatic	*gnosis*	presbyter	works
communities	Gnosticism		

From Paul's Female Colleagues to the Pastor's Intimidated Women

THE OPPRESSION OF WOMEN IN EARLY CHRISTIANITY

WHAT TO EXPECT

One of the most hotly debated issues in modern Christian denominations involves the role of women in the church: should women be ordained, for example, and serve as ministers or priests? This chapter shows that these debates are not only recent but have been going on since the beginning of Christianity. Here we will look at the debates in their earliest stages, considering the role women played in the ministry of Jesus, in the churches of Paul, and in the Christian communities after Paul.

Women played a prominent role in the earliest Christian churches, including those associated with the apostle Paul. They served as evangelists, pastors, teachers, and prophets. Some were wealthy and provided financial support for the apostle; others served as patrons for entire churches, allowing congregations to meet in their homes and supplying them with the resources necessary for their gatherings. Some women were Paul's coworkers on the mission field. Why, then, do most people today think that all the early Christian leaders were men?

This question has generated a number of interesting studies in recent years. Here I will present one of the persuasive perspectives that has emerged from these studies: despite the crucial role that women played in the earliest Christian churches, by the end of the first century they faced serious opposition from those who denied their right to occupy positions of status and authority. This opposition succeeded in pressing Christian women into submission to male authority and obscured the record of their earlier involvement.

WOMEN IN PAUL'S CHURCHES

Despite the impression that one might get from such ancient Christian writings as the Pastoral epistles, women were not always a silent presence in the churches. Consider Paul's letter to the Romans, in which he sends greetings to and from a number of his acquaintances (chap. 16). Although Paul names more men than women here, the women in the church appear to be in no way inferior to their male counterparts. There is **Phoebe**, a deacon (or minister) in the church of Cenchreae and Paul's own patron, entrusted by Paul with the task of carrying the letter to Rome (vv. 1–2). There is **Prisca**, who along with her husband Aquila, is largely responsible for the Gentile mission and who supports a congregation in her home (vv. 3–4; notice that she is named ahead of her husband). There is Mary, Paul's colleague who works among the Romans (v. 6). There are Tryphaena, Tryphosa, and Persis, women whom Paul calls his "coworkers" for the gospel (vv. 6, 12). And there are Julia and the mother of Rufus and the sister of Nereus, all of whom appear to have a high profile in this community (vv. 13, 15). Most impressively of all, there is **Junia**, a woman whom Paul names as "foremost among the apostles" (v. 7). The apostolic band was evidently larger—and more inclusive—than the list of twelve men most people know about.

Other Pauline letters provide a similar impression of women's active involvement in the Christian churches. In Corinth women are full members of the body, with spiritual gifts and the right to use them. They actively participate in services of worship, praying and prophesying alongside the men (1 Cor 11:4–6). In Philippians the only two believers worth mentioning by name are two women, Euodia and Syntyche, whose dissension concerns the apostle, evidently because of their prominent standing in the community (Phil 4:2). Indeed, according to the narrative of Acts, the church in Philippi began with the conversion of Lydia, a woman of means whose entire household came to follow her lead in adopting this new faith. She was the head of her household when the apostle first met her and soon became head of the church that gathered in her home (Acts 16:1–15).

Some women who were associated with Paul's churches came to renounce marriage for the sake of the gospel and attained positions of prominence in their communities. Recall that letters later written in Paul's name speak of such women and try to bring them into submission. Some of these women were "widows," that is, women who had no husband overlord (whether they had previously been married or not). Such women are said to go about telling "old wives' tales" (1 Tim 4:7 and 5:13), possibly stories like the *Acts of Thecla* (see box 18.4) that justified their lifestyles and views. Even in writings

that oppose them, such women are acknowledged to be important to the church because of their full-time ministry in its service (1 Tim 5:3–16).

There is still other evidence of women enjoying prestigious positions in churches, well into the late second century. Some of this evidence derives from Gnostic groups that claimed allegiance to Paul and that were known to have women as their leaders and spokespersons. Other evidence comes from groups associated with the prophet Montanus and his two women colleagues, Prisca and Maximillia, who had forsaken their marriages to live ascetic lives, insisting that the end of the age was near and that God had called his people to renounce all fleshly passions in preparation for the final consummation.

How is it that women attained such a high status and assumed such high levels of authority in the early Christian movement? One way to answer the question is by looking at the ministry of Jesus himself, to see whether women enjoyed a high profile from the very outset of the movement.

WOMEN ASSOCIATED WITH JESUS

We can say with some confidence that Jesus associated with women and ministered to them in public. To be sure, his twelve closest disciples were almost certainly men (as one would expect of a first-century Jewish rabbi). It is largely for this reason that the principal characters in almost all the gospel traditions are men. But not all of them are. In fact, the importance of women in Jesus' ministry is multiply attested in the earliest traditions. Both Mark and L (Luke's special source), for example, indicate that Jesus was accompanied by women in his travels (Mark 15:40–41; Luke 8:1–3), a tradition corroborated by the *Gospel of Thomas* (*Gosp. Thom.* 114). Mark and L also indicate that women provided Jesus with financial support during his ministry, evidently serving as his patrons (Mark 15:40–41; Luke 8:1–3). In both Mark and John, Jesus is said to have engaged in public dialogue and debate with women who were not among his immediate followers (Mark 7:24–30; John 4:1–42). Both Gospels also record, independently of one another, the tradition that Jesus had physical contact

ANOTHER GLIMPSE INTO THE PAST

BOX 18.1 Mary Magdalene

Undoubtedly the most famous early Christian woman was **Mary Magdalene**, who is mentioned in all four of the canonical Gospels as a witness to Jesus' death and resurrection (see, e.g., Matt 27:56, 61; 28:1; Mark 15:40–41, 47; 16:1; Luke 23:49, 55–56; 24:1–9; John 19:25; 20:1–2, 11–18). The epithet "Magdalene" identifies her as coming from the city of Magdala, on the shore of the Sea of Galilee, and is used to differentiate her from the other Marys named in the New Testament (e.g., Jesus' mother and the mother of James; see Matt 24:10).

In addition to her presence with Jesus during his last week, and her observation of the crucifixion and empty tomb, we learn from the Gospel of Luke that Mary Magdalene had been exorcized of seven demons and was one of the women who traveled with Jesus around Galilee, supplying him and his disciples with the funds they needed to live (Luke 8:2–3). Apart from that, not much is said about her in the New Testament. Most people today, of course, think of her as a prostitute, even though there is not a word about this in the New Testament itself (from the biblical epics produced in Hollywood, you would think this was the major point!). Her depiction as a completely disreputable figure does not emerge until nearly 500 years after the New Testament, when she began to be identified as the "sinful woman" who anoints Jesus in Luke 7:36–50. Luke himself does not make this iden-

tification, however—even though he had ample opportunity to do so, given the fact that the story occurs immediately before his reference to Mary Magdalene!

Other later traditions also build on what the New Testament says about Mary Magdalene. In particular, it came to be thought that since she was the first to see Jesus raised from the dead, she must have stood in a particularly close relationship with him. Thus, some Gnostic Gospels indicate that after his resurrection Jesus singled her out for special revelations of the truth that would bring salvation. Some texts go even further, suggesting that the two of them had a rather intimate relationship. In particular, the *Gospel of Philip* indicates that the male disciples were jealous of Mary Magdalene and asked Jesus why he loved her more than them. The precise reason for their dismay? Unfortunately, the details are hard to uncover, since the only copy of this Gospel is full of holes at critical junctures. But it is intriguing to note the sentence immediately prior to the disciples' dismay (*Gosp. Phil.* 63):

> And the companion of the [MISSING WORDS] Mary Magdalene. [MISSING WORDS . . . loved] her more than all the disciples, and used to kiss her often on the [MISSING WORD].

What one might give to know those missing words!

with a woman who anointed him with oil before his Passion (Mark 14:3–9; John 12:1–8). In Mark's account this is an unnamed woman in the house of Simon, a leper; in John's account it is Mary, the sister of Martha and Lazarus, in her own home.

In all four of the canonical Gospels, women are said to have accompanied Jesus from Galilee to Jerusalem during the last week of his life and to have been present at his crucifixion (Matt 27:55; Mark 15:40–41; Luke 23:49; John 19:25). The earliest traditions in Mark suggest that they alone remained faithful to the end: all his male disciples had fled. Finally, it is clear from the Synoptics and John that women followers were the first to believe that

Jesus' body was no longer in the tomb (Matt 28:1–10; Mark 16:1–8; Luke 23:55–24:10; John 20:1–2; *Gosp. Pet.* 50–57). These women were evidently the first to proclaim that Jesus had been raised.

As for the contextual credibility of these traditions, it is true that women were generally viewed as inferior by men in the ancient world, but there were exceptions. Philosophical schools like the Epicureans and the Cynics, for example, advocated equality for women. Of course, there were not many Epicureans or Cynics in Jesus' immediate environment of Palestine, and our limited sources suggest that women, as a rule, were generally even more restricted in that part of the empire with respect

Figure 18.1 Women were allowed places of equality in some of the Greco-Roman philosophical schools, as depicted in this sarcophagus scene in which the pagan philosopher Plotinus is flanked by female disciples.

to their ability to engage in social activities outside the home and away from the authority of their fathers or husbands. Is it credible, then, that a Jewish teacher would have encouraged and promoted such activities?

We have no firm evidence to suggest that other Jewish rabbis had women followers during Jesus' day. But we do know that the Pharisees were supported and protected by powerful women in the court of King Herod the Great. And as we have seen,

there is solid evidence from inscriptions that wealthy Jewish women were sometimes the patrons of synagogues. Unfortunately, the few sources that we have say little about women among the lower classes, who did not have the wealth or standing to make them independent of their fathers or husbands. One consideration that might make the traditions about Jesus' association with women credible, however, is the distinctive burden of his own apocalyptic message. Jesus proclaimed that God was about to intervene in history and bring about a reversal of fortunes: the last would be first and the first last; those who were rich would be impoverished and the poor would be rich; those who were exalted now would be humbled and the humble would be exalted. Jesus associated with the outcasts and downtrodden of society, evidently as an enactment of his proclamation that the kingdom would belong to such as these. If women were generally looked down upon as inferior by the men who made the rules and ran the society, it does not seem implausible that Jesus would have associated freely with them and that they would have been particularly intrigued by his proclamation of the coming kingdom.

Moreover, we should not forget that Jesus urged his followers to begin to implement the ideals of the kingdom in the present in anticipation of the coming Son of Man. For this reason, there may indeed have been some form of equality practiced among the men and women who accompanied Jesus on his itinerant preaching ministry—not as the first step toward reforming society but as a preparation for the new world that was soon to come.

It is possible that the position of women among Jesus' followers while he was alive made an impact on the status of women in the Christian church after his death. This would help explain why women appear to have played significant roles in the churches connected with the apostle Paul, the early Christian churches that we are best informed about. But it would explain these significant roles

WHAT DO YOU THINK?

BOX 18.2   Was Jesus Married with Children?

Because of several "best-seller" books, such as the 1980s classic *Holy Blood, Holy Grail* and the best-selling book of modern times, *The Da Vinci Code*, many people have begun to think that Jesus was probably married, with at least one child. Is this true?

One of the major arguments in favor of this view is that, allegedly, Jewish men at the time were *always* married, and bachelorhood was virtually unheard of. Unfortunately, this is not at all true. We know of numerous single, celibate, adult men from the time of Jesus—for example, the authors of the Dead Sea Scrolls (the Essenes), before Jesus, and the apostle Paul, afterward. What is striking is that both the Essenes and Paul were apocalyptic Jews, expecting the end of all things soon to arrive. For them, the imminent arrival of the Kingdom of God was the best argument against getting married and being tied down to social obligations in the present age: this age is soon to end! Jesus was also an apocalyptic Jew. There is nothing at all implausible about him being single and celibate.

In addition, it is important to point out that in *none* of our Gospels is there ever a reference—not even one reference—to Jesus being married. This is true not only of the Gospels of Matthew, Mark, Luke, and John, it is true of every Gospel that exists from the ancient world—the *Gospels* of *Philip, Mary, Thomas, Peter, Judas*, and on and on. And not only the Gospels! In fact in no ancient Christian literature, of any kind whatsoever, is there any reference to Jesus having a wife. It should be pointed out that the authors of these books had no qualms about mentioning his other relatives: his father, his mother, his brothers, his sisters are all named. If he had a wife, why would she not be named? In light of the fact that there is not a shred of evidence that Jesus was married, and that we know of other apocalyptic Jews like him who were not married, it is very difficult to think of solid grounds for thinking Jesus *was* married. And in fact, there are reasons for thinking that he was not. In an argument that he had with the Sadducees (Mark 12:18–27), Jesus indicates that in the coming kingdom there will be no marriage. Moreover, throughout his ministry he insisted that his followers begin adopting the ways of the kingdom *in the present*. If people were not to be married *then*, and Jesus and his followers were trying to live the life of the kingdom *now*, then it makes best sense that he was already trying to live the "life of the angels"—not married, but single and celibate.

only in part. For a fuller picture, we should return to Paul to consider not only the roles that women played in his churches but also his own view of these roles.

PAUL'S UNDERSTANDING OF WOMEN IN THE CHURCH

The apostle Paul did not know the man Jesus or, probably, any of his women followers. Moreover, as we have seen at some length, many of the things that Paul proclaimed in light of Jesus' death and resurrection varied from the original message heard by the disciples in Galilee. For one thing, Paul believed that the end had already commenced with the victory over the forces of evil that had been won at Jesus' cross and sealed at his resurrection. The victory was not by any means yet complete, but it had at least begun. This victory brought newness of life, the beginning if not the fulfillment of the new age. For this reason, everyone who was baptized into Christ was "a new creation" (2 Cor 5:16). And a new creation at least implied a new social order: "As many of you as were baptized into Christ have clothed yourself with Christ. There is no longer Jew or Greek, there is no longer slave or free, there is no longer male and female; for all of you are one in Christ Jesus" (Gal 3:27–28).

No male and female in Christ—this was a radical notion in an age in which everyone knew that males and females were inherently different. The notion, however, was deeply rooted in the Pauline churches. Modern scholars have recognized that in Gal 3:28 Paul is quoting words that were spoken over converts when they were baptized. No wonder there were women leaders in the Pauline churches. Women could well have taken these words to heart and come to realize that, despite widespread opinion, they were not one whit inferior to the men with whom they served.

Like Jesus himself, however, Paul does not seem to have urged a social revolution in light of his theological conviction (recall our discussion of Philemon). Whether consistent with his own views of equality in Christ or not, Paul maintained that there was still to be a difference between men and women in this world. To eradicate that difference, in Paul's view, was unnatural and wrong. This attitude is

most evident in Paul's insistence that women in Corinth should continue to wear head coverings when they prayed and prophesied in the congregation (1 Cor 11:3–16). A number of the details of Paul's arguments here are difficult to understand and have been the source of endless wrangling among biblical scholars. For example, when he says that women are to have "authority" on their heads (the literal wording of v. 10), does he mean a veil or long hair? Why would having this "authority" on the head affect the angels (v. 10)? Are these good angels or bad? And so on. Despite such ambiguities, it is quite clear from Paul's arguments that women could and did participate openly in the church alongside men—but they were to do so as women, not as men. Nature taught that men should have short hair and women long (at least, that's what nature taught Paul!), so women who made themselves look like men were acting in ways contrary to nature and therefore contrary to the will of God.

For Paul, therefore, even though men and women were equal in Christ, this equality had not yet become a full social reality. We might suppose that it was not to become so until Christ returned to bring in the new age. That is to say, men and women had not yet been granted full social equality any more than masters and slaves had been, for Christians had not yet experienced their glorious resurrection unto immortality. While living in this age, men and women were to continue to accept their "natural" social roles, with women subordinate to men just as men were subordinate to Christ and Christ was subordinate to God (1 Cor 11:3).

WOMEN IN THE AFTERMATH OF PAUL

Paul's attitude toward women in the church may strike you as inconsistent or, at least, as ambivalent. Women could participate in his churches as ministers, prophets, and even apostles, but they were to maintain their social status as women and not appear to be like men. This apparent ambivalence led to a very interesting historical result. When the dispute over the role of women in the church later came to a head, both sides could appeal to the apostle's authority to support their views. On one side were those who urged complete equality

Figure 18.2 Painting of a Christian woman in prayer, from the Catacomb of Priscilla.

submission (1 Tim 2:4). They were to speak out against those who forbade marriage and urged the ascetic life (1 Tim 4:3). They were to silence the women in their churches; women were not to be allowed to tell old wives' tales and especially not to teach in their congregations (1 Tim 4:7). They were to be silent and submissive and sexually active with their spouses; those who wanted to enjoy the benefits of salvation were to produce babies (1 Tim 2:11–13).

The Pastoral epistles present a stark contrast to the views set forth in the *Acts of Thecla*. Is it possible that these epistles were written precisely to counteract such views? Whether or not they were, these letters are quite clear on the role to be played by women who are faithful to Paul and his gospel. The clearest statement is found in that most (in)famous of New Testament passages, 1 Tim 2:11–13. Here we are told that women must not teach men because they were created inferior, as indicated by God himself in the Law. God created Eve second, and for the sake of man; a woman (related to Eve) therefore must not lord it over a man (related to Adam) through her teaching. Furthermore, according to this author, everyone knows what happens when a woman does assume the role of teacher. She is easily duped (by the Devil) and leads the man astray. So women are to stay at home and maintain the virtues appropriate to women, bearing children for their husbands and preserving their modesty. Largely on the basis of this passage, modern critics sometimes malign the apostle Paul for his misogynist views. The problem, of course, is that he did not write it.

Paul does, however, seem to say something similar in his undisputed letters, in the harsh words of 1 Cor 14:34–35. Indeed, this passage is so similar to that of 1 Tim 2:11–15, and so unlike what Paul says elsewhere, that many scholars are convinced that these, too, are words that Paul himself never wrote; rather, they were later inserted into the letter of 1 Corinthians by a scribe who wanted to make Paul's views conform to those of the Pastoral epistles. The parallels are obvious when the two passages are placed side by side (see box 18.3).

Both passages stress that women are to keep silent in church and not teach men. This is allegedly something taught by the Law (e.g., in the story of Adam and Eve). Women are therefore to keep

between men and women in the churches. Some such believers told tales of Paul's own female companions, women like Thecla, who renounced marriage and sexual activity, led ascetic lives, and taught male believers in church. On the other side were those who urged women to remain in complete submission to men. Believers like this could combat the tales of Thecla and other women leaders by portraying Paul as an apostle who insisted on marriage, spurned asceticism, and forbade women to teach.

Which side of this dispute produced the books that made it into the canon? Reconsider the Pastoral epistles from this perspective. These letters were allegedly written by Paul to his two male colleagues, Timothy and Titus, urging them to tend to the problems in their churches, including the problem of women. These pastors were to appoint male leaders (bishops, elders, and deacons), all of whom were to be married (e.g., 1 Tim 3:2–5, 12) and who were to keep their households, including of course their wives, in

BOX 18.3 Similarities between 1 Tim 2:11–15 and 1 Cor 14:34–35

Is it possible that 1 Cor 14:34–35, which argues that women are to be subordinate, was *inserted* into this undisputed Pauline letter by the (pseudonymous) author of the Pastoral Epistles, or by someone who had *read* the Pastorals and agreed with their bias against women? Consider the similarity of the passage with one from 1 Tim:

1 Tim 2:11–15

Let a woman learn in silence with full submission.

I permit no woman to teach or to have authority over a man; she is to keep silent.

For Adam was formed first, then Eve; and Adam was not deceived, but the woman was deceived and became a transgressor.

Yet she will be saved through childbearing, provided they continue in faith and love and holiness, with modesty.

1 Cor 14:34–35

Women should be silent in the churches.

For they are not permitted to speak, but should be subordinate, as the law also says.

If there is anything they desire to know let them ask their husbands at home. For it is shameful for a woman to speak in church.

---

their place, that is, in the home, under the authority of their husbands.

It is not absolutely impossible, of course, that Paul himself wrote the passage that is now found in 1 Corinthians, but as scholars have long pointed out, Paul elsewhere talks about women leaders in his churches without giving any indication that they are to be silent. He names a woman minister in Cenchreae, women prophets in Corinth, and a woman apostle in Rome. Even more significantly, he has already indicated in 1 Corinthians itself that women are allowed to speak in church, for example, when praying or prophesying, activities that were almost always performed aloud in antiquity. How could Paul allow women to speak in chapter 11 but disallow it in chapter 14?

Moreover, it is interesting that the harsh words against women in 1 Cor 14:34–35 interrupt the flow of what Paul has been saying in the context. Up to verse 34 he has been speaking about prophecy, and he does so again in verse 37. It may be, then, that the intervening verses were not part of the text of 1 Corinthians but originated as a marginal

note that later copyists inserted into the text after verse 33 (others inserted it after v. 40). However the verses came to be placed into the text, it does not appear that they were written by Paul but by someone living later, who was familiar with and sympathetic toward the views of women advanced by the author of the Pastoral epistles.

In Paul's own churches, there may not have been an absolute equality between men and women. Women were to cover their heads when praying and prophesying, showing that as females they were still subject to males. But there was a clear movement toward equality that reflected the movement evident in the ministry of Jesus himself. Moreover, Paul's preference for the celibate life (a view not favored by the author of the Pastorals) may have helped promote that movement toward equality, for women who followed his example would not have had husbands at home who could serve as their religious authorities. Indeed, we know of such women from the second and later centuries—ascetics who preferred the freedom of single life to the restrictive confines of ancient marriage.

ANCIENT IDEOLOGIES OF GENDER

The Pauline churches eventually moved to the position embraced by the Pastoral epistles. They restricted the roles that women could play in the churches, insisted that Christians be married, and made Christian women submit to the dictates of their husbands both at home and in the church. It would be easy to attribute this move simply to male chauvinism, as much alive in antiquity as it is today, but the matter is somewhat more complicated. In particular, we need to consider what male domination might have *meant* in an ancient context, for most people in the ancient Roman world thought about gender relations in terms that are quite foreign to us who live in the modern Western world.

People in our world typically consider males and females to be two different kinds of human beings related to one another like two sides of the same coin. We sometimes refer to "my better half" or to "the other half of the human race." In antiquity, however, most people did not think of men and women as different in *kind* but as different in *degree*. For them there was a single continuum that constituted humanity. Some human beings were more fully developed and perfect specimens along that continuum. Women were on the lower end of the scale for biological reasons: they were "men" who had been only partially formed in the womb, and thus they were undeveloped or imperfect from birth. They differed from real men in that their penises had never grown, their lungs had not fully developed, and the rest of their bodies never would develop to their full potential. Thus, by their very nature, women were the weaker sex.

This biological understanding of the sexes had momentous social implications. Ancient Roman society was more forthright than ours in its appreciation of the importance of personal power. It openly revered those who were strong and domineering. Indeed, the virtue most cherished by males was "**honor**," the recognition of one's precedence over others, established chiefly through one's ability to achieve physical, economic, or political dominance. Other virtues were related to how one expressed this domination, for example, by showing courage and "manliness" when it was threatened, and self-control and restraint when it was exercised.

In Roman society, those who were "weaker" were supposed to be subservient to those who were stronger, and women were, by their very nature, weaker than men. Nature itself had set up a kind of pecking order, in which men were to be dominant over women as imperfect and underdeveloped beings, and women accordingly were to be submissive to men. This notion of dominance played itself out in all sorts of relationships, especially the sexual and domestic.

Most people in the Roman world appear to have thought that women were to be sexually dominated by men. This view was sometimes expressed in terms that might strike us as crass; it

Figure 18.3 Statue of a vestal virgin in the Roman forum, circa 70 C.E. The six vestal virgins, among the most prominent women in Roman society, were priestesses who guarded the sacred hearth of Rome and were accorded other special privileges and responsibilities.

was widely understood that men were designed to be penetrators while women were designed to be penetrated. Being sexually penetrated was a sign of weakness and submission. This is why same-sex relations between adult males were so frowned upon—not because of some natural repulsion that people felt for homosexual unions (in parts of the ancient world it was common and acceptable for adult males to have adolescent, and therefore inferior, boys as sex partners), but because such a relation meant that a man was being penetrated and therefore dominated. To be dominated was to lose one's claim to power and therefore one's honor, the principal male virtue.

Women's virtues, on the other hand, derived from their own sphere of influence. Whereas a man's were associated with the public arena of power relations—the forum, the business place, the military—a woman's were associated with the domestic sphere of the home. To be sure, women were extremely active and overworked and burdened with responsibilities and duties, but these were almost always associated with the household: making clothes, preparing food, having babies, educating children, taking care of personal finances, and the like. Even wealthy women shouldered considerable burdens, having to serve as household managers over family, slaves, and employees, while husbands concerned themselves with public affairs.

The domestic nature of a woman's virtues generally required her to keep out of the public eye. At least this is what the Roman men who wrote moral essays for women urged them to do. Women were not to speak in public debates, they were not to exercise authority over their husbands, and they were not to be involved with other men sexually, since this would mean that one man was dominating the wife of another, calling into question the husband's own power and, consequently, his honor.

For this reason, women who sought to exercise any power or authority over men were thought to be "unnatural." When women did attain levels of authority, as was happening with increasing regularity in the Roman world during the time of the New Testament, they were often viewed suspiciously and maligned for not knowing their place, for not maintaining properly female virtues, and for being sexually aggressive, even if their personal sex lives were totally unknown.

GENDER IDEOLOGY AND THE PAULINE CHURCHES

Our theoretical discussion of the **ideology of gender** in the Roman world, that is, of the way that people mentally and socially constructed sexual difference, gives us a backdrop for reconsidering the progressive oppression of women in the Pauline churches. Women may have been disproportionately represented in the earliest Christian communities. This at least was a constant claim made by the opponents of Christianity in the second century, who saw the inordinate number of women believers as a fault; remarkably, the defenders of the faith never denied it. The large number of women followers is not surprising, given the circumstance that the earliest Christian communities, including those established by Paul, were not set up as public institutions like the Jewish synagogues or the local trade associations, which met in public buildings and had high social visibility. Paul established house churches, gatherings of converts who met in private homes (see box 20.5), and in the Roman world, matters of the household were principally handled by women. Of course, the husband was lord of the house, with ultimate authority over everything from finances to household religion, but since the home was private space instead of public, most men gave their wives relatively free reign within its confines. If Paul's churches met in private homes, that is, in the world where women held some degree of jurisdiction, it is small wonder that women often exercised authority in his churches. It is also small wonder that men often allowed them to do so, for the home was the woman's domain. The heightened possibility for their own involvement is perhaps one reason why so many women were drawn to the religion in the first place.

Why, then, did women's roles come to be curtailed? It may be that as the movement grew and individual churches increased in size, more men came to be involved and the activities within the church took on a more public air. People thoroughly imbued with the ancient ideology of gender naturally found it difficult to avoid injecting into the church the perspectives that they brought with them when they converted. These views were a part of who they were, and they accepted them without question as being natural and right. And they could

ANOTHER EARLY CHRISTIAN TEXT

BOX 18.4 The *Acts of Thecla*

The Acts of the Apostles is the only narrative account of the apostles' (postresurrection) activities in the New Testament, but there were numerous accounts written later. These "apocryphal" (i.e., noncanonical) Acts are highly legendary descriptions of the adventures and escapades of individual apostles who take the Gospel throughout the world. And so we have a range of Acts: of Peter, of John, of Andrew, and so on. Among the most famous of the apocryphal Acts is one about a female disciple of Paul named Thecla.

At the beginning of the *Acts of Thecla*, the heroine overhears Paul preaching a message not of salvation through Christ's death and resurrection, but of the need to remain sexually chaste. **Thecla** is enraptured of Paul and his message and converts to be his follower, renouncing her wedding plans (since sex even within marriage is not allowed), much to the consternation of her fiancé and her mother.

These two try to get her to recant, and when she is unwilling, they hand her over to the local authorities for punishment. The account then narrates a series of episodes in which Thecla is put on trial and condemned to death for her refusal to participate in the life of society. But at every point, God intervenes and allows Thecla to escape unharmed. In one particularly famous story, Thecla is forced to face the wild beasts in the arena, and seeing a vat of man-eating seals, she throws herself in, thereby baptizing herself. To protect her from the fierce seals, God sends forth a bolt of lightening that kills them but spares her.

At the end of the narrative Thecla links up once more with Paul, who authorizes her to proclaim the Gospel, which she then does until the end of her long life.

One can see why this narrative would prove attractive especially to women in the early church, who could experience a vicarious liberation from their patriarchal lives (dominated either by their fathers or their husbands) by reading the accounts of Thecla, who applied "Paul's" message of chastity so as to free her from the bonds of marriage and home life to proclaim the gospel of God as a single woman.

always be justified on other, Christian, grounds. For instance, the Scriptures that these people inherited could be used to justify refusing women the right to exercise authority. The Jewish Bible was itself a product of antiquity, rooted in an Israelite world that advocated an ideology of submission as much as the Roman world did, although in a different way.

As a result of the mounting tensions, some Pauline believers, many of them women, we might suppose, began to urge that the views of sexual relations dominant in their culture were no longer appropriate for those who were "in Christ." In reaction to social pressures exerted on them from all sides, these people urged abstinence from marital relations altogether, arguing for sexual continence and freedom from the constraints imposed upon them by marriage. Moreover, they maintained that since they had been set free from all forms of evil by Christ, they were no longer restricted in what they could do in the public forum; they had just as much right and ability to teach and exercise authority as men.

Unfortunately for them, their views never became fully rooted. Indeed, their ideas may have contained the seed of their own destruction, in a manner of speaking. These celibate Christians obviously could not raise a new generation of believers in their views without producing children to train. With the passing of time, and the dwindling of the apocalyptic hope that had produced a sense of equality in the first place, there appeared to be little chance that the ideas so firmly implanted in people by their upbringing could be changed.

Those who advocated the rights of women to exercise authority in the church came to be widely opposed, and probably not only by men. As is true today, in antiquity women were molded as much as men by their culture's assumptions about what is right and wrong, natural and unnatural, appropriate and inappropriate. The proponents of the cultural status quo took the message of Paul (and Jesus) in a radically different direction, different not only from those who advocated a high profile for women in the churches but also from Paul and Jesus themselves. The eschatological fervor that had driven the original proclamation began to wane (notice how it is muted already in the Pastorals), and the church grew in size and strength. More and more it took on a public dimension, with a hierarchy and a structure, a public mission, a public voice, and a concern for public relations. The church, in other words, settled in for the long haul, and the apocalyptic message that had brought women relative freedom from the oppressive constraints of their society took a back seat, taking along with it those who had appealed to its authority to justify their important role in the life of the community.

Women came to be restricted in what they could do in the churches; no longer could they evangelize or teach or exercise authority. These were public activities reserved for the men. The women were to stay at home and protect their modesty, as was "natural" for them; they were to be submissive in all things to their husbands; and they were to bear children and fulfill their functions as the weaker and less perfect members of the human race. The Roman ideology of gender relations became Christianized, and the social implications of Paul's apocalyptic vision became lost except among the outcasts relegated to the margins of his churches, women whose tales have survived only by chance discovery, not by their inclusion in the pages of canonical scripture.

AT A GLANCE

BOX 18.5   Women in Early Christianity

1. Women were actively involved in Jesus' ministry.

2. Jesus evidently did not promote a social revolution for women, but his message of the coming Kingdom of God for the oppressed may have appealed to women who felt they had second-rate status in their world.

3. Women played a prominent role in Paul's churches, as missionaries and leaders; moreover, Paul maintained that in Christ the distinctions between male and female were obliterated.

4. But Paul did not advocate a social revolution for women; instead, he insisted that men and women maintain their distinctive gender roles.

5. After his death, Paul's ambivalence toward women's roles led some church members to stress the equality of women and others to insist on their subjugation to men. The latter perspective soon became dominant in mainstream Christianity.

6. Women may have enjoyed more prominent roles in the Christian communities early in the movement's history because churches met in the home, women's sphere of influence. When churches acquired a more public character, however, men appear to have asserted more fully their gender claims and removed women from positions of authority.

TAKE A STAND

1. Take either side in the following debate. Resolved: Paul's views of women were oppressive.

2. You are in an argument with your roommate who thinks that Christianity has always been bad news for women, and you want to maintain that Jesus himself could be seen as "liberated," someone who supported the independence and significance of women. Make your case.

3. You have read in the newspapers that a particular Christian denomination has voted to forbid women from serving as head pastors (or preachers, or priests) because of the "clear teachings" of the New Testament. How do you respond?

SUGGESTIONS FOR FURTHER READING

Kraemer, Ross. *Unreliable Witnesses: Religion, Gender, and History in the Greco-Roman Mediterranean.* New York: Oxford University Press, 2010. An up-to-date discussion of women and their place in society in the Greco-Roman world, especially in Judaism and Christianity.

Kraemer, Ross, and Mary Rose D'Angelo, eds. *Women and Christian Origins.* New York: Oxford University Press, 1999. An excellent collection of essays dealing with major aspects of women and gender in the New Testament, early Christianity, early Judaism, and the broader Greco-Roman world. Useful as a companion volume in courses on the New Testament and Christian origins.

Lefkowitz, Mary R., and Maureen B. Fant, eds. *Women's Lives in Greece and Rome: A Source Book in Translation.* 2d ed. Baltimore: Johns Hopkins University Press, 2005. An extremely valuable collection of ancient texts illuminating all the major aspects of women's lives in the Greco-Roman world.

McDonald, Dennis. *The Legend and the Apostle: The Battle for Paul in Story and Canon.* Philadelphia: Westminster John Knox, 1983. An intriguing and controversial book that claims that the Pastoral epistles were written to oppose the kinds of views of Paul, highly supportive of women, found in such books as the *Acts of Thecla.*

Osiek, Carolyn, Margaret MacDonald, and Janet Tulloch. *A Woman's Place: House Churches in Early Christianity.* Philadelphia: Fortress, 2005. Using the findings of archaeology and social history, as well as a careful reading of the relevant New Testament texts, the authors discuss the significance of the private home as a space for women in early Christianity. The book covers a large range of social issues related to the daily lives of early Christian women.

Pomeroy, Sarah. *Goddesses, Whores, Wives, and Slaves: Women in Classical Antiquity.* New York: Schocken, 1995. An important study of the changing views and social realities of women in the Greek and Roman worlds.

Schüssler Fiorenza, Elisabeth. *In Memory of Her: A Feminist Theological Reconstruction of Christian Origins.* New York: Crossroad, 1983. A sophisticated, controversial, and highly influential study of the roles women played in the formation of Christianity by a noted feminist New Testament scholar and historian; for more advanced students.

Torjesen, Karen Jo. *When Women Were Priests: Women's Leadership in the Early Church and the Scandal of Their Subordination in the Rise of Christianity.* San Francisco: HarperCollins, 1993. An interesting study of the shifting roles of women in the early Christian churches; particularly suitable for beginning students.

Wire, Antoinette Clark. *The Corinthian Women Prophets: A Reconstruction through Paul's Rhetoric.* Minneapolis: Fortress, 1990. An intriguing attempt to reconstruct the assumptions and views held among the women in the Corinthian congregation who took issue with Paul's perspectives; for more advanced students.

 KEY TERMS

| honor | Junia | Phoebe | Thecla |
| ideology of gender | Mary Magdalene | Prisca | |

Christian Conflicts with Jews and Pagans

HEBREWS AND 1 PETER

WHAT TO EXPECT

With this chapter we move into a consideration of the so-called catholic (or "general") epistles, by looking at the books of Hebrews and 1 Peter. These books deal with two problems encountered by the early Christians. First is the question of how they were to relate to the Jewish religion from which they originally emerged; this problem is taken up by the book of Hebrews, which strives to keep its readers from turning to Judaism by arguing that Christ and the religion he brings are far superior to anything that Judaism has to offer. Second is the question of how Christians were to respond to the persecutions they encountered in the pagan world into which they moved. This is an issue addressed by the book of 1 Peter, which tries to comfort its readers in the midst of their sufferings and to encourage them to remain committed to the faith despite the opposition they were facing.

Now that we have completed our study of the Gospels, Acts, and the letters attributed to Paul, we can move on to explore the remaining books of the New Testament: the **catholic epistles** and the Apocalypse of John. The term "catholic" may cause some confusion for modern readers: contrary to what one might think, these books were not written only by or for Roman Catholics. In this context, "catholic" means "universal" or "general"; for this reason, these books are sometimes called the **"general epistles."** Through the Christian ages, they have been thought to address universal problems experienced by Christians everywhere, as opposed to the letters of Paul, which have been thought to address specific congregations about specific problems.

One of the fruitful ways to go about studying these books is to situate them in a broader historical context to see how they address problems that Christians generally came to experience during the period in which they were written. Many of these problems have already cropped up in our study; they involve the early Christians' relationships with (a) non-Christian Jews, (b) antagonistic pagans, and (c) their own wayward members. In the present chapter we will consider the first two of these relationships; the third will be addressed in Chapter 20.

CHRISTIANS AND JEWS

Although Jesus and his earliest disciples were Jews, and the authors of the New Testament all understood their movement as springing from Judaism, as time went on, conflicts arose between Jews who believed in Jesus and those who did not. Tensions mounted as Jewish Christians began to convert Gentiles to this new faith and to claim that they, too, could be heirs of the promises given to Israel in the Hebrew Scriptures, even without adhering to Jewish customs and practices. The social conflicts that ensued created theological difficulties for the emerging Christian communities: if Gentiles did not have to become Jews in order to be Christians, how were they (and their Jewish-Christian brothers and sisters in the church) to understand themselves in relationship to Judaism?

Before seeing how these issues came to be resolved in one of our early Christian writings, we should begin by examining the more general problem of how early Christians came to understand themselves as a social group that was distinct from Judaism. To use a modern sociological term, this involves the problem of Christian **"self-definition."**

EARLY CHRISTIAN SELF-DEFINITION

Self-definition is a process by which any group of individuals understands itself to be a distinct group. Each of us, of course, belongs to a number of social groups. You are a member of a family; a student at a college or university or professional school; a citizen of a state and a country; perhaps the member of a church, synagogue, or other religious congregation; and possibly a participant in some other academic, religious, or civic group (e.g., a sorority, Campus Crusade, or the Rotary Club). Each of these social networks has ways of understanding and defining itself with respect to both what its members have in common and what makes them different from those who don't belong. These boundaries between insiders and outsiders are part of the group's self-definition.

For some social groups the boundaries are well defined and rigid; for others they are quite loose. For instance, members of a strict fundamentalist Bible church may have a very firm understanding of who is inside and who is outside the body of the faithful. To belong to this church, you may have to hold certain beliefs (e.g., a belief in the Bible as the inerrant Word of God and the literal second coming of Christ) and participate in certain practices (e.g., you must be baptized in this particular church, and you must attend church twice on Sunday and prayer meeting on Wednesday evening). Those who do such things are among the "saved" (insiders) and those who don't are among the "lost" (outsiders).

This rigorous form of self-definition stands in sharp contrast to that found, say, in a liberal Presbyterian church, where members may know why they are Christian and, in general, understand what it means to be Presbyterian, but who do not at all think that they alone are God's chosen or that it would be an irreversible tragedy and unpardonable sin if some of their members were to transfer membership to the Methodist church across the street.

All social groups define themselves by establishing what it means to be a member and how belonging to the group sets a person off from those who do not belong. This has always been the case, as long as human societies have existed. It was certainly true in the early days of Christianity, when one group of Jews understood themselves to be distinct from other Jews (and from everyone else as well) in that they believed that the messiah had come, that he had died and been raised from the dead, and that they could have a right standing before God by faith in him. These beliefs helped to characterize the group and to distinguish it from all other social groups. Bitter conflicts eventually emerged as the group began to define itself more and more rigidly and as those who were outside the community grew hostile toward their beliefs and practices. Opposition drove the group yet further inward as its members began to insist on conversion for admission, practiced distinct initiation rites such as baptism, observed other periodic rituals such as the Lord's Supper, devised distinctive sets of beliefs that were to be confessed by all group members, and condemned those who remained on the outside.

As Christianity developed, it was compelled to define itself not only in relation to the Jewish world from which it emerged but also in relation to the polytheistic world into which it moved and from which it began to draw its greatest number of converts. Sometimes these different aspects of self-definition reinforced each other. Let me point out just one of the many issues involved. As we have seen, Jews were somewhat anomalous in the Greco-Roman world in that (*a*) they maintained that only one God, the God of Israel, was to be worshiped, and (*b*) they adhered to ancient practices that had been ordered by this God as part of his Law, for example, the circumcision of males, Sabbath observance, and dietary restrictions (i.e., these were among the social boundaries of the Jews as a group in the Roman world). Within Roman society, all other people were expected to participate in the cult to the state gods. Jews were exempt because they were an ancient people with ancient customs that forbade such participation.

Along came the Christians, most of them former pagans, who did not appear to be Jewish to most outsiders: they worked on the Sabbath, they ate pork, and their men weren't circumcised. Yet they claimed to worship the God of the Jews and him alone; in fact, they claimed to be the new people of this God. As a result of their monotheism, they refused to worship the state gods. But they had no ancestral traditions to claim—except the traditions of the Jews, most of which they did not even seem to keep (e.g., circumcision, kosher food laws, and so on). If, as was generally accepted in the empire, the gods were angered by those who refused to offer them cult (Jews excepted, given their ancestral traditions), and Christians refused to offer them cult without having any ancestral traditions to fall back on, who would be to blame when the gods sent disaster against the city—an earthquake, famine, epidemic, or the like? You guessed it.

Partially to defend themselves in a world in which nearly everyone knew that a new religion could not possibly be true and in which an exclusivistic cult would certainly not be protected by the state, Christians eventually had to explain how their religion was not recent but venerable with age, as old as Moses and the prophets, the ancient writers of ancient Israel. This act of self-definition was carried out, to some extent at least, for the purpose of public relations, that is, for political gain. If the Christians were the true heirs of the promises of Israel, they had a defense against persecution.

The need for self-defense is just one aspect of the relationship of Christianity to Judaism that drove Christians to develop a sense of group identity. There were other, more internal aspects as well, such as the need for Christians to explain some of the basics of the new faith to converts. How was it that the God who had chosen the Jews to be his people in days of old had now in these recent days chosen a different people, the Christians? How were believers in Jesus related to Jews who did not believe in him? And what was their connection to the Jewish Scriptures?

We have already seen that different Christians answered these questions in different ways—recall our studies of Matthew, Luke-Acts, Galatians, and Ephesians. The differences are magnified even more when we turn to other writing produced by early Christians: the Epistle to the Hebrews.

Figure 19.1   Coin of the emperor Vespasian, which commemorates the conquest of Judea by Titus with the inscription "Judea Taken Captive." The fall of Jerusalem was a significant event in the development of Jewish-Christian relations.

CONTINUITY AND SUPERIORITY: THE EPISTLE TO THE HEBREWS

The Epistle to the Hebrews portrays the Jewish Law as partial and imperfect, unable to accomplish its task of putting people into a right standing before

God. The inadequacy of the old covenant, the book claims, was recognized even by the Old Testament prophets, who predicted that God would establish a new covenant to do what the old one could not. This new covenant was foreshadowed in the legislation of Moses and came to reality only in the work of Jesus. The old has now passed away, and believers must cling to the new.

The Book, the Author, and the Audience

Although Hebrews is normally labeled an epistle, this designation is not particularly fitting. Even though the book has an epistolary closing (13:20–25), there is no epistolary prescript. The author names neither himself nor his addressees, nor does he include an opening prayer, benediction, or thanksgiving on their behalf. Moreover, the author describes his book not as a letter but as a "word of exhortation" (13:22). This is a fair summary of the book's contents, leading most scholars to think that it was originally a sermon or homily delivered by a Christian preacher to his congregation. The author may have composed the sermon to be read aloud (most literature in antiquity was, in fact, read publicly), or possibly he wrote it down after it was delivered orally (from notes?). If it did originate as a sermon, then the epistolary closing with its benediction, exhortation, travel plans, final greetings, and farewell (13:20–25) may have simply been tacked on by its author, or by someone else who read the piece, when he sent it to another community. It is particularly intriguing that Timothy is mentioned at the end (13:23). Are we to infer from this that Paul wrote the sermon?

The book does not claim to be written by Paul; like the New Testament Gospels, it is anonymous. But it came to be included in the canon only after Christians of the third and fourth centuries became convinced that Paul had written it. Modern scholars, however, are unified in recognizing that he did not. The writing style is not Paul's, and the major topics of discussion (e.g., the Old Testament priesthood and the Jewish sacrificial system) are things that Paul scarcely mentions, let alone emphasizes. Moreover, the way this author understands such critical terms as "faith" (11:1) differs markedly from what you find in the writings of the apostle.

It is difficult to say, then, who did write the book. A number of names have been proposed over the years, including such early Christian notables as Barnabas, Apollos, and Priscilla. It is safest, however, simply to accept the pronouncement of a famous Christian scholar of the third century, Origen of Alexandria, who said: "As for who has written it, only God knows."

We are in a better position to say something about the book's audience. The author presupposes that they are Christians who had previously undergone some serious persecutions for their faith, including imprisonment and the confiscation of property (10:32–34), although none of them had been martyred (12:4). From antiquity the book has been entitled "To the Hebrews," but there is some considerable doubt over whether these persecuted Christians were Jews or Gentiles. For instance, when the author reminds them of the instruction they received upon first coming into the fold, he includes such matters as faith in God, belief in the resurrection of the dead, and eternal judgment (6:1–2). Surely Jews attracted to the Christian religion would already have known about such things. It seems more probable, then, that we are dealing with a group of Gentile converts who had experienced some persecution for their Christian faith, possibly (although not certainly) for reasons similar to those sketched earlier, that is, for refusing to worship state gods without having the Jewish roots that would make this refusal acceptable to local state officials.

The author, then, is writing to demonstrate to them that Christianity is superior to Judaism. Possibly he fears that members of his audience are being tempted to convert away from Christianity to non-Christian Judaism, perhaps to escape persecution. To abandon Christ for Judaism, in his judgment, would be a serious mistake. To do so would be to prefer the foreshadowing of God's salvation to salvation itself and to opt for the imperfect and flawed religion of the Jewish Scriptures rather than its perfect and complete fulfillment in Christ. For this author, Christ does indeed stand in continuity with the religion of the Jews as set forth in their sacred writings, but he is superior to that religion in every way, and those who reject the salvation that he alone can provide are in danger of falling under the wrath of God.

The Overarching Theme of the Sermon: The Superiority of Christ

The superiority of Christ and of the salvation he brings is the constant refrain sounded throughout this homily. Consider the following points that the author stresses.

Christ Is Superior to the Prophets (1:1–3). The Jewish prophets were God's spokespersons in former times, but now he has spoken through his own Son, the perfect image of God himself.

Christ Is Superior to the Angels (1:4–11; 2:5–18). The angels mentioned in the Old Testament are God's messengers par excellence, but Christ is his very Son, exalted to a position of power next to God's heavenly throne. Angels are ministers for those destined for salvation, but Christ is the Son of God whose suffering actually brought this salvation.

Christ Is Superior to Moses (3:1–6). Moses was a servant in "God's house," but Jesus is the Son of the house.

Christ Is Superior to Joshua (4:1–11). Joshua gave the people of Israel peace (or "rest") after the Promised Land had been conquered; but as the Scriptures themselves indicate, the people of Israel could not fully enjoy that peace (or "enter into their rest") because they were disobedient. Christ brings a more perfect peace.

Christ Is Superior to the Jewish Priesthood (4:14–5:10; 7:1–29). Like the **Jewish high priests**, Jesus was personally acquainted with human weaknesses that require a mediator before God, but unlike them, he was without sin and did not need to offer a sacrifice for himself before representing the people. He is superior to the priests descended from Levi because he is the one promised in the Scriptures as the priest from the line of Melchizedek (Ps 110:4), the mysterious figure whom Abraham, the ancestor of Levi, honored by paying one-tenth of his goods (Gen 14:17–20). For this reason, Levi himself, as represented by his ancestor, was inferior and subservient to **Melchizedek** and the descendant from his line. If the Levitical priests had been able to make the people of God perfect, God would not

have had to promise to send a priest from the line of Melchizedek into the world. Moreover, Christ is superior to these other priests because they are many, but he is one, and unlike them, he needed to offer his sacrifice only once, not repeatedly.

Christ Is Minister of a Superior Covenant (8:1–13). God promised in the Scriptures to bring a new covenant (Jer 31:31–34), thereby showing that the old covenant with the Jews was outmoded and imperfect. Christ is the minister of this new covenant.

Christ Is Minister in a Superior Tabernacle (9:1–28). The earthly **tabernacle**, where Jewish sacrifices were originally performed, was constructed according to a heavenly model. Unlike the Jewish priests, Christ did not minister in the earthly replica; he brought his sacrifice to heaven, to the real sanctuary, into the presence of God himself.

Christ Makes a Superior Sacrifice (10:1–18). Christ's sacrifice was perfect, unlike those that had to be offered year after year by the Jewish priests. His death brought complete forgiveness of sins; there is therefore no longer any need for sacrifice.

The Method of the Author's Demonstration

Like the author of Matthew, the author of Hebrews bases his understanding of Jesus on the Jewish Scriptures. This may seem somewhat ironic, in view of his insistence that Jesus is superior to anything that the Jewish religion has to offer. But as we have already seen, he was not the only Christian author who used the Jewish Bible to show that the Judaism he knew was inadequate and passé. The apostle Paul, for example, argued that the Jewish Law itself taught his doctrine of justification by faith apart from the Law. The author of Hebrews takes a different tack. He claims that the Scriptures anticipated a future act of God that would surpass everything that had come before. Somewhat like Matthew, he conceptualizes this anticipation in two different ways, as a prophecy that was to be fulfilled and as a foreshadowing that was to be made real.

Prophecy-Fulfillment. On several occasions the author uses predictions of the Jewish Scriptures to show that God had planned something new and better to supplant the Jewish religion. This new something, of course, would stand in continuity with Judaism; otherwise there would scarcely be any reason for the author to quote the Jewish Bible. As something new, however, it would be superior to that which it had been sent to replace. The clearest expression of the author's view comes in his lengthiest citation of the Old Testament (Jer 31:31–34):

> For if that first covenant had been faultless, there would have been no need to look for a second one. God finds fault with them when he says: "The days are surely coming, says the Lord, when I will establish a new covenant with the house of Israel and with the house of Judah . . . for they did not continue in my covenant, and so I had no concern for them," says the Lord. (8:7–9)

He concludes the citation, which continues for three more verses, by saying that "in speaking of 'a new covenant,' [God] has made the first one obso-

lete" (8:13). That is to say, the Scriptures predicted that God would establish a new covenant which would make the older religion, as set forth in the Scriptures themselves, invalid. In the author's judgment, the Scriptural prediction has now been fulfilled in Christ.

Shadow-Reality. The author of Hebrews also understands Christ to be superior to the religion of the Jews to the extent that the reality of a thing is superior to its foreshadowing. On two occasions he makes this claim explicit: both the Old Testament tabernacle (8:5) and the Law itself (10:1) were but "shadows" of another reality; on yet other occasions he appears to presuppose this view without explicitly stating it (9:23–24; 13:10–13).

Scholars have long recognized that the terms "shadow" and "reality" were popular philosophical metaphors that had been developed nearly 500 years earlier by Plato. Plato insisted that things appearing to be real are often only shadows of a

WHAT DO YOU THINK?

BOX 19.1 Divergent Views of Christ in Hebrews

We have seen that sometime during the second century, Christians began to debate whether Jesus was God or man or somehow both. It is fairly easy to see how a book like Hebrews could have been used by all sides in such a debate. On the one hand, there are passages that appear to embrace an exalted view of Christ, more exalted than what is found almost anywhere else in the New Testament. You may have noticed that elsewhere in the New Testament Jesus is rarely, if ever, explicitly called "God" (although he is constantly called "Son of God"). Yet Heb 1:8 presents a quotation of the Psalms in which God is said to be speaking to his Son and calls him "God": "But of the Son, [God] says, 'Your throne, O God, is forever and ever.'"

Is this not an unequivocal statement that Christ himself is God? One difficulty is that the Greek of this verse can be translated in different ways. For example, it could also be rendered: "But of the Son [God] says, 'God is your throne forever and ever.'"

Other passages in Hebrews could be used by the opposite side in the later Christological debates to

show that Jesus was a full flesh-and-blood human. One of the most striking verses is 5:7, which indicates that Jesus went to his death with "loud cries and tears," beseeching God to save him from death, and that he "learned obedience" (meaning that he learned how to obey?) through his suffering. This does not sound like the calm and assured Jesus of some of the Gospel accounts (e.g., Luke and John); here Jesus almost seems to go to the cross kicking and screaming.

Other second- and third-century Christians, of course, could have argued that since Hebrews has both kinds of passages they have to be reconciled in some way, for example, by saying that Jesus started out as a normal human being but became divine at his exaltation (cf. Phil 2:6–10), or that Jesus was at one and the same time both man and God.

How would the author of Hebrews himself have reacted to these debates or reconciled the divergent views that he appears to have written? Regrettably, we will never know.

greater reality. Physical pleasure, for example, has all the appearance of being a superior good; why else would so many people actively pursue it, some of them devoting their entire lives to little else? In itself, though, pleasure is good only in appearance. Witness the hangover, the county jail, and the halfway house. For Plato, the real good is located somewhere outside of bodily pleasure, which is itself, therefore, a mere shadow of reality.

Plato's most famous illustration of this idea is his **Allegory of the Cave**, found in Book VII of his influential dialogue *The Republic*. Let us suppose, says Socrates, the speaker of the dialogue, that there is a cave in which a number of people are chained together on the floor in such a way as to be unable to see anything except what lies in front of their eyes. These prisoners have always lived this way and so do not realize that they are in a cave or that there are other things in the world to be seen. Some distance behind them, unbeknownst to them, is a low half-wall and beyond that a large fire. Between the half-wall and the fire are people carrying puppets in the shapes of plants and animals and humans. The light from the fire casts the shadows of these objects on the wall of the cave that is before the prisoners' eyes. The prisoners themselves can see only the shadows, and when they hear the voices of those who carry the puppets echoing off the wall before them, they naturally assume that it is the images themselves who are speaking. These shadows are the only phenomena that they experience, and they take them to be real—in fact, to be reality in its fullness. For them, these shadows *are* plants, animals, and humans.

What would happen, asks Socrates, if one of these chained persons were set free from his bondage and stood up to look around? He would no doubt be blinded by the bright light; in his terror, he might sit down and beg to be chained again. But if this person's eyes grew accustomed to the light, so that he could see that the images on the wall were actually shadows of puppets, he would then realize how fully his senses had been deceived. What he had taken to be reality were in fact only shadows.

Suppose this person then proceeded to leave the cave and to enter into the light of the sun. A similar sequence of events would no doubt occur. First he would be blinded by the light (in comparison to which the fire in the cave could itself be thought of as only a shadow). Only after his eyes adjusted

would he come to see that not even the puppets had been the real thing, but only imperfect representations of real-life plants, animals, and people. No one who came to this kind of realization would choose to return to the cave to spend the rest of his days watching shadows cast on the wall. Once one has experienced reality, there is no turning back.

For the author of Hebrews, Christ is the reality that was foreshadowed in the Jewish Scriptures. As such, he is superior to anything Judaism has to offer. The author, however, is not concerned merely with making a debating point to an impartial audience. He is writing to Christians, and his ultimate goal is quite clear: he wants to convince his readers that for them there is no turning back to the shadow of Judaism once they have experienced the reality of Christ.

The Goal of the Author's Exposition

Throughout his exposition the author of Hebrews repeatedly exhorts his readers not to fall away from their commitment to Christ. Many of these exhortations are based on the notion that Christ is the reality behind the shadows of the Jewish Scriptures. The Old Testament contains numerous stories of individuals who chose to disobey God. As a rule, the penalties for disobedience were not pretty—being left as rotting carcasses in the wilderness and the like. If this was what happened to people who spurned the imperfect and incomplete revelation of God, asks the author, what gruesome fate awaits those who reject the revelation that is perfect and complete? If rejecting God's servants was bad, what happens to those who reject his Son? The logic of this argument can be easily illustrated: if I was upset when my son played with matches, think how I'd react if he torched the house.

The first exhortation occurs in 2:1–4: "If the message declared through angels was valid, and every transgression or disobedience received a just penalty, how can we escape if we neglect so great a salvation [i.e., provided by Christ]?" The answer: there will be no escape. A similar exhortation appears in 3:7–18: if those who were disobedient to Moses, God's servant, were destroyed in the wilderness, imagine what will happen to those who disobey Jesus, God's Son.

Sometimes these warnings leave less to the imagination, as in the dire and threatening words of 6:1–6, where the author claims there can be no

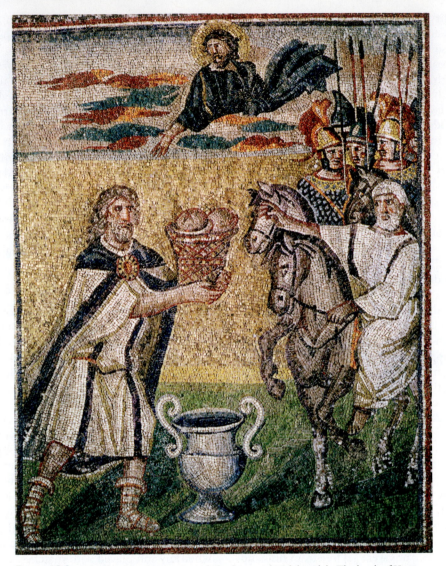

Figure 19.2 A medieval representation of Abraham and Melchizedek. The book of Hebrews indicates that the mysterious figure of Melchizedek, mentioned in Genesis 14 as one to whom Abraham, the father of the Jews, gave a tenth of his goods, was none other than Christ himself.

hope of salvation for those who have "fallen away" after having "been enlightened," that is, for those who leave the faith after once having joined. In the author's opinion, such people are "crucifying again the Son of God and . . . holding him up to contempt" (v. 6). So too in chapter 10:

> If we willfully persist in sin after having received the knowledge of the truth, there no longer remains a

sacrifice for sins, but a fearful prospect of judgment, and a fury of fire that will consume the adversaries (vv. 26–27). . . . It is a fearful thing to fall into the hands of the living God (v. 29).

Why does the author need to give such harsh warnings to people who are members of the congregation? Evidently because some of them were being tempted to fall away. The author does not explicitly state where these people might go after leaving the Christian community, but there can scarcely be any doubt, given everything else that he says about Christ's superiority to non-Christian Judaism. He is afraid that Christians will renounce Christ to join the synagogue, and he's doing everything in his power to stop them.

The author's bottom line is that his readers will inherit the salvation that God has promised only if they remain within the Christian church. And so he exhorts them: "Do not, therefore, abandon that confidence of yours; it brings great reward. For you need endurance, so that when you have done the will of God, you may receive what was promised" (10:35–36). As the Scriptures say, "my righteous one will live by faith" (Hab 2:4, quoted in 10:37). For this author to live by faith appears to mean something different from what it meant for Paul, who also quoted Hab 2:4 (Rom 1:17; Gal 3:11). For the author of Hebrews, faith does not mean a trusting acceptance of Christ's death and resurrection for sins; it means being confident that God will do what he promised. Or in his own more poetic

words, "Faith is the assurance of things hoped for, the conviction of things not seen" (11:1).

Chapter 11 recounts the deeds of the faithful from the Jewish Scriptures, those who lived by and acted on their assurance of that which they had not yet experienced. Jesus himself acted in this way (12:1–2). His followers need to emulate his example. Even though they suffer (as he himself did), they need to remain faithful to God's promises so as to reap their future reward. The book ends with a series of exhortations to love one another, to refrain from sexual improprieties, to obey the community's leaders, and to abstain from false teachings, especially those that promote adherence to the laws of Judaism (13:1–18).

The Epistle to the Hebrews and the Problem of Self-Definition

What was the social context of the author of this book and the readers to whom he made such a strong appeal? Even though we don't know the full story, we can make some plausible stabs at the situation. As we have seen, from its earliest

ANOTHER EARLY CHRISTIAN TEXT

BOX 19.2 The *Letter of Barnabas*

Few early Christian writings were as important or potentially inflammatory as a book called the *Letter of Barnabas*. The book was treasured by many early Christians, some of whom argued that it belonged in the New Testament canon (it was found in some of the earliest New Testament manuscripts). It was allegedly written by the traveling companion of Paul, Barnabas (see Acts 9), and deals with a problem that Paul, too, was concerned about: the relation of Christians and Jews. But the *Letter of Barnabas* has a view of this relationship quite different from that found in the canonical books. Barnabas maintains that Judaism is and always has been a false religion, that Jews have never understood their own laws, and that the Old Testament is therefore a Christian, not a Jewish, book.

One of the interesting elements of Barnabas's argument involves his interpretation of passages

from the Old Testament, in which he shows that the (Jewish) literal interpretation is wrong, because God intended the passages to be taken figuratively. And so he goes through passages concerned with kosher food laws, Sabbath observance, temple worship, and even circumcision, to show that these were not to be followed literally but that they were intended to convey spiritual truths. Sometimes his rejection of literal readings is harsh and his language is vitriolic. The Jews, Barnabas avers, have never been faithful to God and their religion is based on a misreading of their own text, the result of being misled by an evil angel.

The history of anti-Semitism was horrible enough as it was; imagine how much worse it may have been had this book been included among the sacred Scriptures, lending its authority to anti-Jewish attitudes among the Christians.

days the Christian message was closely tied to the apocalyptic notion that the end of the age was imminent, that the forces of evil were on the rise but God would soon intervene on behalf of his people and vindicate their suffering. With the passing of time and the failure of the end to appear, some believers gave up their confidence in this apocalyptic message. Generally, we don't know what happened to such people. Did some of them return to their former gods? Probably. Did some of them maintain their monotheistic devotion to the God of Israel but jettison their faith in Christ as his messiah and join the local synagogue as Gentile "God-fearers"? No doubt some of them did that as well. The author appears fearful that such a conversion (or return) to Judaism might occur among some members of his community.

We don't know where the author's community was located or when he lived. When he conveys greetings from "those from Italy" (13:24), he could mean either "those of us who are presently living in Italy" or "those who hale from Italy but are presently living with us." Some scholars have thought that his references to priests who continually perform sacrifices indicate that the Temple was still standing when he wrote, and therefore that the book must have been written before 70 C.E. Others have pointed out that later Jewish authors also spoke of the Temple in the present tense long

after it was gone and have noted that almost all of the references to the Jewish sacrificial system in the book are drawn from the descriptions in the Old Testament rather than from first-century practice. Moreover, the few explicit references to the community's history suggest a somewhat later date, possibly during the final quarter of the first century. These Christians had earlier suffered persecution but were now experiencing some complacency and possibly some defections.

Whenever he was writing, the anonymous author of Hebrews was concerned to establish appropriate boundaries for his Christian community; that is, he was involved with the problem of Christian self-definition. Even though his community was evidently made up largely of converted polytheists, they understood themselves (or at least the author thought they ought to understand themselves) as the true heirs of the traditions of Israel. They were clearly in conflict with other groups that also claimed these traditions for themselves, in particular, with groups of non-Christian Jews. As we will discuss later in this chapter, non-Christian Jews far outnumbered Christians at this time, and as a rule they found it ludicrous for non-Jews to claim to understand the Jewish religion better than they themselves did.

Nonetheless, the Christian author of Hebrews, whether he himself was Jewish or not, claimed that

BOX 19.3 Hebrews

1. The book of Hebrews is anonymous, although it was eventually admitted into the canon by Christians who thought Paul had written it. Modern scholars are unified in thinking that he did not.

2. The book was probably produced sometime near the end of the first century.

3. It is frequently called an "epistle," but it appears in fact to be a Christian homily or sermon—the earliest one we have, outside those in the book of Acts.

4. It is written for a group of Christians who have experienced persecution. Despite the book's title

("To the Hebrews"), the recipients appear to have been Gentiles.

5. The author's purpose is to convince his listeners not to convert to Judaism.

6. To accomplish this goal, he stresses that Christ and faith in him are superior to anything that Judaism can offer.

7. The author maintains that the Old Testament and the religion it presents are mere foreshadowings of the reality that came into being with Christ.

Christ fulfilled the Old Testament revelation and that his followers were the true people of God. Those outside the Christian faith, whether Jews or Gentiles, could not legitimately claim to be the heirs of the religion espoused by Moses, for that religion looked forward to what was to come. It was but a foreshadowing of the salvation that God had promised in the prophets, a salvation brought in the person of his son Jesus, the messiah. In this sense, the Christian religion was continuous with, but ultimately superior to, the religion of non-Christian Judaism, and Christians were not to yield to the temptation of preferring the foreshadowing of salvation to salvation itself. Those who fell away from their Christian faith would learn first-hand that it is indeed "a fearful thing to fall into the hands of the living God" (10:29).

 ## CHRISTIANS AND PAGANS

Now that we have considered the relationship of Christians to the Jewish religion from which they emerged, we can move to reflect on their relation-

ship to the broader world into which they moved, the pagan world that sometimes tolerated the Christian religion and sometimes attacked it; in particular, we can consider the tensions that arose between Christians and pagans and the early Christian persecutions that sometimes resulted.

The Persecution of the Early Christians

Perhaps as a result of too many bad Hollywood movies, many people have a completely erroneous sense of what it meant to be a Christian in the Roman Empire. It is commonly imagined, for example, that Christians were an immediate and important concern to the upper echelons of the Roman administration, who saw the Christian movement as taking the world by storm and felt constrained to stop it by any means necessary, and therefore launched massive and violent persecutions as a kind of counterattack. In this view, the Roman emperor or senate declared the religion illegal and used the troops and the law courts to the fullest extent possible to repress it. As a result, the Christians went into hiding, meeting secretly

 ## ANOTHER EARLY CHRISTIAN TEXT

BOX 19.4 The Easter Sermon of Melito of Sardis

The anti-Jewish attitudes of some of the early Christians attested already in the New Testament and, say, the *Letter of Barnabas* (see box 19.2) was ratcheted up even higher with the passing of time, as Christianity became a distinctively non-Jewish religion that reacted with considerable antagonism toward Jews who refused to accept Jesus as the messiah. One of the earliest surviving sermons of early Christianity was discovered in the middle of the twentieth century. It is a sermon that was delivered by an important bishop named Melito, of the city of Sardis. It was written near the end of the second Christian century and is intent on showing that since Jesus really was the Passover Lamb who was slain, the Jews are not only guilty for rejecting him: they are guilty for killing him. The sermon is powerful in its rhetoric, but frightening in its vitriol. Here is a small sample.

Pay attention, all families of the nations, and observe! An extraordinary murder has taken place in the center of Jerusalem, in the city devoted to God's law, in the city of the Hebrews, in the city of the prophets, in the city thought of as just And who has been murdered? And who is the murderer? I am ashamed to give the answer, but give it I must. . . . The one who hung the earth in space is himself hanged; the one who fixed the heavens in place, is himself impaled; the one who firmly fixed all things is himself firmly fixed to the tree. The Lord Is insulted. God has been murdered. The King of Israel has been destroyed by the right hand of Israel.

This is the first recorded instance in which the Jewish people are accused by Christians of "deicide," the "murder of God." It was an inflammatory charge, one that would lead to many acts of gratuitous violence against Jews down through the Middle Ages and on into the anti-Semitic actions of modern times.

in the catacombs, conversing only in private, and identifying one another in public through secret signs such as the symbol of the fish.

This view of Christianity in the Roman Empire may make for an indifferent screenplay, but it is far worse from a historical perspective. In fact, Christianity appears to have made only a scant impact on the empire during the first hundred years of its existence. In none of the documents that have survived from pagan authors of the first century of the Common Era—whether histories or philosophical treatises, travelogues or works of fiction, private correspondence or public inscriptions, legal documents or personal notes—in no pagan document of any kind is either Jesus or Christianity mentioned at all. This was not a religion that was on everybody's minds and inspired terror in the hearts of the Roman administration.

I do not mean to say that no one had ever heard of Christianity. People obviously had heard of it, and many of those who did were not kindly disposed toward it. This included at least one of the first-century emperors, as we will see. But the religion was not of major concern to the rulers of the empire or their underlings. During the second half of the first century, it was a minor and insignificant nuisance, a mosquito to be swatted, not a tiger to be tamed.

It was not swatted through an officially enacted empirewide persecution. Contrary to popular imagination, there was no imperial legislation against Christianity and correspondingly no empirewide persecution of the Christians until nearly two centuries after the time of Paul. Not until 250 C.E. did an emperor proscribe the religion and urge persecutions on a large scale, and even then there is some question concerning how massive the scale was. In any event, during the first century Christians were not driven underground and forced to communicate in private and to hide from the authorities in the Roman catacombs.

The Legal Standing of Christians

Christians had the same rights and responsibilities as everyone else in the empire. Starting a new cult was not illegal; it happened occasionally throughout the entire Hellenistic-Roman period. Christians had the right to worship whatever God they chose, even the Jewish God. Furthermore, the Roman authorities did not care whether the Christians who worshiped this God lived and acted as Jews. It was certainly not against any law for Christians to believe and proclaim that Jesus himself was divine, as some of them eventually came to do. As we have seen, most people believed that gods could come to earth in human form, sometimes as great philosophers or powerful rulers. Some people thought that the emperor himself was a god. To proclaim one more person divine was neither sacrilegious nor sinister.

Morever, Christians were within their legal rights to communicate their faith to others, to meet together in private homes, to participate in their own distinctive cultic practices, and to read their sacred Scriptures. Why, then, were Christians like Paul sometimes put in prison, subjected to corporal punishment, and made to stand trial? If they hadn't broken the law, how was it that Christians were found guilty of crimes and punished by torture and imprisonment? To answer the question, we must first visit the Roman legal system.

Roman civil law was extremely sophisticated and nuanced; indeed, it provided the basis for the systems of civil legislation found in European and North American countries today. Disputes over property rights, contractual obligations, financial liabilities, and marriage arrangements were all hammered out by Roman legislators in careful and precise detail. Roman criminal law, on the other hand, was a different matter altogether. Criminal activities were not strictly defined, and punishments were not prescribed by law. In fact, odd though it may seem, neither the Roman emperor nor the Roman senate passed criminal legislation that was binding on all inhabitants of the provincial realms.

The provinces were ruled by governors who were appointed by either the senate or the emperor (depending on whose jurisdiction the province was under). These governors were drawn from the highest ranking officials of the empire, senators and, occasionally, other aristocrats who were judged capable of handling the rule of an indigenous population. The provincial governors had two main responsibilities: to keep the peace and to collect the taxes. They themselves had more than a little stake in these matters, since the governors

Figure 19.3 Many Romans believed that the Roman gods were responsible for their military and political successes, as evident in this silver coin that shows a Roman goddess crowning the memorialized image of a soldier after a victory.

received a cut of the tax money they brought in. Moreover, they were granted nearly absolute power to accomplish their objectives. To assist provincial authorities in their duties, the senate would occasionally pass bills proposing rules of governance; these were not federal laws, however, but more like pieces of official advice. In any situation, the governor was expected to use his best judgment to deal with problems that arose, employing whatever means necessary to maintain public order and maximize revenue collection.

Being able to employ any means necessary gave governors the power of life and death. From a Roman administrative point of view, Pontius Pilate was altogether justified in condemning Jesus to death as a public nuisance. People like Pilate were expected to deal with cases like this with justice when possible and severity when necessary.

This takes us, now, to the minor irritations caused by the Christians and the resultant persecutions that were launched in various localities throughout the early empire. Even though the Christian religion was not illegal, in the strict sense of the term (i.e., there were no laws against it), we know that Christians themselves were frequently involved in socially disruptive and therefore pun-

ishable behavior, as can be seen, for instance, in the accounts in Acts. It was the magistrate's job to resolve the situation by following his best judgment, for example, by punishing parties that caused the disturbance.

Christians as Disturbers of the Peace

What kinds of public disturbances did Christians cause? From our earliest sources we learn that Christians considered their communities of faith to be self-contained groups that made exclusive demands on the individual member. People were to leave behind their former associations to join the church. This involved abandoning their earlier religious affiliations and, if necessary, their own families. Christians claimed that their Lord himself had meant to disrupt the normal family lives of his followers (see box 9.11). From a historical perspective, it is difficult to know whether Jesus actually spoke the words that are attributed to him on this score, but they certainly reflect the realities of the churches that later professed his name:

> Do not think that I have come to bring peace to the earth; I have not come to bring peace, but a sword. For I have come to set a man against his father, and a daughter against her mother, and a daughter-in-law against her mother-in-law; and one's foes will be members of one's own household. Whoever loves father or mother more than me is not worthy of me; and whoever loves son or daughter more than me is not worthy of me. (Matt 10:34–37)

Families were disrupted when one member became a Christian and rejected all family ties in favor of a commitment to the church. Indeed, the Christian church portrayed itself as a convert's new family: believers called one another brother and sister, they had "fathers" and "mothers" in the faith, and God himself was the Father of all.

That this new family of faith was to replace one's real family is evident in such early Christian narratives as Paul's adventures with Thecla, a model convert who left her betrothed to follow the apostle in a life of chastity (see also box 18.4). This religious family opened up new possibilities of life for Christian converts; for those outside, however, the impact was sometimes jarring and disruptive. As you might imagine, the abandoned parents and the men left at the altar were not at all pleased. At least in the apocryphal Acts, they sometimes did something about it by stirring up public opinion against the Christians and demanding judgment from the governor.

The early Christian communities apparently were viewed with suspicion and distrust for other reasons as well. As we have already seen, these communities were closed to outsiders. Closed societies are always seen as suspicious by society at large: What exactly are they trying to hide? When word leaked out concerning the Christians' activities, the news did little to allay other people's fears. It was known that Christians often met with their brothers and sisters either after dark or before dawn to hold a "love feast" (their term for the Lord's Supper), a celebration that included ritual kissing (e.g., see Rom 16:16; 1 Pet 5:14). At this meal they ate the body and drank the blood of the Son of God. Rumors began to fly, and if you can imagine the worst, you won't be far off the mark. Christians were thought to meet under the cloak of darkness in order to hide their despicable deeds from the world. They engaged in wild sex orgies (the love feasts, where the passionate kiss of peace was just the beginning), they committed communal incest with their "brothers and sisters," and most sinister of all, they performed acts of infanticide and ritual cannibalism (eating the son).

These charges may sound ludicrous to us, but they were widely believed by non-Christians in the second century, as evidenced by the fact that Christian authors repeatedly had to defend themselves against them (see box 13.2). Similar charges were leveled against other groups in antiquity as well; evidently one of the common ways to cast aspersions on an unpopular group was to claim that they held nocturnal orgies and ate babies.

Compounding these problems was the fact that Christians refused to participate in local cults and, even worse, in state cults that honored the Roman gods. This refusal was widely seen as treasonous. These were the gods who protected society, who brought peace and prosperity to the empire through the agency of the emperor, who was himself sometimes considered divine in the provinces where Christianity was most successful. In modern terms, failing to worship these gods was

a political statement as much as a religious one, for as we have seen, people in the ancient world didn't separate religion and politics into distinct categories. For them, to spurn the state gods was to repudiate the state.

The earliest Christians were attacked principally for causing public disturbances. This is the consistent testimony of the accounts in Acts and the references in Paul's letters, where followers of Jesus are sometimes subject to mob violence (e.g., Acts 7:54–60; 13:48–51; 14:19–21, 21:27–36; 1 Thess 2:13–16). At other times they suffer an official punishment by order of a Roman magistrate, as indicated, for instance, by Paul's reference to being beaten three times with rods (2 Cor 11:25; see also Acts 16:22). Outsiders evidently considered the followers of Christ to be public nuisances, not the moral, upright citizens one might have expected them to be.

The negative public image of the early Christians can be deduced from the caustic remarks directed against them by pagan authors of the early second century. Thus, for example, the Roman historian Tacitus called Christianity a "pernicious superstition" and claimed that Nero could use Christians as scapegoats for the burning of Rome because of their "hatred of the human race" (*Annals* 15). At about the same time (ca. 115 C.E.), the historian Suetonius described Christians as people who held "to a novel and mischievous superstition" (*Life of Nero* 16). The Roman governor of Bithynia-Pontus, Pliny the Younger, considered the Christians to be "obstinate" and "mad" adherents of a "depraved superstition" and expressed some surprise when he learned that at their community meals they ate ordinary food, possibly because he suspected them of cannibalism (Letter 10 to Trajan). Later authors like the emperor Marcus Aurelius considered Christians to be misguided and hardheaded (*Meditations* XI, 3); the satiricist Lucian portrayed them as irrational, gullible dolts (*Death of Peregrinus*, 11–13).

Official Persecution

This widespread disapproval of the Christians lies at the root of the earliest governmental actions against them. The first full-blown episode appears to have been the persecution under Nero. When Nero's enemies blamed him for the fire that leveled a good portion of the city—a blame that he evidently deserved—he decided to use the Christians in Rome as his scapegoats. According to the Roman historian Tacitus, **Nero** made a public display of Christians, having some of them clothed in animal skins to be eaten by ravenous dogs and others rolled in pitch and set aflame to light his public gardens. Tacitus suggests that Nero could treat the Christians this way with impunity because of the general loathing for them. Nero, however, did not order persecutions of Christians living outside Rome, and more important, he did not punish the Christians of Rome *for being Christians.* He condemned them for arson (even though they were

apparently innocent of the charge). Thus, Christians were accused of committing actual crimes.

Nero may have set a precedent. Christians who were already looked upon with suspicion and hatred increasingly came to be seen as a public problem, and governors in the provinces must have known the disdain that the emperor himself had shown for them. The problems mounted with the passing of time, as Christians grew in number and openly refused to worship the state gods. This becomes clear in the second incident of official persecution that we can speak about with some confidence. In 112 C.E., **Pliny**, the governor of Bithynia-Pontus in Asia Minor, heard complaints about the Christians

---

ANOTHER EARLY CHRISTIAN TEXT

BOX 19.5   The Christian Disruption of the Family: The Case of Perpetua

Early Christians recognized, and sometimes even celebrated, the fact that adherence to their religion could disrupt family lives. For many of them, the Christian church was a new family that replaced their old, biological family. Nowhere can the disruptive possibilities of Christianity be seen more clearly than in the gripping account from the beginning of the third century of the trial and execution of a Roman matron named **Perpetua** and her female slave Felicitas. The first part of the report actually claims to be a private diary that Perpetua kept while in prison awaiting her fate among the wild beasts of a Roman amphitheater in North Africa.

Perpetua reports that she had an infant son whom she had given over to the care of her family. In one of the most powerful and pathetic scenes of the account, her father pleads with her to consider the pain she is causing her loved ones by her senseless determination to die a martyr's death:

> And then my father came to me [in prison], worn out with anxiety. He came up to me, that he might cast me down [from the faith], saying, "Have pity my daughter, on my grey hairs. Have pity on your father, if I am worthy to be called a father by you. . . . Have regard to your brothers, have regard to your mother and your aunt, have regard to your son, who will not be able to live after you. Lay aside your courage, and do not bring

us to destruction; for none of us will speak in freedom if you should suffer anything." . . . And I grieved over the grey hairs of my father . . . and I comforted him saying, "On that scaffold, whatever God wills shall happen. . . ." And he departed from me in sorrow.

> Another day . . . an immense number of people were gathered together. We mount the platform. The rest were interrogated and confessed. Then they came to me and my father immediately appeared with my boy and withdrew me from the step, and said in a supplicating tone, "Have pity on your babe." And Hilarianus the procurator . . . said, "Spare the grey hairs of your father, spare the infancy of your boy, offer sacrifice for the well-being of the emperors." And I replied, "I will not do so." Hilarianus said, "Are you a Christian?" And I replied, "I am a Christian."

> And as my father stood there to cast me down from the faith, he was ordered by Hilarianus to be thrown down, and was beaten with rods. . . . The procurator then delivers judgment on all of us, and condemns us to the wild beasts, and we went down cheerfully to the dungeon. (*Passion of Perpetua and Felicitas* 2)

Perpetua and her slave Felicitas, who had herself given birth just days before the event, were thrown to the wild beasts for confessing to be Christians. A detailed and gory account of the incident was recorded by an eyewitness and forms the final portion of the martyrology called *The Passion of Perpetua and Felicitas.*

in his province and put them on trial. Afterward, he wrote to the emperor **Trajan** to see whether he had handled the situation properly. The letter still survives. In it Pliny tells the emperor that he arrested those suspected of being Christians and forced them to prove their loyalty to the state by paying homage to the images of the emperor and the state gods by offering up incense and wine. He executed those who refused.

Pliny had these people executed not because they worshiped the Christian God—they were free to do that—but because they refused to worship the gods that supported the empire of Rome. Also, Pliny did not punish those who were suspected of having formerly been Christians so long as they were willing to worship the Roman gods. This procedure shows that it was not a crime to have been a Christian (since crimes are punished even after someone stops committing them). The crime was that they were adamant in refusing to worship the state gods. Pliny appears to have recognized that Christians were prevented by their religion from worshiping these gods. For this reason, anyone who persisted in claiming to be a Christian was automatically subject to prosecution.

Trajan gave his full approval to Pliny's procedure in a written reply that also still survives, and governors of other Roman provinces appear to have taken his response to heart. Christians weren't hunted down—Trajan explicitly forbade such a practice—and anonymous accusations were generally disallowed, but when difficulties arose within a community and Christians were thought to be to blame, persecutions erupted, even if for a brief period of time. As the existence of the Christians became more widely known, it

Figure 19.4 Mosaic from a villa in North Africa, showing an animal attacking a man. During the persecutions, Christians were sometimes martyred by wild beasts in the arena.

became increasingly clear that they were (*a*) antisocial, in that they did not participate in the normal social life of their communities; (*b*) sacrilegious, in that they refused to worship the gods; and (*c*) dangerous, since the gods did not take kindly to communities that harbored those who failed to offer them cult. By the end of the second century, the Christian apologist (literally, "defender" of the faith) Tertullian could complain about the widespread perception that Christians were the source of all disasters brought against the human race by the gods:

> They think the Christians the cause of every public disaster, of every affliction with which the people are visited. If the Tiber rises as high as the city walls, if the Nile does not send its waters up over the fields, if the heavens give no rain, if there is an earthquake, if there is famine or pestilence, straightway the cry is, "Away with the Christians to the lion!" (Apology 40)

ANOTHER GLIMPSE INTO THE PAST

BOX 19.6   The Spread of Christianity

Contrary to what many people seem to imagine, the Christian church grew quite slowly in its early years. At the end of the first century, far fewer than 1 percent of the empire's population of 60 million was Christian. But the growth was steady. And it was evidently achieved, according to recent studies, not by large evangelistic campaigns and massive conversions, but via close social networking: a person who converted would explain the benefits of the new religion to family members, friends, and colleagues, some few of whom might themselves convert. With a steady growth rate of 40 percent every decade (the approximate rate of growth for the Mormon church today, as it turns out), the small band of Jesus' followers could become something like 5 percent of the empire by the end of the third century. And then, when the emperor Constantine converted, the numbers rose dramatically, so that by the end of the fourth century, half the empire called itself Christian.

In the early years, what made people decide to give up other forms of worship to accept the Christian God? Older studies claimed that it was because of a widespread spiritual "void" throughout the empire, that the old gods were no longer considered worthy of worship and Christianity arrived on the scene at just the right moment. Archaeological evidence, however, shows that pagan religions were actually thriving in the second and third centuries, with no sign of weakness or malaise.

Some scholars have argued that it was precisely the pagan opposition to Christianity that, somewhat ironically, led to its growth. The logic is that unlike the widely inclusive pagan religions—none of which insisted on having an exclusive corner on the "truth"—Christianity claimed to be the right and the only right religion, and its adherents were willing to die to prove it. According to this view, such stalwart passion for the faith was attractive to potential converts.

Other scholars have noted that the Christian church provided a much-needed social network for people who were otherwise estranged from society, with local Christian communities gathering together at least weekly, considering members of the group all part of a big family, taking care of one another's needs, worshiping and enjoying social occasions together—all of which was attractive to outsiders in a world that didn't provide such intimate social groupings.

Yet other scholars have pointed out that our earliest accounts suggest that outsiders were drawn to belief in Jesus because of the fabulous tales of his power—not just while he was alive, but in the present. People who prayed through him to the one true God had their prayers answered: the sick were healed, the demon-possessed were exorcized, and even the dead were raised. If the "point" of religion was to secure benefits from the divine, and this religion could provide these benefits better than any other, then no surprise that it would attract increasing numbers of adherents.

Fortunately, one does not need to choose among these theories; they (and possibly others you might think of) may all help explain the early success of Christianity in the empire.

ANOTHER EARLY CHRISTIAN TEXT

BOX 19.7 The *Martyrdom of Polycarp*

The only account of an early Christian martyr (someone who is killed for the faith) in the New Testament is the stoning of Stephen in Acts 8. This kind of account became popular among Christians in later times, however, as "martyrologies" came to be written about those who stayed true to their commitment to Christ in the face of public humiliation, torture, and death.

The first surviving martyrology is called the *Martyrdom of Polycarp*, an account of the trial and execution of a famous bishop of the city of Smyrna in Asia Minor (modern Turkey), evidently written by an eyewitness who sent the account to Christians of a nearby community. **Polycarp** was an old man at the time of his arrest—eighty-six years of age, he indicated at his trial. He was arrested on no charge other than being a Christian who propagated the Christian religion in a world that celebrated the pagan gods and that considered Christians to be "atheists" (literally, "without the gods"). At first Polycarp went into hiding to avoid detection, but he

had a dream in which he saw his pillow burning and believed it was a sign by God that he was to be burned at the stake.

When soldiers come to arrest him, he does not resist, but is taken into the arena where the Jewish and pagan mobs are gathered, hungry for blood. The Roman proconsul urges Polycarp to repent and curse Christ, but he refuses, claiming that it is better to do what is right and suffer than to do wrong and be set free. And so the proconsul orders his death at the stake. But God does a miracle for his great saint. The flames do not touch his body but form a kind of sheet around it, and instead of the smell of reeking flesh, a sweet aroma fills the air.

Finally an executioner kills Polycarp with a dagger—but even then the miracles have not ceased. So much blood gushes forth that it extinguishes the fire, and a dove emerges from the saint's side and flies up into heaven—symbolic perhaps of Polycarp's (holy) spirit, returning now to God as a reward for his faithfulness unto death.

Christians, of course, had to devise ways of understanding and reacting to the hatred that confronted them on every side. That is to say, the opposition that Christians faced from the rest of the world drove them to define themselves against it. Sociologists have long recognized that a social group often achieves stronger solidarity and internal bonds of cohesion when faced with an enemy, especially one that is powerful and threatening. Speaking in the most general terms, the opposition and persecution that confronted various early Christian communities strengthened the commitment of their members to one another, since they were compelled to face their adversaries together. It also pushed them to explain to themselves theologically why they, the people of God's special favor, should have to undergo such intense and cruel suffering.

These issues are addressed at length in a number of the early Christian writings, some of which we

have already considered. Next we will examine the book of 1 Peter, written in a context of persecution, a book that can help us acquire further insights into how Christians saw themselves in light of the antagonistic world in which they lived.

CHRISTIANS IN A HOSTILE WORLD: THE LETTER OF 1 PETER

The book of 1 Peter is a kind of circular letter written in the name of the apostle Peter to "the exiles of the Dispersion" in several of the provinces of Asia Minor: "Pontus, Galatia, Cappadocia, Asia, and Bithynia" (1:1). Before considering the question of whether Simon Peter himself actually wrote this letter, we need to learn something about its recipients and their situation.

The Addressees

The author calls his readers "exiles" (1:1) and "aliens" (2:11). Most scholars have understood these to be figurative designations of Christians, whose real home is heaven and who are therefore exiles in this world for the time being. Supporting this interpretation are verses where the author indicates that his readers are in exile only for "a while" (1:17) and that their real allegiance is to their heavenly calling (1:13).

Other scholars, however, have suggested that the addressees really were exiles and aliens in the communities in which they lived, that is, that they were persons who had moved to new communities but were not fully integrated into them. In the Roman world, such "resident aliens" stood on the margins of society, with more legal rights, for example, than slaves but fewer than native-born citizens (with respect, for instance, to the ownership of property). As is often the case with people in our own world who are new in town, especially if they are entering a close-knit community whose families have been together for a long time, these outsiders would no doubt have felt a sense of alienation from their social world.

How should we weigh these two options for understanding the addressees of 1 Peter? On the one hand, resident aliens or foreigners would have been prime candidates for membership in the new churches that were being established by the early Christians. First Peter may well have been addressed to such persons. They stood on the margins of society at large but had been welcomed into a new community of faith in which they could enjoy the benefits of warm fellowship and family ties unavailable to them on the outside. Moreover, this new community was not just any social gathering of like-minded individuals; it was "the household of God" (4:17).

At the same time, it is a little difficult to believe that the author of 1 Peter actually thought that resident aliens were the only people who were Christians in the churches that he addressed (were there no citizens?) or that social outcasts would be the only Christians who would be interested in reading his letter. It is probably best, then, not to press the literal meaning of these designations too far. Many of his addressees may have been resident aliens, but surely not all of them were.

One thing that we can say with relative certainty about the addressees is that, whether or not they were foreigners, they were Christian believers undergoing suffering, and this author is trying to tell them how to deal with it. The word for "suffering" occurs more often in this short letter than in any other book of the New Testament, even more than in the much longer works of Luke and Acts combined. Even where the author is not talking directly about how to handle suffering, he appears to be speaking about it indirectly. Throughout the letter, for example, he urges his readers to live moral lives so that those on the outside can see that they are doing nothing wrong and causing nobody any harm. They are to be obedient slaves, submissive wives, and tender husbands, and they are to obey all governing authority and to be devoted subjects of the emperor. These are not simply pieces of moral advice; they are also guidelines for avoiding persecution from suspicious authorities and for putting to shame those who wrongfully cause abuse.

The Context of Persecution

Those recipients who were literally resident aliens would no doubt have been accustomed to feeling ostracized by society at large. These feelings would have been assuaged to some extent once they joined the Christian community. Here they would have found a home for themselves in the "household of God" (4:17). Joining this new family also would have had a downside, however, in the public opposition that the group evoked.

We have seen that the persecution of Christians in Bithynia-Pontus during the governorship of Pliny erupted at the grassroots level. Correspondingly, 1 Peter indicates that Christians are principally opposed by their former colleagues and friends who "are surprised that you no longer join them in the same excesses of dissipation" (4:4). That is to say, the Christian converts have caused a good deal of consternation for those with whom they used to spend their time. There has been a public outcry, apparently by those who felt abandoned by their former friends (and spouses?), and it may have reached the point of mob violence or administrative intervention. Thus the author speaks of "the fiery ordeal that is taking place among you" (4:12).

The Author's Response

Persecution often functions to solidify the ties that bind a social group together, giving the members of the group a greater sense of cohesion and belonging as they realize they are "all in it together." Although the author of 1 Peter was obviously not versed in modern sociological theory, he was clearly attuned to the social dimensions of suffering as they were being experienced in the communities that he addressed. One of his goals was to keep these communities together, which meant keeping individual members from leaving as the pressure from the outside mounted.

He constantly reminds his readers that they acquired a privileged status when they joined God's household; they were specially chosen by God, they were "sanctified by the Spirit," and they were "sprinkled with [Christ's] blood" (1:2). He wants them to remember that they have been brought into this new family by means of a new birth (1:3, 23) and that they are now children of God their Father (1:14, 17), having been purchased by the precious gift of Christ's blood (1:19). They are the chosen people, set apart from the rest of the world, belonging to God alone (2:9). Indeed, they are the place of God's residence, his own temple, where sacrifices are made to God; at the same time they are the holy priests who make these sacrifices (2:4–9). Clearly these believers are special before God and unique in the world. Indeed, to some extent they are suffering *because* they are so distinct. Outsiders can't fathom why the members of God's house behave so differently, and in their ignorance they lash out at what they don't understand (4:3–5). In this they are driven on by the devil himself, God's cosmic enemy (5:8).

Christians, then, should expect to suffer and should not be surprised when they do so (4:12), for just as Christ suffered, so, too, must his followers (4:13). They must not suffer for doing what is wrong, however, but only for doing what is right. They are therefore to live moral, upright lives (3:14–17; 4:14–15). Moreover, when they suffer in this way, they must be prepared to defend themselves by explaining who they are and what they stand for: "Always be ready to make your defense to anyone who demands from you an accounting for the hope that is in you; yet do it with gentleness and reverence" (3:15–16). By making this kind of defense, Christians will put their enemies to shame (3:17).

Thus the author of 1 Peter is concerned not only to create solidarity in the Christian communities but also, and perhaps primarily, to bring an end to the suffering. He makes precisely this point when he urges his readers to "conduct yourselves honorably among the Gentiles, so that though they malign you as evildoers, they may see your honorable deeds and glorify God" (2:11). His injunctions to moral behavior appear to be designed to win over the skeptical (3:1). In a world in which the Christian community was regarded as antisocial, the believers are to "accept the authority of every human institution, whether of the emperor as supreme or of governors as sent by him to punish those who do wrong and to praise those who do right. For it is God's will that by doing right you should silence the ignorance of the foolish" (3:13–15).

The ultimate reward for those who remain steadfast in suffering will be the salvation that is soon to come (1:1–3, 9). This author has not abandoned the eschatological hope of the earliest Christian communities; he embraces it, confident that God will soon bring the believers' suffering to an end (4:17; 5:10). Who was this author?

The Author of 1 Peter

The book claims, of course, to be written by Peter, the disciple of Jesus, and it suggests that he was writing from the capital of the empire. This is intimated at the close of the letter, where the author says that he has written from "Babylon" (5:13), a code word in early Christianity for Rome, the locus of the evil empire that was opposed to God (see Rev 17:5; 18:2). Peter has been traditionally associated with Rome as its first bishop (i.e., the first pope).

Many scholars, however, doubt that Peter wrote this letter. Virtually the only things that we can say for certain about the disciple Peter is that he was a lower-class fisherman from Galilee (Mark 1:16) who was known to have been illiterate (Acts 4:13). His native tongue was Aramaic. This letter, on the other hand, is written by a highly literate Greek-speaking Christian who is intimately familiar with the Old Testament in its Greek translation and with a range of Greek rhetorical constructions. It is possible of course, that Peter went back to school

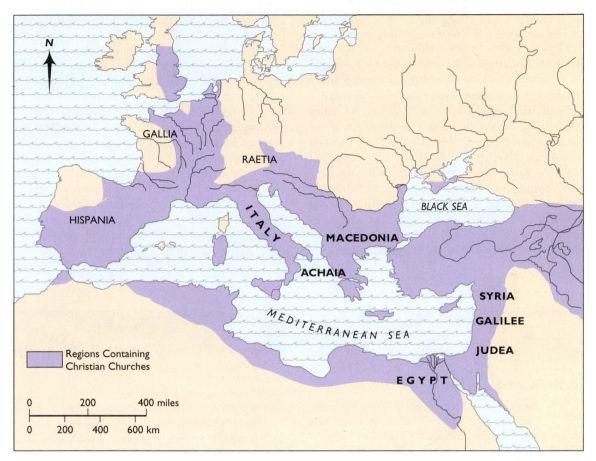

Figure 19.5 The Distribution of Christianity by 300 C.E.

after Jesus' resurrection, learned Greek, became an accomplished writer, mastered the Greek Old Testament, and moved to Rome before writing this letter; but to most scholars, this seems unlikely.

Literacy rates were shockingly low in the world of Jesus and Peter. The most authoritative estimates (see Hezser in Suggestions for Further Reading) indicate that only 3 percent of that population of Roman Palestine could read. Far fewer could write. And far fewer than that could compose literary texts. And even fewer than that could do it in a foreign language (Greek, as opposed to Aramaic). If any Palestinian Jews could compose a book like 1 Peter, it would have been one of the very upper-crust wealthy elite who had the time, leisure, and money for a very advanced education. This does

not sound like the lower-class day laborer Peter. And he could scarcely have gone back to school to learn his letters. There is no evidence of adult education of this kind in antiquity. Nor should one think that as a missionary later in his life, he would have learned enough Greek to allow him to communicate. That may be true (that he eventually could speak faltering Greek), but it would not qualify him to write a highly refined literary composition: training to do so took many years of diligent preparation (as the ancients themselves indicate), something Peter would have no time or money for.

Some have suggested that the letter was actually produced by Silvanus, who is mentioned in 5:12. This is certainly possible as well, but one might then wonder why Silvanus is named not as the author of the letter but only as its scribe (or carrier). Others have thought that Silvanus penned the letter as it was dictated by Peter and that he put Peter's rough dictation into a more aesthetically pleasing and rhetorically persuasive style of Greek. If so, one would still have difficulty accounting for the detailed interpretations of the Greek Old Testament—and, indeed, for most of the detailed argument—without supposing that Silvanus, rather than Peter, was the real author.

I should point out that there are an extraordinary number of pseudonymous writings forged in Peter's name outside the New Testament. In addition to the *Gospel of Peter* that we have already discussed (see box 6.5), there are three apocalypses

attributed to Peter (one of which we will discuss in box 20.7), several "Acts" of Peter, and other Petrine letters. In addition, as we will see, scholars are virtually unanimous in thinking that the book of 2 Peter within the New Testament is pseudonymous as well. On balance, then, it is probably best to regard 1 Peter as yet another example of Christian pseudepigraphy, in which a later author took the name of Jesus' closest disciple to lend authority to his own views.

It is difficult to say, however, when the author would have been writing, or even from where and to whom. If the letter is indeed associated with Asia Minor, as its prescript suggests, it should probably be assigned to the first century, possibly near its end, when persecution of the Christians was on the rise.

AT A GLANCE

BOX 19.8 | Peter

1. 1 Peter claims to be written by Simon Peter, the close disciple of Jesus. Modern scholars have shown reasons to doubt this ascription.

2. It may have been written in Peter's name by a later Christian, living near the end of the first century. If so, it is one of a number of early Christian pseudepigrapha allegedly written by Peter.

3. The book is addressed to Christians in Asia Minor who have been experiencing persecution.

4. The book is written to encourage them in their suffering, to explain why it is happening to them, and to urge them to remain faithful to God in the midst of it, so that they may earn an eternal reward for their wrongful mistreatment.

TAKE A STAND

1. Suppose you are the author of the book of Hebrews, and you are in a conversation with your next-door neighbor, a fellow Christian who is thinking about converting to Judaism. You want to dissuade him. Give him three of your best arguments for why it would be a mistake.

2. Pretend you are a pagan governor of one of the ancient Roman provinces, and you decide that the Christians in your community need to be punished, imprisoned, and possibly executed. Why do you think so? Is there anything the Christians could argue on their

own behalf that would make you change your mind?

3. Choose any writing from early Christianity and show how it reflects a situation in which the author and/or recipients were experiencing persecution.

SUGGESTIONS FOR FURTHER READING

Cobb, L. Stephanie. *Dying to Be Men: Gender and Language in Early Christian Martyr Texts*. New York: Columbia University Press, 2008. A sophisticated study of the early Christian accounts of martyrdom, which tries to show how they portray the deaths of Christians in specifically masculine ways (even for women martyrs); for advanced students.

Dunn, James. *The Partings of the Ways: Between Christianity and Judaism and their Significance for the Character of Christianity*. 2d ed. London: SCM Press, 2011. An important study that explores the factors that led to the separation of Christianity from Judaism to become its own religion.

Elliott, J. H. *A Home for the Homeless: A Sociological Exegesis of 1 Peter, Its Situation, and Strategy*. Eugene, Ore.: Wipf and Stock, 2005. A groundbreaking examination of the communities addressed by 1 Peter from a sociological perspective; for advanced students.

Frend, W. H. C. *Martyrdom and Persecution in the Early Church*. Oxford: Blackwell, 1965. The best full-length study of hostilities against Christians during the first three centuries of the Common Era.

Harrington, Daniel. *What Are They Saying about the Letter to the Hebrews?* Mahway, N.J.: Paulist, 2005. An overview of what scholars now say about the significant historical and literary features of the book of Hebrews; ideal for beginning students.

Hezser, Catherine. *Jewish Literacy in Roman Palestine*. Tübingen, Germany: Mohr Siebeck, 2001. The most thorough and scholarly treatment of every aspect of reading and writing in Palestine at the time of the beginning of Christianity; for advanced students.

Lane Fox, Robin. *Pagans and Christians*. New York: Alfred A. Knopf, 1987. A long but fascinating and often brilliant discussion of the relationship of pagans and Christians during the first centuries of Christianity; for more advanced students.

Lindars, Barnabas. *The Theology of the Letter to the Hebrews*. Cambridge: Cambridge University Press, 1991. A clear account of the theological perspective of Hebrews.

Moss, Candida. *Ancient Christian Martyrdom: Diverse Practices, Theologies, and Traditions*. New Haven, Conn.: Yale University Press, 2012. An exploration of the early texts that describe Christian martyrdoms, which argues that early Christians had a variety of views of what it meant to die for the faith and of whether one should do so.

Perkins, Judith. *The Suffering Self: Pain and Narrative Representation in the Early Christian Era*. London and New York: Routledge, 1995. A brilliant study of early Christian narratives of suffering, which argues that people like Ignatius embraced pain *not* because they were pathological, but because there was a shift in how people in the Greco-Roman world began to see and portray themselves as suffering bodies.

Ruether, Rosemary. *Faith and Fratricide: The Theological Roots of Anti-Semitism*. Eugene, Ore.: Wipf and Stock, 1996. A compelling and controversial study that argues that Christian claims about Jesus, by their very nature, are necessarily anti-Jewish.

Sandmel, Samuel. *Anti-Semitism in the New Testament?* Philadelphia: Fortress, 1978. A clear and interesting discussion, from the perspective of a Jewish scholar, of whether parts of the New Testament should be viewed as anti-Semitic.

Wilken, Robert. *The Christians as the Romans Saw Them*. 2d ed. New Haven. Conn.: Yale University Press, 2003. A popular study of the largely derogatory views of Christians held by several Roman authors; particularly suitable for beginning students.

 KEY TERMS

Allegory of the Cave, Plato's	Joshua	Nero, emperor	self-definition
catholic epistles	*Letter of Barnabas*	Perpetua	shadow-reality
general epistles	*Martyrdom of Polycarp*	Pliny	tabernacle
high priests, Jewish	Melchizedek	Polycarp	Trajan, emperor
		prophecy-fulfillment	

20

Christian Conflicts with Christians

JAMES, 2 PETER, JUDE, AND THE JOHANNINE EPISTLES

WHAT TO EXPECT

The people you argue with the most are usually those closest to you: family, friends, lovers. The same is true with religious communities: they may voice disagreements with people of other religions (Christians with Buddhists, for example), but there are many more disagreements, and often more heated ones, with members of the same religion (Protestants and Catholics, for example, or fundamentalists and liberals).

The same was true in the ancient world. Internal conflict within the early Christian community was frequent and sometimes quite heated, especially in light of its wide-ranging diversity. This chapter considers several general epistles that reflect different areas of conflict—the books of James, 2 Peter, Jude, and the Johannine epistles.

CHRISTIAN CONFLICTS WITH CHRISTIANS

Up to this stage in our examination of the general problems of the general epistles, we have explored two areas of social conflict encountered by the early Christians: those involving non-Christian Jews and those involving pagans. We have seen that these areas of conflict affected more than the external aspects of Christianity; they were profoundly related to certain internal dynamics as well. The Jewish opposition to Christianity, for example, compelled Christians to engage in acts of self-definition as they tried to understand themselves in relation to the religion from which they had emerged and to the people who continued to

embrace it. Not all Christians agreed on the self-definitions that were devised. Pagan opposition also forced Christians to attend to their public image. Church leaders urged their communities to maintain high ethical standards so as to earn the respect of those who suspected the group's motives and activities. Again, not every Christian agreed on what these ethical standards should entail.

We now turn from these external forms of conflict to controversies that raged within the Christian communities themselves. The issues affect not only the general epistles; we have already seen numerous instances of internal Christian conflicts in the other writings we have examined. One need only think of Paul's conflicts with the Judaizing Christians in Galatia or with the "superapostles" in

Corinth, of the Pastoral epistles and the problems of false teaching that they were written to address, or of the Johannine epistles and their attacks on the secessionists from the community. Indeed, it appears that most of our early Christian authors saw as many enemies inside the church as outside.

Internal conflicts arose in no small measure because Christianity was so remarkably diverse in the first two centuries. From the beginnings of this religious movement, believers who insisted that they had a corner on the truth found some of their most energetic adversaries among those who also claimed to be Christian but who advanced a different point of view or promoted a different kind of lifestyle. Only one basic form of Christianity emerged victorious from these conflicts and thereafter declared itself "orthodox," and every major form of modern Christianity—Catholic, Protestant, Eastern Orthodox—traces its roots to this victory. Indeed, the collection of twenty-seven ancient Christian writings that became the sacred canon of Scripture is itself one of the legacies of this victory. During the period we are exploring in this study, however, no New Testament canon had yet come into being, and Christians were by no means in agreement on some of the most basic questions about what to believe and how to live.

We can see some of the conflicts at work in several of the general epistles of the New Testament as well as in other early Christian writings that happen to survive from roughly the same period of time. These books show that the major internal conflicts of the early Christian movement involved ethics, leadership, and doctrine—three areas of concern that were not, of course, mutually exclusive. On the contrary, many early Christians believed that bad leaders introduced false teachings that promoted immoral activities. We have already seen this view reflected in the Pastoral epistles, books that are roughly contemporary with the works we are about to consider: James, Jude, 2 Peter, and the three Johannine epistles.

THE EPISTLE OF JAMES

Of all of the writings that we will be examining in the present chapter, James appears to be the least concerned with corrupt leaders or false teachings

infiltrating the community (but see 3:1–3). Nonetheless, parts of the letter appear to be directed against aberrant notions advanced by Christians known to the author. In particular, it is possible that some Christians had taken Paul's doctrine of justification by faith apart from the works of the Law to mean something that Paul himself did not, namely, that it only mattered what a person believed, not how he or she lived (see box 20.1). James stakes out the opposing position, arguing that true faith will always be manifest in one's life, especially in the ways one treats the poor and the oppressed. To put it in his own words, "a person is justified by works and not by faith alone" (2:24) because "faith without works is dead" (2:26).

The book consists of a series of ethical admonitions to those "who believe in our glorious Lord Jesus Christ" (2:1). It is a letter in form, at least partially: it begins with a prescript that names the author and contains a greeting. There is no epistolary conclusion, however, and the "letter" gives no indication of a specific occasion. It is instead a collection of pieces of good advice to those who "believe in our glorious Lord Jesus Christ" (2:1).

There is some question concerning the identity of the book's author. He gives his name as James, which readers over the centuries have taken to refer to the brother of Jesus, but there is little reason to think that the author is claiming to be that particular James. The name was fairly common in the first century; just within the pages of the New Testament, in addition to the brother of Jesus, we encounter James, the son of Zebedee (Matt 4:21); James, the son of Alphaeus (Matt 10:3); James, the son of Mary (Matt 27:56); and James, the father of Judas (Luke 6:16). If the author of this epistle was James, the brother of Jesus (or was at least claiming to be), it is somewhat strange that he never refers to any personal knowledge of his brother or of his teachings.

The letter that James writes is full of exhortations to his readers, and these strong moral teachings do indeed appear to reflect (although they never quote) traditions of Jesus' own teaching. For instance, believers should not swear oaths, but let their "yes be yes" and their "no be no" (5:12, cf. Matt 5:33–37); loving one's neighbor fulfills the Law (2:8, cf. Matt 22:39–40); and those who are rich should fear the coming judgment (5:1–6, cf. Matt

19:23–24). One of the most striking features of the book, however, is that Jesus himself is scarcely ever mentioned. Apart from 1:1, the epistolary opening, and 2:1, the verse quoted earlier, Jesus makes no appearance at all. What is even more intriguing is that, apart from these two verses, almost none of the ideas in the book is uniquely Christian. The various ethical injunctions have numerous parallels, for instance, in non-Christian Jewish writings, and all the examples of ethical behavior are drawn from stories of the Hebrew Bible (Abraham 2:21, Rahab 2:25, Job 5:11, Elijah 5:17), rather than from the life of Jesus or the activities of his apostles. Even the communities of believers that are addressed appear in Jewish guise—they are described as "the twelve tribes in the Dispersion," and their place of assembly is literally called a "synagogue" (2:2).

For these reasons, some scholars have argued that James is a kind of Jewish book of wisdom (somewhat like the Book of Proverbs but without as many one-liners) with only a thin Christian veneer. According to this opinion, the author took over a piece of Jewish writing and "Christianized" it by adding a couple of references to Jesus.

Not everyone is persuaded by this point of view, however. Many scholars, for example, have observed that a large number of the admonitions in James have close parallels in Matthew's Sermon on the Mount (see the examples cited earlier). In addition, portions of the book relate closely to other teachings of Jesus (compare, for instance, 4:13–15 with Jesus' parable of the rich fool in Luke 12:16–21). How, then, does one account for the general nature of these admonitions, that is, the fact that most of them are not distinctively Christian, *and* for their close similarities to older traditions about Jesus? It may be that the author strung together a number of important ethical admonitions that could be found in a variety of settings, such as Jewish wisdom literature and traditions of Jesus' own teaching, and applied them to the Christian communities that he is addressing.

WHAT DO YOU THINK?

BOX 20.1 Paul and James on Faith and Works

Since the Reformation, scholars have debated whether Paul and James can be reconciled with one another on the fundamental issue of whether a person must "do works" in order to be made right with God, or if, instead, justification comes on the basis of faith alone, without works. On the surface of it, at least, the two do appear to be at odds.

Other scholars have pointed out, however, that Paul and James may mean different things by both "faith" and "works"—that for Paul, faith means a trusting acceptance of Christ's death, which alone makes a person right with God, apart from doing the "works" required by the Jewish Law, whereas James means that one cannot simply have an intellectual acknowledgment of God (= faith for him) but needs to live an appropriate live by doing good deeds (= works for him). If so, then perhaps they do not disagree. What do you think?

Paul

"A person is justified by faith apart from the works prescribed by the law" (Rom 3:28).

If Abraham was justified by works, he has something to boast about, but not before God. . . . Therefore his *faith* was reckoned to him as righteousness.

This is demonstrated by Gen 15:6 (Gal 3:6).

James

"A person is justified by works, not by faith alone" (James 2:24).

"Our ancestor Abraham was justified by works."

This is demonstrated by Gen 15:6 (James 2:23).

James emphasizes that those who have faith need to manifest it in the way they live (1:22–27; 2:14–26). Other recurring themes include the importance of controlling one's "tongue" (i.e., one's speech; 1:26; 3:1–12), the danger of riches for believers (1:9–11; 4:13–17; 5:1–6), and the need to be patient in the midst of suffering (1:2–8, 12–16; 5:7–11). The author, however, is not concerned only with what we might call individual ethics. Near the end of the book he turns to address communal activities within the church as well, giving his readers advice about saying prayers, singing psalms, anointing the sick with oil, confessing sins, and restoring those who have strayed from the faith (5:13–16).

JUDE

A concern for the leadership of the church is addressed in a much shorter letter, one of the shortest of the New Testament. The writer of this one-page epistle names himself Jude (literally, Judas), the "brother of James" (v. 1). As you know, there were early traditions that two of Jesus' own brothers were named Jude and James (Mark 6:3). This author, then, is apparently claiming to be related to the great leader of the Jerusalem church, James, and therefore to be a family relation of Jesus himself.

The letter itself gives scant reason for accepting this ascription, and many critical scholars think that it is another example of early Christian pseudepigraphy. Jesus' brother Jude, of course, would have been a lower-class Aramaic-speaking peasant. Indeed, we learn from sources dating to the second century that Jude's family did not attain social prominence and were therefore, presumably, not well educated: his grandsons were known to be uneducated peasant farmers. The author of this book, on the other hand, was someone who was well trained in Greek and was conversant with a wide range of apocryphal Jewish literature. He quotes, for example, from a lost apocryphal account of the angelic battle over Moses' body (v. 9), and he cites the book of 1 Enoch as Scripture (v. 14). Thus, it does not appear to be likely that Jesus' own brother wrote the book.

The book is concerned with false teachers who have invaded the Christian community:

Beloved . . . I find it necessary to write and appeal to you to contend for the faith that was once for all entrusted to the saints. For certain intruders have stolen in among you, people who long ago were designated for this condemnation as ungodly, who pervert the grace of our God into licentiousness and deny our only Master and Lord, Jesus Christ. (vv. 3–4)

It is hard to know how Christian leaders can be thought to have denied Christ, but it may be that, from the author's perspective, anyone who understands the religion in a way that is significantly different from the way he himself does is liable to this charge. We saw a similar state of affairs in our study of 1 John. Also, just as the secessionists from the Johannine community were thought to have engaged in immoral and illegal activities because of their false beliefs, so the opponents of Jude are chiefly maligned for their licentious and perverse lifestyles. They are "like irrational animals" (v. 10), they engage in "deeds of ungodliness" (v. 15), they are "grumblers and malcontents, they indulge their own lusts, and they are bombastic in speech" (v. 16). The author likens them to the children of Israel, who after escaping from Egypt reveled in wanton acts of disbelief (adulteries and idolatries), and to the inhabitants of Sodom and Gomorrah, who "indulged in sexual immorality and pursued unnatural lust" (vv. 5–7).

From the historians' point of view, it is to be regretted that the author never tells us what these people actually stood for, that is, what they taught and how they lived. Most of the letter is simply filled with invective and name-calling. The author's enemies are "waterless clouds carried along by the winds; autumn trees without fruit, twice dead, uprooted; wild waves of the sea, casting up the foam of their own shame" (vv. 12–13).

It is clear, however, the author feels that his community is in jeopardy from these "worldly people, devoid of the Spirit, who are causing divisions" (v. 19). These false teachers need to realize what happens to those who oppose God and lead his people astray. In the past those who have caused disturbances and promoted immorality among God's people have been confronted with God's judgment. The offenders must take heed and repent, lest they become like the inhabitants of Sodom and Gomorrah, serving "as an example by undergoing a punishment of eternal fire" (v. 7).

ANOTHER EARLY CHRISTIAN TEXT

BOX 20.2 The *Didache*

One of the most significant manuscript discoveries of modern times occurred in 1873, when a Greek scholar named Bryennios found a copy of the *Didache* hidden away in a library in Constantinople. We had known of the existence of this book before—some early Christians considered it canonical—but we did not have it and did not know what was in it. It turns out to be a highly significant text that, among other things, reveals the nature of some of the internal struggles of early Christianity.

The first part of the *Didache* is a set of ethical instructions describing what behaviors Christians ought to engage in and what to avoid. The second part is a kind of church "how-to" manual, which indicates how Christians ought to pray (the "Lord's Prayer," three times a day), fast (on Wednesdays and Fridays, not on Mondays and Thursdays like the Jews), baptize (in cold running water if possible), and celebrate the eucharist (with set prayers that are provided).

The third part of the *Didache* gives instructions about wandering "apostles" and "prophets." Evidently, some Christians were making a living by taking their ministry on the road, sponging off gullible communities who supported them in exchange for their "ministry" of teaching and proclamation. The author of the *Didache* has become alert to the abuses of this system—some of these itinerant preachers are taking advantage of the kind hearts of local congregations, being supported by them while doing no real work themselves.

It appears that the book was written before church structures were in place, with a presiding bishop and presbyters serving beneath him. Like Paul's community in Corinth (where no one was in charge), these communities addressed in the *Didache* needed direction and guidance, a structure to prevent their abuse by Christian scoundrels making a buck off of religion.

We do not know exactly when the pseudonymous author produced his account; most modern scholars date it somewhere near the end of the first century. We do know that the book was used as a source some years later by another pseudonymous author, who produced a similarly vitriolic attack on false teachers who promoted immoral behavior among the Christians. This author wrote in the name of the apostle Peter and produced a letter that was in all likelihood the final book of the New Testament to be written, the epistle of 2 Peter.

2 PETER

For a variety of reasons, there is less debate about the authorship of 2 Peter than any other pseudepigraphon in the New Testament. The vast majority of critical scholars agree that whoever wrote the book, it was not Jesus' disciple Simon Peter. As was the case with 1 Peter, this author is a relatively sophisticated and literate Greek-speaking Christian, not an Aramaic-speaking Jewish peasant. At the same time, the writing style of the book is so radically different from that of 1 Peter that linguists are virtually unanimous in thinking that if Simon Peter was responsible for producing the former book, he could not have written this one. Even more to the point, a major portion of this letter has been taken over from the book of Jude and incorporated into chapter 2. If Jude can be dated near the end of the first century, 2 Peter must be somewhat later. Therefore, it could not have been penned by Jesus' companion Peter, who was evidently martyred in Rome sometime around 64 C.E. during the reign of Emperor Nero.

This letter, then, should probably be included among the large number of pseudonymous writings in the name of Peter, which include the *Gospel of Peter* (see box 6.5) and the *Apocalypse of Peter* (see box 21.3). In this connection, it is striking that the letter was not widely accepted as Peter's, or even known to exist, for most of the first three Christian centuries. There is not a solitary reference to it until around 220 C.E., and it does not appear to have been widely circulated for at least another century after that. It was no doubt included in the canon because the orthodox fathers of the fourth century accepted the claims of its author to be Peter and because it served their purposes in opposing those who promote false teaching.

The author goes out of his way to insist that he is none other than Jesus' disciple—a case, perhaps, of protesting too much. Not only does he begin by naming himself "Simeon Peter, a servant and apostle of Jesus Christ" (1:1), but he proceeds to recount his own personal experience with Jesus on the Mount of Transfiguration, where he beheld for himself Jesus' divine glory and heard God's affirmation of his Son in the voice from heaven (1:17). He assures his reader that he was there to see these things: "We ourselves heard this voice come from heaven, while we were with him on the holy mountain" (1:18). Why does he choose to parade his credentials in this manner? It is probably to con-

vince his readers that he has no need of "cleverly devised myths" to understand Jesus (1:16) since he knows about him firsthand.

This reference to myths may intimate something about the author's opponents. They may be early Gnostics, who use their creative mythologies and genealogies to support their "unorthodox" points of view, for the author goes on to attack people who provide idiosyncratic interpretations of Scripture—a favorite activity of the Gnostics, according to the proto-orthodox church fathers: "First of all you must understand this, that no prophecy of scripture is a matter of one's own interpretation" (1:21). Moreover, the author's opponents appeal to the writings of the apostle Paul, which by this time are evidently in circulation as a collection and are even being considered as "Scripture"—other indications that the letter was written long after the apostle's death. As we have previously seen, the Gnostics took a particular liking to Paul as an authority for their views.

ANOTHER EARLY CHRISTIAN TEXT

BOX 20.3   The *Acts of Peter*

Among the pseudepigrapha connected with the apostle Peter, none is more interesting than the apocryphal *Acts of Peter*, a document that details Peter's various confrontations with the heretical magician Simon Magus (cf. Acts 8:14–24). The narrative shows how Peter outperforms the magician by invoking the power of God. Consider the following entertaining account, in which Peter proves the divine authorization of his message by raising a dead tuna fish back to life:

> But Peter turned round and saw a smoked tunny-fish hanging in a window; and he took it and said to the people, "If you now see this swimming in the water like a fish, will you be able to believe in him whom I preach?" And they all said with one accord, "Indeed we will believe you!" Now there was a fish-pond near by; so he said, "In thy name, Jesus Christ, in which they still fail to believe" [he said to the tunny] "in the presence of all these be alive and swim like a fish!" And he threw the tunny into the pond, and it came alive and began to

swim. And the people saw the fish swimming; and he made it do so not merely for that hour, or it might have been called a delusion, but he made it go on swimming, so that it attracted crowds from all sides and showed that the tunny had become a live fish; so much so that some of the people threw in bread for it, and it ate it all up. And when they saw this, a great number followed him and believed in the Lord. (*Acts of Peter* 5)

In the ultimate showdown between the heretical sorcerer (Simon Magus) and the man of God (Peter), Simon the magician uses his powers to leap into the air and fly like a bird over the temples and hills of Rome. Not to be outdone, Peter calls upon God to smite Simon in midair; God complies, much to the magician's dismay and demise. Unprepared for a crash landing, he plunges to earth and breaks his leg in three places. Seeing what has happened, the crowds rush to stone him to death as an evildoer. And so the true apostle of God triumphs over his enemy, the preacher of heresy.

So also our beloved brother Paul wrote to you according to the wisdom given him, speaking of this as he does in all his letters. There are some things in them hard to understand, which the ignorant and unstable twist to their own destruction, as they do the other scriptures. (3:16)

Unfortunately, the author of 2 Peter does not set forth the actual views of his opponents but simply enters into invective against them. Much of his attack has simply been borrowed from the epistle of Jude. He sees his opponents as "false prophets" (2:1) who engage in acts of flagrant immorality: "They have eyes full of adultery, insatiable for sin. . . . They speak bombastic nonsense, and with licentious desires of the flesh they entice people who have just escaped from those who live in error" (2:14, 18). Moreover, these persons are not outsiders but members of the Christian community who, in the author's judgment, have gone astray to their own destruction:

For it would have been better for them never to have known the way of righteousness than, after knowing it, to turn back from the holy commandment that was passed on to them. It has happened to them according to the true proverb, "The dog turns back to its own vomit." (2:21–22)

One additional piece of information about these Christian adversaries is that they scoff at the traditional apocalyptic belief that the end of the world is imminent. The author assures his readers that the prophets and Jesus himself, speaking through the apostles, predicted that "in the last days scoffers will come scoffing and indulging their own lusts and saying, 'Where is the promise of his coming? For ever since our ancestors died, all things continue as they were from the beginning of the creation'" (3:3–4).

The author goes on to indicate that the end *is* destined to come. Whereas the world had once been destroyed by water, it is now being preserved for destruction by fire. Indeed, this end seems to be slow in coming only for those who measure time in human terms. For God, however, "one day is like a thousand years, and a thousand years are like one day" (3:8)— meaning, one might suppose, that if the end is still 6,000 years away, it is still coming "soon."

The author emphasizes that the end has been delayed to allow all people adequate time to repent and turn to the truth. But the day of judgment is nonetheless destined to come, and when it does, it will appear "like a thief" (3:9). The certainty of this final day should drive people to live "lives of holiness and godliness, waiting for and hastening the coming of the day of God, because of which the heavens will be set ablaze and dissolved, and the elements will melt with fire" (3:11–12).

THE JOHANNINE EPISTLES

The letters of the Johannine community that have made it into the New Testament are not nearly so difficult to read as some of the other books of the New Testament, such as the Gospels. The epistles of 2 John and 3 John take up only a page each, about average for most letters from the ancient world. These, in fact, are the two shortest books of the entire New Testament. One of the first things that may strike you as you read these two letters is that they make full use of the standard conventions of letters that I mentioned earlier. There is therefore little doubt that these two books are actually letters, that is, hand-delivered pieces of correspondence. The letter of 2 John is written by someone who identifies himself as "the elder" to a mysterious person called "the elect lady." In the course of his letter, however, the author stops speaking to this "lady" and begins to address a group of people ("you" plural, starting in v. 6). This shift has led most scholars to assume that the term "elect lady" refers to a Christian community, a group of people who are considered to be the chosen of God. If this assumption is correct, then 2 John is a letter in which a Christian leader (the elder) is addressing problems in a local church of a different community.

The letter of 3 John appears to have the same author. The writing style and many of the themes are the same, and again the author identifies himself as "the elder." In this instance, however, he addresses not an entire community but an individual named Gaius, lending his support to Gaius' side in a dispute that has arisen in the church.

Whereas both of these writings appear to be genuine letters, 1 John does not share their literary conventions. Notice that the author does not introduce himself or address his recipients directly at the outset, nor does he offer a greeting, prayer, or thanksgiving on their behalf. Moreover, at the end there are no closing greetings, well-wishings, final prayers, or even a farewell. On the other hand, the author does speak to his audience as those to whom he is "writing" (1:4; 2:12–14). 1 John is therefore less like an actual letter and more like a persuasive essay written to a community, a treatise intended to convince its recipients to engage in a certain course of action. There are other actual letters from antiquity that served as persuasive essays; this particular one appears to have been sent without the conventions typically found in epistles. Possibly it was sent with a separate cover letter that no longer survives. For the sake of convenience, I will continue to call this book of 1 John an epistle, even though technically speaking it is not.

It is reasonably clear that the author who wrote the letters of 2 and 3 John also produced this essay. Much of the vocabulary and many of the themes are the same, as is the writing style and the historical situation that the book appears to presuppose. Was this author also the one who produced the final version of the Gospel of John near the end of the first century? Scholars have debated the issue

extensively. Today, the majority of scholars believe that this writer was not the author of the Gospel; rather, he was someone living in the same community at a somewhat later time, a person who knew the teachings found in the Gospel and who addressed problems that had arisen in the community after the Gospel had been circulated.

On the one hand, the author of 1, 2, and 3 John seems to understand the Christian faith in terms quite similar to those found in the Fourth Gospel, for a number of themes that are important in the Gospel appear here in the epistles as well (see box 20.4). Yet the writing styles are not the same, and the problems in the community appear to be quite different. As one salient example, the problem of the community's relationship to the Jewish synagogue, one of the primary concerns of the Fourth Gospel, is completely missing from these epistles. Perhaps with the passing of time, the pain of this earlier crisis faded and new problems arose; then a new author, intimately familiar with his community's Gospel and influenced by the ways it understood the faith, wrote to address these problems. This would explain both the similarities of the epistles to the Gospel and the differences. What then can we say about this author and the situation he addressed?

ANOTHER GLIMPSE INTO THE PAST

BOX 20.4   The Gospel and Epistles of John: Some Thematic Similarities

The Johannine epistles share a number of their distinctive themes with the Fourth Gospel, often expressing them in exactly the same words. It seems reasonable to assume, therefore, that all four books derive from the same community, which had developed characteristic ways of understanding its religious traditions.

Among the shared themes are the following:

❖ The images of light and darkness (1 John 1:5–7; 2:9–11; cf. John 8:12; 12:46)

❖ The new and old commandments (1 John 2:7; cf. John 13:34)

❖ Abiding in Christ (1 John 2:27–28; cf. John 15:4, 6)

❖ The command to love one another within the community (1 John 3:11; cf. John 13:34–35)

❖ Being hated by the world (1 John 3:13; cf. John 15:18–19; 17:13–16)

❖ Christ "laying down his life" for others (1 John 3:16; cf. John 10:11, 15, 17–18; 15:12–13)

❖ Christ as the one sent by God into the world out of love (1 John 4:9; cf. John 3:16)

UNDERSTANDING THE JOHANNINE EPISTLES

We can consider these letters as a group of works produced by the same author at roughly the same time. The first is an open letter or persuasive treatise written to a community (1 John), the second a personal letter to the same community (2 John), and the third a personal letter to an individual within it (3 John). There are clues within the letters themselves concerning the historical context that prompted the author to produce them. The first step in the contextual method of interpretation (see p. 188) is to examine these clues and use them to reconstruct the situation.

The most important event in the recent history of this community is that it has experienced a serious rift. The author of 1 John indicates that a faction from within the community has split off from the rest of the group and left in a huff:

> They went out from us, but they did not belong to us; for if they had belonged to us, they would have remained with us. But by going out they made it plain that none of them belongs to us. (1 John 2:19)

Why did this Christian community split, with some members leaving, presumably to start their own congregation? In the next few verses the author designates those who left as "liars" and **"antichrists,"** a word that literally means "those who are opposed to Christ." He then contrasts them with those who have remained, who "know the truth." What do these antichrists believe that makes them so heinous to this author? He indicates that they have "denied that Jesus is the Christ" (2:22). The author's language may appear to suggest that those who have seceded from the community, a group that some scholars have labeled the **"secessionists,"** are Jews who failed to acknowledge that Jesus is the messiah. But they used to belong to the community, that is, they were Christians. In what sense, then, could they deny that Jesus is the Christ?

There are two other places where the author discusses these "antichrists." In 1 John 4:2–3 the author claims that unlike those who belong to God, the antichrists refuse to confess that "Jesus Christ has come in the flesh." A similar statement occurs in 2 John 7, where the antichrists are called "deceivers who have gone out into the world" and are said to deny that "Jesus Christ has come in the flesh." These descriptions suggest the secessionists may have held a point of view that we know about from other sources from about the same period, such as the writings of Ignatius. Ignatius opposed a group of Christians who maintained that Jesus was not himself a flesh-and-blood human being but was completely and only divine. For these persons, God could not have a real bodily existence; God is God—invisible, immortal, all-knowing, all-powerful, and unchanging. If Jesus was God, he could not have experienced the limitations of human flesh. For these people, Jesus only seemed to experience these limitations. Jesus was not really a human; he merely appeared to be.

These Christians came to be known by their opponents as "docetists," a term that derives from the Greek verb for "appear" or "seem." They were opposed by Christian leaders like Ignatius who took umbrage at the idea that Jesus and the things he did, including his death on the cross, were all a show. For Ignatius, Jesus was a real man, with a real body, who shed real blood, and died a real death.

It may be that the secessionists from the Johannine community had developed a **docetic kind of Christology**. In the words of the author, they "denied that Jesus Christ had come in the flesh." If they were, in fact, early docetists, then a number of other things that the author says in these letters make considerable sense. Take, for instance, the opening words of 1 John. Readers who do not realize that the essay is being written because a group of docetic Christians have seceded from the community may not understand why the author begins his work the way he does, with a prologue that in many ways is reminiscent of the Prologue to the Fourth Gospel (with which he was probably familiar):

> We declare to you what was from the beginning, what we have heard, what we have seen with our eyes, what we have looked at and touched with our hands, concerning the word of life—this life was revealed, and we have seen it and testify to it, and declare to you the eternal life that was with the Father, and was revealed to us. (1:1–2)

Once a reader knows the historical context of the epistle, however, this opening statement makes considerable sense. The author is opposing Christians who maintain that Jesus is a phantasmal being without flesh and blood by reminding his audience of their own traditions about this Word of God made manifest: he could be seen, touched, and handled; that is, he had a real human body. And he shed real blood. Thus, the author stresses the importance of Jesus' blood for the forgiveness of sins (1:7) and of the (real) sacrifice for sins that he made (2:2; 4:10).

What led a group of Johannine Christians to split from the community because of their belief that Jesus was not a real flesh-and-blood human being? We have seen that after the community was excluded from the synagogue, it developed a kind of fortress mentality that had a profound effect on its Christology. Christ came to be seen less and less as a human rabbi or messiah and more and more as a divine being of equal standing with God, who came to reveal the truth of God to his people only to be rejected by those who dwelt in darkness. Those who believed in him claimed to understand his divine teachings and considered themselves to be children of God. By the time the Fourth Gospel was completed, some members of the Johannine community had come to believe that Jesus was on a par with God.

It appears that Christians in this community did not stop developing their understandings of Jesus with the completion of the writing of the Gospel. Some of them took their Christology a step further. Not only was Jesus equal with God, he was God himself, totally and completely. Moreover, if he was God, he could not be flesh because God was not composed of flesh; Jesus therefore merely appeared to be a human.

This view proved to be too much for some of the other members of the community; battle lines were drawn and a split resulted. The Johannine epistles were written by an author who thought that the secessionists had gone too far. For this author, Christ was indeed a flesh-and-blood human being; he was the savior "come in the flesh," whose blood brought about salvation from sin. Those who rejected this view, for him, had rejected the community's confession that the man Jesus was the Christ; in his view, they were antichrists.

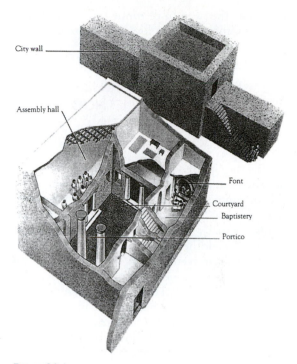

Figure 20.1 Cross-sectional drawing of the earliest Christian church building discovered, a converted house in the eastern Syrian city of Dura.

The charges that the author levels against the secessionists do not pertain exclusively to their ideas about Christ. He also makes moral accusations. He insinuates that his opponents do not practice the commandments of God (2:4), that they fail to love the brothers and sisters in the community (2:9–11; 4:20), and that they practice sin while claiming to have no contact with it (1:6–10). It is possible that, in the mind of the author at least, these moral charges related closely to the doctrinal one. If the secessionists undervalued the fleshly existence of Jesus, perhaps they undervalued the importance of their own fleshly existence as well. In other words, if what really mattered to them was the spirit rather than the flesh, then perhaps they were unconcerned not only about Jesus' real body but also about their own. Thus, they may well have appeared totally uninterested in keeping the commandments that God had given and in manifesting love among the brothers and sisters of the community. This would explain why the author stresses in his letters the need to continue to practice God's commandments and to love one another, unlike those who have left the community.

REFLECTIONS ON THE CONTEXTUAL METHOD FOR UNDERSTANDING THE JOHANNINE EPISTLES

At this stage you may have recognized one of the difficulties in this kind of analysis of the context of the Johannine letters. It is very hard for the historian to know for a fact that the Johannine secessionists actually taught that it was unimportant to love one another and to keep God's commandments. The problem is that the only source we have for the secessionists' views is the author of the Johannine epistles, and he was their enemy.

As we know from other kinds of literature, ancient and modern, it is a very tricky business to learn what people say and do on the basis of what their enemies say about them. Imagine trying to reconstruct the beliefs and practices of a modern politician on the basis of what the opposing campaign says! Sometimes enemies misunderstand their opponents' views, or distort them, or misrepresent them, or draw implications from them that the other party does not.

What, then, do we actually know about the Johannine secessionists? Do we know for a fact that they were docetists who taught others to disobey the commandments and live in sin? No, what we know is that this is how the author of 1 John portrayed them. Some scholars are inclined to accept this portrayal as accurate; others are more cautious and say that we only know how the author himself perceived the secessionists. Others are still more cautious and say that we do not even know how the author perceived them, only how he described them. The issue is not easily resolved, and it is one you need to be alert to as you yourself engage in contextual studies of the New Testament writings.

With these caveats in mind, let me summarize what we can probably say about the historical context of the Johannine letters and then show how these letters can be seen as a response to the situation at hand. There is little to suggest that the author of these letters was intentionally duplicitous in his assessment of his opponents, even though we can never know this for certain. Whether or not his perceptions were correct, then, we can at least say how he perceived the situation. From his point of view, a group of former members of the community had split to form their own group; they taught that Jesus was not a real human being, but only divine; they saw no need to keep the commandments and did not manifest love to other members of the community, and were therefore antichrists and liars; and they continued to be a threat to the community's well-being by deceiving others.

If this is the context, as seen through the eyes of the "elder," what more can we say about the historical occasion of 1, 2, and 3 John? The author was a leader of a community at some distance from the one he addresses in these letters. That he was not in the immediate vicinity is demonstrated by his closing remarks in 2 and 3 John, where he indicates that he will visit soon so as not to be forced to rely on the written word to communicate his views (2 John 12; 3 John 13–14). He appears to have seen himself as having authority over the Christians to whom he writes; that is why he can exhort them to believe and act in the ways that he commands.

1 John would have been a treatise to those in this neighboring church who have not joined the secessionists, written as a kind of open letter to persuade them to remain faithful to the author's position and to see it as standing in true conformity with the tradition that they inherited when they joined the community. 2 John would have been a personal letter to the church urging, in shorter fashion, much the same advice; and 3 John would have been a private letter to an individual in this community giving instruction about a particular aspect of the problem that has arisen.

Scholars have expressed different opinions concerning what had happened to create the need for this final letter, the one most closely related to private letters in antiquity. It appears clear, in any event, that Gaius, the recipient of the letter, is in conflict with another leader in the congregation, Diotrephes, and that this conflict has to do with whether the author of these letters and the representatives he sends to the church should be received as authorities. The author sees Diotrephes as an opponent and Gaius and Demetrius (perhaps the carrier of the letter? v. 12) as allies. It could be that Diotrephes has supported the views of the secessionists and is trying to convert the rest of the church, or it could be that he simply does not like the "elder" who writes this letter, or appreciate his barging in to force his opinions upon the church that meets in his home (see box 20.5). Other options are possible, some of which may occur to you as you yourself engage in the contextual analysis of these letters.

CONFLICTS WITHIN THE EARLY CHRISTIAN COMMUNITIES

In the Christian writings that have survived from the end of the first century and the beginning of the second, we get some sense of the state of Christianity at the close of the New Testament period. The Christian communities were by no means unified at this time. Different Christian leaders and teachers were proclaiming different versions of the faith, and many of them were at serious odds with one another. Christians had different views of how to conduct themselves both within the Christian community and within society as a whole. Some Christians were thought to be engaging in wild, immoral activities and to be promoting such ventures in the church.

As historians of the period we should remember that we have only one side of almost every story. There can be no doubt that the "immoral and corrupt heretics" attacked in surviving writings would have had a lot to say in their own defense. Indeed, they did defend their views and attack their proto-orthodox opponents for propagating error, as we have discovered from the Gnostic writings of the Nag Hammadi library. Regrettably, almost all of the other books produced by advocates of alternative Christian perspectives came to be destroyed on order of their victorious adversaries. Typically, from the ancient world, only the writings of the winners survive.

The authors who later came to be canonized in the New Testament, some of them claiming to be

---

ANOTHER GLIMPSE INTO THE PAST

BOX 20.5   House Churches in Early Christianity

Most people do not realize that for many, many years Christians did not construct church buildings for their services of worship and fellowship. The earliest Christian church building to be uncovered by archaeologists (actually a house that was converted to serve as a church in the city of Dura in Eastern Syria) dates from around the year 250 C.E., well over two centuries after the death of Jesus. The lack of a specially designated sacred space for Christian worship during its first two hundred years made this religion different from almost all others in its world. Pagan cults were centered in temples and shrines, and Jews, of course, worshiped in synagogues (which were themselves sometimes converted homes).

If Christians did not meet in buildings specifically designed for the purpose, where did they meet? References in Paul's letters, the book of Acts, and other early Christian literature show that the early Christian communities were "house churches." Christians gathered together in the private homes of their wealthier members, who alone would have had room to accommodate more than a few persons. One consequence was that the membership and attendance at any given church would have been limited by the size of the house in which they met. Also, within a given city there could have been a number of Christian churches, each possibly with its own leader, who in many cases, presumably, was the person who provided the house.

This situation may shed light on the problem of interchurch conflict addressed in 3 John. It is possible, for example, that Diotrephes owns a relatively large house and meets weekly with a group of Christians, among whom he has assumed the role of leader and patron. Could it be that he sees the "elder" as an interloper who is out of bounds in trying to control what happens within the confines of his own home, among the Christians whom he entertains weekly for a service of worship and fellowship?

apostles, urged their own versions of the faith, their own leaders, and their own systems of ethics. These authors may not have been in full agreement with one another on every point, but most of their differences came to be smoothed over when their books were later collected into a sacred canon of Scripture and read and interpreted only in light of one another. The proto-orthodox Christians chiefly responsible for this canon of Scripture also advocated a church structure that could trace itself back to Jesus and his apostles. In their conflicts with aberrant forms of the religion, these late-first-century and early-second-century believers thus set the stage for the battles over orthodoxy that were to rage throughout the second and third centuries, as different Christian groups representing different understandings of the faith strove for converts both from the outside (through evangelism) and from within.

AT A GLANCE

BOX 20.6   Christian Internal Conflicts

1. Even though some sources, such as the book of Acts, portray the early Christian church as internally harmonious over major points of belief and practice, there were in fact widespread disagreements within Christian communities.

2. The Book of James takes issue with Christians who understood Paul's doctrine of "justification by faith apart from works of the law" to mean that it did not matter what you *did* as a Christian, as long as you believed.

3. Jude and 2 Peter, both of which appear to be pseudonymous, harshly warn against false teachers (whose views are not set forth) who had infiltrated the Christian community and wreaked havoc in their midst.

4. 1, 2, and 3 John were written by a member of the Johannine community, near the end of the first century; the author was not the same person who wrote the Gospel of John, but his theological views were very similar.

5. 1 John is an open letter or persuasive essay; 2 and 3 John are actual letters written to members of a Christian community.

6. The author was particularly troubled by a split in his community, in which some Christians had separated themselves off because of different understandings of Christology. Those who departed had taken the views of the Fourth Gospel to an extreme and had begun to think that Jesus was so divine that he was not at all human.

TAKE A STAND

1. Choose one of the catholic epistles and show how it reveals different Christians, or different Christian groups, at odds with one another. What are the views of each person or group? How do they differ? Why don't they agree?

2. Choose any two authors of the New Testament and argue that on one or two fundamental issues they disagree with each other (whether you happen to think this is true or not). Then state your opinion: are these authors *really* at odds, or do they only seem so on the surface?

3. Return to the book of Acts and discuss its portrayal of the inner harmony of the Christian church. Now consider the books of 2 Peter and Jude and their portrayal of the harmony of the church. In your judgment, do these books have the same view of the matter?

SUGGESTIONS FOR FURTHER READING

Batten, Alicia. *What Are They Saying about the Letter of James?* Mahway, N.J.: Paulist, 2009. An overview of what scholars now say about the significant historical and literary features of the book of James; ideal for beginning students.

Bauckham, Richard. *Jude and the Relatives of Jesus in the Early Church.* Edinburgh: T&T Clark, 1990. An interesting study that argues, among other things, that the epistle of Jude was actually written by Jesus' own brother.

Brown, Raymond. *The Community of the Beloved Disciple: The Lives, Loves and Hates of an Individual Church in New Testament Times.* Mahwah, N.J.: Paulist, 1978. A sketch of the history of the Johannine community, as determined through a careful reading of the Gospel of John and the Johannine epistles.

Chester, Andrew, and Ralph Martin. *The Theology of the Letters of James, Peter, and Jude.* Cambridge: Cambridge University Press, 1994. A nice discussion of the social context and theological perspectives of these catholic epistles.

Ehrman, Bart. *Forged: Writing in the Name of God: Why the Bible's Authors Are Not Who We Think They Are.* San Francisco: HarperOne, 2011. A discussion of all the "pseudepigrapha" of the New Testament, including the books discussed in this chapter, which argues that it is best to understand them as ancient forgeries; for beginning students.

Lieu, Judith. *The Theology of the Johannine Epistles.* Cambridge: Cambridge University Press, 1991. A good discussion of major themes in 1, 2, and 3 John.

 ## KEY TERMS

Acts of Peter	*Didache*	Docetism	secessionists
Christology			

Christians and the Cosmos

THE BOOK OF REVELATION

WHAT TO EXPECT

For most people, the most intriguing but puzzling writing of the New Testament is the book of Revelation, which describes in graphic and highly symbolic terms the cataclysmic events that will transpire at the end of the world. In every generation since the book was written, Christians have argued that its vivid description of catastrophic events would happen in their own day. So far, none of them has been right.

This chapter takes a different approach to the book of Revelation: not asking when its predictions will occur, but seeking to understand the book within its own historical context, as one of the apocalypses written by Christians and Jews in the ancient world. By putting it in its own historical context we will better be able to understand its message of hope for those suffering under the oppressive powers of this world.

The end of the world was near. So proclaimed Jesus, and some years after him, the apostle Paul. And so proclaimed most of the earliest Christians of whom we have any knowledge. The end of time had come, God was about to intervene in history; Christ was soon to return from heaven in judgment on the earth, and people were to repent and prepare for his coming.

With the passing of time, this message lost its appeal in some Christian circles. For the end never did come, and Christians had to reevaluate (or even reject) the earlier traditions that said it would. We have already observed such reevaluations among some of the early Christian authors.

We have noticed, for example, how the Gospel of Luke modifies Jesus' predictions so that he no longer claims that the Son of Man will arrive in his disciples' lifetimes. We have also seen that in several later Gospels, such as John and Thomas, Jesus tells no parables concerning the coming Kingdom of God. We have also observed that among the Christians in Corinth, Jesus' return and the resurrection of the dead became heated questions, as some believers claimed that the divine plan of redemption had already come to completion and that they were already experiencing the full benefits of salvation. Moreover, we have seen that still other Christians, such as those attacked by the author of

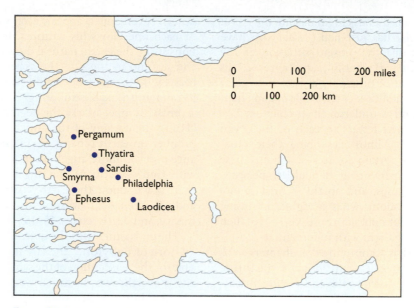

Figure 21.1 The Seven Churches of Asia Minor Addressed in Revelation 2–3.

2 Peter, came to mock the idea that Jesus was soon to return from heaven in judgment.

Nonetheless despite the passing of time and the failure of their hopes to materialize, many Christians remained firmly committed to this belief. It stood at the heart of the message proclaimed by the apostle Paul some twenty years after Jesus himself had died, and by the Gospel of Mark some fifteen years after Paul, by the Gospel of Matthew some fifteen years after Mark, and by 2 Peter some thirty years after Matthew.

The coming of the end was also the fervent conviction of a prophet named John, who lived near the end of the first century. John was a Christian seer who penned a majestic and awe-inspiring account of the end of the world, an account that has spawned endless speculation and debate among those who have continued to await the return of Jesus over the intervening nineteen hundred years. John was not the only Jewish or Christian author to narrate visions of the end of the world. Indeed, the kind of book that he wrote was quite popular among people looking for the heavenly truths that could give meaning to their earthly realities. But none of the other early apocalypses has enjoyed nearly the success of the Apocalypse of John. Indeed, the book of Revelation

continues to serve many Christians today as a kind of blueprint of events that are still to transpire in the future, when the history of the world, as they believe, will be brought to a screeching halt.

THE CONTENT AND STRUCTURE OF THE BOOK OF REVELATION

The title of the book comes from its opening words: "The revelation of Jesus Christ, which God gave him to show his servants what must soon take place" (Rev 1:1). The revelation, or apocalypse (from the Greek word for "unveiling" or "revealing") concerns the end of time; it is given by God through Jesus and his angel to "his servant John" (1:1). The author appears to be known to his readers, who are identified as Christians of seven churches in Asia Minor (1:11). He begins to narrate his visionary experiences by describing his extraordinary encounter with the exalted Christ, the "one like a Son of Man" who walks in the midst of seven golden lampstands (1:12–20).

Christ instructs John to "write what you have seen, what is, and what is to take place after this"

(1:19). In other words, he is to (*a*) narrate the vision of Christ that he has just had ("what you have seen"), (*b*) describe the present situation of the churches in his day ("what is"), and (*c*) record his visions of the end of time ("what is to take place after this"). The first task is accomplished in chapter 1. The second is undertaken in chapters 2–3. Christ dictates brief letters to each of the seven churches of Asia Minor, describing their situations and urging certain courses of action. These churches are experiencing difficulties: persecutions, false teachings, and apathy. Christ praises those who have done what is right, promising them a reward, but upbraids those who have fallen away, threatening them with judgment.

The third task is accomplished in chapters 4–22, which record John's heavenly vision of the future course of history, down to the end of time. Briefly, the narrative unfolds as follows. The prophet is taken up into heaven through a window in the sky. There he beholds the throne of God, who is eternally worshiped and praised by twenty-four human "elders" and four "living creatures" (angelic beings in the shapes of animals; chap. 4). In the hand of the figure on the throne is a scroll sealed with seven seals, which cannot be broken except by one who is found worthy. This scroll records the future of the earth, and the prophet weeps when he sees that no one can break its seals, but one of the elders informs him that there is one who is worthy. He then sees next to the throne a "Lamb standing as if it had been slaughtered" (5:6). The Lamb, of course, is Christ.

The Lamb takes the scroll from the hand of God, amidst much praise and adoration from the twenty-four elders and the four living creatures, and he begins to break its seals (chap. 5). With each broken seal, a major catastrophe strikes the earth: war, famine, death. The sixth seal marks the climax, a disaster of cosmic proportions: the sun turns black, the moon turns red as blood, the stars fall from the sky, and the sky itself disappears. One might think that we have come to the end of all things, the destruction of the universe. But we are only in chapter 6.

The breaking of the seventh seal leads not to a solitary disaster but to a period of silence that is followed by an entirely new set of seven more di-

sasters. Seven angels appear, each with a trumpet. As each one blows his trumpet, further devastations strike the earth: natural disasters on the land and sea and in the sky, the appearance of dread beasts who torture and maim, widespread calamity and unspeakable suffering (chaps. 8–9). The seventh trumpet marks the beginning of the end (11:15), the coming of the antichrist and his false prophet on earth (chaps. 12–13) and the appearance of seven more angels, each with a bowl filled with God's wrath. As the angels each pour out their bowls upon the earth, further destruction and agony ensue: loathsome diseases, widespread misery, and death (chaps. 15–16).

The end comes with the destruction of the great **"whore of Babylon,"** the city ultimately responsible for the persecution of the saints (chap. 17). The city is overthrown, to much weeping and wailing on earth but to much rejoicing in heaven (chaps. 18–19). The defeat of the city is followed by a final cosmic battle in which Christ, with his heavenly armies, engages the forces of the antichrist aligned against him (19:11–21). Christ wins a resounding victory. The enemies of God are completely crushed, and the antichrist and his false prophet are thrown into a lake of burning sulfur to be tormented forever.

Satan himself is then imprisoned in a bottomless pit, while Christ and his saints rule on earth for a thousand years. Afterward, the Devil emerges for a brief time to lead some of the nations astray. Then comes a final judgment, in which all persons are raised from the dead and rewarded for their deeds. Those who have sided with Christ are brought into the eternal kingdom; those who have aligned themselves with the Devil and his antichrist are taken away for eternal torment in the lake of fire. The Devil himself is thrown into the lake, as are finally Hades and Death itself (chap. 20).

The prophet then has a vision of the new heaven and the new earth that God creates for his people. A new Jerusalem descends from heaven, with gates made of pearl and streets paved with gold. This is a beautiful and utopian place where Christ reigns eternal, where there is no fear or darkness, no pain or suffering or evil or death, a place where the good and righteous will dwell forever (chaps. 21–22). The prophet ends his book by emphasizing that his vision is true, and that it will come to fulfillment very soon.

THE BOOK OF REVELATION FROM A HISTORICAL PERSPECTIVE

To most modern readers the Apocalypse of John seems mystical and bizarre, quite unlike anything else that we read. In part, this explains our continual fascination with the book—it is so strange, so unearthly, that its descriptions cannot simply have been dreamed up. Its supernatural feel seems to vindicate its supernatural character.

The historian who approaches the book, however, sees it in a somewhat different light, for this was not the only book of its kind to be written in the ancient world, even if it is the only one that most of us have ever read. Indeed, a number of other apocalypses were produced by ancient Jews and Christians. These works also offer unworldly accounts of happenings in heaven, bizarre descriptions of supranatural events and transcendent realities that impinge on the history of our world, and deeply symbolic visions of the end of time that are given by God through his angels to a human prophet, who writes them down in cryptic and mysterious narratives filled with emphatic claims that they are true and soon to take place.

Some of these other apocalypses still survive, and together they make up a distinct genre of literature. Thus, far from being unique in its own day, the Apocalypse of John followed a number of literary conventions that were well known among Jews and Christians of the ancient world. A historian who wants to understand this one ancient text, then, will situate it in the context of this related literature and explain its important features in light of the literary conventions of the genre.

APOCALYPTIC WORLDVIEWS AND APOCALYPSE GENRE

Apocalypses were written to convey an apocalyptic agenda. Here it is important to be very clear about our terms. Throughout our discussion I have used the term **"apocalypticism"** to refer to an ancient Jewish and Christian worldview that maintained that there were two fundamental components of reality, good and evil, and that everything in the world was aligned on one side or the other (God versus the Devil, the angels versus the demons, life versus death, and so on; see Chapter 9). This dualistic perspective applied to human history: the present age was seen to be evil, controlled by the Devil and his forces, whereas the age to come would be good, controlled by God. According to this view, there was to be a cataclysmic break between these ages, when God would destroy the forces of evil to bring in his kingdom. At that time there would be a judgment of all beings, both living and dead. This judgment was imminent.

Whereas the term "apocalypticism" refers to this worldview, **"apocalypse"** refers to a genre of literature that embodies it. Everyone who wrote a Jewish or Christian apocalypse was obviously an apocalypticist (i.e., he or she embraced the apocalyptic worldview). The reverse, however, is not true: not every apocalypticist wrote an apocalypse. Thus, neither John the Baptist nor Jesus nor Paul, to take three prominent examples, appears to have written a detailed vision of the heavenly realities. The first Jewish apocalypticist to do so, to our knowledge, was the author of Daniel (around 165 B.C.E.), the second half of which contains several brief apocalypses. Other apocalypses written somewhat later include the noncanonical Jewish works of 1 Enoch, 2 Baruch, and 4 Ezra, such as the *Apocalypse of Peter* (see box 21.3).

These apocalypses differ in important ways. Some of their most obvious differences relate to whether they were written by Jews or Christians, since the apocalyptic drama unfolds differently depending on whether or not Jesus himself is the key to the future. One of the things that all these books have in common, however, is that they were evidently written in times of distress and suffering, whether real or perceived. In large measure, apocalypses were books that protested the present order of things and the powers that maintained it; these powers were seen to be inimical to the ways and people of God. These books invariably show that despite the suffering experienced by the people of God, God is ultimately in control and will soon intervene on their behalf. One of the important purposes of these works, then, is to encourage those who are experiencing the forces of evil to hold on and keep the faith. Their suffering is not in vain and it will not last long, for soon they will be vindicated in the glorious climax of history in which God will destroy the forces of evil and exalt those who have remained faithful to him.

Apocalypse as a Genre: General Description

The various Jewish and Christian apocalypses that convey this message share a number of literary features. All these books are first-person narratives by prophets who have been granted highly symbolic visions or dreams. The visions are usually interpreted by a heavenly being who serves as a mediator. For the most part, the visions serve to explain the realities of earth from the perspective of heaven—realities such as the ultimate meaning of life and the future course of earth's history. These narratives always embody a triumphal movement from the painful existence of life here below to the glorious life up above or from the hardships and sufferings of the present to the vindication and bliss of the future.

There are two major kinds of ancient apocalypses. These are not mutually exclusive categories. As you will see, the book of Revelation has aspects of each, although some other apocalypses are of only one type or the other:

1. *Heavenly Journeys.* In this kind of apocalypse, the prophet is taken up into heaven and given a tour of the heavenly realm by an angelic companion, where he beholds symbols and events that have earthly implications. The idea implicit in this kind of apocalypse is that life on earth directly reflects life in heaven; that is, it is somewhat like the earthly shadow of a heavenly reality (cf. our discussion of the Platonic notion of shadow versus reality in Chapter 19).

2. *Historical Sketches.* In this kind of apocalypse, the prophet has a symbolic vision of the future course of history. For example, grotesque beasts might arise out of the sea to wreak havoc on the earth, representing various kingdoms that will come to dominate the people of God (see Daniel 7). The symbolism is often explained to the seer by the heavenly mediator, and through him to the reader.

Apocalypse as a Genre: Specific Literary Features

Despite their wide-ranging differences, the surviving apocalypses typically share specific literary features. The most common of these are the following:

Pseudonymity. Almost all the ancient apocalypses were written pseudonymously in the name of a famous religious person from the past (the book of Revelation is a rare exception). Among the surviving Jewish apocalypses are some claiming to be written by Moses, Abraham, Enoch, and even Adam. We have Christian apocalypses reputedly from the pens of the prophet Isaiah and the apostles Peter, Paul, and Thomas.

Is there a particular reason for authors of apocalypses to hide their identity behind a pseudonym? We have already seen that pseudonymity can help to secure a hearing for one's views, by lending a kind of authority to one's writing that it otherwise could not hope to enjoy. Nowhere is this kind of authority more important than when one is writing a detailed description of heavenly realities that explain the tragedies and suffering of earthly life. Such visions of transcendent truth are obviously not granted to just anybody. It makes sense, then, that authors of apocalypses typically claimed to be famous persons of the past who were renowned for their religious piety and devotion to God. Only to such as these would God reveal the ultimate truths that could unlock the mysteries of human existence.

The use of a pseudonym made particular sense for apocalypses of the historical sketch type. By pretending to be someone living in the distant past, an author could "predict" the future. A typical ploy, then, was to write in the name of a prophet from ancient times to whom was revealed a number of events that were to take place (by the author's time, of course, they already *had* happened). When the author then continued to predict what was soon to happen in his own day—the reader didn't know when this was, of course, since the author claimed to be writing from the distant past—he was naturally granted the benefit of the doubt. That is to say, these future events (from the time of the reader) were just as certain to occur as those

BOX 21.1   The Book of Revelation as Underground Literature

Some readers of the book of Revelation have taken its mysterious symbols to suggest that it was "underground" literature. The symbolic language of the book, according to this interpretation, was used to keep the governing authorities from realizing that they themselves were under attack.

There may be an element of truth in this view, but one might wonder whether a Roman administrator was likely to sit down over the weekend to read a good Christian book. It seems more plausible that the principal function of the symbolism, whether in Revelation or in other apocalypses, lay elsewhere, namely, in the character of the material itself. Indeed, the heavenly secrets are by their very nature not straightforward or banal or subject to empirical demonstration; their mystery and splendor virtually require them to be conveyed in unearthly and bizarre symbols of the higher realities of heaven.

---

that had already happened. The prophet had been right about everything else; surely he was also right about what would come next!

The first apocalypse known to use this technique came to be included in the Hebrew Bible. The book of **Daniel**, allegedly written by the great wise man of the sixth century B.C.E. during the days of the Babylonian captivity, was actually written, in the judgment of almost all critical scholars, sometime during the period of suffering associated with the Maccabean revolt, some 400 years later. No wonder "Daniel" could predict the rise of the Persians and the Greeks, and even more accurately detail events that were to transpire near the time of the Jewish uprising; the author of these "prophecies" lived after they had taken place.

Bizarre Symbolic Visions. Rarely do apocalypses describe the geography of heaven or the events of the future in straightforward and easily understood terms. Instead, they delight in the mystical and revel in the symbolic. The future is envisioned as a series of wild and grotesque beasts that appear on the face of the earth; there are fantastic spectacles, bizarre images, strange figures, mysterious events. The symbols often confuse not only the reader but also the prophet himself, who sometimes presses the angelic mediator for an interpretation of what he has seen. Sometimes the explanation itself is mysterious and subject to a wide range of interpretations.

Violent Repetitions. Apocalypses often convey the mysteries of the heavenly realm through violent repetitions. By this I do not mean that there is always repeated violence in these texts—although there often is—but that the repetitions themselves are violent in that they violate the literal sense of the narrative. That is, apocalypticists often emphasize their points by producing countless repetitions for effect. If one were to take Revelation's descriptions of future disasters literally, for example, there would be no way to map them out chronologically on a time line. As we have already seen, at the breaking of the sixth seal, the sun, moon, and stars are destroyed; surely this is the end—no life could possibly go on existing. But life does go on, and we enter into a new phase of sufferings on the earth with the heavenly lights shining in full force.

What we have, then, is a kind of spiral effect in narrative. The catastrophes that it describes cannot be sketched in linear fashion as if one event necessarily occurred after another. One benefit of this kind of repetition is that it allows the author to employ important numbers known to have mystical qualities. In the book of Revelation, for example, there are three major sets of seven disasters sent from heaven, the number three probably symbolizing fullness and perfection and seven symbolizing divinity—as opposed to six, which is one short of seven, and therefore imperfect (see later on the number of the beast, 666).

Triumphalist Movement. By their nature, apocalypses are designed to provide hope for those who suffer and despair. In the end, God will prevail. The present suffering is intense, and that to come will be yet more intense, but ultimately God will triumph over evil and vindicate his people.

Motivational Function. These books exhort their readers to remain faithful to their religious commitments, to keep true to their faith, and to refuse to give up hope. This point is worth emphasizing: ancient Jewish and Christian apocalypses were written not so much to reveal the precise details of the future as to provide motivation for those who were in danger of growing slack in their commitments and of losing hope in the midst of their suffering. The hope they provided was rooted in the belief that when all was said and done, God was in control of the world and would eventually reward those who remained faithful to him.

Figure 21.2 Roman coin showing the son of the emperor **Domitian** seated on a globe and reaching out to seven stars, with an inscription "To the Divine Caesar." Notice the similarities with the visions found in Revelation, where Christ, too, is a divine being, the Son of God and ruler of the earth, in whose hand are seven stars (e.g., Rev 1:12–16). Interestingly enough, Revelation was written during the time of Domitian, when this coin was minted.

THE REVELATION OF JOHN IN HISTORICAL CONTEXT

The Book of Revelation is virtually unique among apocalypses in that it does not appear to be pseudonymous. The author simply calls himself John without claiming to be a famous person from the past.

Some Christians of the second and third centuries claimed that this John was none other than Jesus' own disciple, the son of Zebedee. Others rejected this notion and as a result refused to admit the book into the Christian canon of Scripture. (If the author had claimed to be that John, the book would probably have to be considered pseudonymous, for reasons we will see momentarily.) One of the ironies of the New Testament is that the Fourth Gospel, which does not claim to be written by someone named John, is called John, whereas the book of Revelation, which does claim to be written by someone named John, is not called by this name. In any event, it can be stated without reservation that whoever wrote the Gospel did not also write this book. For one thing, the theological emphases are quite distinct. In the Gospel of John there is virtually no concern for the coming end of the age (contrast the Synoptics, with their proclamation of the imminent arrival of the Son of

Man); in the book of Revelation the end is nearly the entire concern. Even more important, as recognized even by linguists in early Christianity, the writing styles of these two books are completely different. Detailed studies have shown that the author of Revelation was principally literate in a Semitic language, probably Aramaic, and knew Greek as a second language. His Greek is clumsy in places, sometimes even ungrammatical. This is not at all the case with the Gospel of John, which is written in an entirely different style and therefore by a different author (see box 21.2).

We have already seen that the Fourth Gospel was probably not written by John the son of Zebedee. Is it possible, then, that the book of Revelation was? The difficulty with this view is that parts of the book could scarcely be explained if it were written by Jesus' own disciple. The author, for example, occasionally mentions "the apostles," but he never indicates that he is one of them (e.g., 21:14). Even more intriguingly, at one point in the narrative the prophet sees twenty-four elders around the throne of God (chap. 4). Most interpreters understand these figures to represent the twelve Jewish

ANOTHER GLIMPSE INTO THE PAST

BOX 21.2   The Author of Revelation in the Early Church

Even though the book of Revelation was finally included in the New Testament canon because Christian leaders came to think it had been written by Jesus' disciple, John the son of Zebedee, there were outspoken dissenters. Perhaps the most famous was **Dionysius**, a bishop of the city of Alexandria (Egypt) in the mid-third century, whose remarks about the book have a surprisingly modern feel to them. Dionysius used the author's self-presentation and his Greek writing style to show that he was not the writer of the Fourth Gospel (whom Dionysius assumed was the disciple John). His conclusion? There must have been two different early Christian leaders named John, both of whom were active in Asia Minor, whence both the Gospel and Revelation derived. The following quotations are drawn from Dionysius's writings, as these are quoted by the fourth-century church historian Eusebius (*Ecclesiastical History* 7.25).

> The one who wrote these things (i.e., the book of Revelation) calls himself John, and we should believe him. But it is not clear which John he was. For he doesn't call himself the disciple whom the Lord

loved—as happens often in the Gospel—nor does he say that he was the one who leaned on Jesus' breast or that he was the brother of James, who both saw and heard the Lord. But surely he would have described himself in one of these ways if he had wanted to make himself clearly known. . . . I think [therefore] that there must have been another John living among the Christians in Asia Minor, just as they say that there are two different tombs in Ephesus, both of them allegedly John's.

> The phrasing itself also helps to differentiate between the Gospel and Epistle [of John] on the one hand and the book of Revelation on the other. The first two are written not only without errors in the Greek, but also with real skill with respect to vocabulary, logic, and coherence of meaning. You won't find any barbaric expression, grammatical flaw, or vulgar expression in them. . . . I don't deny that this other author had revelations . . . but I notice that in neither language nor style does he write accurate Greek. He makes use of barbaric expressions and is sometimes guilty even of grammatical error. . . . I don't say this in order to accuse him (far from it!), but simply to demonstrate that the two books are not at all similar.

Patriarchs and the twelve apostles of Jesus (cf. 21:12, 14); among them, of course, would be the two sons of Zebedee. But the author gives no indication that he is seeing himself! It appears, then, that the book was written by some other Christian named John, a prophet who was known to several of the churches of Asia Minor.

It is difficult to know exactly when he wrote this book. Modern interpreters usually appeal to details in some of the visions to pinpoint a date. For example, the Beast of Babylon in chapter 17, which, as we will see, appears to represent the city of Rome, is said to have seven horns on its head. These represent seven "kings," evidently meaning the rulers of Rome (17:9). Five of these are said to have come and gone, and one is currently reigning (17:10). This would presumably mean that the vision was written during the reign of the sixth Roman ruler, but with which ruler should we begin counting—

with the dictator Julius Caesar or with his adopted son, the first emperor, Caesar Augustus? And does this vision date the entire book or simply this portion of it?

On the basis of a detailed study of all such clues in the text, most investigators think that parts of the book were written during the 60s of the Common Era, soon after the persecution of the Christians under Nero. If we begin counting with Julius Caesar, Nero happens to have been the sixth ruler of Rome. He was also one of the author's chief enemies. There are other aspects of the book, however, that suggest that it was not completed until somewhat later, probably around 95 C.E., during the reign of Domitian. For example, the code word "Babylon" (see, e.g., Rev 14:8; 16:9; 18:2) came to be used by Jews to designate Rome as the chief political enemy of God *after* the destruction of Jerusalem in 70 C.E. (e.g., 4 Ezra 3; 2 Baruch 10).

Figure 21.3 Painting of Christ as the Alpha and Omega (Rev 21:6; 22:13), from the catacomb of Commodilla.

Somewhat less complicated is the question of the social context of the book. The author describes the Christian churches of Asia Minor in chapters 2–3. They are persecuted, they have false teachers in their midst, and a number of their members have lost their fervor for their faith, possibly because of the passing of time and the hardships imposed upon them as Christians. Elsewhere in the book we read of extensive Christian martyrdoms (6:5) and find hints that the Christian communities that the author addresses are among the poorer classes, who hate the rich and powerful (18:11–20). In particular, John directs his anger against the political institutions of his day, especially the Roman government, which was responsible for the oppression and suffering of the people of God. In his view, this government will not survive, since God is soon going to destroy it.

In short, Christianity as experienced by this author was an oppressed and persecuted religion. Indeed, interpreters have traditionally maintained that John actually wrote the book while in exile from his homeland because of his Christian proclamation (see 1:9). The churches of his world had suffered from economic exploitation and some Christians had been martyred, but God was going to put an end to it all, and he would do so very soon.

In general terms, Revelation corresponds to the basic description of an apocalypse. It is a firsthand account written by a prophet who has been shown a vision of heaven that explains the realities of earth, a vision that is mediated by angels and full of bizarre and mysterious symbolism. The nature of the book is indicated at the outset in the magnificent vision of the exalted Christ that the prophet describes in chapter 1. Here Christ

ANOTHER EARLY CHRISTIAN TEXT

BOX 21.3 The *Apocalypse of Peter*

One of the most interesting apocalypses from early Christianity is written in the name of Peter (cf. the *Gospel of Peter* and 2 Peter). There are actually three books called the *Apocalypse of Peter* from early Christianity; the one we are interested in here was discovered in the tomb of a monk in 1887 (along with the *Gospel of Peter*; see box 6.5). The reason this discovery sparked such interest is that this text narrates a first-person guided tour of heaven and hell and is, therefore, the oldest surviving ancestor of Dante's *Divine Comedy*.

The account is written in the first person by someone claiming to be none other than Simon Peter. It begins with him discussing with Christ the nature of the end of time and the afterlife. Jesus proceeds to show Peter what the world to come is like, by taking him through the realm of the blessed, where everyone who has sided with God lives in eternal ecstasy, and the realm of the damned, where everyone who has lived a life of sin is subjected to horrific, and graphically described, punishments. As it turns out, habitual sinners are punished in ways that match their crimes, so that liars are hanged by the tongue over eternal flame while, for example, adulterers are hanged by . . . (a different body part) and so on.

One of the overarching points of this fictional narrative is quite clear: in order to avoid the ravaging flames of hell, one needs to side with God and do what is right in this world, before it's too late.

---

appears as "one like a Son of Man" (cf. Dan 7:13–14, where the phrase describes the cosmic judge of the earth) and is seen walking amid the seven golden lampstands (i.e., he is present among the seven churches of Asia Minor, 1:20) with seven stars in his hands (i.e., he himself is in control of the guardian angels of these churches and therefore of the churches' own destinies, 1:20). His appearance is symbolic: among other things, he is a king (wearing a long robe with golden sash, 1:12); he is ancient (with white hair, 1:14); he is the cosmic judge (with eyes like fire, 1:14); he is full of splendor (with feet of burnished bronze, 1:15); he is all-powerful (with a voice of many waters, 1:15); he speaks the word of God (has a two-edged sword coming from his mouth, 1:16); and he is totally overpowering (with a face like the sun, 1:16). The prophet's response to this vision is understandable: he falls down as if dead. But Christ raises him up and commands him to convey both the message of his vision and the truth of what is yet to come. Many other features of the book are also typical of the genre.

Bizarre Symbolism. The symbolic character of John's visions is obvious. Sometimes he himself doesn't understand what he sees and needs an angel to explain it to him (e.g., 17:7). Not everything he says is shrouded in mystery, however. Many of the symbols are not difficult to understand for those who know enough about the Old Testament (e.g., the image of "one like a son of man") or about common images in ancient culture (e.g., eyes of fire). The explanations of other symbols are hinted at in the text. These are among the most interesting features of the book. A few prominent examples will illustrate the process of historical interpretation.

The Great Whore of Babylon. In chapter 17 the prophet is taken into the wilderness to see "the great whore . . . with whom the kings of the earth have committed fornication" (v. 2). He sees a "woman sitting on a scarlet beast that was full of blasphemous names" (v. 3). The woman is wearing fine clothes and jewels and holds in her hand "a golden cup full of abominations and impurities of her fornication" (v. 4). Across her forehead is written the name "Babylon the great." She is "drunk with the blood of the saints and the blood of the witnesses to Jesus" (v. 6).

An amazing vision. Fortunately, the accompanying angel gives enough of an explanation to enable us to interpret its major points with relative ease (though even so some of the details are a bit puzzling). The beast on which the woman is seated is about to descend to the bottomless pit (v. 8); we learn in 20:2 that Satan is about to be thrown into the pit, so this woman, whoever she is, appears to be supported by the Devil. (This is an important point to observe, for the book of Revelation will sometimes interpret its own symbols for the attentive reader.) Who is the woman herself? The beast has seven heads, and we are told that these are seven mountains on which the woman is seated (v. 9). For those who know enough about the world in which the prophet was writing, this will be the only clue that is needed.

WHAT DO YOU THINK?

BOX 21.4 Futuristic Interpretations of the Book of Revelation

One of the most popular ways to interpret the book of Revelation today is to read its symbolic visions as literal descriptions of what is going to transpire in our own day and age. But there are problems with this kind of approach. On the one hand, we should be suspicious of interpretations that are blatantly narcissistic; this way of understanding the book maintains that the entire course of human history has now culminated with us! An even larger problem, however, is that this approach inevitably has to ignore certain features of the text in order to make its interpretations fit.

Consider, as just one example, an interpretation sometimes given of the "locusts" that emerge from the smoke of the bottomless pit in order to wreak havoc on earth in chapter 9. The seer describes the appearance of these dread creatures as follows:

> On their heads were what looked like crowns of gold; their faces were like human faces, their hair like women's hair, and their teeth like lions' teeth; they had scales like iron breastplates, and the noise of their wings was like the noise of many chariots with horses rushing into battle. They have tails like scorpions, with stingers, and in their tails is their power to harm people. . . . (Rev 9:7–10)

According to one futuristic interpretation, these locusts are modern attack helicopters flying forth through the smoke of battle. The seer, living many centuries before the advent of modern warfare, had no way of knowing what these machines really were, and so he described them as best he could. They fly like locusts but are shaped like huge scorpions. The rotors on top appear like crowns, they seem to have human faces as their pilots peer through their windshields, they are draped with camouflage that

from a distance looks like hair, they have fierce teeth painted on their fronts, they are made of steel and so appear to have iron breastplates, the beating of their rotors sounds like chariots rushing to battle, and they have machine guns attached to their tails, like scorpions' stingers.

What could be more plausible? The prophet has glimpsed into the future and seen what he could not understand. We, however, living in the age in which his predictions will come to pass, understand them full well.

The problem is that the interpretation simply doesn't work, because it overlooks some of the most important details of the passage. Consider, for example, what these locusts are actually said to do. The text is quite emphatic: they are not allowed to harm any grass or trees, but only people; moreover, and most significantly, they are given the power to torture people for five months, but not to kill them (9:4–5). Those who are attacked by the locusts will long to die but will not be able to do so (9:6). These locusts can't be modern instruments of war designed for mass destruction because they are explicitly said to be unable to destroy *anything*.

The same problems occur with virtually every interpretation of the book that takes its visions as literal descriptions of events that will transpire in our own imminent future. These approaches simply cannot account for the details of the text, which is to say that they don't take the text itself seriously enough. It is more reasonable to interpret the text within its own historical context, not as a literal description of the future of the earth, but as a metaphorical statement of the ultimate sovereignty of God over a world that is plagued by evil.

For those who don't, the angel makes the matter still clearer in verse 18: "The woman you saw is the great city that rules over the kings of the earth."

The meaning of the vision is now reasonably transparent. The "great city" that ruled the world in John's day was obviously Rome, commonly called the city "built on seven hills" (hence the beast's seven heads). This city, which in the vision is supported by the Devil himself, had corrupted the nations (the whore fornicates with the kings of earth), exploited the peoples of earth (she is bedecked in fine clothing and jewelry), and persecuted the Christians (she is drunk with the blood of the martyrs). Why is the whore called Babylon? This symbol too is clear for those who know the Old Testament, where Babylon is portrayed as the archenemy of God, the city whose armies devastated Judah, leveled Jerusalem, and destroyed the Temple in 587 B.C.E. In Revelation, then, "Babylon" is a code name for the city opposed to God—Rome, God's principal enemy. Like Babylon of old, Rome too will be destroyed (v. 16). Indeed, this is the point of much of the entire book.

The Number of the Beast, 666. Somewhat earlier in the book we are given a description of another beast, which bears a remarkable resemblance to the one we have just observed. According to chapter 13, this other beast arises from the sea and has ten horns and many heads. One of its heads receives a mortal wound that is then healed. The entire world follows this beast, which is empowered by the dragon (i.e., the Devil, 12:9). The beast makes war on the saints and conquers them (13:7). It has power over all the nations of earth (13:7–8), exploiting them economically (13:17) and demanding to be worshiped (13:15). The author concludes his description of this mortal enemy of God with a final identifying mark, given for those "with understanding." The number of the beast is **666** (13:18).

Interpreters have offered numerous explanations of this number over the years (probably more than six hundred and sixty-six of them). Most of these interpreters have been concerned to show that the beast has finally arisen in their own day. Rarely are the interpretations put forth as conjectures, of course, but almost always with the confidence of those who have the inside scoop. Just in modern times, for example, Christian preachers, televangelists, and authors have suggested such tantalizing and diverse candidates as Adolf Hitler, Mussolini, former Secretary of State Henry Kissinger, Pope Paul VI, and Saddam Hussein!

The author of this book, however, was writing for his own day, not for the twentieth or twenty-first century, and he may have had something specific in mind (see box 21.4). In ancient numeral systems, numbers were written by using letters, and conversely, any combination of letters could yield a numerical total. Anyone conversant with gematria would have understood what the author meant by saying that the number of the beast was 666. He was indicating that this was the numerical value of the person's name. An interesting wrinkle in this matter is that some of the ancient Greek manuscripts of the book of Revelation give a different number for the beast. In these documents, it is 616 rather than 666.

How can we make sense of all this? The beast is described as God's enemy, who controls the world, exploits its people, and kills the saints. Given the similarities to the beast in chapter 17, we may not be too far afield to assume that the beast may be another image of the Roman Empire. If so, then the heads would presumably be the rulers of the empire, some of whom demand to be worshiped (as did some of the emperors). One of these heads was mortally wounded, but then healed. What might this mean? Historians have long known of a group of ancient Jewish books called the Sybilline Oracles, which predict that one of the most hated of the Roman emperors, Caesar Nero, will return from the dead to wreak havoc on the earth—making him comparable to one who recovers from a death-inflicting wound. This popular belief may have something to do with the number of the beast. It should be recalled that Nero was seen as the archenemy of the Christians, whom he ruthlessly and unjustly persecuted for setting fire to the city of Rome. Could he have been the beast described in Revelation 13?

Intriguingly, when the name "Caesar Nero" is spelled in Hebrew letters ("Nero" becomes "Neron"), their numerical total is 666. More intriguingly still, the name can be spelled in another way, without a final *n* at the end. The *n* is worth 50 in the Hebrew numerical system. When the alternative spelling is employed, the name adds up to 616.

The author of Revelation is not referring to Hitler or Mussolini or Saddam Hussein or anyone else in modern times. His enemy was Rome and its Caesars. It was Rome that had dominated the other nations of earth, exploited their native populations, and oppressed the people of God; it was the Roman emperor who was worshiped as divine and who persecuted Christians and sometimes put them to death. This book is about how God was going to overthrow this emperor and his empire at the end of time (see especially chaps. 18–19) prior to rewarding his saints with the kingdom in a new heaven and a new earth (chaps. 20–22).

Violent Repetitions. The book of Revelation follows the literary convention of using violent repetitions. It is impossible to take the predictions of this book as a linear, chronological sequence of events that are to transpire at the end of time. The universe caves in on itself in chapter 6, but the pain and agony continue for another thirteen chapters! The author has written for effect, compounding the tribulations and intensifying the sufferings of the last times to show how dreadful things are going to be.

Triumphalist Movement. The narrative moves through tragedy to triumph, through despair to hope. The fundamental point of the narrative is to provide assurance that, regardless of how terrifying the situation may become, God is ultimately in control of it all. The suffering of the present is part of God's plan, and he will vindicate his people by destroying their enemies. When he does so, he will establish a new kingdom on earth in which there will be no more pain, suffering, or death, no more persecution or exploitation, no more disease, famine, or war. There will only be Christ and his kingdom of saints.

Imminence. The author emphasizes at the beginning and end of his work that the events he records are going to happen soon (1:1, 3; 22:6, 10, 12, 20). This emphasis may suggest that the people

Figure 21.4 Coin minted in 71 C.E., showing the city of Rome seated on the seven hills (cf. Rev 17:9).

he addresses are presently undergoing considerable suffering (note the pervasive references to persecution, exploitation, and martyrdom). He is writing to provide them with hope that they will not have to suffer long before the end comes and God intervenes in history to make right all that has gone wrong.

Encouragement and Admonition. Ultimately, Revelation is a book about hope. In some respects, the author's timetable matters less than his overarching message that God is sovereign over this world, appearances notwithstanding, and that he will soon bring his people's suffering to a crashing halt. This message is meant to encourage those who are persecuted and weak, but it is also meant to admonish those who are tempted to abandon ship in view of their present distress. John emphasizes that those who depart from the faith will face a severe judgment, indeed, they will experience eternal torment. Believers must therefore hold on and not cave in, they must keep the faith and never abandon hope, for the end is near, and with it comes a fearful judgment for those who have proved faithless but an eternal reward for those who have stayed true.

AT A GLANCE

BOX 21.5   The Book of Revelation

1. The book of Revelation gives a narrative description of a prophet's vision of what will happen when God brings the world to a cataclysmic end and creates a new heaven and a new earth for his people.

2. The book is best understood within its own historical context as one of the ancient Jewish and Christian apocalypses.

3. Unlike most other apocalypses, it is not pseudonymous: it was written by a Christian prophet named John. This was not, however, John the son of Zebedee.

4. Like other apocalypses, the book is filled with bizarre symbolic visions (whose interpretation the author often intimates), violent repetitions of action, and a movement from catastrophe to triumph.

5. The book is meant to inspire Christians not to give up hope when experiencing suffering, since God will ultimately have the last word and make right all that is wrong.

6. Portions of the book were evidently written in the early 60s under Emperor Nero (who appears to be the antichrist, 666), but it was probably put into final form later, under the emperor Domitian (around 95 C.E.).

TAKE A STAND

1. Your best friend is convinced that the book of Revelation gives a blueprint for what is going to happen in the near future, probably sometime in the next ten years. You want to argue, on the contrary, that the book of Revelation is not predicting what will happen in our future (whether that is your actual view or not). Make your case.

2. Your teacher has asked you to make a class presentation on the book of Revelation as an example of an ancient apocalypse. Outline your presentation.

3. As the local expert on the New Testament, you have been asked to give a ten- to fifteen-minute talk on how to interpret the bizarre symbolism of the book of Revelation (including the whore of Babylon, the beast/antichrist, and 666). Write a sketch of your talk.

 ## SUGGESTIONS FOR FURTHER READING

Aune, David. *The New Testament in Its Literary Environment.* Philadelphia: Westminster, 1987. Includes an insightful discussion of the characteristics of apocalypses and the social world that they presuppose.

Collins, Adela Yarbro. *Crisis and Catharsis: The Power of the Apocalypse.* Philadelphia: Westminster, 1984. A superb introductory discussion of the author, social context, and overarching message of the Apocalypse.

Collins, John J., ed. *Apocalypse: The Morphology of a Genre.* In *Semeia* 14. Missoula, Mont.: Scholars Press 1979. A full-scale investigation of the characteristics of apocalypses; for more advanced students.

(continued)

SUGGESTIONS FOR FURTHER READING *(continued)*

Collins, John, ed. *Encyclopedia of Apocalyticism. Vol. 1: The Origins of Apocalypticism in Judaism and Christianity.* New York: Continuum, 2000. The definitive reference work dealing with everything having to do with early Jewish and Christian apocalyptic thought.

Elliott, J. K. *The Apocryphal New Testament: A Collection of Apocryphal Christian Literature in an English Translation.* Oxford: Clarendon, 1993. An excellent one-volume collection of noncanonical works, including such important apocryphal apocalypses as the *Apocalypse of Peter,* in a readable English translation with brief introductions.

Metzger, Bruce. *Breaking the Code: Understanding the Book of Revelation.* Nashville: Abingdon, 1993. A simple and useful discussion of various understandings of the book of Revelation by a prominent New Testament scholar.

Pilch, J. *What Are They Saying about the Book of Revelation?* New York: Paulist, 1978. A clear overview of modern scholarly insights into major aspects of the book of Revelation.

Pippin, Tina. *Death and Desire: The Rhetoric of Gender in the Apocalypse of John.* Louisville, Ky.: Westminster John Knox, 1992. An intriguing discussion of the female imagery in the book of Revelation and the social world that it presupposes, written from a feminist perspective; for advanced students.

Rowland, Christopher. *The Open Heaven: A Study of Apocalyptic in Judaism and Early Christianity.* Eugene, Ore.: Wipf and Stock, 2002. A major overview of early Jewish and Christian apocalypticism, as evidenced in the surviving texts.

KEY TERMS

666	apocalypticism	Dionysius, bishop	pseudonymity
apocalypse (genre)	Daniel	Domitian, emperor	whore of Babylon
Apocalypse of Peter			

GLOSSARY

666: The "number of the beast" (= antichrist) in Revelation 13; evidently the number is the total of the numerical value of the letters in the antichrist's name. Interpreters think this is a reference to Caesar Nero, whose name, when spelled in Hebrew letters, adds up to 666.

Abraham: A figure from the Old Testament whom God called to be his follower, who in later tradition came to be known as the "Father of the Jews," as all Jews are descended from him.

Achaia: A Roman province in what is now the southern part of Greece, where Paul conducted some of his missionary activities; its capital city was Corinth.

Acts of the Apostles: The fifth book of the New Testament, which narrates the spread of Christianity throughout the Roman world by Jesus' apostles after his death.

Acts of Peter: The legendary account of the missionary exploits of the apostle Peter after the resurrection.

Alexander the Great: The great military leader of Macedonia (356–323 B.C.E.) whose armies conquered much of the eastern Mediterranean and who was responsible for the spread of Greek culture (Hellenism) throughout the lands he conquered.

Allegory of the Cave, Plato's: A famous image from Plato's book, *The Republic*, in which he develops his notion that people here on earth typically experience the mere "shadow" of a greater "reality," until they are enlightened by the truth.

Ancient Biography: An ancient genre of literature that narrated the life of a famous person, usually in chronological sequence, in which the protagonist's major personality characteristics were established at the outset and were displayed in various things she or he said or did throughout life.

Antichrist: Literally, "one who opposes Christ," used (*a*) for anyone who stands against Christ (for example, the "secessionists" mentioned in 1 John, who are called antichrists), (*b*) specifically for the enemy of Christ who will appear at the end of time, according to the book of Revelation.

Antiochus Epiphanes: The Syrian monarch who attempted to force the Jews of Palestine to adopt Greek culture, leading to the Maccabean revolt in 167 B.C.E.

Antipas: Herod Antipas was the son of Herod the Great. Antipas ruled the land of Galilee as a client-king to Rome during Jesus' ministry and is said in the Gospels to have executed John the Baptist.

Antitheses: Literally, "contrary statements," used as a technical term to designate six sayings of Jesus in the Sermon on the Mount (Matt 5:21–48), in which he states a Jewish law ("You have heard it said . . .") and then sets his own interpretation over it ("But I say to you . . .").

Apocalypse: A literary genre in which an author, usually pseudonymous, reports symbolic dreams or visions, given or interpreted through an angelic mediator, which reveal the heavenly mysteries that can make sense of earthly realities.

Apocalypse of Peter: A pseudonymous work that describes a guided tour of heaven and hell given by Jesus to Peter, to reveal to him the blessings of the saved and the eternal torments of the damned.

Apocalypticism: A worldview held by many ancient Jews and Christians that maintained that the present age is controlled by forces of evil, but that these will be destroyed at the end of time when God intervenes in history to bring in his kingdom, an event thought to be imminent.

Apocrypha: A Greek term meaning, literally, "hidden things," used of books on the fringe of the Jewish or Christian canons of Scripture. The Jewish Apocrypha comprises books found in the Septuagint but not in the Hebrew Bible, including 1 and 2 Maccabees and 4 Ezra.

Apollonius of Tyana: A pagan philosopher and holy man of the first century C.E., reported to do miracles and to deliver divinely inspired teachings, a man believed by some of his followers to be a son of God.

Apollos: An apostle who was not one of the original twelve disciples, but a later convert (see Acts 19) and who became a leading figure for the church of Corinth (see 1 Corinthians 1).

Apology: A reasoned explanation and justification of one's beliefs and/or practices, from a Greek word meaning "defense."

Apostle: Generally, one who is commissioned to perform a task, from a Greek word meaning "sent"; in early Christianity, the term was used to designate special emissaries of the faith who were understood to be representatives of Christ. *See also* Disciple.

Apostolic Fathers: A collection of noncanonical writings penned by proto-orthodox Christians of the second century who were traditionally thought to have been followers of the apostles; some of these works were considered Scripture in parts of the early church.

Aquila and Priscilla: A married couple who assisted Paul in his missionary endeavors in the city of Corinth.

Aramaic: A semitic language related to Hebrew that was the native tongue of those who lived in Palestine in the first century, including Jesus.

Areopagus Speech: According to Acts 17, the speech given by Paul to a group of Stoic and Epicurean philosophers on the hill called the Areopagus (meaning "the hill of the god Ares") in Athens.

Aristides, Letter of: A pseudonymous Jewish writing that describes the miraculous translation of the Septuagint (i.e., the Jewish Scriptures in Greek) by seventy-two Jewish scholars.

Associations, Voluntary: In the Greco-Roman world, privately organized small groups of people who shared common interests and met periodically to socialize, enjoy a common meal, and conduct business; two of the best-known types were trade associations (comprised of members of the same profession) and burial societies.

Athanasius: The powerful bishop of Alexandria in the fourth century C.E.; among other things, he was the first to maintain that only the twenty-seven books now in the New Testament were to be considered canonical Scripture, in his 39th Festal Letter.

Augurs: A group of pagan priests in Rome who could interpret the will of the gods by "taking the auspices." *See also* Auspicy.

Auspicy: A form of divination in which specially appointed priests could determine the will of the gods by observing the flight patterns or eating habits of birds. *See also* Divination.

Autograph: The original manuscript of a literary text, from a Greek word meaning "the writing itself."

Baptism: A Christian initiation ritual that originally involved the emersion of a person into water to demonstrate (or accomplish) a union with Christ in his death (thus Romans 6).

Barnabas, Letter of: A letter (wrongly) attributed to Barnabas, the companion of Paul, but actually written around 132 C.E. The letter is harshly anti-Jewish in its content and tone, arguing that Jews have always misunderstood their own law, which was to be interpreted symbolically rather than literally, and that the Old Testament is in fact a Christian rather than Jewish book.

B.C.E. / C.E.: Abbreviations for "Before the Common Era," and the "Common Era," respectively, used as exact equivalents of the Christian designations "before Christ" (B.C.) and "anno domini" (A.D., a Latin phrase meaning "year of our Lord").

Beatitudes: A Latin word meaning, literally, "blessings," used as a technical term for the sayings of Jesus that begin the Sermon on the Mount (e.g., "Blessed are the poor in spirit . . ." Matt 5:3–12).

Belief: *See* Faith.

Beloved Disciple: The nickname for the "disciple whom Jesus loved" in the Gospel of John, who plays a prominent role in the Passion narrative but is never named. Older tradition identified him as John the son of Zebedee and claimed that it was he who wrote the Gospel.

Bishop: The translation of a Greek word that literally means "overseer," referring to a leader of one of the early Christian churches.

Bloody Sweat: Passage in Luke 22:43–44 in which Jesus is said, before his arrest, to have "sweat great drops as if of blood." The passage, found nowhere else in the New Testament, is not present in some of our oldest and best manuscripts of Luke.

Caiaphas: The name of the high priest of the Jews who was the leader of the Sanhedrin, before whom Jesus appeared on trial in the Gospels and who delivered him over, then, to the Roman governor Pontius Pilate.

Canon: From a Greek word meaning "ruler" or "straight edge." The term came to designate any recognized collection of texts; the canon of the New Testament is thus the collection of books that Christians accept as authoritative.

Catholic: From a Greek word meaning "universal" or "general," used of the New Testament epistles James, 1 and 2 Peter, 1, 2, and 3 John, Jude, and sometimes Hebrews (the "catholic" epistles) to differentiate them from the letters of Paul.

Cephas: One of the main leaders of the earliest Christian church in Jerusalem. The name means "rock" and is an Aramaic translation of the Greek word *petros*. According to John 1:42, therefore, Cephas was an alternative name for the apostle Peter.

Charismatic Communities: Communities that understand themselves to be governed by the gifts (= charismata) of the Spirit.

Chloe: A wealthy Christian in Corinth, possibly a patron of the church there, whose slaves appear to have reported to Paul that the community was riddled with problems.

Christ: *See* Messiah.

Christ Hymn (in Philippians): The passage found in Phil 2:6–11 that may have originally been a hymn sung to (or about) Christ, who gave up his divine rights to become human, lowering himself to die on a cross before God exalted him even higher than he had been before.

Christology: Any teaching about the nature of Christ. *See also* Docetism.

Colossae: The town in western Asia Minor (modern-day Turkey) where Onesimus lived and to which the letter to the Colossians is reputedly directed.

Comparative Method: A method used to study a literary text by noting its similarities to and differences from other, related, texts, whether or not any of these other texts was used as a source for the text in question.

Conciliatory Letter: A letter that attempts to bring about a reconciliation after the writer has had a falling out with his readers; used especially in reference to the letter imbedded in 2 Corinthians 1–9.

Contextual Method: A method used to study a literary text first by determining its social and historical context and then using that context to help explain the text's meaning.

Contextual Credibility, Criterion of: One of the criteria commonly used by scholars to establish historically reliable material; with respect to the historical Jesus, the criterion maintains that if a saying or deed of Jesus cannot be credibly fit into his own first-century Palestinian context, then it cannot be regarded as authentic.

Conversion: Literally means a "turning around," used of people who radically change their religious views/beliefs.

Corinth: The capital city of Achaia, where Paul founded a major church that he addresses in 1 and 2 Corinthians.

Cosmos: The Greek word for "world."

Covenant: An agreement or treaty between two social or political parties that have come to terms; used by ancient Jews in reference to the pact that God made to protect and preserve them as his chosen people in exchange for their devotion and adherence to his law.

Cult: The shortened form of *cultus deorum*, a Latin phrase that literally means "care of the gods," generally used of any set of religious practices of worship. In pagan religions, these normally involved acts of sacrifice and prayer.

Cultus Deorum: *See* Cult.

Cynics: Greco-Roman philosophers, commonly portrayed as street preachers who harangued their audiences and urged them to find true freedom by being liberated from all social conventions. The Cynics' decision to live "according to nature" with none of the niceties of life led their opponents to call them "dogs" (in Greek, *cynes*).

Daimonia: A category of divine beings in the Greco-Roman world. Daimonia were widely thought to be less powerful than the gods but far more powerful than humans and capable of influencing human lives.

Daniel: A book in the Old Testament, probably the last one written, which embodies an apocalyptic view of history and which may have been the source for Jesus' teaching of the coming of the "Son of Man" (see Dan 7:13–14).

Dead Sea Scrolls: Ancient Jewish writings discovered in several caves near the northwest edge of the Dead Sea, widely thought to have been produced by a group of apocalyptically minded Essenes who lived in a monastic-like community from Maccabean times through the Jewish War of 66–70 C.E. *See also* Essenes; Qumran.

Deutero-Pauline Epistles: The letters of Ephesians, Colossians, and 2 Thessalonians, which have a "secondary" (Deutero) standing in the Pauline corpus because scholars debate whether they were written by Paul.

Diaspora: Greek for "dispersion," a term that refers to the dispersion of Jews away from Palestine into other parts of the Mediterranean, beginning with the Babylonian conquests in the sixth century B.C.E.

Diatribe: A Greek rhetorical term, referring to a kind of writing in which an author advances his argument by laying out objections and then providing responses to them.

Didache: Significant early Christian writing discovered in 1873 by Bryennios. Dating to around 100 C.E., this is the earliest surviving church manual, which contains ethical teachings, instructions concerning how to conduct affairs of the church, and warnings against itinerant prophets who were abusing the good graces of churches they visited.

Dionysius, Bishop: The second-century bishop of Alexandria who argued that the book of Revelation could not have been written by John, the son of Zebedee.

Disciple: A follower, one who is "taught" (as opposed to an apostle, one who is "sent" as an emissary).

Dissimilarity, Criterion of: One of the criteria commonly used by scholars to establish historically reliable material; the criterion maintains that if a saying or deed of Jesus does not coincide with (or works against) the agenda of the early Christians, it is more likely to be authentic.

Divination: Any practice used to ascertain the will of the gods. *See also* Auspicy; Extispicy.

Docetism: The view that Jesus was not a human being but only appeared to be, from a Greek word meaning "to seem" or "to appear."

Domitian, Emperor: The Roman emperor from 81 to 96 C.E., ruling when the book of Revelation (and other New Testament books) were probably written.

Egyptian, The: A Jewish apocalyptic prophet of the first century C.E. who predicted the destruction of the walls of Jerusalem, mentioned by Josephus.

Enacted Parable: Any kind of physical action that attempts to convey a deeper symbolic meaning, such as Jesus' cleansing of the Temple, which may have

been intended to illustrate his message that the Temple would soon be destroyed.

Epaphras: The man who was reportedly responsible for founding the church in Colossae.

Epaphroditus: The member of the church of Philippi, who brought a monetary gift from the church to Paul and about whom Paul writes in the letter to the Philippians, informing his home church that although he had been ill, he now had recovered.

Epicureans: An ancient group of followers of the Greek philosopher Epicurus, who maintained that the gods were removed from the concerns of human life and so were not to be feared or placated. Happiness came in establishing a peaceful harmony with other like-minded people and enjoying the simple pleasures of daily existence.

Epistles: Another name for "letters" sent in the ancient equivalent of the postal service.

Equestrian: The second-highest socioeconomic class of ancient Rome (below Senator), comprising wealthy aristocrats.

Eschatology: Literally the "study of (or doctrine of) the end times." A technical term that is used to describe notions of what will happen at the "end"—either the end of a person's life or, more commonly, the end of the world.

Essenes: An apocalyptic and ascetic Jewish sect started during the Maccabean period, members of which are generally thought to have produced the Dead Sea Scrolls.

Euodia and Syntyche: Two women in the church of Philippi who were evidently involved in a public argument, whom Paul urges to be reconciled, in his letter to the Philippians.

Expiation: The technical term for the "covering over" of people's sins through a sacrifice to God.

Extispicy: A form of divination in Greek and Roman religions in which a specially appointed priest (haruspex) would examine the entrails of a sacrificed animal to determine whether it had been accepted by the gods.

Faith: For the apostle Paul, faith means a "trusting acceptance" of the work of salvation that God has achieved in the death (and resurrection) of Jesus.

First-Fruit of the Resurrection: The image that Paul uses of Jesus at his resurrection; it is an agricultural term that refers to the first part of the harvest that is gathered in and celebrated before the rest of the harvest is reaped. That Jesus is the "first fruit" indicates that the rest of the harvest (i.e., everyone else) will soon "come in" (i.e., be resurrected soon).

Forgery: The act of writing a work in the name of a famous person in order to deceive one's readers, usually in order to have the writing read.

Four-Source Hypothesis: A solution to the "Synoptic Problem" which maintains that there are four sources that lie behind the Gospels of Matthew, Mark, and Luke: (1) Mark was the source for much of the narrative of Matthew and Luke; (2) Q was the source for the sayings found in Matthew and Luke but not in Mark; (3) M provided the material found only in Matthew's Gospel; and (4) L provided the material found only in Luke.

Fourth Philosophy: A group of Jews that Josephus mentions but leaves unnamed, characterized by their insistence on violent opposition to the foreign domination of the Promised Land. *See also* Sicarii; Zealots.

Friendship Letter: A kind of ancient epistle designed to renew friendship between the writer and his readers.

Fulfillment Citation: The citation of Old Testament Scripture in certain passages of Matthew, where the OT is said to have been "fulfilled" in something that Jesus did or experienced.

Funeral Societies: Ancient voluntary associations that met periodically for social occasions and whose principal purpose involved providing decent burials for members.

Galatia: The region in central Asia Minor (modern-day Turkey) in which Paul established some churches, to whom he directs his letter to the Galatians.

Gamaliel: A famous rabbi of first-century C.E. Judaism.

Gematria: The Jewish method of interpreting a word on the basis of the numerical value of its letters (in both Greek and Hebrew, the letters of the alphabet also serve as numerals.)

General Epistles: *See* Catholic Epistles.

General History: A genre of ancient literature that traced the significant events in the history of a people to show how their character (as a people) was established. Examples of the genre include Josephus's *Antiquities of the Jews* and the Acts of the Apostles.

Genius: A man's guardian spirit (that of a woman was called Iuno).

Genre: Refers to a "kind" of literary text (e.g., a novel, an apocalypse, or a Gospel).

Gentile: A Jewish designation for a non-Jew.

Gnosis: Greek word for "knowledge." *See* Gnosticism.

Gnosticism: A group of ancient religions, some of them closely related to Christianity, that maintained that elements of the divine had become entrapped in this evil world of matter and could be released only when they acquired the secret *gnosis* of who they were and of how they could escape. Gnosis was generally thought to be brought by an emissary of the divine realm.

Golden Rule: The pronouncement of Jesus that you should "do unto others as you would have them do unto you." Similarly worded pronouncements were made by other great religious teachers in the ancient world.

Gospel: The translation of a Greek word that literally means "good news," used of the first four books of the New Testament (and books like them) that narrate the good news of Jesus' life, death, and resurrection.

Gospel of the Nazareans: The Jewish-Christian Gospel written in Aramaic that was very similar to our Gospel of Matthew, without its first two chapters.

Gospel of Peter: A fragmentary account of Jesus' trial, crucifixion, and resurrection, discovered in the tomb of a monk in Egypt; the *Gospel* is more anti-Jewish than those in the New Testament, and it recounts the resurrection event itself (with Jesus emerging from his grave as a giant, with a cross emerging behind him).

Greco-Roman World: The lands (and culture) around the Mediterranean from the time of Alexander the Great to the Emperor Constantine, roughly 300 B.C.E. to 300 C.E. (*see also* box 2.2).

Hanina ben Dosa: A well-known Galilean rabbi of the first century, who was reputed to have done miracles comparable to those of Jesus.

Haruspex: In the Roman religion, a specially trained priest skilled in the practice of extispicy.

Hasmoneans: An alternative name for the Maccabeans, the family of Jewish priests that began the revolt against Syria in 167 B.C.E. and that ruled Israel prior to the Roman conquest of 63 B.C.E.

Hebrew Bible: The Jewish Scriptures, also known as the Christian Old Testament.

Hellenistic World: The term used to refer to the lands around the Mediterranean that were influenced by Greek culture in the wake of the conquests of Alexander the Great.

Hellenization: The spread of Greek language and culture (Hellenism) throughout the Mediterranean, starting with the conquests of Alexander the Great.

Heresy: Any worldview or set of beliefs deemed by those in power to be deviant, from a Greek word meaning "choice" (because "heretics" have "chosen" to deviate from the "truth"). *See also* Orthodoxy.

Herod the Great: Appointed king of Israel, including both Judea and Galilee, by the Romans in 40 B.C.E.; Herod lived until 4 B.C.E. According to the Gospels of Matthew and Luke, it was during his reign that Jesus was born.

High Priest: Prior to 70 C.E., the highest-ranking authority in Judaism when there was no Jewish king, in charge of the operation of the Jerusalem Temple and its priests. *See also* Sadducees; Sanhedrin.

Histories, Ancient: *See* General History.

Historiography: The literary reconstruction of historical events; the writing of history; and the study and analysis of historical narrative.

Holy of Holies: The innermost part of the Jewish Temple in Jerusalem, which was completely empty, but in which God's presence on earth was believed to dwell. No one could enter this room except the High Priest on the Day of Atonement, to make a sacrifice for the sins of the people.

Honi the "Circle-Drawer": A first-century B.C.E. Galilean who was reputed to have done miracles and had experiences similar to those of Jesus.

Honor: The most significant virtue for ancient males, involving the proper use of power and authority and the correct conduct of those who manifested it.

"I am" Sayings: A group of sayings found only in the Gospel of John, in which Jesus identifies himself. In some of the sayings he speaks in metaphor ("I am the bread of life," "I am the light of the world," "I am the way, the truth, and the life"), and other times he identifies himself simply by saying "I am"—a possible reference to the name of God from Exodus 3 ("Before Abraham was, I am"; John 8:58).

Idol: The image of a divine being, usually carved, sculpted, or molded in wood, stone, or metal.

Ideology of Gender: The power relations between males and females and the ideas about these relations that help manifest that power.

Independent Attestation, Criterion of: One of the criteria commonly used by scholars to establish historically reliable material; with respect to the historical Jesus, the criterion maintains that if a saying or deed of Jesus is attested independently by more than one source, it is more likely to be authentic.

Infancy Gospel of Thomas: The early noncanonical Gospel account that describes deeds and experiences of Jesus between the ages of five and twelve.

Infancy Gospels: Noncanonical accounts of the deeds and experiences of Jesus as a child.

Insula: Ancient apartment buildings in which the bottom floor served as a shop for business and the upper floors as living quarters.

Jesus son of Ananias: The prophet figure described by Josephus as living in the 60s C.E., who proclaimed the coming destruction of Jerusalem in the years before the Roman war that leveled the city in 70 C.E.

Jewish Scriptures: *See* Hebrew Bible.

Johannine Epistles: 1, 2, and 3 John, so called because they were traditionally ascribed to John, the son of Zebedee.

Johannine Prologue: The first eighteen verses of John's Gospel, which describe the "Word" of God that was with God and was equal to God, through whom God made the world, and that became flesh in the man Jesus.

Josephus: The first-century Jewish historian, appointed court historian by the Roman emperor Vespasian, whose works *The Jewish War* and *The Antiquities of the Jews* are principal resources for information about life in first-century Palestine.

Joshua: The figure in the Hebrew Bible who was the leader of the children of Israel when they conquered the promised land.

Judaism: The distinctive religion in the Greco-Roman world, which was monotheistic and claimed that God had made a unique covenant with the Jews, who were, in response, to keep the Torah, his law.

Judas Iscariot: The disciple who betrayed Jesus to the authorities; it is not clear what Iscariot means, but it may refer to his village, "man of Carioth."

Judas Maccabeus: The Jewish patriot who led the family responsible for spearheading the Maccabean revolt. *See also* Hasmoneans.

Judicial Model: One of the two principal ways that Paul understood or conceptualized the relationship between Christ's death and salvation. According to this model, salvation is comparable to a legal decision, in which God, who is both lawmaker and judge, treats humans as "not-guilty" for committing acts of transgression (sins) against his law—even though they *are* guilty—because Jesus' death has been accepted as a payment. *See also* Participationist Model.

Julius Caesar: The Roman dictator who was assassinated in 44 B.C.; Octavian (later Caesar Augustus) was his nephew and adopted son.

Junia: The woman mentioned in Rom 16:7 and called there "prominent among the apostles."

Justification by Faith: The doctrine found in Paul's letters (see "Judicial Model"), that a person is "made right" (justified) with God by trusting in the effects of Christ's death, rather than by doing the works prescribed by the Jewish Law.

Justin Martyr: One of the earliest "apologists," Justin lived in Rome in the mid-second century.

L: A document (or documents, written or oral) that no longer survives, but that evidently provided Luke with traditions that are not found in Matthew or Mark. *See also* Four-Source Hypothesis.

Lares: Household deities commonly worshiped in homes throughout the Roman world, thought to protect the home and its inhabitants, and often identified with the spirits of the family's ancestors.

Law, Jewish: The laws, including the Ten Commandments, given by God to Moses according to the books of Exodus, Leviticus, Numbers, and Deuteronomy. Sometimes the entire Pentateuch is referred to as the Law.

Levites: Descendants from the Patriarch Levi, who were Jewish assistants to the priests in the Temple.

Literary-Historical Method: A method used to study a literary text by asking how its genre text functioned in its historical context and by exploring, then, its historical meaning (i.e., seeing how its meaning would have been understood by its earliest readers) in light of its literary characteristics.

Literary Seams: Inconsistencies or discrepancies in a text created when two different sources are spliced together, for example, in the Gospel of John.

Lord's Prayer: The prayer that Jesus taught his disciples ("Our Father . . .") in Matt 6:9–13 (a shorter version is found in Luke 11:2–4).

Love Chapter: The nickname for 1 Corinthians 13, which describes "love" and its role in and importance for the Christian community.

M: A document (or documents, written or oral) that no longer survives, but that evidently provided Matthew with traditions that are not found in Mark or Luke. *See also* Four-Source Hypothesis.

Maccabean Revolt: The Jewish uprising against the Syrians and their king, Antiochus Epiphanes, starting in 167 B.C.E., in protest against the forced imposition of Hellenistic culture and the proscription of Jewish practices such as circumcision. *See also* Hasmoneans.

Macedonia: The northern part of modern-day Greece, where Paul engaged in missionary activities, establishing churches in such cities as Thessalonica and Philippi.

Manumission: The technical term for setting a slave free, usually by paying the owner.

Manuscript: Any handwritten copy of a literary text.

Marcion: A second-century Christian scholar and evangelist, later labeled a heretic for his docetic Christology and his belief in two Gods—the harsh legalistic God of the Jews and the merciful loving God of Jesus—views that he claimed to have found in the writings of Paul.

Markan Priority: The view that Mark was the first of the Synoptic Gospels to be written and was one of the sources used by Matthew and Luke.

Martyrdom of Polycarp: The first account of the trial and execution of a Christian martyr outside the New Testament, written by an eyewitness and sent to Christians of another community; Polycarp had been the long-time bishop of Smyrna in Asia Minor.

Mary Magdalene: One of the female followers of Jesus, who is reported to have been the first to discover his empty tomb.

Meat Offered to Idols: Meat that had been sacrificed to pagan deities and offered, then, for sale for consumption. The Corinthians debated among themselves whether Christians were allowed to eat this meat (see 1 Corinthians 8 and 10).

Melchizedek: A mysterious figure who appears in Genesis 14 as the King of Salem, to whom Abraham made an offering; referred to as a prefiguration of Christ in the letter to the Hebrews.

Messiah: From a Hebrew word that literally means "anointed one," translated into Greek as *Christos*, from which derives our English word *Christ*. In the first century C.E., there was a wide range of expectations about whom this anointed one might be, some Jews anticipating a future warrior king like David, others a cosmic redeemer from heaven, others an authoritative priest, and still others a powerful spokesperson from God like Moses.

Messianic Secret: Reference to a literary feature of the Gospel of Mark, that Jesus regularly attempts to keep his messianic identity secret by urging those he heals, the demons, and his disciples not to reveal to others who he is.

Miracle, Problem of: The "philosophical" problem of miracle is whether or not miracles can ever happen; the "historical" problem of miracle is whether or not miracles—highly *improbable* events—can ever be shown to have happened by historians, who can demonstrate only what *probably* occurred in the past.

Mishnah: A collection of oral traditions passed on by generations of Jewish rabbis who saw themselves as the descendants of the Pharisees, finally put into writing around 200 C.E. *See also* Talmud.

Monotheism: The belief that there is only one God.

Models of Salvation: Ways of understanding how God has brought about salvation. *See* Judicial Model and Participationist Model.

Muratorian Fragment: A fragmentary text discovered in the eighteenth century, named after its Italian discoverer, Muratori, which contains, in Latin, a list of Christian books that its author considered canonical; the canon is usually considered to have been produced in the late second century, in or around Rome.

Mystery Cults: A group of Greco-Roman religions that focused on the devotees' individual needs both in this life and in life after death, so named because their initiation rituals and cultic practices involved the disclosure of hidden things that were to be kept secret from outsiders.

Mysticism, Jewish: Jewish beliefs and practices that were thought to bring about a mystical union with the divine.

Nag Hammadi: The village in upper (southern) Egypt, near the place where a collection of Gnostic writings, including the *Gospel of Thomas*, was discovered in 1945.

Nazareans: An early group of Jewish Christians who maintained their Jewish identity and lifestyles, and insisted that keeping the Jewish Law was essential for salvation. *See Gospel of the Nazareans.*

Nero, Emperor: The Roman emperor from 54–68 C.E., possibly the target of some of the polemic of the book of Revelation and ruler when many of Paul's letters, and possibly his death, are to be dated.

Occasional: Reference to the circumstance that Paul wrote his surviving letters only for certain occasions, in order to deal with problems that had arisen in his churches.

Octavian: The name of the Roman general who became the first emperor, in 27 B.C.E., and who later took for himself the name Caesar Augustus.

Old Testament: *See* Hebrew Bible.

Onesimus: A convert of Paul who was a slave of Philemon, another of his converts, and about whom Paul wrote the letter to Philemon.

Oracle: A sacred place where the gods answered questions brought by their worshipers to the resident holy person—a priest or, more commonly, a priestess—who would often deliver the divine response out of a trance-like state; the term can also refer to the divine answer itself.

Oral Law: The "law" developed by later rabbis that was meant to interpret the "written" law of Moses.

Origen: A Christian philosopher and theologian from early third-century Alexandria, Egypt, who wrote one of the best-known Christian apologies.

Orthodoxy: From the Greek, literally meaning "right opinion"; a term used to designate a worldview or set of beliefs acknowledged to be true by the majority of those in power. *See also* Heresy.

Paganism: Any of the polytheistic religions of the Greco-Roman world, an umbrella term for ancient Mediterranean religions other than Judaism and Christianity.

Painful Letter: A letter written by Paul to the Corinthians that later came to be cut and pasted into what is now 2 Corinthians 10–13.

Paidagogos: A Greek word sometimes translated as "custodian," which refers to a slave in charge of the children of a household, who was expected to watch over their care and to keep them in line.

Palestine: The ancient Roman designation for the land now occupied by Israel.

Papyrus: A reedlike plant that grows principally around the Nile, whose stalk was used for the manufacture of a paperlike writing surface in antiquity.

Parousia: A Greek word meaning "presence" or "coming," used as a technical term to refer to the Second Coming of Jesus in judgment at the end of time.

Participationist Model: One of the two principal ways that Paul understood or conceptualized the relationship between Christ's death and salvation. This model understood sin to be a cosmic force that enslaved people; salvation (liberation from bondage) came by participating in Christ's death through baptism. *See also* Judicial Model.

Partition Theories: Theories of literary composition that indicate a book is comprised of several sources or texts that have been spliced together (e.g., 2 Corinthians or Philippians).

Passion: From a Greek word that means "suffering," used as a technical term to refer to the traditions of Jesus' last days, up to and including his crucifixion (hence the "Passion narrative").

Passover: The most important and widely celebrated annual festival of Jews in Roman times, commemorating the exodus from Egypt.

Pastoral Epistles: New Testament letters that Paul allegedly wrote to two pastors, Timothy (1 and 2 Timothy) and Titus, concerning their pastoral duties.

Pauline Corpus: All the letters of the New Testament that claim to be written by Paul, including the Deutero-Pauline and Pastoral Epistles.

Penates: Household deities commonly worshiped throughout the Roman world, thought to protect the pantry and foodstuffs in the home.

Pentateuch: Literally, the "five scrolls" in Greek, a term used to designate the first five books of the Hebrew Bible, also known as the Torah or the Law of Moses.

Pentecost: A Jewish agricultural festival, celebrated fifty days after the feast of the Passover, from the Greek word for fifty (*pentakosia*).

Perpetua: The Roman matron in North Africa who was arrested on charges of being a Christian and executed for her faith. The *Martyrdom of Perpetua* consists of a diary in her own hand of her trials and time in prison; it includes an account of her martyrdom that was appended by an anonymous editor.

Pesher: An ancient Jewish way of interpreting Scripture, used commonly in the commentaries from the Dead Sea Scrolls, in which a text was explained as having its fulfillment in persons or events of the present day.

Pharisees: A Jewish sect, which may have originated during the Maccabean period, that emphasized strict adherence to the purity laws set forth in the Torah. *See also* Mishnah.

Philemon: A wealthy Christian of Colossae, owner of the slave Onesimus, to whom Paul wrote the letter of Philemon.

Philippi: City in eastern Macedonia, where Paul established a church to which he directed his letter to the Philippians.

Philo: A famous Jewish philosopher who lived in Alexandria Egypt in the first century, who saw the Jewish Scriptures as completely compatible with the insights of Greek philosophy and worked to interpret them accordingly.

Phoebe: A female deacon of the church of Cenchrea, mentioned by Paul in Rom 16:1.

Pliny: Pliny the Younger was a Roman aristocrat who served as governor of Bythinia-Pontus in the early part of the second century; he was one of the first provincial governors known to have persecuted Christians, during the reign of emperor Trajan.

Polycarp: The long-time bishop of Smyrna. *See Martyrdom of Polycarp.*

Polytheism: The belief in many gods. In the ancient world, virtually everyone except Jews was polytheistic.

Pontius Pilate: The prefect (governor) of Judea from 26 to 36 C.E.; he was the one responsible for ordering Jesus' crucifixion.

Presbyter: From a Greek word that literally means "elder," used in reference to a leader of the early church (possibly because originally these were some of the older members of the congregation).

Prescript: The formal beginning of an epistle, normally including the names of the sender and addressees, a greeting, and often a prayer or wish for good health.

Priests, Jewish: Jews descended from Aaron, the brother of Moses, whose job it was to perform the sacrifices and other cultic duties, on a rotating basis, in the temple of Jerusalem.

Prisca: Another name for Priscilla. *See* Aquila and Prisilla.

Prophet: One who speaks words given by means of a revelation from God.

Prophecy-Fulfillment: The idea that God predicted certain events (prophecies) that then occurred (fulfillments). Matthew and Hebrews, for example, both stress that events in Jesus' life were fulfillments of prophecy.

Proto-orthodox Christianity: A form of Christianity endorsed by some Christians of the second and third centuries (including the Apostolic Fathers), which promoted doctrines that were declared "orthodox" in the fourth and later centuries by the victorious Christian party, in opposition to such groups as the Ebionites, the Marcionites, and the Gnostics.

Psalms of Lament: Psalms in the Hebrew Bible in which the author laments his life and what has happened to him; Christians read some of these Psalms as predictive of what was to happen to the messiah and interpreted them in light of what they knew of the suffering of Jesus (e.g., Psalms 22 and 69).

Pseudepigrapha: From the Greek, literally meaning "false writings" and commonly referring to ancient noncanonical Jewish and Christian literary texts, many of which were written pseudonymously.

Pseudonymity: The practice of writing under a fictitious name, evident in a large number of pagan, Jewish, and Christian writings from antiquity.

Q Source: The source used by both Matthew and Luke for the stories they share, principally sayings that are not found in Mark; from the German word Quelle, "source." The document no longer exists, but can be reconstructed on the basis of Matthew and Luke.

Quirinius: According to Luke, the governor of Syria when Jesus was born in Bethlehem.

Qumran: The place near the northwest shore of the Dead Sea, where the Dead Sea Scrolls were discovered in 1946, evidently home to the group of Essenes who had used the Scrolls as part of their library.

Redaction Criticism: The study of how authors modified or edited (i.e., redacted) their sources in view of their own vested interests and concerns.

Redactor: Another name for an "editor."

Redemption: Literally refers to the act of "buying back" someone or something; used to refer to God's salvation in Christ, whose death "bought" the salvation of others.

Rhetoric: The art of persuasion; in the Greco-Roman world, this involved training in the construction and analysis of argumentation and was the principal subject of higher education.

Righteousness: In the writings of the apostle Paul, refers not to good moral character but to a "right" standing before God, achieved for others through the work of Christ.

Road to Damascus: A phrase sometimes used to refer to the conversion of Paul, who saw the resurrected Jesus on his way to the Syrian city of Damascus.

Roman Empire: All the lands conquered by Rome and ruled, ultimately, by the Roman emperor, starting with Caesar Augustus in 27 B.C.E.; prior to that, Rome was a republic ruled by the Senate (*see also* box 2.3).

Sadducees: A Jewish party associated with the Temple cult and the Jewish priests who ran it, comprising principally the Jewish aristocracy in Judea. The party leader, the High Priest, served as the highest ranking local official and chief liaison with the Roman governor.

Samaritans: Inhabitants of Samaria, located between Galilee and Judea, considered by some Jews to be apostates and half-breeds, since their lineage could be traced back to intermarriages between Jews and pagan peoples several centuries before the New Testament period.

Sanhedrin: A council of Jewish leaders headed by the High Priest, which played an advisory role in matters of religious and civil policy.

Scribes, Christian: Literate Christians responsible for copying sacred scripture.

Scribes, Jewish: Highly educated experts in Jewish Law (and possibly its copyists) during the Greco-Roman period.

Secessionists: A reference to the group of Christians who split from the Johannine community over issues of theology and were attacked by the author of the Johannine epistles for refusing to acknowledge that Jesus was a flesh-and-blood human being.

Self-definition: A sociological term used to denote how a group or individual understands itself, especially in ways to differentiate itself from others.

Senators: The highest-ranking members of the Roman aristocracy, comprising the wealthiest men of Rome, responsible for governing the vast Roman bureaucracy during the republic and still active and highly visible during the time of the empire.

Seneca: The famous philosopher of the first century, a tutor of Nero who became one of his close advisers once he became emperor.

Septuagint: The translation of the Hebrew Scriptures into Greek, so named because of a tradition that seventy (Latin: *septuaginta*) Jewish scholars had produced it.

Sermon on the Mount: The sermon found only in Matthew 5–7, which preserves many of the best-known sayings of Jesus (including Matthew's form of the Beatitudes, the antitheses, and the Lord's Prayer).

Shadow-reality: A reference to a motif in the book of Hebrews, originally developed by the Greek philosopher Plato, in which a partial and imperfect experience in this world reflects a greater reality in the true world above. *See* Allegory of the Cave.

Sicarii: A Latin term meaning, literally, "daggermen," a designation for a group of first-century Jews responsible for the assassination of Jewish aristocrats thought to have collaborated with the Romans. *See also* Fourth Philosophy.

Signs: The term used in the Gospel of John to refer to Jesus' miracles, which "signified" who he really was.

Signs Source: A document, which no longer survives, thought by many scholars to have been used as one of the sources of Jesus' ministry in the Fourth Gospel; it reputedly narrated a number of the miraculous deeds of Jesus.

Silvanus: A companion of Paul who coauthored several of his letters.

Sociohistorical Method: A method used to study a literary text that seeks to reconstruct the social history of the community that lay behind it.

Songs of the Suffering Servant: Passages in the Hebrew Bible prophet Isaiah, which describe the sufferings of a servant of the Lord that are endured for the sake of others. In Isaiah, this figure is identified as Israel itself (49:3); early Christian authors understood it to refer to Jesus.

Son of God: In most Greco-Roman circles, the designation of a person born to a god, able to perform miraculous deeds and/or to convey superhuman teachings; in Jewish circles, the designation of persons chosen to stand in a special relationship with the God of Israel, including the ancient Jewish Kings.

Son of Man: A term whose meaning is much disputed among modern scholars, used in some ancient apocalyptic texts to refer to a cosmic judge sent from heaven at the end of time.

Sosthenes: A prominent person in the church of Corinth, according to the book of Acts.

Stephanus, Fortunatus, and Achaicus: Three members of the church of Corinth who delivered a letter to Paul, to which he responds in 1 Corinthians.

Stoics: Greco-Roman philosophers who urged people to understand the way the world worked and to live in accordance with it, letting nothing outside themselves affect their internal state of well-being.

Superapostles: Paul's term (probably sarcastic) for his opponents in Corinth, who emphasize their own supernatural miracle-working powers and wisdom in contrast to Paul's weakness and foolishness.

Superstition: In the ancient world, superstition was understood by the highly educated upper classes as an excessive fear of the gods that drove a person to be excessively scrupulous in trying to avoid their displeasure.

Synagogue: The Jewish place of worship and prayer, from a Greek word that literally means "being brought together."

Synoptic Gospels: The Gospels of Matthew, Mark, and Luke, which narrate so many of the same stories that they can be placed side by side in parallel columns and so "be seen together" (the literal meaning of "synoptic").

Synoptic Problem: The problem of explaining the similarities and differences between the three Synoptic Gospels. *See also* Markan Priority; Q Source.

Tabernacle: The tent made by the ancient Israelites and used by them as a temporary place of worship and sacrifice to God before the Temple was built.

Tacitus: The Roman aristocrat whose *Annals of Rome* detailed the history of the city down to his own day.

Talmud: The great collection of ancient Jewish traditions that comprises the Mishnah and the later commentaries on the Mishnah, called the Gemarah. There are two collections of the Talmud, one made in Palestine during the early fifth century C.E. and the other in Babylon perhaps a century later. The Babylonian Talmud is generally considered the more authoritative.

Tarsus: The city of Cilicia from which, according to the book of Acts, the apostle Paul came.

Temple, Jewish: The impressively large and ornate place of worship for the Jews, located in Jerusalem and considered by some to be the most magnificently constructed holy place in the empire, prior to its destruction in 70 C.E.

Tertullian: A brilliant and acerbic Christian author from the late second and early third century. Tertullian, who was from North Africa and wrote in Latin, is one of the best known early Christian apologists.

Textual Criticism: An academic discipline that seeks to establish the original wording of a text based on the surviving manuscripts.

Thecla: A (legendary) female disciple of Paul whose adventures are narrated in the novel-like work of the second century, *The Acts of Thecla.*

Thematic Method: A method used to study a literary text by isolating its leading ideas, or themes, and exploring them, seeing how they are developed in the text, so as to understand the author's overarching emphases.

Theophilus: The person to whom Luke dedicated both his Gospel and the book of Acts. Theophilus may have been an actual person, possibly a Roman administrator, or the name may be symbolic for the Christian reader (one who "loves God" or who is "loved by God").

Thessalonica: The capital city of Macedonia, a major port in which Paul established a church and to which he directed the letter of 1 Thessalonians.

Theudas: A first-century Jewish apocalyptic prophet (mentioned by Josephus) who predicted the parting of the Jordan River and, evidently, the reconquest of the Promised Land by the chosen people.

3 Corinthians: A letter forged in Paul's name that combats a second-century form of docetic Christology.

Three-storied Universe: Reference to the ancient belief that the entire world (our universe) consists of three spheres: the world below us (where the dead reside), our world here, and the world above (where God dwells).

Timothy: A traveling companion of Paul, with whom he coauthored several letters and to whom the letters of 1 and 2 Timothy are allegedly directed.

Titus, Emperor: The Roman general who was responsible for the destruction of Jerusalem in 70 C.E.; Titus was the son of Vespasian and succeeded him as emperor in 79 C.E.

Titus, Christian: A traveling companion and coworker of Paul to whom the letter of Titus is allegedly directed. Titus was instrumental in reconciling Paul and the church in Corinth, according to 2 Corinthians.

Torah: A Hebrew word that means "guidance" or "direction," but that is usually translated "law." As a technical term, it designates *either* the Law of God given to Moses or the first five books of the Jewish Bible that Moses was traditionally thought to have written—Genesis, Exodus, Leviticus, Numbers, and Deuteronomy.

Trade Organizations: Voluntary associations for persons involved with the same trade. *See* Funeral Societies.

Tradition: Any doctrine, idea, practice, or custom that has been handed down from one person to another.

Trajan, Emperor: The Roman emperor from 98 to 117 C.E., under whose reign Christians were persecuted in Bythinia-Pontus. *See* Pliny.

Undisputed Pauline Epistles: Romans, 1 and 2 Corinthians, Galatians, Philippians, 1 Thessalonians, and Philemon—letters that scholars overwhelmingly judge to be have been written by Paul. *See also* Deutero-Pauline Epistles; Pastoral Epistles.

Vespasian, Emperor: The Roman general who led the assault on the Jews during the Jewish uprising in Palestine in 66 C.E., who then came to be proclaimed emperor in 69 C.E.

Vicarious Suffering: The notion that one person or group can suffer for the sake of and/or in the place of others.

Voluntary Associations: *See* Trade Organizations and Funeral Societies.

Whore of Babylon: An image used in the book of Revelation to refer to the city of Rome. "Babylon" was thought to be the enemy of God's people, since it was the city responsible for the overthrow of Judea in the Hebrew Scriptures; the city is called a "whore" because of its ways of dealing with other countries.

Works: For Paul, "works of the law" refers to practices enjoined on Jews as part of their covenantal relationship with God; for the epistle of James, "good works" refers to the doing of good deeds.

Zadok: A priest during the time of David in the Old Testament, whose descendants were thought by many Jews to be the only legitimate candidates to become the "high priest."

Zealots: A group of Galilean Jews who fled to Jerusalem during the uprising against Rome in 66–70 C.E., who overthrew the reigning aristocracy in the city and urged violent resistance to the bitter end. *See also* Fourth Philosophy.

INDEX

Essenes, 37, 40, 191
   apocalypticism of, 42
   monastic type community of, 41–42
   in Temple, 139–40
Ethics, 19, 48, 148, 217, 321, 323
Euodia and Syntyche, 242–43, 285
Euripides. *See* Alcestis
Eusebius, 341
Evans, Marian, 265
Exclusive commitments, 19
Exodus from Egypt, 31, 53, 81
Exorcism, 121, 142–44
Expiation, 260
Extispicy, 23–24, 24*f*

F

Faith, 327
   of Abraham, 238, 240
   James and Paul on, 322
   justification by, 238, 301, 321
   Romans on, 251–54, 261
False believers, 237
False teaching, 278, 321, 323
Family values, 149, 217
Farewell Discourse, 114, 118, 118*f*
Felicitas, 311
Festival days, 22–23
Field of Blood, 172
First-fruit of the resurrection, 193, 222
Forgery, 265, 266, 267, 271
Fortunatus, 222
Four-source hypothesis, 61, 61*f*
Fourth Gospel. *See* John, Gospel of
Fourth Philosophy, 42, 136
Friendship letter, 210, 242, 243
Fulfillment citation, 81
Funeral societies, 208
Furnish, Victor, 273
Futuristic interpretations of Revelation, 344

G

Gabriel, angel, 101
Gaius, 25, 326, 330
Galatia, 234, 235*f*, 236
Galatians, 5, 185, 186, 233–41
   on Abraham's descendants, 240
   basic issue in, 238–39
   on circumcision, 234–41
   on covenant, 235–36
   on Gentiles, 234–41
   on lawlessness, 240–41
   on Law of God, 234–40
   on love, 240, 243
   occasion and purpose of, 234–36
   Paul's rebuke in, 236
   Paul's response to opponents, 236–41
Galen, 265
Galileans, 174
Gamaliel (rabbi), 190
Gandhi, Mahondas, 11–12
Gematria, 345
Gender. *See also* Women
   ancient ideologies of, 292–93
   ideology and Pauline churches, 293–95
Genealogy
   of Israel, 79
   of Jesus, the Jewish Messiah, 79–81
   in Luke's gospel, 102
   in Matthew's gospel, 82, 100–102
General Epistles, 5, 297
Genius, 20, 21*f*, 22*f*
Genre, 60
   of Acts, 166
   apocalypse, 4, 337–40, 343, 346
   of John's gospel, 113
   of Luke's gospel, 162–63
   of Mark's gospel, 78
Gentiles. *See also* Pagans
   Acts on, 167, 169, 171, 174, 177–78, 180, 218
   circumcision of, 178
   defined, 16
   Ephesians on, 272–73, 275
   Galatians on, 234–41
   Luke's gospel on, 101–3, 107–8, 180
   missionary work among, 91
   Paul as apostle to, 182–214
   Paul's view of, 195, 197
   Romans on, 251–55, 259–62
Gethsemane, Garden of, 70, 71, 122
Gnosis, 277
Gnosticism, 7, 331
   Pastoral epistles on, 282
   2 Peter and, 325–26
   Thomas' gospel and, 73
   1 Timothy and, 277
   Titus, book and, 280
   women and, 285
God. *See also* Kingdom of God
   covenant with Jewish patriarchs, 195
   one true, 206
   righteousness of, Romans on, 253–54
God-fearers, 202
Gods, Roman. *See also* Greco-Roman world;
   Polytheism
   Great, 19–20
   savior, 25
   state, 20, 22, 25, 299–300, 310–12
Golden Rule, 77, 87